Basic Skills in English

7

Contents of the Teacher's Edition

Components of *Basic Skills in English* T2

Significant Features of *Basic Skills in English* T3

Clear, readable presentation for below-level readers T4

Comprehensive coverage of on-level skills T6

Using the Teacher's Edition T8

Other McDougal, Littell Programs T10

Teaching Special Populations T11

Additional Answers: Sentence Diagrams T17

Teaching Special Populations: Specific Suggestions T27

Guidelines for Evaluating Composition T32

Components of *Basic Skills in English*

Student Texts

Red Level
Grade 7

Green Level
Grade 8

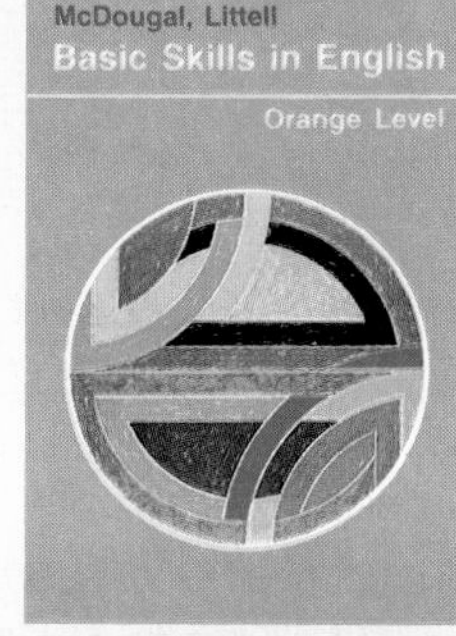

Orange Level
Grade 9

Blue Level
Grade 10

Yellow Level
Grade 11

Purple Level
Grade 12

Teacher's Editions

Practice Books/Duplicating Masters

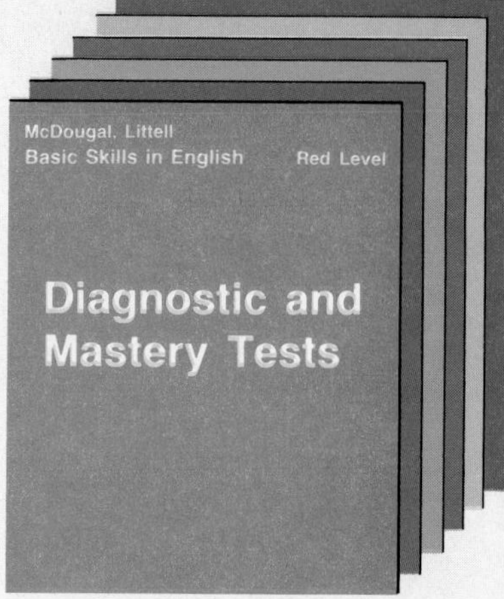

Diagnostic and Mastery Tests

Significant Features of *Basic Skills in English*

The only English series for students reading *below* grade level . . . with content that is *on* grade level!

Ever since its introduction, *Basic Skills in English* has been the only series of its kind—a composition/grammar series for students reading below grade level. It's a program designed to teach all essential skills while helping students learn with confidence and achieve success.

The 1985 edition maintains the tone, format, and clear instruction that teachers praised in the earlier edition. It then builds on this success with more practice exercises, greatly expanded instruction in the process of writing, and new material on study and research skills, speaking and listening, critical thinking, and more. *Basic Skills in English* provides:

Clear, readable presentation for below-level readers

The series offers a controlled reading level, a one-step-at-a-time approach, and success-directed lessons. As a result, students read with ease and master skills gradually, gaining confidence as they progress (see pages T4–T5).

Comprehensive coverage of on-level skills

Students reading below grade level need the same skills and preparation that average students do. That's why *Basic Skills in English* provides thorough instruction in all the language basics: composition, grammar, and related language skills (see pages T6–T7).

Comprehensive coverage of on-level skills

So complete, you can be sure your students will learn all essential English skills.

All students need the same skills, regardless of their reading abilities. That's why *Basic Skills in English* teaches all of the essential concepts and skills that students are expected to master at their grade level. It's a comprehensive program that provides instruction in *all* the language basics: composition; grammar, usage, and mechanics; and related language skills.

Composition

In-depth writing instruction teaches students the skills and techniques they'll need to write effectively:

Process of Writing
Students learn the three stages of the process of writing . . . pre-writing, writing, and revising . . . then use the process consistently throughout the program.

Types of writing
The series teaches students the various elements and techniques that characterize narrative, descriptive, and explanatory writing.

Forms of writing
Students learn and practice the different forms of writing that they will use in school and in everyday life. Lessons on sentences, paragraphs, compositions, reports, and research papers give students the essential skills they need.

Part 5 **Replay**

Revising Your Narrative Paragraph

Here's the Idea After you have written the first draft of your

Part 4 **Time Will Tell**

Writing the First Draft

Part 1 **Tell a Tale**

Pre-Writing: The Narrative Paragraph

Here's the Idea The next four writing sections will teach you how to write different kinds of paragraphs. As you study each type of paragraph, notice that the process of writing is always the same. However, each type of paragraph is developed and organized differently. In this section, you will learn how to develop and organize a **narrative paragraph.**

A narrative tells a story. When you write about an experience at the state fair or your first trip in an airplane, you are writing a narrative. A narrative does not have to be a true story. For example, Rudyard Kipling wrote about a mongoose called Rikki Tikki Tavi, who saves his human and animal friends by slaying two evil cobras. Kipling's story is an imaginary narrative.

When you choose a topic for your narrative paragraph, select a story you can tell well in this length. To help you limit your story, ask questions about it. Ask *who? what? when? where? why?* and *how?* The answers you get will give you the details you need to zero-in on your topic.

After you have selected and limited your topic, think about it. How will you develop your story? Any story, even one brief enough to be told in a single paragraph, is made up of many small incidents or events. Suppose you decided to write about your first ride on a roller coaster. This story would be made up of many events. First, you buy your ticket. Then you wait in line. Finally, it's your turn. You board the roller coaster. These are the kinds of specific details that will help you to tell your story.

A good story also contains sensory details. There are screams as the roller coaster descends. There are the colored lights that decorate the amusement park. There is the smell of popcorn and hot dogs. Details will bring your narrative to life.

106

Grammar, usage, and mechanics

Basic Skills in English offers exceptionally clear, to-the-point instruction in grammar, usage, and mechanics. A flexible handbook format allows for developmental teaching, skills review, and student reference. And each section includes a wealth of varied exercises that are both fun and instructive. The series pays special attention to problems of usage and speech that often present difficulties for less able students.

Part 1 Pairs of Verbs That Are Often Confused

See how the following pairs of verbs are used. Study the difference in their meanings. Avoid making mistakes when you use them.

Can and *May*

Use **can** when you are talking about being able to do something. *Can* has no principal parts. Another form of *can* is *could*.

Use **may** when you are asking or giving permission. *May* is used only as a helping verb. It has no principal parts. Another form of *may* is *might*.

Can you see me?	*Might* we leave early?
Tara *could* not see the screen.	You *may go* to the party.

Exercise Use *can* and *may* correctly.

Number your paper from 1 to 10. Write the correct verb from the two given in parentheses.

1. (May, Can) you write backwards?
2. (May, Can) I help you with anything for the Halloween party?
3. Yes, you (can, may) go to Robert's party.
4. (Can, May) that little stove heat this whole room?
5. (May, Can) Melinda and I go out in the canoe?
6. (May, Can) you read the bottom line without your glasses?
7. A catbird (can, may) imitate other birds.
8. (May, Can) I please be excused?
9. (Can, May) Eduardo go to the par
10. My little brother (may, can) count

392

Related language skills

Separate chapters teach the related skills students need for effective communication and for successful learning in every subject area:

Critical thinking
Topics include distinguishing fact and opinion, avoiding errors in reasoning, and drawing conclusions.

Vocabulary
The series develops skills such as discovering word meaning from context and recognizing word parts.

Levels of language
Students learn about standard and nonstandard English, slang, jargon, regional language, and more.

Life skills
Letters, forms, applications, résumés, and interviews are a few of the topics taught throughout the program.

Study and research
Students learn skills such as following directions, completing research, and preparing for tests.

Speaking and listening
Skills include presenting formal and informal speeches, evaluating speeches, and participating in group discussions.

Part 1 Fact-Finding Mission

Facts and Opinions

Here's the Idea Your mind is like a computer. In it you have stored thousands and thousands of ideas. These ideas may be facts or opinions.

Facts are ideas that can be proved true. They tell about people, things, and events. The following are facts:

1. Many television shows are written by more than one person.
2. President Lincoln signed the Emancipation Proclamation.
3. Vampire bats have sharp, V-shaped teeth.

Facts can be proved in three different ways:

1. Some facts can be proved through observation. You can prove them by using your senses of sight, smell, hearing, taste, and touch. For example, you can use your sense of sight to prove the first fact listed above. All you have to do is watch the credits that follow most television shows.
2. Some facts can be proved by asking an expert. This is someone who has special knowledge, training, or experience. You can prove the second fact by asking a history teacher.
3. Some facts can be proved by checking a reliable written source. A **reliable source** is one you can count on to give you accurate information. You can prove the third fact listed above by reading about vampire bats in an encyclopedia.

Opinions are very different from facts because they cannot be proved true. The following statements are opinions:

1. Everyone should learn to ice skate.
2. Pandas are beautiful and funny.

These statements tell how some people feel about things. Other people might feel differently. That is why these statements can't be proved.

218

As students progress, they build on the success they've already achieved.

Success-directed lessons, a controlled reading level, and a one-step-at-a-time approach combine to make concepts more accessible to students. As a result, they read with ease and master skills gradually, gaining confidence as they progress.

Success-directed lessons

The short, highly-structured lessons are fail-proof . . . every student can achieve success.

Here's the Idea
The main idea of the lesson is presented in a clear, concise manner. Explanations are especially easy to understand.

Check It Out
High-interest examples and models illustrate the main idea of the lesson. Questions help students focus on key points.

Try Your Skill
These highly-structured, success-directed exercises allow students to apply the skill they have learned.

Keep This in Mind
For further reinforcement, a boxed summary highlights the main idea of the lesson.

Now Write
The second exercise is a writing application that gives students independent practice in using the skill.

Part 1 **Sensational!**

Pre-Writing: Using Sensory Details

Here's the Idea A descriptive composition paints a picture with words. It might describe a scene, such as a park in the city. It might describe a thing, such as a cab. It might also describe a person, such as a clown.

Begin planning your word picture by choosing and narrowing a subject. Next, begin gathering sensory details by observing your subject in person or by working from memory. Then list as many sensory details as you can. Ask yourself how your subject looks, sounds, smells, tastes, and feels.

When you finish making your notes, read them over carefully. Cross out any details that will not help you to describe your subject. Then organize your notes in spatial order. Group your details around two or three main ideas. Each of these idea groups will become a paragraph in your composition.

Next, put your main ideas and the details grouped around them into a logical order. You will probably want to use spatial order to show how all the parts of your subject are related.

Check It Out Look at these pre-writing notes.

Topic: Grandma Sarah's apartment

Grandma Sarah and the sea
lives in New Bedford, near harbor—busy
fishing boats—treasures from Grandfather's sailing days

bedroom
four-poster bed, maple, (center),—Chinese clock (red dragons)—oval mirror—sea chests, leather, wood, brass—smells of fresh-washed linen, lavender

favorite corner
window facing sea—colorful seashells—when the window is open, smell of salt and sea—muffled clang of harbor buoy—comfortable rocking chair

174

Popeye, the talking parrot
has a perch near the rocking chair—pale green parrot—loud squawks—"You old sea dog!"

- What senses have been used to gather the details in these pre-writing notes?
- What main ideas have the details been clustered around? How have these idea clusters been organized?

Try Your Skill Below are some pre-writing notes for a descriptive composition about a pizza parlor. Along with the notes are three main ideas. Decide which notes belong with which main idea. Cluster the notes around that main idea.

Main Ideas:	Regina's Pizzeria (outside)	Regina's Pizzeria (inside)	Regina's is the best pizza
Details:	small, old building		10 wooden tables
	red and white checked placemats		crispy crust
			refrigerator for soda
	neon sign		oldies jukebox
	mushrooms, pepperoni		long lines
			creamy cheese

Keep This in Mind

- Gather sensory details to develop your description.
- Group your details around several main ideas.
- Use spatial order to organize your composition.

Now Write Make a list of some people, places, and things that you would like to describe. Choose the one that interests you the most. Use your senses to gather details about your subject. Group your details around several main ideas. Then, organize your main ideas and details in the order you want your reader to notice them.

175

Controlled reading level

While the content of each text is on grade level, the readability has been carefully controlled so that it does not interfere with the concepts.

The language and tone of the instruction is encouraging and conveys confidence in the student's ability. To further motivate students, the text uses lively, high-interest models and exercises.

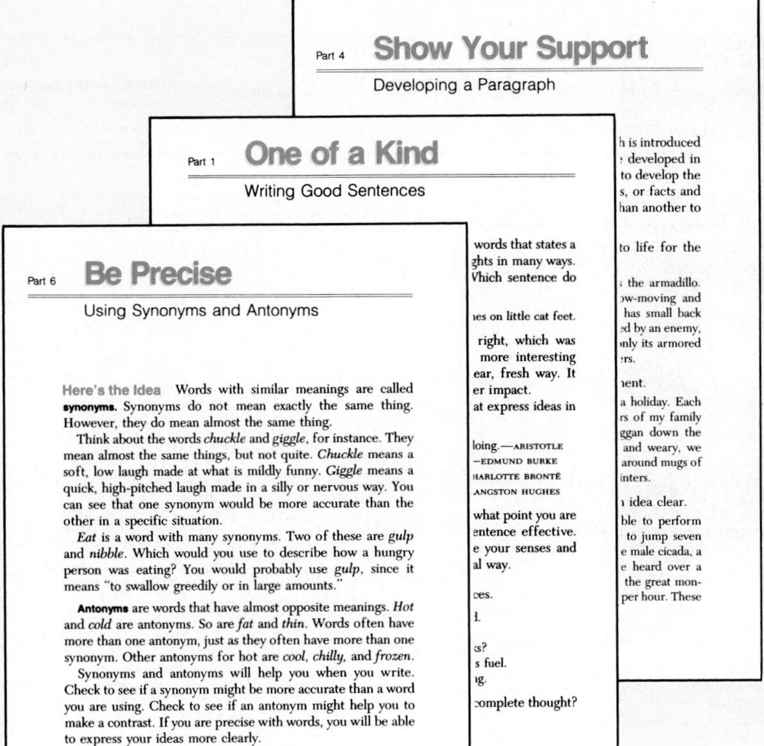

Part 4 **Show Your Support**

Developing a Paragraph

h is introduced
: developed in
to develop the
s, or facts and
han another to

to life for the

; the armadillo.
ɔw-moving and
has small back
ɛd by an enemy,
ɔnly its armored
ɛrs.

ɪent.
a holiday. Each
rs of my family
ggan down the
and weary, we
around mugs of
inters.

ı idea clear.
ble to perform
to jump seven
e male cicada, a
e heard over a
the great mon-
per hour. These

Part 1 **One of a Kind**

Writing Good Sentences

words that states a
ghts in many ways.
Which sentence do

ıes on little cat feet.

right, which was
more interesting
ear, fresh way. It
er impact.
at express ideas in

loing.—ARISTOTLE
—EDMUND BURKE
HARLOTTE BRONTË
ANGSTON HUGHES

what point you are
entence effective.
e your senses and
al way.

ces.
l.

cs?
s fuel.
ıg.

complete thought?

Part 6 **Be Precise**

Using Synonyms and Antonyms

Here's the Idea Words with similar meanings are called **synonyms.** Synonyms do not mean exactly the same thing. However, they do mean almost the same thing.

Think about the words *chuckle* and *giggle*, for instance. They mean almost the same things, but not quite. *Chuckle* means a soft, low laugh made at what is mildly funny. *Giggle* means a quick, high-pitched laugh made in a silly or nervous way. You can see that one synonym would be more accurate than the other in a specific situation.

Eat is a word with many synonyms. Two of these are *gulp* and *nibble*. Which would you use to describe how a hungry person was eating? You would probably use *gulp*, since it means "to swallow greedily or in large amounts."

Antonyms are words that have almost opposite meanings. *Hot* and *cold* are antonyms. So are *fat* and *thin*. Words often have more than one antonym, just as they often have more than one synonym. Other antonyms for hot are *cool, chilly,* and *frozen*.

Synonyms and antonyms will help you when you write. Check to see if a synonym might be more accurate than a word you are using. Check to see if an antonym might help you to make a contrast. If you are precise with words, you will be able to express your ideas more clearly.

Check It Out Read the following sentences.

1. "Be quiet," *said* Tanya, "we don't want them to hear us."
   barked called shrieked whispered
2. Is your job *dull*, or is it ______?" asked Ron.
   busy exciting important valuable

12

One-step-at-a-time approach

Each lesson follows a consistent, manageable format that focuses on one . . . and only one . . . topic at a time.

Single-concept lessons

So that students master skills gradually, lessons focus on a single skill and develop it. Later lessons review and build on the concept, helping students retain what they've learned.

Developmental sequence

Instruction moves logically from the word, to the sentence, to the paragraph, and on to longer types of writing.

Using the Teacher's Edition

The Teacher's Edition for each level provides step-by-step teaching strategies for presenting, developing, reinforcing, and reviewing each lesson.

Full-size student pages

Student pages are reproduced full size for ease in reading.

Objectives

Knowing what the objectives are can make your teaching more directed and purposeful.

Section 6 Objectives

1. To study the steps in the writing process
2. To learn different ways of choosing a subject
3. To understand and apply the process of narrowing a topic
4. To learn how to write direct, interesting topic sentences
5. To learn how to gather information through personal observation, brainstorming, and research
6. To learn how to develop paragraphs by using details, examples, or facts and figures
7. To recognize the four different methods of paragraph organization
8. To understand how to write a first draft
9. To gain skill in writing a paragraph ending that sums up the main idea of the paragraph in an interesting way
10. To understand the purpose of revising and to gain important revising skills

Preparing the Students

Refer once again to the poster developed throughout Section 5. Highlight the main points and explain that in Section 6, students will learn to apply what they have learned about paragraphs.

Additional Resources

Mastery Test — page 19 in the test booklet
Practice Book — pages 26–34
Duplicating Masters — pages 26–34

WRITING SECTION 6

Writing a Paragraph

Part 1 **Stepping Stones**
Writing as a Process

Part 2 **A Matter of Choice**
Pre-Writing: Choosing a Subject

Part 3 **Straight and Narrow**
Pre-Writing: Narrowing a Topic

Part 4 **Direct Contact**
Pre-Writing: Writing a Topic Sentence

Part 5 **Round Up**
Pre-Writing: Developing a Paragraph

Part 6 **Let's Get Organized**
Pre-Writing: Organizing a Paragraph

Part 7 **Blazing the Trail**
Writing the First Draft

Part 8 **Stop Sign**
The First Draft: Ending a Paragraph

Part 9 **Famous Last Words**
Revising Your Paragraph

61

Teaching Special Populations

LD LD students may have great difficulty with Writing Sections 6–18. Some students may be unable to even write more than a sentence or two. Work through these sections slowly and methodically with your LD students.

To arouse interest in and overcome resistance to writing, bring to class pictures (photographs, posters, reproductions of fine art), interesting magazine articles (especially those accompanied by illustrations), exciting stories, and unusual objects. Use these to illustrate different types of writing and as focal points for the students' writing.

Some LD students may find it easier to talk out their sentences and paragraphs than to write them. A tape recorder will enable these students to replay their sentences and perhaps even to improve them.

However you choose to use these writing sections with your LD students, you must modify your expectations. Let your knowledge of your students' abilities be your guide.

ESL ESL students will benefit from frequent brainstorming opportunities. Be sure that they understand suggested ideas and their relation to the subject.

ESL students may need help in locating and using reference materials. You may want to work through Writing Section 20, **Using the Library**, before teaching the writing sections.

Encourage these students to talk about their writing. Pair them with native speakers so that they can check their progress at each stage of the process of writing.

If these students have trouble writing in English, assign a native English speaker to write down what they can express orally.

Preparing the students

The Teacher's Edition suggests ideas for motivating and preparing students prior to every new section.

Additional resources

A detailed list directs you to extra practice, review, and tests.

Teaching special populations

At the beginning of each writing section and at the end of each handbook, the Teacher's Edition explains difficulties faced by the special student. Strategies are presented for helping students for whom English is a second language, students with learning disabilities, and students who speak nonstandard dialicts.

Lesson objectives

Objectives are clearly stated in terms of student performance.

Presenting the lesson

Teaching suggestions stress points to emphasize, possible areas of difficulty, and ways to use the exercises effectively.

Answers

For your convenience, exercise answers are printed on or beside the student page.

Optional practice

Additional ideas are provided for drill, review, or reinforcement.

Part 9

Objective

To understand the purpose of revising and to gain important revising skills

Presenting the Lesson

1. Read aloud and discuss **Here's the Idea.** Have students turn to the contents page for the Handbook section as reference for any questions about mechanics.
2. Discuss **Check It Out.** Read the first draft aloud and then the revised version. Point out how the added details and corrected grammar enhance the paragraph.
3. Assign **Try Your Skill.** Discuss the revisions after the students are finished.
4. Read aloud **Keep This in Mind** and then assign **Now Write.**

Individualizing the Lesson

Less-Advanced Students'

Do the first two sentences in **Try Your Skill** on the board so that the students can see how proofreading symbols are used. Then assign the remainder of the sentences to be corrected individually.

Advanced Students

Have students revise the following paragraph:

Archery can be fun. you need to be strong to do it. Just stringing the bow is difficult, Pulling back on the bow takes strength and consintration. Robin hood made it look so easy. That bullseye seems to get even smaller as you try too hit it with the arrow. You must be careful that the string or arrow does not scrape you're arm as you release.

Part 9 **Famous Last Words**

Revising Your Paragraph

Here's the Idea The third and final step of the writing process is revising. When you revise, you take a fresh look at what you have written. You make changes so that your writing is the best it can be.

At this point, you will have to work very carefully and thoughtfully. First, check your ideas. Be sure your paragraph has a good topic sentence. See that all of your details help to develop the main idea of your paragraph. Are there any unrelated details? Could you add any details that would improve your paragraph?

Next, check the order of your details. Have you chosen a method of organization that suits the kind of paragraph you are writing?

Now look at the ending sentence of your paragraph. Is the ending interesting? Does it work well with the rest of the paragraph? Does it sum up the main idea of your paragraph?

Finally, check the language you have used. Is it direct, lively, and interesting? Try reading aloud what you have written. Sometimes your ears will catch what your eyes miss.

After revising your ideas, your organization, and your language, proofread your work. Be sure you have used correct grammar, capitalization, punctuation, and spelling. Use a dictionary and the Handbook sections of this book to help you proofread your paragraph.

Check It Out Read the following paragraph. Notice how the author has revised it.

- What are some specific things the writer has done to make this paragraph better?

78

At the corner of Elm Street and Fourth Avenue was a house. My friend George and me used to play in it when we were little. The house had boarded up windows and old brick walls. There were a lot of trees around it. On bad days, the wind would rush through the house. George and me would dare each other to go in. We'd give all kinds of excuses not to go in.

Try Your Skill Read the following sentences. Proofread each one for errors in grammar, spelling, punctuation, and capitalization.

1. Black bear's hibarnat every Winter.
2. juan leeped from the truck to the grownd.
3. When you are tired its hard to get up and jog.
4. Put on these Ear muffs on your head.
5. I seen mr. Roberts run toward the gym.

Keep This in Mind

- Revising is the final step in the process of writing.
- Revise your first draft to improve your ideas, organization, and word choice.
- Proofread to find and correct errors in grammar, capitalization, punctuation, and spelling.

Now Write Use what you have learned in this lesson about revising to revise the first draft of your paragraph. When you are satisfied with your paragraph, write it in its final form. Make your work as neat as possible. Proofread the paragraph, reading it aloud one last time. Save your paragraph.

79

Optional Practice

Tell students to exchange with a partner the paragraphs they have been writing, and to check each other's paragraphs for the following:

- Completeness of sentences
- Mechanics such as capitalization and punctuation of sentences and indentation of the paragraph
- Spelling
- A direct, interesting topic sentence
- Sentences that develop the idea in the topic sentence
- An ending that sums up the main idea

Have each student write any suggestions for improvement on a separate sheet of paper.

Extending the Lesson

Introduce the idea of putting out a collection of students' writing. Explain that periodically you will ask for samples of their writing to save for the collection. Encourage students to turn in copies of their completed paragraphs.

On-page teaching suggestions

The text provides ideas for motivating the student, presenting the lesson, and providing enrichment.

Individualizing

Each section provides approaches for adjusting the basic lesson to different levels of ability or skill development.

Extending the lesson

An enrichment lesson or exercise suggests way students can apply the concepts outside of the English classroom.

Guidelines for evaluating composition

Special pages offer guidelines for teaching and evaluating student writing, including an evaluation form.

Other McDougal, Littell Programs

Building English Skills

Building English Skills is the only complete, developmental grammar and composition program for grades 1–12. Skills are developed sequentially from one grade to the next, with each level reinforcing and extending the skills learned earlier.

The McDougal, Littell Literature Series

The *McDougal, Littell Literature* Series for grades 7–12 provides an in-depth presentation of literary types at every level to give students a strong grasp of the possibilities of each genre.

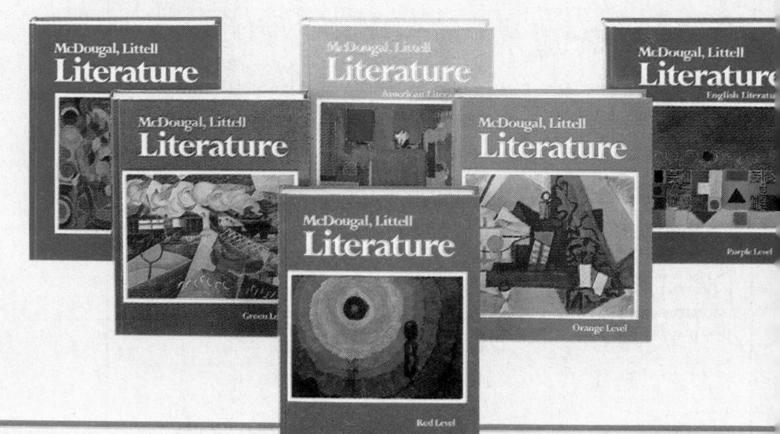

Reading Literature Series

Reading Literature is a new literature program for grades 7–12 that combines high-quality literature selections with developmental instruction in reading skills. The program builds skills in comprehension, reading literature, vocabulary, and writing. In addition, related skills such as study and research, speaking and listening, and critical thinking are reinforced throughout.

Teaching Special Populations

Many classrooms in our society include students with special language needs. Some of these students may have learning disabilities (LD). Others may be learning English as their second language (ESL). Still others may speak a nonstandard dialect of English (NSD). These students are likely to encounter special difficulties in mastering some of the concepts and acquiring some of the skills presented in *Basic Skills in English.*

The purpose of this section is to make the classroom teacher aware of these students and the learning difficulties they may face. A teacher who understands the special needs of these students can make certain that they are not penalized for learning deficiencies beyond their control. At the same time, the teacher will be better equipped to help these students fulfill their potential.

The text for *Basic Skills in English* has been reviewed by consultants whose areas of expertise include the problems faced by LD, ESL and NSD students in the English classroom. Our consultants' general suggestions for adapting *Basic Skills in English* to the special needs of these students are provided on the following pages. Additionally, specific suggestions for teaching special populations are presented at the beginning of each writing section and at the back of this book.

Special Consultants

Rebecca Benjamin, Educational Consultant, Albuquerque, New Mexico

Grace Massey Holt, Instructor of English as a Second Language, California State University, Sacramento, California

Dr. Eleanor Wall Thonis, District Psychologist, Wheatland School District, Wheatland, California

Karen Bustelo Wehle, S.L.D. Teacher, Leon County School District, Tallahassee, Florida

Virginia Woods, Secondary Resource Teacher, Dripping Springs Independent School District, Dripping Springs, Texas

Following are some general strategies for modifying lessons and assignments to help LD, ESL, and NSD students overcome some of their difficulties.

Learning Disabled Students

LD students typically have average or above average potential. However, specific areas of deficiency, which vary from student to student, can make the processing of information and the acquisition of skills difficult. There are many learning problems that can be included under the general heading "learning disabilities."

Specific areas of dysfunction include auditory memory, auditory discrimination, visual memory, visual discrimination, fine motor coordination, gross motor coordination, written expression, and oral expression.

It is important for the teacher to realize that these learning difficulties are beyond the students' control. Learning disabilities may be the result of brain damage, central nervous system dysfunction, mild cerebral palsy, or other physical impairment. Therefore, what may appear to be inattentiveness or an uncooperative attitude on the part of a student may actually be a sign of his or her inability to learn through conventional methods. Nevertheless, learning disabled students can compensate for their handicaps and overcome their problems. This is most likely to occur when teachers understand their students' strengths and limitations and are willing to adjust assignments and the presentation of material to maximize the chances for success.

Whenever possible, the teacher should work with counselors and special education teachers to determine the specific nature of a student's disability. This will allow the teacher to devise strategies for circumventing the disability. Some general strategies that apply to many kinds of learning disabilities are presented here. However, the teacher is encouraged to improvise new methods and to modify material as necessary for individual students.

General Areas of Difficulty

Whatever the nature of a student's disability, there are certain predictable problems that will impede his or her efforts to learn:

1. short attention span
2. poor memory
3. difficulty in generalizing
4. hyperactivity
5. distractability
6. low motivation
7. poor motor coordination

These problems of concentration and memory are usually compounded by low levels of acquired skills:

1. low reading level
2. inability to organize work and ideas
3. laborious and illegible handwriting

General Strategies

There are several strategies the teacher can use to counter learning disabilities.

1. Seat the students in the front of the classroom where there are no obstructions to sight or hearing.
2. Present essential information both orally and in writing. Reinforce written material in the text with oral explanation or with tape recordings made by the teacher, the student, or the student's parents. Write oral instructions and assignments on the board, and provide a written study guide that highlights the key points of oral presentations.
3. Supply visual aids whenever possible, to reinforce

material from the text. Simple charts, diagrams, photographs, and other illustrations may help to clarify the relationships among ideas.

4. Repeat important ideas frequently and begin each lesson with a summary of the material covered the previous day. This will help students to compensate for poor short- and long-term memory. Repeat assignments more than once, and give them both orally and in writing.
5. Demonstrate the correct way to complete an assignment. Work one or more problems on the board, showing the students how to go about answering them. Break down the assignment into steps, and be sure that the order of the steps is clear.
6. Give two grades for written work, one for content and another for mechanics. This two-grade system rewards students for good ideas despite mechanical shortcomings. Do not penalize students with visual disabilities for misspellings.
7. Allow students to answer test questions orally, either directly to the teacher or into a tape recorder. This can help to eliminate the anxiety caused by the prospect of writing under the pressure of time.
8. Help the students find shortcuts so that they can avoid writing long or difficult words repeatedly. When complete words or sentences are unnecessary, devise abbreviatons. For example, use *D.*, *Int.*, *Imp.*, and *E* instead of *Declarative, Interrogative, Imperative,* and *Exclamatory* for completing exercises on the types of sentences. Allow LD students to print rather than write if printing is easier and more legible. You might also suggest that students with writing difficulties learn to type.

Modification of Material

The teacher may find that some modification of the course material in *Basic Skills in English* will be necessary so that learning disabled students can keep pace with the rest of the class.

1. Break long-term assignments into shorter, individual tasks that can be assigned on a step-by-step, short-term basis.
2. Shorten and simplify all regularly assigned work; these students must put extra time and effort into completing their work. When possible, allow the students to select one, or a few, of several questions, topics, or exercises.
3. Simplify the assignments for written paragraphs and compositions, and allow students to work with partners or to put first drafts on tape.
4. If the reading level of a Section is too advanced, explain important vocabulary words and concepts before asking the students to read it.
5. Either supplement or replace difficult terms from the text with simpler ones. For example, when teaching the types of sentences, supplement or replace the terms *Declarative, Interrogative, Imperative,* and *Exclamatory* with words like *Statement, Question, Command,* and *Strong Feeling.*
6. Review "Study and Research Skills" with LD students several times during the year. This chapter will help them to overcome their difficulties in organizing work and ideas.

English as a Second Language

Students whose first language is not English face a number of challenges. These vary in difficulty depending on their native language and culture and their familiarity with American language and culture. In general, speakers of Indo-European languages, such as German and Spanish, will probably have fewer problems learning English grammar and adapting to American culture than will, for example, speakers of Oriental languages. However, most ESL students share one distinct disadvantage: they lack their classmates' years of experience with the English language, experience which is necessary to the thorough understanding of most standard textbooks. For these students, the problems of using textbooks fall into two categories: difficulty with the complexity of language and unfamiliarity with cultural references.

The Sections of *Basic Skills in English* are written at a level that may be difficult for many ESL students. Moreover, the exercises and assignments require students to analyze and manipulate a language that many ESL students will not yet have acquired fully. Once a teacher is aware of these problems, he or she can implement certain techniques for reducing the difficulties ESL students face.

General Strategies for Countering Language Barriers

To help students overcome these difficulties posed by an unfamiliar language, the following strategies may be employed:

1. Introduce new topics at a slower pace, and provide guided practice with increased feedback and monitoring.
2. Read aloud the essential parts of each Section, allowing time for explanation, examples, and the answering of questions.
3. In explaining any abstract concept such as "unity," it is better to go to the specific example first, pointing out the elements that show unity before giving the definition. Beginning from the concrete and particular enables ESL students to follow to the general or abstract.
4. Shorten assignments for these students and allow extra time for the acquisition of concepts.
5. Simplify all activities and exercises linguistically whenever possible. Exercises from intermediate ESL books would be helpful.
6. Build into the activities as many visuals, manipulatives, and concrete experiences as possible. The teacher may have to illustrate and demonstrate meanings as if with small children. However, these aids should not be presented in a condescending manner—the age and intelligence of the students must be respected.
7. Suggest that students work as a group whenever possible. Allowing each student to go through activities with the group before having to do it individually gives him or her enough concrete practice and confidence to try it alone.
8. Correct written exercises and compositions carefully so that students will not continue to practice mistakes.
9. Precede *every* writing activity for ESL students with a similar oral activity; these students must have opportunities to speak and express themselves *before* writing. This procedure provides students with an opportunity to separate the tasks of clarifying ideas and translating them into correct written form.
10. Encourage ESL students to keep journals in English, recording thoughts and impressions without concern for grammar, spelling, and pronunciation. It will help them to develop fluency and build confidence and enjoyment in their writing, and it will free them from anxieties about absolute correctness.
11. To reduce the demands on the teacher's time, recruit advanced students to help the ESL students understand written materials and to monitor their practice.

General Strategies for Countering Culture Differences

The other major problem area for ESL students will be

the many cultural references that appear in the text. Some ESL students will have trouble determining gender from proper names alone. They may also have difficulty understanding references to national holidays, sports, individual teams, famous people, geography, foods, and popular culture. Slang, jargon, and idiomatic expressions are tied directly to a specific culture and are often impossible to translate. The following approaches could alleviate these problems:

1. Encourage class discussion to clarify cultural references and provide general information to the whole class. This and other oral work will greatly facilitate the ESL student's acquisition of English.
2. Encourage discussion of differences and similarities between ESL student's language and English. In covering verb tenses, for example, ask the ESL student to explain how his or her language expresses ideas of time. Such comparisons would benefit the American students by exposing them to aspects of language that are not part of their own linguistic experience.
3. Encourage ESL students to write about their native customs, holidays, geography, celebrities, and foods.
4. Encourage ESL students to read material, at an appropriate level, about specifically American people, places, and events. You might even provide these students with newspapers and popular magazines to read and discuss. This will help them acquire the common stock of information familiar to most Americans.

Speakers of Nonstandard Dialects

Everyone speaks some sort of dialect. The speech of Americans in one section of the country differs in at least some aspects of pronunciation, vocabulary, and grammar from the speech of people in other sections. In addition, certain social, ethnic, and racial groups share a distinct way of speaking. Sometimes, however, the dialect common to a particular group departs so much for the most widely used and accepted dialects that it is termed "nonstandard." It is with students who speak such a dialect that this section is concerned.

Teachers must be aware that nonstandard dialects are legitimate language variations. These dialects follow regular phonological and semantic rules and serve the needs of the speech communities that use them. Speakers of "nonstandard" dialects are not necessarily careless speakers of English, nor should the variant features of these dialects be considered "errors." On the other hand, speakers of these dialects should be led to recognize that they cannot participate fully in mainstream American culture and society without understanding and effectively employing its language, standard English.

General Strategies

The teacher of NSD students should bear in mind that one need not, and indeed should not, eradicate one dialect in order to teach another. Instead, the teacher should implement the following strategies:

1. Encourage students to learn the patterns and usages of standard English for use in contexts where it is considered more appropriate: for academic writing and speech; in job applications and interviews; at work, if co-workers or superiors use standard English.
2. Encourage students to use the dialect that sounds natural both to speaker and listener in informal, casual, and family settings.
3. Tape-record samples of speech from various settings: playing fields, family gatherings, classrooms, committee meetings. Guide students in analyzing the vocabulary, sentence patterns, and grammar

used in these different contexts. This practice will make them see that various forms exist within a single language, each form being appropriate in a certain setting. It has proven to be a non-threatening way to increase all students' awareness of linguistic variation and to demonstrate that shifting from one form of speech to another does not involve a loss of identity.

4. When covering the Writing Sections have the NSD students keep journals, in whatever dialect is natural and comfortable, of thoughts, feelings, impressions, and experiences. Read the journals periodically and comment in writing about potential uses for the material in later compositions. Do not "correct" variations from standard usage or point out misspellings. Such nonjudgmental reading, discussion, and subsequent use of the journal entries will reinforce the lesson that writing in standard English is not abandoning one's identity but communicating it to a wider audience.
5. Establish small-group "workshops" consisting of four or five students, and have them collaborate in making suggestions for revision of written work. This strategy educates all of the students about the various dialects spoken in class.
6. Take note of the areas of grammatical variations that appear in the NSD students' written work, and be prepared to help the students with any problems that arise from these differences. Speakers of so-called Black English, for example, may have trouble with verb usage, for some of the principles of standard grammar and usage do not match their speech patterns. For similar reasons speakers of Hawaiian dialect may encounter difficulties with articles and pronouns. Other groups may have trouble with word order in sentences. Provide extra coaching, more details explanations, and additional practice, until the students have mastered the unfamiliar parts of standard dialect.

Specific suggestions for teaching composition to special populations appear at the beginning of each Composition Section of this book.

Specific suggestions for teaching grammar, usage, and mechanics to special populations appear at the end of this book.

Basic Skills in English

Purple Level

Yellow Level

Blue Level

Orange Level

Green Level

Red Level

JUNIOR HIGH
SUPER

THE McDOUGAL, LITTELL ENGLISH PROGRAM

Basic Skills in English

Red Level

Joy Littell, EDITORIAL DIRECTOR

McDougal, Littell & Company
Evanston, Illinois
New York   Dallas   Sacramento

AUTHORS

Joy Littell, Editorial Director, McDougal, Littell & Company

Edward Hagelin Pearson, Lincoln Junior High School, Park Ridge, Illinois

Kraft and Kraft, Developers of Educational Materials, Newburyport, Massachusetts

CONSULTANTS

Carole B. Bencich, Coordinator of Secondary Language Arts, Brevard County School Board, Rockledge, Florida

Dr. Sheila F. S. Ford, Coordinator for Secondary Language Arts, Spring Branch Independent School District, Houston, Texas

Marietta H. Hickman, English Department Chairman, Wake Forest-Rolesville High School, Wake Forest, North Carolina

Mary Evans Roberts, Supervisor of English and Language Arts, Savannah-Chatham Public Schools, Savannah, Georgia

ISBN: 0-86609-476-8 TE ISBN: 0-86609-477-6

Acknowledgments

Simon & Schuster: for entries from *Webster's New World Dictionary,* Students Edition; copyright © 1981 by Simon & Schuster, Inc. Macmillan Publishing Company: the Handbook section contains, in revised form, some materials that appeared originally in *The Macmillan English Series, Grade 5,* by Thomas Clark Pollock et. al., © 1963 by Macmillan Company. Used by arrangement.
(Acknowledgments are continued on page 604.)

Box 1667, Evanston, Illinois 60204

Composition

WRITING SECTION 1

Words: Building Your Vocabulary 1

Part 1 **It Grows on You** Learning About Language 2
Part 2 **Look Around** Learning Word Meaning from Context 4
Part 3 **Spell It Out** Definition and Restatement 6
Part 4 **Look Again** Using Context Clues: Examples 8
Part 5 **Make It Clear** Learning About Synonyms and Antonyms 10
Part 6 **Get Down to Bases** Learning Word Parts: Base Words 12
Part 7 **Small Beginnings** Learning Word Parts: Prefixes 14
Part 8 **Last, but Not Least** Learning Word Parts: Suffixes 16
Part 9 **Keep Up with the Times** New Language for Special Fields 18

WRITING SECTION 2

Using a Dictionary 21

Part 1 **Look It Up** How To Use a Dictionary 22
Part 2 **Show Me the Way** How To Use Guide Words 25
Part 3 **It's All There** How To Read a Dictionary Entry 27
Part 4 **Does It Fit?** How To Find the Meaning of a Word 30

WRITING SECTION 3

The Right Language at the Right Time 33

Part 1 **Up to Standards** Writing and Speaking Standard English 34
Part 2 **Staying Cool** Using and Misusing Slang 36

WRITING SECTION 4

Writing Better Sentences 39

Part 1 **Put It Together** Learning About Sentences 40
Part 2 **Getting Nowhere** Avoiding Empty Sentences 42
Part 3 **Cut It Out!** Avoiding Padded Sentences 44
Part 4 **All Join Hands** Combining Sentences 46

WRITING SECTION 5

A Look at Paragraphs 49

Part 1 **What Is It?** Learning About Paragraphs 50
Part 2 **United We Stand** Recognizing Unity in a Paragraph 52
Part 3 **What's It All About?** Using a Topic Sentence 54
Part 4 **Follow the Leader** Developing a Paragraph 56
Part 5 **What's in a Name?** Recognizing Three Kinds of Paragraphs 58

WRITING SECTION 6

Writing a Paragraph 61

Part 1 **Step by Step** Writing as a Process 62
Part 2 **What Do You Know?** Pre-Writing: Choosing a Subject 64
Part 3 **In Focus** Pre-Writing: Narrowing a Topic 66
Part 4 **A Better Birdfeeder** Pre-Writing: A Good Topic Sentence 68
Part 5 **Bits and Pieces** Pre-Writing: Gathering Ideas 70
Part 6 **First Things First** Pre-Writing: Organizing a Paragraph 72
Part 7 **Roughing It** Writing the First Draft 74
Part 8 **Saying Goodbye** The First Draft: Ending a Paragraph 76
Part 9 **Icing the Cake** Revising Your First Draft 78

WRITING SECTION 7

The Process of Writing 81

WRITING SECTION 8

The Narrative Paragraph 89

Part 1 **Details, Details** Pre-Writing: Developing a Narrative 90
Part 2 **Then What Happened?** Pre-Writing: Using Chronological Order 92
Part 3 **Who Said That?** Pre-Writing: Choosing a Point of View 94
Part 4 **First, Then, Finally** Writing the First Draft 96
Part 5 **Prance or Trudge?** Revising Your Narrative Paragraph 98

WRITING SECTION 9

The Descriptive Paragraph 101

Part 1 **Observe!** Pre-Writing: Gathering Sensory Details 102
Part 2 **Top to Bottom** Pre-Writing: Using Spatial Order 104
Part 3 **In, Out, and Around** Writing the First Draft 106
Part 4 **The Choice Is Yours** Revising Your Descriptive Paragraph 108

WRITING SECTION 10

The Explanatory Paragraph Telling *How* 111

Part 1 **How Do You Do?** Pre-Writing: Listing the Steps 112

Part 2 **What's Next?** Pre-Writing: Using Step-by-Step Order 114

Part 3 **Watch Your Step!** Writing the First Draft 116

Part 4 **Clear the Way** Revising Your Explanatory *How* Paragraph 118

WRITING SECTION 11

The Explanatory Paragraph Telling *Why* 121

Part 1 **State Your Case** Pre-Writing: Developing an Opinion 122

Part 2 **Save the Best for Last** Pre-Writing: Organizing an Opinion 124

Part 3 **Build Your Case** Writing the First Draft 126

Part 4 **In My Opinion** Revising Your Explanatory *Why* Paragraph 128

WRITING SECTION 12

A Look at Compositions 131

Part 1 **It's a Long Story** Learning About Compositions 132

Part 2 **Decisions, Decisions** Pre-Writing: Choosing a Topic 134

Part 3 **Getting It Together** Pre-Writing: Organizing Ideas 136

Part 4 **First Try** Writing the First Draft 138

Part 5 **Nobody's Perfect** Revising Your Composition 140

Part 6 **Wrap It Up** The Final Copy of a Composition 142

Part 7 **One More Time** Reviewing the Process of Writing 144

WRITING SECTION 13

The Narrative Composition 147

Part 1 **Get Started** Pre-Writing: Planning a Story 148

Part 2 **Action!** Pre-Writing: Plotting a Story 150

Part 3 **What's Your View?** Pre-Writing: Choosing a Point of View 152

Part 4 **First Impressions** Writing the First Draft 154

Part 5 **She Said, He Said** The First Draft: Using Dialogue 156

Part 6 **Go with the Flow** The First Draft: Using Transitions 158

Part 7 **A Second Look** Revising Your Narrative Composition 160

WRITING SECTION 14

The Descriptive Composition 163

Part 1 **It Makes Sense** Pre-Writing: Using Sensory Details 164
Part 2 **Try It Out** Writing the First Draft 166
Part 3 **In Conclusion** The First Draft: Concluding a Description 168
Part 4 **Good, Better, Best** Revising Your Descriptive Composition 170

WRITING SECTION 15

The Explanatory Composition Telling *How* 173

Part 1 **How Is It Done?** Pre-Writing: Listing the Steps 174
Part 2 **One Step at a Time** Pre-Writing: Using Step-by-Step Order 176
Part 3 **Say When** Writing the First Draft 178
Part 4 **Clearly Correct** Revising Your Explanatory *How* Composition 180

WRITING SECTION 16

Writing a Report 183

Part 1 **Narrow-Minded** Pre-Writing: Choosing a Report Topic 184
Part 2 **Just the Facts** Pre-Writing: Gathering Information 186
Part 3 **Order in the Cards** Organizing Notes for a Report 188
Part 4 **Putting It All Together** Writing the First Draft 190
Part 5 **The Finish Line** Revising a Report 192
Part 6 **Consider the Source** Listing Sources 194

WRITING SECTION 17

Clear Thinking 197

Part 1 **A Matter of Facts** Learning About Facts and Opinions 198
Part 2 **Because I Say So** Supporting Opinions 200

WRITING SECTION 18

Using the Library 203

Part 1 **A Good Place To Go** How To Use the Library 204
Part 2 **Pick a Card** How To Use the Card Catalog 207
Part 3 **Look Here!** How To Use an Encyclopedia 210

WRITING SECTION 19

Study and Research Skills 213

Part 1 **The First Step** Understanding the Assignment 214

Part 2 **Stop, Look, and Listen** Following Directions 216

Part 3 **Your Own Space** A Time and a Place To Work 218

Part 4 **Touchdown!** Achieving Goals with a Study Place 220

Part 5 **Five Steps** A Way To Study 222

Part 6 **Get It Down** Taking Notes 224

Part 7 **Get the Picture** Using Graphic Aids 226

Part 8 **Be Confident!** Answering Objective Test Questions 228

Part 9 **Write It Right** Answering Written Test Questions 230

WRITING SECTION 20

Letters and Forms 233

Part 1 **Hi There!** How To Write a Friendly Letter 234

Part 2 **A Good Send-off** How To Prepare Letters for the Mail 237

Part 3 **Thank You** How To Write Social Notes 239

Part 4 **Get Down to Business** How To Write a Business Letter 242

Part 5 **Please Send Me** How To Write a Letter of Request 245

Part 6 **Fill It Up** Filling Out Forms 248

WRITING SECTION 21

Giving a Talk 251

Part 1 **Hear Ye! Hear Ye!** Formal and Informal Talks 252

Part 2 **Explain Yourself** Planning an Informal Talk 254

Part 3 **Be Prepared** Preparing a Formal Talk 256

Part 4 **It's How You Say It** Making a Good Impression 258

Part 5 **Dress Rehearsal** Practicing a Talk 260

Part 6 **Attention!** Learning To Listen 262

Part 7 **The Verdict, Please** Judging a Talk 264

HANDBOOK

HANDBOOK SECTION 1

Learning About Sentences 269

Part 1 **What Is a Sentence?** 270
Part 2 **Different Kinds of Sentences** 273
Part 3 **Punctuating Sentences** 275
Part 4 **Parts of the Sentence** 276
Part 5 **The Simple Predicate, or Verb** 279
Part 6 **The Simple Subject, or Subject of the Verb** 281
Part 7 **The Subject in Unusual Positions** 283
Part 8 **The Subject in Imperative Sentences** 285
Part 9 **Compound Subjects** 286
Part 10 **Compound Predicates** 288
Sentence Patterns Word Order and Meaning 290
Additional Exercises 291
Mixed Review 296
Using Grammar in Writing 298

HANDBOOK SECTION 2

Using Sentences Correctly 299

Part 1 **Avoiding Sentence Fragments** 300
Part 2 **Avoiding Run-on Sentences** 302
Additional Exercises 304
Mixed Review 306
Using Grammar in Writing 307

HANDBOOK SECTION 3

Using Nouns 308

Part 1 **What Are Nouns?** 308
Part 2 **Common Nouns and Proper Nouns** 310
Part 3 **Singular and Plural Nouns** 311
Part 4 **Making Nouns Show Possession** 313
Sentence Patterns The N V Pattern 316
Additional Exercises 317
Mixed Review 319
Using Grammar in Writing 320

HANDBOOK SECTION 4

Using Verbs 321

Part 1 **What Are Verbs?** 321
Part 2 **Main Verbs and Helping Verbs** 326
Part 3 **Direct Objects of Verbs** 331
Part 4 **Linking Verbs** 333
Part 5 **Verb Tenses** 336
Sentence Patterns The N V N Pattern 339
Sentence Patterns The N LV N Pattern 340
Sentence Patterns The N LV Adj Pattern 341
Additional Exercises 342
Mixed Review 344
Using Grammar in Writing 346

HANDBOOK SECTION 5

Using Irregular Verbs 347

Part 1 **Principal Parts of Verbs** 347
Part 2 **Regular Verbs** 348
Part 3 **Irregular Verbs** 349
Part 4 **Practice Pages on Irregular Verbs** 352
Additional Exercises 367
Mixed Review 368
Using Grammar in Writing 369

HANDBOOK SECTION 6

Using Troublesome Verbs Correctly 370

Part 1 **Using the Right Form of *Be*** 371

Part 2 **Using the Right Verb After *There, Here,* and *Where*** 373

Part 3 **Some Confusing Pairs of Verbs** 374

Part 4 **Using Contractions** 379

Part 5 **Using Negatives Correctly** 380

Additional Exercises 383

Mixed Review 385

Using Grammar in Writing 387

HANDBOOK SECTION 7

Using Pronouns 388

Part 1 **Substituting Pronouns for Nouns** 388

Part 2 **Using Pronouns as Subjects** 391

Part 3 **Using Pronouns After Linking Verbs** 393

Part 4 **Using Pronouns as Objects** 394

Part 5 **Using *We* and *Us*** 396

Part 6 **Possessive Pronouns** 398

Additional Exercises 400

Mixed Review 403

Using Grammar in Writing 405

HANDBOOK SECTION 8

Using Adjectives 406

Part 1 **What Are Adjectives?** 406

Part 2 **Articles** 412

Part 3 **Predicate Adjectives** 413

Part 4 **Proper Adjectives** 414

Part 5 **Using Adjectives Correctly** 416

Part 6 **Making Comparisons with Adjectives** 417

Additional Exercises 422

Mixed Review 425

Using Grammar in Writing 427

HANDBOOK SECTION 9

Using Adverbs 428

Part 1 What Are Adverbs? 428
Part 2 Making Comparisons with Adverbs 431
Part 3 Adjective or Adverb? 433
Additional Exercises 437
Mixed Review 439
Using Grammar in Writing 440

HANDBOOK SECTION 10

Using Prepositions and Conjunctions 441

Part 1 What Are Prepositions? 442
Part 2 Objects of Prepositions 445
Part 3 Preposition or Adverb? 449
Part 4 Using Prepositional Phrases in the Right Place 450
Part 5 What Are Conjunctions? 452
Additional Exercises 455
Mixed Review 458
Using Grammar in Writing 461

HANDBOOK SECTION 11

Using the Parts of Speech 462

Part 1 The Parts of Speech 462
Part 2 Using Words as Different Parts of Speech 464
Additional Exercises 467
Mixed Review 468
Using Grammar in Writing 469
Cumulative Review 470

HANDBOOK SECTION 12

Making Subjects and Verbs Agree 472

Part 1 Rules for Making the Subject and Verb Agree 473
Part 2 Special Problems with Subjects 476
Additional Exercises 483
Mixed Review 484
Using Grammar in Writing 485
Cumulative Review 486

HANDBOOK SECTION 13

Using Compound Sentences 487

Part 1 **A Review of the Sentence** 487
Part 2 **What Are Compound Sentences?** 489
Additional Exercises 494
Mixed Review 495
Using Grammar in Writing 496
Cumulative Review 497

HANDBOOK SECTION 14

Diagraming the Sentence 500

Part 1 **What Is Diagraming?** 500
Part 2 **Diagraming Verbs and Their Subjects** 501
Part 3 **Diagraming Subjects in Unusual Order** 502
Part 4 **Diagraming Questions** 503
Part 5 **Diagraming Imperative Sentences** 504
Part 6 **Diagraming Sentences with *There*** 505
Part 7 **Diagraming Compound Subjects and Verbs** 506
Part 8 **Diagraming Sentences Containing Direct Objects** 507
Part 9 **Diagraming Sentences Containing Predicate Nouns** 508
Part 10 **Diagraming Sentences Containing Predicate Adjectives** 509
Part 11 **Diagraming Sentences Containing Adjectives** 510
Part 12 **Diagraming Sentences Containing Possessive Nouns** 512
Part 13 **Diagraming Sentences Containing Adverbs** 513
Part 14 **Diagraming Compound Sentences** 514
Additional Exercises 516
Mixed Review 518
Using Grammar in Writing 519

HANDBOOK SECTION 15

Capitalization 521

Proper Nouns and Adjectives 522
First Words 529
Additional Exercises 536
Mixed Review 538
Using Mechanics in Writing 540

HANDBOOK SECTION 16

Punctuation 541

Using the Period 542
Using the Question Mark 546
Using the Exclamation Point 547
Using the Comma 548
Using the Apostrophe 551
Using the Hyphen 554
Using Quotation Marks 556
Additional Exercises 561
Mixed Review 564
Using Mechanics in Writing 566

HANDBOOK SECTION 17

Spelling 567

Plan Your Study of Spelling 568
Rules for Spelling 571
Homonyms and Other Words Often Confused 577
Additional Exercises 583
Mixed Review 584
Using Mechanics in Writing 585
Cumulative Review 586

Section 1 Objectives

1. To understand that English is a changing language

2. To appreciate the value of context clues in learning the meanings of words

3. To find and use definition and restatement in context to discover word meanings

4. To recognize examples in context that suggest meanings of unfamiliar words

5. To use synonyms and antonyms to express variations in meaning

6. To use base words to understand the meanings of unfamiliar words

7. To learn the meanings and uses of common prefixes

8. To learn the meanings and uses of common suffixes

9. To learn that new technologies change and expand our language

Preparing the Students

Ask students how many vocabularies they have. Explain that they have three—a **listening vocabulary,** a **speaking vocabulary,** and a **reading vocabulary.** The listening vocabulary is the largest, and the speaking vocabulary is the smallest. Tell them that this section will help them to develop techniques for building their vocabularies.

Additional Resources

Mastery Test — Page 11 in the test booklet is recommended for use after teaching the section

Practice Book — pages 1–9

Duplicating Masters — pages 1–9

Words: Building Your Vocabulary

Part 1 **It Grows on You**
Learning About Language

Part 2 **Look Around**
Learning Word Meaning from Context

Part 3 **Spell It Out**
Definition and Restatement

Part 4 **Look Again**
Using Context Clues: Examples

Part 5 **Make It Clear**
Learning About Synonyms and Antonyms

Part 6 **Get Down to Bases**
Learning Word Parts: Base Words

Part 7 **Small Beginnings**
Learning Word Parts: Prefixes

Part 8 **Last, but Not Least**
Learning Word Parts: Suffixes

Part 9 **Keep Up with the Times**
New Language for Special Fields

Teaching Special Populations

LD Learning disabled students will generally require extensive practice and teachers should allow ample time for them to complete exercises. It may be useful to shorten exercises or to tailor them to students' specific needs. Check to see whether students are following instructions correctly. Additional exercises can be found in the Practice Book and under **Optional Practice** and **Extending the Lesson** in the Teacher's Notes for each section.

LD students may experience difficulties when asked to invent their own examples. In the **Now Write** sections, for instance, you may want to monitor progress individually.

ESL Students for whom English is a second language often lack the cultural experience necessary for determining word meanings from context. It will be necessary for you to establish context or help them understand the first meaning of a word before work can be completed.

Though competent native speakers, ESL students may lack alphabetizing skills or may only have used bilingual dictionaries. Whenever you teach word origins, irregular plurals, synonyms, base words, affixes, or compound words, see that students understand terms and examples. Allow extra time for exercises.

NSD For students who speak a nonstandard dialect, pronunciation problems often hinder their ability to find words in a dictionary. Encourage correct pronunciation through drill. When teaching synonyms, ask students to keep a list of the standard words equivalent to nonstandard forms they have used.

Part 1

Objective

To understand that English is a changing language

Presenting the Lesson

1. Read aloud and discuss **Here's the Idea.** Explain that the English language is made up of words from different sources. Some words are borrowed from other languages *(squash* from the Indian word *askutasquash),* some words are compounds *(outback, launchpad),* and some words come from people's names (*sandwich*) or place names (*denim*).

2. Discuss briefly the meanings of words in **Check It Out** that may be unfamiliar to some students.

3. Assign and discuss **Try Your Skill.** You might want the class to first guess at the origin of these words before they use their dictionaries.

4. After the class has completed **Now Write,** discuss the origins of the words in **Check It Out.**

Individualizing the Lesson

Less-Advanced Students

Before assigning any of the exercises, ask students to take out their classroom dictionaries. Review with them where to find the etymology, or history, of a word. (Refer to page 27.) Look up the word *sabotage.* Ask students what language it comes from. Also ask how it came to have the meaning that it has today. Repeat with the word *bacitracin.*

Part 1

It Grows on You

Learning About Language

Here's the Idea English is a living language. Like other living things, it grows and changes. Some words outlive their usefulness and are dropped from the language. From time to time, new words are added. These changes occur in many ways.

Borrowed Words Many English words are borrowed from other languages. English has borrowed words from the American Indian languages (squash), from French (garage), Spanish (cigar), German (noodle), and Dutch (cookie), among others.

Compound Words Other new words come from combining two words. *Motor* and *cycle* for example, were combined to form *motorcycle.* Other examples of compound words are *halfback*, *downtown*, *outdoors*, and *birthday.*

Words from People's Names Sometimes a person's name becomes a word. An example is *sandwich*, named after the Earl of Sandwich. It is believed that he ate such a snack while he gambled so he wouldn't have to leave for meals. Words from the names Charles *Boycott*, Rudolf *Diesel*, Gabriel *Fahrenheit*, and Louis *Pasteur* are also part of the English language.

In these and other ways, words have been added to English. Some of these words are so common today that it is hard to imagine that they were not always used. However, new ideas and inventions need new words. English changes as the world changes.

Building a good vocabulary will help you to express your thoughts and ideas clearly. A good vocabulary will help you communicate better with others.

Check It Out Read the following sentences. Notice the words that have been added to English.

1. Sometimes I *doodle* on my paper.
2. Hamburgers taste better with *ketchup*.
3. A *tornado* picked up Dorothy's house.
4. The pitcher left the *dugout* to warm up in the *bullpen*.
5. Dad's blue *cardigan* is old, but it's still his favorite sweater.

- How is English enriched by these new words?
- How can these words help you to communicate ideas more clearly?

Try Your Skill Read the following English words. Some were borrowed from other languages. Others are compound words or words made from names. Using a dictionary, try to find out how these words came into English.

tea	vampire	anteater	bloomer	zeppelin
pajamas	outfield	watchdog	watt	bookcase

Keep This in Mind

- English is a living language. It changes and grows.
- A good vocabulary will help you to express your thoughts and ideas clearly. It will help you communicate better with others.

Now Write Label your paper **It Grows on You.** Choose any five words that are mentioned but not explained in this lesson. Write the words on your paper. Check the meanings of the words in a dictionary. Then write a sentence using each word. Keep your sentences in your writing folder.

Advanced Students

Have students thumb through their dictionaries and find two new examples of borrowed words, compound words, and words from people's names.

Optional Practice

1. Repeat the **Try Your Skill** exercise on page 3 with these words.

rodeo	sawmill
bloomers	fanjet
backfield	limerick
Fahrenheit	caftan

2. Discuss with students words that have come into being from the name of a product. People refer to a brand name that has been strongly associated with the product and begin to use it as a generic name. Here are some examples.

Kleenex – tissues
Scotch tape – cellophane tape
Jell-o – gelatin
Xerox – copy

Ask the students to think of additional examples.

Extending the Lesson

Each day focus on the origin of one word, drawing from the list below.

hamburger	headlight
shoelace	graham cracker
mackintosh	coyote
popcorn	sled
chocolate	sequoia
hummingbird	teddy bear

Part 2

Objective

To appreciate the value of context clues in learning the meanings of words

Presenting the Lesson

1. Read aloud and discuss **Here's the Idea.** Write the word *context* on the board and make sure students know what it means. Point out that we do not always need to know all of the definitions of a word—just the one needed in a particular sentence or paragraph. Using the context can help the reader understand that meaning of the word.

2. Discuss **Check It Out.** Point out the different types of context clues used.

3. Assign **Try Your Skill.** Discuss the types of clues used by students.

4. Assign **Now Write.**

Individualizing the Lesson

Less-Advanced Students

Using an opaque projector, display a page from the students' science book. Then write a list of preselected words on the board. Ask students if they can determine the meaning of each word from the context.

Advanced Students

Have students select three of the words from the following list and find the meanings in a dictionary. Then they should write a sentence for each word that uses context clues to demonstrate meaning.

mauve	voyage	caribou
lemur	dusk	mansion
sulky	latch	scholar

Part 2

Look Around

Learning Word Meaning from Context

Here's the Idea English has so many words, no one can know all of them. Every reader comes across unfamiliar words from time to time. Sometimes you must look up a word in a dictionary. At other times you don't have to. The context can tell you the meaning.

The **context** of a word is the words and sentences around it. A word's context will often help you figure out what the word means. It may not tell you the exact meaning, but it can give you a general idea.

Read the following example. Try to figure out what the *italicized* word means.

> Australia has some strange native birds, like the *kookaburra*.

You couldn't draw a picture of a kookaburra from the information in this sentence. You do know, though, that it is an Australian bird. The context has helped you understand the meaning of an unfamiliar word.

You cannot always depend on the context to help you with unfamiliar words. Sometimes the context is no help. The example below gives no hints about the meaning of *kookaburra*.

> On the postcard was a picture of a *kookaburra*.

From the information in this sentence, a *kookaburra* could be a mountain, a kind of house, or almost anything.

When you see an unfamiliar word, look for context clues to its meaning. You may find clues in the same sentence as the new word. Sometimes you may have to read two or three sentences to find them. Here is a paragraph that provides context clues.

> You will rarely see pets on a farm. Every animal has a job to do. If a cat is not a good *mouser*, it has no place on a farm.

If you had read the word *mouser* in a list of words, you might not have known what it meant. However, from the context, you can tell it has something to do with a cat's job on a farm. From this you can guess that a *mouser* catches mice.

Check It Out Read the following sentences. Try to figure out what each italicized word means. Use context clues to help you.

1. Jill loves *jalapeños*, which are Mexican hot peppers.
2. The *galleon*, like all large ships, had a crew of hundreds.
3. We heard the *oriole* sing and saw its nest in the tree.
4. Everyone else hurried out, but Elaine *lingered* after class.

- What is the general meaning of each word in italics?
- What context clues helped you figure out the meaning?

Try Your Skill In each of the following sentences, there is a word in italics. Use context clues to figure out what that word means. Write what you think each italicized word means.

1. These streets *intersect*; that is, they cross one another.
2. *Icons*, or religious statues, filled the room.
3. Some blood diseases, like *hemophilia*, are inherited.
4. *Nocturnal* creatures, such as bats, sleep during the day.
5. The pony was not one color; instead, it was *piebald*.
6. If you don't obey the rule, you will be forced to *comply*.

Keep This in Mind

- Context, the words surrounding a word, often gives clues to the meaning of that word.

Now Write Label your paper **Look Around.** List four words you know. Write a sentence using each word. In each sentence, give context clues that would help a reader understand your word. Save the sentences in your folder.

Optional Practice

Repeat the **Try Your Skill** exercise on page 5 with these sentences.

a. The *aspidistra*, a plant of the lily family, has glossy green leaves.
b. Although the children raced down the trails, their mother *ambled* along behind them.
c. Belinda put the *cardamom* on the shelf with the other spices.
d. Some birds *molt;* that is, they shed their feathers before a new growth.
e. David grew beans, carrots, and *kohlrabi* in his vegetable garden.

Extending the Lesson

Have students page through their dictionaries to find five words whose meanings they do not know. Tell them to copy the words and their definitions and then to use each word in a sentence that includes a context clue. You might then play a game in which each student reads the sentences to a partner who must guess the meanings of the unknown words. The student would receive one point for each correct guess.

Part 3

Objective

To find and use definition and restatement in context to discover word meanings

Presenting the Lesson

1. Read aloud and discuss **Here's the Idea.** Remind the class that they encountered these two types of context clues in Part 2, although the clues were not specifically defined.

2. Read and discuss **Check It Out.** Contrast a direct statement of meaning (sentence 1) with a restatement of meaning (sentence 2).

3. Assign and discuss **Try Your Skill.** After completing the exercise, encourage students to check their guesses in a dictionary.

4. Work in a small group with the students who had difficulty in completing **Now Write** successfully.

Individualizing the Lesson

Less-Advanced Students

1. Emphasize the fact that the context clues of definition and restatement are usually preceded by key words or phrases or set off by commas. Read through the sentences in **Check It Out** and **Try Your Skill** aloud. Ask students to identify the key words or phrases or the phrase set off by commas.

2. Make it clear that *or* and commas do not always signal a restatement. Ask students which sentences present a restatement.

Or: Either Bo or Di will help you.
The rotund, or round, man played Santa Claus.

Part 3

Spell It Out

Definition and Restatement

Here's the Idea There are several kinds of context clues. The most direct clues to the meaning of a word are definition and restatement.

In a **definition,** the meaning of a word is given directly.

> We sailed the boat near Longboat Key. A *key* is a low-lying island or reef.

In a **restatement,** the meaning of a word is usually signaled by key words like *or, is called, that is, which is,* or *in other words.* Sometimes the meaning of the word is signaled by a comma or a pair of commas.

> At the zoo we saw a *gnu*, which is a large African antelope.
> Carbon monoxide is a *noxious*, or poisonous, gas.

Writers use definition and restatement to help readers understand unfamiliar words. If you stay alert for context clues, you will learn new words more easily.

Check It Out Read these sentences. Each uses definition or restatement as a clue to the meaning of the italicized word.

1. A mammal that carries its young in a pouch is called a *marsupial*.
2. The horse's coat had a healthy *gloss*, or shine, when it stood in the sunlight.
3. We ate *scrapple*, which is a food made from cornmeal and scraps of pork.
4. Our garden has spiky, colorful flowers called *gladioli*.
5. Jill saw a colony of *gannets*, large white sea birds, on the beach.

- What is the meaning of each italicized word?
- What is the clue in each sentence that signals a definition or restatement?

Try Your Skill Each of the following sentences has one word in italics. You can find context clues that tell what that word means. Write each word and its meaning.

1. A *cowlick* is a patch of hair that sticks up and won't lie flat.
2. I bought a *yucca*, a plant with stiff, pointed leaves.
3. Jim is *indecisive*; that is, he has trouble making up his mind.
4. The *smelt*, a small, silvery fish, has a delicate taste.
5. At first, McCall Junior High seemed like a *labyrinth*, a maze, to me.
6. Our cycling club stayed in *youth hostels*, which are inexpensive places for young travelers to spend the night.

Keep This in Mind

- The most direct context clues to the meaning of a word are definition and restatement.
- A definition or a restatement usually comes after key words or phrases, like *or, is called, that is, which is,* or *in other words*. A definition or restatement may be set off by commas.

Now Write Label your paper **Spell It Out.** List four unusual words that you can define. For example, the words might name special objects, tools, or foods. Imagine that each word you choose is unfamiliar to your reader. Write a sentence for each word. Use definition or restatement in the sentence. Use a key phrase or punctuation to alert the reader. Check your sentences by having a classmate see if your meanings are clear. Save your sentences in your folder.

Commas: He ordered squab, an edible pigeon, for dinner.
Tyler, Texas, is east of Dallas

Advanced Students

1. Ask students to find examples of words defined by the context clues of definition or restatement in their other textbooks. Discuss their examples in class.

2. Ask students to reread **Keep This in Mind.** Then ask them to write a sentence for each of the key words or phrases that introduce context clues.

Optional Practice

Repeat **Try Your Skill** with these sentences.

a. A spy does not want to be *conspicuous*, or easily noticed.
b. *Culottes* are women's pants cut to resemble a skirt.
c. *Calamary*, or squid, is served at that Greek restaurant.
d. The *piton*, which is a metal spike used for mountain climbing, came loose.
e. The audience was *blasé;* that is, they seemed bored with the play.
f. *Quinine*, a substance obtained from cinchona bark, is used to treat malaria.

Extending the Lesson

Ask each student to choose a type of work performed by a relative or acquaintance. Have the student interview the person to learn three or four words unique to the profession. The student should then write a sentence for each new word that contains a definition or restatement type of context clue.

Part 4

Objective

To recognize examples in context that suggest meanings of unfamiliar words

Presenting the Lesson

1. Read aloud **Here's the Idea.** Discuss the meaning of *example* in contexts familiar to the students; for example, food, items of clothing, local buildings, and landmarks.

2. Discuss **Check It Out,** asking students to explain the example in each sentence and to identify the key word or phrase.

3. Assign and discuss **Try Your Skill.** Find the meaning of each italicized word in a dictionary. Discuss how close the students' definitions came to the actual dictionary definitions.

4. Assign and discuss **Now Write.**

Individualizing the Lesson

Less-Advanced Students

Read aloud the following sentences and ask the students to find the key words that indicate context clues in each. Then ask them to give the definition of *pink* as it is used in each sentence.

a. *Pinks* and other flowers filled the vase in the hall.

b. Those shades of *pink* clash, especially that coral color and that hot purple color.

c. The *Pink,* like the other ships, stayed in the harbor until the storm stopped.

Advanced Students

Ask students to reread **Keep This in Mind** on page 9. Then ask them to

Part 4

Look Again

Using Context Clues: Examples

Here's the Idea Another kind of context clue is an **example.** When you read, check to see if an unfamiliar word is explained by one or more examples. The examples may give you a clue to the meaning of the word. Read this sentence.

> *Legumes,* such as peas, beans, and peanuts, are rich in protein.

The context tells you that peas, beans, and peanuts are examples of *legumes*. The words *such as* alert you that one or more examples are used as context clues.

There are several key words and phrases that tell you to look for an example. These include *especially, like, other, this, these, for example, for instance,* and *such as*.

Read two more sentences in which examples give you the meaning of the word *legumes*.

> Many legumes, beans and peanuts *for instance*, are rich in protein.
>
> Include peas, beans, peanuts, and *other* legumes in your diet.

None of these sentences tells you exactly what legumes are. However, they all use examples to make the general meaning of the word clear.

Check It Out Read the following sentences. In each sentence the context clue is an example.

1. *Herbs*, for instance mint and basil, have fragrant odors.
2. *Pit vipers*, such as rattlesnakes and copperheads, are poisonous.
3. The *produce*, especially the lettuce and tomatoes, is always fresh.

- What is the meaning of each of the italicized words?
- Which words or phrases signal an example is used?

Try Your Skill In each sentence, use the context to help you get the meaning of the italicized word. Number your paper from 1 to 5. Then write a definition of each italicized word.

1. *Crustaceans*, including lobsters, crabs, and shrimp, were displayed in a large aquarium.
2. *Quinces*, like many hard fruits, taste best when they are cooked.
3. The *sari* and other items of traditional Indian clothing are often very colorful.
4. *Carbonated* beverages, such as root beer and ginger ale, give some people the hiccups.
5. Guitars, *zithers*, and other stringed instruments are fun to play.

Keep This in Mind

- Examples are sometimes used as context clues.
- Several key words and phrases will alert you to look for an example. These words include *especially, like, other, this, these, for example, for instance,* and *such as*.

Now Write Label your paper **Look Again.** Choose three of the following words to use in sentences: *fish, mammals, board games,* and *vegetables*. Write a sentence using one or more examples as a context clue to the meaning of each of the words you have chosen. Make sure your examples are clear.

Put your work into your folder.

write a new **Try Your Skill** exercise. Here are some suggested words.

dulcimer	okra	marsupial
eaves	echo	ebony
marzipan	sloop	fowl

When students have completed their sentences, discuss them in class.

Optional Practice

Repeat **Try Your Skill** with these sentences.

a. *Citrus* fruits, such as oranges, grapefruits, and lemons, provide Vitamin C.

b. A sailor must be able to make a *clove hitch,* a bowline, a slipknot, and many other knots.

c. Many plants have medicinal uses; foxglove, for instance, provides *digitalis*.

d. *Arachnids,* including black widows, scorpions, and tarantulas, were on display at the science fair.

Extending the Lesson

Below are four words that have different meanings in the United States and in Great Britain. Have students choose one meaning of each word and then write a sentence that contains one or more examples as context clues. Ask volunteers to share their sentences with the class.

boot: type of foot covering (United States)
trunk of a car (Great Britain)

torch: flaming piece of wood (United States)
flashlight (Great Britain)

lift: to raise up (United States)
elevator (Great Britain)

braces: wires worn to straighten teeth (United States)
suspenders (Great Britain)

Part 5

Objective

To use synonyms and antonyms to express variations in meaning

Presenting the Lesson

1. Read aloud and discuss **Here's the Idea.** Write *synonym* and *antonym* on the board along with their definitions. Ask the students for additional examples of synonyms for simple words such as *talk* and *big.* Also ask them for additional pairs of antonyms.

2. Read and discuss **Check It Out.** When the class identifies *slow* as the antonym for *fast*, ask them to suggest synonyms for *slow (deliberate, sluggish, leisurely).* Discuss variations in meaning among these words.

3. Read and discuss **Try Your Skill.** When you feel certain that the students understand how to use precise synonyms and antonyms, assign **Now Write.**

Individualizing the Lesson

Less-Advanced Students

1. Ask students to replace the italicized word in each sentence with a synonym.

a. Carla *drank* her milkshake.
b. That is a *pretty* house.
c. Ted *wrote* something on the paper.
d. The pie was *good.*
e. Marcy *looked* at me over the newspaper.

2. Ask students to complete these sentences with antonyms for the italicized words.

Part 5

Make It Clear

Learning About Synonyms and Antonyms

Here's the Idea Many English words are close to each other in meaning. Such words are called **synonyms.** Synonyms may not mean *exactly* the same thing, however. One of them will usually have a meaning closer to the idea you want to express. Read the following sentence.

Helen ran around the track.

You may want to use a synonym for *ran* in this sentence. The synonym could give more specific information.

Helen **sprinted** around the track.
Helen **jogged** around the track.
Helen **loped** around the track.

Sprinted, jogged, and *loped* all have the same general meaning. They are all ways of running. But each word suggests a different way of running. *Sprinted* suggests that Helen ran at full speed. *Jogged* suggests that she ran at an easy, steady pace. *Loped* suggests that Helen ran with a long, swinging stride. One of these words is the best word to describe how Helen ran.

Knowing **antonyms** will also help you to choose the best words when you write. Antonyms are words with opposite meanings. *Long* and *short* are antonyms. So are *stop* and *go.*

Antonyms are useful when you want to make a contrast in order to emphasize an idea. For example, look at the following sentence: "Roberta was so *generous* that she made me feel *stingy.*" In this sentence, the word *stingy* helps to emphasize the meaning of its antonym, *generous.*

When you write, think about exactly what you want to say. What idea or feeling do you want to give the reader? When these ideas and feelings are clear in your mind, decide which words would best express them.

Check It Out Read the following sentences.

1. Joan is a *fast* walker.
2. Dr. Brown was *quick* to take notice of Martha's symptoms.
3. The deer made a *swift* retreat when Jerry approached it.
4. We noticed a *rapid* change in temperature.
5. Don's remark was *hasty*, and he regretted making it.

- Notice that the word *fast* and its synonyms have their own special meanings. Can you explain each meaning?
- What is an antonym for the word *fast*?

Try Your Skill Decide which synonym would best fit in each blank. Then write the complete sentence.

1. We are studying the art of ______ Rome.
   antique ancient old
2. We need ______ approaches to old problems.
   immature young fresh
3. Our Thanksgiving turkey was ______, not plump.
   little small scrawny
4. The ______ sound of the speaker's voice was soothing.
   loud deep thunderous
5. I heard Kim ______ when I made the same mistake again.
   talk murmur mutter

Keep This in Mind

- Synonyms are words that have similar meanings. Decide which synonym best expresses your idea.
- Antonyms are words that have opposite meanings.

Now Write Label your paper **Make It Clear.** List two synonyms for the word *quick*. Write a sentence for each synonym, using the special meaning of that synonym. Then write antonyms for the words you chose. Use a dictionary or thesaurus to help you. Save your work in your folder.

a. Kim is as *shy* as Kelly is ______.
b. Mark is *scatter-brained*, but Jim is ______.
c. Those peppers are *mild*, but these are ______.
d. Is the lemonade *sweet* or ______?
e. This watch is *cheap;* that one is ______.

Advanced Students

1. Have students write two synonyms for each of the following words.

eat drink child laugh

2. Ask the students to write an antonym for each of these words.

light kind healthy friend

Optional Practice

Using the instructions for **Try Your Skill,** have students complete these sentences.

a. The baby ______ at the top of his lungs.
   whimpered sobbed bawled
b. The weight lifter looked ______.
   wiry stalwart muscular
c. A ______ gently rustled the curtains.
   gale breeze wind
d. The ______ child threw a tantrum.
   sinister evil naughty
e. The perfume has a flowery ______.
   scent odor stench

Extending the Lesson

Give each student a thesaurus, or divide the class into groups and give each group a thesaurus. Explain that a thesaurus is a book of synonyms and antonyms. Then give each student a word to look up. Encourage the students to refer to a thesaurus when they write.

Part 6

Objective

To use base words to understand the meanings of unfamiliar words

Presenting the Lesson

1. Read aloud and discuss **Here's the Idea.** Avoid introducing the terms *prefix* and *suffix* as they will be presented in the next two lessons.

2. Work as a class on **Check It Out.** Help the students to identify the base words in which letters have been dropped or changed.

3. Assign and discuss **Try Your Skill.** Ask the class for further examples of words built on the same base words.

4. Assign and discuss **Now Write.** Some students may choose compound words rather than base words with prefixes and suffixes. Explain the difference. (Each part of a compound word is complete in itself; the syllables added to the beginnings or endings of words have no meanings apart from the base words.)

Individualizing the Lesson

Less-Advanced Students

Explain to students that not all words have added parts. As an example, write *famous* and *family* on the board. Ask for the base words. *Fame* is the base word in famous, and *family* itself is a base word. Give these additional words and ask which are base words with added parts.

trapper, sentence, paper, dive, rewrite, study, common, misspell, reading, unfold

Part 6

Get Down to Bases

Learning Word Parts: Base Words

Here's the Idea One way that language grows is by the addition of word parts to base words. A **base word** is a word on which other words can be built. If you can recognize a base word within a larger word, you will have a good idea what that larger word means.

Some base words have parts added in front of them. The word *untie*, for instance, is built on the base word *tie*. Other base words have parts added to the end of them. *Hopeless* is built on the base word *hope*. A word part added to a base word can change the meaning of the word. A base word may have a word part added at the beginning and at the end. The word *removable* is built on the base word *move*.

Recognizing base words helps you understand the meanings of many unfamiliar words. You may see what appears to be a strange word. If you look again, you may recognize its base word. If you know the meaning of the base word, you can probably figure out the meaning of the entire word. This becomes even easier when you learn the meanings of the word parts that are added to the base words.

Some base words are easy to spot. In the word *joyful*, the base word *joy* is easy to see. In some words, the base word may be harder to see. One letter may be changed or dropped. The word *famous*, for example, is based on the word *fame*. The letter *e* from *fame* has been dropped from the longer word.

When you look for base words, remember that the final letter or letters in base words may be changed or dropped. The word *persuasive* is based on *persuade*. *Beautiful* is based on *beauty*. Sometimes a letter may be doubled when an ending is added. For example, *runner* is based on *run*.

Check It Out Read these three sets of words.

changeable	unlikely	misfit
changeless	likable	fitting
unchanging	likeness	fitness

- Can you find the base words?
- In which words has the spelling of the base words been changed?

Try Your Skill Find the base word in each word listed below. On your paper, write the base word. Remember that the spelling of a base word can change when a word part is added.

1. traveler	11. nonviolent
2. careful	12. rebuild
3. prewash	13. unwanted
4. nonstop	14. eventful
5. harmless	15. unwrap
6. worrier worry	16. preschool
7. misspell	17. unforgettable
8. comfortable	18. boxer
9. reopen	19. sensible sense
10. defenseless	20. unlawful

Keep This in Mind

- Word parts can be added at the beginning or end of a base word to make new words.
- The spelling of a base word may change when an ending is added. Often the final letter is changed or dropped.

Now Write Label your paper **Get Down to Bases.** Open one of your textbooks to any page. Find and copy five words that contain base words. Underline the base words. Then make another word from the same base, and write it on your paper. You may use a dictionary. Save your words in your folder.

Advanced Students

Have students look through their text or a library book and find ten new words that have added beginnings or endings or both.

Optional Practice

Repeat the **Try Your Skill** exercise with these words.

teacher	tireless
fearful	misstep
regain	pregame
presoak	nontoxic
unclear	reliable rely
fighter	carrier carry
nonfat	resharpen
countless	unprofitable
reasonable	retest
masterful	unload

Extending the Lesson

Below is a list of words. Have students write the words in six columns, grouping words that have a common base. At the top of each column, have them write the base word. Encourage them to add words of their own to each column.

happier	happily
unicycle	bicycle
server	certainly
uncertain	joked
unhappiest	service
joking	tricycle
certainty	joker
unlock	relock
reserve	lockable

Part 7

Objective

To learn the meanings and uses of common prefixes

Presenting the Lesson

1. Read aloud and discuss **Here's the Idea.** Write the definitions for *base word* and *prefix* on the board. Suggest that students learn the definitions of the five prefixes introduced in this lesson.

2. Discuss **Check It Out.** Emphasize that prefixes change the meanings of base words.

3. Assign **Try Your Skill.** Review the method for determining whether a word contains a prefix. Work in a small group with students who have difficulty with this exercise.

4. Assign **Now Write.**

Individualizing the Lesson

Less-Advanced Students

1. To help students recognize words with prefixes, write these pairs of words on the board. One has a prefix. The other does not. Ask the students to select the words with prefixes. Then have volunteers draw circles around the prefixes.

mister, misspell
nonactive, none
unity, uncooked
realize, redivide
preschool, presents

2. Before assigning **Try Your Skill,** go through the list of words testing for prefixes. Allow students to complete the exercise independently.

Small Beginnings

Learning Word Parts: Prefixes

Here's the Idea In the last lesson you learned about base words. You learned how to recognize them in longer words. A word part added to the beginning of a base word is called a **prefix.** For instance, the word part *un-* is the prefix in *uncertain.*

There are many different prefixes. The meaning of the prefix changes the meaning of the base word. The prefix *un-* means "not," so *uncertain* means "not certain, doubtful."

Some words may seem to have a prefix, though they do not. The word *under*, for example, does not contain the prefix *un-*. How do you know this? Look at the word. If you cover the letters you think make a prefix, do you have a base word? No, you have only a nonsense syllable, *-der*. Therefore, the word *under* does not have a prefix. Not all words do.

Look at this list of common prefixes. If you learn these prefixes, you will be able to figure out what many words mean.

Prefix	Meaning	Examples
pre-	"before"	preschool
non-	"not"	nonsense
un-	"not"	unhappy
mis-	"wrong"	mistreat
re-	"again"	reappear

Check It Out Notice how these prefixes and base words work together to make new words.

precook — "to cook before"
nonfiction — "not fiction"
uneasy — "not easy"
misjudge — "to judge wrongly"
renew — "to make new again"

- What is the base word in each example?
- Does every prefix change the meaning of the base word?

Try Your Skill Number your paper from 1 to 20. Look at each word below. Decide whether it has a prefix or not. If the word does have a prefix, write the meaning of the prefix plus the base word. For example, next to the word *unhappy* you would write this: not + happy.

1. replay (again + play)
2. misty
3. unfair (not + fair)
4. pressure
5. none
6. receive
7. mispronounce (wrong + pronounce)
8. unity
9. prerecord (before + record)
10. misplace (wrong + place)
11. unskilled (not + skilled)
12. reelect (again + elect)
13. nonswimmer (not + swimmer)
14. ready
15. unnecessary (not + necessary)
16. prejudge (before + judge)
17. recipe
18. nonviolent (not + violent)
19. rebuild (again + build)
20. miserable

Keep This in Mind

- A prefix is a word part added at the beginning of a base word.
- Each prefix has its own meaning or meanings. The prefix changes the meaning of the base word to which it is added.
- Some words appear to have a prefix but do not. Check to see if a base word follows the word part that looks like a prefix.

Now Write Label your paper **Small Beginnings.** Find five words. Each should contain one of the five prefixes you have learned in this lesson. Use a dictionary. List the words on your paper.

Write five sentences, each one using one of the five words you found. Finally, study the words so that you can add them to your vocabulary. Save your sentences in your folder.

Advanced Students

Have students look up in the dictionary the five prefixes introduced in this chapter. Ask them the origin of each prefix. Then point out the great number of words that begin with these prefixes.

Optional Practice

Give students the following lists of prefixes and base words. Instruct them to make as many new words as possible. Ask them to check their work in a dictionary.

mis-	washed
non-	informed
pre-	voter
un-	labeled
re-	painted

Extending the Lesson

1. Have students define each of these prefixes and write two example words using each prefix.

tri- inter- sub-

2. Divide a large sheet of poster paper into five columns. Head each column with one of the prefixes introduced in this lesson. Ask the class to contribute words they learned when doing **Now Write** to the poster. Discuss the meanings of the words and how the prefixes changed the meanings of the base words. Display the completed poster in the classroom. Encourage the students to add words to each column.

Part 8

Objective

To learn the meanings and uses of common suffixes

Presenting the Lesson

1. Read aloud and discuss **Here's the Idea.** Put the definition of *suffix* on the board. Compare it to the definition of *prefix.* (Both are syllables added to base words; both change the meanings of base words.) Encourage the students to memorize the definitions of the five suffixes presented in the lesson.

2. Discuss **Check It Out.** You might want to find the base words with the students before answering the questions in this exercise.

3. Assign and discuss **Try Your Skill.** Note particularly the spelling changes that take place in *penniless, admirable, carrier, lovable, pitiful, runner,* and *generator.*

4. Assign and discuss **Now Write.**

Individualizing the Lesson

Less-Advanced Students

Review with students the spelling rules for adding suffixes to base words. (Handbook Section 17, pages 572–575.) Then have the students combine the following suffixes and base words. Discuss the spelling rules that apply to each case.

glory + ous (glorious) fancy + ful (fanciful)
plan + er (planner) drum + er (drummer)
console + able (consolable) nerve + ous (nervous)

Advanced Students

Have students put the following base words and suffixes together.

Part 8

Last, but Not Least

Learning Word Parts: Suffixes

Here's the Idea A word part added at the end of a base word is called a **suffix.** In the word *wonderful*, the suffix is *-ful.* Like a prefix, a suffix has a meaning of its own. A suffix also changes the meaning of the base word to which it is added.

In this lesson you will study five of the most common suffixes. When you learn the meanings of these five, you will have made a good start toward understanding many words.

Suffix	Meaning	Examples
-er (or **-or**)	"a person or thing that does something"	helper, reflector
-less	"without"	fearless
-able (or **-ible**)	"having this quality, able to be"	washable, sensible
-ful	"full of, having"	hopeful
-ous	"full of, having"	dangerous

When suffixes are added to base words, the spelling of the base word may change. A letter may be dropped from the base word. For example, *cure* becomes *curable*. Sometimes the final letter of the base word will be changed. For example, *beauty* becomes *beautiful*. At other times, the final consonant may double. For example, *swim* becomes *swimmer*. If you are not sure how to spell words when adding suffixes, check the correct spelling in a dictionary.

Check It Out Look at the following words and their definitions. Notice how the suffix and base word work together to make a new word.

winner — "a person or thing that wins"
operator — "a person who operates"
worthless — "without any worth"
reasonable — "having the quality of reason"
horrible — "having the quality of horror"
useful — "having a use"
famous — "having fame"

- Does every suffix change the meaning of the base word?
- In which words is the spelling of the base word changed?

Try Your Skill On your paper write each word below. Next to each, write the base word and the suffix. For example, next to the word *famous*, you would write this: fame + ous. Remember that the spelling of a base word may change when a suffix is added to it.

1. dryer (dry + er)	7. thriller (thrill + er)	13. lovable (love + able)
2. tearful (tear + ful)	8. actor (act + or)	14. pitiful (pity + ful)
3. joyous (joy + ous)	9. homeless (home + less)	15. runner (run + er)
4. counselor (counsel + or)	10. admirable (admire + able)	16. poisonous (poison + ous)
5. penniless (penny + less)	11. breakable (break + able)	17. generator (generate + or)
6. readable (read + able)	12. carrier (carry + er)	18. glamorous (glamor + ous)

Keep This in Mind

- A suffix is a word part added to the end of a base word.
- A suffix changes the meaning of the base word.
- A letter in the base word may be dropped, changed, or doubled when a suffix is added.

Now Write Label your paper **Last, but Not Least.** Write five words, each containing one of the five suffixes you have learned. You may use a dictionary. Then write five sentences, each using one of the five words. Save your work in your folder.

Tell them to check their work in a dictionary.

sin + er (sinner)	flaw + less (flawless)
heart + less (heartless)	basket + ful (basketful)
compose + er (compose)	honor + able (honorable)
beauty + ful (beautiful)	rigor + ous (rigorous)
collect + or (collector)	rely + able (reliable)

Optional Practice

Repeat the **Try Your Skill** exercise with these words.

1. dictator (dictate + or)	9. excusable (excuse + able)
2. studious (study + ous)	10. bountiful (bounty + full)
3. forceful (force + ful)	11. peaceable (peace + able)
4. monotonous (monotone + ous)	12. shapeless (shape + less)
5. preacher (preach + er)	13. vigorous (vigor + ous)
6. valuable (value + able)	14. merciless (mercy + less)
7. educator (educate + or)	15. fistful (fist + full)
8. speechless (speech + less)	

Extending the Lesson

1. Have students define each of these suffixes and write two example words with each.

-ness	-ory	-ence
-ment	-ion	-est

2. Provide each student with an article from a local newspaper. Instruct students to search for words that contain the suffixes introduced in this lesson. As students find words, have them write the words on the chalkboard. Discuss the meanings of the words.

Part 9

Objective

To learn that new technologies change and expand our language

Presenting the Lesson

1. Read aloud and discuss **Here's the Idea.** Ask students to contribute any new words they can think of.

2. Discuss **Check It Out.** Make sure students know what each word means.

3. Assign and discuss **Try Your Skill.** Have students try to figure out if the old and new meanings are related in any way.

4. Assign **Now Write.**

Individualizing the Lesson

Less-Advanced Students

Write only the definitions of all of the technical words used in **Here's the Idea** and **Check It Out** on the board or on ditto sheets. Allow students to refer to the list during the course of the discussion and select the definition that fits each word.

Advanced Students

Have students think of five additional words from either the space industry, or the science and technological fields. Ask them to make matching quizzes. Have the students trade papers and take the quizzes.

Optional Practice

Ask students for the computer-related definitions of these words. Stress the necessity of using an up-to-date dictionary for this assignment.

Part 9

Keep Up with the Times

New Language for Special Fields

Here's the Idea The world around you is constantly changing. People think of new ideas. They invent new machines. They have dreams, and they try to figure out ways to make those dreams become real.

As the world changes, you need to be able to describe the new things in it. The English language grows and changes to help you do so. New words are created. Old words are given new meanings.

The space industry, for example, has added a whole new vocabulary to our language. Can you tell what the following words mean?

countdown	astronaut	zero gravity
liftoff	launch pad	reentry

Computers are changing the world so fast that people speak of the *computer revolution*. The English language has grown to keep up with that revolution. Do you know what each of these terms means?

printout keyboard printer software

Science and technology also add new words to your language. How many of these words do you know?

laser	pacemaker	bionic
videotape	digital	synthesizer

Remember, the world does not stand still. Neither does the English language. If you want to be a part of the modern world, you need to know the new words that describe it.

Check It Out Look carefully at the following words. They are all space, computer, or science and technology terms. Some of them have older, more familiar meanings. Others are made up of two familiar words.

monitor	bioengineering	satellite
bit	booster	ultrasound
printout	word processor	heat shield

- Do you see how English words can take on brand new meanings to describe new ideas and inventions?

Try Your Skill Look up the following words in a dictionary. Write one familiar meaning for each word. Then write each word's space or computer meaning.

instrument used in weaving/spacecraft that makes frequent trips

1. shuttle
2. memory
3. burn to set on fire/firing of a rocket
4. hardware tools made of metal/devices of a computer

to recall/compute parts that recall information

Keep This in Mind

- The English language changes as the world changes.
- English changes in different ways. New words are created, and old words take on new meanings.

Now Write Label your paper **Keep Up with the Times.** Make a list of two space words, two computer words, and two new science and technology words that you know. Next to each word, write its meaning. Share your words with your classmates. Perhaps you and your classmates could make your lists into a *Dictionary of New Language.* Save your work in your folder.

terminal	program
byte	chip
hacker	input

Extending the Lesson

If your school has a computer center, have the students visit. Instruct the students to study the equipment and to look at the computer manual. Have them try to find new computer words.

Section 2 Objectives

1. To learn the general characteristics of dictionaries

2. To learn how to use guide words to locate entries in a dictionary

3. To understand how to interpret the information in dictionary entries

4. To understand that sentence context determines which definition of a word is appropriate

Preparing the Students

Ask students to page through their classroom dictionaries. Have them identify the types of information found in the front and back matter, as well as in the main portion of the book. Use dictionaries that include etymologies.

Additional Resources

Mastery Test — page 12 in the test booklet

Practice Book — pages 10–13

Duplicating Masters — pages 10–13

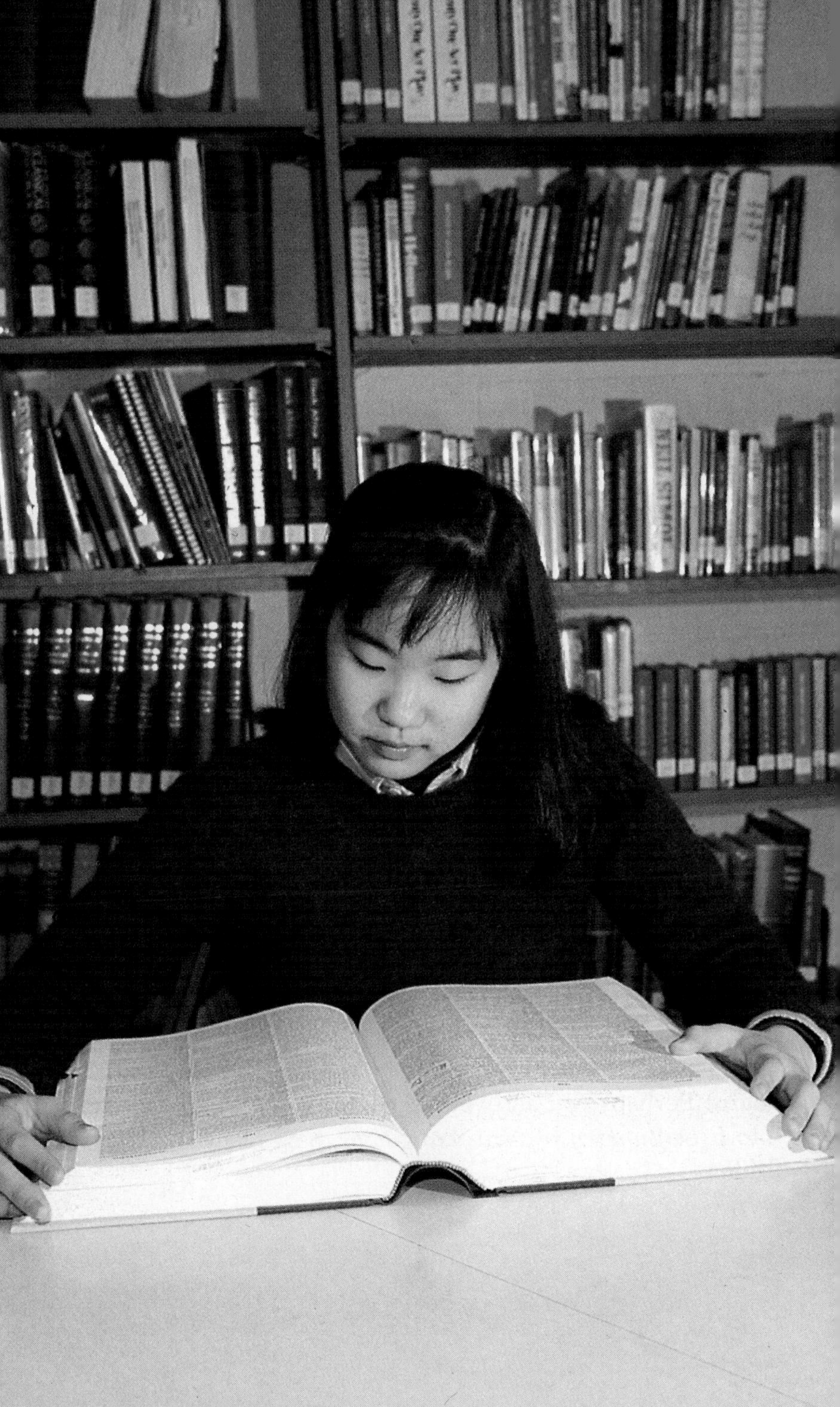

Using a Dictionary

Part 1 **Look It Up**
How To Use a Dictionary

Part 2 **Show Me the Way**
How To Use Guide Words

Part 3 **It's All There**
How To Read a Dictionary Entry

Part 4 **Does It Fit?**
How To Find the Meaning of a Word

Teaching Special Populations

LD Give LD students additional exercises to review alphabetizing skills. Make periodic checks of students' success in finding words in a dictionary.

ESL Pronunciation difficulties may inhibit these students in their efforts to find words in a dictionary. Carefully pronounce each word aloud and have students repeat it after you. Then show students the relationship between diacritical marks, syllables, and how sounds are pronounced. Remember, ESL students may only be familiar with bilingual dictionaries.

Synonyms and nuances of meaning are only apparent to ESL students once they understand the word's primary context. Use contextual examples to demonstrate a word's multiple meanings.

Use pretesting to determine ESL students' knowledge of parts of speech. (See Handbook Sections 3–11.) Remember that certain languages do not permit multiple functions for particular words. If students have trouble understanding words that function in more than one way, provide concrete examples and pair students with native English speakers. Carefully explain dictionary entries for irregular verbs and give students graphic examples.

NSD Ask students to look up the meaning and pronunciation of any unfamiliar words they come across. Encourage NSD students to keep a private list of nonstandard words they often use, together with the standard equivalents.

Part 1

Objective

To learn the general characteristics of dictionaries

Presenting the Lesson

1. Read aloud and discuss **Here's the Idea.** Emphasize that understanding alphabetical order is basic to using a dictionary.

2. Study the dictionary page in **Check It Out.** Compare the symbols and abbreviations used with those used in the classroom dictionary.

3. Assign **Try Your Skill.** Work with those students who made mistakes in alphabetizing.

4. Read **Keep This in Mind** aloud and then assign **Now Write.**

Individualizing the Lesson

Less-Advanced Students

1. For practice in alphabetizing, ask each student to write his or her first name on one side of a piece of paper and last name on the other. Ask each row of students to line up in alphabetical order by first name. Then ask the rows to line up in alphabetical order by last name.

2. Suggest that students either say the alphabet to themselves or write it out and use it when they are alphabetizing long lists of words.

Advanced Students

1. Ask students to alphabetize the following lists of things:

a. the last names of all of the class members
b. the states of the United States of America

Part 1

Look It Up

How To Use a Dictionary

Here's the Idea English has over 600,000 words, more than any other language. Few people know more than a small fraction of them. Everybody needs a dictionary.

What is a dictionary? It is a reference book containing a list of words and information about those words. A dictionary can tell you if a word exists. It can also help you to use words correctly.

The words in a dictionary are listed in alphabetical order. Words that begin with *a* come before words that begin with *b*, and so on. If two words begin with the same letter, they are alphabetized by the second letter. If the first and second letters are the same, the words are alphabetized by the third letter. The following columns of words are in alphabetical order:

admire	hold	schedule	yank
always	holdout	scheme	yarn
at	holiday	school	yawn

There are many kinds of dictionaries. Some dictionaries list only words in special fields, such as music or medicine. Bigger dictionaries may contain more words and a more detailed explanation of each word. The biggest dictionaries, like those on stands in a library, are *unabridged*. That means they contain nearly all the words in the language. An unabridged dictionary is useful when you want to look up an uncommon word.

Most of the time, through, a desk- or pocket-size dictionary, which is *abridged*, will suit your needs. It's helpful to keep one of these handy when you're reading or writing. It will help you to understand difficult words when you're reading. It will also help you to use words correctly when you're writing.

Dictionaries also vary in the ways they are organized and in the kinds of symbols and abbreviations they use. For this reason, it's a good idea to become familiar with the dictionary that you will use most often. Learn how the information for each word is organized. Study the explanatory material in the front of the dictionary to learn what the abbreviations and symbols stand for.

Check It Out Look at this portion of a dictionary page.

firefly 358 **fish and chips**

fire·fly (-flī′) *n., pl.* **-flies′** a small, flying beetle whose lower body glows with a light that goes off and on
☆**fire·house** (-hous′) *n. same as* FIRE STATION
fire insurance insurance against loss or damage resulting from fire
fire·light (-līt′) *n.* light from an open fire
fire·man (-mən) *n., pl.* **-men** **1.** a man whose work is fighting fires **2.** a man who tends a fire in a furnace, locomotive engine, etc. ☆**3.** *U.S. Navy* a nonrated enlisted man whose duties are concerned with the ship's engines, etc. ☆**4.** [Slang] *Baseball* a relief pitcher

FIREFLY (to ½ in. long)

Fi·ren·ze (fē ren′dze) *It. name of* FLORENCE, Italy
fire·place (fīr′plās′) *n.* a place for a fire, esp. an open place built in a wall, at the base of a chimney
fire·plug (-plug′) *n.* a street hydrant to which a hose can be attached for fighting fires
fire·pow·er (-pou′ər) *n. Mil.* **1.** the effectiveness of a weapon in terms of its accuracy and the number of shots it can fire **2.** the number of shots a given unit can fire in a short time
fire·proof (-pro͞of′) *adj.* that does not burn or is not easily destroyed by fire —*vt.* to make fireproof
☆**fire sale** a sale of goods damaged in a fire
fire·side (-sīd′) *n.* **1.** the part of a room near a fireplace; hearth **2.** home or home life
fire station the place where fire engines are kept and where firemen stay when on duty
fire·storm (-stôrm′) *n.* an intense fire over a large area, as one caused by an atomic explosion
fire tower a tower, usually in a forest, where a lookout is posted to watch for fires and give the alarm
fire·trap (-trap′) *n.* a building that would be unsafe in case of fire because it will burn easily or does not have enough exits
☆**fire wall** a fireproof wall for preventing the spread of fire, as from one room to the next
☆**fire·wa·ter** (-wôt′ər, -wät′ər) *n.* [prob. transl. of AmInd. term] alcoholic liquor: now humorous
☆**fire·weed** (-wēd′) *n.* any of various plants that grow readily on cleared or burned-over land
fire·wood (-wood′) *n.* wood used as fuel
fire·works (-wurks′) *n.pl.* **1.** firecrackers, rockets, etc. used, as in celebrations, to produce loud noises or a fancy show of lights: highest in pitch or the leading part —*adv.* **1.** *a*) before any other person or thing [guests are served *first*] *b*) before doing anything else [*first* we had soup] **2.** as the first point [*first*, let me say this] **3.** for the first time [I *first* met him yesterday] **4.** sooner; preferably [when told to beg, he said he'd starve *first*] —*n.* **1.** the first person, thing, class, place, etc. **2.** the first day of the month **3.** the beginning; start [at *first*, I believed him] **4.** a first happening or thing of its kind **5.** [*pl.*] the best quality of merchandise **6.** the winning place, as in a race **7.** the first or lowest forward gear ratio of a motor vehicle
first aid emergency treatment for injury or sudden illness, given while waiting for regular medical care —**first′-aid′** *adj.*
☆**first base** *Baseball* the base on the pitcher's left, the first of the four bases a runner must touch in succession to score a run
first·born (furst′bôrn′) *adj.* born first in a family; oldest —*n.* the firstborn child
first-class (-klas′) *adj.* **1.** of the highest class, rank, quality, etc.; excellent **2.** of the most expensive kind [a *first-class* cabin on a ship] ☆**3.** designating or of mail that is sealed and that carries the highest regular postage rates —**adv.** **1.** with the most expensive accommodations [traveling *first-class*] **2.** as or by first-class mail
first cousin the son or daughter of one's aunt or uncle
first finger the finger next to the thumb
first·hand (-hand′) *adj., adv.* from the original producer or source; direct [a *firsthand* report]
☆**first lady** [*often* **F- L-**] the wife of the U.S. president
first lieutenant a U.S. military officer ranking above a second lieutenant
first·ling (-liŋ) *n.* **1.** the first of a kind **2.** the first fruit, produce, offspring, etc.
first·ly (-lē) *adv.* in the first place; first
first mate a merchant ship's officer next in rank below the captain: also **first officer**
first offender a person found guilty for the first time of breaking the law
first person that form of a pronoun (as *I* or *we*) or verb (as *do*) which refers to the speaker or speakers
first-rate (-rāt′) *adj.* of the highest class, rank, or quality; excellent —**adv.** [Colloq.] very well [I feel *first-rate*]
☆**first sergeant** *U.S. Army & Marine Corps* the noncommissioned officer, usually a master sergeant, serving as chief assistant to the commander of a company, battery, etc.
☆**first-string** (-striŋ′) *adj.* [Colloq.] *Sports* that is the first choice for regular play at a specified position [our *first-string* quarterback]

- How are the words listed?
- What special symbols are used?
- What words are new to you?

2. To give practice in turning quickly to the proper section of a dictionary, have dictionary relay races. Give each row the same list of words and one dictionary. Have the first student look up the first word, write down the page number on which it was found, and pass the dictionary and list to the next student. See which team finishes first. Repeat the exercise with new word lists.

Optional Practice

1. Have students alphabetize each of these lists:

7 granary	9 photogenic	6 sprinkle
6 grammar	6 phosphate	9 sprite
8 grand	2 phoenix	4 springbok
5 grain	5 phonograph	1 sprig
4 graft	4 phonics	3 spring
3 gracious	3 phone	7 sprint
2 grace	1 phobia	10 spritz
1 grab	10 photograph	2 sprightly
10 graph	8 photoflash	8 sprit
9 grape	7 photocopy	5 springer

2. Ask students to write ten words that begin with the letter *n*. Then instruct them to put the words into alphabetical order and to write a short definition for each word. They should check their work in a dictionary.

Extending the Lesson

Have students make a list of the specialized dictionaries that can be found in the local or school library. Tell them to select three and to describe the content of each in one or two sentences.

Try Your Skill On your paper, write each of the following lists in alphabetical order. Then look up one word from each list in a dictionary and write the first meaning given.

1.	2.	3.	4.
3. cake	5. goat	2. none	1. stick
5. easy	3. give	6. now	3. still
1. army	1. get	3. noon	6. stitch
6. friend	6. great	5. note	2. stiff
2. barn	4. glum	1. nod	5. stir
4. duck	2. ghost	4. nose	4. sting

Keep This in Mind

- Dictionaries are reference books that list words alphabetically. They give explanations of each word.
- Have a dictionary nearby when you're reading and writing.
- Become familiar with the organization, symbols, and abbreviations of the dictionaries you use.

Now Write Imagine that you are a person who compiles dictionaries. On your paper, write the title of this lesson, **Look It Up.** Write ten words that begin with the first letter of your last name. Then put the words into alphabetical order.

Write a short definition for each word. Check your work in a dictionary. Save your word lists in your folder.

24

Show Me the Way

How To Use Guide Words

Here's the Idea In most dictionaries there are two **guide words** at the top of each page. They are in large, bold print. The left guide word is the same as the first word at the top of the page. The right guide word is the same as the last word at the bottom of the page. All the other words on the page are arranged alphabetically between the guide words. Look at this top portion of a dictionary page. *Grew* is the first word on the page. What would the last word be?

grew 417 **gripe**

where, formerly, many eloping English couples went to be married **2.** any similar village
grew (groo͞) *pt. of* GROW
grew·some (groo͞′səm) ***adj.*** *same as* GRUESOME
grey (grā) ***adj., n., vt., vi.*** *Brit. sp. of* GRAY
Grey (grā) **1. Charles,** 2d Earl Grey, 1764–1845; Eng. statesman; prime minister (1830–34) **2.** Sir **Edward,** Viscount Grey of Fallodon, 1862–1933; Eng. statesman; foreign secretary (1905–16) **3.** Lady **Jane,** Lady Jane Dudley, 1537–54; queen of England (July 10–19, 1553): beheaded
grey·hound (grā′hound′) ***n.*** [OE. *grighund*] any of a breed of tall, slender, swift hound with a narrow, pointed head and a smooth coat
grid (grid) ***n.*** [short for GRIDIRON] **1.** a framework of parallel bars; gridiron; grating **2.** a network of crossing parallel lines, as on graph paper **3.** a metallic plate in a storage cell for conducting the electric current **4.** an electrode, usually a wire spiral or mesh, for controlling the passage of electrons or ions in an electron tube —☆***adj.*** [Slang] of football

GREYHOUND (28 in. high at shoulder)

☆**grid·der** (grid′ər) ***n.*** [< GRID, *adj.* & GRIDIRON] [Slang] a football player
grid·dle (grid′'l) ***n.*** [< Anglo-Fr. *gridil* < OFr. *graïl* < L. < *craticula*, gridiron < *cratis:* see CRATE] a flat, metal plate or pan for cooking pancakes, etc. —***vt.* -dled, -dling** to cook on a grid-
grill·room (gril′ro͞om′) ***n.*** a restaurant that makes a specialty of grilled foods
grill·work (-wurk′) ***n.*** a grille, or something worked into the form of a grille
grilse (grils) ***n.**, pl.* **grilse, grils′es:** see PLURAL, II, D, 2 [<? OFr. dim. of *gris*, gray] a young salmon on its first return from the sea to fresh water
grim (grim) ***adj.*** **grim′mer, grim′mest** [OE. *grimm* < IE. base *ghrem-*, angry] **1.** fierce; cruel; savage *[war is grim]* **2.** hard and unyielding; relentless; stern *[grim courage]* **3.** appearing stern, forbidding, harsh, etc. *[a grim face]* **4.** frightful or shocking; ghastly *[grim jokes about death]* —see **SYN.** at GHASTLY —**grim′ly *adv.*** —**grim′ness *n.***
gri·mace (gri mās′, grim′əs) ***n.*** [Fr. < OFr. *grimuche*, prob. < Frank.: for IE. base see CHRIST] a twisting of the face in fun or in a look of pain, disgust, etc. —***vi.* -maced′, -mac′ing** to make grimaces —**gri·mac′er *n.***
gri·mal·kin (gri mal′kin, -môl′-) ***n.*** [earlier *gray malkin* (cat)] **1.** a cat; esp., an old female cat **2.** a spiteful or harmful old woman
grime (grīm) ***n.*** [prob. < Fl. *grijm:* for IE. base see CHRIST] sooty dirt rubbed into or covering a surface, as of the skin —***vt.*** **grimed, grim′ing** to make very dirty or grimy
Grimm (grim), **Ja·kob (Ludwig Karl)** (yä′kôp), 1785–1863 & **Wil·helm (Karl)** (vil′helm), 1786–1859; Ger. brothers who worked in language studies and together made a collection of fairy tales

Guide words help you find words quickly. Look at them as you flip the pages searching for your word. Suppose that the word you want is *newt*. First, look for guide words beginning with *n*. Next, look for guide words beginning with *ne*. After that, look for guide words beginning with *new*. Soon you'll come to a page where the left guide word comes alphabetically before *newt*. The right guide word comes alphabetically after *newt*. Now you have found the right page.

Part 2

Objective

To learn how to use guide words to locate words in a dictionary

Presenting the Lesson

1. Read aloud and discuss **Here's the Idea.** Emphasize the importance of knowing how words are alphabetized.

2. Discuss **Check It Out.** Ask students to open the classroom dictionaries and to locate the guide words on several pages.

3. Assign **Try Your Skill.** Select five of the words. Ask students to write the guide words for the pages on which these words appear in their own dictionaries.

4. Read **Keep This in Mind** aloud and then assign **Now Write.**

Individualizing the Lesson

Less-Advanced Students

After discussing **Check It Out,** ask students to take out their classroom dictionaries. Ask them to compare the page layout and the position of the guide words with the sample dictionary page in **Here's the Idea** on page 25. Then ask students to refer to page numbers that you have selected in advance and identify the guide words. For each page, dictate at least three words which the students must identify as being on, before, or after that page.

Advanced Students

1. Ask the students to find the guide words in their dictionaries for the following words: *verse, mirror, photograph, annual,* and *export.*

2. Have the students find the guide words in their own dictionaries for the words in **Try Your Skill.**

Optional Practice

Here are several sets of guide words followed by lists of words. Ask the students to determine if the words on each list fall on, before, or (after) the page on which the guide words appear.

fed/feint	real/rebel
favor	ready
federal	reap
(feisty)	(rebus)
feeler	(rebound)
feature	rear

tart/tattoo

tattle
tar
taste
(taut)
tartar

Extending the Lesson

Use the classroom dictionaries to play a game.

Write a sentence in this pattern: adjective, noun, verb, adverb (for example, *Small cars move quickly*). For each word, give the students these directions:

1. Turn to the page with the guide words _____ and _____. (Insert the guide words on the page for *small.*)
2. Find the word that means _____. (Insert the meaning of *small.*)
3. Write the word.

After doing this four times, the students will have written the entire sentence.

Check It Out Look at the portion of a dictionary page on page 25.

- What are the guide words for this page? Would you find the word *grin* on this page? Which way would you turn the pages to find *great*?

Try Your Skill At the top of a sheet of paper, write the following sets of guide words: *back/boat, break/but, tab/tall,* and *tame/tax*. Look at the list of words below. Find the words that go below each set of guide words. Write them under the correct set in alphabetical order.

brave	tan	tape	bite
tag	take	bark	target
tarnish	brink	tactic	beef
blue	big	tacky	tax
break	breath	bring	taste

back/boat	break/but	tab/tall	tame/tax
back	break	tacky	tan
beef	breath	tactic	tape
big	bring	tag	target
bite	brink	take	tarnish
blue			taste
			tax

Keep This in Mind

- Dictionary guide words show the alphabetical range of words on each page. The left guide word is the same as the first word on the page. The right guide word is the same as the last word on the page.

Now Write Imagine that you are writing a composition about airplanes. You want to look up the following words: *aileron, elevator, fin, fuselage, landing gear, rudder, stabilizer,* and *wing*.

On your paper, write the title of this lesson, **Show Me the Way.** List the words above. Find each word in the dictionary. Next to each word, write the guide words that appear at the top of the page where the word is found.

Save your work in your folder.

It's All There

How To Read a Dictionary Entry

Here's the Idea You know that a dictionary entry gives the meaning of a word. It also gives other helpful information about a word. Take a look at all the information a dictionary entry can give you.

The **entry word** is the word you are looking up. It is in bold type. It is divided into syllables. For example, *mathematics* is entered as **math·e·mat·ics.**

The **pronunciation** of the word is often put inside parentheses following the word. Symbols are used to help you sound out the word. An accent mark tells which syllable to stress. *Science,* for example, appears as (sī′əns).

The **part of speech** is shown by an abbreviation in bold type. For example, *noun* is abbreviated ***n.*** *Adverb* is abbreviated ***adv.*** If you do not recognize an abbreviation, look in the front of the dictionary for an explanation. You will usually find a complete list of the abbreviations used in the dictionary.

If a word can be used as more than one part of speech, the other parts of speech will also be given in the entry.

If a word has **special forms** or **endings,** they will be included next in the entry. For example, the entry for the irregular verb *swim* would include the forms **swam, swum,** and **swimming.** Plural forms are given for nouns.

The **origin,** or **history,** of a word is given next, often in brackets. Symbols and abbreviations are used. The symbol < means "came from." The abreviations *ME.*, *Gr.*, and *L.* stand for "Middle English," "Greek," and "Latin." Look up unfamiliar abbreviations in the complete list at the front of the dictionary.

Part 3

Objective

To understand how to interpret information in dictionary entries

Presenting the Lesson

1. Read aloud and discuss **Here's the Idea.** For each item described, refer to the classroom dictionary. Compare the symbols and abbreviations used there with those presented in the lesson. Most will probably be the same or approximately the same. Highlight any significant differences.

2. Read and discuss **Check It Out.** Compare the sample entry with the same entry in the classroom dictionary.

3. Assign and discuss **Try Your Skill.** Select two of the words. Compare the information in the classroom dictionary with that shown on the sample dictionary page.

4. Read **Keep This in Mind** and then assign **Now Write.**

Individualizing the Lesson

Less-Advanced Students

1. Ask the students to turn to the "Key to Pronunciation" in their classroom dictionaries. Ask them to identify the word represented by each of these respellings.

gadget knock national
(gaj′ it) (näk) (nash′ ə n′l)
(pik′ ′l) (vān) (gʉrl)
pickle vain/vane girl

2. Before answering **Try Your Skill,** ask the students to become dictionary detectives and answer questions *a* through *e* about each of these words: *brass, armadillo, kindergarten, chiffon,* and *tattoo.*

a. How many syllables are in _____?
b. How do you pronounce _____?
c. From what language did the word _____ originate?
d. What parts of speech can _____ be used as?
e. How many definitions are listed for _____?

Advanced Students

1. Ask the students to use their classroom dictionaries to answer the following questions.

a. What is the history of the word *sabotage*? French < *saboter,* to damage machinery by wearing wooden shoes
b. From what language did the word *bandana* originate? Hindi
c. What is the most common meaning of *frieze*? a decoration around a room
d. What is a synonym for the word *opponent*? antagonist
e. What parts of speech are listed for *stare*? verb, noun
f. What words are represented by these respellings?
(kas′ 'l) castle (fō′ nə graf′) phonograph (sēl′ iŋ) ceiling
g. How is *hysteria* divided into syllables? hys·te·ri·a
h. What is the plural of *brother-in-law*? brothers-in-law

2. Ask each student to make up a dictionary quiz including questions that require use of all of the parts of a dictionary entry. Reproduce the student quizzes and use them for additional practice.

Optional Practice

1. Have the students syllabicate these words using the classroom dictionary.

collusion col·lu·sion	flaky flak·y
dromedary drom·e·dar·y	ogre o·gre
accustom ac·cus·tom	militia mi·li·tia
excessive ex·ces·sive	theory the·o·ry
seizure sei·zure	quadrant quad·rant
unanimous u·nan·i·mous	planetarium plan·e·tar·i·um

2. Ask the students to determine the word represented by each of

Definitions are given in a numbered list. Often, the most common definition is given first. Sometimes a word will have a special meaning in one field. The dictionary will show this by naming the field. For example, one definition of *guard* is "*Sports*—to keep an opponent from making a gain or score."

A word may have a special meaning when it is used in speaking or in informal writing. This is a colloquial meaning. The dictionary shows this by using an abbreviation. For example, one definition of *story* is "[Colloq.] a falsehood or fib."

Synonyms and **antonyms** may also be listed. For some words there may also be a *synonymy*—a group of synonyms and their shades of meaning. Or, the notation "**SYN.** *see*" may refer you to another entry.

Entries in one dictionary may differ from entries in another. Become familiar with the way an entry is given in the dictionary you use.

Check It Out

Look at the dictionary entry below.

> **fam·i·ly** (fam′e lē, fam′lē) ***n.,*** *pl.,* **-lies** [L. *familia,* household < *famulus,* servant] **1.** orig., all the people living in the same house; household **2.** *a*) a social unit consisting of parents and their children *b*) the children of the same parents **3.** a group of people related by ancestry or marriage; relatives **4.** all those claiming descent from a common ancestor; tribe or clan; lineage **5.** a group of things having a common source of similar features; specif., *a*) *Biol.* a category that is used in classifying plants or animals and that ranks above a genus and below an order *b*) *Linguis.* a group of languages having a common ancestral language *c*) *Math.* a set of curves, etc. with some shared property —***adj.*** of or for a family

- How many syllables are there in *family*? How many pronunciations are given? What part of speech is *family*? Is it used as any other part of speech? From what language did the word come? What is the most common definition? Are there special meanings for use in particular fields? Are any synonyms given?

Try Your Skill Turn back to the sample dictionary page in the last lesson, **Show Me the Way.** Answer the following questions.

1. How would you pronounce *grimace*? What does it mean?
2. What parts of speech are listed for *grid*?
3. What are the other forms of the adjective *grim*?
4. Where would you find synonyms for *grim*?
5. What is the most common definition of *grid*?

Keep This in Mind

- A dictionary entry contains the meanings of a word. It also contains other helpful information.
- An entry in one dictionary may be different from an entry in another.

Now Write On your paper, write the title of this lesson, **It's All There.** Find the words *back*, *gorilla*, and *uniform* in a dictionary.

Copy two different definitions for each word. Then write a sentence telling any other information you find about each word.

Save your work in your folder.

these respellings, using a dictionary.

exchange	nation	cinder
(iks chānj′)	(nā shən)	(sin′ dər)
(hīt)	(fōt′ ə käp′ ē)	(kwäl′ ə tē)
height	photocopy	quality

3. Have the students find the language from which each of these words originated.

Latin serenade	Arabic giraffe
Greek isometric	Russian samovar
Middle Dutch plug	French lacrosse
Spanish lariat	Old English door

Extending the Lesson

Prepare a worksheet that presents a word as it appears in two dictionaries. Ask specific questions that highlight the differences in symbols and abbreviations. Then ask questions that focus on the information common to both.

Part 4

Objective

To understand that sentence context determines which definition of a word is appropriate

Presenting the Lesson

1. Read aloud and discuss **Here's the Idea.** Make sure that the students understand what *context* means. Ask students to find *glass* in their own dictionaries. Note how the different definitions are presented.

2. Study the entry for *court* in **Check It Out.** Then compare it with the entry in their classroom dictionaries. Have the students use each meaning of the word in a sentence.

3. Assign and discuss **Try Your Skill.** When students demonstrate that they understand the relationship between sentence context and dictionary definitions, assign **Now Write.**

Individualizing the Lesson

Less-Advanced Students

Instead of asking the students to compose their own sentences for all of the definitions of *court,* ask them to tell which definition of *court* fits the context of each of these sentences.

a. The judge presided over traffic *court*. a building where trials are held.
b. Ann lives on Elm *Court*. a short street, often closed at one end
c. There was a fountain in the *court* of the hotel. an uncovered area surrounded by buildings
d. The ambassador was received in *court* by the queen. the palace of a sovereign

Advanced Students

Ask each student to select one of the following words, look it up in the

Does It Fit?

How To Find the Meaning of a Word

Here's the Idea If you see a word that you don't know, you look it up in a dictionary. The word may have several meanings. Which is the right one? Usually the sentence in which you found the word, the context, will help you out.

In each sentence below, the context helps you to know the meaning of the word *glass*.

1. I cannot read without my *glasses*. (In this sentence, *glasses* means "eyeglasses, spectacles.")
2. Would you like a *glass* of strawberry milk? (In this sentence, *glass* means "a quantity of something.")
3. She smiled at her reflection in the *glass*. (In this sentence, *glass* means "a mirror.")

When you look up a word in the dictionary, read through all the definitions given. Try to find the meaning that best fits the word in context.

Check It Out Here is part of a dictionary entry. Study it. Then read the sentence that follows.

> **court** (kôrt) ***n.*** [OFr. <LL. <L. *cohors:* see COHORT] **1.** an uncovered space wholly or partly surrounded by buildings or walls **2.** a short street, often closed at one end **3.** *a)* an area for playing any of several ball games [a tennis *court*] *b)* a part of such an area ☆**4.** a motel: in full, **motorcourt** **5.** *a)* the palace of a sovereign *b)* the family, advisers, etc. of a sovereign, as a group *c)* a sovereign and his councilors as a governing body *d)* any formal gathering held by a sovereign **6.** attention paid to someone in order to get something **7.** courtship; wooing **8.** *a)* a person or persons appointed to examine and decide law cases, make investigations, etc.; judge or judges *b)* a place where trials are held, investigations made, etc. *c)* an assembly or meeting of the judge or judges, the lawyers, and the jury in a law court

We reserved a handball **court** for four o'clock.

- Which definition of *court* fits the context of this sentence?

Try Your Skill Read the entry. Some meanings are for *plug* as a noun, and some are for *plug* as a verb.

> **plug** (plug) ***n.*** [MDu. *plugge*] **1.** an object used to stop up a hole, drain, etc. **2.** *a*) a cake of pressed tobacco *b*) a piece of chewing tobacco **3.** a device, as with prongs that stick out, for fitting into an electric outlet, etc. to make electrical contact **4.** *same as: a*) SPARK PLUG *b*) FIREPLUG **5.** [Colloq.] a defective or shopworn article ☆**6.** [Slang] an old, worn-out horse ☆**7.** [Colloq.] a boost, advertisement, etc., esp. one slipped into the entertainment part of a radio or TV program, a magazine article, etc. **—*vt.* plugged, plug′ging 1.** to stop up (a hole, etc.) with a plug (often with *up*) **2.** to insert (something) as a plug [he *plugged* the putty in the hole] **3.** [Colloq.] *a*) to promote (a song) by frequent performance ☆*b*) to promote with a plug (*n.* 7) **4.** [Slang] to shoot a bullet into **—*vi.*** [Colloq.] to work or study hard and steadily; plod **—plug in** to connect (an electrical device) with an outlet, etc. by inserting a plug in a socket or jack **—plug′ger *n.***

On your paper, write the number of each sentence below. After it, write the meaning from the entry that matches the use of the word *plug*.

1. The painters *plugged* putty into the holes. (vt) 1.
2. This lamp needs a new cord and *plug*. (n) 3.
3. Although math is difficult for Rob, he *plugs* away at it. (v-colloq) 4.
4. The performer *plugged* her new album. (v-colloq) 3.
5. A mechanic replaced the *plugs* and points on the car. (n) 4.

Keep This in Mind

- If you don't know the meaning of a word, look it up. Read all the definitions. The context of the sentence will help you find the right meaning.

Now Write Look up the word *strike* in your dictionary. On your paper, write the title of this lesson, **Does It Fit?** Copy four meanings of *strike*. For each meaning, write a sentence. Save your work in your folder.

dictionary, and write a new **Try Your Skill** exercise. Reproduce these exercises and have the students find the correct answers. Answers will vary.

read	project	plain
jump	game	cut

Optional Practice

Ask students to write down the meanings of the underlined words in these sentences.

a. Sara inherited some stocks and bonds. an interest-bearing certificate
b. The grocery store employees stock the shelves at night. to furnish
c. Joseph enrolled in night school to learn a trade. skilled work
d. The director of the film was disappointed in the rushes. the first prints
e. Laura put the nut on the bolt. a small block with threaded hole
f. People with fair skin should use sunblock. light in color
g. We looked at some cells under the microscope. a small, complex organic unit
h. Dr. Wilkes read an abstract of the article. a summary

Extending the Lesson

Direct students to find five of the following words in the dictionary and to copy two definitions for each.

bat	sand
set	row
play	cut
trip	type
part	grain

Have them use each word in two sentences to illustrate the two definitions. Answers will vary.

Section 3 Objectives

1. To recognize standard and nonstandard English

2. To recognize slang as nonstandard English

Preparing the Students

Give students directions for reading the chapter using nonstandard English. (Example: "O.K., kids, set down in them chairs and open your books to page 34. We going to learn about some awesome language.") Ask the students how those directions differ from the ones you usually give. Explain that this chapter will help them learn when to use standard English.

Additional Resources

Mastery Test — pages 13–14 in the test booklet

Practice Book — pages 14–15

Duplicating Masters — pages 14–15

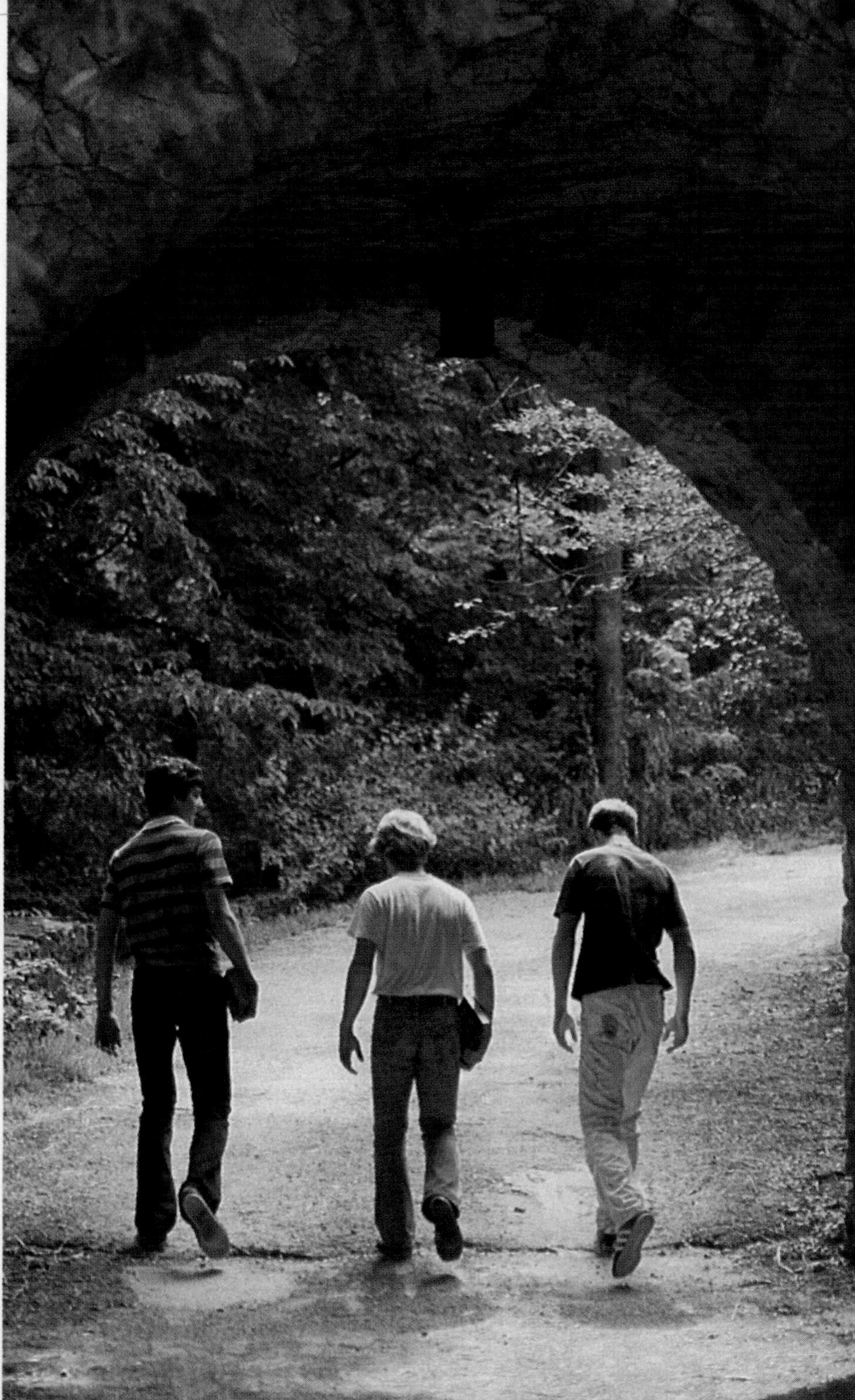

The Right Language at the Right Time

Part 1 **Up to Standards**
Writing and Speaking Standard English

Part 2 **Staying Cool**
Using and Misusing Slang

Teaching Special Populations

LD When necessary, simplify instructions for **Check It Out, Try Your Skill,** and **Now Write.** You may wish to shorten some exercises to make them more easily comprehensible.

ESL Distinguishing standard from nonstandard usage is difficult for ESL students. Provide concrete examples of differences, and particular situations in which each form of usage is appropriate.

Be aware that nonstandard usage by ESL students may derive from their applying foreign grammatical rules to English. For instance, double negatives and verbs at the ends of sentences are correct forms in many languages. Furthermore, some students' nonstandard constructions result from problems with subject-verb agreement. Refer students to Handbook Section 12.

Slang is a cross-cultural phenomenon. Ask ESL students to give examples of slang from their cultures and have them explain when it might be appropriately used.

NSD This section is crucial for students who speak a nonstandard dialect. Even non-standard dialects may conform to grammatical patterns. Be sensitive to students' feelings and emphasize that their usage is neither wrong nor bad. However, stress that there *is* a standard dialect that most people speak.

Demonstrate to NSD students that slang is limiting because not everyone understands it. Use two volunteers to act out a skit employing modern and out-dated slang.

Part 1

Objective

To recognize standard and nonstandard English

Presenting the Lesson

1. Read aloud and discuss **Here's the Idea.** Write the terms *standard English* and *nonstandard English* on the board. Ask students for sentences using nonstandard English. Then ask students to repeat each sentence using standard English. Emphasize that standard English is always acceptable.

2. Discuss **Check It Out.** Refer to Handbook Section 6, **Using Troublesome Verbs Correctly** on pages 370–387 if students need help understanding what is nonstandard about each sentence.

3. Assign and discuss **Try Your Skill.** Refer students to Handbook Section 5, **Using Irregular Verbs,** and Handbook Section 6, **Using Troublesome Verbs Correctly,** if they are having difficulty with the exercise.

4. Read **Keep This in Mind** aloud and then assign **Now Write.**

Individualizing the Lesson

Less-Advanced Students

Do **Try Your Skill** orally. Refer to the appropriate usage rule before attempting each item. (See Handbook Section 6 for 1., 2., 3., and 5. See Section 5 for 4.)

Advanced Students

Add these items to **Try Your Skill.**

6. Can I borrow your calculator?
   May I borrow your calculator? C

Part 1

Up to Standards

Writing and Speaking Standard English

Here's the Idea Do you use the same language with your friends as you do with your teachers? Probably not. Most people speak and write the English language in more than one way.

When you speak before a group or write a paper for class, you probably try to speak as correctly and precisely as possible. In other words, you try to use standard English. **Standard English** follows all of the rules of good grammar and usage. It is the language you use when you want to be understood by everyone. When you use standard English, people tend to listen more carefully to what you have to say.

There is also another type, or "level," of language. It is called nonstandard English. **Nonstandard English** does not follow all of the rules of good grammar and usage. It is often found in friendly letters or casual conversation. Slang is one type of nonstandard English. So are words such as *ain't* and *hisself.* Phrases like *I seen it* and *she gone now* are also nonstandard.

Learn to be aware of the type of language you are using. Remember that nonstandard English is acceptable only in very casual situations. Use standard English in school and in all your writing. Also use it whenever you want to present yourself or your work in the best possible way.

Check It Out Compare these examples.

Standard	Nonstandard
1. *Sit* down and rest.	1. *Set* down and rest.
2. Tim *has gone* to school.	2. Tim *gone* to school.
3. She *doesn't* want to go.	3. She *don't* want to go.
4. I *am* studying for the test.	4. I *be* studying for the test.
5. I didn't learn *anything.*	5. I didn't learn *nothing.*

- What is nonstandard about each sentence in the second column?
- Say the standard sentences to yourself until they sound natural to you.

Try Your Skill Read the following pairs of sentences. Choose the correct standard English sentence in each pair.

1. They were late this morning.
   They was late this morning.
2. Come in and set down.
   Come in and sit down.
3. Ain't it a nice day?
   Isn't it a nice day?
4. I seen the movie already.
   I saw the movie already.
5. He doesn't know anything.
   He don't know nothing.

Keep This in Mind

- Standard English is correct in any situation. Learn to speak and write standard English.

Now Write Make each sentence below show standard usage. Choose the correct word from the two shown in parentheses. Write the complete sentence. Then compare your work with that of your classmates. Correct any mistakes you made. Save your finished work in your folder.

1. They (was, were) hurt badly.
2. Marnee and her sister (aren't, ain't) going to the basketball game.
3. The team doesn't have (no, any) good pitchers.
4. I (saw, seen) the hot air balloon fly away.
5. Frankie (has written, has wrote) me a funny letter.

7. Corey can't find Al nowhere.
   Corey can't find Al anywhere. c
8. I am studying for the quiz. c
   I be studying for the quiz.

Optional Practice

Have the students rewrite these sentences changing the nonstandard English to standard English.

1. They was going downtown. (were)
2. Can't you do nothing right? (anything)
3. I knowed you could do it! (knew)
4. He done the job well. (did)
5. She don't like no jazz. (doesn't, any)

Extending the Lesson

Tape a national news broadcast as an example of standard English, and tape a local rock or country disc jockey as an example of nonstandard English. Play both tapes for the class. Discuss the differences in the language. Also discuss whether or not the language is appropriate for the situation.

Part 2

Objective

To recognize slang as nonstandard usage

Presenting the Lesson

1. Read aloud and discuss **Here's the Idea.** Ask students for examples of current slang. Have them define the slang terms in standard English. Emphasize that although slang can be colorful and descriptive at times, it is nonstandard English and should be used sparingly.

2. Discuss **Check It Out.** Point out that in formal situations you want to make a good first impression. Using standard English is the best way to do that.

3. Assign and discuss **Try Your Skill.** Point out that English has many synonyms both in standard and nonstandard English. Have students complete their answers and decide what is the best standard English for each sentence.

4. Assign **Now Write.**

Individualizing the Lesson

Less-Advanced Students

Allow the students to work in pairs to complete **Try Your Skill.**

Advanced Students

Expand the discussion of slang vs. standard English to show all of the different shades of meaning that can be given by using different words. For example, instead of saying, "That group's music is really *cool*", you might use the words *catchy*, *melodic*, or *original.* Point out that standard English is usually more precise than slang.

Part 2

Staying Cool

Using and Misusing Slang

Here's the Idea Not too long ago, the words *grody* and *far out* were often heard in conversation. Within a few months, however, they were no longer being used. These words, and others like them, are called **slang.** Slang is a type of nonstandard English. It is made up of colorful, descriptive words and phrases. Some slang terms are known by everyone. Some are familiar only to certain groups.

Slang changes rapidly. Most slang terms disappear quickly from our language. The words below were all very popular slang expressions at one time. Do you know what each one means?

groovy	vamoose	bummer	uptight
rap	heavy	marvy	drag

Some slang terms do become permanent parts of our language. *Hot dog,* for example, was once a slang term. Now it is an accepted part of our vocabulary.

Always remember that slang is nonstandard English. Never use slang in a report for school, in a business letter, or when speaking in formal situations. Use it only in casual conversation with your friends.

Check It Out Read the list of activities below.

1. Writing a letter to your principal asking to use the gym for a seventh grade basketball game.
2. Making a phone call to your best friend.
3. Writing an advertisement for a book sale for the junior high classes.

4. Giving an oral report in class.
5. Telling your cousin about the popular styles at your school.

- Which situations require standard English?
- In which situations would slang be acceptable? Why?

Try Your Skill Complete each sentence in two ways. First, complete it with a slang term. Then complete it using standard English. The word or words in parentheses will give you an idea of the types of words you should use.

1. That group's music is really ______. (good)
2. Do you ______ what I'm saying? (understand)
3. His outfit is ______. (in style)
4. This movie ______. (is bad)
5. We ______ last Saturday. (had a good time)

Keep This in Mind

- Slang is current, popular, nonstandard English.
- Slang should never be used in situations that call for standard English.

Now Write Listen to the dialogue on several popular television shows. Write down the slang terms that you hear. Then write down the meaning of each term. Compare your list with the lists of your classmates. What standard English words or phrases could be used in place of these terms? Save your list of slang terms in your folder.

Optional Practice

Have the students write ten slang words that are currently in use. Then have them list two standard English synonyms for each of the slang words.

Extending the Lesson

1. Ask the students to find the slang meanings for these words.

chick	baloney
cat	gravy
way out	hep

2. Bring several slang dictionaries to class and let the students look through them. Discuss some of the entries. Point out that the use of most slang is time specific or situation specific. For example, the terms *hip, far out,* and *groovy* were used in the '70's. *Woody* and *hang ten* are part of a surfer's slang vocabulary. As an extension of this discussion, have the students ask their parents and/or grandparents what slang expressions were popular when they were young. Discuss these expressions in class.

Section 4 Objectives

1. To know the meaning of *sentence*

2. To recognize and to write good sentences

3. To write sentences that do not use needless repetition

4. To write sentences that do not express unsupported opinions

5. To write sentences without using unnecessary words and phrases

6. To combine short sentences into compound sentences using appropriate conjunctions

Preparing the Students

On the chalkboard write these two groups of words:

1. The bark show ball round.
2. The dog gnawed the steak bone.

Discuss the essential difference between these two examples. Sentence 1 does not express a thought, while sentence 2 does. Emphasize that, as with words, sentences are used to communicate. Remind the class that almost everything they learn in school comes to them in the form of sentences.

Additional Resources

Mastery Test — page 14 in the test booklet

Practice Book — pages 16–19

Duplicating Masters — pages 16–19

Special Populations — See special section at the front of this Teacher's Edition.

Writing Better Sentences

Part 1 **Put It Together**
Learning About Sentences

Part 2 **Getting Nowhere**
Avoiding Empty Sentences

Part 3 **Cut It Out!**
Avoiding Padded Sentences

Part 4 **All Join Hands**
Combining Sentences

Teaching Special Populations

LD LD students may require repeated drill and daily practice to help them determine exactly what constitutes a complete thought. To aid students' comprehension, shorten exercises and simplify instructions. Here is an example:

Write three sentences:

1. one that tells what something is,
2. one that tells how to do something,
3. one that tells about an action,

Read over your sentences. Check to be sure that they are clear, complete, and correct. Make corrections before handing them in.

ESL ESL students will need concrete examples of *padding* and *empty sentences*. Show students what specific elements in these sentences make them weak or unclear. Pair students with native English speakers and have them go over examples together.

If ESL students are to improve sentence combining skills they must understand the meaning of the original sentences. Point out the similarity in content and the logical relationship between sentences. Go over various coordinating conjunctions, making sure ESL students understand what logical relationships are signalled by these words.

NSD Use this section to give NSD students extensive practice. The more they are exposed to well-formed sentences, the easier these students will find it to produce good syntax and standard English. Explain that coordinating conjunctions allow writers to convey the relationship between sentence parts.

Part 1

Objectives

1. To know the meaning of *sentence*

2. To recognize and write good sentences

Presenting the Lesson

1. Read aloud and discuss **Here's the Idea.** Write the word *sentence* and its definition on the board.

2. Discuss **Check It Out.** Encourage students to contribute additional examples of powerful sentences. If students seem interested, you may want to make the collection of powerful sentences an ongoing class activity. Emphasize that a good sentence expresses a complete thought in a clear, strong, and direct way.

3. Assign **Try Your Skill.** After discussing students' sentences, you may want to have students revise them.

4. Assign and discuss **Now Write.**

Individualizing the Lesson

Less-Advanced Students

Reduce the number of items. Have each student do only two or three sentences. Discuss them. Use an overhead projector to display each sentence as it is discussed.

If students are having difficulty writing complete sentences, turn to Section One, Part 1, of the Handbook on page 270 for review.

Advanced Students

Have students complete all ten items.

Part 1

Put It Together

Learning About Sentences

Here's the Idea You have seen how a good vocabulary helps you to express ideas clearly. You know that using the right word in the right place can make a big difference. So can using the right word at the right time.

Now you are ready to put your words together in the most effective way. You are ready to create sentences.

A sentence is a group of words that expresses one complete thought. You can use sentences to express many different kinds of ideas. If you write carefully, your sentences can be very powerful. Read these examples of powerful sentences.

> Common sense is not so common.—VOLTAIRE
>
> That it will never come again is what makes life so sweet.
> —EMILY DICKENSON
>
> When one door closes, fortune will usually open another.
> —FERNANDO DE ROJAS

Not every writer can write a sentence that becomes famous. However, you can learn to write good sentences. A good sentence states an idea in a clear, direct, and lively way.

Check It Out Read the following sentences.

1. A junk is a flat-bottomed Chinese boat.
2. The pale moon rose over the snow-capped mountains.
3. We have a haunted telephone.
4. Computers can do almost anything.
5. The Mahoney family celebrates Christmas in July.

- Does each sentence express a complete thought?
- Is each sentence clear and direct?

Try Your Skill Read the ten sentences below. Each one asks you to tell about something. Choose five directions to follow. Write a single sentence to answer each direction. Try to make each sentence clear, direct, and lively. Use details from your memory or your imagination.

1. Tell one event that happened in this class.
2. Describe your favorite object.
3. Explain one way to cheer someone up.
4. Explain what a best friend is.
5. Explain why a person should get enough sleep.
6. Tell how you came to school this morning.
7. Describe how your head feels when you have a cold.
8. Explain what a broom does.
9. Explain why people should vote.
10. Tell one of your favorite wishes.

Keep This in Mind

- A sentence is a group of words that expresses a complete thought.
- A good sentence expresses an idea clearly and directly.

Now Write Write five sentences. Write a sentence that tells how to do something. Write one that describes something. Write one that tells what something is. Write one that tells why something should be done. Finally, write one that tells about some action.

Try to write sentences that you would enjoy reading. When you've written your sentences, read them over. Are they clear and direct? Are they strong? If not, rewrite them. Save your work in your folder.

Optional Practice

Make a collection of short newspaper articles without their headlines. Give one to each student. Have each student write a clear, direct, lively sentence to serve as the headline for his or her article. Discuss them in class.

Extending the Lesson

Collect ten or fifteen magazine photographs in which the action or subject matter is nonspecific (or use a series of color slides). Display the photos. Ask each student to choose three and to write a sentence about each. The sentence should tell how to do something related to the photo; describe or identify what is pictured; or tell about an action. Provide time for students to share their sentences.

Part 2

Objectives

1. To write sentences that do not use needless repetition

2. To write sentences that do not express unsupported opinions

Presenting the Lesson

1. Read aloud and discuss **Here's the Idea.** Emphasize that both types of sentence errors described can be corrected with the addition of specific information.

2. Discuss **Check It Out,** helping the students to understand that sentences 1, 4, and 5 contain repetitions and that sentences 2 and 3 give unsupported opinions.

3. Assign **Try Your Skill.** Remind students that a sentence with an unsupported opinion can be corrected in one sentence, two sentences, or possibly three or more sentences. Discuss students' answers.

4. Assign **Now Write.**

Individualizing the Lesson

Less-Advanced Students

Before having students correct the sentences in **Try Your Skill,** discuss them as a class. Decide what is wrong with each one. Then ask students to improve them individually.

Advanced Students

Add these items to the **Try Your Skill** exercise.

7. The room was dark, and there wasn't any light.
8. Self-confidence is an important attitude.

Getting Nowhere

Avoiding Empty Sentences

Here's the Idea Some sentences get nowhere. They are written as sentences, but they do not say anything. Such groups of words are called **empty sentences.**

There are two kinds of empty sentences. The first repeats an idea from an earlier sentence, or states one idea twice.

> I was thirsty and I wanted something to drink.

If you are thirsty, it is understood that you want something to drink. The sentence above needlessly repeats the same idea. A sentence like this can be revised by adding more information.

> I was thirsty because I had eaten a bag of salty pretzels.

The second kind of empty sentence gives an unsupported opinion. The writer makes a strong statement that captures a reader's attention, but leaves the reader asking "Why?"

> Most TV news programs are second-rate.

Such strong statements must be supported with details. These details may be facts, reasons, or examples. Supporting evidence may be given in the same sentence or in following sentences.

> Most TV news programs are second-rate because newscasters act like entertainers, not like journalists.
>
> Most TV news programs are second-rate. Newscasters devote too little time to explaining news events. Instead, they try to entertain.

When you give an opinion, you must also give a reason for your opinion. Otherwise, your writing will seem empty. Your readers may not agree with you, but at least they will know *why* you think as you do.

Check It Out Read the following empty sentences.

1. The forest was quiet because there wasn't a sound.
2. You should always try to eat a good breakfast.
3. Exercise can be enjoyable.
4. I didn't like the movie because it was terrible.
5. This record is broken, and it is unplayable.

- Which sentences repeat an idea? Which sentences give an unsupported opinion?
- How could you improve these empty sentences?

Try Your Skill Copy the following sentences. Decide why each one is empty. Then try to improve each sentence.

1. The wind was freezing, and I was cold.
2. My feet were sore from walking, and they hurt.
3. The city is the best place to live.
4. We shouldn't waste our natural resources.
5. The book was so dull that it bored me.
6. Writing is the most important skill you will ever learn.

Keep This in Mind

- There are two kinds of empty sentences. One kind repeats an idea. The other kind states an opinion without supporting it.
- Improve sentences that repeat an idea by taking out the repeated idea. Complete sentences that give an opinion by supporting the opinion with facts, reasons, or examples.

Now Write Read some advertisements in magazines and newspapers. Find two examples of empty sentences. Write down the sentences. Then write why you think each one is empty. Finally, improve each sentence. Save your work in your folder.

9. Sky-diving is a dangerous sport.
10. The water was boiling, and it was very hot.

Optional Practice

If students are having difficulty correcting empty sentences, teach each kind separately. Have students correct these empty sentences.

Sentences with Repeated Ideas

1. I sipped the ice water, and it was icy cold.
2. Marty got all the answers right, and he got a perfect score.
3. The baby was crying, and she was upset.

Sentences with Unsupported Opinions

1. Everyone should take vitamins.
2. Reading is a necessary skill.
3. Bicycle safety rules are important.

Extending the Lesson

Divide the class into two groups. Have each of the students in one group write one good sentence, following the guidelines presented in Part 1. Have each of the students in the other write an empty sentence. Collect the sentences and type them on a ditto master, mixing up the good and bad sentences. Duplicate them and return them to the class. Have each student identify the good sentences and rewrite the empty sentences to correct them.

Part 3

Objective

To write sentences without using unnecessary words and phrases

Presenting the Lesson

1. Read aloud and discuss **Here's the Idea.** Emphasize that sentences should be as direct as possible.

2. Compare the padded and improved sentences in **Check It Out.** Ask students to pick out the excess words and phrases in the padded sentences.

3. Assign and discuss **Try Your Skill.** Compare different versions of each group of sentences. Work in a small group with the students who had difficulty with this exercise. Have them examine the words in each sentence to determine which should be eliminated.

4. Assign and discuss **Now Write.**

Individualizing the Lesson

Less-Advanced Students

Do item one of **Try Your Skill** orally. If necessary, work in a small group with students who are having difficulty. Have them examine the words in each sentence to determine which should be eliminated.

Advanced Students

Have each student write two padded sentences. Then have students exchange papers and rewrite the sentences, eliminating the padding.

Optional Practice

Have students rewrite the following paragraph eliminating any unnecessary words or phrases.

Part 3

Cut It Out!

Avoiding Padded Sentences

Here's the Idea Every word in a sentence should say something about the main idea of the sentence. Some sentences will be longer than others. However, a good sentence should have no extra words.

Sentences that contain useless words or phrases are called padded sentences. A padded sentence is not clear and direct. It takes too long to get to the point. Padded sentences can be improved by trimming. Read the following example.

> Due to the fact that I didn't have shoes on, I couldn't go into the museum.

The phrase *due to the fact that* is unclear. It adds nothing to the sentence. It gets in the way of the main idea. The sentence could be improved by leaving out the padding.

> Because I didn't have shoes on, I couldn't go into the museum.

Phrases such as *you know, you see, what I mean to say is,* and *well, what I think is* are sometimes used in conversation. However, they don't help you to state ideas clearly. You should avoid them when you write and speak.

Remember that padding gets in the way of your ideas. Good writers revise their work to leave out unnecessary words.

Check It Out Read the following pairs of sentences. Notice how each padded sentence has been revised.

Padded — What I mean to say is that I agree.
Improved — I agree.

Padded — I am going to write about whales, which are not fish, but mammals.
Improved — Whales are not fish, but mammals.

Padded What I want to do is catch the four o'clock bus.
Improved I want to catch the four o'clock bus.

- Do you notice how much clearer and more direct the improved sentences are?

Try Your Skill Decide which sentences are padded in each of the following groups. Copy each padded sentence. Draw a line through each unnecessary word or phrase. Then write the improved sentences.

1. What I want to say is that bees are social insects. They live together in large groups. Each insect in the group has one job to do.
2. Never go to bed angry. The reason that you shouldn't is because your anger may keep you awake or give you nightmares. Then your night will be as bad as your day was.
3. What I think is that Willie Mays was one of the greatest ballplayers of all time. He played twenty-two seasons in the major leagues. Mays had a career batting average of .302 and hit 660 home runs.

Keep This in Mind

- A padded sentence has more words than are necessary to express an idea.
- Leave out words and phrases that add nothing to the idea in a sentence.

Now Write Improve the following padded sentences by rewriting them.

Well, you see during World War II, Navajo Indians sent secret messages for the United States Marines. You see they used a code that substituted the Navajo names of animals for military terms. On account of the fact that the Navajo language is so varied, the enemy never broke the code.

I feel that bananas are a very healthy food. Well, you see, bananas are high in potassium and low in fat and cholesterol. On account of the fact that they are high in sucrose, they are a good energy source. What I mean to say is that bananas are good and good for you.

Extending the Lesson

Explain that padded sentences are common in informal conversation. Direct students to make a note of sentences in which they hear padding. After a specified period of time—perhaps two or three days—discuss the most commonly heard types of padding.

Part 4

Objective

To combine short sentences into compound sentences using appropriate conjunctions

Presenting the Lesson

1. Read aloud and discuss **Here's the Idea.** Write the words *and, but,* and *or* on the chalkboard. Explain that these words are called *conjunctions* and that the job of a conjunction is to join either words or sentences together.

2. Discuss **Check It Out.**

3. Assign and discuss **Try Your Skill.**

4. Read **Keep This in Mind** as a review. Then assign **Now Write.**

Individualizing the Lesson

Less-Advanced Students

1. Before assigning **Now Write,** discuss which conjunction would be appropriate for each pair of sentences. Then have students complete the exercise individually or in pairs.

2. Have students read the combined sentences aloud. Point out the choppiness of the short sentences and the smoothness of the combined sentences.

Advanced Students

Have each student write one pair of short sentences and instructions for combining them, such as those in **Try Your Skill.** Reproduce the items on ditto paper and have students combine the sentences.

Part 4

All Join Hands

Combining Sentences

Here's the Idea You know that a sentence states a complete idea. Sometimes you may write two or more short sentences that have similar ideas. These sentences can often be combined. The new sentence will include the ideas stated in the shorter sentences.

Sometimes two sentences contain similar ideas that are equally important. You can combine sentences like these by using a comma and the word *and.*

Diane plays the flute. Her brother plays the piano.
Diane plays the flute**, and** her brother plays the piano.

Other sentences may state contrasting ideas of equal importance. You can combine sentences like these with a comma and the word *but*.

Ted barely finished the test. He got the highest grade.
Ted barely finished the test**, but** but he got the highest grade.

Sometimes, two sentences state a choice between ideas. You can combine sentences like these with a comma and *or.*

We can wait for the bus. We can start walking.
We can wait for the bus **, or** we can start walking.

Check It Out Read the following sentences.

1. Do you want to order Chinese food, or should we make some?
2. Jean mopped up the water, and Andy called the plumber.
3. The work was hard, but the results were worth it.

- Which sentence combines closely related ideas of equal importance?
- Which sentence combines contrasting ideas of equal importance?
- Which sentence combines ideas of equal importance and offers a choice between them?

Try Your Skill Combine each pair of sentences. Follow the directions in parentheses.

1. Nick brought the camera. Sheila took all the pictures. (Join with **, but.**)
2. The wind was brisk. The water was rough. (Join with **, and.**)
3. Did Inspecter Clouseau know the truth? Was he only guessing? (Join with **, or.**)

Keep This in Mind

- Use a comma and *and* to combine sentences that express closely related ideas of equal importance.
- Use a comma and *but* to combine sentences that express contrasting ideas of equal importance.
- Use a comma and *or* to combine sentences that offer a choice between ideas of equal importance.

Now Write Combine the following pairs of sentences, using **, and** or **, but** or **, or.**

1. Joyce chopped the vegetables. Adam sliced the cheese.
2. Aluminum is lighter than steel. It is more expensive.
3. Lisa weeded the garden. I watered the plants.
4. The metal must be painted. It will rust.
5. The shoes fit. They don't feel comfortable.

Optional Practice

Follow the instructions for **Now Write.** Then have students explain why they chose the conjunctions that they used.

1. President Reagan delivered the speech. One of his speechwriters wrote it.
2. Ezra assembled the picnic table. Andy stained it.
3. Lois caught the fish. Carol cleaned it.
4. Turn off the water. The tub will overflow.
5. Mike plays the tuba. Felix plays the trombone.

Extending the Lesson

Make copies of an interesting article from an encyclopedia. Distribute these, and have students read through the article, underlining examples of combined sentences. Check their work as a group. Have students explain why each particular conjunction was used.

Section 5 Objectives

1. To understand the basic elements of a paragraph

2. To recognize unity, or the lack of it, in a paragraph

3. To learn the purpose of a topic sentence in a paragraph

4. To learn three ways to develop a paragraph

5. To study the three kinds of paragraphs: narrative, descriptive, and explanatory

Preparing the Students

The material in Section 5 is the next step in the logical progression from words to sentences to groups of sentences. Open the lesson by showing several examples of paragraphs from different classroom sources. Note the indentation of the first sentence in each paragraph. Explain that a paragraph is more than a group of sentences and that students are going to learn what makes a paragraph a special way of expressing ideas.

Additional Resources

Mastery Test — pages 16–17 in the test booklet

Practice Book — pages 20–24

Duplicating Masters — pages 20–24

A Look at Paragraphs

Part 1 **What Is It?**
Learning About Paragraphs

Part 2 **United We Stand**
Recognizing Unity in a Paragraph

Part 3 **What's It All About?**
Using a Topic Sentence

Part 4 **Follow the Leader**
Developing a Paragraph

Part 5 **What's in a Name?**
Recognizing Three Kinds of Paragraphs

Teaching Special Populations

LD LD students may need specific, simplified examples to understand the relationship between constituent parts of a paragraph. Review **Try Your Skill.**

Clarify the instructions throughout this section. The instructions for **Now Write** in Part I, for instance, can be rewritten as follows:

> Look at paragraph 1 above. Find the two sentences that do not belong and underline them. Rewrite the paragraph, leaving out the sentences you have underlined.

LD students may also have difficulty distinguishing between the three types of paragraphs. Give extra examples of each type and have them tell what features of these paragraphs mark them as explanatory, descriptive, or narrative.

ESL Make sure that ESL students fully understand the content of the sample paragraphs. In **Now Write**, Part 3, for instance, you might want to explain briefly about the history of native American peoples. Be sure to explain the terms and concepts used in the sample paragraphs as well as the terms used in the instructions. Finally, give extra examples and topics related to students' own cultural experience.

NSD Make sure that NSD students have extensive practice in this section. Some forms of nonstandard dialect tend to obscure the logical connection between sentences, so show NSD students where the unity and coherence of their paragraphs can be improved. Also, NSD students often avoid using details and examples. Point out to them the important function of these items.

Part 1

Objective

To understand the basic elements of a paragraph

Presenting the Lesson

1. Read aloud and discuss **Here's the Idea.** Write the word *paragraph* and its definition on the chalkboard. Ask the students to identify the one main idea in each group of sentences.

2. Discuss **Check It Out.**

3. Assign and discuss **Try Your Skill.** Refer students to the definition of a paragraph you have written on the chalkboard. Tell them to check this definition as they decide whether each group of sentences is or is not a paragraph.

4. Read **Keep This in Mind** and then assign **Now Write.** Remind the students to follow paragraph form.

Individualizing the Lesson

Less-Advanced Students

1. For **Check It Out** and **Try Your Skill,** read through each paragraph orally. First ask students to state the main idea of each. Then analyze each group, one sentence at a time, to see if all of the sentences support the main idea.

2. Give the students additional practice with the following paragraph. Have them find the main idea and then determine if all of the sentences support that idea.

Peter Carl Fabergé, a jeweler at the turn of the century, is best known for his Easter eggs. His eggs are not the commonplace eggs we find on Easter morning.

Part 1

What Is It?

Learning About Paragraphs

Here's the Idea You want your reader to understand what you have to say. Your reader will understand your ideas if you organize them well. The basic tool for organizing ideas in writing is the paragraph.

What is a paragraph? A **paragraph** is a group of sentences that work together. Each sentence says something about one main idea.

Read each of the following groups of sentences. See if the sentences in each group work together.

1 Kit knew that she had to warn her friend. She snatched her cloak from the peg and, carrying her leather boots in her hand, crept down the stairs. She dared not try to unbolt the great front door. Instead, she tiptoed cautiously through the cold company room into the back chamber. She let herself out the shed door into the garden. She could hear shouts in the distance. Slipping hurriedly into her boots, she fled along the roadway.

—ELIZABETH GEORGE SPEARE

2 The young boy turned over on the thin mattress as the summer sun edged its way over the East River. The sun moved slowly. It spread a soft, gray light down the boy's face, and he was awakened. His eyes opened quickly, hurrying sleep away. He lay still a moment, smelling and hearing the morning all around him.

3 You can create your own T-shirt design. Use a plain T-shirt, a piece of cloth, an apple, a stiff paintbrush, and textile paint in any colors of your choice. Begin by slicing an apple in half lengthwise. Brush a thick layer of textile paint over the cut side of the apple halves. Press the apple, paint side down, on a piece of cloth. Keep practicing until you have it just right. Then print your T-shirt.

Check It Out Look again at the three groups of sentences above. The first group tells a story. The second group describes a person. The third explains a process. Are they all paragraphs?

- Does each group of sentences deal with one idea?
- Does every sentence in each group say something about the main idea?

Try Your Skill Below are two groups of sentences. One is a paragraph. One is not. Read each group and decide which one is not a good paragraph. Write a sentence or two explaining why that group of sentences does not make a good paragraph.

1 I'll never forget the championship game of the baseball season. That night our family had fried chicken for dinner. Chicken is my favorite food. There were two outs in the last inning and I was batting. I like batting better than fielding. We were behind, but the tying run was at third base. Unfortunately, I popped the ball up to the infield for the final out.

2 To change a flat tire, first secure the emergency brake, then loosen the nuts on the wheel rim. Next use the jack to raise the car. Then replace the flat tire with the spare. Turn the nuts until they are almost tight. Finally, lower the car and tighten the nuts.

Keep This in Mind

- Each paragraph should deal with one main idea.
- Every sentence in the paragraph should say something about the main idea.

Now Write Find one of the groups of sentences in **Try Your Skill** that does not make a good paragraph. Look it over, using **Keep This in Mind** as a guide. Find the sentences that do not belong. Copy the remaining sentences in the form of a paragraph. Put your paragraph into your folder.

His eggs were made of gold, platinum, and enamel. They were decorated with precious gems. These elaborate and expensive eggs were made for Russian royalty.

Advanced Students

Have the students either write or find samples of good paragraphs. Read the paragraphs aloud. Have the students state the main idea in each one. Discuss how each sentence supports the main idea.

Optional Practice

Follow the directions for **Try Your Skill.**

1. The armadillo is a strange-looking animal. It has two armored plates on its back. The plates are connected by movable bands. It has a pointy, armored snout and a long tail. Although it is really a gentle animal, the armadillo's appearance is frightening.
2. Eating an ice cream cone at the beach can be messy. The beach near our house is great. First of all, the ice cream drips down your hand. Also, sand blows around and gets in the ice cream. The lake water is refreshing. There is always the danger that the ice cream will fall off the cone. Perhaps lemonade would be a better treat for cooling off at the beach.

Extending the Lesson

Have the students make a collection from magazines and newspapers of the three kinds of paragraphs discussed in the section: *narrative*, *descriptive*, and *explanatory*. Have them underline the main idea of each paragraph. Then have the students make a bulletin board display of the paragraphs.

Part 2

Objective

To recognize unity, or the lack of it, in a paragraph

Presenting the Lesson

1. Read aloud and discuss **Here's the Idea.** Write the term *unity* and its definition on the chalkboard.

2. Discuss **Check It Out.** Analyze the paragraph, sentence by sentence, to illustrate that the paragraph does have unity. All of the sentences support the main idea that Tracy Austin achieved greatness at an early age.

3. Assign and discuss **Try Your Skill.** Have students discuss what the main idea of each paragraph is before they begin this exercise.

4. Read **Keep This in Mind** and then assign **Now Write.**

Individualizing the Lesson

Less-Advanced Students

1. Do the first paragraph of **Try Your Skill** orally. Have the students identify the sentence that states the main idea as well as the sentence that does not belong in the paragraph. Allow the students to work in pairs to complete the exercise.

2. Work in a small group with any students who were unable to complete **Try Your Skill** successfully. Choose one of the four paragraphs in that exercise. On the chalkboard, write the first sentence. Determine as a group the idea of that sentence. Do this with each sentence of the paragraph. Students should be able to easily identify the sentence that does not work with the others.

Part 2

United We Stand

Recognizing Unity in a Paragraph

Here's the Idea You have learned that a paragraph is a group of sentences that work together. This means that all of the sentences tell about one main idea. When all of the sentences in a paragraph work together to express one main idea, the paragraph has **unity.**

Check It Out Read this paragraph:

> Tracy Austin is one of the few athletes who achieved greatness at an early age. By the age of ten, she had won age-group titles in national tennis tournaments. She was one of the youngest contenders ever to play at Wimbledon. In 1981, Austin became the youngest woman ever to win the U.S. Open, beating such tennis greats as Chris Evert Lloyd and Martina Navratilova. She was just sixteen years old at the time.

- Do all of these sentences work together? Do they all tell about one main idea? Does this paragraph have unity?

Try Your Skill Here are four paragraphs without unity. In each, one sentence does not work with the others. Write the sentence in each paragraph that does not belong.

1 I guess I've been on every kind of diet ever invented. Many books on diets have been published recently. I remember the time I resolved to eat only fruit and cottage cheese. I gained three pounds, and to this day I hate the sight of cottage cheese. Then there was the B diet: boiled eggs and bananas. I ate so many bananas that I felt like King Kong. The trouble was, I was still shaped like him, too.

2 Thomas Jefferson and Alexander Hamilton did not get along. The tall, red-headed lawyer from Virginia had little use for the ideas of the smaller, dark-complexioned former lawyer from New York. The two disagreed on the idea of democracy. Jefferson was in favor of it, Hamilton against it. They disagreed, too, on which group the national government should favor—farmers, or those who owned factories and businesses. Hamilton was killed in a duel.

3 My cousin and I learned most of our family's history by playing in Grandmother's attic. In one corner stood a brass-bound trunk, filled with dolls once treasured by aunts and mothers. Grandfather's World War I uniform hung on a metal rack, along with once-stylish dresses. The clothing now is much more comfortable than it was thirty years ago. When we played with the toys our mothers had played with, or dressed up in the old-fashioned clothes, we felt that the past was truly part of our lives.

4 Senses are so basic that all animals have them, but not all animals use their senses in the same way. Many people have lost their sense of hearing. A frog's eye, for instance, does not see a fly as we see it. In fact, a frog won't spot a fly at all unless the fly moves. Put a frog into a cage with dead insects, and it will starve.

Keep This in Mind

- All of the sentences in a paragraph should work together. They should all say something about the main idea. Then a paragraph has unity.

Now Write Label your paper **United We Stand.** Choose one of the paragraphs from **Try Your Skill** that does not have unity. Look at the sentence on your paper that does not belong with the others. Now write the paragraph so that it has unity. Save your paragraph in your folder.

Advanced Students

In addition to discussing the unity of the paragraphs in **Try Your Skill,** discuss what kind of paragraph each is. Also, begin to discuss the style of writing in the paragraphs. Point out that the first paragraph is humorous. Ask the students how the writer achieved that effect.

Optional Practice

Find the main idea and the sentence that does not belong in each paragraph.

1. The triathlon is a grueling competition. There are three difficult events—swimming, bicycling, and running. Swimming burns up more calories than almost any other activity. For example, in the Ironman triathlon, the contestants swim 2.4 miles. Then they bicycle for 112 miles. Finally, they run 26.2 miles. Only athletes in the best shape consider this sport.

2. Winter in the Midwest is unpredictable. One year there is a record snowfall, and the next year there is barely any snow. One year the temperature stays below zero for a month, and the next year the weather is 70° in February. One year the pipes froze in many homes.

Extending the Lesson

Ask each student to bring in a paragraph copied from a book or magazine. Using an opaque projector, study the paragraphs in class. Have the students identify the main idea of each paragraph. Discuss whether or not each paragraph has unity.

Part 3

Objective

To learn the purpose of a topic sentence in a paragraph

Presenting the Lesson

1. Read aloud and discuss **Here's the Idea.** Emphasize that a topic sentence states an idea that is developed in the rest of the paragraph. Use the paragraph in **Check It Out** as an example.

2. Assign and discuss **Try Your Skill.** Point out how all the other sentences in these paragraphs just give examples of the idea in the topic sentence (examples of biting cold piercing my body, examples of pleasant and unpleasant things about early railroads, etc.).

3. Read **Keep This In Mind** and assign **Now Write.**

Individualizing the Lesson

Less-Advanced Students

Help the students choose the topic sentence for group 1 in **Try Your Skill.** Allow them to work in pairs to complete the exercise.

Advanced Students

Have the students write each group of sentences in **Try Your Skill** as a paragraph. Tell them to underline the topic sentence. Discuss their paragraphs and why they organized them as they did.

Optional Practice

Write the topic sentence for each of the following groups. Then write each group as a paragraph.

Part 3

What's It All About?

Using a Topic Sentence

Here's the Idea To write a paragraph that has unity, you must have a **topic sentence.** The topic sentence tells what the paragraph is about. It states the main idea in a clear and interesting way. The topic sentence is often the first sentence in a paragraph.

There are two good reasons for using topic sentences. First, a topic sentence helps you to keep track of your ideas. Make sure that all of your sentences tell about the main idea stated in the topic sentence. Then you will not make the mistake of bringing in unrelated ideas. All your sentences will work together. Second, the topic sentence helps your readers. It tells them what the paragraph is going to be about.

Check It Out Read the following paragraph.

> When Manolo was nine he became aware of three important facts in his life. First, the older he became, the more he looked like his father. Second, he, Manolo Oliver, was a coward. Third, everyone in the town of Arcangel expected him to grow up to be a famous bullfighter, like his father. —JAMES RAMSEY ULLMAN

- Does this paragraph have a topic sentence?
- Does the topic sentence state what the paragraph is about?

Try Your Skill Write the topic sentence from each group.

1. (a) My toes became numb inside my boots.
   (b) As I walked home, the biting cold pierced my body.
   (c) Even under a heavy jacket, my skin had goosebumps.
   (d) My face felt as if it would never thaw.
   (e) I exhaled in huge bursts of steamy fog.

2. (a) In first-class sections, there were elegant dining cars, homey parlor cars, and comfortable sleepers.
(b) However, dust from the plains swept over the passengers.
(c) Railroads brought new speed to travel.
(d) In addition, floods and blizzards often destroyed sections of track, causing delays.
(e) Early railroads were both enjoyable and unpleasant.

3. (a) She applied it to everything I did.
(b) Sometimes she'd say it barely loud enough to hear, and I'd stop and think about what I was doing.
(c) At other times she'd write it on a piece of paper and put the paper where I'd be sure to find it.
(d) "An ounce of prevention is worth a pound of cure" was my grandmother's favorite saying.
(e) I used to tease her about her "all-purpose" advice, but I never questioned the wisdom of that advice.

Keep This in Mind

- Be sure that every paragraph has a topic sentence.
- Be sure that the topic sentence states clearly what the paragraph is about.

Now Write Look at the sentences below. They all tell about one main idea. However, they do not have a topic sentence. Write a clear and interesting topic sentence that states the main idea these sentences tell about. Share your topic sentence with your classmates. Save your paragraph in your folder.

Our English language includes *skunk* and *pecan* from the Algonquin Indians. *Persimmon* came to us from the Powhatan Indians of Virginia. *Moose* came into English from the Narragansett tribes, *woodchuck* from the Cree Indians, and *toboggan* from the Micmacs of New England.

1. a. When he was very young he published a book of drawings about a lost cat.
   b. He was born on February 29 in the leap year 1908.
   c. The painter Balthus has led an interesting life.
   d. In the '30's he made a living by designing stage sets.
   e. Now some people consider him the greatest living painter.
2. a. The carat refers to the size of a diamond: a carat is 1/142 ounce.
   b. The value of a diamond is determined by the carat weight, cut, clarity, and color of the stone.
   c. Clarity refers to the visibility of flaws in a diamond.
   d. The cut refers to the shape of the stone.
   e. The term color is self-explanatory; the colorless diamonds are the most valuable.

Extending the Lesson

Help students choose the best topic sentence for each of the following topics.

1. **Topic:** the damage done by a storm
   a. We awoke to a scene of destruction.
   b. Our dog is afraid of thunder and lightning.
   c. Storms sometimes strike unexpectedly.
2. **Topic:** how to mow a lawn
   a. Last summer Roy started a lawn-mowing business.
   b. Mowing a lawn correctly involves four simple steps.
   c. I love the smell of freshly cut grass.

Part 4

Objective

To learn three ways to develop a paragraph

Presenting the Lesson

1. Read aloud and discuss **Here's the Idea.** Discuss each example. Ask the students to identify the details in paragraph 1, to explain the example in paragraph 2, and to cite the facts and figures in paragraph 3.

2. Read and discuss **Check It Out.** Have the class list the examples used to support the topic sentence.

3. Assign and discuss **Try Your Skill.**

4. Read **Keep This in Mind** and then assign **Now Write.**

Individualizing the Lesson

Less-Advanced Students

After completing **Try Your Skill,** give the students additional practice identifying ways paragraphs are developed. Use these sample paragraphs from other parts of the chapter.

a. *Details:* Steinbeck paragraph in Part 5, page 58.

b. *Examples:* Tracy Austin paragraph in Part 2, page 52.

c. *Facts and Figures:* **Now Write** paragraph in Part 3 on page 55.

Advanced Students

Have the students think of topics that could be developed by details, examples, and facts and figures. Have them write one topic sentence for each.

Part 4

Follow the Leader

Developing a Paragraph

Here's the Idea The sentences that follow a topic sentence should tell about the main idea of the paragraph. That means that these sentences should add important information about the main idea. This information can include **details, examples,** and **facts and figures.**

Details can be used to develop a topic sentence.

My uncle's stall in the market is a feast for the senses. The aromas of sweet strawberries and pungent onions rise above the rows of lettuce in every shade of green. Uncle Max shouts, "Get your berries, two pints a dollar," waving his arms to signal the crowds to come take a look. He tumbles potatoes into a scale which responds with creaking springs and a rattling chain, while the black arrow swings downward–one, two, three pounds.

An **example** develops the topic sentence in this paragraph:

Dolphins can solve simple problems. At Marineland of Florida, gates separate the dolphins' small pools from the big show pool. One night some dolphins must have wanted to play in the big pool. They figured out how to use their snouts to open the gates.—*National Geographic World*

Facts and figures are used to develop the topic sentence in this paragraph:

The open mouth of a killer whale is a frightening sight. An adult may have as many as fifty teeth. The teeth are cone-shaped, three inches long and one inch in diameter. They curve inward toward the throat and interlock when the jaw is closed. The teeth are used for grasping, ripping, and tearing food, but not for chewing. The food is swallowed whole or in large chunks.

—SEYMOUR SIMON

Check It Out Read this paragraph about the Mayan Indians.

The Mayan Indians excelled in many fields. They created pyramid-shaped buildings, covered with stone carvings and filled with painted murals. They developed a written language based on pictures and used it to write books. They created a number system that included zero. But their greatest accomplishment was their calendar. It was as accurate as ours is today.

- Is the topic sentence developed by details? Is it developed by examples? Is it developed by facts and figures?

Try Your Skill Find and write the topic sentence in this paragraph. Write whether it is developed by details, examples, or facts and figures.

Even in a small area of the desert there can be a tremendous variation in temperatures. Temperatures on the ground are often 30 to 60 degrees higher than air temperatures in the shade. The National Park Service has recorded some astounding ground temperatures in Death Valley. In 1974 a reading of 176° was recorded and in 1978 a reading of 182°. In 1972 a reading of 201° was recorded. This is almost the boiling point of water.

Keep This in Mind

- The main idea of a paragraph can be developed by using details, an example, or facts and figures.

Now Write Find the topic sentence in the following paragraph and write it. Then write whether the topic sentence is developed with details, examples, or facts and figures.

A white mare galloped west along the strand against the fierce spring wind. Her tail was stretched out stiff and motionless. Flecks of foam dropped from her jaws with each outrush of her breath. Her wide-open nostrils were blood red. Hailstones, carried slantwise at a great speed by the wind's power, struck with a loud noise against the canvas of her saddle. —LIAM O'FLAHERTY

Optional Practice

Discuss the best way to develop each of these topic sentences.

a. An egg is a marvelous creation.
b. Chicago has adorned its streets and plazas with works of art.
c. Jabba the Hutt is one of the ugliest monsters in movie history.
d. The amount of exercise you do determines the number of calories you burn in a day.
e. The lobby of the old hotel was cozy.

Extending the Lesson

Discuss with the class two different ways of developing a paragraph about lighthouses. First, give the students the following topic sentence:

The lighthouse on Gull's Beak Point is the largest lighthouse in the world.

Discuss how facts and figures could be used to develop the rest of the paragraph.

Then give students this topic sentence:

My visits to the lighthouse on Sailor's Cliff have always been exciting.

Discuss how the paragraph could be developed with an example of an exciting event during one of the visits.

Part 5

Objective

To study the three kinds of paragraphs: narrative, descriptive, and explanatory

Presenting the Lesson

1. Read aloud and discuss **Here's the Idea.** Ask the class for suggestions about subject matter that might be covered in each of the three types of paragraphs. For example, stories about people or animals are narratives; describing people, places, or things are descriptions; recipes and directions are explanatory.

2. Read and discuss **Check It Out.** Emphasize that paragraph 1 creates a word picture with many details and that paragraph 2 recounts an incident in time sequence.

3. Assign and discuss **Try Your Skill.**

4. Read **Keep This in Mind** and then assign **Now Write.** Remind the class that two types of paragraphs are arranged in time sequence—the narrative paragraph and the "how-to" kind of explanatory paragraph.

Individualizing the Lesson

Less-Advanced Students

Do **Try Your Skill** orally. Ask students to turn back to paragraphs 1-3 on page 50 of Part 1. Decide whether each is narrative, descriptive, or explanatory.

Advanced Students

Ask the students to find an example of each type of paragraph in a

Part 5

What's in a Name?

Recognizing Three Kinds of Paragraphs

Here's the Idea When you write, you may want to tell a story. You may want to describe someone or something. You may want to explain. For each of these times you would use one of the three kinds of paragraphs: narrative, descriptive, or explanatory.

A **narrative** paragraph tells a story about something or someone. It tells that story in the same order that it happened.

A **descriptive** paragraph is a picture drawn with words. It appeals to your senses of sight, sound, taste, smell, and touch.

An **explanatory** paragraph explains something as clearly as possible. It may tell "how" or "why." A "how" paragraph explains what is to be done first, what is to be done next, and so on through all the steps in a process. A "why" paragraph gives reasons why something is so. It begins with an idea or an opinion. Then it is expanded with reasons that tell why the idea or opinion is true.

You will learn more about narrative, descriptive, and explanatory paragraphs in Sections 8–11.

Check It Out Read the following paragraphs.

1 In the roads where the teams moved, the dirt crust broke and the dust formed. Every moving thing lifted the dust into the air. A walking man lifted a thin layer as high as his waist. A wagon lifted the dust as high as the fence tops and an automobile boiled a cloud behind it. The dust was long in settling back again.

—JOHN STEINBECK

2 Keith was suspicious when he opened the front door. No one was supposed to be home, but he had heard strange, shuffling noises. Then some lights in the kitchen went off. Keith was worried. He headed towards the door. Suddenly his friends burst into the room. "Surprise! Happy birthday!" they shouted. Then Keith laughed.

- Do these paragraphs tell stories, describe, or explain? Are they narrative, descriptive, or explanatory?

Try Your Skill Read each paragraph. Write whether it is narrative, descriptive, or explanatory.

1 Dean had invented a new kind of pizza. On the bottom was a thick, crispy crust. On top of the crust were tangy tomatoes, then juicy sausage and pepperoni. Next came a second layer of tomato-covered crust to make a double-decker pizza. Thick, gooey cheese topped the creation.

2 All people would be happier as pet owners. Whether the pet is a dog, a rabbit, or a hamster, it is fun to watch and to play with. In its own way, a pet shows affection. In addition, it can teach its owner how to care for other living things. Certainly, no one is lonely with a pet.

Keep This in Mind

- A narrative paragraph tells a story.
- A descriptive paragraph describes someone or something.
- An explanatory paragraph explains "how" or "why."

Now Write Below is a list of topics. For each topic, write *Narrative, Descriptive,* or *Explanatory* to show the kind of paragraph you would write for it. Then, briefly explain why. Label your paper **What's in a Name?** Save it in your folder.

my father's garden
why I enjoy hiking
my first airplane ride
how to make papier mâché
why I like spring
Lake Geneva in winter
how to sail a boat
the surprise of my life

textbook, magazine, or newspaper. Discuss their examples in class.

Optional Practice

Follow the directions for **Try Your Skill.**

1. Writing a report is a step-by-step process. First you must decide on an interesting topic. Then you have to gather and organize information on the topic. Writing the first draft is the next step. Revising and rewriting it are the final steps. The result should be an interesting, well-written paper.

2. I will always remember my first swim in the ocean. As I walked down to the beach, the sea seemed to be running away from me. When I waded in, I could feel the undertow. I plunged into the water and came up with a mouthful of salt water. Nobody had warned me how terrible the ocean tastes!

Extending the Lesson

Give the students the following topic sentences.

1. The Sun Coach Company unveiled a solar-powered car.
2. Long ago, deep in the Russian forest, there lived a monster with a problem.
3. The eighth grade needs a newspaper of its own.
4. Last Saturday dawned sunny and warm.

Discuss the possible content of the paragraphs that might develop these topic sentences. Ask students to explain whether each paragraph would be narrative, descriptive, or explanatory.

Section Objectives

1. To learn the three stages in the writing process: pre-writing, writing the first draft, and revising
2. To learn what makes a good subject
3. To learn how to find a good subject
4. To learn when and how to narrow a topic
5. To learn how to write good topic sentences
6. To learn how to gather information to develop a topic
7. To learn the three basic ways to organize a paragraph
8. To learn how to write a first draft of a paragraph
9. To learn how to write good concluding sentences
10. To learn how to revise a first draft

Preparing the Students

Remind the students that they studied paragraphs in Section 5. Ask them to recall this information:

1. The definition of a paragraph
2. The meaning of paragraph unity
3. The function of a topic sentence
4. Three ways of developing paragraphs
5. Three kinds of paragraphs

Explain that in this Section they are going to apply what they learned to paragraphs of their own.

Additional Resources

Mastery Test — page 18 in the test booklet

Practice Book — pages 25–33

Duplicating Masters — pages 25–33

Writing a Paragraph

Part 1 **Step by Step**
Writing as a Process

Part 2 **What Do You Know?**
Pre-Writing: Choosing a Subject

Part 3 **In Focus**
Pre-Writing: Narrowing a Topic

Part 4 **A Better Birdfeeder**
Pre-Writing: A Good Topic Sentence

Part 5 **Bits and Pieces**
Pre-Writing: Gathering Ideas

Part 6 **First Things First**
Pre-Writing: Organizing a Paragraph

Part 7 **Roughing It**
Writing the First Draft

Part 8 **Saying Goodbye**
The First Draft: Ending a Paragraph

Part 9 **Icing the Cake**
Revising Your First Draft

Teaching Special Populations

LD Writing Sections 6–18 may pose considerable difficulties for LD students. Teachers should allow more time to guide students individually through the stages of writing. Try to modify your expectations as to what constitutes error-free writing, and judge each student's progress according to his or her capability. See that LD students keep rough drafts in a file, and ask them to bring the drafts to each session.

Enliven the writing process by including interesting secondary material: pictures (photographs, advertisements), stories, magazine articles (especially those containing illustrations), and short films can all be used. Ask students to respond verbally to the secondary material, then use their responses as an occasion for writing.

ESL Go through certain steps as a group before asking ESL students to proceed with writing. Brainstorming exercises, when conducted first with the whole group, will boost students' confidence and their understanding of what is required.

ESL students may have trouble locating and using reference materials. It may help to work through Section 18, **Using the Library,** before doing writing sections.

NSD For NSD students, writing is stressful because it highlights "errors." Stress the importance of first drafts. Emphasize that all writers use a form of dialect or shorthand in their own drafts. Students should understand that they may construct first drafts in their own dialects. During revision they can standardize nonstandard expressions.

Part 1

Objective

To learn the three stages in the writing process: pre-writing, writing the first draft, and revising

Presenting the Lesson

1. Read aloud and discuss **Here's the Idea.** Write the three stages of the writing process on the chalkboard.

2. Discuss **Check It Out.** Ask students what the result would be if any of the stages of the process of writing were left out. Then ask them what would happen if the stages were done in a different order.

3. Assign and discuss **Try Your Skill.** Do this exercise as an in-class discussion. Encourage students to find the purpose behind writing with a plan.

4. Read **Keep This in Mind.** Then assign **Now Write.**

Individualizing the Lesson

Less-Advanced Students

Do **Try Your Skill** as a class. Write the answers to the first three questions on the board for reinforcement.

Advanced Students

Add these items to **Check It Out.**

7. improves the adjectives in the paragraph
8. corrects errors in punctuation
9. narrows the subject
10. decides how to support the topic

Optional Practice

Ask the students to think of situations in the adult world or in their

Part 1

Step by Step

Writing as a Process

Here's the Idea You have learned that a paragraph is a group of sentences that work together to express one main idea. You know that the main idea of a paragraph can be developed with details, examples, or facts and figures. You also know that a paragraph can tell a story, describe someone or something, or explain something. Now you are ready to start writing some paragraphs of your own.

You may have some questions as you get ready to write. What will you write about? Where will you get your ideas? Once you have begun, how can you improve what you have written? You can find the answers to these questions if you follow a plan when you write. This plan is called the **process of writing.**

The process of writing has three stages. The first stage is **pre-writing.** Pre-writing is all of the planning that you do before you write. This includes choosing a subject, gathering ideas, and putting those ideas into a logical order.

The second stage of the writing process is **writing the first draft.** This is your first attempt to put your ideas down on paper. At this stage you use the ideas you have gathered and organized to write a rough version of your paragraph.

The third and final stage of the writing process is **revising.** *Revise* means "to look over again in order to improve." At this stage of the writing process you try to make your paragraph better.

The lessons in this chapter will show you how you can use the writing process to improve your writing.

Check It Out Here are some things a writer does when writing a paragraph.

1. organizes ideas
2. corrects spelling errors
3. chooses a subject
4. puts ideas in sentence form
5. gathers information
6. improves sentences

- Which of these activities are part of pre-writing? writing the first draft? revising?

Try Your Skill Answer these questions about the writing process.

1. How many stages are there in the writing process? What is each stage called?
2. Name some things you would do during pre-writing.
3. What is the purpose of a first draft?
4. What is the reason for revising what you have written?

Keep This in Mind

- **Pre-writing** includes all the planning you do before you write.
- **Writing the first draft** is the stage where you write a rough version of your paragraph.
- **Revising** is the stage where you improve what you have written.

Now Write In order to become better at something, you have to practice. One of the best ways to get practice in writing is by keeping a journal. A *journal* is a notebook that you write in every day. It is a place where you can write about the things you do, think, or feel.

Get a notebook that you can use as your journal. Try to write in it each day. For today, write down the most interesting thing that you saw or did last week. Include as many details as you can.

lives where written work must be produced. Discuss the pre-writing steps that must be accomplished for each task. (Examples: a newspaper article, a report for the P.T.A., a letter to the editor, etc.)

Extending the Lesson

Read a well-written paragraph to the class. Discuss all of the steps that the writer took to complete the paragraph. Repeat with other paragraphs.

Part 2

Objectives

1. To learn what makes a good subject

2. To learn how to find a good subject

Presenting the Lesson

1. Read aloud and discuss **Here's the Idea.** Ask the students to summarize what makes a good subject. Then write the two ways to find subjects on the chalkboard. Explain that *brainstorming* is a free association technique. One word or topic suggests another. Practice brainstorming with one of these topics: climate, games, music, or clothes.

2. Discuss **Check It Out.** Point out which of the ideas would make good subjects and which would not and why.

3. Assign and discuss **Try Your Skill.** Do one of the topics first as a class activity.

4. Read **Keep This in Mind.** Then assign **Now Write.** Tell students that they may use one of the subjects discovered in **Try Your Skill.** Also, remind them to read through their journals to look for possible subjects.

Individualizing the Lesson

Less-Advanced Students

Have several brainstorming sessions as a class before assigning **Try Your Skill.** If the class has difficulty with brainstorming, allow the students to work in small groups to complete **Try Your Skill.**

Part 2

What Do You Know?

Pre-Writing: Choosing a Subject

Here's the Idea Have you ever stared at a blank piece of paper and grumbled, "I can't think of *anything* to write about?" Choosing a good subject for a paragraph or a composition can be hard. You can make the job easier, however, by learning what a good subject is and how to find one.

A good subject is something that interests you and is important to you. A good subject is also something that you know about.

Knowing what makes a good subject is the first part of choosing something to write about. The second part is knowing where to look for ideas. Here are two ways you can find good subjects to write about.

Journal Writing In your journal you write about your ideas, your feelings, and your experiences. These are subjects that interest you and are important to you. They are also subjects you know something about. Read over what you've written in your journal. You'll find many good writing ideas there.

Brainstorming Brainstorming is an enjoyable way to search for a subject. You can do it by yourself or with friends. Start out with a general idea such as *school*. Then build on that idea by writing down everything about school that comes into your mind. As you brainstorm, you will probably think of several subjects, such as "the food in the cafeteria," "the time the frog escaped from biology lab," and "why I like gym."

Check It Out Here is what one student wrote in his journal during a brainstorming session on the subject *sports*.

- Do you see how brainstorming can lead from one idea to another?
- Can you find some subjects in these notes that this student might write about?

Try Your Skill Here are four very general subjects. Choose one, and spend about fifteen minutes brainstorming about it. As you brainstorm, make notes in your journal. Try to find two or three good subjects among the ideas you wrote down.

school   friends   family life at home   hobbies

Keep This in Mind

- Choose a subject that is important to you and that you know something about.
- Use journal writing and brainstorming to help you find good subjects for writing.

Now Write In the next few lessons you will be writing a paragraph of your own, one step at a time. Your first step, of course, is to choose a subject. Use what you have learned in this lesson to help you. When you have chosen your subject, write it on a piece of paper. Save it in your folder.

Advanced Students

Assign more than one brainstorming topic for **Try Your Skill.**

Optional Practice

Have the students examine their journals and select one or two subjects for writing. Discuss their choices. Point out which would make good subjects and which would not. Explain your reasons.

Extending the Lesson

Practice brainstorming using stimuli other than words. For example, play different pieces of music and ask students to write down whatever comes to their minds. As an alternative, use the sense of smell. Bring in jars filled with "smelly" things and let the smells suggest topics to the students.

Part 3

Objective

To learn when and how to narrow a topic

Presenting the Lesson

1. Read aloud and discuss **Here's the Idea.** Point out that the answers to the questions to ask in narrowing a topic are covered in the sample paragraph, and that the topic sentence is also drawn from the answers to those questions.

2. Do **Check It Out** as a class activity. Help the students to translate their ideas into specific topics.

3. Assign and discuss **Try Your Skill.** When students have mastered the skill of narrowing a topic, assign **Now Write.** Check each student's proposed topic.

Individualizing the Lesson

Less-Advanced Students

Do one of the **Try Your Skill** items as a class. Then assign only one to be completed individually.

Advanced Students

Give the students the following topics. Ask them which of the topics are narrowed enough to be covered in one paragraph and which are not. Have the students narrow the topics that are too broad.

sneakers	trees
Dutch elm disease	trains
waxing a car	T.V. commercials

Optional Practice

For further practice in determining whether a topic is specific enough,

Part 3

In Focus

Pre-Writing: Narrowing a Topic

Here's the Idea Choosing a subject is the first step in writing a paragraph. Sometimes, however, you may choose a subject that is too broad or general to be covered well in a single paragraph. You will need to narrow your subject. This means that you will have to make it more specific.

The subject "vacations," for example, is too general. If you tried to write a paragraph about it, you might end up with something dull like this:

> I like vacations. I like being out of school. It's fun to go different places and do fun things. I wish my vacations were longer.

The subject "vacations" needs to be narrowed. One way to narrow a subject that is too general is by asking questions about it. Such questions might begin with *who, what, when, where, how,* and *why*.

Vacations

Who? me
What? learned to ski
When? last winter
Where? Toll House slopes, Stowe, Vermont
How? lessons, practice
Why? outdoor fun?

Now the general subject "vacations" has been narrowed to "my first attempts at skiing." Narrowing the subject in this way could lead to an interesting paragraph like this one:

I've discovered that learning to ski can be a painful experience. When my family took a winter vacation to Stowe, Vermont, I decided to take skiing lessons. For five days, I climbed up the Toll House slopes and strapped on my skis. Each time, I soon found myself sliding along on my back or tumbling into a tree. On the sixth day, I sat and watched everyone else make it look easy.

Check It Out Now it's your turn to work with the general subject "vacations." Try to narrow it to a more specific topic. Jot down your ideas.

- Did you narrow the subject by asking *who? what? when? where? how?* and *why*?
- Can your narrowed topic be covered in one paragraph?

Try Your Skill Choose two of the general subjects below. Narrow each one by answering the questions *who? what? when? where? how?* and *why?*

family traditions	best friends
school rules	cafeteria food
my pet	gym class

Keep This in Mind

- Choose a subject that you can cover well in one paragraph.
- Narrow general subjects by asking *who? what? when? where? how?* and *why?*

Now Write Think about the subject you chose in **What Do You Know?** Narrow that subject by asking *who? what? when? where? how?* and *why?* Write your narrowed topic in your journal.

give the students the following pairs of topics.

1. outer space—the moons of Venus
2. how robins build their nests—birds
3. I don't get along with our toaster—appliances
4. movies—*The Return of the Jedi*

Ask the class to identify the topic in each pair that is the more specific and to explain why the other one is too broad to be covered in one paragraph.

Extending the Lesson

Read several well-written paragraphs to the class. Ask the students to identify the general topic. Then ask them to explain how it was developed. Have them determine whether the questions *who, what, when, where, how,* and *why* are answered. (The **Check It Out** paragraph on page 79, Part 9 of this section, is a good example for this purpose.)

Part 4

Objective

To learn how to write good topic sentences

Presenting the Lesson

1. Read aloud and discuss **Here's the Idea.** Emphasize the importance of directness.

2. Discuss the topic sentence in **Check It Out.** Work with the class to write the sentence in various ways.

3. Assign and discuss **Try Your Skill.** Have students explain why these sentences are poorly written.

4. Read **Keep This in Mind** and then assign **Now Write.**

Individualizing the Lesson

Less-Advanced Students

Do the **Try Your Skill** exercise together instead of individually.

Advanced Students

Have the students rewrite these general topic sentences to make them more specific. Tell them to refer to **Here's the Idea** to help them improve these sentences.

1. Pizza is good.
2. Checkers is a nice game.
3. Camping can be fun.
4. Dogs are interesting.

Optional Practice

Have the students explain what is wrong with each of these topic sentences. Then have them rewrite the sentences to make them direct, interesting, and informative.

1. I think that football is a dangerous sport.

A Better Birdfeeder

Pre-Writing: A Good Topic Sentence

Here's the Idea Once you've narrowed your topic, you will have a good idea of what you want to write about. To make your idea clear to your reader, you will write a topic sentence for your paragraph.

A topic sentence states the main idea of a paragraph. It tells the reader what the paragraph is going to be about. When you write a topic sentence, keep the following points in mind.

A good topic sentence is direct and interesting. Avoid unnecessary words in your topic sentence. These are words that introduce *you* instead of your topic. Don't write sentences like these:

I am going to write about birdfeeders.
My paragraph is about how dolphins talk to each other.

Instead, write direct and interesting statements like these:

Building a birdfeeder takes just three easy steps.
Dolphins have their own special language.

A good topic sentence is informative. Your topic sentence should give specific information about your paragraph. Don't write general statements like these:

Playing baseball can be exciting.
Cheetahs run fast.

Instead, write specific and informative statements like these:

I'll never forget my first pony league home run.
The cheetah is the fastest land animal in the world.

Check It Out Read this topic sentence.

In this paragraph, I'm going to write about why I like sports.

- Does this topic sentence avoid extra words that introduce you and not the topic?
- Is this topic sentence interesting?
- Does this topic sentence give specific information?

Try Your Skill Below are four poorly-written topic sentences. Rewrite two of them. Make each topic sentence direct and informative.

1. I want to tell you about my best friend George.
2. It is my opinion that school should be closed on Wednesdays.
3. My paragraph is going to be about the hardships of the early sailors.
4. I think I can tell you in this paragraph how to fry a fish.

Keep This in Mind

- A topic sentence should be direct, interesting, and informative.
- Avoid extra words in a topic sentence that introduce you and not the topic.
- Give specific information in a topic sentence.

Now Write Think about the topic you narrowed in the last lesson, **In Focus.** Now write a good topic sentence that tells what your paragraph is about.

Writing a good topic sentence may take some time. Be patient. Try writing several different topic sentences. Which one does the best job of stating your main idea? Choose the best topic sentence. Be sure it is direct, interesting, and informative. Save your topic sentence in your folder.

2. Cats are curious.
3. My paragraph is about how to tune up a car.
4. Marathons are long races.

Extending the Lesson

Have students read the opening sentences of magazine articles and newspaper features to find several good examples of topic sentences. Suggest *National Geographic World* and *Cricket* as possible sources. Ask several students to share their examples with the class. Display the best examples in the classroom.

Part 5

Objective

To learn how to gather information to develop a topic

Presenting the Lesson

1. Read aloud and discuss **Here's the Idea.** As a review, list the three kinds of information used to develop topics on the chalkboard. Then list the three ways discussed to gather information.

2. Discuss **Check It Out.** Point out that there could be more than one answer to this question. Ask students if the writer could also develop the main idea with examples or facts and figures.

3. Assign and discuss **Try Your Skill.** Have students explain *why* they decided to use one kind of information.

4. Read **Keep This in Mind** aloud. Then assign **Now Write.**

Individualizing the Lesson

Less-Advanced Students

Do one of the items from **Try Your Skill** as a class. Allow the students to work in pairs to complete the exercise.

Advanced Students

Add these items to the **Try Your Skill** exercise.

6. Peter Carl Fabergé was a famous jeweler.
7. Fishing is a challenging sport.
8. The first day of high school is an exciting experience.

Part 5

Bits and Pieces

Pre-Writing: Gathering Ideas

Here's the Idea The topic sentence introduces the main idea of a paragraph. The sentences that follow the topic sentence *develop* that main idea. That is, they add information that tells about the main idea. This information may be descriptive details. It may be examples, or facts and figures.

One way to gather information for a paragraph is through **personal observation.** Suppose that you want to describe the cafeteria at school. You would go to the cafeteria and write what you see, hear, smell, taste, and so on. These are the descriptive details you would use to develop your main idea.

Another way to gather information is by **brainstorming.** Perhaps you are writing a paragraph about all the rules a student has to follow at school. Think about your subject and write down all of the examples, incidents, and ideas that come into your head. These details will help you to explain your main idea when you write your paragraph.

A third way to gather information is by **doing research** in the library. Maybe you want to write a paragraph about how fast some animals can travel. You would find the facts and figures you need to explain your main idea by looking up different animals in an encyclopedia.

Check It Out Read these pre-writing notes.

Uncle Dom's Butcher Shop

Smells: · sausage, sawdust, cheese

Touch: · rough, greasy butcher blocks

· cold display cases / razor-sharp knives

Sights: · rows of steaks, chops / mounds of ground beef
· Uncle Dominick—his gold tooth in front
· freezer cases (chrome and glass)
Sounds: · knives being sharpened
· meat cleaver on butcher block
· slap of meat on the scale
· slicer

- How do you think these descriptive details were gathered?

Try Your Skill Here are four topic sentences. Read each one and decide what kind of information is needed to develop it. Would you use descriptive details, examples, or facts and figures? Would you gather this information through personal observation, brainstorming, or research?

1. Paramedics help people in many kinds of emergencies.
2. My neighbor's kitchen is a most comfortable room to be in.
3. Television programs get sillier each year.
4. Chicago has some of the world's tallest buildings.

Keep This in Mind

- You can gather ideas through personal observation, by brainstorming, and by looking things up.
- The kind of ideas you gather depends on what your paragraph is about.

Now Write Gather some ideas and information for your paragraph. First read your topic sentence. Then ask yourself what kind of information you need to develop it: descriptive details, examples, or facts and figures. Use personal observation, brainstorming, or research to gather this information. Write your information. Save your notes in your folder.

Optional Practice

Have students select one of the following general topics and write three topic sentences—one to be developed with facts and figures, one with examples, and one with descriptive details.

cooking	television	skyscrapers
farming	restaurants	cars

Write the following example on the board for them, first.

Topic: Fishing

Facts & Figures: Sport fishing in Michigan has become more popular.

Example: The first fish I caught actually caught me.

Descriptive Details: A gar is an unusual-looking fish.

Extending the Lesson

Have each student bring a sample paragraph to class. Use an overhead projector or duplicate the paragraphs. Discuss what kind of material was used in each to support the topic sentence. Also discuss how the writer probably went about gathering that information.

Part 6

Objective

To learn the three basic ways to organize a paragraph

Presenting the Lesson

1. Read aloud and discuss **Here's the Idea.** Write the three ways to organize a paragraph on the chalkboard. Have the students look back to Section 5 and examine the sample paragraphs in each part. Then have the students explain how each one is organized. As an alternative, bring in three paragraphs that illustrate the different ways to organize a paragraph and discuss them with the students.

2. Discuss **Check It Out.** Make sure the class understands that it is the purpose of the paragraph that determines the organization.

3. Assign and discuss **Try Your Skill.** Ask students what the purpose of the paragraph is.

4. Read **Keep This in Mind** and then assign **Now Write.**

Individualizing the Lesson

Less-Advanced Students

Allow the students to work in pairs to complete **Try Your Skill.**

Advanced Students

Have the students determine which method of organization would be best for each of these topics.

- the benefits of a college education
- how to make deep-dish pizza
- the advantages of owning a dog
- a sunset over the ocean
- a new car

Part 6

First Things First

Pre-Writing: Organizing a Paragraph

Here's the Idea Once you have gathered information for your paragraph, you must make another decision. How should this information be arranged?

There are basically three ways to organize information in a paragraph. The method you choose will depend on the purpose of your paragraph. One way is to arrange details in *the order that they happened or should happen.* This is called **chronological order.** You would choose this order if your purpose were to tell a story or explain how to do something.

A second way to organize details is to arrange them in *the order that a viewer would notice them.* This is called **spatial order.** You would use this order if your purpose were to describe something—the objects in your room, for example.

A third way to organize details is to arrange them in **the order of their importance.** You might start with the least important idea and work toward the most important. Or you could do just the opposite. You would use this kind of order if some of your ideas are more important than others.

When you are organizing the details for a paragraph, choose an order that fits the type of paragraph that you are writing.

Check It Out Read the following paragraph.

> Making a delicious chocolate milkshake is as easy as one, two, three. First, drop two scoops of creamy vanilla ice cream into a blender. Second, add about one cup of milk and as much chocolate syrup as you like. Third, blend the ingredients at high speed for a minute or two. Now pour the milk shake into a chilled glass, and enjoy a mouth-watering, warm-weather treat!

- What is the purpose of this paragraph?
- In what order have the details been arranged?

- Does the arrangement fit the purpose of the paragraph?

Try Your Skill Here are some pre-writing notes for a paragraph explaining how to paint a bike. Organize the notes so that a good paragraph can be written from them. Remember to choose an order that fits the purpose of the paragraph. When you have finished, write the kind of order that you used.

- finally, wax the newly-painted bike
- after primer dries, spray on metal paint
- begin by cleaning bike with steel wool
- before applying metal paint, spray on coat of primer paint
- after sanding, use masking tape to cover all parts you don't want to paint
- when bike is clean, sand all parts you want to paint
- when metal paint dries, remove masking tape

Keep This in Mind

- The details in a paragraph can be organized in three ways:
  1. chronological order, or the order in which they happened or should happen.
  2. spatial order, or the order in which a viewer would notice them.
  3. the order of their importance.
- Details should be organized to fit the type of paragraph you are writing.

Now Write Look over the details you gathered in the last lesson, **Bits and Pieces.** Organize these details so that you can write a good paragraph from them.

First ask yourself what type of paragraph you are writing. Then choose an order that fits your purpose. Save your organized details in your folder.

Optional Practice

Follow the directions for **Try Your Skill.**

- Ms. Gertie rode into town
- boots covered with mud from the fields
- gray, frizzy hair
- wide leather belt with a silver buckle
- wore an old plaid flannel shirt
- tan, weathered face
- had on faded blue jeans

Extending the Lesson

Have students find examples of paragraphs in magazines or newspapers using each method of organization. Have them bring the samples in and make a bulletin board display.

Part 7

Objective

To learn how to write a first draft of a paragraph

Presenting the Lesson

1. Read aloud and discuss **Here's the Idea.** Emphasize that the purpose of a first draft is to get the writer's ideas on paper. Explain that a first draft is not the final product; it will be improved and rewritten for the final copy.

2. Discuss **Check It Out.** Point out the differences between the pre-writing notes and the first draft. Explain that at any stage in writing, changes can be made to improve the paragraph.

3. Assign and discuss **Try Your Skill.** This would be a good time to go over each student's work and discuss it with him or her individually. Always point out the things that a student has done well, not just what needs improvement.

4. Read aloud **Keep This in Mind.** Then assign **Now Write.**

Individualizing the Lesson

Less-Advanced Students

Help the students develop their topic sentences to get them started on their first drafts.

Advanced Students

Using an opaque projector, display and discuss the students' first drafts. Have them check for strong topic sentences and suitable organization of details. Then review the first drafts for grammatical and mechanical errors.

Part 7

Roughing It

Writing the First Draft

Here's the Idea All the work you've done on your paragraph up to now has been part of pre-writing, the first stage of the writing process. Now you are ready to begin the second stage of the process, **writing the first draft**.

The first draft is the first time you write your ideas down in paragraph form. It is a chance for you to experiment. You may find out as you write your first draft that your topic sentence is weak. If that is the case, go ahead and rewrite it. You might decide that the order of your details needs to be changed. Feel free to move them around. You may even discover that you need more information. If so, stop writing and look for more details. Remember, your first draft is not your final paragraph. You can change it as much as you want to. You may even write several drafts before you are satisfied with your paragraph.

As you write your first draft, concentrate on explaining your ideas as well as you can. Don't worry about whether a word is spelled correctly, or whether you need a comma in a sentence. You will have time later on to fix your spelling and punctuation. Skip lines as you write so you will have room to make corrections.

Check It Out Read this first draft. It was written from the pre-writing notes on pages 70–71.

> My favorite place to spend a Saturday afternoon is my uncle Dominick's butcher shop. I love the smell of the sausages and cheeses. Uncle Dom is always smiling and talking to the customers. Aunt Christina is there too. She arranges the steaks into rows

in the display cases. I can hear the knives click as she sharpens them. The customers always tell her say hello to your family. Everybody is friendly. That's why I like my uncle Dom's butcher shop.

- Does this first draft have a clear topic sentence?
- Does this draft use ideas from the pre-writing notes on pages 70–71?
- Has the writer added any new details to the draft that weren't in the pre-writing notes?

Try Your Skill Look over the pre-writing notes that you organized in **Try Your Skill** on page 73. Use your organized notes to write a first draft of a paragraph about painting a bike. Write a topic sentence for the paragraph. Remember, you can add new details if you want to.

Keep This in Mind

- A first draft is the first written version of your paragraph.
- A first draft is a chance for you to experiment with your ideas.
- When you write a first draft, don't worry about spelling and punctuation. Just get your ideas down in paragraph form.

Now Write Take out your organized notes from the last lesson, **First Things First.** Write a first draft of your paragraph. Don't be afraid to change your ideas as you write. Feel free to experiment. Remember to skip lines as you write. Save your first draft in your folder.

Optional Practice

Assign another first draft using the details from the **Optional Practice** exercise in Section 6, Part 6 on page 73.

Extending the Lesson

Ask the students if they know of any careers that use writing skills (author, newspaper reporter, script-writer, textbook writer, lawyer, business consultant, etc.). Explain that writers make many drafts of their work before it is ready to be written in its final form.

Explain that if something is to be published, editors review the drafts of writers' works and make suggestions for improvement. Introduce the students to the standard proofreading symbols. They can usually be found in a good dictionary. (Also see page 85.) Assign a group of students to make a large poster illustrating the marks and hang it in the classroom for future use.

Finally, use the proofreading symbols when correcting the first drafts written by the students.

Part 8

Objective

To learn how to write good concluding sentences

Presenting the Lesson

1. Read aloud and discuss **Here's the Idea.** Emphasize that a good ending sentence should relate in some way to the sentences that precede it. Discuss the paragraph in **Check It Out.** Ask for suggestions about ideas that might be included in a revised final sentence. One possibility is to note the connection between the word *gopher* and the phrase *go for.*

2. Assign **Try Your Skill.** Remind the class to follow the guidelines summarized under **Keep This in Mind.**

3. Assign **Now Write.** Encourage students to write several versions of endings before writing a final conclusion.

Individualizing the Lesson

Less-Advanced Students

Have students do **Try Your Skill** as an in-class exercise.

Advanced Students

Have each student revise his or her concluding sentence for the paragraph on painting a bike (**Try Your Skill,** Part 7). Also, if he or she did the **Optional Practice** in Part 7, have each student revise that concluding sentence.

Optional Practice

Add a good concluding sentence to the following paragraph.

Part 8

Saying Goodbye

The First Draft: Ending a Paragraph

Here's the Idea Once you have written your ideas in paragraph form, your first draft is nearly finished. All that it needs is a good ending sentence.

A good ending sentence should follow naturally from what you have already written. It should tie the paragraph together by summing up the main idea. The ending sentence should not add any new information to the paragraph.

A good ending sentence should also be interesting. Don't just repeat your topic sentence. Put a new twist on your words. Try to make your ending as interesting as your beginning.

Check It Out Read the following paragraph.

> My friend George is a "gopher." George works for his father during the summers. George and his father build and repair houses. Most of the time, George's father does the carpentry. When he needs nails, he yells, "George, go for the nails." When he wants coffee, he says, "George, go for some coffee." George is my best friend.

- Does the paragraph have an ending sentence?
- Does the ending sentence follow naturally from the rest of the paragraph? Does it sum up the idea of the paragraph?
- Is the ending sentence interesting? Explain your answer.

Try Your Skill Revise the ending sentences of these two paragraphs. Be sure each ending sentence sums up the main idea of the paragraph. Try to make each ending sentence interesting.

1 Susan joined the sea of subway riders. Clutching her purse, she went down the escalator. She was pushed along with the crowd, first to the ticket booth and then to one of the screeching trains. Once inside, she saw that there was no chance of getting a seat. The subway was powered by electricity.

2 Homemade gifts are the best gifts. Not only are they less expensive than bought gifts, but they can also be more personal. Homemade gifts show that the giver cares, because they require time, energy, and creativity. They are appreciated more than gifts that are bought from a store. I made my own Christmas gift two years ago.

Keep This in Mind

- A paragraph should have an ending sentence.
- A good ending sentence is interesting and sums up the main idea of the paragraph.
- A good ending sentence should not add any new information to the paragraph.

Now Write Reread your first draft. Write an ending sentence that is interesting and that sums up the main idea of the paragraph. Save your draft in your folder.

Swimming is almost a perfect exercise. It gets the heart and lungs working, so it is a good aerobic workout. Swimming also tones and firms the muscles. Moreover, it does not put any stress on the joints of the body.

Extending the Lesson

Have the students find examples of well-written paragraphs in books, magazines, or newspapers. Each student should select one paragraph and copy it, deleting the concluding sentence. Have the students exchange paragraphs and add concluding sentences. Compare the students' sentences with those written by the original author. Have students use **Keep This in Mind** when evaluating the sentences.

Part 9

Objective

To know how to revise a first draft

Presenting the Lesson

1. Read aloud and discuss **Here's the Idea.** Have the students write a checklist of the steps in the revision process.

2. Discuss **Check It Out.** In particular, point out the improvement in the details and in the language used in the revised paragraph.

3. Assign and discuss **Try Your Skill.** A good way to compare revisions is to duplicate examples of students' work.

4. Read **Keep This in Mind.** Then assign **Now Write.**

Individualizing the Lesson

Less-Advanced Students

Do **Try Your Skill** as a classroom activity.

Advanced Students

Have the students revise the paragraph written for **Try Your Skill,** Part 6 (painting a bicycle) for additional practice.

Optional Practice

Have the students revise this first draft.

The weight-lifter was huge. he was over six-feet tall. his bald head gleemed in the lights. his shoulder and arm muscles rippled when he moved. his legs were strong. and muscular too. He was realy a site.

Part 9

Icing the Cake

Revising Your First Draft

Here's the Idea You have finished writing your first draft. Now you are ready to begin the last stage of the writing process: **revising.**

The purpose of revision is to improve what you have written. All writers have to revise their first drafts. They know that careful revision will make their writing the best it can be.

When you begin revising your rough draft, first work on your ideas. Then work on your organization. Check to see that your paragraph begins with a good topic sentence. Be sure all of the details you have used help to develop the main idea of your paragraph. Look at the arrangement of those details. Does the order make sense? See that you have ended your paragraph with a good ending sentence.

When you are sure that your ideas are strong and in good order, look at the language you have used. Is it lively? Is it interesting? Does it make your paragraph come alive for your readers? Replace any dull language that you find.

Finally, you will want to proofread your draft. Is your grammar correct? Have you used capital letters where they are needed? Have you used the right punctuation? Are all of the words spelled correctly? Use a dictionary and the Handbook sections of this book if you need help.

When you are satisfied that your revised paragraph is as good as it can be, make a final copy of it. Proofread this final copy one last time to correct any mistakes.

Check It Out Read this revised version of the first draft on pages 74–75.

My favorite place to spend a Saturday afternoon is my uncle Dominick's butcher shop. I love the smell of the spicy sausages and the sharp cheeses. Uncle Dom is always smiling as he talks to his customers. His gold tooth gleams in the bright white light. Aunt Christina helps out, too. She arranges the steaks and chops into neat rows in the shiny display cases. I can hear the click and scrape of the knives as she sharpens them. The customers always tell her, "Say hello to your family." Everybody is so friendly. Who wouldn't enjoy a place as warm and happy as my uncle Dom's butcher shop?

- How is this version different from the one on pages 74–75? Why is it better?

Try Your Skill Revise this draft. Improve the topic sentence. Add interesting details. Replace any dull language. Add a good ending sentence. Compare your revision with those of your classmates.

The best time is lunch. We all go from class to the lunchroom. Sometimes we bring lunch from home. Then we can trade. Sometimes we buy lunch. Everyone talks about what to do after school. There is music on the loudspeaker.

Keep This in Mind

- When you revise, try to improve your ideas, organization and word choice.
- Proofread to correct any errors in grammar, capitalization, punctuation and spelling.

Now Write Revise your first draft. Use the guidelines you studied in this lesson. When you are satisfied with your revision, make a good copy of your paragraph. Save your paragraph in your folder.

Extending the Lesson

Assign a group of students to make a poster (or a bulletin board display) of a checklist for the revision process. Hang it in the classroom for future reference.

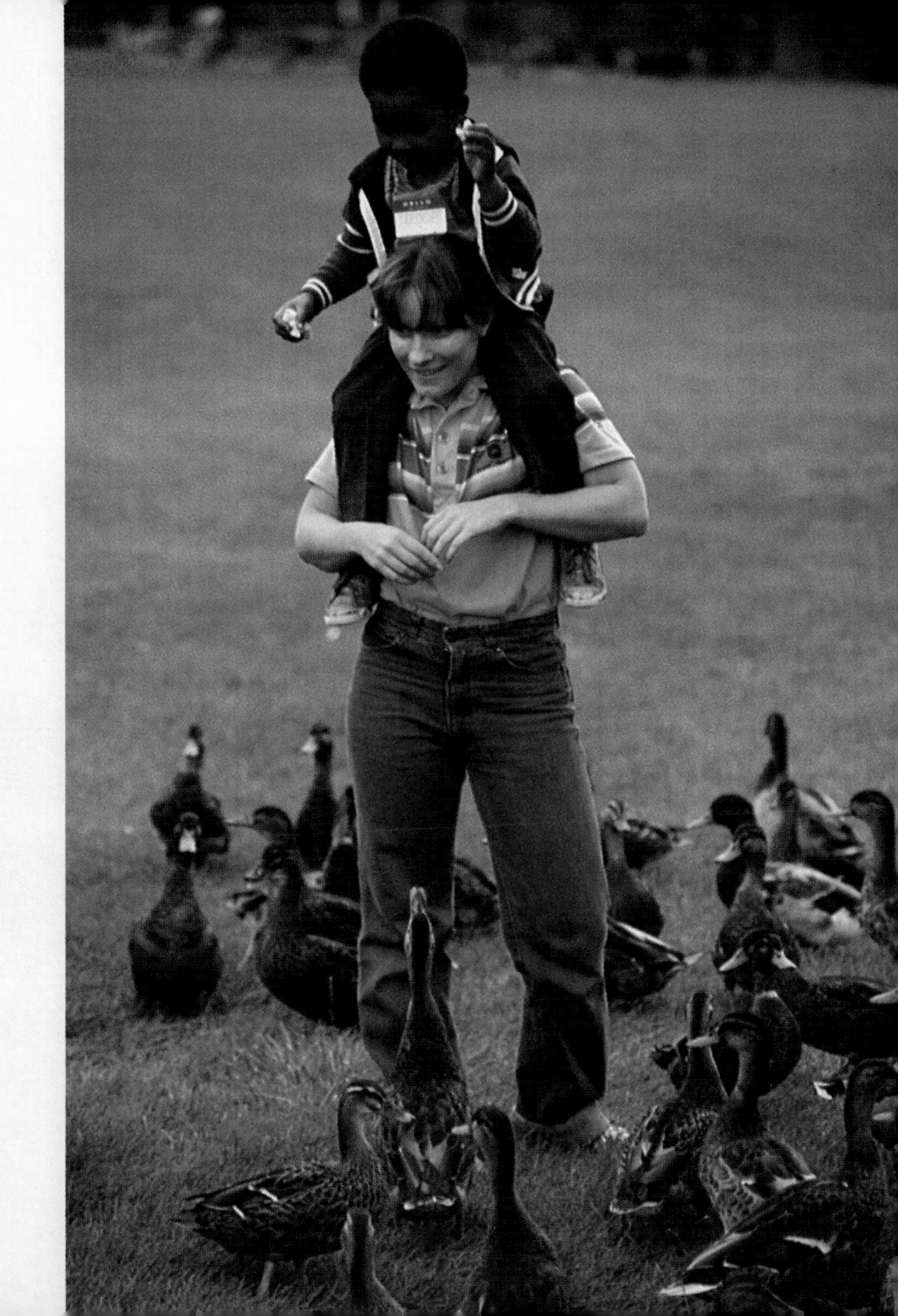

The Process of Writing

Teaching Special Populations

LD See **Teaching Special Populations,** page 61.

ESL Students may benefit from being paired with a native English speaker for some of the pre-writing steps. Make periodic checks of students' spelling, capitalization, grammar, and punctuation. Provide additional practice whenever necessary. Be prepared to accept sentences that are unimaginative but grammatically correct.

NSD See **Teaching Special Populations,** page 61.

Section Objectives

1. To review the stages of the process of writing

2. To understand and correctly use proofreading symbols

Presenting the Lesson

This section is a review of the process of writing presented in Section 6. The three stages in the writing process are explained again, and a sample paragraph is presented in its various stages of development. There are no exercises for students to complete.

This section can be used as a culminating activity for Section 6. The concepts presented should be reviewed with the class, and the writing samples should be studied in detail. In the pre-writing notes, point out the details that will be omitted. Ask the students why the writer chose to delete these details. Then ask the students to study the way in which the details have been organized. Have the students explain why chronological order is right for this topic. Then read the first draft.

Ask the students to suggest changes that they think would improve the paragraph. Stress the importance of revising to your students. Be sure they understand that revising is more than just fixing misspellings or adding missing punctuation. Revising is a chance to improve the entire paragraph or composition, including its ideas and organization.

Review the list of questions on page 85. Have the students practice using the proofreading symbols in the chart on page 85. Finally, compare the first draft to the revised

The Process of Writing

In the last section, you learned about the three main stages in the process of writing. You learned how to choose and narrow subjects. You learned how to gather and organize information during pre-writing. You learned how to write a first draft, and how to revise.

Now you can begin practicing your writing skills. In the next few sections, you will be writing many different kinds of paragraphs and compositions. However, no matter what kind of writing you do, the process of writing remains the same.

In this lesson, you will review the process of writing from beginning to end. First, read about each step in the process. Then look at the example that shows how one student followed each step.

Pre-Writing Sometimes you write in response to an assignment. Sometimes you choose to write in order to communicate something that is important to you. No matter what or why you write, you will find the pre-writing, or planning, stage to be very important.

Before you write, you may want to brainstorm for subject ideas. Perhaps you have kept a journal. Look through it for interesting subjects to write about. When you choose a subject, narrow it. That is, make it specific enough so that it can be covered well in a given length.

Jot down some notes and ideas about your topic. These notes may include lists of descriptive details, examples, or facts and figures that you can use to develop your topic. You can gather this kind of information through personal observations, by brainstorming, or by using the library.

When you have gathered enough details, you need to organize them. You may not need to use all of the information you have collected. Look over your details and cross out any that do not relate directly to your main idea. Then arrange your details in the best order for the kind of writing you are doing. Three kinds of order you might use are chronological order, spatial order, and the order of importance.

Pre-Writing

You list possible topics and choose one.

topics

Rocky to the vet — Red Sox win — history test — the beach — moving day

You list details, choose the most important ones, and organize them.

details

① Rocky needed shots
⑥ rabbit on a leash
② Rocky hides under bed (he knew!)
⑦ four cats
⑧ heartworm (false alarm)
④ smell of disinfectant
③ Rocky won't get in car
~~spotless office~~
⑤ pet photos on wall
~~collie on way to surgery~~
⑨ Rocky gets doggie treat
~~smiling assistant~~

Writing the First Draft At this point in the process of writing, you are ready to write your first draft. Simply put your pencil to paper and write. Don't try to make anything perfect at this stage. Don't worry about spelling or punctuation. Let whatever happens, happen. Just put your ideas down in para-

copy. Ask the students to point out the specific changes that have been made in the revised copy. Be sure they understand the symbols used.

You may want to introduce your students to some or all of the following revising techniques.

Peer evaluation—Students critique each other's writings in small group sessions.

Conference—Oral evaluations by the teacher concentrate on both strengths and problems.

Editorial group—Students are assigned the roles of author, editor, and proofreader and work together on an assignment.

Group questioning—After one student in a group reads a piece of writing aloud, the other students ask questions focusing on what they still want to know about the subject.

Clinics—In workshops, students with similar writing problems receive instruction from the teacher.

Tutoring—A student who is weak in some area is paired with a student who is stronger in the same area.

A second use for this section is as a reference tool. Before an important writing assignment, either review this section with the class, or have students review it individually.

Additional Resources

Practice Book — pages 34–35.

Duplicating Masters — pages 34–35.

graph form, following the order you decided on. You will have time later to revise. Skip lines as you write, so that you will have space to make corrections.

Writing the First Draft

You write a paragraph about your topic.

I had to take Rocky to the vet for his shots. I knew I was in for trouble. I had to drag him out from under the bed. He refused to get in the car. At the office, we waited to see the doctor. The office smelled like disinfectant. There were pet photos on the wall. In the waiting room was a lady with four cats. A boy had a rabbit on a leash he was shaking. When the doctor looked at Rocky, he thought Rocky might have a case of heartworm. It was a false alarm. After his shots, Rocky got a doggie treat. He couldn't get out of the doctor's office fast enough. And that was my trip to the vet with Rocky.

84

Revising At this stage of the process, you have to check what you have written. You should read your first draft carefully and decide how you can make it better. Here are some questions you should ask yourself about your first draft.

1. Have I written a topic sentence? Is it interesting, direct, and informative?
2. Have I included enough details to develop my topic?
3. Do all of my details tell about the main idea of the paragraph?
4. Have I organized my details well?
5. Have I used lively, interesting language?
6. Have I written a strong ending?

As you answer these questions, you will discover how to improve what you have written.

Proofreading Proofreading is the last stage of revising. Check your draft to see that you have used correct grammar, capitalization, punctuation, and spelling. Use the Handbook sections of this textbook and a dictionary to check your work.

As you revise your first draft, use the following proofreading marks to show your corrections and changes.

Proofreading Symbols

Symbol	Meaning	Example
∧	add	would ∧ gone (have)
≡	capitalize	United states
/	make lower case	our club President
∾	reverse	thier
℘	take out	finished the the race
¶	make new paragraph	....be over. ¶ New ideas
⊙	period	....and stop ⊙ Before we
∧	add comma	Red, blue and green are

Here is how the paragraph about Rocky was revised.

Revising

You rewrite.

You express your idea in a different way.

When Mom said   , my collie ,
I had to take Rocky to the vet
     yearly
for his shots, I knew I was in for
     First,
trouble. I had to drag him out
     my   Then,
from under ~~the~~ bed. ~~He~~ he refused to
     to
get in the car. At the office, we
waited to see the doctor. The office
smelled like disinfectant. ~~There were~~
~~pet photos on the wall.~~ In the
     sat
waiting room ~~was~~ a lady with four
fat   They hissed at Rocky, and he barked right back.
cats. A boy had a rabbit on a leash.
     The rabbit
~~he~~ was shaking. When the doctor
     examined
~~looked at~~ Rocky, he thought Rocky
might have a case of heartworm. It
turned out to be   he got
~~was~~ a false alarm. After his shots,
     was given   Then he dragged me to the door.
Rocky ~~got~~ a doggie treat. ~~He couldn't~~
~~get out of the doctor's office fast~~
     a trip to the vet with Rocky can be an
~~enough.~~ ~~And that was my trip to~~
exhausting experience.
~~the vet with Rocky.~~

86

Making the Final Copy Finally, when you are satisfied that your writing is clear and correct, make a final copy. Write carefully. Make your work as neat as possible.

When you have finished your final copy, proofread it one last time. If you discover a mistake, correct it neatly.

Final Copy

When Mom said I had to take Rocky, my collie, to the vet for his yearly shots, I knew I was in for trouble. First, I had to drag him out from under my bed. Then, he refused to get into the car. At the office, we waited to see the doctor. The office smelled like disinfectant. In the waiting room sat a lady with four fat cats. They hissed at Rocky, and he barked right back. A boy had a rabbit on a leash. The rabbit was shaking. When the doctor examined Rocky, he thought Rocky might have a case of heartworm. It turned out to be a false alarm. After he got his shots, Rocky was given a doggie treat. Then he dragged me to the door. He couldn't get out of the doctor's office fast enough. A trip to the vet with Rocky can be an exhausting experience.

You can learn to write only by writing. Whenever you write, follow the steps in the writing process that you have learned. Each time you write, you will be learning something about writing and about yourself.

Section 8 Objectives

1. To develop the details of a narrative paragraph by using the guide questions *who? what? where? when? why?* and *how?*

2. To understand and apply the concept of chronological order in a narrative paragraph

3. To understand the concept of point of view

4. To distinguish between first-person point of view and third-person point of view

5. To use transitions to show time sequence

6. To check for sufficient details, chronological order, good transitions, and consistent point of view when revising a narrative paragraph

7. To use strong, specific verbs

Preparing the Students

Read aloud selected paragraphs from a book with strong narrative qualities. *The Incredible Journey* by Sheila Burnford is such a book. Review the meaning of *narrative paragraph.* Explain that in the next five lessons the students will learn to write narrative paragraphs of their own.

Additional Resources

Mastery Test — page 19 in the test booklet

Practice Book — pages 36–40

Duplicating Masters — pages 36–40

The Narrative Paragraph

Part 1 **Details, Details**
Pre-Writing: Developing a Narrative

Part 2 **Then What Happened?**
Pre-Writing: Using Chronological Order

Part 3 **Who Said That?**
Pre-Writing: Choosing a Point of View

Part 4 **First, Then, Finally**
Writing the First Draft

Part 5 **Prance or Trudge?**
Revising Your Narrative Paragraph

Teaching Special Populations

LD See **Teaching Special Populations,** page 61.

ESL Pay particular attention to the sections on chronological order and emphasize the vocabulary related to time. Give students numerous contextual examples of the change of form in third-person singular present tense verbs. Combine these exercises with practice in using the third-person point of view.

NSD See **Teaching Special Populations,** page 61.

Part 1

Objective

To develop the details of a narrative paragraph by using the guide questions *who? what? where? when? why?* and *how?*

Presenting the Lesson

1. Read aloud and discuss **Here's the Idea.** Write the definition of *narrative paragraph* on the chalkboard. Then ask the students to suggest possible topics for narrative paragraphs.

2. Read and discuss **Check It Out.** Then ask *who? what? where? when? why?* and *how?* about one of the topics suggested by the students. Write these pre-writing notes on the chalkboard or use an overhead projector.

3. Assign and discuss **Try Your Skill.** If students have trouble answering the questions, tell them to try the *brainstorming* technique. Explain that after they come up with many details, they can then choose those that relate to their topics.

4. Read **Keep This in Mind.** Then assign **Now Write.**

Individualizing the Lesson

Less-Advanced Students

Before assigning **Try Your Skill,** read the students a sample narrative paragraph. (See Writing Section 5, Part 5 and the TE for that section to find examples.) Then do the **Try Your Skill** exercise as a class.

Part 1

Details, Details

Pre-Writing: Developing a Narrative

Here's the Idea No matter what kind of paragraph you write, the three stages that make up the process of writing always remain the same. The choices you make at each stage of the process, however, will change. You want to make choices that best suit the kind of paragraph you are writing. In this section you will learn about some of the choices you might make as you develop a narrative paragraph.

A **narrative paragraph** tells a story. When you choose a subject for this type of paragraph, choose an interesting or exciting event. You might, for example, write about something that happened to you on a weekend camping trip or in your science class. You could also write a story that you make up, such as a space adventure.

When you have chosen a subject for your narrative paragraph, you must gather supporting ideas to develop your story. The best way to develop a narrative paragraph is to use **specific details.** These should be vivid, interesting details. They should make the story seem real to your readers.

You can find details to develop your story by doing what newspaper reporters do. Reporters ask *who? what? when? where? why?* and *how?* to discover the details that make up a story. Ask yourself these same questions about the story you want to tell. The answers to these questions will give you the details you need to write a good narrative paragraph.

Check It Out Read these pre-writing notes for a paragraph about a toboggan ride.

90

Who? Chris, David, Drew, and I
What? tobogganing for the first time
Where? Bemus Woods, twenty-foot high slide, six-foot long toboggan
When? last weekend, during subzero cold, −13°
Why? to try a new daredevil challenge
How? bundled like mummies, laughing and shrieking

- Do you see how asking *who? what? when? where? why?* and *how?* can help you to find vivid, interesting details for your narrative paragraph?

Try Your Skill Read the topics listed below. Ask *who? what? when? where? why?* and *how?* to gather specific details for one of the topics. List as many details as you can.

1. a sports event I attended
2. a birthday party
3. a funny incident in class

Keep This in Mind

- Develop narrative paragraphs by using specific details.
- The details for a narrative paragraph can be gathered by asking *who? what? when? where? why?* and *how?*

Now Write Choose one of the two topics you did not use in **Try Your Skill.** Narrow the topic to a specific event you can tell about in one paragraph. Ask yourself questions to gather vivid, specific details that will make the story seem real to your readers. Save your pre-writing notes in your folder.

Advanced Students

Add these topics to **Try Your Skill.** Have each student gather specific details for two topics.

4. a highlight of a trip
5. the scariest thing that ever happened to me

Optional Practice

Repeat **Try Your Skill** with these topics.

1. the best entertainment I've ever seen or heard
2. my most embarrassing moment
3. a funny incident at home

Extending the Lesson

Have each student find an example of a well-written narrative paragraph from a book, magazine, or newspaper. Have each student answer the questions *who? what? where? when? why?* and *how?* for his or her paragraph. Read and discuss the narrative paragraphs in class.

Part 2

Objective

To understand and apply the concept of chronological order in a narrative paragraph

Presenting the Lesson

1. Read aloud and discuss **Here's the Idea.** Study the sample paragraph. Ask students to list the events that are described in the paragraph.

2. Read and discuss **Check It Out.** Emphasize the main events in the narrative to reinforce the concept of chronological order.

3. Assign **Try Your Skill.** Ask students to point out the words that tell them the time sequence ("Before dinner," "To end the evening," "The evening began," etc.)

4. Assign **Now Write.**

Individualizing the Lesson

Less-Advanced Students

1. Work in a small group with students who have not mastered chronological order. Give them a simple topic that will naturally fall into a time sequence. You might suggest one of the following:

a. Getting dressed for very cold weather
b. Walking home from school (select one day)
c. The final minutes of an exciting game
d. A day when everything goes wrong

Ask each student to list four or five things that happened. Note that the events should be in chronological order. You may or may not direct the group to complete their paragraphs.

Part 2

Then What Happened?

Pre-Writing: Using Chronological Order

Here's the Idea After you have gathered details for your narrative paragraph, the next important pre-writing step is deciding how to organize those details. Remember, narrative paragraphs tell stories. As the narrator, or person who tells the story, you will want to tell your story in the same order that the events took place. This type of organization is called **chronological order.** *Chronological* means "arranged in the order of time."

Use a natural time sequence to organize the details of your story. Tell what happened first, what happened next, and so on. This will help the reader understand the story.

Look at this narrative paragraph. Notice that the events are told in the same order that they happened.

> He crawled through the doorway. He pulled the ankle flaps of his new winter moccasins up and tied them tightly. He fastened the thongs of the snowshoes firmly around his toes and around his ankles. He moved out onto the snow with wide, swinging steps and flapped his arms to make his blood flow fast and warm. It was good to be out in the open again, not just to push to the stream for water or to the storehouse for food, but out in the open and free to swing anywhere throughout his canyon.
>
> —JACK SHAEFER

Check It Out Now read this narrative paragraph:

> Huck began to dig and scratch now. Some boards were soon uncovered and removed. They had concealed a natural chasm which led under the rock. Tom got into this and held his candle as far under the rock as he could, but said he could not see to the end of the rift. He proposed to explore. He stooped and passed

under; the narrow way descended gradually. He followed its winding course, first to the right, then to the left, Huck at his heels. Tom turned a short curve, by and by, and exclaimed: "My goodness, Huck, looky here!"

—MARK TWAIN

- In what kind of order are the details of this narrative arranged? How do you know?

Try Your Skill Arrange the following pre-writing notes into a chronological order.

- My grandparents' 50th wedding anniversary party was wonderful.
- Before dinner, my grandparents opened gifts from friends and family.
- To end the evening, the band played polkas and waltzes.
- The evening began with everyone shouting "Surprise!" as my grandparents walked through the door.
- Then, there was a huge meal with a special cake for dessert.
- After dinner, my father gave a toast to the couple.

Keep This in Mind

- In a narrative paragraph, use chronological order to organize details.

Now Write Look at the topic you chose and the pre-writing notes you gathered in the last lesson, **Details, Details.** Organize these notes in chronological order. Save your organized notes in your folder.

2. Ask students to write one-paragraph summaries of television programs, films, or books. Guide them in choosing examples that have strong story lines.

Advanced Students

Have the students select one of these topics and write a set of pre-writing notes for it. Remind the students that the notes are to be in chronological order.

1. my first (bus, plane, train) ride
2. a good time with my friends (brother, mom, dad, etc.)
3. a visit to an interesting place

Optional Practice

Follow the directions for **Try Your Skill.**

1 • The Arts Festival was a huge success.
4 • During lunch time a local jazz quartet played.
5 • After lunch, local artists set up booths around the stage area to display their work.
2 • The festival began with a parade down Main Street to the park.
3 • In the morning, a mime troupe performed.
6 • During the afternoon the high school drama group performed a series of one-act plays.

Extending the Lesson

Either perform a pantomime yourself or help several students prepare and perform one for the class. Then have the students list, in chronological order, the events that happened in the pantomime. Discuss the students' lists of details. (Possible pantomime topics: eating out in a restaurant, going to the beach, walking a dog, etc.)

Part 3

Objectives

1. To understand the concept of point of view

2. To distinguish between first-person point of view and third-person point of view

Presenting the Lesson

1. Read aloud and discuss **Here's the Idea.** To illustrate the concept of point of view, draw a diagram of a car accident on the chalkboard. Explain that the description of what happened would differ according to the point of view used. One driver's story might differ from the other's, and the story of an eyewitness might be slightly different from both of the drivers' stories.

When you discuss the difference between first-person and third-person point of view, read examples of each to the class. (A good source for examples illustrating point of view is the short story section of the students' literature text.)

2. Read **Check It Out.** Ask students to tell you which pronouns are used in each paragraph. Then have them discuss the questions asked.

3. Assign and discuss **Try Your Skill.**

4. Read **Keep This in Mind** aloud. Then assign **Now Write.**

Individualizing the Lesson

Less-Advanced Students

Have the students identify the point of view in these pairs of topic sentences. Stress that the use of one or the other point of view can

Part 3

Who Said That?

Pre-Writing: Choosing a Point of View

Here's the Idea You have chosen a story to tell. You have gathered and organized the details you need to tell your story. Before you can begin writing the first draft of your narrative, however, you have one more decision to make. You must choose a point of view.

Point of view means the eyes and mind through which something is written. You may decide to use first-person point of view or third-person point of view.

When you use **first-person point of view,** you use the first-person prounoun *I*. *I* becomes the person telling the story. The reader can see and know only what *I* sees, knows, and thinks about. You will usually use the first-person point of view when you write about things that happened to you. You may also use first person in an imaginary story. In an imaginary story, you can let *I* be the main character, or any character.

When you use **third-person point of view,** you often use the third-person pronouns *he* and *she*. The narrator is not part of the story. You use the third-person point of view to tell about things that happened to other people.

Choose the point of view that best suits the type of narrative you are writing. Be sure to use the same point of view throughout your paragraph.

Check It Out Read the following paragraphs.

1 I wished that my first day of school at Hunter Junior High had been my last. Because I had transferred from a school three hundred miles away, I knew no one. The large building with its maze of halls confused me. Worst of all, no one talked to me or even smiled. I wondered if I would always feel like a stranger.

2 When Jane spotted a glowing mass in the dark sky, she shouted a warning to her friend Anita. She dived to the ground and pulled Anita with her. The reddish disc seemed to come closer. The girls blinked. Then the painful light disappeared. As they got up, Jane said she had never believed in flying saucers.

- Which of these paragraphs uses first-person point of view? Which uses third-person? How do you know?

Try Your Skill Copy this paragraph twice. The first time, fill in the blanks with the correct pronouns for the first-person point of view. The second time, use correct pronouns for the third-person point of view

_______ sat on the bleachers, nervously tapping _______ feet and twisting the jersey of _______ uniform around _______ finger. The coach was calling out the names of the kids who had made the varsity squad. _______ knew _______ tryout had gone well, but there were so many talented players in the gym that day. Suddenly, _______ heard it. The coach was calling _______ name. _______ leaped to _______ feet and let out a whoop. _______ dream had just come true.

Keep This in Mind

- With first-person point of view, the first-person pronoun *I* is used. *I* tells the story.
- With third-person point of view, the third-person pronouns *he* and *she* are used. The narrator is not a part of the story.

Now Write Think about the narrative paragraph you have been developing throughout these lessons. Decide whether you want to write it using first-person point of view or third-person point of view. Write your decision on the paper where you organized your pre-writing notes. Save these notes in your folder.

change the whole story.

1. a. He walked proudly down the dusty street to meet the stagecoach. third-person
   b. I walked stiffly down the dusty street, nervously awaiting the arrival of the stagecoach. first-person
2. a. I ate a good breakfast and tried to get mentally prepared for the tennis match. first-person
   b. She ate a good breakfast on the day of the tennis match. third-person

Advanced Students

Have the students imagine a trial. Ask them to write down as many points of view as they can think of from which the trial might be described. Ask them to state whether the point of view would be first-person or third-person.

Optional Practice

To reinforce the idea that *I* in first-person point of view can be any character, describe the following situation:

A boy walks into a room and plops down on a chair. The chair breaks.

Ask the students to write about what happened in the following ways:

1. Through the eyes of the boy
2. Through the eyes of a dog in the room
3. Through the eyes of the chair

Extending the Lesson

Have the students read the first paragraphs of the short stories in their literature texts. Ask them to identify the point of view used in each story.

Part 4

Objective

To use transitions to show time sequence

Presenting the Lesson

1. Read aloud and discuss **Here's the Idea.** Then ask a student to tell the class what he or she has done so far today. Have the class listen for transitional words and phrases.

2. Read and discuss **Check It Out.** List the transitional words and phrases on the board as students identify them. Ask students if they can think of any other transitional words they can substitute for those on the board. Point out how many words and phrases can help show time order.

3. Assign **Try Your Skill.** Provide time for students to share their comic strip ideas. Identify the transitional words used by each student.

4. Read **Keep This in Mind** aloud. Then assign **Now Write.**

Individualizing the Lesson

Less-Advanced Students

Allow the students to work in pairs to complete **Try Your Skill.**

Advanced Students

Have students watch a half-hour television show—either a dramatic show or a comedy. Then ask them to write a narrative paragraph summarizing the plot of the show. Remind the students to use transitional words and phrases.

Part 4

First, Then, Finally

Writing the First Draft

Here's the Idea All the work you've done so far has been part of the pre-writing stage. You are now ready for the next stage, writing the first draft. This is where you write your ideas in paragraph form for the first time.

As you write your first draft, remember that you are telling a story. In order to tell the story as it happened, you need special words and phrases to help you to show time order. These words and phrases are called **transitional words.**

Good transitional words show your readers when things happened in your story. Read this list of transitions.

first	now	at the beginning	before
then	soon	in the middle	after
next	later	at the end	by the time

As you write your first draft, include some of these transitional words. Also, use any other words and phrases, such as *suddenly* or *a few minutes later,* that help show time order.

Check It Out Read the following narrative paragraph.

> Yesterday I headed the supermarket's "Ten Most Wanted" list. First, because I entered the store through the exit door, I set off the burglar alarm. Then I slipped and fell into a pyramid of citrus, sending grapefruit flying. Afterward, I was so nervous that I dropped a dozen eggs. Finally, I didn't bring enough money to pay for my groceries. Needless to say, I was not the supermarket's favorite customer that day.

- Find the transitional words. Do they help make the story clear?
- Do the transitional words show time-order?

Try Your Skill Stories can be told with pictures as well as with words. Comic strips usually combine words with pictures. Some comic strips tell stories in pictures only. Here is one.

You are going to add words to these pictures. Tell what happens, frame by frame. Describe the action. Try to keep the humor of the cartoon.

First, jot down notes on your paper for each frame. Number each note to match the number of the frame it refers to.

Now write a few good transitional words for each frame. These should help you tell the story in the correct order. Use these transitional words along with your notes when you write about the cartoon.

Keep This in Mind

- Transitional words that show time-order help to make a narrative clear.

Now Write Write the first draft of your narrative paragraph. Use the details you gathered. Put these details in the order you decided on. Use transitional words to show time order.

Don't worry about grammar, spelling, or punctuation as you write. Just get your ideas down on paper in paragraph form. Save your first draft in your folder.

Optional Practice

Make a copy of this paragraph for the students. Have them underline the transitional words and phrases. Remind the students to refer to the list of transitions on page 96.

My first solo sailing excursion was a disaster. In the first place, I forgot to put the centerboard down. No wonder I couldn't get the boat to turn! Secondly, I didn't fasten one of the lines securely, and one of the sails started flapping in the breeze. Next, I wasn't paying attention, and I got hit in the head with the boom. Then, for my finale, I managed to capsize the boat. It was on that fateful day that I earned my nickname—"Landlubber!"

Extending the Lesson

Describe the following situation.

A boy has a dentist appointment. He is nervous, He has a funny feeling in his stomach. He imagines terrible things that are going to happen to him. He fixes a snack, but he can't eat it. He rides his bike to the dentist's office.

Ask students to write a narrative paragraph, in a time sequence, based on this situation. Encourage them to add additional information where they think it is necessary. Instruct them to use at least four transitional words or phrases from the list on page 96.

Part 5

Objectives

1. To check for sufficient details, chronological order, good transitions, and consistent point of view when revising a narrative paragraph
2. To use strong, specific verbs

Presenting the Lesson

1. Read aloud and discuss **Here's the Idea.** Have the students write the four questions to ask when revising narrative paragraphs in their notebooks. Then tell them to add a fifth question: "5. Have I used strong, specific verbs?" Emphasize that students should use action verbs wherever possible and that they should use a rich variety of specific verbs rather than general verbs.

2. Read and discuss the paragraph in **Check It Out.** To emphasize the value of specific action words, reread the paragraph, substituting linking verbs and general verbs for the italicized verbs.

3. Assign and discuss **Try Your Skill.** Refer students to a dictionary or thesaurus for ideas for verbs to use in place of *walk*.

4. Read **Keep This in Mind** and then assign **Now Write.**

Individualizing the Lesson

Less-Advanced Students

Before assigning **Try Your Skill,** have the students suggest synonyms for several common verbs (*said, ate,* etc.). Discuss the shades of meaning of the different synonyms.

Part 5

Prance or Trudge?

Revising Your Narrative Paragraph

Here's the Idea When you revise your narrative paragraph, you want to make it the best it can be. Here are some questions you should ask yourself as you revise your narrative.

1. Have I included enough details to tell my story well?
2. Are my details arranged in chronological order?
3. Have I included transitional words to show time order?
4. Have I used the same point of view throughout?

One other thing you should look at as you revise is your choice of verbs. You can make your narrative come alive by using strong, specific verbs.

Some verbs, like *trudge* and *prance,* are strong and show action. Linking or state-of-being verbs, such as *is, become,* and *seem,* are weaker. It is stronger to write "Mary *won*" than "Mary *was* the winner."

You will also want to use verbs that are specific rather than general. For example, think of all the ways to say *look* that are more interesting and more specific. A detective, for example, might *spy, snoop, pry,* or *peep.* The detective might also *stare, survey, inspect,* or *examine.* Any one of these verbs is stronger and more specific than *look.*

As you revise your narrative paragraph, replace weak, general verbs with strong, specific ones.

Check It Out Notice the verbs in this paragraph.

> The skydiver *ignored* her fear. She *leaped* from the hatch of the plane and *arched* her body for a free fall. Her arms and legs *stretched* spiderlike. Suddenly, she *whirled* to the right, then the left, and *looped* backwards. She *had sailed* through a figure-eight stunt. Then, she *popped* her parachute.

- How do the verbs in italics make this narrative paragraph come alive?

Try Your Skill Imagine that you walked to school on Monday and Friday last week. On Monday you were facing a tough math test. On Friday you were looking forward to videotaping a class play. Copy the following paragraph twice. The first time, write about Monday morning. Then write about Friday morning. Use strong, specific verbs to express your different moods on these two mornings. Compare your paragraphs with your classmates'.

On (Monday, Friday) morning, I ______ out the door on the way to school. I ______ around the corner and ______ down the street. When the light changed, I ______ across the street. I ______ up the school steps. The bell was ringing as I ______ into class.

Keep This in Mind

When revising a narrative paragraph:

- Use enough specific details to tell the story.
- Use clear chronological order and strong transitional words.
- Use the same point of view throughout.
- Use strong, specific verbs.

Now Write Revise your first draft. First follow the guidelines presented in this lesson. Then proofread your draft. Be sure you have used correct grammar, capitalization, punctuation, and spelling. When you are satisfied that your narrative is the best it can be, make a final copy. Save your narrative paragraph in your folder.

Advanced Students

In addition to the **Try Your Skill** exercise, have the students rewrite this paragraph using strong, active verbs. Remind them to avoid using linking verbs.

The leaders in the parade were the band. A majorette walked in front of the band doing baton tricks. A group of cowboys on black stallions came after the band. Then a group of clowns walked down the street playing tricks on each other. A string of huge circus elephants came after the clowns. Next came the cages holding lions and tigers. What a way to begin the circus!

Optional Practice

Have the students replace the underlined verb in each sentence with a stronger verb.

1. Alisa <u>walked</u> through the garden.
2. Loren <u>ate</u> his dinner hungrily.
3. "Don't you ever do that again!" <u>said</u> Mr. Engle.
4. The child <u>talked</u> during the entire plane ride.
5. The batter <u>hit</u> the ball.

Extending the Lesson

Give the students some practice with a thesaurus. Have them look at the following list of general verbs. Then ask them to make a list of specific verbs for each general verb. Finally, have each student choose one of the verb lists and write a sentence using each of the specific verbs.

say talk lift put
eat sing like laugh

Section 9 Objectives

1. To use sensory details to develop descriptive paragraphs

2. To use spatial order to organize details for a descriptive paragraph

3. To use transitional words that tell *where*

4. To check descriptive paragraphs for strong sensory details, clear spatial order, and good transitions

5. To use vivid, specific adjectives in a description

Preparing the Students

Review the definition of a descriptive paragraph as a word picture that appeals to the senses. Read again the two sample descriptive paragraphs in Section 5, Part 5, pages 58–59.

Additional Resources

Mastery Test — page 20 in the test booklet

Practice Book — pages 41–44

Duplicating Masters — pages 41–44

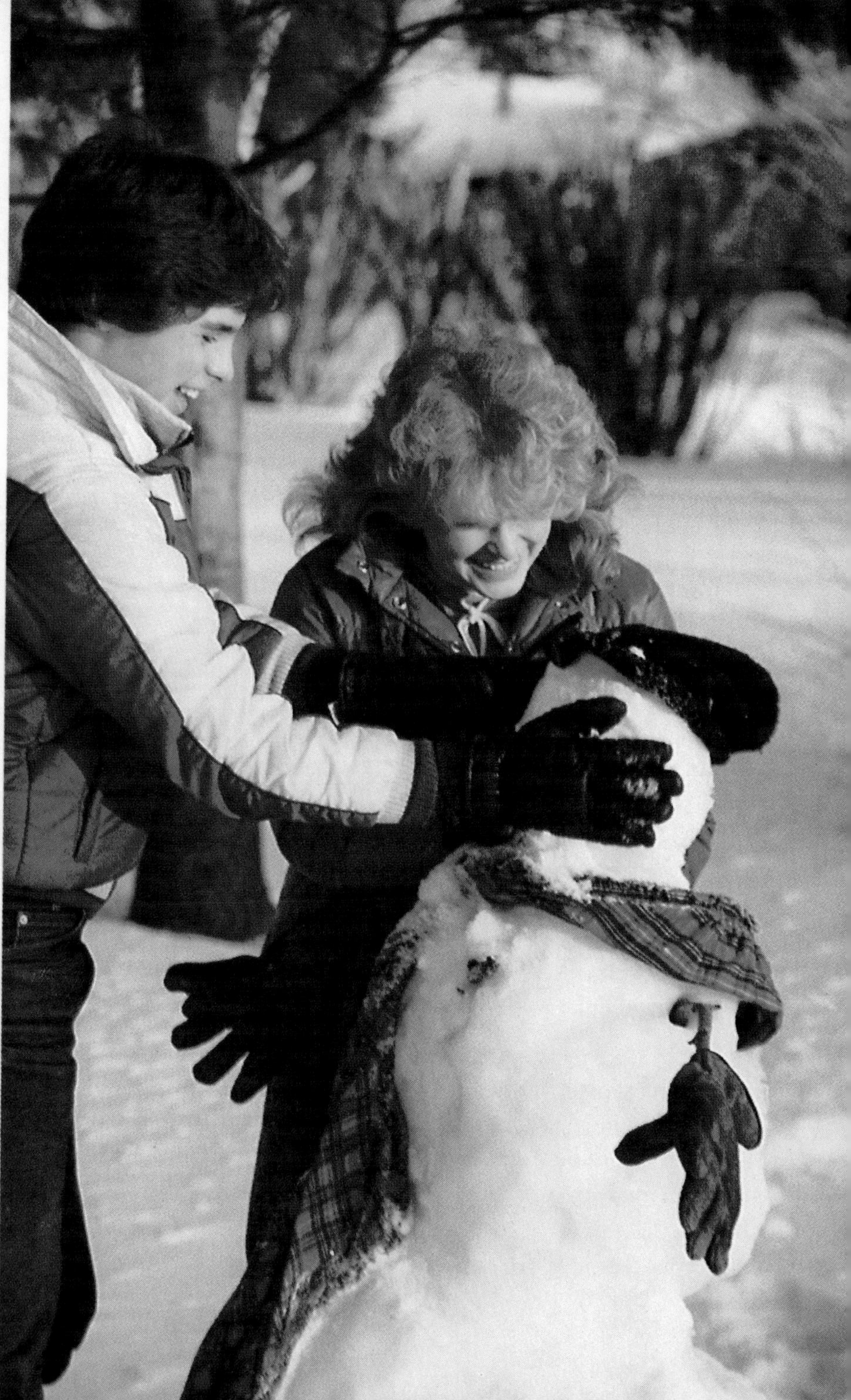

The Descriptive Paragraph

Part 1 **Observe!**
Pre-Writing: Gathering Sensory Details

Part 2 **Top to Bottom**
Pre-Writing: Using Spatial Order

Part 3 **In, Out, and Around**
Writing the First Draft

Part 4 **The Choice Is Yours**
Revising Your Descriptive Paragraph

Teaching Special Populations

LD See **Teaching Special Populations,** page 61.

ESL ESL students' limited vocabulary may hamper them when they attempt to write descriptive passages. Concentrate your exercises on vocabulary associated with the senses. Give students concrete examples of different textures, smells, sounds, or tastes, and have them describe the experiences in complete sentences. Ask ESL students to share sensory words from their native languages and have them find equivalent words in English. Remember that some languages have a wider or narrower range of sensory words than English. For instance, some languages do not distinguish between colors such as red and orange, while others have words describing many different shades of white.

Also, employ exercises that develop concepts and vocabulary associated with spatial order. Pair students with partners and have them issue instructions to one another using words that indicate spatial relationships (*above, below, to the right, inside,* and so on). Show students a large poster or photograph and have them use these words to describe where the objects in the picture are in relation to each other.

NSD See **Teaching Special Populations,** page 61.

Part 1

Objective

To use sensory details to develop descriptive paragraphs

Presenting the Lesson

1. Read aloud and discuss **Here's the Idea.** As a class, list the sensory details that apply to the students' cafeteria. Put each detail under its proper sense (sight, smell, taste, etc.).

2. Discuss **Check It Out.** Ask the students to explain to which sense each detail appeals.

3. Assign **Try Your Skill.** Explain that memories of sensory experiences are just as valid as direct experience. Ask students what other sensory details come into their minds as they imagine each listed sensation.

4. Read **Keep This in Mind** aloud. Then assign **Now Write.**

Individualizing the Lesson

Less-Advanced Students

Actually bring in the items listed for **Try Your Skill** to give the students some stimuli for writing descriptive words. (Make a tape of a football game.) In addition to discussing the assigned descriptions, ask the students what other sensory details can be used to describe each object. (Example: the feel of a tennis ball, the sound of potato chips being eaten, the feel of soap when it is dry or when it is wet, etc.)

Part 1

Observe!

Pre-Writing: Gathering Sensory Details

Here's the Idea When you write a descriptive paragraph, you are painting a picture with words. You want your reader to get to know the person, place, or thing you are describing as well as you know it. Once you have chosen a subject for your descriptive paragraph, how can you make that subject come alive for your readers?

The best way to develop a descriptive paragraph is through the use of sensory details. **Sensory details** tell about things that can be seen, heard, felt, tasted, and smelled. Sensory details can help paint a clear, real picture for your readers.

You can gather sensory details for your descriptive paragraph through **observation.** For instance, you might want to describe a place, such as the school cafeteria. Go to that place, or close your eyes and picture the place in your mind as clearly as possible. Write down the things you *see*. List the noises you *hear*. Make notes about how the food *tastes*, how the cafeteria *smells*, how objects in the cafeteria *feel* (greasy table, hot soup). When you have finished making your notes, you will have gathered many good sensory details. These details will make your readers feel as if they are right in that cafeteria with you.

Check It Out Read this descriptive paragraph.

> Just as we were getting weary, we spotted a clear stream. The banks surrounding the stream were carpeted in thick, spongy moss. Shallow water bubbled and gurgled as it rushed across rocks. Sunlight glistened off the clear water. We hurriedly filled our cups and found the water numbingly cold. It tasted fresh as a

liquid icicle. We dipped our burning feet into the blue water, resting them on the sharp stones that lined the bottom of the stream. We inhaled the crisp mountain air, lightly scented with the perfume of spring's first wildflowers.

- What sensory details are included in this descriptive paragraph?

Try Your Skill Use your senses to create specific, lively descriptions. Try to imagine each of the sensations listed below. Then write two vivid words or phrases to describe each one.

1. the smell of soap
2. the feel of your hairbrush
3. the sounds of a football game
4. the taste of potato chips
5. the way a tennis ball looks
6. the taste of an orange
7. the way your nose looks
8. the feel of sand

Keep This in Mind

- When you write a descriptive paragraph, develop your description with sensory details.
- Gather sensory details through observation or memory.

Now Write Think about some possible subjects for a descriptive paragraph. Make a list of persons (your best friend, a passenger on a bus), places (a locker room, a crowded beach), and things (a race car, a camel) you might want to describe.

Choose one of these as the subject of your descriptive paragraph. Observe your subject. Gather as many sensory details as you can about it. List each detail under the sense it is related to. Save your list of sensory details in your folder.

Advanced Students

Ask the students for examples of words that relate to each of the senses. For example, *bright* relates to sight, *booming* to hearing, and *coarse* to touch. Ask the students to begin a five-part chart with words in each category of the senses. They can use the chart for reference.

Optional Practice

Explain that although foods are usually described by tasting and smelling, they also have hearing, touch, and sight appeal. Direct students to choose one food and to list details in all five sense categories. Then have them choose a second food that is as much the opposite of the first food as possible.

Extending the Lesson

Duplicate the following paragraph for your students. Ask them to pick out the sensory images and the words that trigger them. Students can look through their literature texts for examples of paragraphs that contain sensory images.

> Juan was dazzled by the marketplace. Each seller's stall was sheltered from the burning sun by a roof of brightly colored cloth. Within each stall the sellers' wares were displayed. One woman sold only apples—tart Jonathans and sweet Paula Reds. Another sold flowers—tall, multicolored gladioli, fragrant roses, and golden daffodils. An elderly gentleman offered red and green cabbages from his wrinkled, leathery hands. From every corner of the marketplace Juan could hear the shouting. "Potatoes here!" and "I've got chickens, best in the market!" and "Get your bananas here—ten cents a pound!"

Part 2

Objective

To use spatial order to organize details for a descriptive paragraph

Presenting the Lesson

1. Read aloud and discuss **Here's the Idea.** Point out that the word *spatial* comes from the root word *space*. In a descriptive paragraph, the writer must find an orderly way to describe how things relate to each other in the space being described.

Point out that the details in the example paragraph are arranged from the front to the back of the squirt gun.

2. Discuss **Check It Out.** Ask the students how else this paragraph might have been arranged.

3. Assign and discuss **Try Your Skill.**

4. Read **Keep This in Mind** aloud. Then assign **Now Write.**

Individualizing the Lesson

Less-Advanced Students

Before assigning the **Try Your Skill** exercise for independent work, do one example with the entire group. List the details to be used on the chalkboard. Then decide on a spatial order and organize the details accordingly. Emphasize that no one method of organization is necessarily better than another. It depends on what is being described.

Advanced Students

Bring in pictures of famous buildings, natural wonders, or landmarks. Have each student choose one. Instruct each student to study his or

Part 2

Top to Bottom

Pre-Writing: Using Spatial Order

Here's the Idea When you organized the details of your narrative paragraph, the order you needed to use was clear. You wanted to tell your story in the same order that it really happened. How should you arrange the sensory details for your descriptive paragraph?

Whenever you describe something, you want your readers to see it in a special way. You should organize your details in the order that you want your readers to notice them. Start with the first detail you want them to notice. Then add the other details as they relate to this first one. This is called **spatial order.** Using spatial order, you might describe your subject from top to bottom, side to side, front to back, or near to far.

For example, you might be describing the driver of a bus. What do you want your readers to notice first? Her drab, brown uniform? Her friendly smile? Her strong, clear voice? What did *you* notice first? Then continue your description, leading your readers from one detail to another in the order that you want your readers to see them.

Read this descriptive paragraph. Notice how the details are organized.

> Professor Lookit invented a unique squirtgun. The barrel and trigger below it pump water like any other water pistol. From the bottom of the grip, a rubber tube runs down to a balloon-like tank, which is filled with water. At the side of the tank is a plug for filling. The main advantage of this gun is that it gives more squirts with fewer refills.

Check It Out Read this description:

My family calls my dresser "Danny's dump." The top of the dresser is usually piled high with clothes, sports equipment, and a few leftover snacks. The top drawer is jammed so full of old comic books that I can't open it. The drawer below has socks and T-shirts spilling out over the sides. I leave the bottom drawer open for my dog's bones, toys, and scraps. My dresser might not be orderly, but I know where everything is.

- How does this description use spatial order?

Try Your Skill Make notes for a description of someone or something in your classroom. First observe your subject, listing as many sensory details as you can. Then put these details into the order you would want a reader to notice them.

Keep This in Mind

- Use spatial order to organize the sensory details for your descriptive paragraph.
- Put your details in the order that you want your readers to notice them.

Now Write Look over the sensory details you gathered in the last lesson. Decide the order in which you want your readers to notice them. Then arrange the details in that order. You may want to try several different arrangements until you find one that best suits your subject. Save your organized details in your folder.

her picture and list sensory details that describe it. Then have him or her arrange the details in the order that would help the reader to picture the object clearly. An optional extension of this exercise is to have the students actually write the descriptive paragraphs.

Optional Practice

Bring in copies of famous cartoon characters. Ask each student to choose one and to list sensory details to describe that character. Then instruct the students to organize their details in a good spatial order.

Extending the Lesson

Show the class a series of slides or poster-size prints that picture animals, places, and objects. For each, discuss the following:

1. The four or five main areas to be described
2. The logical starting place
3. The logical order in which to appeal
4. Key words and phrases that indicate spatial relationships among the main areas

Part 3

Objective

To use transitional words that tell *where*

Presenting the Lesson

1. Read aloud and discuss **Here's the Idea.** Point out that many of the transitional words are prepositions. Ask students to use some of the words and phrases in sentences.

2. Read **Check It Out.** Ask students to identify the transitions in the paragraph.

3. Assign and discuss **Try Your Skill.**

4. Assign **Now Write.** Remind the class that the purpose of a first draft is to get all of the important ideas on paper.

Individualizing the Lesson

Less-Advanced Students

Do all of the pre-writing steps for **Try Your Skill** as a class. Start by deciding what order should be used. Ask the students what item should be described first. Once the students have decided if they are going to describe the front of the room from left to right or right to left or top to bottom or some other order, write the details in order on the chalkboard. Then discuss which transitional words or phrases should be used. Have the students complete the paragraph independently.

Advanced Students

Have students improve this paragraph by adding transitional words

Part 3

In, Out, and Around

Writing the First Draft

Here's the Idea Now that you have organized your sensory details, you are ready to write the first draft of your descriptive paragraph. As you write your first draft, remember that you want your readers to see your subject in a special way. Try to make your description as clear as possible.

If you think you need to make some parts of your description clearer, you may want to add transitional words. When you wrote your narrative paragraph, you used transitional words to tell *when*. In a descriptive paragraph, you use transitional words to tell *where*.

Here are some examples of transitional words and phrases used in description:

in	ahead of	down	to the right
on	outside	by	back and forth
above	downstairs	front	at the end of
under	close to	north	side by side
behind	between	east	in back of

Look at how this description of a dog uses transitional words and phrases to show spatial order.

My dog Duke came inside last night looking as if he had lost a major battle. On top of his head two patches of fur were missing. Over one ear was a long scratch, and his matted tail hung down behind him. He limped because he was holding his injured left rear leg up under his belly. Duke needed first aid and my kindly attention.

Check It Out Now read this description of a dungeon:

The prisoner found himself in a dark, musty cell. A tiny vent high on the wall in front of him was the only opening. A leaky pipe above him dripped onto an iron cot, and a puddle of foul water stood in the center of the cell. Insects skittered around the edges of the dirt floor. He shivered in disgust, as the solid iron door slammed behind him.

- What transitional words in this descriptive paragraph tell *where*?

Try Your Skill Write a brief description of the objects in the front of your classroom, including anything on the wall. Use transitional words from the list in this lesson to make your description clear. Compare your description with those of your classmates.

Keep This in Mind

- To make your description clear, use transitional words that tell *where*.

Now Write Write the first draft of your descriptive paragraph. Describe your subject as you want your readers to see it. Use transitional words to make your description clear. Save your first draft in your folder.

and phrases.

The mountain looked majestic. There was snow on it. The skiers glided down the mountain on ski runs. There were forests of pine trees on the mountain. A frozen stream ran to the valley. The lodge, a comfortable, warm cabin, awaited the skiers.

Optional Practice

Repeat the **Try Your Skill** exercise. Bring in pictures of famous paintings and have the students write descriptions of them. Remind them to use transitional words and phrases.

Extending the Lesson

Have students pretend that they are salespeople. They are to write a paragraph for a brochure describing the wonderful features of their product. Remind the students to use good transitions. (Possible product topics: a new car, a super-deluxe vacuum cleaner, a sophisticated camera, a collapsible baby stroller, a calculator/watch/alarm, etc.)

Part 4

Objectives

1. To check descriptive paragraphs for strong sensory details, clear spatial order, and good transitions

2. To use vivid, specific adjectives in a description

Presenting the Lesson

1. Read aloud and discuss **Here's the Idea.** Have the students copy the three questions to ask themselves when revising a description. Then have them add question number four: "Have I used strong, specific verbs and vivid adjectives?"

2. Discuss **Check It Out.** Look at the paragraph, sentence by sentence, to find all of the verbs and adjectives used in the description.

3. Assign and discuss **Try Your Skill.** Make sure students have access to a dictionary for this exercise.

4. Read **Keep This in Mind** and then assign **Now Write.**

Individualizing the Lesson

Less-Advanced Students

1. For the **Try Your Skill** exercise, do the first half orally.

2. Break the **Now Write** exercise into segments. Have the students write the first drafts independently. Then work with each student individually to revise his or her paragraph. Then have the students make their final copies independently.

Part 4

The Choice Is Yours

Revising Your Descriptive Paragraph

Here's the Idea As you revise your descriptive paragraph, remember that you are trying to paint a word picture for your readers. Here are some questions to ask yourself to help make your description better.

1. Have I used strong sensory details in my description?
2. Are the details arranged in the order that I want my readers to notice them?
3. Have I used transitional words to make my description clear?

Another way you can improve your description is through your word choice. Be sure you use strong, specific verbs. Also pay special attention to your use of adjectives. Adjectives, you will remember, are words that describe. They can help your descriptive paragraph come alive for your readers.

You must choose adjectives carefully. There is usually one adjective that says just what you want to say better than any other word. For example, if you were describing a big park, you might use the adjective *big*. However, you could also describe the park as *huge, enormous, large, sprawling, gigantic, vast,* or *immense.* Always search for the best adjectives to make your description clear.

Be careful not to overuse adjectives in your descriptive paragraph. Too many adjectives can make your writing wordy. There is no need to say "the dark, inky, black sky," when "the inky sky" says just what you want to say.

Check It Out Read the following description.

> The steamy jungle teemed with life. Monstrous trees were home to agile monkeys and colorful parrots. Long, thick snakes

slithered along low-lying branches. Exotic frogs hopped from limb to limb. Graceful flying squirrels launched themselves from treetops and glided to the forest floor. The air was filled with the harsh cries, sudden screeches, and excited babble of a thousand strange creatures.

- Name some vivid adjectives and strong, specific verbs that are used in this paragraph. Do you see how these words make this description more interesting?

Try Your Skill Beside each number below, there are three adjectives that have similar meanings. Number your paper from 1 to 8. Arrange the adjectives from the weakest to the strongest. For example, you would rearrange the adjectives *frightened, uneasy, terrified* to *uneasy, frightened, terrified.* Look up any words you are not familiar with.

1. hot, warm, blistering
2. cold, cool, freezing
3. beautiful, pretty, gorgeous
4. soggy, damp, soaking
5. huge, enormous, large
6. blackness, shady, dark
7. love, adore, like
8. thunderous, noisy, loud

Keep This in Mind

When revising your descriptive paragraph:

- Use strong sensory details.
- Arrange details in the order that you want the reader to notice them.
- Use transitional words that tell *where.*
- Use strong, specific verbs and vivid adjectives.

Now Write Revise the first draft of your descriptive paragraph, using the guidelines in this lesson. When you are satisifed that your description is as clear as it can be, proofread it. Correct any errors in grammar, capitalization, punctuation, and spelling. Then make a final copy. Save this final copy in your folder.

Advanced Students

Have the students rewrite this paragraph using strong, specific verbs and vivid adjectives. If necessary, they may change the sentence structure.

We walked through the outdoor market. At the flower stall, bees flew around the flowers. The fruit vendor's stand held apples, oranges, bananas, pineapples, mangoes, and papayas. Farther along the street was a man weaving baskets. The baskets for sale were behind him. Walking throughout the market were children carrying trays of sweets to sell. The bake shop sold bread. At the end of the street there was a café that sold coffee and rolls. The market was a good place to shop.

Optional Practice

Have the students list as many adjectives as they can to describe the following nouns. Compare the students' choices.

ballerina	chair
quarterback	rose
car	hair
eggs	horse

Extending the Lesson

Direct each student to find a paragraph that vividly describes a setting. You will need to provide books for the students to use or help them locate books in the library. Have them identify the strong, specific verbs and the vivid adjectives used in the descriptions.

Section 10 Objectives

1. To know that an explanatory *how* paragraph explains a process

2. To use a step-by-step order to organize an explanatory *how* paragraph

3. To use transitional words to make an explanation clear

4. To revise an explanatory *how* paragraph so that the process being explained can be clearly understood

Preparing the Students

Discuss with the class instances in which they have read and followed directions. Encourage a variety of responses. Explain that in the following four lessons they are going to learn to write good directions of their own in paragraph form.

Additional Resources

Mastery Test — page 21 in the test booklet

Practice Book — pages 45–48

Duplicating Masters — pages 45–48

The Explanatory Paragraph

Telling *How*

Part 1 **How Do You Do?**
Pre-Writing: Listing the Steps

Part 2 **What's Next?**
Pre-Writing: Using Step-by-Step Order

Part 3 **Watch Your Step!**
Writing the First Draft

Part 4 **Clear the Way**
Revising Your Explanatory *How* Paragraph

Teaching Special Populations

LD See **Teaching Special Populations,** page 61.

Make sure you go over the meaning of terms and concepts as they appear in the text. Remind students of the importance of step-by-step order and natural time order.

ESL Some of the topics and exercises (Part 1, **Try Your Skill,** for instance) may rely on cultural experience which is foreign to your ESL students. Try to adapt these examples and include topics which are appropriate to ESL students' background (how to construct an origami sculpture, how to make burritos, how to wrap parcels securely for international mailing, and so on).

Make doubly sure that students understand the vocabulary associated with time. Devote extra attention to those students whose native languages may not include such words.

NSD See **Teaching Special Populations,** page 61.

When students experience difficulty, have them work with a standard English speaker and translate rough notes in nonstandard dialect into explanatory paragraphs that use standard English. Stress the fact that misunderstandings often arise when nonstandard dialect is used for explaining a process, giving directions, and so on.

Part 1

Objective

To know that an explanatory *how* paragraph explains a process

Presenting the Lesson

1. Read aloud and discuss **Here's the Idea.** Explain that writing a paragraph is one way to explain a process. Other ways include listing and numbering the steps, drawing pictures and writing the directions next to them, and demonstrating and explaining the steps.

2. Read and discuss **Check It Out.** Point out that the pre-writing notes only include the materials that are needed to build the tree house, not the steps to build it.

3. Assign and discuss **Try Your Skill.** Point out that most of the humor of the explanation comes from a lack of details and mixed up and incomplete steps.

4. Read **Keep This in Mind** aloud. Then assign **Now Write.**

Individualizing the Lesson

Less-Advanced Students

Do the **Try Your Skill** exercise as a class. Then, with the help of the students, write a good set of pre-writing notes explaining how to make a pizza.

Advanced Students

Have students make a set of pre-writing notes explaining either how to build a tree house or how to make a pizza. Compare and discuss their notes in class.

Part 1

How Do You Do?

Pre-Writing: Listing the Steps

Here's the Idea Some paragraphs tell a story. Other paragraphs give a description. Still other paragraphs present an explanation. A paragraph that explains is called an **explanatory paragraph**. When such a paragraph explains how *something is done* or *how something happens,* it is called an explanatory *how* paragraph.

Sometimes an explanatory *how* paragraph tells how to do something. You might write a how-to paragraph to explain how to type a message on a computer, how to shoot a free-throw, how to make a pizza, or how to play a flute.

An explanatory *how* paragraph can also tell how something happens or how something works. This kind of paragraph might explain how a cell divides, how snow is formed, how volcanos erupt, or how a caterpillar becomes a butterfly.

Whether you are explaining how to do something or how something happens, or works, you are explaining a process. A process is made up of a series of steps. The details you gather for your pre-writing notes should include all of these steps. As you record these steps, be sure you don't leave any out. Also, make each step simple and specific. Otherwise, your readers won't understand your explanation.

Check It Out Read the following pre-writing notes for a paragraph explaining how to build a tree house.

need a big tree
get lots of scrap lumber
tree must have strong branches
ladder for climbing up tree
need nails and a hammer
get a saw

- Do these notes for an explanatory *how* paragraph include all the steps needed to explain how to build a tree-house? What other details should be included?

Try Your Skill A six-year old child gave the following explanation of how to make pizza. Explain what is wrong with these directions. On your paper, list at least three errors.

Pizza
½ of white cheese
1 full thing of red gravy
A lot of dough

Get the dough into a circle about size 14. Then throw it up in the air over your head.

Cook the gravy for a couple of hours or minutes. Then put it on the dough with a cookin' spoon—and pat it all around.

Take your gold square thing that makes the cheese all crumble up.

Then put on the gravy and cook it for a real long time.

If you don't get it out on time, it gets kind of blackish, but you still have to eat it.

Have it in the summer with ice cream.—*Smashed Potatoes*

Keep This in Mind

- An explanatory *how* paragraph can explain how to do something. It can also tell how something happens or works.
- An explanatory *how* paragraph must include all of the steps of the process being explained.
- Each step must be simple and specific.

Now Write Think of a simple process that you would like to explain. You might explain how to do something or how something happens or works. Make a list of all the important steps that are a part of the process. Save your list in your folder.

Optional Practice

Have students make a list of the steps involved in one of these processes.

- making scrambled eggs
- feeding a baby a bottle
- mowing a lawn
- waxing a car
- making a photocopy
- changing a bicycle tire
- taping a TV show on a VCR

Extending the Lesson

Have the students bring their science books to class. Instruct each of them to find an example of a paragraph that explains a process (how something is done or how something happens). Read and discuss the paragraphs in class.

Part 2

Objective

To use a step-by-step order to organize an explanatory *how* paragraph

Presenting the Lesson

1. Read and discuss **Here's the Idea.** Emphasize that the pre-writing notes for a *how* paragraph must include all of the steps in the process to be explained. Also, emphasize that all of the steps must be in the right order.

2. Discuss **Check It Out.** Point out that step-by-step order is a natural time order. The events in the paragraph are listed in the order in which they are to be done.

3. Assign and discuss **Try Your Skill.** Explain that certain words help point out the step-by-step order (*first, after spraying, newly painted,* etc.).

4. Read **Keep This in Mind** aloud. Then assign **Now Write.**

Individualizing the Lesson

Less-Advanced Students

Either do the **Try Your Skill** exercise with the class or allow students to work in pairs to complete it.

Advanced Students

Have students select one of these games. Then have them research the game to see how it is played. As a final product, have them list the steps of the "process" of the game in a natural time order.

soccer	rugby
polo	bocce ball
cricket	croquet

What's Next?

Pre-Writing: Using Step-by-Step Order

Here's the Idea In an explanatory *how* paragraph, you need to explain a process step-by-step. You must start with the first thing that happens or that must be done. Then you must follow that with the next step, and so on. Having a step out of order could confuse your reader as much as leaving out a step.

If you were explaining how to play Frisbee, you would not start out by saying "To catch a Frisbee, you should . . . ." Catching is the last step in the process. Instead, you would begin by first explaining how to hold a Frisbee properly. Then you would explain how to throw it and, finally, how to catch it. That would be the correct step-by-step order to explain how to play Frisbee.

Step-by-step order is very much like the chronological order you used when you wrote a narrative paragraph. In both cases you need to use a natural time order to organize your paragraph.

Check It Out Read the following paragraph.

> Sewing a button on clothing is a simple task. First, gather a needle, straight pins, scissors, and thread that matches the color of the clothing. Second, remove any loose threads where the button used to be. Thread your needle. Next, mark the space for the button with a straight pin. Then, put the button in place and hold it there with one hand. Now, with your other hand, sew in and out of the holes in the button until it is firmly attached. Finally, knot the thread on the underside of the clothing. Snip the thread close to the clothing.

- Does this explanatory *how* paragraph explain a process step-by-step?
- Are the steps listed in natural time order?

Try Your Skill Read the following pre-writing notes. They are for a paragraph that explains how to build a jar garden. Organize them into step-by-step order.

Making a Jar Garden

1. drop plants into jar and cover roots with soil using long stick
2. lightly mist newly planted plants with a sprayer
3. to prepare jar, put a layer of charcoal on bottom of jar
4. add light potting soil on top of pebbles using paper funnel
5. set garden in a sunny spot
6. cover charcoal with clean, small pebbles
7. after spraying, add tiny decorative rocks or ornaments to newly planted garden
8. take plants out of original pots and shake roots clean
9. screw the top on your new jar garden
10. first choose a large water bottle or jar with narrow lip

Keep This in Mind

- In an explanatory *how* paragraph, explain a process step-by-step.
- Organize the steps in the natural time order of the process.

Now Write Using the notes you gathered in the last lesson, **How Do You Do?**, organize your explanatory *how* paragraph. Place your notes in step-by-step order. Make sure all of your steps are in the correct order. Save your organized notes in your folder.

Optional Practice

Have students organize these pre-writing notes into step-by-step order.

How To Write a Letter Requesting Merchandise

4 • State what you want to order in the body of the letter.
1 • In the upper right hand corner of the page write your name, your address, and the date.
2 • Starting on the left side of the page below your address, write the name and address of the business to whom you are writing.
5 • Explain in the body of the letter how you will pay for your order.
3 • Use a colon after the salutation, or greeting.
6 • Place a comma after the complimentary close.
7 • Sign your name clearly.

Extending the Lesson

Ask each student to make a simple design using triangles, rectangles, and circles. Then have students write instructions, in step-by-step order, on how to draw their designs. To see if the instructions are complete and specific, have the students try drawing each other's designs from the instructions.

Part 3

Objective

To use transitional words to make an explanation clear

Presenting the Lesson

1. Read aloud and discuss **Here's the Idea.** Compare this list of transitions to the list on page 96 (Section 8, Part 4). Explain that both narrative paragraphs and explanatory *how* paragraphs use natural time order.

2. Discuss **Check It Out.**

3. Assign and discuss **Try Your Skill.** Tell students not to use the same transitional words and phrases over and over. Tell them to try to find transitions other than *first* and *second.* Ask for some suggestions before they begin to write.

4. Read **Keep This in Mind** aloud. Then assign **Now Write.**

Individualizing the Lesson

Less-Advanced Students

Find the topic sentence and arrange the sentences in the **Try Your Skill** paragraph in step-by-step order as a class. Then review the list of transitions on page 116. Have the students complete the exercise independently.

Advanced Students

Have the students improve this paragraph by adding transitions.

The American Bird Banding Association puts identification bracelets on birds to help learn about their migration patterns. The birds have to be caught. They are weighed. Their wing measurement is taken. The bander records this information as well as the

Part 3

Watch Your Step!

Writing the First Draft

Here's the Idea As you write the first draft of your explanatory *how* paragraph, you want to be careful to make your explanation as clear as possible. Remember to include all of the important steps. Be sure you follow the order you decided on in the last lesson. Try to make each step in your explanatory paragraph simple and specific.

Another way you can make your explanation clear is by using transitional words. Transitional words can help you to show your reader how the steps in your explanation are related to each other. Transitional words can show which step comes first, which comes second, and so on. If two steps in the process you are explaining happen at the same time, transitional words can help you to make that idea clear.

Here is a list of transitional words. Use them as you write your first draft to help make your explanation clear.

first	then	at first
second	now	to start with
third	when	after that
fourth	while	at the same time
next	until	the next step
last	finally	at last

Check It Out Read the following paragraph.

Scrambled eggs make a delicious light meal that is easy to prepare. First, gather the necessary utensils. You need a mixing bowl, an egg beater or wire whisk, a spatula, and a frying pan. Second, collect the ingredients. You need eggs, milk, butter, salt, and pepper. The third step is to break the eggs into the bowl. Use one egg for each person you are serving. Next, add a small amount of milk, and beat the mixture until it is fluffy. Then, over low heat, melt a tablespoon of butter in the frying pan. Add the eggs. Cook the eggs slowly until they are firm. While they cook, mix them a few times with the spatula. Finally, season them with salt and pepper and serve hot.

- What transitional words and phrases in this explanatory *how* paragraph help to make the explanation clear?

Try Your Skill The sentences below belong in a paragraph, but their order has been jumbled. First of all, find the topic sentence and write it on your paper. Then write the remaining sentences of the paragraph in step-by-step order. Finally, fill in the blanks with precise transitional words to show the order.

_______, get a group of hardy bikers together.
_______, enjoy the fresh air and scenery _______ you are traveling.
Bike trips are fun, but they require careful planning.
_______, have the group use maps to plan each day's routes.
_______ you set out, have the group check the brakes, gears, and tires on all the bikes.
_______, make a list of needed supplies and _______ gather them together.

Keep This in Mind

- In an explanatory *how* paragraph, use transitional words and phrases to make your explanation clear.

Now Write Using your organized notes from Part 2, write the first draft of your explanatory *how* paragraph. Include all of the important steps in the right order. Use transitional words to help make your explanation clear. Save your first draft in your folder.

species, sex, and age of the bird. An identification band is placed on the bird's leg. The bird is released. If the band is recovered, the information about the bird's travel patterns and life span is recorded by the U.S. Fish and Wildlife Service.

Optional Practice

Have the students add transitions to improve this paragraph.

Even a person without a green thumb can grow an avocado plant. Select a ripe avocado. Halve it and remove the pit. Allow the pit to dry for a day. Remove the brown skin that covers the pit. Plant the avocado pit, with the larger end down, half way into the soil in your pot. Leave the top exposed. Water the pit with warm water. Keep it moist. Within a month the seed will split, and the plant will begin to grow.

Extending the Lesson

On the chalkboard, write the names of simple outdoor games that the students play now or have played at one time. These will probably include hopscotch, red rover, red light, kick the can, statue, hide and seek, jump rope games, and games using marbles. Invite additions from the class.

Divide the class into partners. Assign a game to each pair of students. Direct them to write a paragraph telling how to play the game and to write the final copy on a 3 x 5 index card. Collect the cards into a card file and present it to a class of younger children.

Part 4

Objective

To revise an explanatory *how* paragraph so that the process being explained can be clearly understood

Presenting the Lesson

1. Read aloud and discuss **Here's the Idea.** Have the students copy the revision checklist for explanatory *how* paragraphs into their notebooks.

2. Read and discuss **Check It Out.** Have the students ask the four questions to use when revising an explanatory *how* paragraph as they discuss this paragraph.

3. Assign and discuss **Try Your Skill.** Remind students that their revision must be in a step-by-step time order. Ask students for suggestions of transitions that would help make this order clear.

4. Read **Keep This in Mind** aloud. Then assign **Now Write.**

Individualizing the Lesson

Less-Advanced Students

As a class, develop pre-writing notes for the topic "how to play checkers." List all of the steps, make sure the steps are simple and specific, check that the steps are in the proper order, and note transitions that would make the explanation clear. After completing these pre-writing steps as a class, have each student, working independently, write a paragraph explaining "how to play checkers." Work individually with each student to help him or her revise the paragraph.

Part 4

Clear the Way

Revising Your Explanatory *How* Paragraph

Here's the Idea After you have written the first draft of your explanatory *how* paragraph, read it carefully. Remember that your purpose is to explain a process to your readers as simply and as clearly as you can. Here are some questions you should ask yourself as you read your first draft. If you can't answer *yes* to a question, then you will have to revise that part of your first draft.

1. Have I included all of the important steps in the process I am explaining?
2. Have I arranged those steps in a natural, step-by-step time order?
3. Have I made each step simple and specific?
4. Have I used transitional words to make my explanation clear?

You might want to ask one of your classmates to read your first draft. Ask him or her to answer the four questions above. The answers you get will help you to know how you should revise your first draft.

Check It Out Read the following explanatory *how* paragraph.

> It's easy to play checkers. First, get the right kind of board and playing pieces. One player is red. The other player is black. You have to move the pieces across the board. You try to jump your opponent's pieces that are in front of you. At the other side of the board, your pieces are crowned. Then you win.

- Is this a good explanatory *how* paragraph? Explain your answer.

Try Your Skill Revise the paragraph in **Check It Out.** Make it as clear as possible. Use the guidelines in this lesson as you revise. When you are finished, compare your revision with those of your classmates.

Keep This in Mind

When you revise an explanatory *how* paragraph:

- Include all the important steps.
- Arrange the steps in natural time order.
- Make each step simple and specific.
- Use transitional words to make your explanation clear.

Now Write Read your first draft carefully. Revise it, using the guidelines in this lesson. Remember to proofread your draft to be sure you have used correct grammar, usage, capitalization, punctuation, and spelling. When you have finished your revision, make a good copy of your explanatory *how* paragraph. Save this final copy in your folder.

Advanced Students

Have the students select one of the following listed topics (or a personal choice), make pre-writing notes, and then write a first draft. Using an opaque projector, discuss each draft. Have the students ask the four questions from page 118 about each paragraph. Then have the students revise their paragraphs.

- how to bowl
- how to score a bowling game
- how to open a combination lock
- how to change a bicycle tire
- how to build a fire
- how to make popcorn

Optional Practice

Have the students revise this explanatory *how* paragraph

How To Make Greasepaint

Making your own greasepaint for Halloween make-up is easy. You mix the cornstarch and water together. You need 1 teaspoon of cornstarch, ½ teaspoon of water, ½ teaspoon of cold cream, and food coloring. Stir in the cold cream. You also need a small dish and a spoon. Add the food coloring a drop at a time. Now you are ready to paint your face!

Extending the Lesson

Have the students make a bulletin board display of *how* paragraphs collected from newspapers, magazines, books, games, and recipes.

Section 11 Objectives

1. To express strong, specific opinions in writing

2. To support opinions with logical reasons and accurate facts

3. To organize supporting reasons and facts from the least important idea to the most important idea

4. To use transitional words in stating opinions and in presenting reasons

5. To conclude an explanatory *why* paragraph with a sentence which summarizes the opinion and supporting reasons

6. To revise an explanatory *why* paragraph to make it clear and convincing

Preparing the Students

Ask the class questions such as these: What is the best flavor of ice cream? What is the best television program? Who is the most outstanding living American? Point out that when answering these questions, the students are expressing opinions orally. In this lesson they are going to learn to express them in writing.

Additional Resources

Mastery Test — page 22 in the test booklet

Practice Book — pages 49–52

Duplicating Masters — pages 49–52

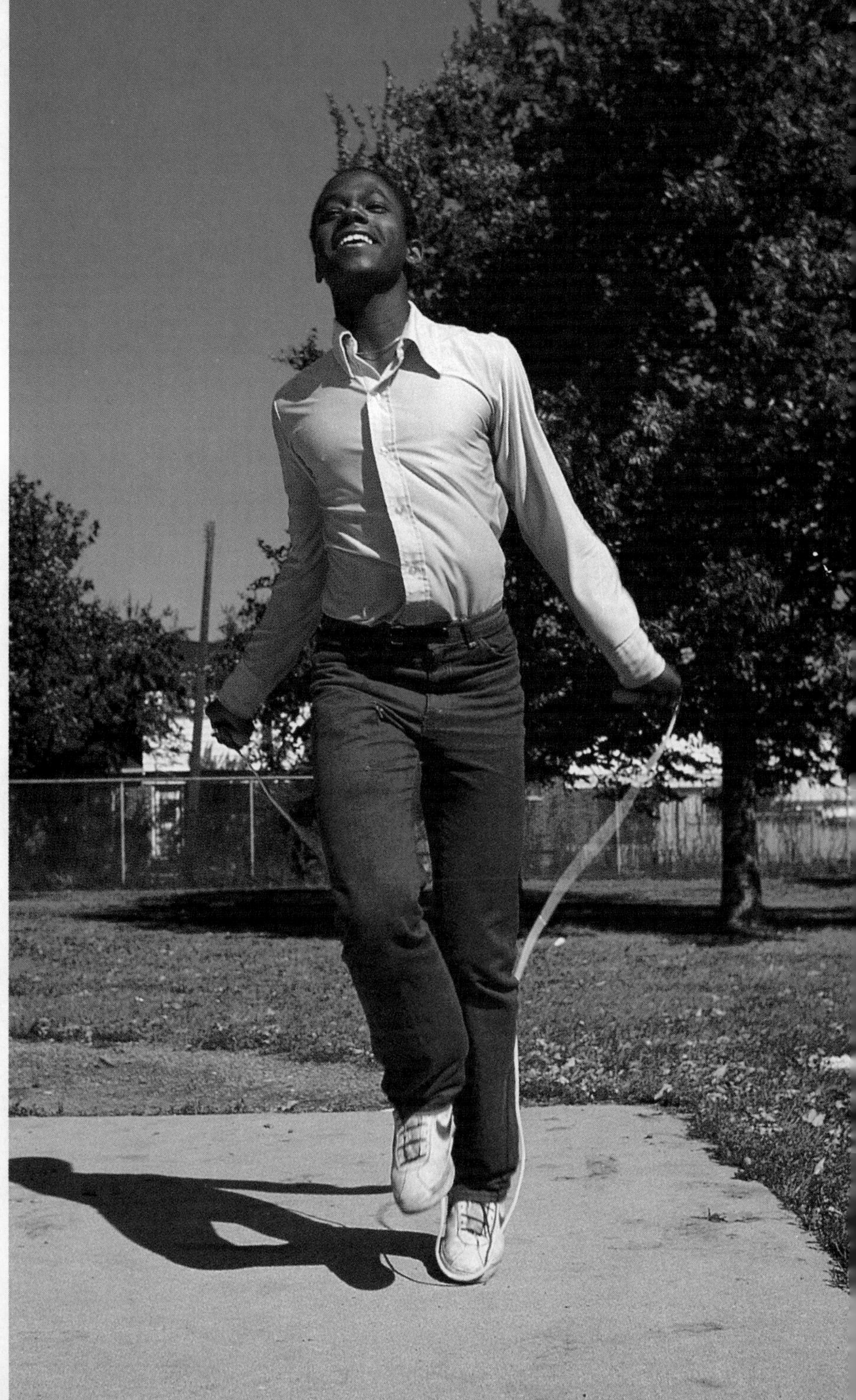

The Explanatory Paragraph

Telling *Why*

Part 1 **State Your Case**
Pre-Writing: Developing an Opinion

Part 2 **Save the Best for Last**
Pre-Writing: Organizing an Opinion

Part 3 **Build Your Case**
Writing the First Draft

Part 4 **In My Opinion**
Revising Your Explanatory *Why* Paragraph

Teaching Special Populations

LD See **Teaching Special Populations,** page 61.

ESL When writing explanatory paragraphs, many ESL students have difficulty with modals. Some languages express mood by using inflected verbs, so alert students to the need for separate words in English.

Some ESL students are subject to stricter standards of decorum than their peers, and they may thus be unwilling to state firm opinions in their own writing. They may also consider it impolite to disagree with the teacher. Encourage these students by starting them on uncontroversial topics such as sports and food.

Make sure that ESL students understand the vocabulary associated with sequence and order of importance.

NSD See **Teaching Special Populations,** page 61.

Part 1

Objective

1. To express strong, specific opinions in writing

2. To support opinions with logical reasons and accurate facts

Presenting the Lesson

1. Read aloud and discuss **Here's the Idea.** Discuss briefly the difference between fact and opinion. Use the following statements to contrast the two.

The Logan School has a lunch program. (fact)

The school lunch program should be eliminated. (opinion)

Ask the students for additional examples.

2. Read and discuss **Check It Out.** Identify the opinion and the reasons and facts that support it.

3. Assign and discuss **Try Your Skill.** Tell students that if they need reasons or facts to support their opinion, they can use an encyclopedia or other research book to find good supporting information.

4. Read **Keep This in Mind** and then assign **Now Write.**

Individualizing the Lesson

Less-Advanced Students

Write a set of pre-writing notes for one of the **Try Your Skill** opinions as a class. Then have the students select one of the remaining opinions and develop it independently.

Advanced Students

Explain to the students that in a debate two people hold different opinions about the same topic. The

Part 1

State Your Case

Pre-Writing: Developing an Opinion

Here's the Idea How do you feel about math, your uncle Harry, spinach, softball, or the school lunch program? Having strong feelings or beliefs about things is only natural. Expressing your opinion is something you do often.

The purpose of an explanatory *why* paragraph is to present your opinion in writing. You may want to explain why something is so, or why it should be changed. In either case, the first pre-writing step is to make your opinion clear in your own mind so that it will be clear to your readers. You can do this by writing a sentence that states your opinion simply and directly. Later, when you write your first draft, you can use this statement as the topic sentence of your paragraph.

Here are some typical statements of opinion.

The school lunchroom should serve food from other countries.

All students should take science classes.

Now you have to make your readers understand why you hold this opinion. To do this, you have to list specific reasons or facts to support your opinion. Your reasons must sound logical. Your facts must be accurate. Here are some examples of good supporting reasons and facts.

Opinion: The school lunchroom should serve food from other countries.

Reasons/Facts: Food teaches us about other cultures.

We have many foreign students in our school: 10% are from Asia, 15% are from Latin America, 5% are from India.

Having their own food served in the lunchroom will make foreign students feel more at home.

It's interesting to try different foods.

Check It Out Read the following paragraph.

Students should be allowed to use calculators in math class. Calculators are not a form of cheating. Even with a calculator, a student must know what to do to solve a problem. The calculator simply saves time by doing the addition, multiplication, subtraction, or division. It does this quickly and accurately. Since electronics is the way of the future, today's students should keep pace. They should use the most efficient method, the calculator.

- Does this paragraph state an opinion clearly?
- Is the opinion supported with logical reasons and accurate facts?

Try Your Skill Below are three opinions that could be developed in explanatory *why* paragraphs. Choose one opinion and develop some pre-writing notes for it. List at least three logical reasons or accurate facts to support it.

1. Smoking is dangerous to your health.
2. All students need to learn computer skills.
3. A balanced diet is important to good health.

Keep This in Mind

- In an explanatory *why* paragraph, you present and support an opinion.
- Use logical reasons and accurate facts to support the opinion.

Now Write Title a piece of paper "I Believe." Then do some brainstorming. Write down your opinions on different subjects. List as many opinions as you can.

Choose one opinion you would like to write about. In your pre-writing notes, list all the reasons and facts you can think of to support your opinion. Be sure your reasons are logical and your facts accurate. Save your pre-writing notes in your folder.

winner of a debate is the person who provides the best reasons and facts in support of his or her opinion. Ask the students to select one of these opinions and write three reasons or facts for the *pro* side and three reasons or facts for the *con* side.

- All students should/should not learn a foreign language.
- The Olympic Games should/should not have one country as a permanent home.
- Schools should/should not cut after-school activities to save money.

Optional Practice

Follow the directions for **Try Your Skill.**

1. The Olympics should include professional athletes.
2. School should be in session all year.
3. A ______ makes a good pet.

Extending the Lesson

Study examples of opinions expressed in print. Bring in copies of editorials and letters to the editor. Read them to the class. Ask students to identify the opinion expressed in each one. Then discuss how each opinion is or is not supported.

Part 2

Objective

To organize supporting reasons and facts from the least important idea to the most important idea

Presenting the Lesson

1. Read aloud and discuss **Here's the Idea.** Then reread the **Check It Out** paragraph on calculators from Part One on page 123. Ask the students if the reasons and facts are arranged from the least important to the most important idea.

2. Study the sample paragraph in **Check It Out.**

3. Assign and discuss **Try Your Skill.** Explain to the class that sometimes it is difficult to tell which reason or fact is more important than another. Ask them how they decided on the order for these reasons and facts.

4. Read **Keep This in Mind** aloud. Then assign **Now Write.**

Individualizing the Lesson

Less-Advanced Students

Some students may need help in finding a topic on which to express an opinion. Give them the following questions. Discuss the answers. Point out the possible topics generated by the discussion.

1. What environmental problems are found in your neighborhood? Noise or air pollution? Litter? Which affects your life the most?
2. Do you have regular chores to do at home? Do you think you should have them?

Part 2

Save the Best for Last

Pre-Writing: Organizing an Opinion

Here's the Idea Now that you have a list of supporting reasons and facts, you have to decide how to present them. You want your reasons to have the greatest impact on your reader. One good method is to save your strongest reasons until the end. This method of organization is called **least important to most important idea.** When you use this type of organization, you leave the most convincing reason fresh in your reader's mind.

For example, below are three reasons why private cars should be banned from large cities.

1. Pleasant pedestrian malls could replace some streets.
2. Energy is saved when people use public transportation.
3. Air pollution would be reduced, and cities would be healthier places to live.

The first reason is a good one, but it isn't as important to the nation as the second reason, saving energy. The last reason is probably the most important of all, since it affects people directly. We are all concerned about our health. You can see that these reasons have been listed in order, from the least important to the most important.

Check It Out Read the following explanatory paragraph.

> More junior high schools should offer soccer. A fast-moving game, soccer is fun to play and to watch. Soccer is also inexpensive for a school, since it requires little equipment. Most important, soccer is a sport that anyone of any size can play. For all these reasons, soccer is a popular sport all over the world. Junior high school students should have a chance to try it.

- Is the opinion supported by specific facts or reasons?
- Is the evidence given in order of importance, from the least important to the most important?

Try Your Skill In the last lesson, **State Your Case,** reasons were listed that support the opinion "The school lunchroom should serve food from different countries." Organize these reasons from the least important to the most important. Compare your organization with that of your classmates. Save these organized notes in your folder.

Keep This in Mind

- The most convincing way to organize an explanatory *why* paragraph is to list reasons and facts in the order of their importance. Start with the least important idea and end with the most important.

Now Write In the last lesson, **State Your Case,** you chose an opinion to write about. Then you listed reasons and facts to support that opinion. Now arrange these reasons or facts in the order of their importance. Save your organized list in your folder.

Select one of the topics and develop it with the students. Remind them to organize the reasons and facts from the least important to the most important.

Advanced Students

Have students take out the debate topics they chose and the reasons and facts that they wrote to support them, both *pro* and *con* (Part 1, **Advanced Students**). Then ask students to arrange those facts and reasons from the least important idea to the most important idea.

Optional Practice

Have students arrange these facts and reasons from the least important idea to the most important idea.

Topic Sentence: People should not use table salt.

3 • Consuming too much salt can raise the blood pressure in some people, which is dangerous.

2 • Prepared foods already contain a lot of salt.

1 • Other herbs and spices can be used to flavor food.

Extending the Lesson

Ask students to think about things they would like to buy or do. They can be things the students have always dreamed of doing (for example, joining a circus) or things that have recently become important (for example, buying a pair of roller skates). Ask the students to write pre-writing notes stating three reasons why they should have their wish. Remind the students to arrange their ideas from the least important idea to the most important idea.

Part 3

Objectives

1. To use transitional words in stating opinions and in presenting reasons

2. To conclude an explanatory *why* paragraph with a sentence which summarizes the opinion and supporting reasons

Presenting the Lesson

1. Read aloud and discuss **Here's the Idea.** Ask the students to think of example sentences that use the two types of transitions.

2. Discuss **Check It Out.** Before answering questions, have the students identify the transitional words used in the paragraph.

3. Assign and discuss **Try Your Skill.** Have students go over their paragraphs to see if they used the first person in their topic sentences.

4. Read **Keep This in Mind** aloud. Then assign **Now Write.**

Individualizing the Lesson

Less-Advanced Students

Begin the **Try Your Skill** exercise working as a class. Review how the reasons are organized and ask the class to suggest transitions to be used for each. Then allow students to write their first drafts independently. Remind them to write a strong ending sentence for the paragraph.

Advanced Students

Have students write a first draft of a paragraph using one of their debate topics, either the *pro* or the *con*

Part 3

Build Your Case

Writing the First Draft

Here's the Idea An explanatory *why* paragraph has two purposes. One is to present your opinion. The other is to give good reasons that support your opinion. Keep these two purposes in mind as you write your first draft.

You present your opinion in your topic sentence. Write a clear, direct sentence that tells your readers how you feel about a subject. Do not, however, use the first person in your topic sentence. Don't write "I think . . ." or "I believe . . ." or "In my opinion. . . ." When you state an opinion, your reader already knows that it is what you think.

In the body of your paragraph, offer reasons and facts to support and develop your topic sentence. As you write, use transitional words to help make your opinion clear. Here are some transitional words you may find helpful. One kind helps you to state reasons and facts. The other kind helps you to put your reasons and facts in the order of their importance.

To State Reasons and Facts:	because, so, since, therefore, as a result, if (something) . . . then (something)
To Put in Order of Importance:	the first reason, second, more important, most important, finally

Finally, you want to end your paragraph with a strong ending sentence that sums up your opinion and your reasons.

Check It Out Read this paragraph.

The highway speed limit should not be raised from 55 miles per hour. The first reason is that passengers can see more and are more relaxed at slower speeds. More important, lower speeds save fuel because engines are working efficiently. Most important, if motorists drive slowly they have more time to react to dangerous situations and lives will be saved. The savings in headaches, fuel, and lives speak strongly for keeping the speed limit at 55 miles per hour.

- Does the topic sentence state an opinion clearly?
- Which transitional words and phrases show the reasons? Which show their order of importance?
- Does the concluding sentence sum up the argument?

Try Your Skill Write a first draft using the pre-writing notes you organized in the **Try Your Skill** section of **Save the Best for Last.** Be sure that the opinion is stated in the topic sentence. Use transitional words in the body of the paragraph. Write a strong ending sentence. Save the first draft in your folder.

Keep This in Mind

- State your opinion in the topic sentence.
- Use transitional words that show the supporting reasons and facts and their order of importance.
- Sum up your argument in the ending sentence.

Now Write Using your organized notes from the last lesson, write a first draft of your explanatory *why* paragraph. State your opinion in the topic sentence. Use clear transitional words. Write a strong ending sentence. Save your first draft in your folder.

side (continued from **Advanced Students,** Part 2). Remind them to write a strong concluding sentence. Then have students read their paragraphs in class. Read them by topic, *pro* and *con.*

Optional Practice

Direct students to rewrite this paragraph using transitional words. Also, have them write a strong ending sentence for the paragraph.

Table salt should be eliminated from your diet. Other spices and herbs can flavor food. Prepared foods have a lot of salt in them. Eating too much salt can raise the blood pressure in many people, which is dangerous.

Extending the Lesson

On the chalkboard, write the opinions expressed by the students in their paragraphs. Eliminate duplications. Direct the students to choose one of the opinions and to write an opinion expressing the opposite point of view. Ask them to write reasons in support of their opinions. If students seem to need more practice in paragraph writing, have them complete their paragraphs.

Part 4

Objective

To revise an explanatory *why* paragraph to make it clear and convincing

Presenting the Lesson

1. Read aloud and discuss **Here's the Idea.**

2. Discuss **Check It Out.** Point out the transitional words and the strong ending sentence.

3. Assign **Try Your Skill.** List the six questions from **Check It Out** on the board as a reminder of what to look for when revising.

4. Read **Keep This in Mind** aloud. Then assign **Now Write.** Emphasize the importance of proofreading the paragraph before making a final copy.

Individualizing the Lesson

Less-Advanced Students

For the **Try Your Skill** exercise have the students exchange papers, read their partner's paragraph, and suggest revisions. Remind the students to ask the six questions to help revise an explanatory *why* paragraph. Then return the papers and have the students make the necessary revisions. Work with students individually if they seem to be having difficulty with the task.

Advanced Students

When the students complete the **Try Your Skill** revision, have them revise their debate topic paragraph (continued from **Advanced Students,** Part 3).

Part 4

In My Opinion

Revising Your Explanatory *Why* Paragraph

Here's the Idea When you revise the first draft of your explanatory *why* paragraph, try to make it clearer and more convincing. Ask yourself the following questions as you revise.

1. Have I presented my opinion clearly and directly in the topic sentence?
2. Have I supported my opinion with reasons and facts?
3. Are my reasons logical? Are my facts accurate?
4. Have I arranged my details from the least important to the most important idea?
5. Have I used transitional words to state my reasons and organize them?
6. Does my ending sentence sum up my opinion and reasons?

You may want to ask a friend to read your paragraph. Ask your friend to tell you if your opinion is presented clearly and strongly and if you have supported your opinion with good reasons and facts.

Check It Out Read the following explanatory *why* paragraph.

> All bicyclists should be required to wear safety helmets. Each year, thousands of cyclists are injured in accidents. Because many riders do not wear helmets, they suffer serious head injuries. As a result, some of these riders are paralyzed for the rest of their lives. Some even die from their injuries. If more bicyclists wore safety helmets, then fewer riders would suffer serious and sometimes fatal head injuries.

- Does the topic sentence state the writer's opinion clearly and directly?
- Are the reasons and facts arranged from the least important to the most important?
- What transitional words has the writer used to help state the reasons and facts?
- Does the ending sentence sum up the argument?

Try Your Skill Revise the first draft you wrote in **Build Your Case** about serving food from different countries in the lunchroom. Follow the guidelines presented in this lesson.

Keep This in Mind

When revising your explanatory *why* paragraph:

- State your opinion clearly and directly in your topic sentence.
- Use logical reasons and accurate facts to support your opinion.
- Use transitional words to state your reasons and to show the order of their importance.
- Be sure your concluding sentence sums up your argument.

Now Write Revise the first draft of your explanatory *why* paragraph using the guidelines presented in this lesson. Proofread your paragraph for correct grammar, usage, capitalization, punctuation, and spelling. Neatly rewrite your revised paragraph. Save this final copy in your folder.

Optional Practice

Have the students read this paragraph and identify its problems. Then have them revise the paragraph. Remind them to use the revision guide on page 128.

> I believe that school should be held twelve months a year. We no longer are primarily a farming society. Students do not have to help with the planting and harvesting in the summer. There would be less juvenile delinquency if adolescents were in school all year. Holding school all year would be efficient. The school buildings would not sit vacant all summer. Besides, school can be fun.

Extending the Lesson

Write an editorial page with the class. Have students select topics that are important to them and write paragraphs expressing their opinion. Also, have the students write headlines to title their paragraphs. After they have completed their revisions, compile and photocopy this editorial page. Distribute it to students.

Section 12 Objectives

1. To know the three parts of a composition—introduction, body, and conclusion

2. To select and narrow a topic for a composition

3. To support the topic of a composition with details, examples, and facts and figures

4. To organize the ideas for a composition into groups of notes of paragraph length

5. To capture the reader's interest with the introduction of a composition

6. To use transitions between paragraphs to help the reader move from one idea to another in the body of a composition

7. To summarize the ideas presented in the conclusion of a composition

8. To give a composition an interesting title

9. To revise the rough draft of a composition, improving the ideas, the organization, and the word choice

10. To proofread the rough draft of a composition for errors in grammar, capitalization, punctuation, and spelling

11. To know and use the guidelines for a final copy of a composition

12. To review the process of writing a composition

Preparing the Students

Review the main characteristics of a paragraph:

1. It is a group of sentences about one idea.
2. It has a topic sentence that states the main idea.

A Look at Compositions

Part 1 **It's a Long Story**
Learning About Compositions

Part 2 **Decisions, Decisions**
Pre-Writing: Choosing a Topic

Part 3 **Getting It Together**
Pre-Writing: Organizing Ideas

Part 4 **First Try**
Writing the First Draft

Part 5 **Nobody's Perfect**
Revising Your Composition

Part 6 **Wrap It Up**
The Final Copy of a Composition

Part 7 **One More Time**
Reviewing the Process of Writing

3. It has sentences that develop the main idea.
4. It is one of three kinds: narrative, descriptive, or explanatory.

Explain that a composition is similar to a paragraph in many ways.

Additional Resources

Mastery Test — pages 22-23 in the test booklet

Practice Book — pages 53-59

Duplicating Masters — pages 53-59

Teaching Special Populations

LD See **Teaching Special Populations** , page 61.

ESL Devote extra time to explaining general terms such as *introduction, body, conclusion,* and *composition* to ESL students. Always provide specific examples of each item. Also, have students identify these constituent elements in several complete compositions so that they understand the difference between *paragraph* and *composition*. Stress to students that pre-writing and the use of first drafts allows them to put down thoughts in a rough form without fear of criticism.

NSD See **Teaching Special Populations,** page 61.

Part 1

Objective

To know the three parts of a composition—introduction, body, and conclusion

Presenting the Lesson

1. Read aloud and discuss **Here's the Idea.** Write the definition of *composition* on the chalkboard.

2. Discuss the sample composition in **Check It Out.** Explain that it is a descriptive composition and that the main idea is developed with details.

3. Assign and discuss **Try Your Skill.**

4. Read **Keep This in Mind** aloud. Then assign **Now Write.**

Individualizing the Lesson

Less-Advanced Students

Study additional examples of well-written compositions. (Use student-written compositions from your files.) Have students express the main idea in each composition. Then have them identify the introduction, the body, and the conclusion in each.

Advanced Students

Explain that compositions, like paragraphs, can be narrative, descriptive, or explanatory. Read examples of each kind to the students and have them identify the type of composition. Also, have the students express the main idea of each composition and identify the introduction, body, and conclusion in each.

Part 1

It's a Long Story

Learning About Compositions

Here's the Idea There are times when you cannot say everything you want to say in one paragraph. You may have a long story to tell or a lot of information to present. A subject that is too big for a paragraph may be just right for a composition.

A **composition** is a group of paragraphs that tell about one idea. A composition has three parts: an introduction, a body, and a conclusion.

The **introduction** is a paragraph that tells what the composition is about. The introduction does the same job in a composition that the topic sentence does in a paragraph.

The **body** of a composition is made up of paragraphs that develop the main idea. The main idea can be developed with descriptive details, examples, or facts and figures.

The **conclusion** of a composition is a paragraph that sums up the important ideas in the composition. The conclusion does the same job as the ending sentence of a paragraph.

Check It Out Read the following composition.

The Jacobs' Specialty

At first glance, there doesn't seem to be much that's special about the Jacob family. However, something sets them apart from every other family I know. It's their refrigerator.

From the outside, the refrigerator looks like a big, white box next to the sink. Open the door, though, and the inside is unlike anything you've ever seen before. Every shelf and space is always crammed with tempting foods. The top shelf has colorful containers of pickles, jelly, cold meats, milk, and juices. The middle shelf is always heaped with plates of sandwiches. The bottom shelf is packed with cheeses, homemade breads, and fruit of every kind.

Getting an invitation to the Jacobs' house is like being invited to a banquet. One day the snack might be ham and Swiss on rolls with sharp dill pickles on the side. Another day, it might be rich cream cheese on thick slices of rye bread. On a rainy Saturday, the feast might include homemade pizza.

Whenever I think of that refrigerator, I think of the Jacob family itself. Every member of that family is friendly, generous, and affectionate. Everyone seems to contribute something to the comfort of family and friends. I guess that makes the family special. Their hearts are as open as their refrigerator door.

- What is the main idea of this composition?
- Which part is the introduction, which is the body, and which is the conclusion?

Try Your Skill Write which part of a composition you think this paragraph is. Write the reasons for your answer.

A good-luck charm may be anything from a rabbit's foot to a shiny penny. It's not the shape or size that matters. What counts is that the owner believes in the charm. That belief gives confidence, and confidence often assures success. In that respect, anyway, good-luck charms have really worked.

Keep This in Mind

- A composition is a group of paragraphs that tell about one idea.
- A composition has three parts: an introduction, a body, and a conclusion.

Now Write Write a paragraph that explains what a composition is. In your paragraph, define the term *composition*. Tell how many parts a composition has. Tell what each part does. Be sure your paragraph has a good topic sentence and an ending sentence. Save your paragraph in your folder.

Optional Practice

Follow the instructions for **Try Your Skill,** using these paragraphs.

A. Another way to invest money is to buy stocks. Some stocks are secure investments. They are called "blue-chip" stocks. Other stocks are less secure. They are "speculative" stocks. It is wise to learn something about the market and stocks before investing your money in the stock market. body

B. Careful landscaping can also help you save energy. Evergreens around the house cut the winter winds. Leafy trees near the house shade it in summer yet allow the sun to warm it in winter. Bushes and trees are practical as well as pretty! body

Extending the Lesson

Read to the class a simple fable that is presented in five or six paragraphs. Note that it is a narrative composition. Ask students to identify the introduction, the body, and the conclusion of the fable and to list the events that are described in the body.

Part 2

Objective

To narrow a topic for a composition

Presenting the Lesson

1. Read aloud and discuss **Here's the Idea.** Ask students to suggest composition topics. Practice narrowing the suggested topics so that each can be covered in a four or five paragraph composition.

2. Discuss **Check It Out.**

3. Assign and discuss **Try Your Skill.** Be sure students understand that several good topics can result from narrowing one general subject.

4. Read **Keep This in Mind** aloud. Then assign **Now Write.**

Individualizing the Lesson

Less-Advanced Students

Do one of the **Try Your Skill** topics as a class before having students select one to do independently.

Advanced Students

Have students select more than one topic to develop for the **Try Your Skill** exercise.

Optional Practice

Give this list of topics to students. Have them decide which are suitable for a short composition, which are too narrow, and which are too broad. Then have them narrow each of the topics that is too broad for a short composition.

- the U.S. National Parks
- a description of a dime

Part 2

Decisions, Decisions

Pre-Writing: Choosing a Topic

Here's the Idea The first step in planning a composition is choosing a topic. You want to choose a topic that you are interested in and that you know something about. You also want to choose a topic that you can cover thoroughly in four or five paragraphs.

One place you might find ideas for your compositions is in your journal. Perhaps you made some notes about topics that you later decided were too long for just one paragraph. You might use them now for compositions. The books, magazines, and newspapers that you read might also suggest some composition ideas to you. Finally, you may want to discuss some possible topics with your classmates or do some brainstorming.

Once you have chosen a subject to write about, you may have to narrow it. Even though a composition is longer than a paragraph, some subjects are still too general to be covered well in a short composition. One way to narrow a topic is to ask questions such as *who? what? where? when? how?* and *why?* about it. The answers to these questions will give you information to make your topic more specific.

For example, the subject, "a challenging adventure," is too general. By asking the questions *who? what? where? when? how?* and *why?* about this subject, you might come up with narrowed topics like these:

–the time Sandy and I hiked from the rim of the Grand Canyon down to the canyon floor
–winning the canoe race last summer at camp
–when Rob and I explored the old Hickock coal mine in Lester County

Check It Out See how one writer narrowed a general subject to a more specific topic by asking questions.

General subject — an outdoor adventure
Who? — Rob and I, with the Portland Hiking Club
What? — camping trip
Where? — Acadia National Park
When? — summer vacation July, 1985
How? — open-air camping
Why? — to see what living outdoors for a week is like
Specific topic — my week-long camping trip to Acadia National Park with the Portland Hiking Club in July, 1985

- How is the specific topic different from the general subject?

Try Your Skill Each of these subjects is too general for a composition. Choose one. Then ask *who? what? where? when? how?* and *why?* about it. Write the answers below the subject. Then use your notes to write a specific topic.

a big surprise	a difficult challenge
a long, hard day	a new invitation
a real accomplishment	a funny incident

Keep This in Mind

- Choose a topic that is interesting and that you know something about.
- Narrow your topic so that it is specific enough to be covered well in a composition.

Now Write Choose a subject that is suitable for a composition. Narrow your subject by asking *who? what? where? when? how?* and *why?* Then write a specific topic. Save your topic in your folder.

- good aerobic exercise for everybody
- my first piano lesson
- flowers to grow indoors
- automobiles
- movies
- building a birdhouse

Extending the Lesson

Most students have written compositions without defining them as such. These probably include reports for social studies and science classes, directions for doing or making things, and book reports. Discuss the class's experience in composition writing. Focus particularly on the kinds of topics involved.

Part 3

Objectives

1. To support the topic of a composition with details, examples, and facts and figures

2. To organize the ideas for a composition into groups of notes of paragraph length

Presenting the Lesson

1. Read aloud and discuss **Here's the Idea.**

2. Read and discuss **Check It Out.** Then, as a class, develop and organize pre-writing notes for another topic. (topic suggestion: the town's 4th of July celebration; possible groups of notes: parade, games, concert, picnic, fireworks, etc.)

3. Assign and discuss **Try Your Skill.**

4. Read **Keep This in Mind** aloud. Then assign **Now Write.**

Individualizing the Lesson

Less-Advanced Students

Give students the two main ideas for the **Try Your Skill** exercise (1. Who the first settlers were, and 2. Why the first settlers came to America). Then have them organize the details under the main ideas.

Advanced Students

Explain to students that topics can be developed in more than one way. For example, a composition about a 4th of July celebration could be organized around the main ideas "morning activities," "afternoon activities," and "evening activities." As

Getting It Together

Pre-Writing: Organizing Ideas

Here's the Idea Once you have chosen and narrowed your topic, you must gather ideas for your composition. These ideas will include specific details, sensory details, examples, and facts and figures. You can gather these ideas through brainstorming, personal observation, and research in a library.

Before you can use the ideas you gather to write your first draft, you must organize them. Look at your pre-writing notes. Which notes seem to belong together? That is, which notes seem to be about the same main ideas? Try to group your pre-writing notes around two or three main ideas. Each group of notes can then become a paragraph in the body of your composition.

Check It Out Look at these pre-writing notes for a composition about soccer.

–oldest sport
–I lift weights for strength
–Roman soldiers brought game to England
–you must kick or bounce ball into opponent's goal
–world's most popular game
–only goalkeeper can touch ball with hands
–players always running
–boys and girls can play
–players need good physical conditioning
–players use feet, bodies, heads to move ball

These notes could be grouped around three main ideas:

History
oldest sport
Roman soldiers brought game to England
world's most popular game

Players
boys and girls can play
I lift weights for strength
players always running
players need good physical conditioning

Rules
players use feet, bodies, and heads to move ball
only goal keeper can touch ball with hands
you must kick or bounce ball into opponent's goal
2 teams of 5 to 11 players

- What three main ideas are these notes grouped around?
- Do you see how each group of notes could be developed into a paragraph?

Try Your Skill Read the following pre-writing notes for a composition about the early settlers in America. Decide what two main ideas these notes could be grouped around.

came to make a better life
some were adventurers
came to make a fortune
came to find religious freedom
some were criminals
some were persecuted minorities

Keep This in Mind

- Gather ideas for your topic through brainstorming, personal observation, or research in a library.
- Organize your ideas by grouping them around several main ideas. Use each grouping as a paragraph in your composition.

Now Write Make a list of pre-writing notes for the topic you chose in the last lesson, **Decisions, Decisions.** Then group your notes around two or three main ideas. Save your notes.

an alternative, it could be organized around the ideas "the parade," "the games," and "the fireworks." Have students select one of the following topics and make a set of pre-writing notes for it. Remind students to organize their notes into groups of ideas. Each group should be the foundation for a paragraph. Discuss the students' notes in class.

after-school activities
kinds of sports
family traditions
kinds of games
a healthy diet

Optional Practice

Have students read these pre-writing notes about spring yard work. Then have them decide what three main ideas these notes should be grouped around.

- the grass should be fertilized
- plant flower seeds
- trim dead branches from trees
- add peat moss to soil in flower beds
- rake lawn to remove dead grass
- pull any weeds in lawn
- turn over soil in flower beds
- spray trees for insects
- fertilize trees

Extending the Lesson

Go to the school library. Have each student find an example composition in a magazine. Using an opaque projector, discuss each example. Determine the main idea of each composition. Then have the students identify the groups of ideas developed in each.

Part 4

Objectives

1. To capture the reader's interest with the introduction of a composition

2. To use transitions between paragraphs to help the reader move from one idea to another in the body of a composition

3. To summarize the ideas presented in the conclusion of a composition

4. To give a composition an interesting title

Presenting the Lesson

1. Read aloud and discuss **Here's the Idea.** Reread the **Check It Out** composition from Part One on page 132. Discuss each part. Did the writer capture the reader's interest in the introduction? Does each body paragraph cover a separate topic? Does the conclusion summarize the composition?

2. Discuss **Check It Out.** Refer the students to the pre-writing notes on page 136.

3. Assign and discuss **Try Your Skill.**

4. Read **Keep This in Mind** aloud. Then assign **Now Write.**

Individualizing the Lesson

Less-Advanced Students

Do the **Try Your Skill** exercise as a class. In addition, break down the **Now Write** exercise into smaller tasks. First have students write the introductions. Discuss them and suggest improvements. Do the same with the body paragraphs and the conclusions of their compositions.

Part 4

First Try

Writing the First Draft

Here's the Idea Once you have organized your ideas, you can begin writing your first draft. Remember that this draft is just your first attempt to put your ideas into paragraphs. As you write, you may take out some ideas or add new ones. You may even change your organization. Don't worry about details such as grammar, punctuation, or spelling. You can make any necessary corrections when you revise your composition.

As you write your first draft, remember the three parts of a composition and the purpose of each part.

Introduction Your first paragraph introduces your composition. This paragraph should capture your reader's interest. It should also let the reader know what you will be writing about.

Body The body of your composition is made up of paragraphs that develop your topic. Each group of ideas from your pre-writing notes will become a paragraph in your composition. Each of these paragraphs should have its own topic sentence.

Arrange the paragraphs and the ideas within them logically. You can use chronological order, spatial order, or the order of importance. Use transitional words and phrases within and between paragraphs to make your ideas flow smoothly.

Conclusion End your composition with a concluding paragraph. The conclusion may be a summary or a general statement about your story, description, or explanation. The conclusion may also be just a group of sentences that clearly signal an ending to the idea you have developed. Be sure not to introduce any new ideas in your concluding paragraph.

When you have finished writing the first draft, give your composition an interesting title.

Check It Out Read the following first draft.

I found out that soccer is the most popular game in the world. It is also the oldest sport. The Chinese played the game over 2,000 years ago. Roman soldiers played the game, to. They brought it to England when they conquered England. I play soccer on our school team.

In the game, players use their feet, bodies, and heads to move the ball. The only ones who can touch the ball with their hands are the goalkeepers. Each team tries to put the ball into the opponent's goal to get points. I like to play goalie.

Boys and girls can play this game. It is a very active game. They need to be in good physical condition.

Soccer is a popular game. It has lasted so long because it is easy to learn and is a game everyone can take part in and enjoy.

- Has the writer made each group of ideas from the pre-writing notes into a paragraph?
- Are the ideas in a logical order?
- Has the writer added any new ideas that weren't in the pre-writing notes? Has the writer taken out any ideas?

Try Your Skill Reread the first draft of the composition on soccer. What are some things you could do to improve this first draft? Discuss your idea with your classmates.

Keep This in Mind

- Your rough draft should have an introduction, a body, and a conclusion.
- Organize the paragraphs and the ideas within them logically.

Now Write Use your organized ideas to write a first draft of your composition. Make sure you have an introduction, a body, and a conclusion. Be sure the paragraphs are arranged logically. Give your composition a title. Save your first draft.

Advanced Students

Have students rewrite the soccer composition from **Check It Out,** incorporating any suggested improvements.

Optional Practice

Have students write an introduction for a composition describing their town's 4th of July celebration. Remind students to write the paragraph so that it not only introduces the topic, but that it also catches the reader's attention.

Extending the Lesson

Take copies of several well-written compositions from your files or from books or magazines. Copy them, but eliminate the conclusions. Discuss the introductions, point out the logical organization of the body paragraphs in each, and find the transitions used in each composition. Then have students select one of the compositions and write a conclusion for it.

Part 5

Objectives

1. To revise the rough draft of a composition, improving the ideas, the organization, and the word choice

2. To proofread the rough draft of a composition for errors in grammar, capitalization, punctuation, and spelling

Presenting the Lesson

1. Read aloud and discuss **Here's the Idea.**

2. Before discussing **Check It Out,** reread the rough draft of the composition on soccer on page 139. Then read and discuss **Check It Out.**

3. Assign and discuss **Try Your Skill.**

4. Assign **Now Write.** Remind students to proofread their compositions after they have made their revisions.

Individualizing the Lesson

Less-Advanced Students

Work individually or in small groups with students to help them revise the first drafts of their compositions.

Advanced Students

Have students select partners and exchange their compositions. Direct the students to use the guidelines on page 140, and to make suggestions for improvements on their partner's paper. Have students discuss their suggestions with each other. Repeat the exchanging process for proofreading after the revisions are made.

Part 5

Nobody's Perfect

Revising Your Composition

Here's the Idea All writers, even experienced ones, have to revise their first drafts. When you revise, you can improve your ideas, your organization, and your word choice. You can correct any errors you find in grammar, capitalization, punctuation, and spelling. Revising helps you to make your composition better than it was when you first wrote it.

Here are some questions you should ask yourself as you revise.

1. Have I included enough details to develop my topic? Are there any unrelated details that should be taken out?
2. Have I organized my details around two or three main ideas?
3. Is my introductory paragraph interesting? Does it tell the reader what my composition is about?
4. Does each paragraph in the body contain details about just one main idea? Are the paragraphs and the ideas within them arranged logically?
5. Have I written a strong concluding paragraph that sums up the ideas in my composition?
6. Have I used good transitional words to lead the reader from one idea to another?
7. Have I used verbs that are strong and specific? Have I used vivid adjectives?

Check It Out Notice how the first few paragraphs of the composition on soccer have been revised.

- Do you see how these paragraphs have been improved through revision?

¶ *There was a time when football, baseball, and basketball were the only sports Americans cared about. Now soccer has joined the big three as one of the country's most popular sports.*

~~I found out that~~ soccer is the most popular game in the world. It is also the oldest sport. The Chinese played the game over 2,000 years ago. Roman soldiers played the game, to. They brought *the game with them.* ~~it to England~~ when they conquered England, ~~I play soccer on our school team.~~

In *soccer,* ~~the game,~~ players use their feet, bodies, and heads to move the ball. The only ones who can touch the ball with their hands are the goalkeepers. Each team tries to kick or bounce the ball into their opponent's goal to get points. ~~I like to play goalie.~~

Try Your Skill Use proofreading symbols (See Section 7, p. 85) to correct the errors in these sentences.

1. We new that it nearly ten o clock.
2. Independence Day is a Major holiday in the united states.
3. My Brother and Sister found there shoes in the closest.

Keep This in Mind

- Revise your composition to improve your ideas, organization, and word choice.
- Proofread your composition to correct errors in grammar, capitalization, punctuation, and spelling.

Now Write Use the guidelines in this lesson to revise the first draft of your composition. Save the revised copy.

Optional Practice

Have students proofread this paragraph.

When I go upstairs in my aunt lils attic, I feel like I am stepping into history. not only does she have boxes full of pictures and books, but also trunks ful of old cloths. In addition, the attic itself is cluttered with peices of furniture from my Grandmothers house. That attic is a wonderfull place to spend a rainy afternoon

Extending the Lesson

Arrange a cooperative project with one of the departments or teachers in your school. For example, have the social studies or science teacher assign a composition and help students research their topics. Then, in the language arts class, help students to organize their notes, write their rough drafts, revise them, and make final copies.

Part 6

Objective

To know and use the guidelines for a final copy of a composition

Presenting the Lesson

1. Read aloud and discuss **Here's the Idea.** List the guidelines on the board. You may also bring up the fact that some people prefer to type their papers. Explain that typed papers must be neat, too. They should be typed on white, unlined paper.

2. Discuss **Check It Out.**

3. Assign and discuss **Try Your Skill.**

4. Assign **Now Write.**

Individualizing the Lesson

Less-Advanced Students

Reproduce a composition that has been carelessly copied (sloppy handwriting, misplaced title, no margins, scratch-outs, etc.). For practice, give each student a copy and have him or her rewrite it using the guidelines for a final copy.

Advanced Students

Have students look through their writing folders and critique their final copies. Do they meet the standards for a good final copy? If they do not, have students discuss the problems. Then have each student select his or her worst paper and make a better final copy.

Part 6

Wrap It Up

The Final Copy of a Composition

Here's the Idea You have put a great deal of effort into writing your composition. However, you are not quite finished. Now you have to write your **final copy.** This is the only copy of your composition that your readers will see. Therefore, it is important to take your time with this final step in the writing of your composition.

Always write your final copy on clean, white, lined paper. Use a pen, not a pencil. Put your name, the subject, and the date in the upper right-hand corner of your paper. On the second line of your paper, center the title for your composition.

Copy each line of your composition carefully. Include all of the changes you made when you revised your composition. Leave at least one inch on the right and left sides of the paper for a margin. Leave at least one line blank at the bottom of your paper. Write on only one side of a piece of paper. If you need more than one sheet, number each sheet after the first one in the center at the very top.

When you are done, proofread your final copy one last time. Use a single line to cross out any errors you find. If you have made more than three or four mistakes, you may want to rewrite your composition. Remember, you want your final copy to be as neat as possible.

Check It Out Look at this beginning of the final copy of the soccer composition.

- Does this final copy follow the guidelines presented in this lesson?

Melissa Kim
English
January 11, 1985

A Lasting Sport

There was a time when football, basketball, and baseball were the only sports Americans cared about. Now soccer has joined the big three as one of the country's most popular sports.

Soccer is already the most popular game in the world. It is also the oldest sport. The Chinese played the

Try Your Skill Write the answers to these questions about the final copy of a composition.

1. What kind of paper should you use?
2. What three pieces of information are written at the top of the first page?
3. Where is the title written?
4. How should errors be corrected?
5. If you use more than one sheet of paper, where should you put the numbers 2, 3, and so on?
6. How wide a margin should you leave on the left and the right sides of the paper?

Keep This in Mind

- The final copy of your composition should be neat and free of errors.

Now Write Use the guidelines in this lesson to write a final copy of your composition. Make sure this copy is as free from errors as you can make it. Save your final copy in your folder.

Optional Practice

Collect or write copies of compositions with errors (one written on colored paper, one written in pencil, one with no title, one with no margins, one with illegible writing, etc.). Ask students to identify the problem with each composition.

Extending the Lesson

Have students, working in small groups, make posters illustrating and explaining what the final copy of a composition should look like. For reference, hang the posters in study halls, classrooms, and the library.

Part 7

Objective

To review the process of writing a composition

Presenting the Lesson

Read aloud and discuss the *Guidelines for Writing a Composition.* It will serve as a review for the previous six sections. In addition, it can be used as a reference tool for the students during the process of writing any further compositions.

Extending the Lesson

Ask students to suggest other writing activities that could be added to each section of the guidelines.

Part 7

One More Time

Reviewing the Process of Writing

In the following sections, you will be writing many different kinds of compositions. Remember, no matter what kind of composition you write, the process of writing remains the same. Below is a checklist of steps for writing a composition. Refer to this checklist often as you write your compositions.

Guidelines for Writing a Composition

Pre-Writing

- Choose a topic that interests you and that you know something about. Narrow the topic so that you can cover it well in the assigned length of your composition.
- Gather details that you can use to develop the topic.
- Group similar details together around two or three main ideas.
- Organize those details into an order that suits the type of composition you are writing.

Writing the First Draft

- Begin your composition with an interesting introductory paragraph that tells the reader what your composition is about.
- Follow the introduction with the body of your composition. Use your organized details to develop your topic. Each group of details will be a paragraph in the body of your composition.
- Use transitions to lead the reader from one idea to another.

- Add, take out, and reorganize ideas if you need to.
- Finish your composition with a concluding paragraph that sums up your ideas.
- Add an interesting title to your composition.

Revising

- Be sure your composition has an introduction, a body, and a conclusion.
- Check to see that you have included enough details to develop your topic.
- The paragraphs and the ideas within them should be organized logically.
- Each paragraph should have a topic sentence that presents the main idea of that paragraph.
- Use effective transitional words to make your ideas flow smoothly.
- Make sure you have used vivid language.
- Proofread to find and correct errors in grammar, capitalization, punctuation, and spelling.

Final Copy

- Rewrite your composition neatly in ink on white, lined paper.
- Write your name, subject, and the date in the upper right-hand corner of your paper.
- Proofread your final copy one last time. Neatly correct any errors you find.

145

Section 13 Objectives

1. To know the elements of a narrative composition: setting, characters, plot, conflict, and ending

2. To use specific details and chronological order when plotting a story

3. To review the meanings of first-person and third-person limited point of view

4. To learn the meaning of third-person omniscient point of view

5. To know the purpose of each part of a narrative composition—the introduction, the body, and the conclusion

6. To know how to use dialogue in a narrative composition

7. To use transitions within and between the paragraphs of a narrative composition

8. To know and use the guidelines for revising a narrative composition

Preparing the Students

Review the definition of a narrative paragraph, a paragraph that tells a story in chronological order. Explain that a narrative composition is a group of paragraphs telling a story in chronological order. Emphasize that a narrative composition can be fiction or nonfiction. In other words, it can relate an imaginary story or a true story.

Additional Resources

Practice Book — pages 60–66
Duplicating Masters — pages 60–66

The Narrative Composition

Part 1 **Get Started**
Pre-Writing: Planning a Story

Part 2 **Action!**
Pre-Writing: Plotting a Story

Part 3 **What's Your View?**
Pre-Writing: Choosing a Point of View

Part 4 **First Impressions**
Writing the First Draft

Part 5 **She Said, He Said**
The First Draft: Using Dialogue

Part 6 **Go with the Flow**
The First Draft: Using Transitions

Part 7 **A Second Look**
Revising Your Narrative Composition

Teaching Special Populations

LD See **Teaching Special Populations**, page 61.

ESL Use concrete examples to demonstrate the meaning of *setting, characters, plot,* and *conflict*. It might also be useful to have students translate folk tales from their native cultures and identify narrative elements in these stories.

Ask native English speakers to play the part of first- and third-person narrators and have ESL students identify the respective points of view.

Give ESL students plenty of practice in punctuating dialogue. Hand out copies of a narrative cartoon, for example, and have students transcribe correctly the dialogue between characters. Review Handbook Section 17, pages 556–558, as a group. Additional exercises on punctuating dialogue can be found in the Practice Book.

NSD See **Teaching Special Populations,** page 61.

Use narratives incorporating dialogue to reinforce standard usage amongst NSD students. Though students will frequently want to write narratives using characters from their own mileau, they should be encouraged to also include standard forms of dialogue. Make sure students understand that it is only in the context of written dialogue that nonstandard dialect is acceptable.

Part 1

Objective

To know the elements of a narrative composition: setting, characters, plot, conflict, and ending

Presenting the Lesson

1. Read aloud and discuss **Here's the Idea.** Write the five elements of a narrative on the chalkboard. Then read students a short story from a student literature text or magazine. Ask students to identify the elements of a narrative in the story.

2. Discuss **Check It Out.** If necessary, redefine each part of a narrative.

3. Complete **Try Your Skill.** Encourage the students to have fun with this activity. The more creative the story the better. The point is to show students how the five parts work together to make a story.

4. Read **Keep This in Mind** aloud. Then assign **Now Write.**

Individualizing the Lesson

Less-Advanced Students

Give students some experience identifying conflicts. Read a collection of news stories which describe various kinds of conflicts (mayor vs. city council, citizens of Utah vs. flood waters, etc.). Explain that news articles can be a type of real narrative. Ask students to identify the conflict in each article.

Advanced Students

In addition to developing one story plan as a class in **Try Your Skill,** have each student write his or her own story plan.

Part 1

Get Started

Pre-Writing: Planning a Story

Here's the Idea Narrative compositions tell stories. Some narratives tell stories about events that really happened. Others tell stories that happened only in the writer's imagination.

Whether real or imaginary, a narrative has to have a point. It is not just a series of events. A narrative should tell a story that the reader can become involved with. The story should tell the reader something about the way people think, feel, and act.

A narrative must also have a setting. The **setting** is where and when a story takes place. The setting may be real or imaginary. The setting may be any time in the past, present, or future. Your story might begin, "As night fell, we were still 3,000 feet from the top of Mount Everest." Describing the setting of your story with specific details will help your readers see what you have imagined.

Narratives must also have **characters.** Your characters can be people or animals. Describe your characters carefully to your readers. What does a character look like? What does his or her voice sound like? How does the character behave?

A good narrative also has an interesting plot. The **plot** of a story is made up of the events that take place. Usually, the plot centers around a conflict. The **conflict** in a story is some problem that a character struggles with. A character might struggle with a fear, such as a fear of the dark. A character might struggle with another character—in a basketball game, for example. A character might also struggle with nature, during a blizzard or alone in a forest.

Finally, like any composition, a narrative has an ending. The **ending** of a narrative brings the story to a close. The conflict is settled, and the reader is satisfied that the story has been brought to a reasonable conclusion.

Check It Out Look at these pre-writing notes for the plan of a narrative.

Setting	Beech river, an August afternoon
Characters	me and my sister Blanca
Plot	Blanca and I go rafting on the Beech river; my raft overturns, and I nearly drown.
Conflict	me against the icy water and swift currents of the river
Ending	I manage to drag myself to safety along the river-bank.

- Do these pre-writing notes include all of the important parts of a narrative?

Try Your Skill Along with your classmates, develop a plan for an imaginary story. Where will the story take place? Who will the characters be? What is the plot? What is the conflict? How will the story end?

Keep This in Mind

- A narrative composition tells a story with a point.
- A good narrative has a setting, characters, plot, conflict, and an ending.

Now Write Think about some stories you would like to tell. These stories may be real or imaginary, serious or humorous. Remember, each story should have a point. It should tell about characters who face and overcome a conflict. Make a list of all your story possibilities and save it in your folder.

Optional Practice

Ask students to select a fairy tale that they enjoyed as a child. Have them name its characters and describe its setting, plot, and major conflict.

Extending the Lesson

Provide students with a number of short stories. Either use their literature anthology or stories found in student literature or reading magazines in the school library. Divide the class into small groups. Assign each group a story to read. Then have students identify the elements of a narrative in that story. Have each group report its findings to the class.

Part 2

Objective

To use specific details and chronological order when plotting a story

Presenting the Lesson

1. Read aloud and discuss **Here's the Idea.** Review the definitions of **plot** and **chronological order.** Ask students to look at the pre-writing notes in **Check It Out,** Part 1 on page 149. Ask students what other details might be added to the plot.

2. Discuss **Check It Out.**

3. Assign and discuss **Try Your Skill.**

4. Read **Keep This in Mind** aloud. Then assign **Now Write.**

Individualizing the Lesson

Less-Advanced Students

Either divide the class into small groups or have students work in pairs. Have each group select one of the following topics and make a set of pre-writing notes developing the plot. Remind students to determine the major conflict in the story.

- an explorer is lost in the jungle
- during a blizzard the electricity is cut off in your house
- a spy is captured by the enemy
- a spaceship carrying three astronauts malfunctions

Advanced Students

Have students read the following introduction to a narrative composition. Then have them make a set of pre-writing notes to develop the plot of the narrative. Remind students to

Part 2

Action!

Pre-Writing: Plotting a Story

Here's the Idea Have you ever gone to a movie and then described what happened for some friends who hadn't seen it yet? Whether you realized it or not, you were telling your friends the plot of the story. Plot, as you learned in the last lesson, is all of the events of a story.

Once you have an idea for a narrative composition, you have to plot your story. That is, you have to gather together all of the events that you want to tell about. If you are telling a real story, make notes about everything that happened. Try to remember specific details about each event. These might include names, dates, places, and times. They might also include sensory details. Be sure all of your details are accurate. Plotting an imaginary story calls for the same kind of information. The only difference is that the events and details are not real, but made up.

As you write down the events that tell your story, you must be sure they are arranged in the order that they happened. This is called chronological order. Chronological order makes it easy for the reader to follow the action of your story.

Check It Out Look over these pre-writing notes for a narrative composition.

1. We are camping at Beech river. *River Park campground* / *hot August day*
2. Blanca and I decide to go rafting.
3. We forget our life jackets back at the camp, but go in anyway.
4. I paddle to middle of river and get carried away by current. *Blanca waves her arms at me from shore*

5. I get caught up in a stretch of rapids.
6. Raft overturns—I'm thrown in river. < water like icicles / can't catch breath
7. Rapids tumble me around. < I think I'm drowning. / My arms feel heavy as lead.
8. I'm knocked against rock; can't hold on. — rocks feel slippery
9. I reach for tree branch and hold on.
10. I pull myself ashore. < choking, exhausted / Blanca screaming my name in distance—too weak to answer

- Are these notes arranged in chronological order?
- Do you notice how the writer added details to the list of events?
- Do you see how the writer has grouped her notes into paragraphs?

Try Your Skill Practice recalling events and arranging them in the order that they happened. Make a list of everything that you did last Saturday. Remember as many details as you can. Then arrange the items on your list in chronological order.

Keep This in Mind

- Plot is the events that tell a story.
- Arrange the events that make up your plot in chronological order.

Now Write In the last lesson, **Get Started,** you made up a list of possible stories to tell. Choose the one you like best and make some pre-writing notes about it. Arrange your notes in chronological order. Save your pre-writing notes.

use chronological order.

Hiking in the mountains is an exhilarating experience. The air is fresh, the scenery is beautiful, and the trails are challenging. However, as my friend and I found out on our last camping trip, hiking can also be dangerous.

Optional Practice

Show the class a short narrative movie. (If there are none available, use a cartoon or tape a short dramatic television show.) Have the class list the events of the plot in chronological order.

Extending the Lesson

Explain to students that sometimes true stories are more interesting than fiction. Also discuss the fact that many fiction writers base their stories on true events. Have each student read the newspaper and find an article that could be the basis for a good composition, either real or imaginary. Then have each student develop the plot for his or her chosen story. Discuss the pre-writing notes in class.

Objectives

1. To review the meanings of first-person and third-person limited point of view

2. To learn the meaning of third-person omniscient point of view

Presenting the Lesson

1. Read aloud and discuss **Here's the Idea.** Emphasize the differences among the three points of view, particularly between the third-person limited and the third-person omniscient points of view.

2. Read and discuss **Check It Out.** The pronoun *I* identifies paragraph 1 as first-person point of view; the description of Blanca's realization identifies paragraph 2 as third-person omniscient point of view.

3. Assign **Try Your Skill.** Remind the class to use the pronoun *I* when writing with the first-person point of view, and to include descriptions of Steve's feelings when using the omniscient point of view.

4. Assign **Now Write.**

Individualizing the Lesson

Less-Advanced Students

Give students additional practice recognizing the three different types of point of view. Have them identify the point of view used in each of these groups of sentences.

1. Sally pedaled her bike home furiously. She was angry that she had to miss the soccer game to babysit for her brother. third-person omniscient
2. I paddled the canoe across the lake to visit the neighboring camp. first-person

Part 3

What's Your View?

Pre-Writing: Choosing a Point of View

Here's the Idea Now you must decide how to tell your story. One thing that affects your story is **point of view.**

In the **first-person point of view,** the story is told through the eyes of one character. This character is identified by the pronoun *I*. *I* is the narrator, the person who tells the story. The reader knows only what this character knows. Use this point of view when you are writing a story in which you are a character.

A story can also be told from the **third-person point of view.** This point of view uses the pronouns *he* and *she*. There are two types of third-person point of view—limited and omniscient (om•ni′•shunt). In the **third-person limited point of view,** the narrator is not a character in the story. Like a radio announcer at a baseball game, the narrator tells what he or she sees. The narrator never gives his or her opinion about what is happening in the story. The readers never know what the characters are thinking or feeling unless the characters themselves say so. This point of view works well for stories with many characters and much action.

The second type of third-person point of view is called **third-person omniscient.** Omniscient means "all-knowing." Just as in third-person limited, the omniscient narrator is not a character in the story. However, the omniscient narrator knows everything that is going on in the story. The omniscient narrator knows what the characters are thinking and feeling. This point of view allows the writer to choose which details to emphasize and which to keep hidden.

Check It Out Read the introductions below.

1 Last summer, on a warm August afternoon, my sister Blanca and I decided to go rafting on the Beech River. Our family was

camping at River Park. Blanca and I dragged our small rubber rafts a half mile to the river's edge. That's when Blanca realized we had left our life jackets back at camp.

2 Last summer, on a warm August afternoon, Tina and Blanca Vazquez decided to go rafting on the Beech River. Their family was camping at River Park. Tina and Blanca dragged their small rubber rafts a half mile to the river's edge. That's when Blanca realized they had left their life jackets back at camp.

- What is the point of view of each paragraph?

Try Your Skill This paragraph uses the third-person limited point of view. Rewrite it twice, once using the first-person point of view, and the second time using the third-person omniscient point of view.

Steve sat on the stubbly grass surrounding the basketball court. Five other boys his age were playing on the court. They shouted and joked with each other, but paid no attention to Steve. Steve sat stiffly. He never took his eyes off the game.

Keep This in Mind

- In the first-person point of view, the reader knows only what the main character sees and feels.
- In the third-person limited point of view, the reader can see and hear only what the narrator describes.
- In the third-person omniscient point of view, the reader knows everything—thoughts, feelings, and actions.

Now Write Look over your pre-writing notes from the last lesson, **Action!** Decide which point of view would help you to tell your story best. On the same page with your notes, write the point of view you have chosen. Save your notes.

3. Lauren passed Eric in the hall. They didn't speak, but she gave him a note. third-person limited
4. Aaron wished he were anywhere but in his science class. He was not prepared for the test. third-person omniscient

Advanced Students

Read three classic stories, each using one of the three points of view. (For example, use "The Tell-Tale Heart" by Edgar Allan Poe for first-person, "The Flying Machine" by Ray Bradbury for third-person limited, and "An Occurrence at Owl Creek Bridge" by Ambrose Bierce for third-person omniscient.) Discuss the possible reasons why each author chose that point of view.

Optional Practice

Follow the directions for **Try Your Skill.**

It was Karen's turn to bat. The bases were loaded, and there were two outs. The crowd was cheering for her. She wiped her brow. Then she took a few practice swings and walked up to the plate.

Extending the Lesson

Have students find examples of stories written from different points of view. Provide students with magazines and short story collections for their search.

Part 4

Objective

To know the purpose of each part of a narrative composition—the introduction, the body, and the conclusion

Presenting the Lesson

1. Read aloud and discuss **Here's the Idea.** For reinforcement, write the three parts of a narrative composition on the board. Next to each part write its function in the composition.

2. Discuss **Check It Out.**

3. Assign **Try Your Skill.** Compare students' conclusions to see how each of them resolved the conflict.

4. Read **Keep This in Mind** aloud. Then assign **Now Write.**

Individualizing the Lesson

Less-Advanced Students

Begin the **Try Your Skill** exercise with a discussion of possible resolutions of the conflict. Once several possibilities have been proposed, have the students write a conclusion for the composition.

Advanced Students

Have students write a good introductory paragraph for one of the following topics (or one of their own). First of all, though, have students decide on the major conflict and write notes for the plot of their story. Remind students that an introduction must set the scene and introduce the characters.

- a spy stealing secret documents
- a baseball player hitting the winning home run

Part 4

First Impressions

Writing the First Draft

Here's the Idea A narrative composition has the same parts as any composition. A narrative has an introduction, a body, and a conclusion.

In a narrative composition, the **introduction** usually sets the scene and introduces the characters. The introduction may also present the conflict, although the conflict is often presented in the body. Make your introduction interesting for your readers. Use sensory details to set the scene. Include specific details to describe your characters.

The **body** of a narrative presents the plot of the story. As you write your first draft, use the plot to develop the conflict. Don't simply *tell* your readers that a character is struggling with a problem. *Show* the conflict developing. *Show* how your characters react to it.

In the **conclusion** of a narrative, the conflict is solved, and the story is brought to a close. Be consistent about time sequence, characterization, and point of view. If you have been describing an event in the past, don't leap to the present in your conclusion. If your character has been timid, don't make her or him aggressive. If you've been using the first-person point of view, use it in your conclusion. Make your conclusion interesting. It is the last impression you leave with your reader.

Check It Out Read this introduction.

> It was a fine summer morning in downtown Milwaukee. The breeze off Lake Michigan was cool, and the air was surprisingly clear. Melvin Marvel, the world famous magician, was whistling to himself as he braked for a light. Looking in his rearview mirror, Melvin saw—or thought he saw—an enormous white rabbit sitting in the back seat.

- Does this introduction set the scene?
- Does this introduction introduce the characters?
- What sensory and specific details are included?

Try Your Skill Read this story in need of a conclusion. Find the conflict in the body. Then write a conclusion for this narrative that solves the conflict and brings the story to a close.

Jim Allen leaped up the steps and bolted into the house.

"What is it, Jim?" his mother called.

Jim moaned, "My telescope has to be mounted and ready for display in the science fair tomorrow morning."

"You promised to cut the lawn today," his mother said.

From his room, Jim shouted that he just couldn't do it.

Jim's mother said that he would have to keep his promise.

Jim flopped on his bed to think. What should he do? Suddenly the phone rang. Jim ran to answer it. It was his friend Ken.

Ken was stuck five miles outside of town. He had spent his last quarter on the call. He begged Jim to come and get him.

Jim tried to explain his own predicament.

"Please, Jim," Ken interrupted. "I have to be at work soon."

Jim turned to his mother. He had a difficult decision to make.

Keep This in Mind

- The introduction in a narrative sets the scene and introduces the characters.
- The body of a narrative presents events that tell the story and develop the conflict.
- The conclusion of a narrative solves the conflict and brings the story to a close.

Now Write Begin writing the first draft of your narrative. Just write the introduction. Be sure to set the scene and introduce the characters. Use specific and sensory details. Try to capture your readers' attention. Save your work in your folder.

- diving off the high dive for the first time
- running in a marathon

Optional Practice

Either find or write an example of a well-written narrative composition. Reproduce it without the conclusion. Give each student a copy and have him or her write a conclusion for it. Remind students that a good conclusion solves the conflict and brings the story to a close.

Extending the Lesson

Ask students to read the introductions to several stories and to select the one they think is the most effective. Ask them to tell whether it introduces the characters and setting; to identify whether the story will be a mystery, adventure, science fiction, or some other genre; and to describe the mood created by the paragraph. Emphasize the great variety among story beginnings.

Part 5

Objective

To know how to use dialogue in a narrative composition

Presenting the Lesson

1. Read aloud and discuss **Here's the Idea.** Write the definition of *dialogue* on the board. Then turn back to the **Try Your Skill** exercise in Part 4 on page 155 to see an example of a narrative composition that uses dialogue. Find all the words used instead of *said*. Also, point out the difference between a direct quotation and an indirect quotation. Review the correct form for writing dialogue on pages 556–559 of the Handbook.

2. Discuss **Check It Out.**

3. Assign and discuss **Try Your Skill.**

4. Read **Keep This in Mind** aloud. Then assign **Now Write.**

Individualizing the Lesson

Less-Advanced Students

Have students rewrite this paragraph in the proper form. Also, have them substitute better words for *said* throughout.

> Our Halloween short-cut through the cemetery was a walk that I won't ever forget. I'm scared said Mickey so softly that I could hardly hear her. What are you afraid of? I said. There aren't any ghosts, you goof. Well, then, what is making that swish, swish, swish sound I'm hearing? Answer that one if you're such an expert on ghosts Mickey said. I'm sure there's a logical explanation for the noise I said. Well, I'm not sticking around to find out what it is. Let's run said Mickey.

Part 5

She Said, He Said

Writing the First Draft: Using Dialogue

Here's the Idea Narratives almost always include people, and people like to talk. That is why a narrative often includes dialogue. **Dialogue** is the conversation between characters.

Dialogue is important in a narrative. For example, the things a character says can tell the reader what the character is like. Dialogue can also help the writer to tell the story. Instead of the writer telling the reader what happened, a character can tell the reader through dialogue.

Whenever you write dialogue, try to use language that suits the speaker. If a teenager is speaking, use the kind of words a teen would use. Don't use the same kind of language for the teenager's father. If one of your characters is a bully, be sure he uses a bully's words and way of speaking.

Dialogue always includes words that tell who is speaking, such as *she said* or *Tom said*. Try to use a word other than *said* whenever a different word would suit the speaker. For example, if a character is angry, you might write *She shouted*. If a character is embarrassed, your could write *he mumbled* or *he whispered*.

Always begin a new paragraph whenever a different speaker talks. Be sure to put the quotation marks around the speaker's exact words. To learn more about the correct form for quotation marks, see Handbook Section 16, pages 556–559.

Check It Out Read this dialogue.

> "We better go back," Blanca said.
>
> "What?" I said. "You're going to walk all that way for a dumb life jacket?"

"You know what Mom and Dad say," Blanca replied. "They never let any of us go boating without our life jackets."

"Look," I said. "You can swim and so can I. Nothing's going to happen. Let's go."

We paddled close to the shore for a while. Then I decided to head for the middle of the river.

"Be careful," Blanca shouted. "The water looks choppy out there."

- What does this dialogue tell you about Blanca? About her sister?
- How does this dialogue help the writer to tell the story?
- Does the language suit the characters? Give examples.

Try Your Skill Rewrite this narrative using dialogue.

My friend Sammy and I were playing basketball when he said to me that he's never been to the beach at night. I told him that it's great and we should go. Then he said that his parents might not let him. I told him that we could ask them and that my parents would take us. Sammy said that was neat and I said that we should go ask them. We ran off to ask Sammy's parents.

Keep This in Mind

- Dialogue is conversation between characters.
- Dialogue can show what a character is like. It can also help to move the story along.

Now Write Continue writing your first draft. Include dialogue that will help you to tell your story. Save your first draft in your folder.

Advanced Students

Give students a scene from the script of a play. Read it with them. Explain that the dialogue is written next to the character's names, and that the stage directions are written in parentheses. Have students rewrite the scene in the form of a narrative. Remind them to use the proper form and to use words other than *said* when explaining who is speaking.

Optional Practice

Have students rewrite this narrative using dialogue.

Elise and Derrick were weeding the garden when he said he needed to earn some money. Elise wanted to know why he needed money. Derrick said that he wanted to save for the class trip to Washington, D.C. Elise thought for a while. Then she said that she had a plan—they could start a gardening business. Derrick said that that sounded like a good idea. Then he said that they should start looking for some customers.

Extending the Lesson

Find examples of stories that use dialogue. Read them to the students. Explain that the way a person speaks tells something about him or her. Also, point out that dialogue can make a narrative more dramatic.

Part 6

Objective

To use transitions within and between the paragraphs of a narrative composition

Presenting the Lesson

1. Read aloud and discuss **Here's the Idea.** Emphasize that transitional words make a sequence of events clear. Explain that students use transitional words without thinking when relating things that happened.

2. Help the class to identify the transitions within paragraphs in **Check It Out** (*as, as soon as, once, again and again*). Do the same for transitions between paragraphs (*as, soon, just then, suddenly*).

3. Assign and discuss **Try Your Skill.** When students have mastered the use of transitions, assign **Now Write.** Remind the class to revise and proofread carefully.

Individualizing the Lesson

Less-Advanced Students

Before assigning **Now Write,** have students look over their pre-writing notes. Tell them to jot down, in the margins, the possible transitional words that they could use. Then work individually with students as they begin to write the first drafts of their narrative compositions.

Advanced Students

Have students find an example of narrative writing from a newspaper, magazine, or book. Ask them to copy the passage, underlining the transitions used within paragraphs, and circling the transitions used between paragraphs.

Part 6

Go with the Flow

The First Draft: Using Transitions

Here's the Idea Narratives are usually told in **chronological order.** To make the order clear, you should use transitional words and phrases.

You have used transitional words such as *first, then, next, later, soon,* and *afterwards* within narrative paragraphs. It is also important to use transitional words between paragraphs. These transitional words help your story to flow smoothly from paragraph to paragraph. Examples of paragraph transitions are *later that day, by noon,* and *when I got home.*

Check It Out Read the body and conclusion of the narrative composition about Blanca and her sister.

As I neared the middle of the river, the current pushed my small raft faster and faster. I tried to turn back but the current was too strong. I saw Blanca waving her arm at me. She got smaller and smaller as my raft raced down the river.

Soon I heard a low roar ahead. I knew that meant rapids. The rapids weren't very big, but my little rubber raft was no match for them. As soon as I reached the first waves, the raft overturned. I was thrown into the bubbling water.

The river was icy cold. I could barely catch my breath. I tried to swim, but the rapids kept pulling me under. I banged up against big rocks. Once, I grabbed on and almost pulled myself up on a large rock, but the water pulled me back. My strength was almost gone.

Just then I noticed some low hanging tree branches up ahead. If I could grab them, I might be able to pull myself to shore. I reached up and grabbed a branch. The river tried to drag me away, but I held on. Slowly, I dragged myself along the branch toward the shore. Again and again the river tried to snatch me.

Suddenly, I felt solid ground under my feet. Choking, I crawled the last few yards to the shore. In the distance, I heard Blanca screaming my name. But I was too exhausted to answer her. All I could think about was how lucky I was to be alive and how foolish I had been. I had beaten the river this time. I hoped I would never have to try again.

- What transitional words are used between paragraphs?
- What transitional words are used within paragraphs?

Try Your Skill Rewrite the paragraph below. Arrange the sentences in correct time sequence. Use transitional words and phrases to make the time sequence clear.

I put a sandwich and an orange in a bag for lunch. I woke up too late to eat breakfast. I was so hungry that my stomach growled in class. I saw that I had forgotten my lunch at home. My family was shocked to see how much I ate at dinner.

Keep This in Mind

- Use transitional words to show time order within paragraphs and between paragraphs.

Now Write Finish writing the first draft of your narrative composition. Remember to include transitional words and phrases to show time order. Be sure your conclusion solves the conflict. Save your first draft in your folder.

Optional Practice

Have students follow the instructions of **Try Your Skill.**

[2] I put on my ski vest. [1] My first time water-skiing was comical. [3] I got into the lake and tried to put on my skis. [8] I remembered to let go of the tow rope so that I wouldn't be dragged underwater behind the boat. [6] The skis kept crossing in front of me. [5] I yelled "Hit it!" to signal the boat driver that I was ready. [4] The driver threw me the tow rope. [7] I went flying out of the water, but *I* "hit it" a moment later—right on my face. [9] I decided to try a dryer, slower sport.

Extending the Lesson

Locate a five or six-paragraph biography or account of an historical event. Rearrange the paragraphs. Make a copy for each student in the class. Direct students to underline each transitional word or phrase and then to number the paragraphs in the right order.

Part 7

Objective

To know and use the guidelines for revising a narrative composition

Presenting the Lesson

1. Read aloud and discuss **Here's the Idea.** Study the composition about Blanca's rafting accident in its entirety and see if it meets the guidelines on page 160. (The introduction is on pages 152–153 in Part 3, **Check It Out;** the next section is the dialogue in Part 5, **Check It Out** on pages 156–157; and the remainder of the composition is in Part 6, **Check It Out** on pages 158–159.)

2. Discuss **Check It Out.** Point out that the author uses words to show spatial relations so that the reader can follow Alice's chase. Also point out the use of dialogue. Lastly, discuss the suspense that is created in the paragraph.

3. Assign and discuss **Try Your Skill.**

4. Assign **Now Write.**

Individualizing the Lesson

Less-Advanced Students

Work individually with students during the revision process. Read each student's paper and discuss with him or her what changes should be made.

Advanced Students

Discuss the value of peer critiques with students. Explain that sometimes what is not obvious to a writer can be seen by a reader with an objective point of view. Emphasize that criticisms should be con-

Part 7

A Second Look

Revising Your Narrative Composition

Here's the Idea You know that your first draft isn't your final composition. You can change it as much as you like until it is just right. The following questions will help you to see where your first draft needs to be changed. Use these questions to help you revise your narrative composition.

1. Does my introduction set the scene and introduce the characters?
2. Have I included all of the events I need to tell my story?
3. Are the events arranged in chronological order?
4. Do the events in the body of my narrative develop the conflict?
5. Have I used the same point of view throughout my story?
6. Have I included dialogue that moves my story along and tells about the characters?
7. Have I used transitional words within paragraphs and between paragraphs to show time order?
8. Does my conclusion solve the conflict and bring the story to a satisfactory close?

Remember to proofread your narrative to find and correct any errors in grammar, capitalization, punctuation, and spelling. Pay special attention to the punctuation you used for dialogue. You can find the correct form for punctuation of dialogue on pages 556–559 in the Handbook.

Check It Out Read the following paragraph from a narrative.

Alice was not a bit hurt, and she jumped on to her feet in a moment. She looked up, but it was all dark overhead. Before her was another long passage, and the White Rabbit was still in sight, hurrying down it. There was not a moment to be lost. Away went Alice like the wind, and was just in time to hear it say, as it turned a corner, "Oh, my ears and whiskers, how late it's getting!" She was close behind it when she turned the corner, but the Rabbit was no longer to be seen. She found herself in a long, low hall, which was lit up by a row of lamps hanging from the roof.

—LEWIS CARROLL

- What are some of the things that make this a good narrative?

Try Your Skill Proofread the following dialogue. Find and correct any errors in capitalization and punctuation.

It looks like rain," Bob said.

"Let's hope it holds off" his sister said. "Dad says we've got to get these crops in".

"Dad really loves farming," Bob said.

It's his life, "his sister said, "I guess he hopes it will be ours someday, too.

Keep This in Mind

- Your first draft is not a final copy. Revise your first draft until it is as good as you can make it.

Now Write Revise your narrative composition. Use the guidelines in this lesson to help you. When you are satisfied with your narrative, make a final copy. Save your narrative composition in your folder.

structive—they should suggest improvements. For example, a critic should not say, "This conclusion is awful." Instead, he or she should say, "Summarize the main ideas of the composition here."

After discussing student evaluations, have students work in pairs to revise their compositions. Remind them to use the checklist on page 160.

Optional Practice

Select a fable and read it to the class. Ask the eight questions in the guidelines for revising a narrative composition. See if the fable meets these standards.

Extending the Lesson

Compile students' narrative compositions into booklets. First of all, group them according to fiction or nonfiction. Then divide them into sub-groups according to the type of story. For example, fiction could be divided into adventure, mystery, science fiction, etc. Nonfiction could be divided into adventure, humor, family life, etc. Once the class has grouped the compositions, discuss possible titles for the booklets. Break the class into small groups. Assign a booklet to each group. Have each group design a cover and bind the booklet.

Section 14 Objectives

1. To use sensory details in a descriptive composition

2. To know the functions of the three parts of a descriptive composition—the introduction, the body, and the conclusion

3. To use transitional words that tell *where* to make a description clear

4. To write a conclusion that pulls together main ideas and that includes personal reactions

5. To know and use the guidelines for revising a descriptive composition

Preparing the Students

Select two or more descriptive passages that include sensory details. Ask students to close their eyes while you read the descriptions. Ask them to concentrate on the mental pictures created by the descriptions. Discuss what students "saw" in their minds.

Additional Resources

Practice Book — pages 67–70

Duplicating Masters — pages 67–70

The Descriptive Composition

Part 1 **It Makes Sense**
Pre-Writing: Using Sensory Details

Part 2 **Try It Out**
Writing the First Draft

Part 3 **In Conclusion**
The First Draft: Concluding a Description

Part 4 **Good, Better, Best**
Revising Your Descriptive Composition

Teaching Special Populations

LD See **Teaching Special Populations,** page 61.

ESL See **Teaching Special Populations,** page 101.

For practice, place a variety of small objects in a bag and have students determine by touch alone what the items are. Ask students to describe the shape and texture of the objects, using complete sentences. Give students additional lists of words that describe sensory impressions. Have them write out new words on vocabulary cards and keep them on file.

NSD See **Teaching Special Populations,** page 61.

Part 1

Objective

To use sensory details in a descriptive composition

Presenting the Lesson

1. Read aloud and discuss **Here's the Idea.** As a class, practice listing sensory details that describe different people or places (a barn, a cosmetics salesperson, a gym, a bakery, etc.). Also, discuss how each set of pre-writing notes should be arranged. Review the definition of *spatial order*.

2. Discuss **Check It Out.**

3. Assign and discuss **Try Your Skill.**

4. Assign **Now Write.**

Individualizing the Lesson

Less-Advanced Students

Allow students to work in pairs to complete the **Try Your Skill** exercise.

Advanced Students

Have students write pre-writing notes describing a futuristic house. Discuss with students what a house might look like and contain in one hundred years. After students have brainstormed and written a list of sensory details, ask them to arrange the details in spatial order.

Optional Practice

Bring color pictures of interesting places, people, and things to class. Have each student select one picture and make a list of sensory details that describe that picture. Then have students arrange the details in spatial order.

Part 1

It Makes Sense

Pre-Writing: Using Sensory Details

Here's the Idea A descriptive composition paints a picture with words. Therefore, the first step in planning a descriptive composition is choosing a person, place, or thing that is interesting enough to describe in detail.

Once you have selected a subject, you must begin gathering supporting details. The more vivid and specific your details are, the better your word picture will be. To find vivid details, use each of your senses.

Not every object or scene affects all the senses. Food can be tasted, but it is not often heard. You can see a tree, but you wouldn't taste it. However, you should try to use as many of your senses as possible as you gather details for your description. Here are some questions you might ask for each sense.

Sight: What colors do I see? what shapes? what sizes?

Touch: Is it hot or cold? rough or smooth? dry or oily?

Sound: What sounds do I hear? What words best describe each sound?

Smell: What do I smell? Are the odors strong or weak? pleasant or unpleasant?

Taste: Is the taste pleasant or unpleasant? Is it sweet, sour, salty, spicy, or bitter?

When you have finished making your notes, read them over carefully. Cross out any details that do not seem important to your description. Add new ones as you think of them. Then arrange your details in spatial order. This is the order that you want your reader to notice them.

Check It Out Look at these pre-writing notes.

Topic my science lab
science lab, most exciting room in school
odors of gas, strange smelling chemicals
noise: click of brass weights, hum of pump in fish tank
special equipment
classroom: teacher's demonstration table (front)
supply cabinet (left), tropical fish tank (right)
my table: Bunsen burner (left), test tubes (right)
sink, chrome faucets (center)
balance: horizontal bar, chains, pans and weights

- What senses have been used in gathering these pre-writing notes?
- How is the writer organizing the details?

Try Your Skill Make some pre-writing notes for a descriptive composition about the classroom you are in or for any other room in your school. Gather as many sensory details as you can. Then arrange the details in the order that you want the viewers to notice them.

Keep This in Mind

- Gather sensory details to develop your description.
- Arrange your details in the order that you want the viewers to notice them.

Now Write Choose a person, place, or thing to describe in your descriptive composition. Use your senses to gather details that will make your description vivid. Arrange your details in the order that you want your reader to notice them. Save your organized pre-writing notes in your folder.

Extending the Lesson

Have three or four students each dress in costume as a distinct character and present a monologue, in character, to the class. (Suggestions: a bag lady, a rock star, a salesperson, etc.) After the presentations, ask students to choose one of the characters and make a list of details describing him or her. Have students arrange the details in spatial order.

Part 2

Objectives

1. To know the function of the parts of a descriptive composition—the introduction, the body, and the conclusion

2. To use transitional words that tell *where* to make a description clear

Presenting the Lesson

1. Read aloud and discuss **Here's the Idea.** Write the three parts of a compositon on the chalkboard. Next to each write the function of that part in a descriptive composition. Then review the list of transitional words that tell *where*. Ask students for additional examples.

2. Discuss **Check It Out.**

3. Assign **Try Your Skill.** When students have completed their introductions, share them with the class.

4. Read **Keep This in Mind** aloud. Then assign **Now Write.**

Individualizing the Lesson

Less-Advanced Students

As a class, write an introduction to a descriptive composition before assigning **Try Your Skill.** Use your classroom as the topic. Start by listing sensory details.

Advanced Students

Have students also write the body paragraphs for the descriptive composition about the home economics classroom. Remind students to use transitional words that tell *where* to make the description clear.

Part 2

Try It Out

Writing the First Draft

Here's the Idea As you write the first draft of your descriptive composition, picture in your mind the person, place, or thing you are describing. This will help you to write a vivid description for your readers.

Remember that your composition must have three parts. The first paragraph is the **introduction.** This paragraph contains a topic sentence. It tells the reader who or what you are describing. The introduction should be interesting. It should make the reader want to read on.

The paragraphs that follow the introduction are called the **body.** The body contains all of the sensory details that develop the description. These details are grouped around two or three main ideas. Each main idea is a paragraph in the body. For example, in the body of a composition that describes a person, one group of details might tell about the person's physical features. Another group might describe the person's clothes.

The final paragraph of your description is the **conclusion.** The conclusion sums up all of the ideas in your composition.

You can make your description clear by using transitional words that tell *where*. Some of these words are *behind, near, beside, in front of, inside, on top of, under,* and *to the left.*

Check It Out Read this introduction.

> Our science lab is the most exciting classroom in school. Something is always happening there. As we work, we can smell the chemicals. We hear gas hissing from the compressor in the back closet. Water splashes in the sink near the window. Test tubes clink all around the room. Everywhere in the lab we are busy with special equipment, like Bunsen burners, test tubes, and balances.

- What is the topic sentence in this introduction?
- What transitional words have been used to make the description clear?

Try Your Skill Below are pre-writing notes for an introduction to a descriptive composition. Using these notes, along with details from your imagination, write an introduction.

Topic	our home economics classroom
Introduction	home ec. room—4 superkitchens in 1 sounds—pots and pans, water, laughing mouth-watering smells—blueberry muffins, bread good tastes—pizza, apple pie stainless steel sinks (along one wall) storage cabinets (back) wall of windows (to courtyard) counter space (wall near door) stove—where something good is cooking (?)

Keep This in Mind

- In a descriptive composition, the introduction presents the person, place, or thing being described.
- The body contains sensory details that develop the description.
- The conclusion sums up the description.
- Use transitional words that tell *where* to make your description clear.

Now Write Use your pre-writing notes from the last lesson to write the first draft of your descriptive composition. Be sure your introduction is interesting and has a strong topic sentence. Use transitional words to make your description clear. For now, just write the introduction and the body. Save your first draft in your folder.

Optional Practice

Give students the following topic sentences. Ask them to describe other details that might be included in an introduction. Then have students complete an introductory paragraph for one of the topics.

1. The lake looked cool, calm, and tempting.
2. The box was opened to reveal Ralph the Robot.
3. My room was more than just messy.

Extending the Lesson

Have students study several examples of well-written descriptive compositions from your files. Discuss the effectiveness of the introduction, the body paragraphs, and the conclusion. In addition, ask students to point out the transitional words that show *where*.

Part 3

Objective

To write a conclusion that pulls together main ideas and that includes personal reactions

Presenting the Lesson

1. Read aloud and discuss **Here's the Idea.** Highlight the two characteristics of a strong conclusion.

2. Read and discuss **Check It Out.** Note that the main ideas in the composition are given personal interpretations. For example, the composition describes special equipment; the conclusion states that working with the equipment is challenging.

3. Assign and discuss **Try Your Skill.** Work with those students who need further help in integrating main ideas and personal reactions.

4. Assign **Now Write.**

Individualizing the Lesson

Less-Advanced Students

Have students do the **Try Your Skill** exercise as a class. Then work with students individually to help them write the conclusions of their descriptive compositions.

Advanced Students

Bring a print of a famous work of art to class. (It should be complicated enough to need a composition to describe it.) With the class, formulate a set of pre-writing notes describing the painting or sculpture. Arrange the details in a logical spatial order. Then have students write a conclusion for the composition.

Part 3

In Conclusion

The First Draft: Concluding a Description

Here's the Idea A descriptive composition should have a strong, clear ending. Your reader should know that the composition is finished.

First, look at the topic sentences for each of the paragraphs in the body of your composition. These are the ideas that you used to develop your topic. Think about how you can pull all of these ideas together to summarize the main idea of your composition. Try to state your ideas in a different way. Don't just copy them.

Second, think about why you are telling the reader about your topic. Why is it interesting or important to you? You can share your feelings in such a way that the reader will feel as close as you do to your subject. In this way, the conclusion will strengthen the main idea of your composition. This main idea was stated in the topic sentence of your introduction.

Sometimes it's possible to end your description on a light or humorous note. Let your attitude about the topic be your guide.

Check It Out Read the conclusion below.

> Each day in the science lab is a new experience. The sounds and smells are exciting. Working with all the special equipment is challenging. I'm improving my skills every day. Some day I hope to be a research scientist. Then I will be able to work in a lab every day.

- How does the writer feel about the science lab?
- Does the conclusion pull all the main ideas in the composition together?

Try Your Skill Look at the pre-writing notes in **Try Your Skill** on page 167. Use these notes, along with any other details you can imagine, to write a conclusion. Compare your conclusion with those of your classmates.

Keep This in Mind

- In the conclusion to a descriptive composition, tell how you feel about what you are describing.
- The conclusion should summarize the ideas in the composition.

Now Write Read the first draft you wrote in the last lesson. Then write a good conclusion to your descriptive composition. Save your first draft in your folder.

Optional Practice

Make copies of a well-written descriptive composition, but omit the conclusion. Have students read the incomplete composition and then write a conclusion for it.

Extending the Lesson

Review this section, using the students' own work. Select and duplicate two compositions. Tell students to do the following for each of them.

a. Identify the introduction, body, and conclusion.
b. Circle the transitional words that indicate spatial order.
c. In one sentence, describe the spatial order followed.
d. Underline the topic sentence for the entire composition with a colored pencil.
e. Underline the sensory details.
f. In one sentence, describe how the writer feels about what he or she is describing.

Part 4

Objective

To know and use the guidelines for revising a descriptive composition

Presenting the Lesson

1. Read aloud and discuss **Here's the Idea.** Using an anonymous student composition for an example, have the class answer each of the questions in the guidelines.

2. Discuss **Check It Out.** Refer students to page 85 to review the proofreading symbols.

3. Assign and discuss **Try Your Skill.**

4. Assign **Now Write.**

Individualizing the Lesson

Less-Advanced Students

Work with students individually during the revision process in **Now Write.** Suggest improvements and help students revise their compositions accordingly.

Advanced Students

For **Now Write,** have students exchange compositions and critique each other's paper using the guidelines on page 170. Remind students to use constructive criticism. Then have students discuss the comments with each other. Finally, have them revise their compositions.

Optional Practice

Have students revise this descriptive composition. Remind them to use the guidelines in this lesson. Also, remind them to proofread it for errors in grammar, capitalization,

Part 4

Good, Better, Best

Revising Your Descriptive Composition

Here's the Idea You already know that a descriptive composition paints a word picture. Your goal is to make the person, place, or thing you are describing seem real to your reader. You want your description to be clear and strong. As you read over your first draft, ask yourself if you have achieved your goal. Here are some other questions to help you revise your first draft.

1. Have I collected good sensory details to develop my description? Are all the words and details as specific as I can make them?
2. Have I organized my details in the order that I want my readers to notice them?
3. Have I used transitional words that tell *where*?
4. Is my introduction interesting? Does it contain a topic sentence that presents the person, place, or thing I am describing?
5. Does each paragraph in the body have a strong topic sentence that presents the main idea of that paragraph?
6. Does my conclusion sum up all of the ideas in my composition? Does it tell the reader how I feel about my topic?

When you are satisfied that your ideas and your organization are the best they can be, proofread your composition. Find and correct any errors in grammar, capitalization, punctuation, and spelling. Then make a final copy of your composition, following the guidelines on pages 142–143.

Check It Out Notice how this paragraph from a descriptive composition has been revised.

Whenever my Dad wants to escape the house he only has to go retreat to the basement. Dad has a place where my brothers and sisters and the telephone can't find him. Dads workroom is his castle.

- What types of revisions has the writer made to the ideas in this paragraph? How have these changes improved the description?
- What errors in capitalization, punctuation, or spelling have been corrected?

Try Your Skill Here is more of the rough draft you looked at in **Check It Out.** Continue to revise this descriptive composition. Use the guidelines in this lesson. Remember to proofread for errors in grammar, capitalization, punctuation, and spelling. Compare your revision with those of your classmates.

Dad keeps his tools their, he has his power saw, drill press, and lathe. He has a workbench covered in junk. jars of stuff are on the wall. He always got some project sitting around.

Dad got a chair and hassock in the room. He got our old T.V. there, a lamp and even keeps a refrigerator full of things to eat.

Dad locks the room unless he's there. When hes there he doesn't like to be disturbed. I guess even dad's need a place to go.

Keep This in Mind

- Revise your descriptive composition to make the description vivid, real, and strong.

Now Write Use the guidelines in this lesson to revise the first draft of your composition. When you are pleased with the composition, make a final copy. Save it in your folder.

punctuation, and spelling.

"What a honey!" is the way my older brother describes the second-hand car he just bought. To the average observer, the car looks like a slightly rusting 1969 red Ford Mustang. As my brother explained to me, though, there is more to it than meets the eye.

"Why," he said, "just look under the hood. theirs a 302 engine in there! He pointed out the new battery. All of the belts and hoses are new, he said.

the body is in great shape," he said, ignoring the rust spots. he pointed out the sleek look of the fast-back design. He said the bumpers and chrome strips were in excellent condition Brand new tires.

The interior was in good condition. The leather upholstery was clean and unripped. the carpeting was covered with mats. The dashboard was sparkling clean.

All in all, it was probably a good buy The mechanical parts of the car seem to be in good shape. The car is nice looking both inside and out. The real test will be if it starts every morning.

Extending the Lesson

Have students make illustrations to accompany their compositions. Then make a display of the compositions and illustrations.

Section 15 Objectives

1. To prepare to write an explanatory *how* composition by identifying the steps in the process being explained

2. To develop an explanatory *how* composition in step-by-step order.

3. To use transitional words and phrases to clarify the order of the steps in a process

4. To know and use the guidelines for revising an explanatory *how* composition

Preparing the Students

Recall for the class the various topics they selected as subjects for explanatory paragraphs (Section 10). Point out that these topics were limited enough to be covered in one paragraph. Explain that for many common topics (washing a car, providing a dog-walking service, planning a party, starting a class newspaper) one paragraph would not be adequate. A group of paragraphs—a composition—is needed.

Additional Resources

Mastery Test — page 20 in the test booklet

Practice Book — pages 71–74

Duplicating Masters — pages 71–74

The Explanatory Composition

Telling *How*

Part 1 **How Is It Done?**
Pre-Writing: Listing the Steps

Part 2 **One Step at a Time**
Pre-Writing: Using Step-by-Step Order

Part 3 **Say When**
Writing the First Draft

Part 4 **Clearly Correct**
Revising Your Explanatory *How* Composition

Teaching Special Populations

LD See **Teaching Special Populations,** page 61.

ESL Work with students to produce a comprehensive list of transitional words and phrases that reflect temporal order. (Some examples can be found on pages 96 and 178.) Make sure students understand the contextual meaning of these items and then have them use the words in sentences. As a final exercise, ask one student to perform a simple action (such as walking across a room to hang up a coat), then have ESL students describe the action using as many transitional words and phrases as possible. Be sure students understand the two important functions of transitions: to indicate time and to help readers get from one idea to the next or from one paragraph to the next.

NSD See **Teaching Special Populations,** page 61.

Part 1

Objective

To prepare to write an explanatory *how* composition by identifying the steps in the process being explained

Presenting the Lesson

1. Read aloud and discuss **Here's the Idea.** Choose a simple task that can be done in the classroom (covering a book, changing a typewriter ribbon, etc.). Demonstrate it and ask students to list all of the steps in the process.

2. Study the notes in **Check It Out.** Point out that the directions are organized into four basic steps and that each step is developed with specific details.

3. Assign and discuss **Try Your Skill.**

4. Read **Keep This in Mind** aloud. Then assign **Now Write.**

Individualizing the Lesson

Less-Advanced Students

Before assigning the **Try Your Skill** exercise, write a set of pre-writing notes in class for an equally easy topic (making popcorn, sewing a button, etc.).

Advanced Students

Substitute more difficult processes for the process in the **Try Your Skill** exercise. Allow students to research the process that they choose. Here are some suggestions.

- how to make tacos
- how snow forms
- how to get a Social Security card
- how to make an overseas telephone call

Part 1

How Is It Done?

Pre-Writing: Listing the Steps

Here's the Idea An explanatory *how* composition explains the steps in a process. You might explain how to do something, such as how to use a CB radio or how to build a model rocket. You could also explain how something happens, such as how an island is formed. Finally, you might tell how something works, such as an air conditioner. Choose a subject that you know about and could explain well.

When you have chosen a subject, gather supporting details. These details will be all of the steps that make up the process you are explaining. As you gather your details, you will want to be sure you don't leave out any important steps. If you do, your readers won't understand the process. You will also want to be sure that each step in the process is explained simply and clearly.

Check It Out Read these pre-writing notes.

How To Make Vegetable Soup

select vegetables

firm, fresh
4 or 5 different kinds
different colors, different flavors

preparation

need sharp knife
clean, peel, cut into bite-sized pieces
use cutting board

cooking

vegetables
beef or chicken broth
simmer one hour

season and serve

season to taste
serve with bread and cheese

- What process do these steps explain?
- Have any important steps been left out?
- Is each step worded simply and clearly?

Try Your Skill Make some pre-writing notes to help you explain how to make a peanut butter and jelly sandwich. Be sure to include *all* of the steps. Each step should be worded simply and clearly. Compare your notes with those of your classmates.

Keep This in Mind

- Explanatory *how* compositions explain the steps in a process. They explain how to do something or how something happens or works.
- List all of the steps that make up the process. Don't leave out any steps.
- Explain each step in the process simply and clearly.

Now Write Choose a process that you would like to explain. Make a list of all of the important steps in the process. Save your notes in your folder.

Optional Practice

Have students make pre-writing notes to plan an explanatory composition on one of the following topics. Allow time for the students to research the topics.

- how to cheer someone up
- how a butterfly develops
- how to make candles
- how a cell divides
- how to set up a fish tank

Extending the Lesson

Gather and display in the classroom a variety of "how to" books. Point out that the directions in the books are presented step-by-step and include specific details. Encourage students to examine the books for topics.

Part 2

Objective

To develop an explanatory *how* composition in step-by-step order

Presenting the Lesson

1. Read aloud and discuss **Here's the Idea.** Remind the class that the three-part organization suggested parallels the three basic parts of a composition—introduction, body, and conclusion.

2. Study the sample pre-writing notes **Check It Out.**

3. Assign **Try Your Skill.** Explain that the paragraphs are out of order, but not the sentences within the paragraphs.

4. Read **Keep This in Mind** and then assign **Now Write.**

Individualizing the Lesson

Less-Advanced Students

Help students to organize the steps in this process into step-by-step order.

Planting a Pineapple

3 • Let the pineapple top rest a day or two before planting it.
4 • Put stones in the bottom of a clay pot for drainage.
5 • Make a soil mixture of ½ potting soil, ¼ humus, and ¼ coffee grounds.
1 • Cut off the green top of the pineapple.
8 • Give the plant a lot of water.
2 • Leave about an inch of fruit on the pineapple top.
7 • Fertilize the crown of the pineapple plant with a weak solution of fertilizer.
6 • Bury the pineapple top so that the soil comes up to the crown.

Part 2

One Step at a Time

Pre-Writing: Using Step-By-Step Order

Here's the Idea A good way to organize an explanatory *how* composition is to follow this plan: introduction, steps in the process, and conclusion.

One sentence of the introduction should serve as the topic sentence for the composition. Suppose that your topic is how to prepare vegetable soup. The topic sentence might be "Vegetable soup is good for you, delicious, and easy to prepare."

In the paragraphs that follow the introduction, give a step-by-step explanation. You might divide the making of vegetable soup into getting the ingredients, preparing the vegetables, and cooking the soup. Each of these steps would become a separate paragraph. You would then develop each paragraph with specific details from your pre-writing notes. Arranging the steps of a process in the order they are supposed to happen is called **step-by-step order.**

You might develop the concluding paragraph from the final step, seasoning and serving the soup. Your concluding paragraph could also be a summary of the process you explained.

Check It Out Look at these pre-writing notes for an explanatory composition about how a tornado forms.

time of year—spring
time of day—usually afternoon or early evening
temperature—hot, humid

1. big thunderclouds appear (thunder heard in distance)
2. one cloud becomes very dark and dense
3. bottom of cloud starts to twist around
4. twisting produces a funnel cloud that reaches for ground

5. heavy rain and hail falls—much lightning
6. funnel cloud begins to hiss
7. funnel cloud touches ground—hiss becomes a loud roar
8. funnel cloud stirs up big cloud of dust—begins dancing along ground.

- Do you see how these notes have been arranged in correct step-by-step order?

Try Your Skill Below is the body of a composition explaining how to take pictures of stars. However, these three steps are not organized correctly. Write them in correct step-by-step order.

Then point your camera at the stars. Center it on the North Star, which appears as the most stable star in the sky. Next, set your camera for a time exposure of one hour or more.

Begin by choosing a clear night for your photography. Find an open field that is away from lights and buildings. When you have a clear view of the stars, mount your camera on the tripod.

During the exposure, sit back and let the camera do its work. Your only job is to avoid bumping or shaking the camera.

Keep This in Mind

- Organize the details of the process you are explaining in correct step-by-step order.

Now Write Arrange your pre-writing notes from the last lesson, **How Is It Done?,** in step-by-step order. Save your organized notes in your folder.

Advanced Students

Coordinate a project with the social studies teacher. Have students do some research and list all of the steps in step-by-step order for one of these processes.

- how a bill becomes a law in the U.S. Congress
- how the Electoral College chooses a president
- how to become a U.S. citizen
- how an ordinance for your city is made into a law

Optional Practice

Have each student write the steps for a process in scrambled order. Students can then exchange papers and try to list the scrambled steps in the correct order.

Extending the Lesson

Discuss with students various ways that they might earn money. (*Good Cents, every kid's guide to making money* by The Amazing Life Games Company is a good source of ideas.) List the five or six most feasible ideas. Divide the class into groups of four or five students. Assign each group a money-making idea. Direct them to list the steps involved in implementing the ideas and to add details for each step.

Part 3

Objective

To use transitional words and phrases to clarify the order of the steps in a process

Presenting the Lesson

1. Read aloud and discuss **Here's the Idea.** Emphasize the importance of transitions to show time order.

2. Read and discuss **Check It Out.** Help students to identify the transitional words used within the paragraphs in the composition from **Try Your Skill** in Part 2 (*when, next*) and also between the paragraphs (*then, begin,* and *during*).

Then read the introduction and the conclusion of the composition on making soup. Point out that the last sentence of the introduction tells the reader that the "few simple steps" will follow in the body. The conclusion begins with the transitional phrase *In a short time.* Within the concluding paragraph the transition *After* is used.

3. Assign and discuss **Try Your Skill.**

4. Read **Keep This in Mind** aloud. Then assign **Now Write.** Explain that students have probably used many transitional words already.

Individualizing the Lesson

Less-Advanced Students

For additional practice recognizing the use of transitions, have the students find the transitions used in the two **Here's the Idea** paragraphs in Part 1.

Work with students individually as they write the rough drafts of their **Now Write** compositions.

Say When

Writing the First Draft

Here's the Idea As you write your first draft, be sure to include all of the steps in the process you are explaining. Tell about each step in the correct order. To make the order in your composition as clear as possible, use transitional words and phrases. These are words and phrases that tell *when.* Look at the examples below.

first	the next step	when	before
second	after that	finally	as soon as
then	at the same time	last	afterwards

Transitional words can help make the order of ideas in the paragraph clear. Transitional words can also link paragraphs. They work like a bridge to carry the reader from the main idea of one paragraph to the main idea of the next.

As you write the first draft of your explanatory composition, include transitional words to help make your explanation clear.

Check It Out Review the body of the explanation you corrected in the last lesson. Which transitional words are used within each paragraph? Which ones link the three paragraphs?

Now, read these two paragraphs. They are the introduction and conclusion of a composition on making soup. Notice how they are linked to the body of the composition.

Introduction

What food warms your insides and brings a smile to your face? What tastes great for lunch on a chilly day? Homemade soup. It's everyone's favorite. Vegetable soup is especially nutritious, delicious, and easy to prepare. You can make it by following a few simple steps.

Conclusion

In a short time, the vegetables will become tender and full of flavor. After you have adjusted the seasonings, serve this easy-to-make meal in big bowls. Crusty bread and cheese are good with this soup. Anyone who tastes this hot, hearty, healthful treat will want seconds. People everywhere love vegetable soup.

- What transitional words are used in these two paragraphs?
- Are there any transitional words that link the introduction or the conclusion to the body? What are they?

Try Your Skill Below is a paragraph about how clouds are formed. There are no transitional words. Copy the paragraph. Make the order in the paragraph clear by adding clear transitional words. Use several different ones.

_______ rain water soaks into the soil. _______ underground water seeps into small streams. _______ the streams empty into rivers. _______ the rivers flow into lakes and oceans. _______ the water from large bodies of water evaporates into the air.

Keep This in Mind

- In an explanatory composition, use transitional words that tell *when*. They help make the step-by-step order clear.
- Transitional words can be used within paragraphs and between paragraphs.

Now Write Write the first draft of your explanatory *how* composition. Remember to include a strong topic sentence in your introductory paragraph. Use transitional words within and between paragraphs. Be sure the steps in the process you are explaining are simple and specific. Make your explanation as clear as possible. Save your first draft in your folder.

Advanced Students

Using the pre-writing notes from **Check It Out,** (pages 176–177), have students write the rough draft of a composition explaining how a tornado forms. Instruct students to concentrate on using transitional words and phrases to clarify the steps in the process.

Optional Practice

Have students organize the following pre-writing notes into step-by-step order. Instruct them to decide which notes belong together as paragraphs. Then have students suggest transitions to be used between paragraphs and also within each paragraph. Answers may vary.

- Try to use comfortable chairs.
- Choose the table cloth.
- Each place should be set properly.
- The knife, blade inward, and then the spoon are placed to the right of the dinner plate.
- The napkin may either be placed under the fork or in a napkin ring on the plate.
- The fork or forks go to the left of the dinner plate.
- Select a centerpiece.
- The dinner plate is centered.
- Consider the comfort of the guests when setting a table.
- Place the water glass above the plate and to the right.
- Avoid setting a place that will "bump" the guest into a table leg.
- Choose the candlesticks and holders.
- The table should look attractive.

Extending the Lesson

Collect directions for popular board and outdoor games, card games, and magic tricks. Have students identify the transitional words in each set of directions.

Part 4

Objective

To know and use the guidelines for revising an explanatory *how* composition

Presenting the Lesson

1. Read aloud and discuss **Here's the Idea.** Using an opaque projector, show one or more sample explanatory *how* compositions from your files. Have students ask the questions in the guidelines about each composition.

2. Discuss **Check It Out.**

3. Assign and discuss **Try Your Skill.**

4. Read **Keep This in Mind** aloud. Then assign **Now Write.**

Individualizing the Lesson

Less-Advanced Students

Work with students individually during the revision process. Using the revision guidelines, help students to find and improve the weak parts of their compositions.

Advanced Students

Allow students to work in pairs to revise their papers. Remind them to use constructive criticism when discussing each other's composition. Lastly, have students review the guidelines on page 145 for making a final copy.

Optional Practice

Make copies of a poorly written explanatory *how* composition. Have students revise and proofread it. Remind them to use the guidelines on page 180.

Part 4

Clearly Correct

Revising Your Explanatory *How* Composition

Here's the Idea When you write the first draft of your explanation, you usually write it very quickly. You don't worry about proper grammar, capitalization, punctuation, or spelling. In your haste you might even forget one of the steps that explain the process to your reader. That is why it is important to revise your explanatory *how* composition. You want to make sure your explanation is clear, complete, and correct.

Here are some questions that can help you to revise the first draft of your explanatory *how* composition.

1. Did I write a strong, clear topic sentence in my introductory paragraph?
2. Did I include *all* of the steps in the process I am explaining?
3. Are my details arranged in step-by-step order? Does each paragraph tell about a different step?
4. Is each step explained simply and clearly?
5. Did I use transitional words that tell *when* to link sentences and paragraphs?
6. Does each paragraph in the body of my composition have a topic sentence?
7. Does my conclusion sum up the process I have been explaining?

After you have used these questions to revise your composition, proofread it. Find and correct any errors in grammar, capitalization, punctuation, and spelling.

Check It Out Read this paragraph from an explanatory *how* composition.

Do you know how to make raisins? Raisins are dried grapes. Workers pick only grapes that have thick skins. When the grapes have dried out almost completely, they are raisins. They dry easily in the sun. The grapes are picked in August. They are spread on clean paper in the sunshine to dry.

- Does this paragraph need revision? Why?

Try Your Skill Revise the paragraph in **Check It Out.** Use the guidelines in this lesson to help you. Compare your final copy to those of your classmates.

Keep This in Mind

- When revising your explanatory *how* composition, be sure you have included all of the steps. Also make sure that your explanation is clear.
- Proofread your composition to find and correct any errors in grammar, capitalization, punctuation, and spelling.

Now Write Using the guidelines in this lesson, revise the first draft of your explanatory *how* composition. When your revision is complete, make a final copy. Save your composition in your folder.

Extending the Lesson

Have students group their *how* compositions by similar subjects. For each group of compositions, have students make a booklet, title it, design a cover for it, and then bind it.

If the topics are too diverse to group the compositions into booklets, have each student make an illustration to accompany his or her paper. Display the compositions and illustrations in the classroom.

Section 16 Objectives

1. To know how to choose and narrow a topic for a report

2. To know where to find information for a report

3. To know how to take notes from written sources

4. To organize notes for a report around several main ideas

5. To write an introduction, body paragraphs, and a conclusion for a report

6. To improve a report by revising it and making a final copy

7. To name sources in a bibliography at the end of a report

Preparing the Students

Ask students to give examples of reports that they read in everyday life (newspaper articles, book reports, etc.). Point out that reports are like compositions in some ways. The writer follows the same process of writing: pre-writing, writing a rough draft, revising it, and making a final copy. Also, a report has an introduction, body paragraphs, and a conclusion.

A report is always based on factual information. Consequently, during the pre-writing stage the writer must do research to gather facts.

Explain that in this section students will learn how to write reports.

Additional Resources

Mastery Test — page 24 in the test booklet

Practice Book — pages 75–80

Duplicating Masters — pages 75–80

Writing a Report

Part 1 **Narrow-Minded**
Pre-Writing: Choosing a Report Topic

Part 2 **Just the Facts**
Pre-Writing: Gathering Information

Part 3 **Order in the Cards**
Organizing Notes for a Report

Part 4 **Putting It All Together**
Writing the First Draft

Part 5 **The Finish Line**
Revising a Report

Part 6 **Consider the Source**
Listing Sources

Teaching Special Populations

LD See **Teaching Special Populations,** page 61. Remember that many LD students are slow readers and so you will have to supply simplified reference materials.

ESL These students may be intimidated by the quantity of reading necessary for writing a research paper. Work carefully with students during the research stage and offer them shorter, simplified reference materials. Review summarizing skills with the students and emphasize the necessity of keeping complete notes.

Assist ESL students in choosing topics that relate to their particular cultural backgrounds. Even those students whose English skills are severely limited can conduct some form of research on a cultural topic. For instance, students could interview family members, friends, even shopowners, about some aspect of shared cultural history. Have ESL students with similar linguistic and cultural backgrounds share ideas for topics. In the revision stage, pair ESL students with native English speakers.

NSD See **Teaching Special Populations,** page 61.

Part 1

Objective

To know how to choose and narrow a topic for a report

Presenting the Lesson

1. Read aloud and discuss **Here's the Idea.** Emphasize the difference between a composition and a report. Then mention other general topics and have students suggest report topics (insects, vitamins, space travel, dogs, sports, etc.).

2. Discuss **Check It Out.**

3. Assign and discuss **Try Your Skill.**

4. Read **Keep This in Mind** aloud. Then assign **Now Write.**

Individualizing the Lesson

Less-Advanced Students

Work with students individually to help them select and narrow suitable report topics.

Advanced Students

Take students to the library and have them browse through periodicals and other reference materials to get ideas for report topics.

Optional Practice

Follow the instructions for **Try Your Skill,** using these examples.

my favorite movie
the first Apollo space mission
windsurfing
opera
how a microwave oven works
my experience with pets
the skyscrapers of Chicago
termites

Part 1

Narrow-Minded

Pre-Writing: Choosing a Report Topic

Here's the Idea A report, like any other composition, is a group of paragraphs about one topic. There are two important differences between a standard composition and a report, however.

First, most compositions include opinions, your feelings about a topic. A report, however, deals only with facts. Facts are statements that can be proven true. To learn more about facts and opinions, read Section 17, **Clear Thinking.**

A second difference is that a report is written from information gathered from outside sources. These outside sources may include encyclopedias, books, and magazine and newspaper articles. The purpose of a report is to use the information you gather from these outside sources to inform your readers about your topic.

The first step in preparing to write a report is choosing a topic. You must be careful to choose a topic that is not too general. You should be able to cover your topic well in the assigned length of your report. A topic such as "The History of Coal" is much too general for a short report. You could easily write a whole book about it. If you wanted to write a report about coal, better topics might be "Inside a Coal Mine" and "How Coal Is Formed."

Check It Out Read these two paragraphs.

1 The purple martin is a small, sparrow-like bird that lives in eastern Canada and the United States. It is known for its strange nesting behavior. The purple martin nests mainly in birdhouses which people build for it. Biologists and bird-watchers have seen purple martins nesting in trees on rare occasions, but these birds usually depend on people to build houses for them.

2 Miguel looked out his bedroom window and saw the thunderstorm approaching. He was terrified. Huge gray clouds rolled across the sky, throwing shadows over the red tile rooftops of the town. Suddenly, a flash of lightning lit up the sky. Miguel waited nervously for the thunder to follow. When it did, it was as if all the doors in the world had just slammed shut.

- Which paragraph contains information gathered from an outside source?
- Which paragraph is from a report? How can you tell?

Try Your Skill Below is a list of topics. Write which topics would be good for a report. Remember, a good report topic should not be too general. It must also be a subject that can be explained with facts gathered from outside sources. Discuss your choice with your classmates.

the history of rock music	my favorite television program
the battle of Bunker Hill	magic through the ages
the Civil War	the German shepherd dog
tropical fish	my dog Ralph

Keep This in Mind

- A report is based on information gathered from outside sources.
- A report uses facts to inform the reader.
- A report does not include the writer's feelings or opinions.

Now Write Think about some possible topics for a report. Write them down as they come to mind. Remember, a good topic is specific. It will be supported with facts that you gather from outside sources. Choose the topic that you most want to write about. Write it down and keep it in your folder.

Extending the Lesson

Explain to students that they have probably already written reports. Discuss papers that they have written for science, social studies, and other subjects. If possible, make a collection of student reports and display it in the classroom.

Part 2

Objectives

1. To know where to find information for a report

2. To know how to take notes from written sources

Presenting the Lesson

1. Read aloud and discuss **Here's the Idea.** If possible, hold the class in the library. Review with students where the card catalog is and how nonfiction is classified and arranged on the shelves. Also point out where periodicals, encyclopedias, and other reference books are kept. If necessary, review use of the *Readers' Guide to Periodical Literature.*

2. Discuss **Check It Out.** Point out that the note card only mentions the title of the source. More detailed information about the source should be written on the source card.

3. Assign and discuss **Try Your Skill.** Remind students to take notes in their own words. Explain that using a writer's exact words without giving him or her credit is called *plagiarism.*

4. Read **Keep This in Mind** aloud. Then assign **Now Write.**

Individualizing the Lesson

Less-Advanced Students

Structure the **Now Write** exercise more rigidly. Require three sources for the report: one encyclopedia article, one book, and one magazine article. Explain to students that they do not necessarily have to read an entire book to gather information. Remind them to use the table of

Part 2

Just the Facts

Pre-Writing: Gathering Information

Here's the Idea Once you have chosen a topic for your report, you will need to find information about it. A good place to look is an encyclopedia. Other sources are books, magazines, and newspapers. You will find all these sources in your school and community libraries. To learn how to find information in a library, see Section 18, **Using the Library.**

As you research your topic, you will want to copy important facts to use in your report. Use note cards for your notes. Here are some guidelines for making note cards.

1. Use a separate 3 x 5 note card for each fact or idea.
2. Write down where the fact or idea came from. Write down the name of the source and the page number the information was on.
3. Take notes in your own words. **Do not copy sentences directly from your source.** It is not acceptable to use another writer's work word-for-word.
4. Make a separate "source card" for each source you use. On this card, write down the following information for each type of source. You will need this information when you list your sources in Part 6.

Book: author, title, publisher, date published

Magazine: author of article (if there is one), title of article, name of magazine, date published, page number of article.

Encyclopedia: title of article, name of encyclopedia, volume number, page number of article, date published

Newspaper: author of article (if there is one); title of article; name of newspaper; date published; section, page, and column number of article

Check It Out Read the information on this note card.

> The skeletons of many small ocean creatures make up the material known as coral.
> Source— The World We Live In page 115

- Does the note card include one important fact?
- Does the note card list the source of information?

Try Your Skill Read the following paragraph. Make two or three note cards to help prepare a report on hamburgers.

> The hamburger originated in Russia, where medieval Tartars ate raw meat scraped and shredded with a dull knife and seasoned with salt, pepper, and onion juice. German sailors picked up the dish at Russian ports and brought the recipe back to their home base at Hamburg. Finicky Hamburgers, not used to eating their meat raw, took some of the red out of their tartar steak by broiling the meat. Thus, the hamburger steak was born.
>
> —*The People's Almanac #2* page 956

Keep This in Mind

- As you research your report, write the important information in your own words on note cards.
- Make a source card for each source you use.

Now Write Go to the library and find two or three sources for your report. Read each source carefully. Make note cards for the important facts and ideas you find. Make source cards, too. Save your cards in your folder.

contents and the index of a book to locate specific information. Use class time for the research so that you can assist those students having difficulty locating sources of information.

Advanced Students

Discuss the issue of credibility with students. Point out that an article in a scientific journal would be more credible than one found in a weekly news magazine or newspaper.

Also discuss the strengths and limitations of various sources. Encyclopedia articles have the advantage of being easy to find. However, they are usually general, and they may not be up-to-date. A newspaper article is current, but many times it is only a reporting of something published elsewhere. Point out that it is usually best to consult the original source.

Optional Practice

Make a copy of a brief article from a magazine. Also copy the cover. Have students read the article and make notes on it. Ask them to make five note cards and also a source card.

Extending the Lesson

Explain to students that *paraphrasing* means to put something in your own words. Notes must be paraphrased unless they are to be used in a direct quotation with credit given to the author.

Copy several paragraphs from an encyclopedia entry. Have students paraphrase them.

Part 3

Objective

To organize notes for a report around several main ideas

Presenting the Lesson

1. Read aloud and discuss **Here's the Idea.** As a practical suggestion, tell students to use rubberbands or envelopes to keep their notes separated.

2. Discuss **Check It Out.**

3. Assign and discuss **Try Your Skill.**

4. Assign **Now Write.**

Individualizing the Lesson

Less-Advanced Students

Allow students to work in pairs to complete the **Try Your Skill** exercise.

Advanced Students

After students have organized their note cards into piles according to the main ideas, introduce the concept of outlining a report. Do not dwell on the mechanics of outlining. Concentrate on having students state the main ideas and list the details for each main idea.

Optional Practice

Have students sort these notes about prairie dogs according to main ideas. Then have them write sentences to state the main idea of each group of facts. Order may vary.

- Prairie dogs live in the Great Plains of the U.S.
- Prairie dogs, whose name in Greek means "mouse dog," make a barking noise.

Part 3

Order in the Cards

Organizing Notes for a Report

Here's the Idea You will find it easier to write your report if you have planned it carefully. Organizing your information is an important step in planning your report.

Begin to organize your information by reading through the note cards you have made. You will discover that some of them tell about one main idea and that others tell about a different main idea. Separate the cards into several piles. Each pile should contain cards with information about one main idea.

For example, you might be writing a report about the Pilgrims at Plymouth, Massachusetts. You might find that your note cards had information about three main ideas. These ideas are (1) why the Pilgrims went to Plymouth, (2) how they got there, and (3) how they lived at Plymouth. Each of these main ideas could be a paragraph in your report. You would separate your cards into three piles that match the three main ideas. The cards in the pile about how the Pilgrims lived at Plymouth might include note cards with this information:

1. The Pilgrims found much game to hunt for food.
2. Pilgrims made clothing from the skins of animals they trapped.
3. Indians helped Pilgrims plant corn and other vegetables.

Group your other cards in the same way.

As you organize your information, you may find some cards that do not belong with any others. If this happens, you probably will not want this information in your report.

Check It Out Each of these sentences describes the main idea of one pile of note cards for a report about the pilgrims at Plymouth. You should write sentences like these to describe the main idea of each group of cards.

1. The Pilgrims left England and sailed to America to escape being put in jail because of their religious beliefs.

2. The Pilgrims sailed across stormy seas, on the *Mayflower*, and landed at Plymouth.

3. The Pilgrims hunted and trapped animals for food and clothing, and farmed with the help of Indians.

- Do you see how each one of these sentences might serve as the topic sentence of a paragraph in a report about the Pilgrims?

Try Your Skill Below are nine facts from note cards on the Pilgrims. Put each fact into one of the following groups: (1) why the Pilgrims went to Plymouth, (2) how the Pilgrims got to Plymouth, and (3) how the Pilgrims lived at Plymouth. Find one fact that does not belong in any group.

- Indians helped the Pilgrims to plant corn and vegetables.
- The *Mayflower* had to cross stormy seas to reach America.
- Most of the Pilgrims refused to belong to the Church of England.
- Many people became seasick on the voyage.
- Pilgrims made clothing from the skins of animals they trapped.
- Plymouth is a popular tourist town today.
- The Pilgrims found much game to hunt for food.
- It took the *Mayflower* sixty-five days to cross the Atlantic.
- The English government arrested people who would not join the Church of England.

Keep This in Mind

- Organize your note cards by grouping together cards that tell about the same main idea.

Now Write Read over your note cards. Organize them into a few main ideas. Write a sentence that describes each main idea. Keep your sentences and your notes in your folder.

- The prairie dog is a rodent.
- A prairie dog burrow has both an entrance and an exit.
- Prairie dogs have short brown fur.
- Prairie dogs communicate with their posture.
- Some types of prairie dogs have white tails and some have black tails.
- Scientists think that prairie dogs have special calls for making threats, signaling distress, and sounding an alert.
- A sitting-up-and-looking-around posture is probably signaling for others to pay attention.
- The nesting chamber of a burrow is where the prairie dogs sleep and where the young stay.
- When a prairie dog jumps into the air with his forelimbs up and his head back, he is signaling an all-clear from danger.
- Prairie dogs have tiny ears and plump-looking bodies.
- Turning bays in burrows allow the prairie dogs to escape from predators.
- Prairie dogs also have an all-clear whistle.

Extending the Lesson

With students, create and duplicate a checklist to use for the process of organizing a report. The list might include the following:

- Reread note cards.
- Group notes by common ideas.
- Omit cards with irrelevant facts.
- Do more research, if necessary.
- Write a sentence expressing the main idea of each group of facts.
- Decide in which order to develop the main ideas.

Part 4

Objective

To write an introduction, body paragraphs, and a conclusion for a report

Presenting the Lesson

1. Read aloud and discuss **Here's the Idea.** Emphasize the importance of a strong introduction for a report and of clear topic sentences for the body paragraphs.

2. Discuss **Check It Out.** Ask students to find the topic sentence in each paragraph.

3. Assign **Try Your Skill.**

4. Read **Keep This in Mind** aloud. Then assign **Now Write.** After they have completed their rough drafts, have students write titles for their reports.

Individualizing the Lesson

Less-Advanced Students

Do the **Try Your Skill** exercise as a class. If time permits, have students write the third body paragraph about the Pilgrims independently.

Advanced Students

For the **Try Your Skill** exercise, have students complete the report on the Pilgrims. They should write two further body paragraphs and the conclusion. Also have them write a title for the report.

Optional Practice

Have students select one of the main ideas from the **Optional Practice** exercise in Part 3 and write a

Part 4

Putting It All Together

Writing the First Draft

Here's the Idea After you have organized your notes, you are ready to begin writing the first draft of your report. The report has three parts—an introduction, a body, and a conclusion. The introduction tells the reader what your report is about. The body develops each main idea of the report with details. The conclusion sums up the important information in the report.

The introduction will be the first paragraph of your report. This paragraph will introduce your subject. Don't begin by saying "In my report I want to tell about . . . " or "My report is about . . . " Instead, write an interesting, informative first sentence. You may want to present some facts from your note cards in the introduction. Notice how the first paragraph in **Check It Out** presents the subject of a report on the Pilgrims.

As you write the paragraph for the body of your report, include topic sentences. You might want to use the topic sentences you wrote when you grouped your note cards in separate piles. Use your cards to add details to each paragraph.

Your report should end with a clearly written conclusion. The conclusion should sum up the information in your report in one brief paragraph.

Check It Out Read the introduction and first paragraph of the body of a report about the Pilgrims at Plymouth Colony.

In 1620, a group of colonists left England to search for religious freedom in a new land. They arrived at a point along the shore of Cape Cod Bay in Massachusetts. The colonists named the place Plymouth, after the town of Plymouth in England. They called themselves Pilgrims, a name that refers to people who go on religious journeys.

The Pilgrims left England and sailed to America to escape being jailed because of their religious beliefs. At this time in history, the English government arrested people who would not join the Church of England. Most of the Pilgrims refused to belong to the Church of England. They wanted to live where they could worship in freedom. They decided to leave England and set sail for America.

- Does the introduction tell who this report is about? Is it interesting and informative?
- Are all of the facts in the first paragraph of the body about one main idea? What is that main idea?

Try Your Skill Go back to the **Try Your Skill** section in the last lesson, **Order in the Cards.** Review the notes you grouped together about the Pilgrims' trip to America. Use these notes to write a second paragraph for the body of the report in **Check It Out** about the Pilgrims at Plymouth Colony.

Keep This in Mind

- A report has an introduction, a body, and a conclusion.
- The introduction tells what your report is about.
- The body develops the topic with facts from your note cards.
- The conclusion sums up the information in your report.

Now Write Write the first draft of your report. Use your note cards and the topic sentences you wrote in Part 3. Make sure you have a clear introduction, body, and conclusion. Don't worry about spelling, punctuation, or grammar at this point. Just try to present your ideas clearly. Save your first draft in your folder.

body paragraph for the report on prairie dogs.

Extending the Lesson

Using an overhead projector, display samples of well-written reports from your files. Have students examine all of the parts of the reports. Have them ask the following questions. Is the introduction interesting? Do the body paragraphs each develop one main idea? Are the topic sentences for the body paragraphs clear and well-written? Does the conclusion sum up the report?

Part 5

Objective

To improve a report by revising it and making a final copy

Presenting the Lesson

1. Read aloud and discuss **Here's the Idea.** Emphasize the importance of checking the accuracy of the facts used in the report.

2. Discuss **Check It Out.** Point out the fact that the revised version uses more specific details than the original. Also, stronger verbs have been used in several places.

3. Assign and discuss **Try Your Skill.**

4. Read **Keep This in Mind** aloud. Then assign **Now Write.**

Individualizing the Lesson

Less-Advanced Students

Work with students individually or in small groups to help them proceed through each step of the revision process for their reports.

Advanced Students

Allow students to work in pairs during the revision process. Have partners exchange papers and note cards. Instruct students to suggest improvements to each other for the content and organization of the reports. Also, have them proofread the papers.

Optional Practice

Have students revise and proofread the first four paragraphs of the following report on prairie dogs. Supply students with the facts from

Part 5

The Finish Line

Revising a Report

Here's the Idea When you have finished the first draft of your report, you will want to revise it. Take time to read your report and think about it carefully.

Because a report is written from facts, it is important that the facts be correct. Also, be sure all of your ideas are clearly expressed. If a sentence seems unclear, rewrite it.

Be sure that your report is well organized. Make sure the introduction tells what your report is about. See that the body develops your topic with good details. Be sure the conclusion sums up the report.

Proofread your report for errors in grammar, capitalization, punctuation, and spelling. Neatly copy your report in its final form. Proofread it for errors one last time.

Check It Out Read this paragraph. Notice the revisions.

The pilgrims' first winter at Plymouth was a difficult one. ~~It was very cold.~~ They suffered from terrible cold and heavy snowstorms. The ~~people~~ colonists ~~had made~~ built houses out of light, wooden boards that did not keep out the cold winds. Their crops failed and many people were hungry. By spring, nearly half the colony had died from ~~sickness.~~ influenza, pneumonia, and starvation.

- Did the writer make this a better paragraph by adding details and improving word choice?
- Did the writer correct all spelling and punctuation errors?

Try Your Skill Read the following paragraph. Proofread it to find and correct the errors in grammar, capitalization, punctuation, and spelling. Check for sentences that are unclear. If you find one, rewrite it.

Mount Everest is the highest mountan in the world. It is five miles above sea level. The peak is in the Himalaya range, along the boundry's of china and nepal, north of india. Mount Everest was named for Sir George Everest, the Englishman who discovered it:

Keep This in Mind

As you revise your report, ask yourself these questions:

- Is my information accurate?
- Are my ideas stated clearly? Could I add more details or improve my word choice?
- Is my organization logical?
- Is my grammar, usage, spelling, punctuation, and capitalization correct?

Now Write Use the guidelines in this lesson to revise your report. Check your facts for accuracy. Be sure your ideas are clear. Check your organization. Look for errors in grammar, capitalization, punctuation, and spelling. Make a final copy of your report and proofread it one last time. Neatly correct any errors you find. Save your report in your folder.

the **Optional Practice** exercise in Part 3 of this section. Remind them to check the accuracy of the facts. Then have students write a concluding paragraph for the report and make a final copy. Answers will vary.

Prairie dogs are cute little rodents that live in the Great Lakes states of the united states. they have tiny ears and plump-looking furry brown bodies Some have white tails and some have black. these little creatures have amazeing living quarters and communication systems.

Prairie dogs, whose Greek name means "mouse dog," make a barking noise. They make difrent sounds for difrent reasons.

Prairie dogs also use "body language." They're posture is a way of communicating. When they sit up and look around, they are signaling the others to pay attention. They also jump into the air with their forelimbs up and their heads back. This action signals an all clear.

Prairie dogs live in complex burrows tunneled beneath the ground. These burrows have separate entrances and exits. They also have turning bays to help the prairie dogs escape from predators. The main chamber of the burrow is the nesting chamber. Where the prairie dogs sleep and where the young stay.

Extending the Lesson

Make a collection of various style guides for term papers and reports. Examine them with students and then put them on display.

Part 6

Objective

To name sources in a bibliography at the end of a report

Presenting the Lesson

1. Read aloud and discuss **Here's the Idea.** Point out the punctuation used for each type of listing. Then on the chalkboard write out a formula for each type of listing (i.e., Book: *author's last name* comma *author's first name* period *book title* period *book publisher* comma *year of publication* period).

2. Discuss **Check It Out.**

3. Assign and discuss **Try Your Skill.**

4. Read **Keep This in Mind** aloud. Then assign **Now Write.**

Individualizing the Lesson

Less-Advanced Students

Allow students to work in pairs to complete the **Try Your Skill** exercise.

Advanced Students

Have students find five more sources of information on the topic of their report. Have them make a second bibliography with these sources and title it "For Further Research."

Optional Practice

Repeat the directions for **Try Your Skill.**

1. a magazine article titled "Mysteries of Bird Migration" by Allan C. Fisher, Jr., published on pages 154–193 of the August 1979 issue of *National Geographic*

Part 6

Consider the Source

Listing Sources

Here's the Idea Whenever you write a report, you need to tell your readers where you got your information. You must list your sources on a separate page. This list of sources is called a **bibliography**. It tells where to look up more information about your topic. Each source in the bibliography is called an entry.

Look at the source cards you made in Part 2, **Just the Facts**. These cards contain all of the information you need to write a bibliography. Arrange these cards in alphabetical order, according to the author's last name. If no author is mentioned in the source, use the first main word of the title. Now write your bibliography. Here are the correct forms to use.

Book: Cooke, Alistair. *America*. Alfred A. Knopf, 1973.

Encyclopedia: "Jupiter." *The World Book Encyclopedia*. Volume 11, pp. 162–164, 1983.

Magazine: Desauteb, Paul. "Majestic Jewels Find New Setting at Smithsonian." *Smithsonian*. June 1974, pp. 36–43.

Newspaper: Idaszak, Jerome. "Seeing Yosemite Off the Beaten Trail." *Sun-Times*, 10 January 1984, Sec. A, p. 41, Cols. 1–3.

Check It Out Look at the following bibliography.

Bibliography

Dillon, Frances. *The Pilgrims*. Doubleday, 1973.

"Plymouth Colony." *World Book Encyclopedia*. Volume 15, pp. 518–521, 1967.

Schultz, F. L. "Thanksgiving Pilgrim Style." *American History Illustrated*. Nov. 1982, p. 17.

White, Paul. "Plymouth Revisited." *Chicago Tribune*, 18 September 1984, Sec. B., p. 3, Col. 1.

- Is all of the necessary information included in each entry? Is the information for each entry in the correct order? Are the entries arranged in correct alphabetical order?

Try Your Skill Write a bibliography entry for each source below. Follow the correct form for each type of source. Then put the entries in correct alphabetical order.

1. an encyclopedia article titled "Mesa Verde" by Herbert E. Kahla in the *World Book Encyclopedia*, 1967, page 344, Volume 13
2. a book titled *A Talent for Detail* by Peter Daniel, published in 1974 by Harmony Books
3. a magazine article titled "Fighting the New Slavery" by Michael Serrill, published on p. 99 of the September 19, 1983 issue of *Time*
4. a newspaper article titled "Shuttle Mission a Success" by Victor Vazquez, in the *Herald Tribune* on Oct 9, 1985, in Section A, page 2, columns 1–4

Keep This in Mind

- The last page of your report should be a list of your outside sources.
- Encyclopedias, books, magazines, and newspapers each have their own form in a bibliography.
- Put your sources in alphabetical order by the author's last name. If no author is mentioned, use the first main word of the title.

Now Write Make a list of sources for your report. Follow the samples you studied in this lesson. Write your sources in alphabetical order on a separate sheet of paper titled *List of Sources.* Put this page at the end of your report.

2. an encyclopedia article titled "Puffins" in *The World Book Encyclopedia*, 1984, pages 779–780, Volume 5
3. a book titled *Is It Bigger Than a Sparrow?* by Barbara Brenner, published in 1972 by Alfred A. Knopf, Inc.
4. a newspaper article entitled "Birds of a Feather" by Marcia Byline in the *City Chronicle* on November 3, 1984, in section B, page 7, column 1

Extending the Lesson

Provide students with copies of *Time* or *Newsweek* magazines and ask them to read passages showing that factual reports can be lively and interesting.

Section 17 Objectives

1. To differentiate between a fact and an opinion

2. To support an opinion with facts

Preparing the Students

Explain to students that in our modern world we are bombarded with information all day long. Radio, television, newspapers, magazines, billboards, and other people all have "messages" for us. We, as receivers of the information, must be able to evaluate that information and decide whether or not to accept it as true. We must use our thinking skills to question things that we see, read, and hear.

Tell students that this section will help them learn how to evaluate what they see, hear and read. Also, it will help them to present their own ideas more convincingly.

Additional Resources

Mastery Test — page 25 in the test booklet

Practice Book — pages 81–82

Duplicating Masters — pages 81–82

Clear Thinking

Part 1 **A Matter of Facts**
Learning About Facts and Opinions

Part 2 **Because I Say So**
Supporting Opinions

Teaching Special Populations

LD These students may find it difficult distinguishing between facts and opinions, so provide extra practice in testing statements through personal observation or through the use of reliable sources. Provide students with a set of statements and ask them to check the validity of these propositions in an encyclopedia. Help students in identifying particular words that signal the presence of opinions.

ESL To some ESL students, the distinction between facts and opinions in English may appear to be a subtle one. Give students numerous concrete examples. Go over passages together in class and demonstrate how facts can be supported by personal observation or by reference to reliable sources. Identify opinions as such and have students underline supporting facts, if there are any. Let the students offer examples of facts and opinions from their own experiences.

NSD Without being too critical, point out to NSD students that nonstandard dialect can obscure the factual content of a passage or the relationship between opinions and supporting details. Give students extra practice in listing supporting facts.

Part 1

Objective

To differentiate between a fact and an opinion

Presenting the Lesson

1. Read aloud and discuss **Here's the Idea.** Write the terms *fact* and *opinion* and their definitions on the chalkboard for emphasis. Ask each student to state a fact. Then ask how each statement of fact can be proven true.

2. Discuss **Check It Out.**

3. Assign and discuss **Try Your Skill.** Have students give reasons for choosing one method of proof over another.

4. Read **Keep This in Mind** aloud. Then assign **Now Write.**

Individualizing the Lesson

Less-Advanced Students

Do the first two items of the **Try Your Skill** exercise with the class. Then have students complete the exercise independently.

Advanced Students

Add these items to the **Try Your Skill** exercise.

5. The garage sale is a fund-raiser for the Pep Club of the junior high school. F
   No one should sell merchandise from door to door. O
6. Opossums are ugly. O
   Opossums are nocturnal animals. F
7. Liver is nutritious because it supplies iron to the body. F
   Liver tastes awful. O
8. The dance tickets are too expensive. O
   Tickets to the dance are $20.00. F

Part 1

A Matter of Facts

Learning About Facts and Opinions

Here's the Idea Facts and opinions are an important part of our lives. We read them in books, magazines, and newspapers. We hear them on radio and television. We exchange them when we talk to family and friends. It is important, therefore, to learn how to use facts and opinions correctly.

The first step in understanding facts and opinions is to learn the difference between them. A **fact** is a statement that can be proved true. Look at the following statements. Each is a fact.

1. The sun rises in the east.
2. In 1543, Copernicus showed that the earth traveled around the sun.
3. President Franklin Roosevelt had polio.

Facts can be proved true in different ways. Statement 1 can be proved true by **personal observation**. You can watch a sunrise and check the direction with a compass. In the same way, if someone says, "It's raining," you can look out a window to see if that statement is true. If it is, the statement is a fact.

Another way to prove that a statement is true is by checking a **reliable source**. An encyclopedia is one reliable source. You can prove that statements 2 and 3 are true by reading what an encyclopedia says about Copernicus and Roosevelt.

Another type of reliable source is a person who has special knowledge about a subject. You could find out if statement 3 is true by asking someone who has studied Roosevelt's life. You could also ask someone who was alive at the same time as Roosevelt and who knew about him.

An **opinion** is different from a fact. Opinions cannot be proved true. An opinion tells what someone believes or feels about something. If you say, "The country is a better place to live than the city," that is just your opinion. It is not a fact.

Check It Out Read the following statements.

1. Mt. Everest is the highest mountain in the world.
2. Basketball is a boring sport.
3. Students should have a long summer vacation because they work so hard during the rest of the year.
4. The state flower of Georgia is the Cherokee rose.

- Which of these statements can be proved true?
- Which of these statements are opinions? How do you know?

Try Your Skill Read each pair of statements. In each pair, which statement is the fact and which is the opinion? Would you use personal observation or a reliable source to prove that each fact is true?

1. Your hair is blond.
   Blond hair is the prettiest type of hair.
2. Winter is the best season.
   Forty inches of snow fell in our city last winter.
3. It rained all day yesterday.
   Rainy days are depressing.
4. Everyone in the world should learn English.
   More people speak Mandarin than any other language.

Keep This in Mind

- A fact is a statement that can be proved true.
- An opinion tells what someone believes or feels. An opinion cannot be proved true or untrue.

Now Write Write down two opinions that you have heard people express about teenagers. Then write down two facts about teenagers. Compare your opinion and facts to those of your classmates. Did anyone confuse an opinion with a fact? Title your paper **A Matter of Facts.** Save it in your folder.

Optional Practice

Read the following statements. Decide which are facts and which are opinions. Then state how you could prove the facts to be true.

F 1. Samuel Clemens's pen name was Mark Twain.
F 2. Smoking is harmful to your health.
O 3. Watching baseball on T.V. is dull.
F 4. Kareem Abdul-Jabbar used to be known as Lew Alcindor.
O 5. Rubies are the most beautiful jewels in the world.
O 6. Every child should have a pet.
F 7. Charles Lindbergh's airplane was called *The Spirit of St. Louis*.
F 8. Presidential elections are held every four years in America.

Extending the Lesson

Bring in old newspapers to class. Have each student find a headline that is a statement of fact and one that is an opinion. Read and discuss them in class.

Part 2

Objective

To support an opinion with facts

Presenting the Lesson

1. Read aloud and discuss **Here's the Idea.** Have each student state an opinion and then give two supporting facts.

2. Discuss **Check It Out.**

3. Assign and discuss **Try Your Skill.** Point out that advertisers do not rely only on logic to sell their products. They also use subtle emotional appeals. "If you use our product, you will be rich, famous, beautiful, etc." Explain that this is done with both words and pictures.

4. Read **Keep This in Mind** aloud. Then assign **Now Write.**

Individualizing the Lesson

Less-Advanced Students

Before assigning **Try Your Skill,** show students sample advertisements, one with an opinion supported by facts and one with an unsupported opinion. Then have each student find one ad of each type.

Advanced Students

Have each student invent a product. Then have students create magazine ads to explain the features of their products. Remind students to support their opinions with facts.

Part 2

Because I Say So

Supporting Opinions

Here's the Idea Everyone has the right to state his or her opinions. However, opinions by themselves are not very convincing. An opinion needs support. It should have facts to back it up. Read the following opinion:

Sudzy Soap is the best detergent for your clothes.

This is the opinion of the makers of Sudzy Soap. It is the way they feel about their product. It is the way they want *you* to feel. By itself, though, this opinion isn't at all convincing. It is not supported by any facts that tell *why* Sudzy Soap is the best. Here's how the makers of Sudzy Soap might back up their opinion to make it more convincing:

Opinion: Sudzy Soap is the best detergent for your clothes.

Supporting fact: It has strong ingredients to clean the clothes of active young people.

Supporting fact: It easily removes grease, food stains, and ground-in dirt.

Remember, the more supporting facts an opinion has, the more convincing it is. Whenever you write an opinion, include facts to back it up. Whenever you read or hear an opinion, look for supporting information that explains *why*.

Check It Out Read the following discussion.

"I think that multiple-choice tests are the worst kind," said Jackson.

"Nope," said Marcia. "It's got to be short-answer tests that are the worst. I hate short-answer tests!"

"You're both wrong," sighed Terry. "Essay tests are the hardest. You have to read the questions so carefully. You have to organize your time. You have to give so many details. Essay tests are definitely the hardest!"

- What is the opinion of each student? Which student supports his or her opinion with facts? What are those facts?

Try Your Skill Look at advertisements in newspapers or magazines. Find advertisements that contain opinions. Try to find two opinions that are supported with facts, then find two that are not well supported. Bring your ads to class and talk about them with your classmates. Are the supported or unsupported opinions more convincing? Why?

Keep This in Mind

- To be convincing, an opinion must be supported by facts.
- The facts that support an opinion should tell *why*.

Now Write Think for a while about some things you believe or feel strongly about. Write several opinions that state your beliefs or feelings. Choose one of your opinions and write a short paragraph about it. State your opinion in the topic sentence. Then support your opinion with facts. Title your paper **Because I Say So**. Save it in your folder.

Optional Practice

Make copies of several editorials or letters to the editor from a newspaper. Have students underline the opinion that is expressed in each editorial. Then instruct them to underline each supporting fact. Discuss how well each writer has supported his or her opinion.

Extending the Lesson

Have students critique the critics. Ask each student to bring in either a movie review, a book review, or a restaurant review. Ask students to state the critic's opinion about the movie, book, or restaurant. Then discuss what facts he or she uses to support that opinion.

Section 18 Objectives

1. To understand and use the classification systems for fiction and nonfiction books

2. To understand the library's card catalog and to use it to find books

3. To know how to locate information in an encyclopedia

Preparing the Students

Discuss briefly the many different kinds of reading, viewing, and listening materials found in a library. These include books, magazines, pamphlets, newspapers, pictures, and records. If your local library offers services such as story hours, tutoring, a community bulletin board, films, and writing and craft classes for children and adults, describe these for the students as well. Emphasize that the library has something for everyone.

Additional Resources

Mastery Test — page 26 in the test booklet

Practice Book — pages 83–85

Duplicating Masters — pages 83–85

Using the Library

Part 1 **A Good Place To Go**
How To Use the Library

Part 2 **Pick a Card**
How To Use the Card Catalog

Part 3 **Look Here!**
How To Use an Encyclopedia

Teaching Special Populations

LD This is an important section for LD students since it teaches essential skills such as organization and categorization. Work through all of the sections in class with your students. Whenever possible, use actual library materials or take the whole group to the library. Use concrete, obvious examples to demonstrate the concepts presented in this lesson.

ESL The library can be a formidable place for ESL students. Once they understand the way it functions, however, a library can enrich their cultural experience considerably. Provide as much library practice as possible. Conduct numerous tours of the library with your students, and have them make simple floor plans of its layout. In fact, you may want to teach this section in the library itself rather than in a classroom.

By having actual experience with library materials your students will quickly improve their research techniques. From time to time you should check to make sure students are coping with the alphabetizing skills necessary for using the card catalog and other reference works.

NSD Teach this section in the library itself if possible. Make sure students are coping with the necessary alphabetizing and categorizing skills.

Part 1

Objective

To understand and use the classification systems for fiction and nonfiction books

Presenting the Lesson

1. Read aloud and discuss **Here's the Idea.** Show students a number of fiction books from the library. Emphasize that these books are arranged according to the first letter of the author's last name. Then have a student put the fiction books in correct shelf order. Next show some examples of nonfiction books. Point out the call numbers on the spines. Then have a student put the nonfiction books in correct shelf order.

2. Point out that many fiction authors have written more than one book. Explain that books by the same author are arranged alphabetically by title. Point out that the words *a, an,* and *the* do not count as first words. Also explain that under the Dewey Decimal System, there are many books with the same Dewey Decimal number. When two books have the same number, they are arranged alphabetically by the author's last name within that number.

3. Discuss **Check It Out.** Use the categories on page 204 for reference.

4. Assign and discuss **Try Your Skill.** When students can differentiate between fiction and nonfiction books and can identify title and author, assign **Now Write.** Have them record the call numbers of the nonfiction books.

Part 1

A Good Place To Go

How To Use the Library

Here's the Idea Almost anything you might want to read for pleasure or research is available in your school or public library. Do you know where to find what you want? Do you know how materials are arranged?

The books in the library are divided into two groups, **fiction** and **nonfiction.** Fiction books are arranged alphabetically on the shelves according to the author's last name. For example, *Johnny Tremain*, written by Esther Forbes, would be shelved under **F.**

Most libraries arrange nonfiction books according to the **Dewey Decimal System.** This system puts books into ten general categories. Each category has its own set of numbers. Nonfiction books are arranged numerically on the library shelves by their Dewey Decimal number. The ten categories are listed below.

000–099	**General Works**	(encyclopedias, almanacs)
100–199	**Philosophy**	(conduct, psychology)
200–299	**Religion**	(the Bible, mythology)
300–399	**Social Science**	(economics, law, education, government)
400–499	**Language**	(languages, grammar, dictionaries)
500–599	**Science**	(mathematics, biology, chemistry)
600–699	**Useful Arts**	(farming, cooking, sewing, television, business)
700–799	**Fine Arts**	(music, photography, games, sports)
800–899	**Literature**	(poetry, plays)
900–999	**History**	(biography, travel, geography)

On the spine of each nonfiction book is its **call number.** This number includes the Dewey Decimal number and other information. Look at the example below. Notice the information included in the call number.

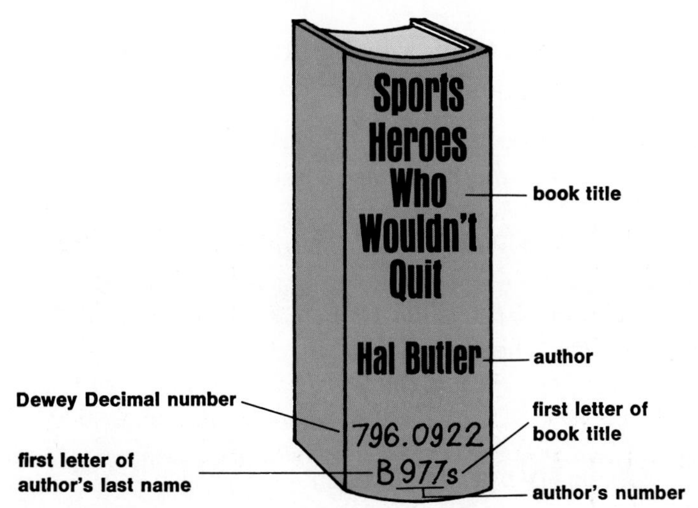

Check It Out Look at the spines of the books represented below.

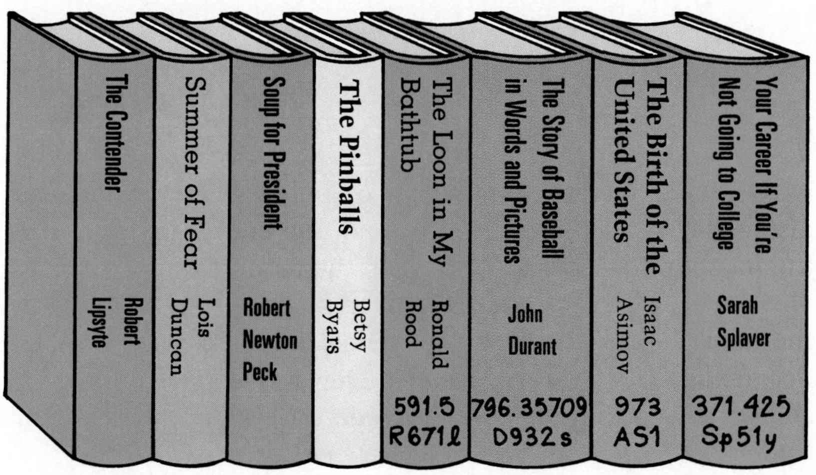

Individualizing the Lesson

Less-Advanced Students

1. To give extra help in alphabetizing, ask students to arrange these authors' last names in alphabetical order: Cormier, Conford, Dickens, Dixon, Corbett, Dahl, Corcoran, Danziger.

2. To give extra help with the Dewey Decimal System, ask students to arrange these call numbers in the order in which they would be found on the shelf: 635.965, 629.13, 613.85, 612.3, 636.1, 635.955, 629.4, 599.09, 614.47, 599.744.

Advanced Students

1. Give each student five to ten strips of paper to represent book spines. Have students use a library and write the titles and authors of fiction books on the strips. Mix up the strips. Then have each student take five to ten strips and arrange them in alphabetical order by author. Repeat the exercise with nonfiction books. Remind students to include the call number on the spine. As a final exercise, divide students into two groups. Have one arrange all of the fiction strips on the bulletin board in proper shelf order and have the other group arrange all of the nonfiction book strips.

2. Ask students to write five topics of interest to them. Then ask them to refer to page 204 and assign the general Dewey Decimal category that applies to each topic.

Optional Practice

Ask students to find the general Dewey Decimal category for each of these books. Refer to the chart on page 204.

Sports Question and Answer Book
The Story of the Laser
Historical American Landmarks
Bulfinch's Mythology

Extending the Lesson

1. Take students to the school library. Give students a diagram of the library, including each set of bookcases. Ask them to label each bookcase *fiction* or *nonfiction.* If it is fiction, label the letters included (for example, A-F). If it is nonfiction, label the call numbers included (for example, 700-820).

2. Have students research and report on the Library of Congress categories. Compare them to the Dewey Decimal System categories.

- How can you tell if books are fiction or nonfiction?
- What is the general Dewey Decimal category of each nonfiction book?
- How can the call numbers and authors' names on the spines help you find these books?

Try Your Skill Decide which of the following books are on the fiction shelves and which are on the nonfiction shelves.

1. *May I Cross Your Golden River?* Paige Dixon
2. *Facts About the Presidents,* Joseph Nathan Kane, R973.0992 K131f
3. *Fitzgo: The Wild Dog of Central Park,* Paul Wilkes, 636.7 W652f
4. *Dear Lovey Hart, I'm Desperate,* Ellen Conford
5. *The Cay,* Theodore Taylor
6. *Riders of the Wind: The Story of Ballooning,* 629.13322DW1

Keep This in Mind

- Library books are divided into two groups, fiction and nonfiction.
- Fiction books are filed alphabetically by the author's last name.
- Nonfiction books are classified in ten general categories. Each nonfiction book has its own call number to show where it can be found on the shelves.

Now Write Go to your school or public library. Find one history book, one science book, and one encyclopedia. Write the name of each book. Also write the author, if there is one. Now write the call number exactly as it appears on the spine of the book. Check the Dewey Decimal numbers on page 204. See if the book has the kind of Dewey Decimal number it should have according to its subject. Save your work in your folder.

2

Pick a Card

How To Use the Card Catalog

Here's the Idea When you're looking for a book in the library, the **card catalog** is the place to start. Every book in the library is listed there, at least three times.

Every book is recorded on an **author card,** a **title card,** and at least one **subject card.** All three cards give the call number of the book in the upper left corner. The same number appears on the binding of the book. The number determines where the book is located on the shelves.

All three cards contain the same information, but the information is arranged differently on each card. All three cards tell the publisher, the date of publication, and the number of pages in the book. There is also a notation telling whether the book has illustrations. Sometimes, there is a short description of the book or mention of other books on the same topic.

On an **author card,** the author's name is at the top. The author's name is written with the last name first. Author cards are arranged alphabetically by the author's last name.

Author Card

793.8
R972g

Rydell, Wendy
The great book of magic: including 150 mystifying tricks you can perform/
by Wendy Rydell, with George Gilbert.—New York: H. N. Abrams, c. 1976.
271 p.: ill. (some col.); 28 cm.
Bibliography: p. 264

Part 2

Objective

To understand the library's card catalog and to use it to find books

Presenting the Lesson

1. Read aloud and discuss **Here's the Idea.** Analyze in detail the sample author card. Explain that the same information is included on the other two cards. Note the differences among the top lines of the cards. Point out that the library system does not capitalize words in a title.

2. Discuss **Check It Out.**

3. Assign and discuss **Try Your Skill.** To achieve uniformity, you may wish to ditto enough cards for the class.

4. Assign **Now Write.** Read the instructions aloud. Ask students which types of cards they will be using to complete this assignment.

Individualizing the Lesson

Less-Advanced Students

1. Make copies of six to ten card catalog cards and give them to students. (If that is impossible, use an opaque projector.) Look at the first line of each card. Ask students to identify which type of card each one is. Point out the title, the author, and the call number on each card.

2. Ask students what letter they would look under to find each of the following items. Then ask what kind of card they would be using for each—title, author, or subject.

a. a book by Russel Baker

b. a book titled *A Day No Pigs Would Die*

c. a book about tides
d. the life story of Dwight Eisenhower
e. a book titled *The Right Stuff*

Advanced Students

1. Repeat the **Try Your Skill** exercise on page 209 using this information.

a. *Lord of the Flies,* William Golding
b. *The First Book of Caves,* Elizabeth Hamilton, 551.44
c. *Wild Cats,* Peggy D. Winston, 599.74
d. *I Am the Cheese,* Robert Cormier
e. *The Supreme Court,* Gerald White Johnson, 347.9

2. Have students find the following information using the card catalog.

a. Name two books written by Robert Silverberg.
b. Find a book about the Civil War. How many pages does it have? What is its call number?
c. Write the title of a book about dinosaurs. Is the book illustrated? What is the call number?
d. Who wrote the book *The Red Pony?*
e. Write the title and author of a book about automobiles. What is its call number?

Optional Practice

Describe the following situations for the class. Ask students to explain, in two or three sentences, how they would locate the books needed in each situation.

1. You enjoyed *Julie of the Wolves* very much. You want to read more books by the same author, but you can't remember her name.
2. You enjoy reading about the stars and planets. Someone has told you that Isaac Asimov has written several good books on the subject.

On a **title card,** the title comes first. Title cards are alphabetized according to the first word of the title. However, if *A, An,* or *The* is the first word in a title, look for the title card under the first letter of the second word in the title. For example, you would find *The Great Book of Magic* filed under the letter *G.*

Title Card

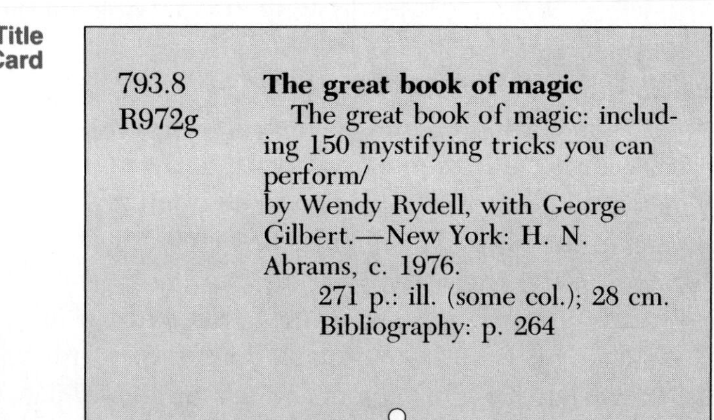

793.8
R972g

The great book of magic
The great book of magic: including 150 mystifying tricks you can perform/
by Wendy Rydell, with George Gilbert.—New York: H. N. Abrams, c. 1976.
271 p.: ill. (some col.); 28 cm.
Bibliography: p. 264

On a **subject card,** the subject is at the top. In the card catalog, the subject card is arranged alphabetically by the first word of the subject. The subject may be written in capital letters or in red.

Subject Card

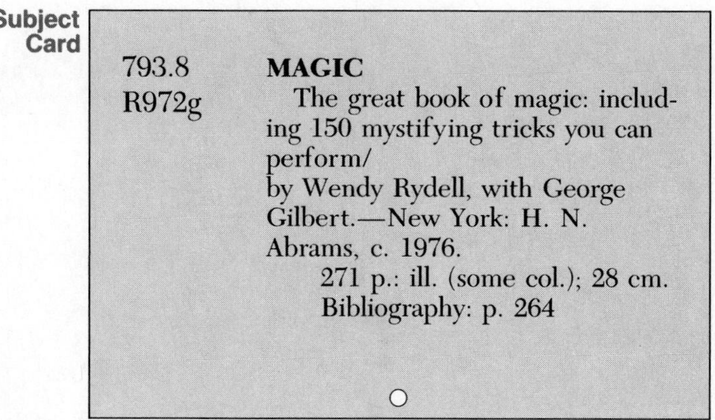

793.8
R972g

MAGIC
The great book of magic: including 150 mystifying tricks you can perform/
by Wendy Rydell, with George Gilbert.—New York: H. N. Abrams, c. 1976.
271 p.: ill. (some col.); 28 cm.
Bibliography: p. 264

Check It Out Look at the three sample cards shown. Answer the following questions.

- Under what letter of the alphabet would each card be filed?
- Where could you look for more books by Wendy Rydell?
- Where would you find more books on magic?

Try Your Skill Below are the title, author, and call number for a book about magic. On a sheet of paper, draw three rectangles to represent file cards. Use the information below to make an author card, a title card, and a subject card.

The Illustrated History of Magic, by Christopher Milbourne, 793.8 C4666m

Keep This in Mind

- Every book in a library is listed in the card catalog, on at least three different cards—author, title, and subject.
- Each card records the call number, the author, the title, and other important information about the book.

Now Write Write the name of your favorite fiction author.

Next, think of a subject you're interested in. It might be a hobby, a sport, a person, or an art form. Write it on your paper.

Go to the card catalog in your school or public library. Find two books by the author you have chosen and two books on the subject you have chosen.

On your paper, make a rectangle to look like a file card. Copy the information from one of the cards into the rectangle.

Save your work in your folder.

3. You must do a report on the life cycle of a frog. You need at least two books on this subject.

Extending the Lesson

Arrange a class visit to a local library with a computerized catalog. Show the students how to use the terminals to find a specific author, title, and subject.

209

Part 3

Objective

To know how to locate information in an encyclopedia

Presenting the Lesson

1. Read aloud and discuss **Here's the Idea.** Use a class set of encyclopedias to illustrate each major point.

2. Discuss **Check It Out.** Find each topic in the class set of encyclopedias. Note the guide words at the top of each page.

3. Assign and discuss **Try Your Skill.** Have students check their answers by locating the information in the class set of encyclopedias.

4. Assign **Now Write.**

Individualizing the Lesson

Less-Advanced Students

Make a list of three topics for each volume of the classroom encyclopedia. Give one volume to each student and assign the appropriate topics. Ask students to find each article and write down the page number and the guide words for each.

Advanced Students

Have students make up their own encyclopedia quizzes like the one in **Try Your Skill** on page 211. Tell them to make answer keys for their quizzes. In addition to the key word and the number of the encyclopedia volume, they should include the page number on which each article begins and the guide words on the page.

Reproduce the quizzes, and have students use them for practice in using the encyclopedia.

Part 3

Look Here!

How To Use an Encyclopedia

Here's the Idea A good way to begin any search for information is to look in an encyclopedia. An **encyclopedia** contains articles on many different subjects. The articles are arranged alphabetically by subject. On the spine of each volume you will find a single letter or guide letters to tell you what subjects are covered in it. Look at the set of encyclopedias arranged below.

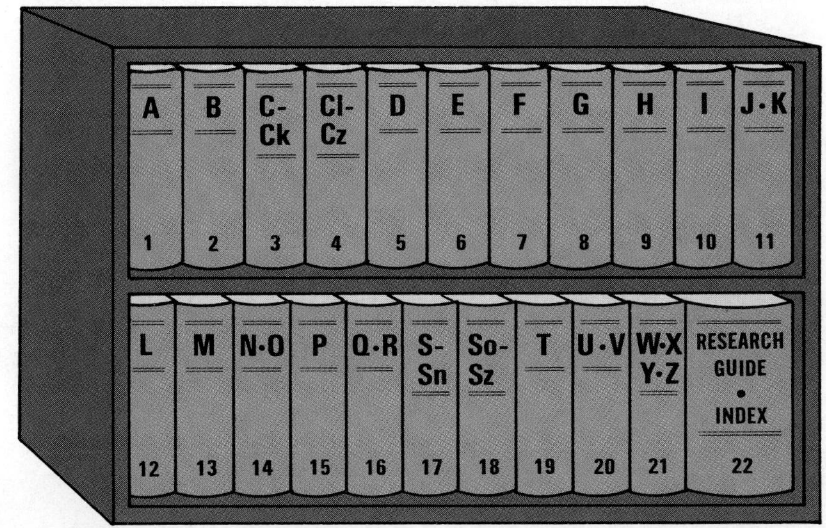

If you want to look up *magic*, for instance, first find the volume that contains subjects beginning with *M*. Then, look up the word *magic* in that volume, just as you would in a dictionary. Each page has guide words just as a dictionary does.

A major article in an encyclopedia is often divided into parts. Each part has a subtitle. When you need information on a specific topic, you usually don't have to read every word of the article. Just look under the appropriate heading. For example, you wouldn't need to study an entire article on the United States to find out about the Battle of Gettysburg. You might look in the section on *History* under *The Civil War*.

An article may also tell you where to look for further information, or provide a list of books for further reading.

Different encyclopedias have different reading levels. Read an article in several encyclopedias. Find the one that is easiest for you to understand. Try *Collier's Encyclopedia*, *Brittanica Junior Encyclopedia*, or *World Book Encyclopedia*.

Check It Out Look at the sample encyclopedia shown at the left. Answer the following questions.

- In what volume would you find information about New Zealand? Theodore Roosevelt? volcanoes? Mexico?

Try Your Skill Use the sample encyclopedia pictured in **Here's the Idea.** Write the key word in each question that tells you where to look in the encyclopedia. Next to the key word write the number of the volume in which you would look.

1. What is the name of the largest crater on the moon?
2. Was the game of lacrosse invented in North America?
3. Where does the tradition of Halloween come from?

Keep This in Mind

- An encyclopedia contains articles on many subjects. The articles are arranged alphabetically.
- Use key words to find articles on your topic.

Now Write Write the same nonfiction subject you chose for the last lesson, **Pick a Card.** Find an encyclopedia article on your subject. List the following information: the name of the encyclopedia, the number and guide letters, the guide words, related articles, and the titles of any recommended books.

Optional Practice

Follow the directions for **Try Your Skill** on page 211.

1. When was Sputnik launched?
2. What are the major exports from Argentina?
3. Is the coral snake poisonous?
4. Was Mary Cassatt an American or a French painter?
5. When was the first Model T Ford automobile produced?

Extending the Lesson

1. Prepare a list of ten topics from students' science and social studies texts. Tell students to follow the directions for **Now Write.** Give the class several days to complete the activity.

2. Have students survey the different sets of encyclopedias in the school and/or public library. Ask them to answer the following questions:

How many volumes are there? Is there a yearbook? Is there an index? How large is the type face? Are there illustrations? Are the articles easy to understand? Are additional resources listed after the articles?

Discuss the students' findings in class.

Section 19 Objectives

1. To understand assignments and to record them in an assignment notebook

2. To follow spoken and written directions carefully

3. To know what makes a good study space

4. To know how to develop a study plan

5. To understand and use the SQ3R study system

6. To take clear and effective notes from a talk or from a written work

7. To use graphic aids to understand information

8. To know how to answer objective test questions

9. To know how to answer test questions that require written answers

Preparing the Students

Ask students if this situation sounds familiar: it is Thursday night, and Max has a math test Friday morning, an essay exam in English on Friday afternoon, and a social studies report due on Monday. He also forgot to read an article for his science class. He is unprepared and feeling overwhelmed!

Explain that crisis situations like the one described can be avoided. All students need to do is to learn the proper study skills and to apply them. That is what this chapter is about.

Additional Resources

Practice Book — pages 86–94

Duplicating Masters — pages 86–94

Study and Research Skills

Part 1 **The First Step**
Understanding the Assignment

Part 2 **Stop, Look, and Listen**
Following Directions

Part 3 **Your Own Space**
A Time and a Place To Work

Part 4 **Touchdown!**
Achieving Goals with a Study Plan

Part 5 **Five Steps**
A Way To Study

Part 6 **Get It Down**
Taking Notes

Part 7 **Get the Picture**
Using Graphic Aids

Part 8 **Be Confident!**
Answering Objective Test Questions

Part 9 **Write It Right**
Answering Written Test Questions

Teaching Special Populations

LD Remind the students that they should read *all* the directions before starting a project. To reinforce this point, ask students to follow a set of instructions such as this:

> Take a piece of plain white paper. On it, draw a simple map of how to get from your house to the nearest public library. Mark the position of your home with an **X** and the library with a **Y.** On the inside of the folded paper, write a short description of how to get to the library. Before starting, fold the paper in half. Draw your map on the outside.

Also emphasize Part 8. Give students timed practice tests, pointing out that they will be able to answer more questions in a set time if they answer the easy ones first.

ESL Some of the suggestions in this chapter may be difficult for your ESL students to carry out. If some ESL students live in crowded conditions, they may find it difficult to locate a quiet study space. They may also have to work long hours after school or care for family members.

Try to compensate for these problems by giving students flexible assignment dates. Devote more time to in-class work and make sure that students are aware of study areas in local public libraries.

NSD To make the language of research assignments and test questions more familiar to NSD students, give them extra practice in reading directions. Make doubly sure that students are aware of the meanings of words commonly used in test questions (*discuss, compare, describe, summarize,* and so on).

Part 1

Objective

To understand assignments and to record them in an assignment notebook

Presenting the Lesson

1. Read aloud and discuss **Here's the Idea.** Poll the class to see how many students use an assignment notebook. Ask students to get an assignment notebook or to set aside a section of a class notebook for assignments.

2. Discuss **Check It Out.**

3. Assign and discuss **Try Your Skill.**

4. Read **Keep This In Mind.** Ask the students to write the following four questions in the front of their assignment notebooks. These are questions that they should ask themselves each time that they are given an assignment. 1. What kind of assignment is it? 2. What is the final product? 3. What supplies do I need? 4. When is the assignment due?

5. Assign **Now Write.**

Individualizing the Lesson

Less-Advanced Students

Before assigning **Now Write,** draw a sample assignment notebook sheet on the board. Practice with several assignments such as the following, asking for volunteers.

a. Read Chapter 14 of your U.S. history text. Write out the answers to the even-numbered study questions. The papers are due tomorrow.

Part 1

The First Step

Understanding the Assignment

Here's the Idea Your schoolwork presents you with many challenges. You can meet these challenges if you learn good study and research skills. These skills will help you to learn your lessons well and prepare good papers and projects.

The first step in learning to do good schoolwork is understanding the assignments you are given. Whenever you are given an assignment, write it down immediately. Use a special section of your notebook or a separate assignment book. First write the subject. Then write exactly what you are supposed to do. Finally, write the date the assignment is given. Also write the date it is due. Here is an example.

Subject	Assignment	Date Given	Date Due
English	Memorize myths pp. 22-24	10-8	10-11
Math	Review Chapter 8. Do exercises pp. 182-183	10-8	10-9
Science	Read Chapter 5 pp. 80-95	10-8	10-12

Before working on the assignment, ask some questions.

1. **What kind of assignment is it?** Will you have to read, study, memorize, write, answer questions or build?
2. **What should the final product be?** Will it be a composition, answers to exercises, a skit, a lab report, or a speech?
3. **What will I need?** Will you have to look at certain books in the library? Will you need any special supplies?
4. **When is the assignment due?** How many days will you have to finish the assignment?

Check It Out Read the following sample English assignment.

> Collect at least five magazine advertisements that include famous people. Paste the ads in your notebook. The notebooks will be due on Friday.

- What two things does the assignment ask you to do?
- What will the final product be?
- What will you need to complete the assignment?
- When is the assignment due?

Try Your Skill Read the sample math assignment below. What type of assignment is it? What will the final product be? What special supplies will you need?

> By Thursday, read the chapter on measurements in your math book. Then measure any two rooms in your house. Use both yards and meters. Write these measurements down in your notebook.

Keep This in Mind

- When you are given an assignment, be sure you understand what kind of assignment it is. Know what the final product should be. Know what supplies you may need. Also know when the assignment is due.
- Enter the details and due dates of your assignments in an assignment notebook.

Now Write On your paper, draw a page from an assignment book like the one on page 214. Make four columns. Title the columns *Subject, Assignment, Date Given,* and *Date Due*. Look at the two assignments presented in **Check It Out** and **Try Your Skill.** Enter them in your "assignment notebook." Save your work in your folder.

b. Collect fifteen different kinds of leaves. Bring them to biology class on Friday for identification.

Advanced Students

As a continuation of **Now Write,** have each student make up three assignments for various subjects. Ask students to trade papers and write the assignments on their **Now Write** papers. Remind them to ask for clarification if any important information is missing or if they do not understand the assignment.

Optional Practice

Ask students to apply the points from **Keep This in Mind** to these assignments and to find out what information is lacking.

a. Read the article "Interest Rates" and write a one-paragraph summary of it.

b. Find some poems. We will discuss them in class tomorrow.

Extending the Lesson

Require students to use an assignment notebook for class. Check it periodically.

Part 2

Objective

To follow spoken and written directions carefully

Presenting the Lesson

1. Read aloud and discuss **Here's the Idea.** Apply the guidelines for "Listening to Spoken Directions" to this sample set of directions: "Read page 47 of your science book and then answer study question number 5 for tomorrow." Have students jot down the assignment as you speak. Check their notes for accuracy. Then discuss the steps in the assignment and the key words in each step.

2. Discuss **Check It Out.**

3. Assign and discuss **Try Your Skill.** Point out that not reading all of the directions thoroughly before beginning an assignment may mean doing unnecessary work.

4. Assign **Now Write.**

Individualizing the Lesson

Less-Advanced Students

1. Make copies of simple sets of directions (i.e., recipes, board games, etc.). Ask students to underline the key words in the directions.

2. Scramble the order of the steps in a recipe or some other set of instructions. Ask students to put the steps in the proper order.

Advanced Students

Ask each student to write a set of directions for a simple task like putting air in a tire, sewing a button on a

Part 2

Stop, Look, and Listen

Following Directions

Here's the Idea Knowing how to follow directions is important whether you are traveling to a new city, learning to work a computer, or doing your homework. In order to understand an assignment completely, you must learn to follow directions carefully. Directions may be spoken or written.

These guidelines will help you follow *spoken* directions:

Listening to Spoken Directions

1. Pay careful attention to what is being said.
2. Notice how many steps there are in the directions. Also notice the order in which the steps should be completed.
3. Listen for the key word in each step, such as *read, answer, write, organize,* or *memorize*.
4. Ask your teacher to explain any step you do not understand.
5. Write down the directions as you hear them.

These guidelines will help you to follow *written* directions:

Reading Written Directions

1. Read *all* of the directions carefully before you begin the assignment.
2. Ask your teacher questions if there is any part of the assignment that you do not understand.
3. Assemble the books and other materials that you will need before you begin.
4. Break down the assignment into steps. Organize these steps in the order that you will complete them.

Check It Out Read the directions for this sample assignment.

Choose a city in another state or country that you would like to visit. Find a picture of something in that city. Get the pictures from a magazine, or copy a picture out of a book. List three reasons why you would like to visit this city.

- Do you understand exactly what you will need to hand in? Do you know what form the project should be in? If not, what questions could you ask to make these directions clearer?
- How would you break down this assignment into steps?

Try Your Skill Read and follow this set of directions.

1. Write five words that describe your personality.
2. List three things about yourself that you would like to change.
3. Remember that you should be reading all of the directions completely before beginning. Now ignore directions 1 and 2. Copy the "Reading Written Directions" chart on a piece of paper.

Save your work in your folder.

Keep This in Mind

- Read or listen to *all* of the directions before you begin working.
- Ask questions if there is any part of the directions that you do not understand.

Now Write Follow this three-step direction:

On a piece of paper first draw a circle. Then draw a square inside the circle. Finally draw a triangle on top of the circle.

Now, make up your own three-part direction about drawing simple shapes. Be prepared to read your directions to your classmates. See how well they follow your directions.

shirt, etc. Discuss the directions in class. Refer to **Keep This in Mind** on page 217.

Optional Practice

1. Make up the assignments for an entire week. Read them aloud to the class and ask students to take notes. See how accurately they listen to and record the directions.

2. Bring a set of Tinker Toys to class. Divide the class into small groups. Have each group first make a simple construction and then list directions on how to construct it. Trade directions and see if the other groups can rebuild the construction from the directions.

Extending the Lesson

Have students bring to class various types of directions. Some suggestions are exercise and fitness guides, household repair books, craft books, board games, etc. Discuss the examples in class. Are they easy to follow? Are the steps in logical order? What are the key words?

217

Part 3

Objective

To know what makes a good study space

Presenting the Lesson

1. Read aloud and discuss **Here's the Idea.** Emphasize the importance of the "Requirements for a Good Study Space."

2. Read and discuss **Check It Out.**

3. Assign and discuss **Try Your Skill.**

4. Assign **Now Write.**

Individualizing the Lesson

Less-Advanced Students

1. Divide students into groups. Help each group plan and present a skit that shows a specific study problem.

2. Work individually with students who cannot apply the suggestions in the lesson because of unusual home situations. Urge students to develop the habit of regular library study.

Advanced Students

Have students write "Dear Abby" letters describing real or fictional study problems. Let the class play Abby and solve the problems in discussion.

Optional Practice

Do a practice exercise on concentrating. Give each student a brief poem. Keep the classroom distraction-free. Allow ten or fifteen minutes and ask students to memorize the poem.

Part 3

Your Own Space

A Time and a Place To Work

Here's the Idea You plant a vegetable garden in a sunny spot during the spring. You play football in an open field when there's enough light for you to see the ball. Studying also requires a special place and time.

At home you can put a table or a desk in your room or some other quiet place. At school you would use the library or a study hall. At the public library you can usually find a table in a quiet corner. No matter where you find your study space, you should be sure that it meets the following requirements.

Requirements for a Good Study Space

1. **It should be quiet.** You should not be disturbed by TV, radio, the telephone, or other noises.
2. **It should be well lit.** Poor lighting can strain your eyes and give you headaches.
3. **It should be neat and well-organized.** You should not have to search for books, papers, or other materials.
4. **It should be properly equipped.** You should always have a supply of paper, pens, and pencils handy. Your study space should also have a dictionary.

Check It Out Here are six possible study spaces.

1. A desk in a bedroom. There is also a shelf for books and a drawer for pencils, paper, and other study tools.
2. The student cafeteria during lunchtime.
3. A table in the dining room after dinner. Your books and study tools are neatly arranged on this table.
4. The living room floor in front of the television set.
5. A table or desk in the library. The table has enough space for your books and materials.
6. Your bed. The radio is on nearby to relax you.

- Which of these spaces would be good places for studying? Which would not be good places? Explain why you think so.

Try Your Skill Rate the place where you study by answering the following questions.

1. Do you sit at a table or a desk?
2. Is the light good for studying?
3. What noises can you usually hear?
4. Are your books and supplies neatly organized?
5. Do you have all of the books and other study tools that you need?

Compare your answers to the requirements for a good study space that are listed on the previous page. Rate your place of study as:

A. Excellent (needs no improvement)
B. Fair (needs some improvement)
C. Poor (needs much improvement)

Keep This in Mind

- A study area should be a quiet, well-lit, and neat place.
- A study area should always have paper, pens, pencils, and a dictionary.
- Establish a regular time each day to study.

Now Write On a clean piece of notebook paper, list four places in your home, in school, or at the public library that are good for studying. Also list the times that these places are available and convenient for you. Then, describe a study place that you think would be ideal. Save your paper in your folder.

Extending the Lesson

Have students make a checklist of requirements for a good study space. Refer to page 218 for "Requirements for a Good Study Space" and to the questions in **Try Your Skill** on page 219. Make copies. Then divide students into groups and send them to evaluate each study area in the school. After each area is rated, have students draft suggestions for improvements, if necessary.

219

Part 4

Objective

To know how to develop a study plan

Presenting the Lesson

1. Read aloud and discuss **Here's the Idea.** Emphasize the distinction between short- and long-term goals.

2. Discuss **Check It Out.**

3. Assign and discuss **Try Your Skill.**

4. Assign **Now Write.** Refer to **Keep This in Mind** on page 221.

Individualizing the Lesson

Less-Advanced Students

1. Before assigning **Try Your Skill,** break down the following long-term goal on the board.

> In a notebook, make a collection of dried flowers and leaves. Label as many of these as you can.

2. Allow students to work in pairs or small groups to complete **Try Your Skill** and **Now Write.**

Advanced Students

Have students write an actual study plan for themselves for the next week.

Optional Practice

Break down these long-term goals into short-term goals.

a. Draw a map of Africa. Label each country with its main agricultural products, industries, imports, and exports.

b. Make an insect collection of at least 25 insects. Mount them in a display box and identify them.

Part 4

Touchdown!

Achieving Goals with a Study Plan

Here's the Idea If you plan your time carefully you will be able to complete all of your school assignments by their due dates. The best way to plan your time well is to set long-term and short-term goals.

At the end of each day see which assignments are due the next day. These assignments are your **short-term goals.** You should set aside some time every day to complete these assignments.

The assignments that will take longer than one day to complete are your **long-term goals.** Break these assignments down into shorter tasks. Then decide which task needs to be done first, which should be done second, and so on.

Suppose you have to write a report about panda bears. You might break up this long-term goal into the following tasks:

1. Go to the library and find two books.
2. Read the sections on panda bears in these books.
3. Take notes on the important information.
4. Organize the notes into an outline.
5. Write the first draft.
6. Revise the first draft.
7. Make a final copy.

Now you need to develop a study plan. A **study plan** is a schedule of all of your daily activities. It includes your social activities, as well as your school activities and homework. A study plan helps you to schedule your long- and short-term goals around your other daily plans. Make a study plan whenever you have a long-term goal to complete.

Check It Out Notice how the research report about panda bears has been scheduled in this study plan.

Monday	Tuesday	Wednesday	Thursday	Friday	Saturday	Sunday
Library	Research pandas Guitar lesson	Outline report Swim practice	Write first draft	Dinner, Aunt Nancy's	Revise draft Swim meet	Make final copy of report
Panda report due	Read history chap. 5	Review history chapter	History test Council meeting	Free	Movie with Kevin	Review math problems

- Do you see how the work on this report has been scheduled so that it can be completed on time?
- Did you notice that the student realized there were some nights no work could be done?

Try Your Skill Break up the following long-term goal into several tasks. Arrange them in the order they need to be done.

Make a notebook that tells about five Greek or Roman myths. Find a book on these myths in the library. Read it and select five myths. Then write your version of the five myths, including a picture for each.

Keep This in Mind

- Set aside a daily block of time for completing short-term goals.
- Break down all long-term goals into small tasks. Then put those tasks in a logical order.
- Make a study plan to schedule your study time.

Now Write Make a two-week study plan like the one on this page. Show your regular activities. Break down the following assignment into several tasks. Fit them into your schedule. The assignment is to write a paragraph that describes a person from history. Pretend that this was assigned Monday, and is due Friday. Save your work in your folder.

Extending the Lesson

Distribute copies of the calendar page for the month to students. Tell them to keep them in their assignment notebooks to use for making study plans. Continue this practice monthly if it helps students to get organized.

Part 5

Objective

To understand and use the SQ3R study system

Presenting the Lesson

1. Read aloud and discuss **Here's the Idea.** Write SQ3R and the words the abbreviation stands for on the board. Emphasize that reading comprehension is improved when there is a purpose for reading. By making a list of questions to answer, the reader has a purpose.

2. Discuss **Check It Out.**

3. Assign and discuss **Try Your Skill.**

4. Assign **Now Write.**

Individualizing the Lesson

Less-Advanced Students

1. Using students' social studies or science texts, practice turning titles into questions.

2. Allow students to work in pairs on **Try Your Skill.**

Advanced Students

Either copy an article or assign a chapter from the students' social studies or science text. Ask students to read the material using the SQ3R study method. Discuss the questions they formulate and their answers.

Optional Practice

Bring a collection of newspaper articles to class. Give one to each student. Ask students to read the articles using the SQ3R study

Part 5

Five Steps

A Way To Study

Here's the Idea Most of your assignments include reading and studying. You can learn to study more effectively if you use a regular study method. One such method is called **SQ3R**. SQ3R stands for the five steps that make up this study method. The five steps are **s**urvey, **q**uestion, **r**ead, **r**ecite, and **r**eview.

SQ3R	
Survey	Look over the material to get a general idea of what it is about. Read the titles, the subtitles, the introduction, and the summary. Look at any illustrations.
Question	Make a list of questions that you should be able to answer at the end of your reading. These include any questions provided by your teacher or given at the end of the chapter. You can also turn titles, topic sentences, and illustrations into questions.
Read	Identify the main ideas in each section that you read. Try to find the answers to the questions you wrote.
Recite	Recite your answers to the questions. Write brief notes to help you remember these answers. Also take notes on other important ideas.
Review	Quickly read over your notes to review the main ideas of what you read.

Check It Out Look at the questions that follow these titles.

"Five Steps: A Way to Study"
—What are the five steps?

"Learning to Follow Directions"
—How can I learn to follow directions?

"Croc's and 'Gators: Two Dangerous Reptiles"
—What is dangerous about crocodiles and alligators?

- Do you see how titles can be turned into questions?

Try Your Skill Apply the SQ3R method to the following passage on alligators and crocodiles. Write and answer the questions you think up. Make notes about any other important information.

Croc's and 'Gators: Two Dangerous Reptiles

Alligators and crocodiles are both ugly and dangerous. Crocodiles are more likely to kill humans than are alligators. However, alligators will attack when cornered. Both types of reptiles and their related species are the last living link to the prehistoric dinosaur-like reptiles.

Physical Differences Crocodiles have narrower heads and sharper snouts than alligators. They have two teeth which are always visible. Alligators' teeth cannot be seen when their mouths are closed.

Geographic Differences Crocodiles are found near swamps, rivers, and lakes in Africa, Asia, Australia, Madagascar, and the Americas. Alligators are found in the southeastern United States and in the Yangtze River region of China. Alligators prefer to live near fresh water.

Keep This in Mind

- The five steps of the SQ3R method are **s**urvey, **q**uestion, **r**ead, **r**ecite, and **r**eview.
- Use the SQ3R method to study for all your classes.

Now Write Apply the SQ3R method to the next lesson, **Get It Down.** Write your questions, answers, and notes on notebook paper. Save your work in your folder.

method. Have each student discuss the questions he or she formulated before reading and then discuss the main ideas of what was read.

Extending the Lesson

1. Introduce the SQ3R study method to your colleagues if they are not already familiar with it. Ask that they encourage their students to use it when reading material for their classes.

2. Have students make posters explaining the SQ3R study method. Place one in every classroom and study hall in the school.

Part 6

Objective

To take clear and effective notes from a talk or from a written work

Presenting the Lesson

1. Ask students to review their **Now Write** papers from Part 5. Ask for a volunteer to summarize the main ideas from this section.

2. Read aloud and discuss **Here's the Idea.** See how well each student took notes on this section for **Now Write,** Part 5.

3. Discuss **Check It Out.** Write a sample set of notes on the board.

4. Assign and discuss **Try Your Skill.**

5. Read **Keep This in Mind** aloud and then assign **Now Write.**

Individualizing the Lesson

Less-Advanced Students

1. Allow students to work in pairs to complete **Try Your Skill.**

2. Read a simple paragraph or give a mini-lecture to students. Ask them to take notes. Check the notes in class.

Advanced Students

1. Have students read a chapter in their social studies or science book and take notes on it. Compare students' notes and discuss them in class.

2. Make a tape of a famous speech or of a recent speech given by a politician. Play it for students and ask them to take notes on it. Discuss their notes.

Part 6

Get It Down

Taking Notes

Here's the Idea Your schoolwork presents you with much new information. One way to learn this information is to take notes. Notes help you to understand what you read and hear. They help you to locate the main ideas in the material. The notes you take can also become a good study guide for later review.

Keep your notes in a notebook. This notebook should be divided into sections for each subject. Write the date and the subject at the top of each page of notes. A good notebook will include the main ideas covered in class. It will also include the notes and questions that you write when you read your textbooks.

When you take notes while someone is talking, you should listen for clues that can tell you what information is important. These clues include phrases like "The main point is . . . ," "Most importantly . . . ," and "To summarize. . . ." Write this important information in your notebook.

When you take notes as you read, you should include all the main ideas, key words, and definitions that you come across. Also, write down the answers to any questions that you think of while you read.

The notes you take do not have to be complete sentences. That would take too much time. Instead, write phrases and key words that will help you remember the main ideas. Use abbreviations whenever you can. You might want to circle or put a star next to the most important information in your notes. Be sure you write your notes neatly and clearly. That way you will have no trouble reading them when it's time to review.

Check It Out Notice the important ideas in this passage on myth.

Myths are legends that explain things about people and nature. The characters in myths are usually gods and goddesses with special powers. Sometimes they look like humans; sometimes they take the shape of animals. However, they all show human emotions, such as love, hate, and jealousy.

- If you were to take notes on this paragraph, what important ideas would you include?

Try Your Skill Take notes on the following paragraph. Compare your notes with those of your classmates.

There are two basic types of myths. **Creation myths** tell about the beginning of the world and how the different creatures first came to be. **Explanatory myths** try to tell *why* certain things exist or how they began.

Keep This in Mind

- Notes can help you to study and remember information.
- Write your notes in phrases, not sentences.
- Use abbreviations to save time and space.
- Only take notes on the most important facts and ideas.

Now Write Look through an encyclopedia in your school library. Select a one- or two-paragraph passage on a subject that interests you. Take notes on this passage. Follow the suggestions in this lesson for taking good notes. Save your notes in your folder.

Optional Practice

1. Repeat **Try Your Skill** on page 225 with this paragraph.

Stalactites and stalagmites are easy to tell apart, and their names are easy to remember; a stalactite—the one that contains the letter *c* —clings tightly to the *c*-eiling; a stalagmite—the one that contains the letter *g*—grows from the *g*-round. Both of these words come from the Greek language and mean 'oozing out in drops' and 'dripping.' That is exactly what stalactites and stalagmites are—drops and drips.

-Elizabeth Hamilton

2. Repeat **Try Your Skill** with **Here's the Idea** from Part 1 of "Using the Library" (page 204).

Extending the Lesson

Assign either oral or written research reports. After students select a topic, they are to refer to three sources for information. They should have a set of notes for each source. These are to be turned in either with a written report or after an oral report is given.

Part 7

Objective

To use graphic aids to understand information

Presenting the Lesson

1. Read aloud and discuss **Here's the Idea.** Write the types of graphic aids discussed on the chalkboard. Then ask students where they have encountered these kinds of graphic aids.

2. Discuss **Check It Out.**

3. Assign and discuss **Try Your Skill.**

4. Assign **Now Write.** Point out that the graph in **Check It Out** is a bar graph.

Individualizing the Lesson

Less-Advanced Students

Divide the class into five groups, one for each type of graphic aid. Give the groups old magazines and newspapers. Ask each group to find examples of one type of graphic aid. Then have them make a poster displaying the best examples of their type of graphic aid. Hang the posters in the classroom.

Advanced Students

Ask students to make graphic aids to illustrate the following sets of facts.

a. School enrollment figures: 1969, 1,200 students; 1974, 1,000 students; 1978, 800 students; 1982, 700 students

b. Percentage of girls and boys enrolled in gymnastics: girls, 65%; boys, 35%

Part 7

Get the Picture

Using Graphic Aids

Here's the Idea Some of the information you learn in school is presented in words. Other information is presented through illustrations, maps, diagrams, photographs, and tables. These **graphic aids** present information clearly and quickly.

Photographs and illustrations can often show ideas better than words can. Read the captions that appear with these pictures. The captions may contain important information.

Diagrams help you to identify parts of an object. They may also show you how each part is related to the other parts.

Maps are drawings of areas of land and water. A map can give many facts about an area. A map might tell about population or annual rainfall. It could also tell about the height of mountains or the depth of lakes and oceans.

Tables and charts present groups of facts. The information in a table or chart is usually set up in columns.

Graphs are special charts that show how one fact is related to another. To understand a graph, you must first read the title. Next read the key to any symbols in the graph. Finally, read the information inside and along the sides of the graph.

Check It Out Study these graphic aids. Then ask yourself these questions.

- Which graphic aid is an illustration? a diagram? a map? a table? a graph?
- What is the metal part of a saddle called?
- Which Indian tribe lived in Alberta?
- During which year were the *least* gold records awarded to albums? To singles?

Homelands of Indian Tribes

Tribe	Homeland
Apache	Arizona, New Mexico
Blackfoot	Montana, Alberta, Saskatchewan
Cherokee	Georgia, North Carolina, South Carolina
Navaho	Arizona, New Mexico
Potawatomi	Illinois, Michigan, Wisconsin

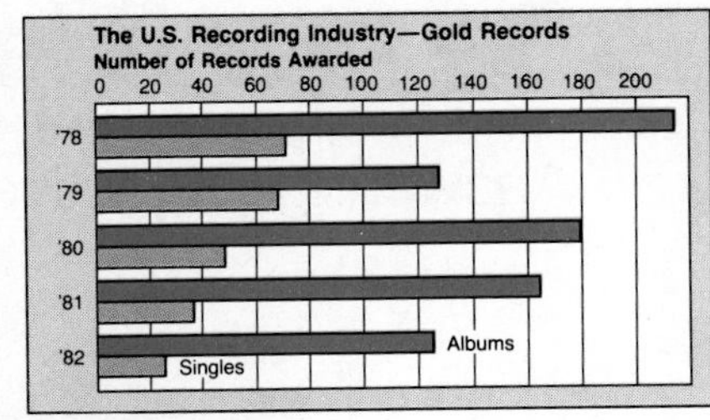

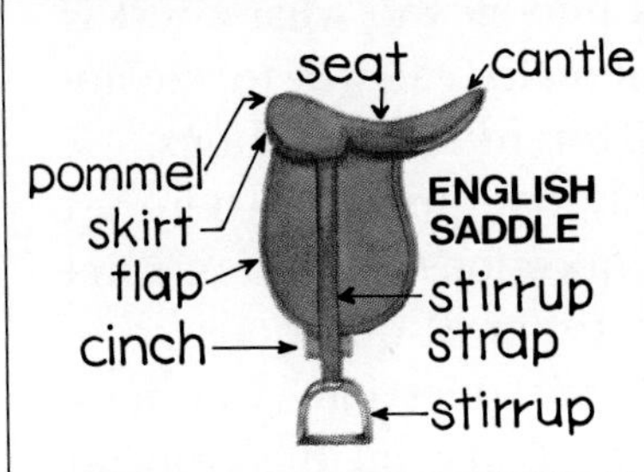

Try Your Skill What type of graphic aid would you use to present each type of information listed below? Choose from diagram, map, chart and table, graph, and photograph.

1. The location of the five time zones
2. How to assemble a model airplane
3. How a cumulus cloud differs from a cirrus cloud
4. Attendance at seven football games

Keep This in Mind

- Graphic aids can present information clearly.
- Read the title, abbreviations, and explanations accompanying a graphic aid.

Now Write Draw a bar graph that displays these facts about the percentage of people who speak different languages around the world: Indo-European, 48%; Siro-Tibetan, 23%; Black African, 7%; Japanese and Korean, 4%. Save your graph.

c. The controls on a television set and how they are turned or pushed

d. Directions from your school to another school

Optional Practice

Make copies of graphic aids found in students' social studies textbooks. Using an opaque or an overhead projector, discuss them with the class.

Extending the Lesson

Coordinate a report with either students' science or social studies teachers. Require that the report include several graphic aids. Grade the report for organization, mechanics, and the use of graphic aids. Then have each student make a corrected copy of his report and submit it to the science or social studies teacher for a grade on the content of the report.

Part 8

Objective

To know how to answer objective test questions

Presenting the Lesson

1. Read aloud and discuss **Here's the Idea.** Point out that the time element is important when taking tests. Remind students to skip questions that are too difficult, and to return to them after completing the rest of the test. Also discuss the fact that sometimes separate answer sheets are used. Show students a sample answer sheet. Discuss the importance of marking the answers in the proper places.

2. Discuss **Check It Out.** Mention that sometimes matching tests have extra items in Column B.

3. Assign and discuss **Try Your Skill.**

4. Read **Keep This in Mind** aloud and then assign **Now Write.**

Individualizing the Lesson

Less-Advanced Students

If your school gets copies of weekly reading magazines, borrow a set. Read one of the articles to the class and then assign the objective comprehension questions. Repeat with several other articles. Discuss the types of questions used.

If your school does not get a reading magazine, read a brief story or article to the class. Then give students an objective test on the content.

Part 8

Be Confident!

Answering Objective Test Questions

Here's the Idea The better you understand what a test is, the easier it will be for you to do well on it. One way to become more confident is to learn about different test questions.

Objective test questions have only one answer. There are three main types of objective test questions. Here are some guidelines to help you answer these types of questions.

Multiple Choice In a multiple choice question, you must choose the best possible answer out of several that you are given. Be sure to read all of the choices before you decide which one is the best answer.

Which of the following cities is *not* one of the ten windiest cities in the United States?
(A) Omaha (B) Chicago (C) Buffalo (D) Boston (E) Dallas

True-False This kind of test question asks you to decide whether a statement is *true* or *false*. Words like "always," "never," "all," or "none" often make a statement false.

The Taj Mahal was ordered built by an
Indian ruler as a final resting place for his wife. T

Matching In a matching question, you are given two lists. You must match items in one list to similar items from the other list. Match those items that you are sure of first. That will make it easier for you to match the items you are unsure of.

Match column A to column B.

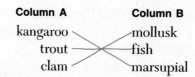

Column A	Column B
kangaroo	mollusk
trout	fish
clam	marsupial

Check It Out See how the following questions are answered.

1. True-False questions are always true. ___F___
2. Multiple Choice questions always have:
   (A) one answer that sounds almost right
   (B) one best answer
   (C) all correct answers
3. Match the tests in column A with their types of answers in column B.

A.	B.
matching	a circled or written letter
true-false	a line leading to its match
multiple choice	T or F

- Do you see how different types of questions require different types of answers?

Try Your Skill Read an encyclopedia article on a subject that interests you. Use it to make up two examples of each of the following types of questions: true-false and multiple choice. Include the answer to each question.

Keep This in Mind

- Taking tests will be easier if you learn how to recognize and answer different kinds of questions.
- Always read a test question completely before answering it.

Now Write Write an objective test that asks questions about your school. Write three true-false questions and three multiple choice questions. Write a matching question with a list of four academic subjects in one column and four humorous descriptions of the subjects in a second column. Exchange tests with a classmate. See how well you can answer the questions.

Advanced Students

Prepare an objective test on language arts material that students have already studied. (Include all three types of test questions discussed.) Set a time limit and have a separate answer sheet. Administer the test and then discuss the results as a review.

Optional Practice

Repeat the **Try Your Skill** exercise, but have students make separate answer keys. Use the new tests either for individual or for group practice.

Extending the Lesson

Divide the class into small groups. Have each group write an objective test for one of the chapters in the language arts book. Instruct the groups to make separate answer keys. Either make a class file or make individual copies of the chapter tests for each student. These can be used for chapter reviews.

Part 9

Objective

To know how to answer test questions that require written answers

Presenting the Lesson

1. Read aloud and discuss **Here's the Idea.** Write the three types of written test questions on the board.

2. Discuss **Check It Out.** Stress that answers to a written test question must follow the rules of good grammar, capitalization, punctuation, and spelling.

3. Assign and discuss **Try Your Skill.**

4. Read **Keep This in Mind** aloud and then assign **Now Write.**

Individualizing the Lesson

Less-Advanced Students

For **Try Your Skill,** reduce the number of questions of each type to one.

Advanced Students

For **Try Your Skill,** increase the number of questions to be written. Also ask for essay questions.

Optional Practice

Collect samples of old tests requiring written answers from your files and from other teachers in the school. Using an opaque projector, show them to the class. Discuss the kinds of questions asked and how to answer them.

Part 9

Write It Right

Answering Written Test Questions

Here's the Idea Some test questions require written answers. Study these examples.

Completion or **Fill-in-the-Blank** For this kind of test question, you add the correct word or phrase to an incomplete sentence. If the word or phrase comes at the end of the sentence, add the correct punctuation. If it comes at the beginning of the sentence, capitalize the first letter.

Short Answer A short answer test question asks you to write a one- or two-sentence answer. Answer the questions in complete sentences. Capitalize and punctuate correctly.

Essay An essay test question requires you to write an answer of one or more paragraphs. Before you write, do some prewriting. Find out what the question asks. Words such as "explain" or "describe" are clues. List and organize your ideas on scratch paper. Be sure each paragraph has a good topic sentence.

Check It Out See how these questions are answered.

1. The earliest examples of cave art have been found in *France.*.

2. What are the two most heavily populated cities in the world?

The two most heavily populated cities in the world are Tokyo and Mexico City.

3. Explain why water is important to the human body.

Water is necessary to the human body. Over fifty percent of all body cells are water. Water dissolves vitamins and carries them throughout the body. Water helps control body temperature.

- Do you see how each of these types of questions should be answered?

Try Your Skill Read an encyclopedia article on a subject that interests you. Use it to make up two examples of completion questions and two examples of short-answer questions. Write the answer to each question. Use the proper form.

Keep This in Mind

- A completion question asks for a word or phrase.
- A short-answer question asks for one or two sentences.
- An essay question asks for one or more paragraphs.

Now Write Answer the following essay test question:

Describe three study and research skills you have learned. Explain why each one is important.

Use correct composition skills in your answer. Capitalize and punctuate correctly. Save your essay in your folder.

Extending the Lesson

Ask each student to select a chapter from his or her science or social studies book and to write three essay questions to accompany the chapter. Duplicate the questions and make an essay test question file. For practice, ask each student to select a question and answer it.

Section 20 Objectives

1. To know the five main parts of a friendly letter

2. To use the correct form for preparing and addressing an envelope

3. To know the purposes of and formats for invitations and thank-you notes

4. To know and use the correct form and content for a business letter

5. To know the purpose and the form of a letter of request

6. To know guidelines for filling out forms completely and correctly

Preparing the Students

Discuss briefly the types of things communicated through letters—for example, friendly greetings, complaints about products, opinions expressed in letters to an editor, and requests for tickets or free samples. Explain that because letters have different purposes, they require different forms, which is the subject of the following lessons.

Additional Resources

Mastery Test — pages 27–28 in the test booklet

Practice Book — pages 95–100

Duplicating Masters — 95–100

Letters and Forms

Part 1 **Hi There!**
How To Write a Friendly Letter

Part 2 **A Good Send-off**
How To Prepare Letters for the Mail

Part 3 **Thank You**
How To Write Social Notes

Part 4 **Get Down to Business**
How To Write a Business Letter

Part 5 **Please Send Me**
How To Write a Letter of Request

Part 6 **Fill It Up**
Filling Out Forms

Teaching Special Populations

LD Whenever possible, supplement instructions with demonstrations of how to write and prepare letters for mailing. You may want to amend or simplify some instructions. For example, in Part 6, tell students to first write answers on a separate piece of paper then copy the information onto the form.

ESL Conventions governing letters differ from society to society. For instance, many cultures do not use the block and modified block form of American business letters. They may also have different conventions for spacing addresses or writing dates, numerals, and salutations. The terse tone of business letters in the U.S. would be considered very rude by some cultures, as would the comparative informality of address in American friendly letters. Discuss such differences in class, and have ESL students read their letters to partners who are native English speakers.

NSD Use this section to help your NSD students practice using standard English. Stress that slang and other forms of nonstandard usage are particularly inappropriate in business letters. Have students write a variety of letters, making sure they use standard English.

Part 1

Objective

To know the five main parts of a friendly letter

Presenting the Lesson

1. Read aloud and discuss **Here's the Idea.** As each part is described, point it out in the sample letter in **Check It Out.** Highlight punctuation and capitalization.

2. Assign and discuss **Try Your Skill.**

3. Assign **Now Write.** Remind students to follow the model presented in **Check It Out.**

Individualizing the Lesson

Less-Advanced Students

Review the capitalization and punctuation rules that apply to letters. Then have students rewrite the following letter parts in the correct form using the correct capitalization and punctuation.

a. 756 broadway avenue glendale utah 84047 april 5 1985

b. dear margaret

c. sincerely yours steve

d. 14 state street chicago illinois 60100 june 8 1985

e. your friend jim

f. dear mr. alvarez

Advanced Students

Have students rewrite the following friendly letter using the correct form. Remind students to indent paragraphs and to use correct capitalization and punctuation.

1411 elm street villa grove illinois 61956 march 15 1985 dear joan Thank you for your letter. I really enjoyed

Hi There!

How To Write a Friendly Letter

Here's the Idea A **friendly letter** is a letter that you write to someone you know. It should be interesting, neat, and easy to read. A friendly letter should seem as natural as a conversation. Share your feelings. Ask questions. Talk about subjects that interest you. Keep your language lively and specific.

A friendly letter has five main parts: the *heading*, the *salutation* or greeting, the *body* or main part, the *closing*, and the *signature*.

The **heading** appears in the upper right corner of the page. It includes your address and the date.

The **salutation** is the part of the letter where you say "hello." In a friendly letter, the salutation might say "Dear Alec" or "Hi Juan." The salutation begins with a capital letter and is followed by a comma.

The **body,** the main part of the letter, starts on the next line. In the body of the letter you talk to your friend. If the letter is lively, it will make your friend feel as though you were there in person. The first word of the body is indented. Each new paragraph of the body is indented, too.

The **closing** says "goodbye." In a friendly letter the closing might say "Your friend" or "Best wishes." It is written on the line below the last sentence of the body. The closing begins with a capital letter and is followed by a comma.

The **signature** is the last part of your letter. Skip a line after the closing and write your name in line with the first word of the closing. When you are writing a friendly letter to someone you know well, use your first name as your signature. Otherwise, sign your full name.

Check It Out Read the friendly letter below.

- What details make this letter interesting?
- Identify the five parts of this letter. Notice when each part appears in the letter.

361 Newton Road
New York, New York 10001
March 11, 1985

Hi Juan,

It sure was good to hear from you. I'm glad to hear you are doing so well in math this year. After the trouble you had with it last year, I'm sure you must be feeling relieved.

School has been hard for me this year. I have five main subjects, including French.

One bright spot has been the school paper. I have been doing drawings for it this year and am really enjoying it. Who knows, maybe next year I'll have my own comic strip. Keep in touch, and let me know when you're coming to New York again. I'll throw a big party for you when you visit!

Your friend,
Marty

hearing about your trip to California. The school year is going well for me. I enjoy all of my classes, but my favorite is science. We are going to dissect a frog next week. I have been keeping busy after school, too. I am on the soccer team, and we have practice three afternoons a week. So far our team is undefeated. Write me soon. I want to hear about your school activities. your friend lauren

Optional Practice

1. Have students rewrite these return addresses using the correct form.

a. 2100 s. holland avenue san mateo california 94002 march 19 1985

b. 1792 waunatta drive orlando florida 32789 july 20 1985

c. 5050 wright terrace skokie illinois 60077 november 5 1985

2. Ask students to jot down notes on what they have done in the last week or so. Have them use the notes to write a letter to a friend.

Extending the Lesson

Write students' names on separate slips of paper. Have each student draw a name and write a friendly letter to that person. When the person "receives" the letter, he or she should write and "send" an answer in reply.

Try Your Skill Here's a friendly letter that has some problems. Read the letter and decide what's wrong with it. Compare the form of this letter with the letter on page 235. Write a few sentences explaining what should be changed.

27 Whitcomb Street
Price, Utah 84501
January 5, 1985

dear Ronnie,

Happy New Year. I miss you. I hope you can make it out here this year. School is OK. Not much news to tell. I just wanted to say hello.

Sincerely, Gerry

Keep This in Mind

- Friendly letters should be lively and neat.
- Friendly letters should follow the correct form. The heading, salutation, body, closing, and signature should each be written correctly.

Now Write Write **Hi There!** at the top of your paper. Then write a friendly letter to a friend or relative. Be sure you use correct form. Save your letter in your folder.

236

A Good Send-off

How To Prepare Letters for the Mail

Here's the Idea Once you've written your letter, fold it neatly. Use an envelope that matches the width of your letter. Carefully insert the letter into the envelope. Seal the envelope.

Follow these steps for preparing your envelope:

1. Address the envelope. Add your return address.
2. Double-check all numbers to make sure they are in the proper order.
3. Include the correct five-number ZIP code. If you do not know the correct ZIP code, look it up in your telephone directory or call your local post office.
4. Put a stamp on your envelope.

Addressing the envelope accurately will get your letter to the right place. Get in the habit of checking your letters and packages for accuracy. Call your local post office if you need more information.

Check It Out Look at the envelope below.

Ms. Gwen Linehan
1607 Stratford Street
Big Sky, MT 59716

Dr. Samuel Collins
147 Barnes Road
Farwell, NE 68838

Part 2

Objective

To use the correct form for preparing and addressing an envelope

Presenting the Lesson

1. Read aloud and discuss **Here's the Idea.** Demonstrate the correct way to fold a letter.

2. Discuss the sample envelope in **Check It Out.** Emphasize completeness in both the mailing address and return address.

3. Assign **Try Your Skill.** Remind students to capitalize and punctuate the addresses correctly.

4. Assign **Now Write.** Provide business-size envelopes.

Individualizing the Lesson

Less-Advanced Students

1. Do the first item of **Try Your Skill** together. Write it on the chalkboard or use an overhead projector.

2. Have students fold an 8½ × 11 inch piece of blank paper into thirds horizontally. Each third will represent an envelope. Have them write their home address as the return address on the first one, the school address in the second one, and a classmate's address in the third. Then have them address these "envelopes" to different people.

Advanced Students

Have students address envelopes to three family members or friends. They should use their own addresses for return addresses. Then show students where they can find ZIP code information in the local telephone directory.

Optional Practice

Follow the instructions for **Try Your Skill** on page 238.

a. Debby Russell, P.O. Box 1268, Vail CO 81657
b. Mr. and Mrs. Martin Klein, 73 River Drive, Glenview IL 60025
c. Ray Stone, 1213 Gilmore Street, Long Beach, CA 90815
d. Betsy Benson, 203 Charter Road, Austin, TX 78712
e. Mr. Howard Holmgren, 17 Skyline Drive, Tampa, FL 33603

Extending the Lesson

1. Procure a complete list of the two-letter state abbreviations used by the post office. Make a copy for each student to keep in his or her usual letter-writing place.

2. Arrange a tour of the local post office so the class can see how letters are processed. Emphasis should be on the difference between the processing of letters that are addressed correctly and the processing of those that are not.

- To whom is the letter being sent? Who sent the letter?
- How could you check to be sure that the state abbreviations and ZIP codes are correct?

Try Your Skill Write each of the addresses below as it should appear on an envelope. Also write a return address.

1. Kate Lawrence, 24 Hampton Road, New Orleans, LA 70118
2. Mr. and Mrs. Peter Donovan, 7318 Skyline Drive, Washington, D.C. 20008
3. Anthony Colelli, 4325 Broadway Boulevard, Apartment 2-C, Oakland, CA 94602
4. Martha Woodworth, 7 Churchill Lane, Durham, NH 03824
5. James O'Shea, 281 Chestnut Street, Phoenix, Arizona 85040

Keep This in Mind

- Prepare your letter correctly. Fold your letter neatly, and use an envelope that matches the width of the letter
- Check addresses for neatness and accuracy. Check abbreviations of states and correct ZIP codes.
- Put your return address on the envelope.

Now Write Take out the friendly letter you wrote in the last lesson, **Hi There!**

On another piece of paper, write the title of this lesson, **A Good Send-off.** Draw a rectangle to represent an envelope. Address it as though you were going to mail it to your friend.

Copy your work onto a real envelope. Fold your letter and put it into the envelope. Put a stamp on the envelope.

Mail your letter. Save your sample envelope in your folder.

Thank You

How To Write Social Notes

Here's the Idea Invitations and thank-you notes are both short forms of friendly letters. They use the same five parts. The heading may be shortened to include only the date.

An **invitation** should include all the information that the other person needs. Tell what kind of occasion you are inviting him or her to. Tell where and when it will take place. Sometimes you wish to know whether or not the person will attend. Then write *R.S.V.P.* at the bottom of the invitation. *R.S.V.P.* is an abbreviation for a French phrase that means "please reply."

Whenever you receive an invitation, answer as soon as possible. Thank the person for inviting you. Then tell the person whether or not you can accept the invitation. If you can't accept it, express your regrets and give a short explanation.

There are two kinds of **thank-you** notes. One kind of thank-you note is usually written after you have received a present. If a gift was mailed to you, the thank-you note tells the sender that the gift arrived. It also thanks the person for being kind. If you liked the gift, say so. If you didn't like it, you can still thank the sender for her or his thoughtfulness and effort.

Another kind of thank-you note is called a **bread-and-butter** note. This kind of letter thanks someone for his or her hospitality. You would write a bread-and-butter note after you stayed overnight at someone's house.

Both kinds of thank-you letters should show your appreciation for what another person has done for you. Also, both kinds of letters should be written as soon as possible after you receive a gift or someone's hospitality.

Part 3

Objective

To know the purposes of and the formats for invitations and thank-you notes

Presenting the Lesson

1. Read aloud and discuss **Here's the Idea.** Emphasize the differences in content among the three types of social notes described.

2. Read and discuss the thank-you note in **Check It Out.**

3. Assign and discuss **Try Your Skill.** When students have mastered the form of the thank-you note, assign **Now Write.**

Individualizing the Lesson

Less-Advanced Students

Use an overhead or an opaque projector and show students examples of invitations, reply notes, and thank-you notes. Ask students to identify each type of social note. Point out the format for each. Emphasize that the important aspect of an invitation is including the *what, when* and *where*. For thank-you notes, the important element is showing appreciation.

Advanced Students

1. Have each student write an invitation to a barbeque at his or her house starting at noon on the Fourth of July. Discuss the invitations in class.

2. Have the students select one of the following situations or think of one on their own and write an appropriate thank-you note.

a. Write to your pen-pal overseas, and thank him or her for an unusual gift.

b. You are president of a local fan-club. Write and thank your favorite rock star for sending you an autographed T-shirt.

Optional Practice

1. Have students write an invitation to a party that they would like to host. Then have students exchange invitations and write notes of reply.

2. Write the names of gifts on pieces of paper. Give a "gift" to each student. Have students write thank-you notes to you.

3. Ask each student to imagine that a friend has thrown a surprise party for him or her. Have each student write a thank-you note to that friend.

Extending the Lesson

As a class, decide on a project or activity that might be shared with another class. Suggest as possibilities an interesting bulletin board or display, a play the students have prepared, or an exhibit of student writing. Decide on time and place. Then direct each student to write an invitation to a member of the other class.

Check It Out Read the social note below.

February 8, 1985

Dear Mr. and Mrs. Cullen,

You were very nice to let me spend last weekend with you. I want you to know how much I appreciate it. I had never been on roller skates before, and that by itself was a great treat.

I hope you get the chance to visit me in Jonesboro sometime. Then your family can stay here, and I can return the hospitality. Thanks for everything.

Sincerely,
Hank Reidell

- What type of social note is this? How is the form of this letter different from the friendly letter shown in **Hi There!** in this section?
- What words and phrases are used to express appreciation in this letter?

Try Your Skill Read the thank-you note on the next page. Then rewrite it, correcting any errors that you find.

Dear Ms. Bert,

Thanks for the sweater. It is not really my favorite color, but it's a nice sweater. I guess you didn't know that I don't like blue. Hope everyone is fine at your house.

Robin

Keep This in Mind

- Social notes include invitations and thank-you notes. They are short forms of friendly letters. They have a heading, a salutation, a body, a closing, and a signature, in that order.
- An invitation should tell *what, when,* and *where.*
- Thank-you notes thank people for the thoughtfulness of their gifts and their hospitality.

Now Write Label your paper **Thank You.** Imagine that one of your relatives has sent you a pair of purple sneakers for your birthday. Another has sent you a book by your favorite author. Write a short thank-you note to each relative.

Save your thank-you notes in your folder.

241

Part 4

Objective

To know and use the correct form and content for a business letter

Presenting the Lesson

1. Read **Here's the Idea.** Use the letter in **Check It Out** to illustrate modified block form. Show students an example of block form.

2. Assign and discuss **Try Your Skill.** Note the brevity and directness of the body content.

3. Assign **Now Write.** Remind students that block form is used for typewritten letters only.

Individualizing the Lesson

Less-Advanced Students

Ask students to rewrite these inside addresses correctly.

a. Ms. Myra Berkley 25 York Road Elmhurst Illinois 60126

b. The Computer Store 1900 Webster Boulevard St. Louis Missouri 63140

c. Alumni Association Emerson Building Partridge College Dubuque Iowa 52001

Advanced Students

Have students rewrite this business letter in modified block form. Remind them to indent new paragraphs and to use proper capitalization and punctuation.

[illegible]025 downey avenue monterrey california 93940 april 3 1985 mr. jack emmert goldtree realty company 1715 clark street aptos california 95003 dear mr. emmert I am a student at Monterrey Junior High School. The school is sponsoring a career day on

Part 4

Get Down to Business

How To Write a Business Letter

Here's the Idea Many times you will need to write a letter asking for information, ordering a product, or complaining about a product. Such letters are called **business letters.**

Business letters may be written in *modified block form* or *block form.* In the modified block form, the paragraphs are indented, and the closing and signature are in line with the heading, just as in a friendly letter. This form may be used for both handwritten and typed business letters.

The *block* form for a business letter is used only when the letter is typewritten. All the parts of the letter begin at the left margin. The paragraphs are not indented. Instead, there is a double space between paragraphs.

Both forms of a business letter include an inside address. An **inside address** is the name and address of the business or person you are writing to. The inside address is placed above the salutation. It begins at the left margin. If you are writing to a specific person, use *Dear* and the person's name in the salutation. Otherwise, use a general greeting, such as *Dear Sir or Madam.* All salutations begin two lines after the inside address and end with a colon (:).

Always be brief and to the point in a business letter. It's a good idea to make a copy of a business letter for your records. If you make a copy, mail the original.

Check It Out Look at the business letter on page 243.

- What is the purpose of this business letter?
- Identify the six parts of the letter.
- Is this letter written in block form or modified block form?

39 Hastings Street
Dodge City, Kansas 67801
February 5, 1985

Sales Manager
Old West Nostalgia Shop
4736 Madison Street
Elko, Nevada 89801

Dear Madam or Sir:

My hobby is collecting items related to the American West. My favorite hero is Wild Bill Hickok, who, like me, spent most of his life in Kansas.

Please send me the catalog of your collection called "Heroes of the West." I am enclosing $2.95 for the catalog, plus $1.00 postage.

Yours truly,
Mary Lou Taylor

May 15 of this year. We are inviting local businesspeople to discuss their jobs with the students. We would be honored if you could attend and explain various careers in real estate. Please inform me of your decision at your earliest convenience. I am looking forward to hearing from you. Respectfully Douglas Chandler

Optional Practice

1. Give each student one of the yellow pages from an old phone book. Ask students to use addresses from the pages to write the beginnings of three business letters, including a heading, an inside address, and a salutation for each. Remind them to use the modified block form.

2. Have students write to the sales manager of an imaginary company asking for the latest catalog. Let students choose either block or modified block style.

Extending the Lesson

Get a copy of a catalog of U.S. Government publications. Select several free items and list them on the chalkboard. Direct each student to choose one publication and to write a letter requesting that it be sent to him or her. Encourage students to prepare envelopes and to mail their letters.

Try Your Skill Below are the six parts of a business letter. On your paper, write them in the correct modified block form. Use the correct punctuation.

Heading

14 Boundbrook Road
Nutley, New Jersey 07110
March 13, 1985

Signature

Thomas Presti

Body

Please send me two dozen personalized pencils. Use my full name on each. Enclosed is my check for $6.50 to cover the cost of the pencils, handling, and postage.

Closing

Yours truly

Salutation

Dear Sir or Madam

Inside Address

Sales Manager
Conway Stationery Company
2149 Northern Avenue
East Orange, New Jersey 07019

Keep This in Mind

- Business letters are written to request information, order products, or complain about products. They should be brief and to the point.
- The six parts of a business letter are the *heading*, the *inside address*, the *salutation*, the *body*, the *closing*, and the *signature*.
- *Block* and *modified block* are two forms for a business letter.

Now Write On your paper, write the title of this lesson, **Get Down to Business.** Choose a company in your city or town. Imagine that you are going to write a business letter to that company. Write the heading and the inside address for such a letter. Be sure to use the proper form. Save your work.

244

Please Send Me

How To Write a Letter of Request

Here's the Idea One type of business letter requests information. It should be brief and to the point. The more specific your request is, the easier it will be for the reader to reply. Be sure to include all the necessary information.

Explain *what.* Ask only for the information you need. If you want a timetable for flights between Chicago and Houston, name the two cities. If you also want a list of fares, don't forget to say so.

Explain *when*. If you plan to fly to Houston on June 19, say so.

Explain *why*. Sometimes you may want to tell briefly why you are writing. You might say "I am writing a report on weather forecasting. I need some information from your company to make my report complete."

Always be polite and appreciative. Remember that you are asking someone for help.

Check It Out Read the letter of request on page 246. Then answer these questions.

- Is this letter of request brief and polite?
- Is all the necessary information requested? Does it explain *what, when,* and *why*?

Try Your Skill On page 247 is a letter of request. It has some problems. First, read the letter carefully. Then rewrite the letter. Use the correct form. Be brief, specific, and polite.

Part 5

Objective

To know the purpose and form of a letter of request

Presenting the Lesson

1. Read aloud and discuss **Here's the Idea.** Emphasize that the request should specify *what, when,* and sometimes *why*.
2. Discuss the sample letter in **Check It Out.** Note the business letter format. Discuss which parts express *what, when,* and *why*.
3. Assign and discuss **Try Your Skill.** Remind students to capitalize and punctuate the six parts of the letter correctly.
4. Assign **Now Write.** Allow class time to discuss the replies, if any.

Individualizing the Lesson

Less-Advanced Students

Before assigning **Try Your Skill,** compose a letter of request with students and write it on the board. Select one of the topics from the exercise for advanced students.

Advanced Students

Have students write a letter of request for one of the following items. Remind them to use proper business letter form.

a. Request information about vacation spots in Michigan from the Michigan Travel Bureau, P.O. Box 30226, Lansing, Michigan 48909.
b. Request a catalog from the U.S. Cavalry Store, Inc., 1375 North Wilson Road, Radcliff, Kentucky 40160. The cost for the catalog is $3.00.

c. Request a free catalog of recorded books from Books on Tape, Box 7900, Newport Beach, California 92660.

d. Order a sample issue of *CATS* Magazine. The cost is $1.75. The address is *CATS* Magazine, Department 80, P.O. Box 83048, Lincoln, Nebraska 68501

Optional Practice

Have students look through the advertisements in a magazine and write a letter requesting more information about a particular product. They should invent any details necessary to complete the six parts of the letter.

Extending the Lesson

Choose several local landmarks or companies that students might enjoy visiting. Have them write to the places, asking for information about organized tours or arrangements that can be made. Remind them to keep the key questions *what? when?* and *why?* in mind.

76 Linden Lane
Kankakee, Illinois 60901
April 14, 1985

Midwest Airways
188 Lake Towers
Chicago, Illinois 60607

Dear Sir or Madam:

Please send me your June 1985 timetable for flights between Chicago, Illinois, and Houston, Texas. I also need a listing of all available rates.

My local travel agency has run out of timetables. They suggested that I contact you directly.

Thank you for your help.

Yours truly,
Sarah Kaplan

Keep This in Mind

- Business letters of request should be brief, specific, and polite.
- Ask only for the information you need. Include *what, when,* and *why.*

Sales Manager
Kelly Flagpole Company
Morristown, New Jersey
07960

13 Ross Way
Prospect, Kentucky 40059
June 25, 1985

Dear Sir,

Well, we finally did it. We bought a flag that's too big for our pole. Now we need a new pole.

A guy at my V.F.W. post told me you sell aluminum and wooden poles. He said your prices were higher than your poles. How much would a thirty-foot pole cost?

If I ordered it right away, when could you guarantee delivery? I'll need it by the Fourth.

I'll expect your answer in three days at the latest, as I don't have much time to waste.

Edgar T. Welsh

Now Write On your paper, write the title of this lesson, **Please Send Me.** Write a letter to your local representative in Congress. Ask your representative to explain how he or she feels about an issue that is important to you. You may also want to ask how he or she voted on key issues. Address an envelope for your letter and mail it. Save your reply in your folder.

247

Part 6

Objective

To know guidelines for filling out forms completely and correctly

Presenting the Lesson

1. Read aloud and discuss **Here's the Idea.** Stress the importance of being prepared before filling out a form. For example, often job applications ask for the names and addresses of references. Also point out that, in addition to completing forms, other documents may be needed to complete an application. For example, a library may require something showing proof of residency. In order to get a social security number you must show a birth certificate. It is wise to ask ahead of time if there is any special information or documentation needed before going to fill out forms.

2. Discuss **Check It Out.** Point out the specific instructions to print. Also point out the areas that are not to be filled in.

3. Assign **Try Your Skill.**

4. Assign **Now Write.**

Individualizing the Lesson

Less-Advanced Students

Make copies of several rebate offers, offers for premiums, or contest applications printed by manufacturers. (The coupon rack in the supermarket is a good source for these.) Fill in the first form together. Have students complete the additional forms independently.

Part 6

Fill It Up

Filling Out Forms

Here's the Idea Learning to fill out a form correctly is an important skill. You will be filling out many different forms during your life. For example, you need to fill out a form to get a library card or a social security number. You need a filled out form to go on a school field trip. Study the following guidelines. They will help you to fill out forms correctly.

1. Skim the form. Look it over quickly to learn what kind of information is needed. The form might ask for information that you won't know and will have to find. For instance, a bicycle registration form might ask for the serial number of your bike. It will be helpful for you to have this information on hand before you begin filling out the form.

2. Read the directions carefully. Look for important guidelines. For instance, you may be asked to give your last name first on the form. Or the form may request that you print rather than write.

3. Be sure you have the right kind of writing tool. Most forms request pen and ink. Other forms, however, may require a pencil. Occasionally, you may be asked to type the requested information.

4. Fill out the form line by line. This way, you will be sure that you have completed every item on the form.

5. Proofread the completed form. Have all of the lines been filled in? Is all of the information correct? Are all of the words spelled correctly?

Check It Out Examine this bicycle registration form.

- Have all the directions been followed?
- Have items on the form been answered completely?
- Has the form been filled in carefully and neatly?

VILLAGE OF SCHAUMBURG, IL **No.** ______ (Do not write in this space)

POLICE 555-3586

PERMANENT BICYCLE REGISTRATION

(Please print)

FEE $.25 **Serial No.** JM389170-5

Licensee Vasquez (Last name) Carmen (First name) A. (Middle initial)

Address 1407 W. Rose Court, 31044

School Sally Ride Elementary

Phone 914-0273 **Age** 12

Make Schwinn Sportabout

Special Markings: Blue with silver lettering

Signature X Carmen Vazquez

For Police use only. Do not write below this line.

Date Issued ______ **Issued By** ______

Try Your Skill Copy the form in **Check It Out.** Fill it out as if it were a real form.

Keep This in Mind

- Skim the form before you fill it out. Know what information is needed.
- Read all instructions carefully. Use the correct writing tools. Proofread the completed form.

Now Write Get an application form for a library card. Complete this form using the guidelines in this lesson.

Advanced Students

Reproduce a sample job application and have students fill it out.

Optional Practice

Collect a variety of application forms that students will eventually be exposed to (social security application, bank account application, driver's license application, health insurance forms, life insurance application, credit card application, income tax forms, leases, etc.). Use an opaque projector and study them with the class. For additional practice, make copies of some of the forms and have students fill them out.

Extending the Lesson

Ask students to gather and list personal information (date and place of birth, chronological list of schools attended and dates of attendance, hobbies, social activities, physician's name and phone number, brief health history) often required on forms. Have students keep the list for their own use.

Section 21 Objectives

1. To differentiate between a formal talk and an informal talk

2. To know how to prepare for an informal talk

3. To know how to prepare for a formal talk

4. To know how to deliver a talk successfully

5. To practice a talk before presenting it to an audience

6. To know how to be a good listener

7. To know the guidelines for judging the content and the presentation of a talk

Preparing the Students

Explain that speaking to an audience does not come naturally to most people. Also, many people do not know how to be good listeners. This section will instruct students how to prepare for both informal and formal talks. It will also help them to present their talks well. Finally, it will explain the importance of being attentive listeners.

Additional Resources

Mastery Test — page 29 in the test booklet

Practice Book — pages 101–107

Duplicating Masters — pages 101–107

Giving a Talk

Part 1 **Hear Ye! Hear Ye!**
Formal and Informal Talks

Part 2 **Explain Yourself**
Planning an Informal Talk

Part 3 **Be Prepared**
Preparing a Formal Talk

Part 4 **It's How You Say It**
Making a Good Impression

Part 5 **Dress Rehearsal**
Practicing a Talk

Part 6 **Attention!**
Learning To Listen

Part 7 **The Verdict, Please**
Judging a Talk

Teaching Special Populations

LD Some students with emotional problems, speech problems, or behavioral problems, will not be able to cope with the demands of making speeches. Do not force these students to participate. Modify, shorten, or omit parts of this section in accordance with each student's disability.

ESL Public speaking will help ESL students practice syntax and pronunciation. However, they may also be very self-conscious about making mistakes. Start by having these students address a group of their ESL classmates. When their confidence develops they can speak in front of the whole class.

Work individually with students when they are preparing their talks. Though you should not expect perfect grammar, usage, or pronunciation, you can help ESL students by concentrating on a few particular problems such as syntax and organization. Encourage students to widen the range of their vocabulary.

It often helps to have ESL students memorize and deliver a short passage from a work of literature or some other secondary source.

Remember that body language varies from society to society. Eye contact and certain gestures are considered rude in some cultures. Alert students to these differences. To make ESL students feel more at ease, ask them to speak on some unique apect of their indigenous cultures.

NSD Nonstandard dialect relies on nonstandard pronunciation. Have NSD students read to their peers daily, and point out to students any pronunciation mistakes.

Part 1

Objective

To differentiate between a formal talk and an informal talk

Presenting the Lesson

1. Read aloud and discuss **Check It Out.** Ask students to cite examples of formal talks that they have heard. Also ask for additional examples of the four types of informal talks.

2. Discuss **Check It Out.**

3. Assign and discuss **Try Your Skill.**

4. Read **Keep This in Mind** aloud. Then assign **Now Write.**

Individualizing the Lesson

Less-Advanced Students

Do the **Try Your Skill** exercise as a class. Also, help students get started on the **Now Write** exercise by giving them an example of a situation that might require a talk.

Advanced Students

If you have access to a videotape machine, have students prepare and perform examples of each type of informal talk. Tape the presentations and play the tape for the class. Discuss the talks. If you do not have a videotape recorder, either tape record the talks or have students present the talks directly to the class.

Optional Practice

Ask students to determine whether each topic is for a formal talk or an informal talk. Have them explain their choices.

Part 1

Hear Ye! Hear Ye!

Formal and Informal Talks

Here's the Idea Many people get nervous when they have to speak in front of others. Their hands get moist and their mouths go dry. Has this ever happened to you? The best way to overcome this nervousness is to learn good speaking skills.

There are two main types of talks. A **formal** talk covers a subject in some depth. It is usually fairly long. Most formal talks are written out before-hand. An oral report about the causes of the Revolutionary War would be a formal talk. So would a talk explaining why you want to run for a class office. You will learn more about formal talks later in this chapter.

An **informal talk** is much shorter than a formal speech. It is usually used to pass on information quickly. There are four main types of informal talks.

Informal Talks

Type of Talk	Purpose	Examples
Announcements	to tell what has happened or what will happen	telling about a meeting at school inviting people to a party
Directions	to tell how to do something or how to get somewhere	explaining to a friend how to get to the public library
Introductions	to introduce someone	introducing a speaker at the PTA
Demonstrations	to show how to do something	showing someone how to roller skate backwards

Check It Out Think about each of the following situations.

1. Carly's cousin Michele is coming to visit from another town. Carly has to tell Michele how to get to her house from the airport.
2. The Boy Scouts are having a pancake brunch. They want everyone in the neighborhood to find out about it.
3. Lena is walking with her grandmother when they meet Lena's math teacher.

- Which type of talk should be used in each situation?

Try Your Skill Which of these situations calls for a formal talk? Which calls for an informal talk? Write your answers.

1. Jessie was asked to give a ten-minute talk to her class. The talk would be about ways students can earn money. She planned to talk about babysitting, delivering newspapers, and doing yard work.
2. The student council from Jefferson Junior High wanted to cut down on bicycle accidents. The council invited one of the city's traffic officers to speak to the school at a special safety assembly.
3. The eighth grade class wanted to decorate a float for the Columbus Day parade. Mr. Pinsker, the art teacher, said he'd show them how.

Keep This in Mind

- A formal talk tells about a subject in some depth. It is usually long and may be written out.
- An informal talk is short. Informal talks include announcements, directions, introductions, and demonstrations.

Now Write Make a list of situations at school that might require a talk. Try to list at least five situations.

What type of talk would be best for each situation? Write your answers. If an informal talk is called for, tell which kind. Save your list in your folder.

1. Marnie must explain to the students in the Agriculture Club how to take a cutting from a plant.
2. Lionel must introduce the mayor, who is a guest speaker, to the student council.
3. Jackson must give a talk to his history class explaining the causes of the Civil War.
4. Sandy must give the details of a homecoming celebration over the public address system during homeroom period.
5. Betsy will report on trends in modern art to the art history club.

Extending the Lesson

Tape excerpts of formal and informal talks. Play them for students. Have them identify the excerpts as formal or informal talks. If a talk is informal, have students identify which kind of informal talk it is. (Suggestions for taping: a presidential address, a news bulletin, an introduction on a talk show, an editorial on a news show, a cooking demonstration, etc.)

Part 2

Objective

To know how to prepare for an informal talk

Presenting the Lesson

1. Read aloud and discuss **Here's the Idea.** Then write the four types of informal talks on the chalkboard. As a review, ask the students how they would prepare for each one.

2. Discuss **Check It Out.** Ask for a volunteer to prepare and make the announcement.

3. Assign and discuss **Try Your Skill.**

4. Assign **Now Write.**

Individualizing the Lesson

Less-Advanced Students

Before assigning **Try Your Skill,** work as a class and prepare a set of directions. Ask students to plan directions telling how to get from your classroom to the gym. Repeat the process with other places in school: the principal's office, the cafeteria, the library, etc.

Advanced Students

Give each of the students a road map of the United States. Have each student select two cities and then prepare a set of directions telling how to get from one city to the other. Allow students to present their talks. Have the audience check out the directions for accuracy on their maps.

Optional Practice

1. Have students prepare a simple demonstration on one topic.

Part 2

Explain Yourself

Planning an Informal Talk

Here's the Idea Informal talks are the most common type of talk. You make them every day, both in and out of school. An informal talk is short. However, you must still do some planning if you want it to turn out well.

Announcements. When you make an announcement, you must include *who, what, when, where,* and *why* in your talk. Perhaps you have to announce the next meeting of the ice-skating club. First, find out all the details. Then you might say, "Next Saturday, February 10, the Ice-Skating Club will meet at the Rainbow Ice Rink, 205 Salem Street. The time of the meeting is 1:00 p.m. The members will be treated to a demonstration by Olympic team member Marge Paxson."

Directions. When you give directions, you must give clear, specific information. If someone asks you how to get to the Rainbow Ice Rink for the meeting, first think through the directions. Then you might say, "Take Main Street north to Salem Street. Turn left and walk two blocks. The Rainbow Rink is on the right side of the street, next to the bank."

Introductions. Introductions must be polite and informative. The best way to introduce someone is to talk to that person first. Try to find out some interesting facts about him or her. Suppose that you have to introduce the special guest at the ice-skating club meeting. You talk with her and find out that she won her first figure-skating medal when she was thirteen. You could mention this in your introduction.

Demonstrations. When you give a demonstration, present the steps of the process one at a time. Figure out the steps before you give your talk. Make sure that you don't leave out important information. You may also need to find or to make some props. Suppose that you have been asked to demonstrate a figure eight at the Rainbow Rink. You would probably practice first and then plan what you will say. You might also want to make a diagram to help your audience understand what you are demonstrating.

Check It Out Read about the following situation.

The student council is trying to raise money to buy books for the junior high school. They decide to have a car wash. The cost will be one dollar per car. The members plan to wash the cars in the school's parking lot. The car wash will be held on Saturday afternoon, October 17, between one and four o'clock. The members announce the car wash at the next PTA meeting.

- What information should be included in the student council's announcement?

Try Your Skill Plan some directions telling how to get to school from your house. List the directions in step-by-step order. Make sure that you don't leave out any details. Have a friend or relative listen to your directions. Ask whether the information is clear and correct. Rework the directions if they are unclear or incomplete.

Keep This in Mind

- An informal talk requires some background work.
- Gather all of the information you need to make your talk clear and complete.

Now Write Choose a partner from your class. Get some background information about your partner. Put together an interesting introduction. Make some notes for the introduction. Then introduce your partner to the class. Keep your notes in your folder.

- how to play tic-tac-toe
- how to play paper, stone, scissors
- how to play hangman

2. Make a list of famous people. Instruct each student to select and do research on one of them and then to prepare an introduction. Have students "introduce" the celebrities in class. (Suggestions: Sandra Day O'Connor, Mother Teresa, Henry Kissinger, John Glenn, Jane Goodall, Sir Georg Solti, Sally Ride, Luciano Pavarotti, Beverly Sills, etc.)

Extending the Lesson

Have each student bring a game to class. Ask each student to read the directions to his or her game and then prepare a talk explaining how to play it. Have students present their talks in class.

Part 3

Objective

To know how to prepare for a formal talk

Presenting the Lesson

1. Read aloud and discuss **Here's the Idea.** Write the basic steps for preparing a formal talk on the chalkboard.

2. Discuss **Check It Out.**

3. Assign and discuss **Try Your Skill.**

4. Read **Keep This in Mind** aloud. Then assign **Now Write.**

Individualizing the Lesson

Less-Advanced Students

Have students do **Check It Out** with a partner. Have them discuss their choices with the whole class.

Advanced Students

Have students narrow each of these topics so that it would be suitable for a formal talk. Then have them write a title for each topic and state the purpose of the talk.

sports bicycles
snakes newspapers
food first aid
pets hobbies

Optional Practice

Have students write three specific topics for each of these general topics. The purpose of each should be different—one should inform, one should entertain, and one should persuade.

dogs cats cars exercise food

Part 3

Be Prepared

Preparing a Formal Talk

Here's the Idea If you have given a formal talk in class, you know that this kind of talk calls for a great deal of preparation.

Planning a formal talk is just like planning a composition. You follow the same pre-writing steps. Take the time to prepare properly. If you do, the content of your talk will be better. You will also feel more confident about what you have to say.

Steps for Preparing a Formal Talk

1. Choose an interesting topic. If the topic is interesting to you, it will be easier for you to make it interesting for your audience. Be sure the topic is not too broad or too narrow. You can't talk about the entire history of baseball in five minutes. However, you might be able to discuss some of the qualities that make a winning baseball team.

2. Know your audience. Whom will you be speaking to? How much does your audience know about your topic?

3. Decide on your purpose. What do you want the end result of your speech to be? Do you want your speech to inform, to entertain, or to persuade?

4. Gather your information. The information you need for your speech might come from your experience, or from talking with others. You can also find information by reading. Make sure the information you collect fits your topic, audience, and purpose. Write useful details and ideas on note cards.

5. Organize your information. Put the information on your note cards into a logical order. Choose an order that fits the content and purpose of your talk. Leave out any information that is not important to your main idea.

Check It Out Gary was gathering information for a talk about hurricanes. His main idea was how hurricanes are formed. He had only five minutes for his talk. His notes included this information:

hurricanes get started over oceans	hurricanes are violent tropical storms
water must be warm	clouds gather around an "eye"
air pressure must be low	
hurricanes are given names	

- Which notes will Gary need for his talk?
- Which notes are not important to Gary's main idea?

Try Your Skill Choose the topic that would make a good talk for each of the following audiences. Next to each choice, write why you chose that topic for that audience.

Audience	Topic
the Outdoors Club	raising healthy and happy pets
PTA	how to choose good hiking boots
dog owners	school fund-raising techniques

Keep This in Mind

- Plan a formal talk the same way you plan a composition.
- Decide on a topic, purpose and audience.
- Gather necessary information. Take notes.
- Organize your information.

Now Write Think about some topics that would be good for a formal talk. Choose the one you like the best. Gather the information you need to give an interesting talk. Write that information on note cards. Then arrange the information in a logical order. Save your organized notes in your folder.

Extending the Lesson

Prepare a selection of introductions taken from famous speeches. Sources include: *Classic Speeches: Words That Shook the World*, Richard Crosscup; *The World's Greatest Speeches*, Lewis Copeland; *American Public Addresses*, Albert Craig Baird; *Treasury of the World's Great Speeches*, Houston Peterson. Present the introductions to the class. Ask students to identify the purpose of each speech from its introduction.

Part 4

Objective

To know how to deliver a talk successfully

Presenting the Lesson

1. Read aloud and discuss **Here's the Idea.** Then you present a brief talk to the class and deliberately deliver it poorly. Mumble, don't look at the audience, stand stiffly, use a visual aid that the audience can't read, etc. Then ask the students to discuss how you could improve the delivery of your talk.

2. Discuss **Check It Out.**

3. Assign **Try Your Skill.**

4. Read **Keep This in Mind** aloud. Then assign **Now Write.**

Individualizing the Lesson

Less-Advanced Students

Gather a collection of short humorous poems (Ogden Nash, Shel Silverstein, etc.). Have each student select one, memorize it, and present it to the class. (Allow students to refer to a copy of the poem, if necessary.) Review the basics of a good delivery before beginning the presentations.

Advanced Students

To give students practice speaking before the class, have each of them select his or her favorite book and prepare a brief talk on it. Explain that the book talk should include the title and author of the book, what it is about, and why it is his or her favorite.

Part 4

It's How You Say It

Making a Good Impression

Here's the Idea "That was a terrific speech!" Have you ever said this? If so, try to remember what made the speech seem so good? Was it just the topic and the arrangement of ideas? Or was it also the *way* the speaker gave the talk?

Whenever you speak, you are not just presenting your ideas. You are also presenting yourself. How you look and how you sound are just as important as what you say. Remember each of the following points:

1. Be sure to look at your audience. This is called **eye contact**. Try to make your audience feel that you are talking to them, not *at* them. Keep your expression pleasant. If you are using notes, look at them only when necessary. Don't bury your face in them.
2. Your **posture** is also important. Don't slouch or let your head hang down. If you stand tall, you will look confident. However, don't stand stiffly. Take a deep breath and relax.
3. Use your **voice** well. The audience wants to hear what you are saying. Be sure your voice is not too loud or too soft. Don't mumble. Speak clearly and slowly. There is no need to rush.
4. Use **gestures** when you speak. Your face and hands can help emphasize important ideas. Smile when you say something funny. Point to stress a fact or detail. Don't fiddle with your hair or play with your notes as you talk. Keep your gestures natural. This will help you appear confident and relaxed.
5. If you use **visual aids** in your talk, use them well. For example, if you use a projector, be sure you know how to run it. If you use a poster, be sure that it is large enough so that everyone can read it.

Check It Out Read the following descriptions:

The announcer introduced Mr. Fred Martin, the candidate for city council. Mr. Martin got up to speak, holding his notes tightly. He looked at the ceiling. He started reading his speech. He talked quickly and softly. The audience grew restless.

Ms. Jackson was presenting the annual report to her company's board of directors. She stood up straight. She looked directly at her audience. She appeared confident. Her voice was clear and easy to understand. She used a large poster to illustrate her talk.

- What did Mr. Martin do wrong? How could he improve his talk?
- Do you think Ms. Jackson's talk was a success? Why?

Try Your Skill Think of something funny that happened to you lately. Tell a friend about it. As you speak, pretend you are giving an informal talk. Look your listener in the eye. Think about the way you are standing. Use natural gestures. Finally, concentrate on speaking slowly and clearly.

Keep This in Mind

- When you present a talk, look at your audience.
- Use good posture, but try to look relaxed.
- Speak slowly in a clear voice.
- Use natural gestures.

Now Write Look over the five guidelines to good speaking discussed in this chapter. Decide how well you could follow each set of guidelines. Do you use your voice well? Do you stand straight? Can you use natural gestures? Write down the areas in which you might need work. Save this list for use in the next part.

Optional Practice

Give students practice delivering brief talks. Have each student look up one of his or her heroes in an encyclopedia and organize a talk on this personality. Instruct students to select a purpose for their talk. For example, the purpose of the talk "Jane Goodall and the Chimpanzees" is probably to inform. However, "The Beatles, the Greatest Singing Group in the World" is probably to persuade.

Extending the Lesson

If possible, videotape a variety of people in formal speaking situations: a news anchor, a commentator, a citizen replying to an editorial, the principal addressing the P.T.A., the president speaking to the nation, etc. Discuss the delivery of each speaker. Use the points in **Here's the Idea** as a checklist.

Part 5

Objective

To practice a talk before presenting it to an audience

Presenting the Lesson

1. Read aloud and discuss **Here's the Idea.** Write the three guidelines for practicing a talk on the chalkboard.

2. Discuss **Check It Out.**

3. Assign and discuss **Try Your Skill.**

4. Assign **Now Speak.**

Individualizing the Lesson

Less-Advanced Students

Arrange to have students deliver their talks to you privately for practice. Make suggestions for improvements to students so that they can work on their talks before presenting them to the entire class.

Advanced Students

Videotape students' talks. Play them back to students and allow them to critique both the content and the delivery of their own speeches.

Optional Practice

Instruct students to write out their talks word-for-word before presenting them. Explain that although this step may not be necessary, it is a helpful one in preparing to present a talk. When their talks are written out, students can easily examine them and question the content just as they would for a composition. Is the

Part 5

Dress Rehearsal

Practicing a Talk

Here's the Idea Good speakers always practice their talks. This gives them a chance to polish their material. It also helps them become more familiar with it. You should allow time for practice, too. The better you know your speech, the more comfortable you will be with it.

Guidelines for Practicing a Talk

1. **Read through your notes several times**. This will help you see whether you have all the necessary information. It will also help you to see if your notes are organized properly. You want to be sure that your notes are a good guide for what you want to say.

   As you read your notes, you will also become more familiar with your talk. Then you won't have to depend on your note cards. Remember, you don't have to *memorize* your talk word for word. However, you shouldn't just read it, either.

2. **Practice your talk aloud a number of times**. First, practice your talk in front of a mirror. Notice your expression and the gestures you use. Check your posture. Do you look relaxed? Are your movements natural?

   Record your speech on a tape recorder, if you can. Does your voice sound pleasant? Do you sound interested in what you are saying? Try to improve the way you speak as you practice.

3. **Present your talk to family and friends**. Ask them about the way you look and sound. Ask them how you can improve your talk. Use their suggestions to make your talk better. Finally, practice your talk one last time.

Check It Out Read how this student prepares his talk.

Kim enjoys photography. He decided to give a talk on his hobby for an art project. After Kim gathered and organized his information, he read his notes several times. Then he read them out loud, practicing how he would say them. Next, Kim practiced his talk in front of a mirror. Finally he presented his talk to his parents. After listening to their comments, he decided he was ready to give his talk.

- Do you think Kim's talk will be a success? Why?

Try Your Skill Look over the guidelines for practicing a talk. Then write two more suggestions that would help a student to practice a talk. Discuss your suggestions with your classmates.

Keep This in Mind

- Practice your talk before you give it.
- Work to improve the content of your talk. Also work on the way you deliver it.

Now Speak Use the guidelines in this lesson to practice the talk you prepared in Part 3. When you feel confident, give your talk to the class.

introduction interesting? Are facts arranged logically? Are transitions used to help the listener follow along easily? Does the conclusion sum up the talk?

Once students have completed their revisions, have them read their talks aloud several times. Then have them practice the talks using only their notes, not the written scripts. Explain that although it is helpful to write out a talk word for word, a good speaker never reads his or her talk to the audience.

Extending the Lesson

Invite a member of the local Toastmaster's Club to speak to the students. Explain that it is an organization specifically designed to help adults overcome their fear of public speaking.

Part 6

Objective

To know how to be a good listener

Presenting the Lesson

1. Read aloud and discuss **Here's the Idea.** However, instead of having the students follow along in their texts, have them just listen to you read the section. Give them a purpose for listening. Tell them to listen for ways to be a good listener. Then, when you have finished, ask them to write down the "Guidelines for Good Listening." Also, comment on how well they, from a speaker's point of view, listened to you.

2. Discuss **Check It Out.**

3. Assign **Try Your Skill** when you present Part 7. Instruct the students to take notes. Explain that notes do not have to be extensive. They should be used to outline the general structure of a talk and to jog the listener's memory. Review **Get It Down,** pages 224–225 with the class.

4. Assign and discuss **Now Speak.**

Individualizing the Lesson

Less-Advanced Students

Give students practice sharpening their listening skills. Give them a brief talk, and then quiz them on the content. Repeat the procedure with other items—play a song, read a poem, or reread the school's daily announcements. After each, quiz students.

Advanced Students

Discuss how to take notes from a speaker. Explain that an outline form

Part 6

Attention!

Learning To Listen

Here's the Idea Knowing how to give a talk is an important skill. So is knowing how to listen to one. If you are a good listener, you will get more out of what you hear. You will be able to pick out important ideas and information.

Read the following guidelines. They can help you become a better listener.

Guidelines for Good Listening

1. Find a place where you can easily see and hear the speaker.
2. Give your complete attention to the speaker. Don't whisper to those around you or talk back to the speaker. Don't fidget or cause other distractions.
3. *Show* the speaker that you are listening. Look at the speaker. Keep an alert expression on your face. This will show that you are interested in what the speaker has to say. Take notes if you need to.
4. Listen for the speaker's main ideas. Try to pick out the important information the speaker has to give. Listen for key words and phrases like *first, next, for example, most importantly* and *let me point out*.

Check It Out Read how one class listens to a talk.

The school assembly had just let out. Mr. Garrett was upset with his class's behavior. He said that they were not good listeners.

"Some people slouched in their seats," he said. "Others booed and hissed when Ms. Lacey said something they didn't like.

"No one sat in the first two rows of seats. Some students were holding their own conversations during the entire talk. And why didn't anyone applaud when the talk was finished?"

- These students were not good listeners. What did they do wrong? What rules of good listening could they have used?

Try Your Skill As your teacher presents the next lesson, practice your listening skills. Give the teacher your complete attention. Show that you are listening and interested. Try to pick out the main ideas.

Keep This in Mind

- It is important to be a good listener.
- Give your full attention to whomever is speaking. Show that you are interested.
- Listen for the main idea.

Now Speak Look through the daily newspaper or a news magazine. Find an article you think would be interesting to your class. Read the article to your classmates. Ask them to list the main idea of the article. Have them tell you about the most important details. Were they good listeners? Try your own listening skills as you listen to other students' presentations.

is usually used because a listener cannot possibly write down every word a speaker says. Notes should include the main ideas and important details. Also stress the importance of reviewing notes after a speaker is finished. The notetaker can clarify or expand the notes while his or her memory is fresh.

Give students practice taking notes. Tape a speech and play if for students. Have them take notes. Replay the speech and have students check their notes against it.

Optional Practice

Videotape (or tape record) a news broadcast. Play it for students and instruct them to listen carefully. Discuss the main ideas presented in each news story.

Extending the Lesson

Discuss other situations where being a good listener is important: when receiving instructions, when talking to friends, when watching a movie, etc. Point out that courtesy is always part of being a good listener. The good listener is courteous both to the speaker and to the people around him or her.

Part 7

Objective

To know the guidelines for judging the content and the presentation of a talk

Presenting the Lesson

1. Read aloud and discuss **Here's the Idea.** Present a short talk to the class and then ask the students to evaluate it using the guidelines.

2. Discuss **Check It Out.**

3. Assign and discuss **Try Your Skill.**

4. Assign **Now Write.**

Individualizing the Lesson

Less-Advanced Students

Do the **Try Your Skill** exercise as a class.

Advanced Students

Instead of judging the presentation of one newscaster, have students judge and compare the performances of the major competing local or national newscasters. Discuss students' conclusions in class.

Optional Practice

Have students repeat their talks, incorporating any improvements they have made since the first presentation after Part 5. Make evaluation forms and have each student evaluate each speaker. Give each speaker the evaluation forms for his or her talk. Discuss the evaluations with each student individually.

Part 7

The Verdict, Please

Judging a Talk

Here's the Idea It is important to be polite when you are part of an audience. As a listener, you may be asked to judge the speaker's talk. To do this, you must listen to *what* is said. This is the **content.** You must also watch for *how* the ideas are said. This is the **presentation.** When you judge a talk, be fair to the speaker.

Guidelines for Judging a Talk

CONTENT

Topic:	Did the speaker make the main point of the speech clear?
Purpose:	What was the purpose of the speech? Was it to inform, to persuade, or to entertain? Did the speaker succeed in his or her purpose?
Development:	Was enough information presented about the subject? Was there any unnecessary information?
Organization:	Was the information well organized? Did the ideas flow logically?

PRESENTATION

Eye Contact:	Did the speaker look directly at the audience?
Posture:	Did the speaker stand up straight? Did he or she appear relaxed?
Voice:	Was the speaker's voice easy to hear?
Gestures:	Were the speaker's gestures natural?
Preparation:	Did the speaker know the talk well?

Check It Out Read about this student's talk.

LaDonna gave a talk in class about dolphins. Her purpose was to explain how intelligent dolphins are. First she explained how easily dolphins can be trained. Then she told about how dolphins talk to one another. Finally, she mentioned that scientists are trying to learn the dolphins' language so that people can talk to these amazing animals.

As LaDonna talked, she looked right at her audience. She looked at her note cards only a few times. She spoke slowly and clearly. She smiled when she told how some dolphins like to tease their trainers. LaDonna seemed to enjoy her speech as much as her audience did.

- LaDonna's teacher gave her an A in Content and an A in Presentation. What things did LaDonna do right?

Try Your Skill Judge the presentation of a television newscaster. Use the guidelines on the previous page. Write down the things the newscaster did right and the things he or she did wrong. Give the newscaster's presentation a grade: *good, fair,* or *needs improvement*.

Keep This in Mind

When you judge a talk, listen carefully to the content of the speech. Also notice the speaker's presentation.

Now Write Make out an evaluation form for judging a speaker. On the top half of your paper write *Content*. Then write the five categories listed in heavy type under *Content* on page 264. Draw a line and write *Presentation*. List the five categories shown under that heading on page 264. When you judge a talk, mark *Good, Fair,* or *Needs Work* next to each category. Save your evaluation form in your folder.

Extending the Lesson

Sponsor a speech contest with the student council or one of the clubs in the school. Select an appropriate topic and arrange for an appropriate prize (i.e., Topic: "The Importance of Sports Programs for Girls"; Prize: season tickets to the girls' basketball games). Have your class evaluate the speakers and select a winner using the "Guidelines for Judging a Talk."

31

Handbook

Section 1	Learning About Sentences	269
Section 2	Using Sentences Correctly	299
Section 3	Using Nouns	308
Section 4	Using Verbs	321
Section 5	Using Irregular Verbs	347
Section 6	Using Troublesome Verbs Correctly	370
Section 7	Using Pronouns	388
Section 8	Using Adjectives	406
Section 9	Using Adverbs	428
Section 10	Using Prepositions and Conjunctions	441
Section 11	Using the Parts of Speech	462
Section 12	Making Subjects and Verbs Agree	472
Section 13	Using Compound Sentences	487
Section 14	Diagraming the Sentence	500
Section 15	Capitalization	521
Section 16	Punctuation	541
Section 17	Spelling	567

A detailed Table of Contents for the Handbook appears in the front of this book.

Learning About Sentences

How would you invite a friend to a picnic? How would you identify yourself on the telephone? How would you ask for the shirt you want at a store?

Without thinking, you would put words together to make sentences. The clearest way to get your ideas across to someone else is to use sentences.

Section Objectives

1. To identify a sentence and to differentiate between fragments and sentences

2. To distinguish the four kinds of sentences—declarative, interrogative, imperative, and exclamatory—and to understand their purposes

3. To use proper end punctuation for the four kinds of sentences

4. To identify the two parts of the sentence: subject and predicate

5. To identify the simple predicate, or verb

6. To identify the simple subject, or subject of the verb

7. To identify the subject in unusual positions

8. To be aware of the understood subject in imperative sentences

9. To identify compound subjects

10. To identify compound predicates

Preparing the Students

Discuss the importance of communication in everyday life. Ask students to name both written and spoken situations where clear communication is necessary. Read page 269 and discuss the questions.

Additional Resources

Diagnostic Test — page 1 in the test booklet

Mastery Test — pages 31-34 in the test booklet

Additional Exercises — pages 291-297 in the student text

Practice Book — pages 111-121

Duplicating Masters — pages 111-121

Special Populations — See special section at the front of this Teacher's Edition.

Part 1

Objective

To identify a sentence and to differentiate between fragments and sentences

Presenting the Lesson

1. Read and discuss page 270. Ask students to define the word *fragment*. Point out that a fragment of any kind is always a piece or a part of something else. It is not whole or entire in itself. Relate the discussion to the words *complete* and *incomplete*. You may put the headings *Fragments* and *Complete Things* on the board and ask students to give examples. Have them complete the sentence

"A _____ is part of a _____"
to verify their examples.

Examples:

Fragments	*Complete Things*
nose	face
baseball player	team
fragment	sentence
brick	wall

2. Read and discuss page 271.

3. Assign and discuss Exercises A, B, and C on page 272. You may want to have students change the fragments in Exercise C to sentences.

Individualizing the Lesson

Less-Advanced Students

To illustrate the need for complete sentences, use a "Note in the Snow" exercise. Have each student write several one-sentence notes they might pass to a friend. Then tell them to pretend that the notes were dropped in the snow and partially

Part 1 What Is a Sentence?

Read the four groups of words below. Each group expresses a complete thought or idea. Each group of words is a sentence. Notice that each sentence begins with a capital letter.

1. Richard made a belt.
2. Greg is a goalie.
3. Laura was handed the trophy.
4. The gym class played volleyball.

A sentence is a group of words that expresses a complete thought.

Sentence Fragments

Read these groups of words. Can you tell whether each group is a sentence?

1. The girls went to the park.
2. Dominic and his brother.
3. Played in the snow.

Maybe you are not sure whether these groups of words are sentences. Here are two questions to help you decide whether a group of words is a sentence:

Who or what did something? Does the group of words tell who or what did something?

What happened? Does the group of words tell what happened?

If a group of words answers both of these questions, it expresses a complete thought. The group of words is a sentence.

If a group of words does not answer both questions, it does not express a complete thought. The group of words is a **fragment.**

Making Sure Sentences Are Complete

Now return to the three groups of words shown earlier and test them for complete thoughts.

Example 1 The girls went to the park

Who or what did something?	What happened?
The girls	went to the park.

This group of words answers both questions. You know, then, that it is a sentence. It expresses a complete thought.

Example 2 Dominic and his brother

Who or what did something?	What happened?
Dominic and his brother	

Does this group of words answer both questions? No, it does not. You can see that it is not a sentence. It is a fragment. It tells only part of a thought. You can add words to this fragment to make a whole sentence.

Who or what did something?	What happened?
Dominic and his brother	planted a garden.

Example 3 Played in the snow

Who or what did something?	What happened?
	Played in the snow

Does this group of words answer both questions? No, it does not. Like Example 2, it is not a sentence. It is a fragment. You can also add words to this fragment to make a sentence.

Who or what did something?	What happened?
The black kitten	played in the snow.

destroyed. Students should rewrite the sentences as fragments, leaving out essential information. Examples: "Meet me in the gym." becomes "Meet me in" or "Jack really likes Jenny" becomes "Jack really likes . . ." After reading the notes aloud, the group should discuss the frustration that resulted.

Advanced Students

Have the students write as many different completions for the fragments in Exercises A and B, on page 272, as they can. Encourage them to be original but logical.

Optional Practice

Put the following list on the board, or make up a worksheet. Instruct the students to identify each item as a sentence or a fragment.

F 1. The newspaper reporter
S 2. It is raining
F 3. The lamp on the wooden table
F 4. Jumped over the hurdle
S 5. This picture needs a frame
F 6. Tomatoes, onions and cheese
S 7. My birthday is next Tuesday
F 8. Rabbits in their cages
F 9. The large oak tree near our front porch
S 10. Mandy winked at me
F 11. Peeled and cut the apples
S 12. The ducks swam slowly
F 13. Spilled apple juice on the floor
S 14. The baby cried
S 15. A fragment is not a sentence

Extending the Lesson

Put each of the following fragments on a separate index card. Tell the class they are going to play "Who Dunit?", combining fragments to make complete sentences. (This can be done as teams.) Point out that while several combinations may work, ie. "The sleeping cat . . . flashed on and off," only one will make good sense.

A. the clever detective
1. was taking careful notes
B. the angry cook
2. said dinner was getting cold
C. the confused artist
3. looked for his paint brushes
D. the smoke from the fireplace
4. smelled of pine logs
E. the light in the dining room
5. flashed on and off
F. Tina, the sleeping cat,
6. woke up and licked her paws
G. Butch, the huge dog,
7. started barking at the moon
H. the phone on the mantle
8. began to ring loudly
I. the large picture window
9. suddenly crashed into pieces
J. the nervous butler
10. nearly dropped his tray
K. the old mansion
11. had over twenty rooms
L. the silent maid
12. never said a word
M. the nearsighted writer
13. sat cleaning his glasses
N. Robbo, the clown,
14. kept making silly jokes
O. the little girl
15. just hugged her doll

Exercises **Write complete sentences.**

A. For each group of words you must answer the question *What happened?* to make a complete sentence. Write the whole sentence. There are many possible correct answers.
Answers will vary.

1. The boy with the camera
2. An angry dog
3. My two sisters
4. The TV show
5. Most birds

B. For each group of words you must answer the question *Who or what did something?* to make a complete sentence. Write the whole sentence. There are many possible correct answers. Answers will vary.

1. talked on the phone
2. made a spinach salad
3. found an old coin
4. likes football
5. played in the band

C. Number your paper from 1 to 10. Write *Sentence* after each number that stands before a sentence. Write *Fragment* after each number that stands before a fragment.

S 1. We built a bookshelf
F 2. The lifeguard
F 3. An anthill in the yard
S 4. Our class planned a field trip
F 5. Carved the turkey
F 6. Rides a bike to school
S 7. Our hamster is loose
S 8. Alice dived into the lake
F 9. Makes jewelry out of beads
F 10. The cattle rancher

Part 2 Different Kinds of Sentences

You use sentences for several different reasons. Sometimes you want to tell something. Sometimes you want to ask something. Sometimes you want to tell someone to do something. Sometimes you want to show how strongly you feel about something. There is a different kind of sentence for each of these four purposes. Every sentence that you read or write is one of these four different kinds.

The Declarative Sentence

A declarative sentence tells or states something. Use a period **(.)** at the end of a declarative sentence.

> Tomorrow is my birthday.

The Interrogative Sentence

An interrogative sentence asks a question. Use a question mark **(?)** at the end of an interrogative sentence.

> Do you enjoy basketball?

The Imperative Sentence

An imperative sentence makes a request or gives directions. Use a period **(.)** at the end of most imperative sentences.

> Pass the salt, please.

The Exclamatory Sentence

An exclamatory sentence shows strong feeling. Use an exclamation point **(!)** at the end of every exclamatory sentence.

> Our house is on fire!

Part 2

Objective

To distinguish the four kinds of sentences—declarative, interrogative, imperative, and exclamatory—and to understand their purposes

Presenting the Lesson

1. Read and discuss page 273. Ask students to supply additional examples for each type of sentence and also to explain when each type would be used. Here are some sample explanations: *declarative,* to tell someone where I am going; *interrogative,* to ask my mother if I can visit a friend after school; *imperative,* to tell my brother to leave me alone; and *exclamatory,* to show pain when I pinch my finger. If students know any of the four types of sentences by other names (*statement* for *declarative, exclamation* for *exclamatory*), show the relationship of those names to the ones in the text.

2. Assign and discuss Exercises A and B on page 274.

Individualizing the Lesson

Less-Advanced Students

Point out that the speaker's tone of voice is often the clue to the kind of sentence being said. Write the following sets of sentences on the board and have the students say them aloud and then identify the kind of sentence.

It's snowing.
Is it snowing yet?
It is snowing at last!
Go away, snow.

What great fireworks those are!
I like fireworks.
When do the fireworks start?
Put down those fireworks.

Advanced Students

Have the students construct one of each type of sentence for the following subjects. Answers will vary.

A football game
Lunchtime
Wet paint
Computers

Optional Practice

Put the sentences below on the board. Have students divide a paper into four columns: *Declarative*, *Interrogative*, *Imperative*, and *Exclamatory*. Have them decide which group each sentence belongs to, and put the number of that sentence in the proper column.

Int 1. Are you going out after dinner?
Imp 2. Put the boxes in the back of the car.
E 3. What a great movie that was!
D 4. I need to buy some notebooks.
Imp 5. Be quiet.
Int 6. Will you help me carry the box?
D 7. My sister works after school.
Int 8. Does your brother have a job?
D 9. I'd like fruit salad for dessert.
E 10. What a hot day this is!

Extending the Lesson

Have the students construct several four-sentence conversations using each of the types of sentences. Be sure to have them identify the speakers.

Examples:
Mom: Who messed up this room?
Son: I don't think it's a mess.
Mom: Clean it now.
Son: That's not fair!

Exercises Recognize the four kinds of sentences.

A. Number your paper from 1 to 10. Write *Declarative*, *Interrogative*, *Imperative*, or *Exclamatory* to tell what kind of sentence each is.

Example: Are you going shopping Saturday?
Interrogative

1. What good luck you always have! E
2. Do you have roller skates? Int.
3. Tom has been taking piano lessons for two years. D
4. When will the train arrive? Int.
5. Aim for the center of the target. Imp.
6. Tomorrow is my birthday. D
7. Are you telling me the truth? Int.
8. Guess the right number. Imp.
9. Ouch, that hurt! E
10. Hurry up. Imp.

B. Number your paper from 1 to 10. Write *Declarative*, *Interrogative*, *Imperative*, or *Exclamatory* to tell what kind of sentence each is. Then add the mark of punctuation that belongs at the end of each sentence.

1. The rocket took off on time. D
2. Have you ever seen the circus? Int.
3. What a terrific game it was! E
4. Ken erased the chalkboards. D
5. How cold it is today! E
6. My family took a vacation in Virginia. D
7. What a mess we made with the paint! E
8. Have another piece of this delicious bread. Imp.
9. Where does the bike trail end? Int.
10. Watch out! E

Part 3 Punctuating Sentences

Punctuation marks are important signals in reading and writing. Use the correct signals in your writing. Follow the signals when you read. Remember these rules:

1. **Use a period after a declarative sentence.**

   We will have a school assembly tomorrow.

2. **Use a question mark after an interrogative sentence.**

   Did you enjoy that book?

3. **Use a period after most imperative sentences.** If the imperative sentence expresses strong feeling, use an exclamation point.

   Give me the hot chocolate, please. Don't spill it!

4. **Use an exclamation point after an exclamatory sentence.**

   The Tigers win again!

Exercises Punctuate sentences correctly.

A. Copy these sentences. Use the correct punctuation mark at the end of each sentence.

1. How funny the monkey looks!
2. What is the name of that movie?
3. Turn on the radio, please.
4. Are you going on the bike trip?
5. Henry, read a story to the class.
6. Marcia hit a home run.
7. What an exciting game it was!
8. What time is it now?
9. Our class went to the museum.
10. Please open the window.

Part 3

Objective

To use proper end punctuation for the four kinds of sentences

Presenting the Lesson

1. Read and discuss page 275. Have students read the sample sentences aloud with expression. Discuss the different kinds of sentences and why different end punctuation is necessary for the reader.

2. Assign Exercises A and B on pages 275 and 276. When discussing them, it may be helpful to have students read the sentences aloud.

Individualizing the Lesson

Less-Advanced Students

Find four pictures from magazines which lend themselves to the different types of sentences. Have students tell which type of sentence fits each picture. They should write and punctuate a sentence for each.

Advanced Students

Ask students to find an example of each of the four kinds of sentences used in radio or television commercials. Have them write out and punctuate two examples of each, to be read aloud in class.

Optional Practice

Have students find examples of the different kinds of end punctuation in their other textbooks. Have them list nine examples (three for each) and after each sentence write what type of sentence it is. Tell students they should be ready to explain why the end marks were used.

Extending the Lesson

Using heavy paper or cardboard, draw a period, a question mark, and an exclamation point on separate sheets. Color the shapes so they can be seen from a distance. Show them to students and have them do the same. Put the following six sentences on the board without end punctuation.

1. The bear growled .
2. I like guitar music .
3. Watch out for the dangerous car !
4. She has two older brothers.
5. Can you play ball after school?
6. What a colorful picture that is!

Ask different students to read each sentence the way they think it should sound. Have other students hold up the correct punctuation card to match student's reading. Point out how intonation affects the meaning of the sentence.

Part 4

Objective

To identify the two parts of the sentence: subject and predicate

Presenting the Lesson

1. You might want to discuss how the two parts of a sentence that fit together are like two pieces of a puzzle that fit together. One part without the other is incomplete. Both parts are needed to make a sentence.

Build on what students have al-

B. Copy these sentences. Use the correct punctuation mark at the end of each sentence.

1. We went to a carnival.
2. Can you answer the question?
3. Stop it!
4. Do you have a ballpoint pen?
5. I found a birthday gift for Mother.
6. Try the vanilla milkshake.
7. Please come to my house after school.
8. Does Ellen wear glasses?
9. What a surprise this is!
10. I watched the baseball game.

Part 4 Parts of the Sentence

Every sentence has two parts. One part of the sentence is the **subject.** The subject answers the question *Who or what did something.*

Take another look at these sentences from **Part 1.**

1. Richard made a belt.
2. Greg is a goalie.
3. Laura was handed the trophy.
4. The gym class played volleyball.

Can you find the subject in each of these sentences? Find the answer to the question *Who or what did something* or *What is the sentence about.* Here are the subjects:

1. Richard
2. Greg
3. Laura
4. The gym class

The other part of the sentence is the **predicate.** The predicate tells something about the subject. The predicate tells *What the subject did, What the subject is,* or *What happened to the subject.*

First, see if you can find the predicates in the sample sentences by yourself. Then look at the following chart to find out if you were right.

Subject	Predicate
1. Richard *(who)*	made a belt. *(what the subject did)*
2. Greg *(who)*	is a goalie. *(what the subject is)*
3. Laura *(who)*	was handed the trophy. *(what happened to the subject)*
4. The gym class *(what)*	played volleyball. *(what the subject did)*

The subject of a sentence tells who or what did something, or what the sentence is about.

The predicate of a sentence tells what the subject did, what the subject is, or what happened to the subject.

A group of words is not a sentence unless it has a subject and a predicate.

Here are three new sentences. Which words in each sentence are the subject? Which words are the predicate? Check your answers against the chart that follows.

That big dog is a collie.
My older sister planted the garden.
Dave's math book fell into a puddle.

Subject	Predicate
That big dog	is a collie.
My older sister	planted the garden.
Dave's math book	fell into a puddle.

ready learned. If necesary, review the discussion in Part 1 concerning what a complete sentence is and how it is different from a fragment. Review especially the two basic questions (page 270) used to decide whether or not a sentence is complete.

2. Read and discuss pages 276 and 277.

3. Assign and discuss Exercises A and B on page 278. For each sentence, ask students to tell you who or what did something and what that person or thing did. Make sure students understand what a subject and a predicate are.

Individualizing the Lesson

Less-Advanced Students

Discuss in detail the subject/predicate chart on page 277. Be sure that the students clearly understand the usefulness in developing their own chart of this kind. Then when assigning Exercise B, ask the students to make a similar chart for the first five sentences.

It may also be helpful to do at least the first half of Exercise A as a group activity before assigning it for individual completion.

Advanced Students

Have students rewrite the sentences in Exercise A by changing the subjects. In Exercise B, have them change the predicates.

Optional Practice

On a worksheet, list the following eight subjects on the left and eight predicates on the right. Have the students draw a line from each subject to a predicate that will complete the thought. They should then write each complete sentence.

Subject	Predicate
1. Our doctor	tuned her guitar. 5
2. That dog	chose the photograph for the cover. 4
3. School	is kind and friendly. 1
4. They	is my favorite. 7
5. The musician	baked a sausage casserole. 6
6. The chef	has a flat tire. 8
7. That purse	will be closed for a few days. 3
8. His truck	can shake hands. 2

Extending the Lesson

Discuss some of the students' favorite sports. Ask them to write five sentences expressing five things that happen during the playing of a particular sport. Have them draw one line under the subject of each sentence and two lines under the predicate.

Examples: A football player runs with the football.
The crowd cheers at the touchdown.
The linebacker tackled the runner.

Exercises Find subjects and predicates.

A. Copy these sentences. Draw a vertical line between the subject and the predicate of each sentence.

Example: The red wagon | makes squeaky noises.

1. My friends | went to the beach.
2. The fierce tiger | growled in his cage.
3. Don | raced on roller skates.
4. Chris | is the pitcher.
5. Aunt Beth | has many strange plants.
6. The baby | reached for her bottle.
7. The first show | began at two o'clock.
8. Our neighbors | built a treehouse.
9. A baby robin | flew from the nest.
10. Susan | told a good joke.

B. Copy these sentences. Draw a vertical line between the subject and the predicate of each sentence.

Example: The girls | hiked through the park.

1. The small airplane | landed in a field.
2. A team of horses | pulled the wagon.
3. My brother's favorite holiday | is Halloween.
4. The runners | lined up.
5. Our family | watched the fireworks from the porch.
6. Ms. Adams | did a backflip for the class.
7. Snow | fell all day.
8. Mark | found a dollar in the hall.
9. My sister | makes her own clothes.
10. Doug Henning | performed many magic tricks.

Part 5 The Simple Predicate, or Verb

You have learned about the two parts of the sentence. The subject part is called the **complete subject.** The predicate part is called the **complete predicate.**

The complete subject may be short or long. It includes all the words that tell who or what did something.

The complete predicate may also be short or long. It includes all the words that tell what happened.

Complete Subject	Complete Predicate
The girl	played.
The tall girl with glasses	played basketball at the Y.

In each complete predicate, one part is more important than the rest. This part is the **verb.** A verb is a word that can tell of an action. It can also tell that something *is*. Both of the sentences above have the same verb: *played*. The verb is sometimes called the **simple predicate.** In the rest of this book, we will speak of it as the *verb*.

Finding the Verb

The verbs in these sentences are underlined.

The children <u>fell</u> on the ice.
Scott <u>knew</u> the answer.

Some verbs tell of an action you can see.

The quarterback <u>dropped</u> the ball.
The lion <u>jumped</u> through a hoop.

Part 5

Objective

To identify the simple predicate, or verb

Presenting the Lesson

1. Read pages 279 and 280 and discuss the different kinds of verbs. Ask students to give further examples of the two types of action verbs. Emphasize that usually the verb follows the subject. Stress that in Part 1 of this section, when students answered the question, *What happened?* in a sentence, they were talking about the verb. If necessary, review Part 1.

2. Assign and discuss Exercise A on page 280. You might remind students to use the questions on page 277 to help them locate the verbs. Assign and discuss Exercise B on pages 280 and 281.

Individualizing the Lesson

Less-Advanced Students

On the board, write the list of verbs below. Have students make two columns on a sheet of paper, one headed *Action*, the other *State-of-Being*. Tell them to decide what kind of verb each one is, and then to write it in the correct column. Verbs: *grabbed, saw, is, laughed, raced, signaled, were, has been, repair, broke, seemed, expressed, awoke, are, bounced, appeared, collected, am, spill, will be, sang, ate, was.*

Advanced Students

Ask the students to think about a particular hobby they enjoy or have enjoyed. Then have them write ten sentences about it, five containing action verbs and five containing state-of-being verbs. Remind them that the list of verbs on page 280 may help.

Optional Practice

Have the students find the verb in each of the following sentences and identify them as action or state-of-being.

A 1. The party started at eight.
SB 2. The moon is full tonight.
A 3. Geese fly south for the winter.
A 4. The video arcade has new games.
A 5. The tired boy crawled into bed.
SB 6. The fans are very rowdy.
A 7. Boston has many traffic circles.
A 8. We exercise every morning.
SB 9. This medicine is not bitter.
A 10. The cat ate my homework.

Extending the Lesson

Each sentence pair below uses a particular word two ways. In one of the sentences, the underlined word is a verb. In the other it is not. Have the student choose the sentence in each pair whose underlined word is a verb.

1. a. The charge for the meal was low.
   b. The cavalry charged up the hill. v
2. a. Run home and get your baseball mitt. v
   b. He scored a run in the first inning of the game.
3. a. That light is too bright.
   b. Light a match. v
4. a. Please set the alarm clock. v
   b. I bought a paint set.
5. a. They drive to Florida every year. v
   b. The drive home seemed long.

Once the students have completed this exercise, have them write five similar pairs of sentences.

Other verbs tell of an action you cannot see.

My mother heard the baby's cry.
I remember all the words of that song.

- Verbs that tell of an action are called **action verbs.**

Another kind of verb tells that something *is*.

I am a student. Your desk is new.

- Verbs that tell that something *is* are called **state-of-being verbs.**

Here are some of the most common state-of-being verbs:

is	am	were	has been	seem
are	was	will be	have been	look

A verb is a word that tells of an action, or that tells that something *is*.

Exercises Find the verb.

A. Write the verb in each sentence.

1. Ms. Morgan writes with a quill pen.
2. My uncle is a test pilot.
3. The Apollo spacecraft went to the moon.
4. Margie rested before the race.
5. Three penguins waddled toward the water.
6. The sky looked pink and orange.
7. The zookeeper feeds the lions at noon.
8. The truck took garbage to the dump.
9. Our club planted flowers in the square.
10. Adam hoped for better luck.

B. Write the verb in each sentence. After the verb, write *Action* or *State-of-Being* to tell what kind of verb it is.

SB 1. That flag is colorful.

A 2. Valerie's dog (performed) a new trick.
A 3. Two girls (paddled) the canoe.
A 4. The lizard (darted) up a tree.
A 5. Our class (published) a newspaper.
SB 6. Father (seems) impatient.
A 7. Eli (used) the microphone.
SB 8. The Girl Scouts (are) at camp.
A 9. Indians (made) these beautiful necklaces.
SB 10. The fans (were) happy about the victory.

Part 6 The Simple Subject, or Subject of the Verb

In each complete subject, one part is more important than the rest. This part is sometimes called the **simple subject.** Another name for it is the **subject of the verb.** The subject of the verb tells *who* or *what* about the verb.

In the examples below, the subject of the verb is printed in *italics*.

Complete Subject	Verb
The *clock*	stopped.
The old *clock* on the shelf	stopped.

Finding the Subject of the Verb

To find the subject of the verb, first find the verb. Then put *who* or *what* before the verb to make a question.

Examples: Monkeys escaped from the zoo.
Verb: *escaped*
Who or what *escaped?* *monkeys*
Monkeys is the subject of *escaped.*

Part 6

Objective

To identify the subject of the verb

Presenting the Lesson

1. Read and discuss pages 281 and 282. You might remind students that they are familiar with subjects of sentences (Part 4). Now they are to look more closely and pick out the one word that tells *who* or *what.* Point out that in most sentences the subject comes before the verb, but that other words may come between them.

2. It may be helpful to do Exercise A on pages 282 and 283 with the students. Assign and discuss Exercise B. You may want to review the purpose of a subject in a sentence during the discussion.

Individualizing the Lesson

Less-Advanced Students

Some students may have difficulties finding the subject. Remind them to first find the action or state-of-being verb, and then to ask *who* or *what* before the verb. Have students work through Exercise A as a group. Then assign Exercise B for individual completion.

Advanced Students

Have students provide new subjects for the sentences in Exercise A and new predicates for the sentences in Exercise B. Remind them that their new sentences should be interesting but logical.

Optional Practice

Point out that added words give more detail to a subject and make the sentence more interesting. Have the students "feed" the following "starved sentences" by adding to the subject only. Answers will vary.

1. The sandwich was tasty.
2. The clown did many tricks.
3. My pajamas are new.
4. The lake was still.
5. A tornado was spotted.
6. The robber was caught.
7. My brother is very strong.
8. The sail was torn.
9. This soup is too hot.
10. My bike needs a new tire.

Extending the Lesson

Use this activity only with those students who understand the difference between the subject and the verb.

Have students write two sentences for each of the following words, first using the word as a simple subject and then using the word as a verb: Answers will vary.

box plant light play trap

Three young monkeys escaped from the zoo.

Verb: *escaped*
Who or what *escaped?* *monkeys*
Monkeys is still the subject of the verb.

See if you can find the verb, and then the subject of the verb, in this example.

Students from our class acted in the play.

Did you find the action verb *acted?* The subject tells you *who* acted. What is the subject?

Did you say the *students* acted? *Students* is the subject of the verb *acted*.

In the next example, look for a state-of-being verb. Then find the subject of the verb.

Victor's blue jacket is on the chair.

Did you find the state-of-being verb *is?* The subject tells you *what* is. Did you say the *jacket is? Jacket* is the subject of the verb *is*.

Exercises Find the verb and its simple subject.

A. Find the verb and its simple subject in each sentence. Write the subject before the verb. Draw a vertical line between them.

Example: The ski slopes were crowded.
slopes | were

1. High waves tipped the sailboat.
2. Juanita added three books to her library.
3. Three jugglers in the main ring tossed hoops into the air.
4. My new gloves are waterproof.
5. Tom Sawyer found a secret hideout.
6. Jocelyn was her sister's bridesmaid.
7. A large group sang carols.

8. Six climbers from Nevada reached the mountaintop.
9. The desert seems endless.
10. Our parrot speaks Spanish.

B. Follow the directions for Exercise A.

1. Outside, hailstones fell.
2. Melinda leaped over the fence.
3. David is sick with the flu.
4. The American flag has fifty stars.
5. The pickers handled the fruit gently.
6. Dr. Mendez taped my wrist.
7. Tomatoes grow in our garden.
8. Today we had a fire drill.
9. A stray dog slept on the back steps.
10. The sweater with yellow and orange stripes is mine.

Part 7 The Subject in Unusual Positions

In most sentences the subject comes before the predicate. Sometimes, though, the subject does not come before the predicate. Where is the subject placed in each of the sentences below?

Example 1 The rocket soared toward the planet Venus.

Verb: *soared*
Who or what *soared?* the *rocket*

Rocket is the subject of the verb. It is placed before the verb near the beginning of the sentence.

Example 2 Toward the planet Venus the rocket soared.

Rocket is still the subject of the verb. It is still placed before the verb. It is now near the end of the sentence.

Part 7

Objective

To identify the subject in unusual positions

Presenting the Lesson

1. Read and discuss pages 283 and 284. Emphasize that even when the subject and verb change positions in a sentence, the students should still use the same procedure for finding verbs and subjects that they learned earlier in the section.

2. It may be helpful to do Exercise A on page 284 with the students. Assign and discuss Exercise B on pages 284 and 285.

Individualizing the Lesson

Less-Advanced Students

When working Exercise A as an oral group activity, students should

283

first identify the simple subject and verb in each sentence. They should write only those two words in normal word order. Assign Exercise B for independent completion.

Advanced Students

Explain to the students that sentence parts are often placed in unusual positions for the sake of emphasis. In the following sentences the emphasis changes slightly, but the subject is the same in each. Have students identify the subject.

Under the sofa I found that old, green blanket.

I found that old, green blanket under the sofa.

That old, green blanket I found under the sofa.

The students can then write similar groups of sentences, changing the position of the subject.

Optional Practice

Have the students follow the directions for Exercise A on page 284 using these sentences.

1. In front of the mirror stood Kate. Kate/stood
2. On the railing sat the birds. birds/sat
3. Up the ladder hurried the fireman. fireman/hurried
4. Into the hoop I threw the ball. I/threw
5. During the night the rain came. rain/came
6. Over the fence jumped Rover. Rover/jumped
7. Through the tunnel the train rushed. train/rushed
8. In the woods the mushrooms grew. mushrooms/grew

Extending the Lesson

Have the students rearrange the following Mother Goose rhymes, placing the verb and the subject in new positions. The sentences must still be grammarically correct. Point out that the meaning will remain the

Example 3 Toward the planet Venus soared the rocket.

In this sentence, the subject is still *rocket,* but it has been moved again. Now it is placed after the verb.

When you are looking for the subject in sentences like examples 2 and 3, follow the usual steps. First, find the verb. (*What happened?*) Then put *who* or *what* before the verb to make a question.

Example: During the movie we ate some popcorn.
Verb: *ate*
Who or what *ate?* *we* ate

Exercises Find the subject in unusual positions.

A. Find the verb and the subject in each sentence. Write the subject before the verb. Draw a vertical line between them.

Example: In the drawer are two pencils.
pencils | are

1. Down the hill ran José.
2. In the early evening, fireflies appeared.
3. On the top branch sat a crow.
4. From the trees fell the colorful leaves.
5. Down came the rain.
6. Into the hall the band marched.
7. Up into the tree sailed the balloon.
8. Into the water fell our money.
9. Out of the dark came a strange sound.
10. Across the range the cowboys rode.

B. Follow the directions for Exercise A.

1. Around the barnyard waddled a goose.
2. Out into the night went the cat.
3. After the storm a rainbow appeared.

4. Into the pond jumped a frog.
5. Over the apple orchard sailed a beautiful kite.
6. In front of the store Mom waited.
7. Through the gate came a hay wagon.
8. Across the snow whisked the sled.
9. Above the clouds the jet soared.
10. At the front of the parade marched the mayor.

Part 8 The Subject in Imperative Sentences

An imperative sentence makes a request, or gives directions or orders. Study these examples of imperative sentences. Look for the subjects.

Switch off the light.
Turn left at the gas station.
Don't throw the pencil.
Finish your test.

In each of these sentences, the subject is not stated. The subject is understood to be *you*. *You* is the person or group being spoken to.

(You) Switch off the light.
(You) Turn left at the gas station.
(You) Don't throw the pencil.
(You) Finish your test.

Exercises Find the subject.

A. Write the subject and the verb in each of the following sentences. If the subject is not given in the sentence, write it in parentheses before the verb.

Example: Wait here for me.
(You) Wait

(You) 1. Try it again, please.
(You) 2. Taste this soup.

same in each example. Answers will vary.

1. Little Miss Muffet sat on a tuffet.
2. Jack and Jill went up the hill.
3. This little pig went to market.
4. The cow jumped over the moon.
5. The pig flew in the air.
6. Old Mother Hubbard went to the cupboard.
7. Little Tommy Tucker sings for his supper.
8. Humpty Dumpty sat on the wall.

Part 8

Objective

To identify the subject in imperative sentences

Presenting the Lesson

1. Read and discuss page 285. Ask students for further examples. Ask them how many different subjects there are for imperative sentences. Point out that knowing that *you* is the only subject makes it much easier to find.

2. You may want to do Exercise A on pages 285 and 286 with the students. Assign and discuss Exercise B on page 286.

Individualizing the Lesson

Less-Advanced Students

To reinforce the concept of *you* as the subject, have students go over these sentences aloud, adding *you* in the right place. They should identify the verb.

1. Pick up that litter.
2. Shut the door.

3. Don't walk on the grass.
4. Hand in your papers.
5. Now hear this.
6. Tell me what happened.
7. Don't move.
8. Line up quickly.

Advanced Students

Give the following directions to students: Imagine you are assisting the teacher in a first grade classroom. You are helping him take children to a play. Write ten imperative sentences telling them how to behave. Leave a space before each sentence. Then write the understood subject *you* in that space.

Extending the Lesson

Have each student write three imperative sentences that tell another student to do something in the classroom. Call on two students. The first student reads one of his sentences, and the second follows the direction. Point out that whenever they wish to issue an instruction, they will be using an imperative sentence, and the subject will be understood as "you."

Part 9

Objective

To identify compound subjects

Presenting the Lesson

1. Read and discuss pages 286 and 287.

You may wish to discuss the meaning of *junction* and how it is

3. Karen took the message.
(You) 4. Have a second baked potato.
(You) 5. Stay in your seats.
6. I like crisp, sweet apples.
(You) 7. Look at that fancy car.
(You) 8. Add one cup of flour to the mixture.
(You) 9. Read chapter 2 for tomorrow.
10. Those boys need help with the ladder.

B. Follow the directions for Exercise A.

1. Astronomers watch for unusual stars.
(You) 2. Bait your hook this way.
(You) 3. Speak a little louder, please.
(You) 4. Save some money for your bus fare.
5. Careful shoppers compare prices.
(You) 6. Do your best.
(You) 7. Sing with the music.
8. Rosa entered the science contest.
(You) 9. Use fine sandpaper for this job.
(You) 10. Buy your tickets at the box office.

Part 9 Compound Subjects

When two or more subjects are used with the same predicate, they are called a **compound subject.** The word *compound* means "having more than one part." Read these two sentences:

Subject	Predicate
Jennifer	played softball.
I	played softball.

Since the predicates are the same, you can join the two sentences. Now the subject has two parts.

Subject	Predicate
Jennifer and I	played softball.

In the new sentence, the word *and* joins the two parts of the subject. The word *or* can also be used to join parts of a subject. (A word that is used to join words or groups of words is called a **conjunction.**)

Look at these sentences with compound subjects:

Carrie and *Jake* left the meeting early.
Sausage or *pepperoni* tastes good on pizza.

When you combine three or more subjects in a compound subject, use commas to separate them. Place the conjunction before the last subject.

Example: Our summer *cottage,* the *dock,* **and** a *rowboat* suffered damage in the hurricane.

Exercises Find compound subjects.

A. Find the verb and its compound subject in each of the following sentences. Write the subjects first and then the verb. Draw a line between them.

Example: Dan, Bob, and Ginny came to my house.
Dan, Bob, Ginny | came

1. The brakes and seat on my bike are new.
2. Suzanne or Richard presents the first speech.
3. Posters and lockers line the hallway.
4. Bacon, lettuce, and tomato make a tasty sandwich.
5. The horse and rider avoided the highway.
6. A chair and a phone were the only props.
7. Karen and Joyce shared a milkshake.
8. The manager and the umpire disagreed on the call.

used in other contexts (highway junction, telephone junction box, electrical junction) and relate that to *conjunction.* You may also find it of value to discuss the word *compound* in other areas (a chemical compound, a building compound, a compound fracture) and relate the meaning to compound subjects.

2. Assign and discuss Exercises A and B on pages 287 and 288.

Individualizing the Lesson

Less-Advanced Students

Some students may have some difficulty identifying compound subjects. Give them the following list and tell them to write *C* after the sentence if the subject is compound and *S* if the subject is simple.

S 1. Our school has a great soccer team.
C 2. Justin and Derek are captains.
C 3. Our school and Central school played a game yesterday.
S 4. We won by three goals.
C 5. Carol, Jack, and Jenny led the cheering.
S 6. They did cartwheels and kicks.
C 7. After the game, Carol and Jack were hoarse.
S 8. Our team is now in first place.

Advanced Students

Have the students find and copy examples of compound subjects from other textbooks.

Optional Practice

Have students write ten sentences, using the following pairs of words as compound subjects.

Answers will vary.

1. rain, hail
2. lizard, iguana
3. Ramon, Kim

4. clown, magician
5. speed-skating, skiing
6. squid, octopus
7. Mars, Jupiter
8. earthquakes, volcanoes
9. mustard, relish
10. Willy Nelson, Emmylou Harris

Extending the Lesson

Rewrite each of the following sentence pairs as a single sentence with a compound subject.

Tom and Amy earned an A in math.
1. Tom earned an A in math.
   Amy earned an A in math.

My aunt and my cousin visited the Grand Canyon.
2. My aunt visited the Grand Canyon.
   My cousin visited the Grand Canyon.

The rabbit and the gerbil ate the lettuce.
3. The rabbit ate the lettuce.
   The gerbil ate the lettuce.

Many rainstorms and windstorms occur in April.
4. Many rainstorms occur in April.
   Many windstorms occur in April.

Part 10

Objective

To identify compound predicates

Presenting the Lesson

1. Read and discuss pages 288 and 289. Point out the similarities in the use of conjunctions and commas between compound subjects and compound predicates.

2. Assign and discuss Exercises A and B on page 289.

Individualizing the Lesson

Less-Advanced Students

Have the students write a sentence for each of the following sets

9. Jenkins, Tortini, and Owens scored runs.
10. Corn, wheat, and soybeans are the main crops of this farm.

B. Follow the directions for Exercise A.

1. Gymnasts and dancers performed at parents' night.
2. The principal and the teachers planned new courses.
3. Rain and winds whipped the countryside.
4. Ponies and cows grazed in the field.
5. Radio, TV, and newspapers reported the crime.
6. Bob or Regina found the books.
7. Colorado, Utah, and Vermont have many ski resorts.
8. The police and paramedics raced to the scene.
9. Palms and ferns need a lot of light.
10. Vic, Al, and Kelly listened to a new album.

Part 10 Compound Predicates

When two or more predicates are used with the same subject, they are called a **compound predicate.** The parts of a compound predicate are joined with a conjunction.

Often you can combine two or more sentences by using a compound predicate.

Subject	Predicate
I	sat at the table.
I	ate my breakfast.

Subject	Predicate
I	sat at the table and ate my breakfast.

When you combine three or more predicates in a compound

predicate, use commas to separate them. Place the conjunction before the last predicate.

Example: Jean *rehearsed the part, tried out,* **and** *won a role in the class play.*

Exercises Find compound predicates.

A. Write the compound predicates in each of the following sentences.

1. Laurie watched TV and did her homework.
2. Rob rode the bus and went to the zoo.
3. Ellen dropped the bat and ran to first base.
4. The car skidded on the ice and hit the sign.
5. Our cat caught a mouse and brought it inside.
6. I grabbed my coat and ran to the store.
7. Tina drew a picture and gave it to her mother.
8. Beth raced down the court and shot a basket.
9. Mike read a story and wrote a report.
10. Tony learned a new dance and taught it to us.

B. Follow the directions for Exercise A.

1. The campers pitched their tent and cooked supper.
2. Ed writes folk songs and plays them on his guitar.
3. Jane cut her jeans and made them into shorts.
4. A friend took a brush and painted with me.
5. Joe gets his allowance on Friday and spends it right away.
6. Les took the test and passed it.
7. The tennis instructor explained a serve and demonstrated it.
8. Joanie sorted the mail and delivered it.
9. Terry made a sandwich and cleaned the kitchen.
10. Tom joined the game and played third base.

of words, using them as the verbs in a compound predicate. Answers will vary.

1. laughed, played
2. leaped, jumped
3. whistled, howled
4. boiled, bubbled
5. screamed, cried
6. crashed, broke

Advanced Students

Ask the students to write a description of a game they enjoy playing. At least five of these sentences should contain compound predicates.

Optional Practice

Have the students label the following sentences CP for compound predicates or SP for simple predicates.

CP 1. We cleaned and carved the pumpkin.
SP 2. Robins carry sticks and string to their nests.
CP 3. The children squealed and giggled during the magic show.
CP 4. After dinner we sat and sang around the campfire.
SP 5. We ate nuts and raisins for our snack today.

Extending the Lesson

Have the students copy the following sentences, adding commas and conjunctions to separate the parts of each compound predicate.

1. The pony turned, ran, and jumped the fence.
2. We brush, comb, and bathe our dog.
3. The dragon kite floats, twists, and trails its streamers in the air.
4. The barber clips, cuts, and trims hair.
5. I washed, peeled, and sliced the apples.

Sentence Patterns

Objective

To recognize the usual word order of sentences

Presenting the Lesson

1. Ask the class to listen carefully and follow the instructions below. Read them no more than twice, and wait for the students to figure them out.

1. Book your hold up.
2. Hand raise your other.

Discuss why they had difficulty understanding the directions.

2. Read and discuss page 290.

3. Assign and discuss the Exercise on page 290.

Optional Practice

Put the list below on a worksheet. Tell students to unscramble the words in each, and write them in two different orders for two correct sentences. You may wish to set a time limit, and have students work in groups to see which group can finish first. Answers will vary.

1. Pencil the on the book is. The pencil is on the book.
2. Introduced the magician his assistant. The magician introduced his assistant.
3. Fights the bull matador the. The matador fights the bull.
4. Is friend my Sally. Sally is my friend.
5. Protected dog the the boy. The dog protected the boy.
6. Game big today is the. The big game is today.
7. Waved Sally Jacob at. Sally waved at Jacob.
8. Rat big bit pig the. The big rat bit the pig.
9. Men nurses are some. Some nurses are men.

Sentence Patterns Word Order and Meaning

A sentence is a group of words. However, not every group of words is a sentence. For example, read these word groups. Which one makes sense?

Pete fast ran. Pete ran fast. Ran Pete fast.

The only group that sounds right is the second group. Its words are in the order you are used to hearing. You would say that its words are in the right order for a sentence. A good sentence must have the right word order.

Sometimes a group of words has more than one right order. Read these two sentences. They contain the same words. The words are simply in different order.

Carrie told Brad. Brad told Carrie.

Each word order sounds right. Each tells an idea. However, changing the word order changes the idea. The difference in word order makes an important difference in meaning.

Exercise Change the word order and meaning.

Read each sentence. Then change the order of the words to change the meaning. Write each new sentence on your paper.

1. Herb called Sylvia. Sylvia called Herb.
2. The rug hid the dirt. The dirt hid the rug.
3. Some dogs chase cats. Some cats chase dogs.
4. Bob wrote to my sister. My sister wrote to Bob.
5. Jeanne called the principal. The principal called Jeanne.
6. Tom knows Monica. Monica knows Tom
7. Julio thanked the coach. The coach thanked Julio.
8. The Cubs beat the Mets. The Mets beat the Cubs.
9. Carol heard Dan. Dan heard Carol.
10. The car hit the bus. The bus hit the car.

ADDITIONAL EXERCISES

Learning About Sentences

A. Recognizing Sentences Number your paper from 1 to 10. Write *Sentence* or *Fragment* for each of the following groups of words to show what each group is. (Use after page 272.)

F 1. The deer on the highway
S 2. Maggie slipped
S 3. Craig borrowed the tape measure
F 4. Swam across the lake
F 5. Our rivals from across town
S 6. Nora filled the wheelbarrow
F 7. Finished the history assignment
F 8. John and his three cousins
S 9. The arrow hit the bull's-eye
S 10. Ms. Lee directed the play

B. Kinds of Sentences For each of the following sentences, write *Declarative*, *Interrogative*, *Imperative*, or *Exclamatory* to show what kind it is. (Use after page 274.)

Int. 1. Have you opened your presents?
Imp. 2. Try this new dessert.
D 3. James forgot his social studies book.
E 4. How deep the snow is!
Int. 5. Where did you find that eraser?
D 6. Two inches of rain fell last night.
Imp. 7. Take the 4:30 train.
D 8. Andrew Wyeth did that painting.
Imp. 9. Don't forget the meeting.
E 10. What a surprise that was!

Additional Exercises

These Additional Exercises may be used for additional practice of the concepts presented in this Section. Each exercise focuses on a single concept, and should be used after the page number indicated in parentheses.

Review

If you have not assigned these Additional Exercises before this time, you can also use them as an excellent Section Review.

C. Punctuating Sentences Copy these sentences. Add the correct punctuation mark to each. (Use after page 276.)

1. Did you meet my brother?
2. Wendy packed a picnic lunch.
3. Don't forget your watch.
4. What is the capital of Maryland?
5. How cold it was this morning!
6. Dad took us to the zoo.
7. Bring your chess game.
8. My cousins live on that farm.
9. Watch out!
10. Where are you going?

D. Subjects and Predicates Copy these sentences. Draw a vertical line between the subject and the predicate of each sentence. (Use after page 278.)

1. My cousin | plays the violin.
2. Our team | uses that locker room.
3. Lou | washed the car.
4. Mr. Dickens | is the new coach.
5. A coin | fell behind the counter.
6. Trisha | parachuted from the small plane.
7. Dogs | are intelligent animals.
8. The blizzard | stopped the air traffic.
9. The campers | left at dawn.
10. Dr. O'Connell | removed the heavy cast.

E. Verbs Write the verb in each sentence. (Use after page 281.)

1. The jets roared overhead.
2. Laura is the head of the committee.

292

3. Brad baked apple-raisin bread.
4. Chris painted the garage.
5. The suspect seemed nervous.
6. Ducks swam in the pond.
7. Luis was the president of his class.
8. Bees swarmed around the picnic table.
9. Clay dunked the ball through the hoop.
10. This bread seems stale.

F. Subjects and Verbs Find the verb and its simple subject in each sentence. Write the subject before the verb. Draw a vertical line between them. (Use after page 283.)

1. Katie made a bookshelf. Katie | made
2. The store on Saxon Avenue has a sale on T-shirts. store | has
3. Our teacher tells very funny stories. teacher | tells
4. Juanita plays the drums. Juanita | plays
5. Grapes are my favorite snack. grapes | are
6. The carnival was fun. carnival | was
7. My parents framed the drawing. parents | framed
8. The new theater opens tomorrow. theater | opens
9. The trees in the park are maples. trees | are
10. Jeff repaired the typewriter. Jeff | repaired

G. Subjects in Unusual Positions Find the verb and its subject in each sentence. Write the subject before the verb. Draw a vertical line between them. (Use after page 285.)

1. In the hallways Bob hung posters. Bob | hung
2. Over the mountains the eagle soared. eagle | soared
3. Down the path galloped the horse. horse | galloped
4. In the middle of the gym was a trampoline. trampoline | was
5. Through the grass slithered the snake. snake | slithered

293

6. During the storm the lights dimmed. lights | dimmed
7. Over the roof sailed the baseball. baseball | sailed
8. Around the bend a deer appeared. deer | appeared
9. Throughout the night the snow fell. snow | fell
10. Into the store trotted the beagle. beagle | trotted

H. Subjects in Sentences Find the verb and its subject in each of the following sentences. Write the subject before the verb. Draw a vertical line between them. If the subject is not stated, write it in parentheses. (Use after page 286.)

1. Begin with the third chapter. (You) | Begin
2. Marsha drew that picture. Marsha | drew
3. Look for a good picnic spot. (You) | Look
4. Try one of these cheese puffs. (You) | try
5. My father winds this clock every day. father | winds
6. Bring your raincoat. (You) | Bring
7. Be here at 5:00 P.M. (You) | Be
8. The boys weeded the garden. boys | weeded
9. Water those plants carefully. (You) | Water
10. Larry returned the books. Larry | returned

I. Compound Subjects Write the compound subjects in each of the following sentences. (Use after page 288.)

1. James or Judy told the principal.
2. The field and bleachers were wet.
3. Marigolds, zinnias, and daisies grew in the garden.
4. Marge and Tony sang a duet.
5. The streets and sidewalks were slippery.
6. Tom, Charlie, and Bill met at the gym.
7. Tennis and golf are his favorite sports.
8. Mushrooms, sausage, and onions covered the pizza.

294

9. Lisa and Beth wrote the play.
10. Apples, oranges, and bananas filled the basket.

J. Compound Predicates Write the compound predicates in each of the following sentences. (Use after page 289.)

1. The dog growled at Jeff and snapped at me.
2. Karl washed the windows and dusted the furniture.
3. The club planned the picnic and made the arrangements.
4. Barb made some popcorn and ate it.
5. The vase fell from the ledge and shattered on the floor.
6. Dad washed the walls, painted the ceiling, and vacuumed the carpets.
7. Jill poured the juice and sliced the bread.
8. The audience rose from their seats and applauded the actors.
9. George sealed the letter and mailed it.
10. The player caught the football and ran for a touchdown.

295

Mixed Review

These exercises provide review of the concepts presented in this Section. Each exercise challenges the students to apply several of the skills they have acquired during previous study. Because the "mixed" feature of these activities makes them more difficult, the teacher may wish to have less-advanced students do them orally or in small groups.

MIXED REVIEW

Learning About Sentences

A. Recognizing fragments and kinds of sentences Read the groups of words below. If a group of words is a fragment, write *Fragment*. If a group of words is a sentence, write *Declarative, Interrogative, Imperative,* or *Exclamatory* to show what kind it is. Punctuate each sentence.

F 1. Sean and his pet hamster
Int. 2. What is the score?
F 3. Gave her report to the class
F 4. The tall, thin man
D 5. Darlene opened her locker.
D 6. Giant fir trees lined the road.
E 7. How surprised we were!
F 8. Washed their bikes
Imp. 9. Close the door, please.
Int. 10. Is today your birthday?

B. Finding subjects, predicates, and verbs Copy the following sentences. Draw a vertical line between each subject and predicate. Then underline each verb.

1. The band | played a joyous march.
2. Two trains | pulled into the station.
3. Justin | rode the elevator.
4. Dad | waited in the car.
5. Kelly's umbrella | is pink and green.
6. Our parents | made the costumes.
7. Ginger | looked under her chair.
8. Lightning | split the old oak tree.
9. Mr. Jennings | is my uncle.
10. Dark clouds | hid the sun.

C. Finding the verb and its subject In some of these sentences, the subject is before the verb. In others, the verb is first. Copy each sentence. Underline the subject once and the verb twice. If a subject is understood, write it in parentheses.

1. Three clowns rode the elephant.
2. After dinner we watched a special on TV.
3. Santa Fe is the capital of New Mexico.
4. (You) Turn the record over.
5. Barbara hit a home run.
6. Down the alley rolled the tennis ball.
7. The boys studied the old map.
8. Across the finish line came the bikes.
9. (You) Listen to this melody.
10. My old brown boots are too small.

D. Finding compound subjects and compound predicates Label two columns on your paper *Compound Subject* and *Compound Predicate.* Number your paper from 1 to 10. Write the compound subjects and compound predicates from each sentence in the proper columns. Not every sentence will have both.

1. Mary and Tom boarded the plane.
2. We talked and laughed for hours.
3. The pots and pans are washed and dried.
4. Wisconsin, Michigan, and Minnesota have long winters.
5. Kyle shopped for the food and cooked the dinner.
6. Peg found my wallet and returned it.
7. Robins, sparrows, and bluejays visit our birdfeeder.
8. The scouts and their leader hiked into the woods and camped there.
9. The storm raged all night and stopped at dawn.
10. Chip and Molly have birthdays next week.

297

Using Grammar in Writing

These challenging and enjoyable activities allow the students to see how the concepts of grammar, usage, and mechanics may be applied in actual writing situations. Each exercise is designed to allow students practice in several of the skills they have acquired in this Section. The activities also provide opportunities for students to write creatively about a wide variety of interesting and unusual subjects.

USING GRAMMAR IN WRITING

Learning About Sentences

A. Imagine that NASA has announced that it will send a young person into space. You are amazed to learn that you have been chosen. Write a letter to NASA, accepting the assignment. Express your excitement at being chosen. Ask any questions you have. Use at least one declarative sentence, one imperative sentence, one interrogative sentence, and one exclamatory sentence. When you are finished, draw a vertical line between the subject and the predicate of each sentence.

B. Following is an imaginary letter that was written to an advice columnist. Rewrite the letter. Correct any sentence fragments that you find. Then pretend you are the columnist and write an answer to the letter. In your answer, include one sentence that has a compound subject. Also include one that has a compound predicate.

> Dear Gabby,
>
> Every time I play games or sports. I lose. Even my little sister beats me. At checkers. If I fly a kite. It gets tangled up. In a tree. I even think my dog is smarter than me. I'm crazy. About a pretty red-haired girl, and she couldn't care less. Can you give me some advice?
>
> Tired of losing,
> Charlie Brown

C. There's going to be a party at your house right after school. Some of your classmates will need directions to get to your house. Write a paragraph that tells how to get from your school to your home. Underline each imperative sentence that you use. In parentheses, write the subject of each imperative sentence.

HANDBOOK SECTION 2

Using Sentences Correctly

You know that a sentence expresses a complete thought.

The papers fell on the floor.

Some groups of words do not express a complete thought. They express only part of a thought. These groups of words are called **sentence fragments.**

Example: The papers on the floor.

Sometimes two or more sentences are written as one sentence. This is called a **run-on sentence.**

Example: The papers fell on the floor some blew away.

See how clear these ideas are when separate sentences are used.

The papers fell on the floor. Some blew away.

Section Objectives

1. To recognize and avoid sentence fragments

2. To recognize and avoid run-on sentences

Preparing the Students

Put the following examples and paragraph on a worksheet. Have students identify the examples that make sense. Ask them to tell what is wrong with the others. Without prompting, see if they recognize the three examples with incomplete thoughts.

1. Called it a strike.
2. The infielder walked to second base.
3. A double play in the second inning.
4. Over the fence.
5. We won.

Next, have students read this paragraph aloud and tell what is wrong with it. Do they recognize that it is missing punctuation? Can they tell where more punctuation is needed and why?

There were runners on first and second. the umpire called the next pitch a strike. Then the batter hit a hard ground ball down the third base line. The third baseman made a spectacular catch. he threw to second; the second baseman threw to first just in time. That made three outs. it was all over.

Explain that this chapter will help students become aware of two common errors in sentence structure and punctuation that were demonstrated on the worksheet. Read and discuss the introduction to the section on pages 299 and 300.

Additional Resources

Mastery Test — Pages 35-36 in the test booklet

Additional Exercises — pages 304-306 in the student text

Practice Book — pages 122-124

Duplicating Masters — pages 122-124

Special Populations — See special section at the front of this Teacher's Edition.

Part 1

Objective

To recognize and avoid sentence fragments

Presenting the Lesson

1. Read and discuss page 300. If necessary, review the discussion of the word *fragment* from Section 1.

2. You may find it helpful to do Exercise A on pages 300 and 301 with the class. Assign and discuss Exercises B and C on page 301.

Individualizing the Lesson

Less-Advanced Students

Ask the students to read the following paragraph. They should locate the fragments and rewrite them as complete sentences. Sentences will vary.

Yesteday I helped my dad make soup. A surprise for Mom. We boiled some beef bones. Added lots off vegetables. Carrots, peas, tomatoes, and onions. We didn't have any celery. Simmered for one hour. It smelled great. Best soup ever made.

Always write sentences carefully. Avoid using fragments and run-ons. In this section, you will be able to practice writing sentences correctly.

Part 1 Avoiding Sentence Fragments

A sentence fragment tells only a part of a thought. For example, a fragment may tell only *who*.

Example: The tall boy in the band

A fragment may tell only *what happened*.

Example: Played the guitar for us

A fragment may tell only *where*.

Example: At the party

Each of these sentence fragments tells only part of an idea. None of these fragments states a complete thought.

A sentence that is written correctly, however, always expresses a complete thought.

Examples: The tall boy in the band played the guitar for us at the party.
The boy played the guitar.

Exercises Recognize sentence fragments.

A. Read each of the following groups of words. Write *Sentence* or *Fragment* to tell what each group is.

S 1. The film crew built the scenery
F 2. Took photographs on vacation
F 3. A terrific hockey game

F 4. Three books on the library shelves
S 5. Our class went to the museum
F 6. Hung from the ceiling
S 7. Ruby interviewed Steve Garvey
F 8. Assignments on the blackboard
S 9. We climbed a rope ladder
S 10. Margo looks like her older sister

B. Follow the directions for Exercise A.

F 1. A magazine about cars
S 2. Several girls won scholarships
S 3. The bell rang
F 4. Appeared in a TV series
S 5. Scientists study animal behavior
F 6. Predicted rain
S 7. Carla bought new jeans
S 8. A stranger peered through the window
F 9. Only one car in the garage
F 10. Makes oatmeal cookies with raisins

C. Writing Make sentences from these fragments. Add whatever is needed to make each thought complete. Write each sentence on your paper. Answers will vary.

1. ten pages in the math book
2. long, curly hair
3. turned three cartwheels
4. the girls in the chorus
5. an art fair next week
6. the icy streets
7. ate a slice of watermelon
8. pasted photos into a scrapbook
9. one of the new tape recorders
10. the canoe in the water

Advanced Students

Ask the students to make the fragments in **Optional Practice** into complete sentences. Sentences will vary.

Optional Practice

List the following fragments on the board or on a worksheet. Tell students to write *who, what,* or *what happened* for each one, depending on which question the fragment answers.

1. the leaky carton what
2. the exhausted runner who
3. beat on the drums what happened
4. started the motor who
5. the pioneers of the plains who
6. was collecting rare stamps what happened

Extending the Lesson

This activity should provide some humorous combinations but it should also stress that a fragment is not a complete idea. If a writer wants to express a sensible idea, he must complete every sentence.

Divide the class into four groups. Have each group write five fragments. The first group's fragments should answer the question *who* (preferably common nouns), the second the question *what,* and the third and fourth the question *what happened.* Call on students, at random, to read one fragment each from their lists. Alternate each student from group one or two with a student from group three or four to produce a complete sentence from the two fragments. Make sure students realize that the silly sentences give a hint of the confusion that can result from careless use of fragments in written work.

Part 2

Objective

To recognize and avoid run-on sentences

Presenting the Lesson

1. You may wish to review what a good sentence does: it expresses one complete idea. Stress particularly that it is important to write clear sentences because a writer is not present to explain the meaning to a reader. Have different students write individual sentences about a picture in one of their texts, describing it to someone who cannot see it. Use this experience as an example of how much care is needed to express thoughts clearly.

2. Read and discuss page 302. Stress the importance of avoiding run-ons by thinking of each idea separately and using end marks to show the separations.

3. You may wish to do Exercise A on pages 302 and 303 with students to check their understanding. Assign Exercises B and C.

Individualizing the Lesson

Less-Advanced Students

Point out to students that although it may seem that we speak in run-ons, we pause and stop when speaking to make the meaning clear. In writing, however, it is absolutely necessary to use correct punctuation to separate ideas. Have each student write one example of a run-on sentence on the board. Then, have the class suggest where the sentence-break should be, and add punctuation.

Part 2 Avoiding Run-on Sentences

A run-on sentence is two or more sentences written as one. These sentences are often joined incorrectly by a comma. Run-ons are confusing because they tell more than one complete thought. See how confusing these examples are:

> The campers sat around a fire they sang songs.
> Dan scrubbed the porch, Marcy weeded the garden.

Now see how clear the ideas are when each sentence expresses just one complete thought:

> The campers sat around a fire. They sang songs.
> Dan scrubbed the porch. Marcy weeded the garden.

Whenever you write, be careful to put just one complete thought in each sentence. End each complete thought with a period, question mark, or exclamation point. Begin each new sentence with a capital letter.

Exercises Recognize run-on sentences.

A. Some of the following sentences are run-on sentences. Some are correct sentences. Read each sentence. Write *Correct* or *Run-on* to tell what each one is.

R 1. Three clowns were riding on one donkey, they pushed each other off.
C 2. Lillian and Darren raced to the car.
R 3. I had a piano lesson for one hour then my teacher played a piece for me.
R 4. Yesterday we played baseball Judy scored three runs.
C 5. Everyone recited the Pledge of Allegiance.
C 6. Melvin had tomato soup and a cheese sandwich for lunch.
R 7. It rained on Labor Day, we had our picnic inside.

R 8. Jeff answered an ad in the paper he got a guitar.

C 9. Adelle played chess with her father every night last week.

R 10. The 4-H Club met Tuesday after school, a speaker told about a contest.

B. Follow the directions for Exercise A.

R 1. I have two younger brothers, they are twins.

C 2. Janet delivers papers each morning.

C 3. My friends from camp exchange letters.

R 4. My brother catches fireflies he keeps them in a jar.

R 5. Last year we planted a tree, it's in the back yard.

R 6. We picked bouquets of tulips and daffodils, we placed them in the dining room.

C 7. Aunt Meg knits sweaters for everyone in the family.

C 8. Rick knows the capital city of every state.

R 9. Luis likes corn and broccoli, he is a good cook.

C 10. Cassie filled the bookcase with mystery novels.

C. Writing Read each run-on sentence. Then rewrite each one, using correct capitalization and punctuation.

1. Jorge swam twenty laps, he felt tired.
2. Lisa trains animals she is good at it.
3. The Browns have a big family there are ten children.
4. Ms. Lake has a ranch she breeds cattle.
5. The beekeeper was working at the honeycomb he was collecting honey.
6. The cat climbed a tree, we rescued him.
7. The group hiked near the stream they stopped for a swim.
8. Jody paddled the canoe, she traveled downstream.
9. Do sharks swim close to shore have you seen one?
10. The race cars sped down the track, many people watched the race.

Advanced Students

Select a lively passage, without dialogue, from one of the students' literature books. Write out this passage on a worksheet, or on the board, running some of the sentences together. Have the students indicate which are the run-ons, and where the punctuation should be.

Optional Practice

Tell the students that four of the following sentences are run-ons, and one is correct. They are to identify the run-on sentences and to tell where the division | should be between the two ideas.

R 1. Did you find a glove | I lost mine.

R 2. The baseball went over the fence | it landed in the garden.

R 3. Those books are due at the library | I want to get some more.

R 4. The dog is barking | the cat is howling.

C 5. I need to buy a birthday present for my friend.

Extending the Lesson

Have the students pretend that they are editors of a newspaper column. They are to correct the run-ons in the following letter.

Dear Sybil,

I had the most awful experience yesteday I just had to tell you about it maybe you will print my letter. At noon the dogs next door starting barking, and I had to call the neighbors to complain that usually does the trick. There was no answer so I went over and rang the doorbell then I noticed that someone had broken into the house. Someone was still inside I nearly fainted. It was my neighbor's son he had come home without his keys. What a relief I'll be more careful next time.

Signed,
Relieved

Additional Exercises

These Additional Exercises may be used for additional practice of the concepts presented in this Section. Each exercise focuses on a single concept, and should be used after the page number indicated in parentheses.

Review

If you have not assigned these Additional Exercises before this time, you can also use them as an excellent Section Review.

ADDITIONAL EXERCISES

Using Sentences Correctly

A. Sentences and Fragments Write *Fragment* or *Sentence* for each of the following groups of words to show what each group is. (Use after page 301.)

S 1. A strong current pulled our boat.
F 2. An all-day bike trip.
F 3. A red notebook with a picture of Charlie Brown on the front.
S 4. Fans lined up at the gates.
F 5. Bought fresh orange juice.
S 6. Cross-country skiing has become popular.
F 7. A long pass from the forty-yard line.
S 8. Cathy wore her new clogs to school.
S 9. The boys made ice cream for the party.
F 10. Studied the chapters in the science book.

B. Sentences and Run-ons Write *Correct* or *Run-on* for each of the following groups of words to show what each group is. (Use after page 303.)

R 1. Vera hit a slapshot, it landed in the net.
C 2. The road with the narrow bridge was flooded.
R 3. The boys found a cave, they crawled in.
R 4. The nurse gave me a shot it didn't hurt.
C 5. The bowling ball is in my locker.
R 6. TV programs get Emmy awards, movies get Oscars.
C 7. These windows face the sun.
R 8. Jenny rode the horse it needed exercise.
C 9. The drawer was full of photographs.
C 10. Skaters glided around the rink.

C. Sentences, Fragments, and Run-on Sentences Write *Fragment, Sentence,* or *Run-on* for each of the following groups of words to show what each group is.

R 1. Carol worked on the engine, she finally fixed it.
F 2. The jacket hanging in my locker.
R 3. Van takes piano lessons, George takes voice lessons.
S 4. Dennis borrowed your bike.
S 5. A helicopter flew along the shore.
F 6. The last day of school.
R 7. The potatoes burned, the fish was too dry.
S 8. Return these books to the library.
F 9. Asked several questions about the movie.
S 10. The sky grew cloudy.

305

Mixed Review

These exercises provide review of the concepts presented in this Section. Each exercise challenges the students to apply several of the skills they have acquired during previous study. Because the "mixed" feature of these activities makes them more difficult, the teacher may wish to have less-advanced students do them orally or in small groups.

MIXED REVIEW

Using Sentences Correctly

A. Identifying sentences, fragments, and run-on sentences Write *Fragment*, *Sentence*, or *Run-On* for each of the following groups of words. Then, correct fragments by adding words to make complete sentences. Correct run-ons by using the correct capitalization and punctuation to show where each complete thought begins and ends.

S 1. The cellar door was left open.
F 2. My aunt, uncle, and six cousins. Sentences will vary.
R 3. We practiced all morning; now our act is perfect. (N)
F 4. Slept until nine o'clock. Sentences will vary.
S 5. Don't eat before the race.
F 6. A scary spy story. Sentences will vary.
R 7. Evan's birthday is March 26; he will be thirteen. (H)
S 8. The movie follows the cartoons.
R 9. Have you read this book? would you like to borrow it? (W)
F 10. Worked until seven o'clock. Sentences will vary.
S 11. Hope recited her poem.
S 12. Everyone met at Jean's house.
R 13. Kate collected pine cones; she put them in a basket. (S)
F 14. The old house on the corner. Sentences will vary.
S 15. I need thirty-five cents.

B. Correct fragments and run-on sentences Copy this paragraph. Correct any fragments or run-on sentences.

Corrections will vary. Suggested corrections below.

Last Saturday night was no ordinary evening for me. (It was m)My first baby-sitting job. It began at six o'clock. It ended at ten. During that time I fed, chased, and bathed three children and a dog. (I a)Also put them to bed. Why is it called baby-*sitting*? I never sat down at all!

USING GRAMMAR IN WRITING

Using Sentences Correctly

A. Imagine that you woke up in the middle of the night. You had just had a vivid dream. You wanted to remember the dream, so you reached for a pencil and pad of paper. In the dark you scribbled down your dream. The next morning, here is what you read:

> I was on a giant roller coaster I got to the top of the highest hill when I looked over I saw next to me Darth Vader was I scared Just then we started down-hill we were going so fast I was breathless all I could hear was Darth Vader's loud steady breathing suddenly the car flew off the track and plunged to earth but earth had disappeared I was floating among the stars Darth Vader was laughing a horrible, hollow laugh.

Rewrite your dream. Add the correct punctuation. Be sure you leave no fragments or run-on sentences.

B. Below is a group of sentence fragments. Use at least four of the fragments to write a short paragraph about why it is good to have a sense of humor. Change all of the fragments to complete sentences. You can use the fragments in any order you like.

not always easy	an example
able to laugh	better than complaining
if you're upset	rather than cry
at your own mistakes	a comedian

Using Grammar in Writing

These challenging and enjoyable activities allow the students to see how the concepts of grammar, usage, and mechanics may be applied in actual writing situations. Each exercise is designed to allow students practice in several of the skills they have acquired in this Section. The activities also provide opportunities for students to write creatively about a wide variety of interesting and unusual subjects.

307

Section Objectives

1. To understand the concept of a noun and to identify nouns in sentences

2. To differentiate between common and proper nouns

3. To differentiate between singular and plural nouns, and to form plurals correctly

4. To form and use possessive nouns correctly

5. To recognize the basic word order in the NV sentence pattern

Preparing the Students

Discuss a picture showing people and objects. Ask students to tell you who or what is in the picture. Tell them that each answer is a noun.

Additonal Resources

Diagnostic Test — page 2 in the test booklet

Mastery Test — pages 36–37 in the test booklet

Additional Exercises — pages 317–319 in the student text

Practice Book — pages 125–129

Duplicating Masters — pages 125–129

Special Populations — See special section at the front of this Teacher's Edition.

Part 1

Objective

To understand the concept of a noun and to identify nouns in sentences

Using Nouns

Part 1 What Are Nouns?

The words you use to name things are called **nouns.**

Look around you. Who is sitting near you? What is the name of your school? What street or road is it on? What city or town do you live in? The words that you use to name these things are nouns.

Nouns are words that name persons, places, or things. Read these examples:

Persons: Greg Luzinski, firefighter, pilot, Diana
Places: frontier, New York City, ranch, playground
Things: tree, Rocky Mountains, pizza, Frisbee

Some nouns, like those listed on page 308, are names of things that you can see. Other nouns are names of things that you cannot see. Here are some nouns that name things you cannot see.

idea courage loneliness peace

Exercises Find nouns.

A. Number your paper from 1 to 10. List the nouns in each sentence below.

1. Stacy saw the fireworks last July.
2. A surfer rode a huge wave.
3. A new band performed at the fair.
4. My brother has excellent eyesight.
5. My cousin lives on a farm in Iowa.
6. Jason plays the piano and the trombone.
7. The Dodgers will play in the World Series.
8. Keith has a picture of the Golden Gate Bridge on his notebook.
9. Ms. Mason told a story about the first Thanksgiving.
10. Robert does chores around the house and earns an allowance.

B. Writing This exercise will show you how often nouns are used in writing and in discussion. On your paper, make four lists of nouns according to these directions. Answers will vary.

1. Copy the names of five characters from short stories or novels.
2. Copy five nouns from your science book or math book.
3. List five names of foods.
4. List five names of places you have visited or read about.

Presenting the Lesson

1. Read and discuss pages 308–309. Point out that certain words can fit into two classes. For example, *ranch* can be considered a place or a thing.

2. Assign and discuss the exercises on pages 309–310.

Individualizing the Lesson

Less-Advanced Students

Ask the students to look around the classroom and make a list of objects that they can see. Then point out that these are all nouns. Remind the students that nouns can also name things or qualities that cannot be seen.

Advanced Students

Point out that there are some words that are both nouns and verbs, i.e. *spring, hit, fish.* Many sports have words that can be used as verbs and nouns, for example, *kick*, *ski*, *dive*. Have the students choose two or three sports and then make a list of such words. Remind them that the function of the word in a sentence determines whether it is a noun or verb.

Optional Practice

Have the students list the nouns in these sentences.

1. May is my favorite month.
2. The birds sing in the trees.
3. Flowers bloom in gardens.
4. There is no more cold or snow.
5. We play games at the park.
6. Activities at school increase.
7. My family goes on picnics.
8. Sometimes we go to the lake.

Part 2

Objective

To differentiate between common nouns and proper nouns

Presenting the Lesson

1. Read and discuss page 310. Ask students for more examples of common and proper nouns.

2. Assign and discuss the exercise on page 310. Discuss why proper nouns need to be capitalized.

Individualizing the Lesson

Less-Advanced Students

Before doing the exercise, give the students the following list of words and have them respond to each word with a particular proper noun: uncle, ocean, month, country, day, store, book.

Advanced Students

Ask the students to list the following proper nouns, capitalizing the correct words: 5 cities, 5 TV shows, 5 holidays, 5 states, 5 famous Americans.

Optional Practice

Ask the students to circle the proper nouns and underline the common nouns in the following sentences.

1. Jerry fell into Salt Creek.
2. Our dog bit Tom, the mailman.
3. Main Street has new lights.
4. The Byrds moved to Utah.
5. The Titanic sank after it hit an iceberg in the Atlantic.

Part 2 Common Nouns and Proper Nouns

The noun *student* names any person. *Cecilia* names one particular student.

The noun *city* names any place. *San Francisco* names one particular city.

The noun *car* names any thing. *Ford* names one particular car.

A common noun is a general name for a person, place, or thing. A common noun begins with a small letter.

A proper noun names a particular person, place, or thing. A proper noun always begins with a capital letter.

Many proper nouns are made up of two or more words, such as *Atlantic Ocean* and *Grand Canyon National Park*. When the proper noun has several words, capitalize all the important words. You do not have to capitalize *of*, *on*, or *the*.

Exercise Find common nouns and proper nouns.

On your paper, make two columns. Label one column *Common Nouns* and the other column *Proper Nouns*. Write each word below in the appropriate column. Remember to begin every proper noun with a capital letter.

C 1. person
C 2. city
P 3. washington [W]
P 4. ms. steele [M, S]
C 5. paper
P 6. timothy [T]
C 7. principal
C 8. college
P 9. africa [A]
P 10. lake superior [L, S]
P 11. maria [M]
C 12. post office
P 13. england [E]
C 14. building
P 15. mr. ruiz [M, R]
P 16. chicago [C]
C 17. dentist
P 18. elm street [E, S]
C 19. cat
P 20. the chicago tribune [C, T]

Part 3 Singular and Plural Nouns

What is the difference between the words in these pairs?

astronaut	cake	idea	town
astronauts	cakes	ideas	towns

You can see that the words are almost the same, but that they have different endings. The bottom word in each pair has an *-s* added. What difference does that *-s* make in the meaning of the words? The *-s* changes the *number* of persons, places, or things that the word names.

A noun that names just one person, place, or thing is called a **singular noun.** A noun that names more than one person, place, or thing is called a **plural noun.** (All the nouns in the top line of the word pairs are *singular*. All the nouns in the bottom line are *plural*.) Changing a word from singular to plural is called forming the plural of the noun.

Here are seven rules for forming the plurals of nouns:

1. To form the plural of most nouns, just add an *-s*.

stick**s**	cow**s**	bike**s**	drink**s**
stone**s**	dog**s**	skate**s**	snack**s**

2. When the singular noun ends in *s, sh, ch, x,* or *z*, add *-es*.

circus**es**	ash**es**	fox**es**
class**es**	lunch**es**	waltz**es**

3. When the singular ends in *o*, add *-s*.

studio**s** radio**s** stereo**s** banjo**s**

Exceptions: For the following nouns ending in *o*, add *-es*:

echo**es** hero**es** tomato**es** potato**es**

4. When the singular noun ends in *y* with a consonant before it, change the *y* to *i*, and add *-es*.

fly → fl**ies**	penny → penn**ies**
pony → pon**ies**	candy → cand**ies**

Part 3

Objective

To differentiate between singular and plural nouns, and to form plurals correctly

Presenting the Lesson

1. Read and discuss page 311 through Rule 1. Point out the relationship between the words *single* and *singular* to help students understand singularity of nouns. Ask students to look around the classroom and give other examples of plurals formed by adding only an *s*.

2. Go over Rules 2 to 7 on pages 311 and 312 with the students. Ask them why simply adding *s* to the examples in Rule 2 would cause problems in pronunciation.

3. Read and discuss page 312. If students have access to dictionaries, have them look up each word listed under Rule 7.

4. Assign and discuss Exercises A and B on page 313. Have students check their answers to Exercise B in the dictionary.

Individualizing the Lesson

Less-Advanced Students

To give students more practice in forming plurals, have them name ten or more animals not mentioned in the lesson. Write the singular form on the board. Then have the students write the plural form on the board. Refer to the rules in the text if necessary. The same exercise may be done with plants or foods.

Advanced Students

Suggest that students write a

paragraph describing a trip to the store using at least 10 plural forms. Have them use the rules in the textbook and a dictionary to check the spelling of the plurals.

Optional Practice

Have the students follow the directions for Exercise A using the following words:

3 1. rodeo-rodeos
2 2. dish-dishes
4 3. daisy-daisies
2 4. wax-waxes
1 5. arcade-arcades
3 6. echo-echoes
7 7. child-children
5 8. calf-calves
1 9. monkey-monkeys
7 10. ox-oxen
5 11. gulf-gulfs
1 12. gerbil-gerbils
7 13. louse-lice
2 14. six-sixes
6 15. sheep-sheep
5 16. chief-chiefs
2 17. waltz-waltzes
4 18. fly-flies
4 19. baby-babies
2 20. tax-taxes

Extending the Lesson

After students have studied all the rules on pages 312 and 313, have a spelling bee using only plural nouns. Divide the class into teams, and have the teams stand in lines. Dictate words from the following word list, from the text, or from the students' other work. Any student misspelling a word must sit down. Alternate teams. The winning team will be the one with the most students standing at the end.

If you wish to make this more difficult, use singular nouns and have the students say the plural form and then spell it.

Word List. *Rule 2:* crosses, boxes, churches, catches, benches, crashes, wishes, dishes, splashes, dresses, touches, flashes, patches, glasses, guesses, mixes, passes, pushes, masses, circuses, bunches, porches,

5. For most nouns ending in *f* or *fe*, add *-s*. For some nouns ending in *f* or *fe*, however, change the *f* to *v* and add *-es* or *-s*.

belief → beliefs	thief → thieves	leaf → leaves
chief → chiefs	knife → knives	half → halves
roof → roofs	wife → wives	shelf → shelves
dwarf → dwarfs	life → lives	elf → elves

6. Some nouns are the same for both singular and plural.

deer trout sheep moose salmon

7. Some nouns form their plurals in special ways.

mouse → mice	man → men	tooth → teeth
goose → geese	woman → women	foot → feet
	child → children	

Using a Dictionary To Find Plurals

Here is a dictionary entry for the word *echo*. Notice that the entry shows the plural ending, *-oes*. (The plural noun is *echoes*.) Most dictionaries show the plural form of a noun if the plural is formed in an irregular way. When you are not sure how to form the plural of a noun, look up the noun in a dictionary.

---

ech•o (ek′ō) ***n.***, *pl.* **-oes** [< L. < Gr. *ēchō*] **1.** *a)* the repetition of a sound that occurs when sound waves are reflected from a surface *b)* a sound so made **2.** *a)* any repetition or imitation of the words, ideas, etc. of another *b)* a person who repeats or imitates in this way **3.** sympathetic response **4.** a radar wave reflected from an object, appearing as a spot of light on a radarscope —[**E-**] *Gr. Myth.* a nymph who pined away for Narcissus until only her voice remained —***vi.*** **-oed, -o•ing** **1.** to be filled with echoes *[*the long hall *echoed* with their laughter*]* **2.** to be repeated as an echo *[*his words *echoed* in the valley*]* —***vt.*** **1.** to repeat (the words, ideas, etc.) of (another) **2.** to repeat or reflect (sound) from a surface

---

Exercises **Form the plurals of nouns.**

A. Number your paper from 1 to 10. Copy each pair of nouns below. Then write the number of the rule that tells how the plural was formed.

3	1. piano → pianos	7	6. tooth → teeth
5	2. roof → roofs	3	7. tomato → tomatoes
1	3. doctor doctors	5	8. life → lives
2	4. tax → taxes	6	9. moose → moose
4	5. party → parties	2	10. bench → benches

B. Write the plural form for each of these nouns.

women 1. woman	dwarfs 6. dwarf	trout 11. trout	copies 16. copy
knives 2. knife	radios 7. radio	noises 12. noise	mice 17. mouse
sheep 3. sheep	watches 8. watch	halves 13. half	teams 18. team
girls 4. girl	children 9. child	potatoes 14. potato	sandwiches 19. sandwich
candies 5. candy	boys 10. boy	gases 15. gas	leaves 20. leaf

Part 4 Making Nouns Show Possession

Study these examples.

These are my sister's skates.
(Who owns the skates?)
Sally's mother called.
(Whose mother called?)
This is the boy's hat.
(Who owns the hat?)

What has been added to the nouns *sister, Sally,* and *boy?* Adding *'s* makes the nouns show ownership, or possession. Words such as *sister's, Sally's,* and *boy's* are **possessive nouns.**

A possessive noun shows possession of the noun that follows.

watches, inches, peaches, searches, scratches, sandwiches, expresses, kisses, riches. *Rule 3:* zoos, taboos. *Rule 4:* armies, countries, cries, families, histories, parties, stories, worries, babies, industries, puppies, cookies, bakeries, daddies, enemies, replies. *Rule 5:* wives, halves, chiefs.

Part 4

Objective

To form and use possessive nouns correctly

Presenting the Lesson

1. Discuss the meaning of the word *possession.* Show that besides indicating ownership (the car of my brother), it can also refer to a relationship (the sister of Bob) or other connection (the friend of my uncle). *Possess* could also mean "to use" (the crib of the baby), or simply "to have" (the collar of the dog). Ask students for the shorter way of saying each of these phrases and discuss the idea of possession in each:

the saw of the lumberjack, the ox of Paul Bunyan, the bridle of the horse, the business partner of my aunt, the daughter of my cousin.

2. Read and discuss page 313.

3. Read and discuss pages 314 and 315. Stress that a possessive form is made by adding to a noun which is already singular or plural.

4. You may want to do Exercise A on page 315 with the students. Have them read each sentence aloud with the possessive form, then spell the posssessive noun correctly. Assign and discuss Exercise B.

Individualizing the Lesson

Less-Advanced Students

Have students rewrite each of the following phrases, using the possessive form.

Example: the growl of the bear
the bear's growl

1. the daughter of the woman (the woman's daughter)
2. the chattering of the birds (the birds' chattering)
3. the coat of the person (the person's coat)
4. the stunts of the acrobats (the acrobats' stunts)
5. the wild pitch of the pitcher (the pitcher's wild pitch)
6. the shovels of the workmen (the workmen's shovels)
7. the roller skates of my friend (my friend's roller skates)
8. the dive of the stuntwoman (the stuntwoman's dive)

Advanced Students

Give students the following list of nouns. Have them write the possessive for each and then supply something that belongs to the noun.

Example: Noun = Manuel
Manuel's gloves

Nouns: Father's, the cat's, the wall's, my teacher's, the lions', the lady's, the ladies', Mr. Blair's, the battle's, the thief's, the mouse's, the mice's, my sister's. Phrases will vary.

Making Singular Nouns Show Possession

To make a singular noun show possession, add an apostrophe and *s*.

Singular Noun	Possessive Noun
mechanic	mechanic's
James	James's
Ms. Roberts	Ms. Roberts's

Making Plural Nouns Show Possession

There are two rules to remember for making a plural noun show possession.

1. If the plural noun ends in *s*, simply add an apostrophe after the *s*.

Plural Noun	Possessive Noun
workers	workers'
nurses	nurses'
dentists	dentists'

2. If the plural noun does not end in *s*, add an apostrophe and an *s* after the apostrophe.

Plural Noun	Possessive Noun
men	men's
women	women's
children	children's

Adding the Apostrophe

Look at these words. See where the apostrophe is added.

the girl's project	This means a project belonging to one girl.
the girls' project	This means a project belonging to more than one girl.

If you are not sure where to add the apostrophe, write the word by itself first. Then follow the rules.

Exercises **Make nouns show possession.**

A. Copy the following sentences. Make the underlined words show possession.

1. Rosa team beat Dwayne team yesterday. Rosa's/Dwayne's
2. In my uncle shop they sell men and ladies clothes. uncle's/men's/ladies'
3. Bonnie team won the spelling match. Bonnie's
4. Tammy little sister got lost in the store. Tammy's
5. Where are the children toys? children's
6. My two brothers clothes were all over the floor. brothers'
7. The girl books fell out of the car. girl's
8. The doctor gently felt the dog paw. dog's
9. I left my sweater at the dentist office. dentist's
10. Richard hobby is collecting ballplayers autographs. Richard's/ballplayers'

B. In each sentence one noun is underlined. Write the noun. Then add an apostrophe or an apostrophe and *s* to make the noun show possession.

1. We found Ramon bike in the basement. Ramon's
2. There are two girls coats in the closet. girls'
3. One man hat blew into the street. man's
4. It was "Ladies Day" at Yankee Stadium. Ladies'
5. The children library closes at five o'clock. children's
6. We found George mittens. George's
7. Which department sells babies cribs? babies'
8. Where are the women tickets? women's
9. I lost my father pen. father's
10. Pam and Sue were studying Jenny notes. Jenny's

Optional Practice

Have the students add apostrophes to the possessives in the following sentences.

1. Juan's book was on Dan's desk.
2. The teachers' meeting is at 4 P.M.
3. Have you seen Rachel's mother?
4. The car's brakes were faulty.
5. The school's gymnastics team is the best in the state.
6. The radio club's fundraiser is selling Krasners' cookies.
7. Are the Thomases' kittens still lost?
8. These children's toys are safe.

Extending the Lesson

Put the phrases below on the board or on a worksheet. Have students identify the possessive nouns. Then have students divide a paper into two columns, headed *singular* and *plural*. Ask them to write the base noun of the possessive in the correct column. You may also want to review the rules for forming plural nouns (Pages 311–312).

Examples: 1. my grandmother's hat
2. the horses' hoofs

	Singular	*Plural*
1.	grandmother	
2.		horses

- P a. the thieves' getaway car thieves
- P b. the chiefs' fire helmets chiefs
- S c. the fox's footprints fox
- S d. the class's play class
- P e. the women's tennis racquets women
- P f. the winners' trophies winners
- S g. the barber's scissors barber
- S h. the team's final score team
- S i. the lizard's tongue lizard
- P j. the boys' socks boys
- S k. my friend's hamster friend
- P l. the cars' horns cars

Objective

To recognize the basic word order in the NV sentence pattern

Presenting the Lesson

1. Read and discuss page 316. As the chart indicates, the noun part of each sentence includes not only the noun identified as the subject, but also all the modifiers of that noun (as in *This camera*). The verb part includes the verb and its modifiers, if any (as in *works easily*). The students should be able to identify the point at which a sentence can be divided into these two parts.

2. Assign and discuss Exercise A. It is suggested that the class do Exercises B and C together.

Optional Practice

The following lengthy sentences are basic NV pattern sentences. Ask students to identify the break between the noun part and the verb part.

1. That old rusty car in the junk yard | can still run.
2. The hot tomato and mushroom sauce | was cooking on the stove.
3. All the fire engines | rushed quickly to the scene of the explosion.
4. Nearly everyone in our class | went to the picnic.
5. The dense fog in the harbor | swirled around the boats.
6. Half the burritos in the pan | were sold in the first five minutes of the fair.
7. The telephone | has been busy for quite some time.
8. He | will be here soon.

Sentence Patterns The N V Pattern

In an English sentence, words are put together in a certain order to make sense. The word order in most sentences follows a pattern. In this book you will study four **sentence patterns.**

Every sentence has a subject and a verb. The subject is usually a noun. In this chart, *N* stands for the noun in the complete subject. *V* is the verb in the complete predicate.

N	V
Diana	stumbled.
My brother	waited.
This camera	works easily.

The word order in these sentences follows a pattern. That pattern is noun-verb, or N V, and is called the **N V pattern.**

Exercises Use the N V pattern.

A. Make a chart like the one above. Label one column *N*. Label the other column *V*. Write these sentences on the chart.

1. Rain (N) | fell (V).
2. Katy (N) | bats (V) next.
3. The bus (N) | stopped (V).
4. Scott (N) | laughed (V).
5. The green vase (N) | shattered (V).
6. The train (N) | started (V) slowly.

B. Copy this chart. Complete each sentence in the N V pattern. Sentences will vary.

N	V
1. ________	listened.
2. ________	worked carefully.
3. The sun	________.
4. ________	turned around.

C. Write five sentences in the N V pattern. Sentences will vary.

ADDITIONAL EXERCISES

Using Nouns

A. Recognizing Nouns Write the nouns in each of the following sentences. (Use after page 309.)

1. Mark ate tacos for dinner.
2. That artist shows talent.
3. The boat sailed beneath the bridge.
4. Bob gave Joe two tickets to the performance.
5. The Guggenheim Museum is in New York City.
6. Gerry likes hamburgers with mustard and relish.
7. A colorful glider swooped silently over the crowd.
8. Meg sewed the patches into a quilt.
9. Milwaukee is a city on the shores of Lake Michigan.
10. The music came from the radio in the kitchen.

B. Finding Proper Nouns Write the proper nouns in each of the following sentences. Capitalize them. (Use after page 310.)

1. Leslie and mark play baseball with their friends. M
2. Have you crossed the brooklyn bridge in new york? B B N Y
3. Joan and her family moved from montana to california. M C
4. In the last game, the pirates beat the cardinals. P C
5. Mr. lynch drove his plymouth through the mountains. L P
6. That man crossed the atlantic ocean in a sailboat. A O
7. The train for atlanta leaves in the morning. A
8. Ms. martin explained the long chapter. M
9. Her family drove from louisville to chicago. L C
10. The philippine islands are in the pacific ocean. P I P O

C. Forming Plurals Write the plural form of each underlined noun in these sentences. (Use after page 313.)

1. Her brother visited the movie studio. studios
2. The woman owned the bookstore. women

Additional Exercises

These Additional Exercises may be used for additional practice of the concepts presented in this Section. Each exercise focuses on a single concept, and should be used after the page number indicated in parentheses.

Review

If you have not assigned these Additional Exercises before this time, you can also use them as an excellent Section Review.

3. Robert searched the library shelf for the book. shelves
4. The chef made the sandwich with rye bread. sandwiches
5. The baby played with the toys. babies
6. Salmon swim upstream. salmon
7. The workers repaired the damaged roof. roofs
8. The box of books fell from the rickety table. boxes
9. Bev's mouse ate cheese and crackers. mice
10. Rick lost his ski on the ski lift. skis

D. Forming Possessives Write the possessive form of each underlined noun. (Use after page 315.)

1. the teachers meeting teachers'
2. Jess part in the play Jess's
3. a cartoonist drawings cartoonist's
4. the players pictures in the paper players'
5. all the boys uniforms boys'
6. the children playground children's
7. the dog collar dog's
8. Ms. Burns car Ms. Burns's
9. the cities budget cities'
10. the typist notepad typist's

318

MIXED REVIEW

Using Nouns

A. Finding nouns and identifying proper nouns Copy the following sentences. Underline all the nouns. If a noun is proper, capitalize it.

1. Amy is moving to hazel crest drive.
2. St. paul is the capital of minnesota.
3. My family drove our camper through the smoky mountains.
4. Donna is studying history at boston college.
5. What foods are eaten during passover?
6. Dale has tickets for the game on saturday.
7. This movie stars clint eastwood.
8. Our library has the new book by beverly cleary.
9. The girls want to play monopoly.
10. The wildlife of africa must be protected.

B. Using plurals and possessives of nouns Copy the following sentences. For each sentence, choose the correct word from the two in parentheses.

1. The principal needs three (copys, copies) of the letter.
2. Two (halfs, halves) make a whole.
3. The (boy's, boys') arm is broken.
4. James has two loose (tooth's, teeth).
5. Ms. Lewis is our (team's, teams) coach.
6. Cheryl lightly touched the (piano's, pianos) keys.
7. The (childrens', children's) department is on the third floor.
8. (Gina's, Ginas') aunt is a doctor at that hospital.
9. That (girl's, girls') hobbies are painting and coin collecting.
10. There are about forty (sheep, sheeps) in that herd.

Mixed Review

These exercises provide review of the concepts presented in this Section. Each exercise challenges the students to apply several of the skills they have acquired during previous study. Because the "mixed" feature of these activities makes them more difficult, the teacher may wish to have less-advanced students do them orally or in small groups.

Using Grammar in Writing

These challenging and enjoyable activities allow the students to see how the concepts of grammar, usage, and mechanics may be applied in actual writing situations. Each exercise is designed to allow students practice in several of the skills they have acquired in this Section. The activities also provide opportunities for students to write creatively about a wide variety of interesting and unusual subjects.

USING GRAMMAR IN WRITING

Using Nouns

A. Most of our names have a special meaning. For example, the name Debby means "bee" in the Hebrew language. The name Richard originally meant "strong king." What do you know about your name? Try to find out what it means and what language it comes from. Look in the dictionary or in a book about names. Your school or local librarian will help you.

Write a paragraph about your name. Tell what language or country it came from. Also tell what the name means and why it was chosen for you. If there are other forms of your name, write those too.

If you wish, tell whether or not you like your name. If you would rather have another name, what is it, and why? Underline each noun that you use in your paragraph. Underline common nouns once and proper nouns twice.

B. One of your friends has suggested that several of you have a garage sale. At a garage sale, you sell things you don't need anymore. It is a way to make some extra spending money. Make a list of twenty items you would put in the sale. Make your list specific. Include names of games, sports equipment, items of clothing, comics, records, and so on. Underline any proper nouns in your list. Circle any plural nouns. Put a star next to any possessive nouns.

C. Now write an ad about the garage sale that would run in your local newspaper. Give the time, the date, and the location of the sale. Also, mention some of the most interesting items that you have to sell.

Using Verbs

Part 1 What Are Verbs?

Read these sentences. What do the underlined words tell you?

Roberto hit a home run. Vera ran to the store.

The underlined words tell what each person did. They tell about action. Words that tell about action are called **action verbs.**

Action Verbs

Some verbs tell about action you can see, such as *hit* and *ran.* Other verbs tell about action you cannot see, as in these examples:

Sarah worried about the test.
Tony wants a new jacket.
I have two dollars.
The jury believed the witness.

Section Objectives

1. To identify verbs as either action or state-of-being verbs

2. To differentiate between main verbs and helping verbs, and to recognize and use them correctly

3. To understand the function of direct objects and to identify them in sentences

4. To understand the concept of linking verbs, and to identify them and the words linked to the subject

5. To recognize and use the present, past, and future verb tenses

6. To recognize the basic word order in the N V N sentence pattern

7. To recognize the basic word order in the N LV N sentence pattern

8. To recognize the basic word order in the N LV Adj sentence pattern

Preparing the Students

Display a picture showing action or use a picture from a textbook. Discuss what is happening. During the discussion, list any action or state-of-being verbs that the students use. Explain that this section will help them use verbs correctly.

Additional Resources

Diagnostic Test — page 3 in the test booklet

Mastery Test — pages 39–42 in the test booklet

Additional Exercises — pages 342–345 in the student text

Practice Book — pages 130–138

Duplicating Masters — pages 130–138

Special Populations — See special section at the front of this Teacher's Edition.

Part 1

Objective

To identify verbs as either action or state-of-being verbs

Presenting the Lesson

1. In addition to what is presented in the text, there are other ways to identify a verb. These ways, listed below, are based on what linguists have discovered about the structure of a word and the order of words in a sentence. It is suggested that the information below be used to point out additional ways in which verbs function.

Ways To Identify Verbs

1. Look for words that change their forms to show past time.

Present	Past
walk	walked
eat	ate

2. Look for words that follow helping verbs (forms of *be, do,* and *have,* and helping verbs like *can, could, shall, will, may, might,* and *must*).

3. Look for words with the following endings or suffixes:

-ify (identify) *-ize* (realize)

4. Look for words that fit the blank in this test sentence:

Please _____ .

2. Read and discuss page 321. Ask students for examples of both types of action verbs.

3. Assign and discuss Exercises A and B on page 322.

4. Read and discuss page 323. Ask students to identify the state-of-being verbs in the following sentences:

Exercises Find action verbs.

A. Write the action verb in each sentence.

1. The hikers lost their way in the fog.
2. Jennifer agreed with Rick about the plans for the dance.
3. Marty has two younger brothers.
4. Jim wished for a sunny day.
5. Members of Congress make laws.
6. Linda climbed the maple tree.
7. Luis expected a call from his uncle in San Juan.
8. The band marched onto the field at half-time.
9. Jessica traveled through Oregon last summer.
10. The actors painted their faces with makeup.

B. Think of an action verb that will complete each sentence below. Copy the sentences, filling in each blank with an action verb. Many different answers are possible for each sentence.

Answers will vary.

Example: Toby _____ the ball.

Possible answers: Toby caught the ball.
Toby threw the ball.
Toby held the ball.
Toby hit the ball.

1. The class _____ at the old joke.
2. Aunt Suzanne _____ a new sweater.
3. Several people _____ on the crowded beach.
4. A silver fox _____ over the fence.
5. Gina _____ her new fountain pen.
6. Anita _____ down the hall.
7. The two brothers _____ .
8. The conductor _____ tickets.
9. We _____ for the signal to begin our cheer.
10. The scientists _____ an Arctic expedition.

Verbs That State That Something Is

Not all verbs tell about action. Some verbs state that something *is*. The underlined verbs in these sentences say that something *is*. They are called **state-of-being verbs.**

I am a student.	The girls were happy.
John is my brother.	The weather was bad.
We are late.	We will be on time.

The most common state-of-being verbs are these:

is	am	were	being
are	was	be	been

Other state-of-being verbs include these:

look seem become taste smell feel

I feel sick.	The juice tasted good.
Jill became a dancer.	Ed seems surprised.

Verbs are words that tell about an action or state that something *is*.

Exercises Use action verbs and state-of-being verbs.

A. Write the verb in each of the following sentences. Some are action verbs, and some are state-of-being verbs.

1. The Dodgers are her heroes.
2. The boys were still hungry.
3. Aaron bought his ticket for the concert.
4. Pam argued with her sister about clothes.
5. The new hardware store opens tomorrow.
6. My cousin is a stunt driver.
7. John and Flo sang together.
8. Lisa climbed the spiral staircase.
9. Dan imagined a trip to Mars.
10. A butterfly sailed in the wind.

a. This art project is difficult.
b. My scissors are not sharp.
c. I am very careful with paints.
d. The directions were clear.
e. The final product will be a mobile.

5. It is suggested that Exercise A on page 323 be done as a class activity. Then assign and discuss Exercises B and C on page 324.

6. Read and discuss pages 324 and 325.

7. You may wish to do Exercise A on page 325 with the class. Assign and discuss Exercise B.

Individualizing the Lesson

Less-Advanced Students

Point out to students that state-of-being verbs can be compared to an equal sign in arithmetic. A sentence with a state-of-being verb can be compared to an equation.

$3 + 3 = 6$
three and three *are* six.
Joshua = a tall boy.
Joshua *is* a tall boy.

Remind students that no action is involved.

You may wish to encourage students to memorize the basic state-of-being verbs *am, is, are, was, were, be, being,* and *been.* These are to be used to complete the following sentences. Have students write in the correct verb above the equal sign. Some of the answers will vary.

1. We = very good friends.
2. I = a hungry boy.
3. Those girls = members of the tennis team.
4. Last year they = the state champions.
5. Shana and Joyce = the best doubles players at our school.

6. Your sister = very good in the class play.
7. My math teacher = Ms. Kane.
8. The baby = naughty this morning.
9. The horses = all beautifully groomed for today's show.
10. New Mexico = a perfect place to study Indian culture.

Advanced Students

Have students write complete sentence answers to the following questions. The answer to the first question should contain a state-of-being verb. The answer to the second question should contain an action verb and may be more than one sentence long. Answers will vary.

1a. How many people are in your family?
1b. What do they do on Sundays?
2a. What is the name of your favorite sports figure?
2b. Why is he/she your favorite?
3a. Where were you after school yesterday?
3b. What did you do there?
4a. What is the title of your favorite book?
4b. What happened at the end of the book?

Optional Practice

To further clarify the difference between action and state-of-being verbs, give students the following pairs of sentences. Have them fill in an appropriate verb and label it *A* or *SB*. Answers will vary.

1. This class ______ very large.
2. This class ______ a present to the teacher.
3. Someone ______ sandwiches for us.
4. The sandwiches ______ very tasty.

B. Number your paper from 1 to 10. Write the verb in each of the following sentences. After the verb, write *Action* or *State-of-Being* to tell what kind of verb it is.

A 1. Juan plays the drums in the school band.
A 2. Gino's parents own a toy store.
SB 3. Gloria is the class clown.
A 4. I made a puppet for my niece.
A 5. The sparrow injured its wing.
SB 6. The parade is at noon.
A 7. Max hid in the basement during the thunderstorm.
SB 8. The weather was beautiful.
A 9. Karen enjoys mystery novels.
A 10. The basketball landed in the bleachers.

C. Follow the directions for Exercise B.

SB 1. This popcorn tastes too salty.
A 2. Mike's sister works at the ice cream shop.
SB 3. Your suitcase feels very light.
SB 4. The hotel seems old.
A 5. George likes country music.
A 6. Liz chopped wood for the fire.
SB 7. A conch is a large shell.
SB 8. Hutchinson was a fine player.
A 9. My brother collects arrowheads and fossils.
A 10. Joey and Maria planned the class trip.

Using Verbs in Sentences

Look at these groups of words. They do not express complete ideas. They are not sentences. What words are missing?

Kevin sick   We the zoo every year

These are not sentences because they do not have verbs.

When you add verbs, you can make sentences like these:

Kevin *was* sick.   We *visit* the zoo every year.

Remember that every sentence must have a verb.

Exercises Use verbs in sentences.

A. Writing Read the following groups of words. If a word group is a sentence, write *Sentence*. If it is not a sentence, add a verb. Then write the complete sentence. There are many correct ways to finish each sentence.

Answers to 1, 2, 4, 7, 10 will vary.

1. The quarterback the ball.
2. Heidi a mountain girl.
3. S 3. A plane landed on the lake.
4. Rosy a yellow scarf.
5. S 5. The elevator stopped.
6. S 6. Apples are my favorite fruit.
7. Amy her shoes in the closet.
8. S 8. We play soccer in that field.
9. S 9. *The Wiz* was a play and a movie.
10. The crowd the national anthem.

B. Follow the directions for Exercise A.

Answers to 1, 3, 4, 7, 9 will vary.

1. Where the water fountain?
2. S 2. Al put posters on the wall.
3. A crabapple sour.
4. The Broncos in the fourth quarter.
5. S 5. The girls rode their bikes.
6. S 6. My collie sleeps near my bed.
7. The farmer the grain.
8. S 8. A tire makes a good swing.
9. Many people turkey on Thanksgiving.
10. S 10. The firefighters opened the fire hydrant.

SB 5. Ed _____ class president last year.

A 6. Ed _____ that students should have more activities.

A 7. I _____ when I see spiders.

SB 8. I _____ afraid of spiders.

SB 9. My family _____ usually together on weekends.

A 10. My family _____ games at the forest preserve.

SB 11. Laura _____ a professional dancer.

A 12. Laura _____ with the Civic Ballet Company.

A 13. That dog _____ at me.

SB 14. That dog _____ mean.

SB 15. High winds _____ a danger to the peach crop.

A 16. High winds _____ off the roof of our shed.

Part 2

Objective

To differentiate between main verbs and helping verbs, and to recognize and use them correctly

Presenting the Lesson

1. Read and discuss pages 326 and 327. Make sure students understand the difference between the predicate and the verb. The predicate includes *all* the words that tell what happened, while the verb includes *only* the main verb (either action or state-of-being) and its helping verbs. They should become familiar with the helping verbs listed in the text so that they can find them easily in a long predicate.

Point out that the one-word verbs students have already studied are grouped with main verbs. Some students may have the false belief that a verb is always only one word. Make sure that they see the need for helping verbs in the sample sentences. Stress that the function of the verb as a whole remains the same.

2. Ask students to point out the main verbs and the helping verbs in these sentences:

HV MV
The dog is barking loudly.
HV MV
The dog has barked loudly all night.

3. Assign and discuss Exercises A and B on page 327.

4. Read and discuss page 328. Ask students to give other examples of sentences using main verbs that need helping verbs.

5. You might wish to do Exercise

Part 2 Main Verbs and Helping Verbs

Most of the verbs you have studied so far have been just one word: *hit, is, ran,* and *climbed,* for example.

Many verbs are made up of more than one word. Notice the verbs in these sentences.

Betsy *walked* home.
Betsy *is walking* home.
Betsy *has been walking* home.

Steven *called* you.
Steven *was calling* you.
Steven *might have called* you.

When a verb is made up of more than one word, the last word is the **main verb.** The other words are called **helping verbs.**

Helping Verb +	Main Verb =	Verb
	walked	walked
is	walking	is walking
has been	walking	has been walking
	called	called
was	calling	was calling
might have	called	might have called

The most common helping verbs are forms of *be, have,* and *do*:

be—am, is, are, was, were
have—has, have, had
do—does, do, did

These words can also be used by themselves as main verbs.

Used as Helping Verb	**Used as Main Verb**
Janet *was visiting.*	Janet *was* in Indiana.
Ralph *does like* math.	Ralph *does* his work.

These are other helping verbs that can be used with main verbs:

be	been	shall	could	would	might
being	can	will	should	may	

A verb may be a single word. A verb may also be a group of words, made up of a main verb and one or more helping verbs.

Exercises Find main verbs and helping verbs.

A. Make two columns. Label the first column *Helping Verbs*. Label the second column *Main Verb*. Write the parts of the verb for each of these sentences in the correct column.

Example: That car should have stopped for the bus.

Helping Verbs	**Main Verb**
should have	stopped

1. Ernest has [HV] eaten [MV] some fudge.
2. Tomorrow we will [HV] be [HV] going [MV] to the museum.
3. One horse was [HV] leading [MV] the parade.
4. Lorraine is [HV] carrying [MV] her catcher's mitt.
5. The trip should [HV] have [HV] ended [MV] sooner.
6. Stephanie does [HV] like [MV] the new apartment.
7. We may [HV] wash [MV] the car today.
8. They could [HV] have [HV] arrived [MV] on time.
9. Julio has [HV] been [HV] painting [MV] with poster paints.
10. Our teacher had [HV] explained [MV] the experiment before.

B. Writing Write five sentences. Each sentence should have a main verb and one or more helping verbs. Underline the main verb in each sentence once. Underline the helping verbs twice. Answers will vary.

A on pages 328 and 329 with the class. Then assign and discuss Exercise B on page 329.

6. Read and discuss page 329. Stress that separation of the helping verb from the main verb does not change the meaning of the whole verb.

7. Assign and discuss Exercises A and B on page 330.

Individualizing the Lesson

Less-Advanced Students

1. Before students work on the exercises, be certain they recognize that certain forms of helping verbs and main verbs are used together. Remind them that they have been using these verbs in everyday spoken language, and that this lesson simply sorts out and labels the verbs they know. Point out that time and other conditions often dictate what form of verb should be used.

Ask students to put the verb *talk* after each of the helping verbs on page 327. Then turn back to the forms of *be, have,* and *do* on page 326. Using the word *talk* after each helping verb, have students notice how the form changes, necessitating the "ing" or "ed" ending. If needed, continue with the words *play, bake,* and *paint*.

2. Give special attention to the three-column chart in the middle of page 326. Review it thoroughly before assigning the exercises on page 327. Make sure students realize that sometimes more than one helping verb is used before the main verb. Have them see how many helping verbs can be put before the word *eating* (was, were, will be, is, are, has been, have been, had been, shall have been, will have been, could have been, should have been, would have been, may have been, might have been, must have been).

Advanced Students

It is important for students to understand how different helping verbs change the meaning of a sentence. Have students vary the following sentences by changing verb forms and helping verbs. Remind them to use the list of helping verbs on page 327. Have them do at least two variations of each sentence.

Answers will vary.

Example:

original sentence: We are washing the windows now.

variations: We should have washed the windows last week.

We might be washing the windows tomorrow, too.

We have washed all the windows.

1. We have chased all the flies out of the tent.
2. The girls have been swimming for hours.
3. Julio fished down by the lake.
4. The wind is blowing everything around the campsite.
5. There may be some rain tonight.

Optional Practice

Have students follow the directions for the Exercises on page 330, using these sentences. Let students know that verbs used as helping verbs in some sentences are used as main verbs in other sentences.

HV MV
1. Did the baby crawl up the stairs?

HV MV
2. The racer has run many times before.

MV
3. The carpenter did a good job on the repairs.

Some Verbs Need Helping Verbs

Read these three sentences:

We *ate* the cheese.
We *eaten* all of the chicken.
We *eating* crackers now.

Something is wrong with the last two sentences. What can you add to make them sound right? You can add helping verbs.

We **have** *eaten* all of the chicken.
We **are** *eating* crackers now.

Four of the verbs that you use very often must be used with helping verbs. They are *been, done, gone,* and *seen.* Verbs with the *-en* ending, like *chosen* or *ridden,* must be used with helping verbs. Verbs with the *-ing* ending, like *sitting* and *talking,* must be used with helping verbs. There are many other verbs that must be used with helping verbs. You will learn more about them in **Section 5.**

Exercises **Add helping verbs.**

A. Read each of these sentences. If the sentence is correct, write *Correct.* If the verb needs a helping verb, write a helping verb and the main verb. There may be more than one right helping verb. Suggested answers follow for 1, 3, 4, 7, 9, 10.

Example: Ms. Lorne waiting at the bus stop.
was waiting

1. The groundhog seen its shadow. has seen, had seen
2. A huge truck has swept the streets. C
3. We playing hockey. are playing, were playing
4. The vase broken by accident. was broken, has been broken
5. Superman rescued the miners. C
6. Babe Didrikson was a great athlete. C

7. A lady walking the tightrope. is walking, was walking, will be walking

C 8. The girl was running down the alley.

9. We been listening to a Donna Summer album. have been listening, had been listening

10. I using your ruler. am using, was using, have been using

B. Follow the directions for Exercise A. Suggested answers follow for 1, 3, 5, 6, 7, 9, 10.

1. Barb ridden a bronco. has ridden, had ridden

C 2. Millions of years ago, dinosaurs roamed the earth.

3. The class learning about government. is learning, was learning

C 4. Alec had a strange dream.

5. My sister Carmen chosen the records. has chosen, had chosen

6. A new movie theater opening soon. is opening, will be opening

7. We leaving for Boston tomorrow. are leaving, will be leaving

C 8. Costumes were stored in a trunk.

9. That dog bitten our mail carrier. has bitten, had bitten

10. Listeners guessing the punch lines. were guessing, are guessing

Separated Parts of the Verb

Sometimes another part of the sentence comes between the helping verb and the main verb.

> Ezra **may** not **pitch** today.
> Joanne **will** probably **stay** for dinner.
> The gate **should**n't **have been locked** last night.

Not and the ending *n't* are never part of the verb, although they do change the meaning of the verb.

In questions, there are usually one or more words between the helping verb and the main verb.

Does this bicycle **need** oil?	**Have** you **been listening?**
Were you **looking** for me?	**Is** Dad **painting** in the garage?

4. We are (MV) members of the school baseball team.
5. My friend has (MV) a unicycle.
6. The dogs are (HV) swimming (MV) in the water.
7. The lions have (MV) locks on their cages.
8. The seals have (HV) been (HV) fed (MV) already.
9. I should (HV) have (HV) taken (MV) more pictures.
10. That car alarm has (HV) been (HV) ringing (MV) all night.
11. Someone should (HV) have (HV) turned (MV) it off by now.
12. The wind might (HV) have (HV) set (MV) off the alarm.
13. I may (HV) call (MV) the police.
14. Now I can (HV) no longer hear (MV) it.
15. Perhaps I shall (HV) get (MV) a good night's sleep after all.

Extending the Lesson

1. Ask students to bring in a short newspaper or magazine article. Have them underline the helping verbs and put a box around each main verb.

2. If any class members speak or are studying other languages in addition to English, ask them whether the corresponding verb forms in the other language are created by the use of separate helping verbs, by changes to the main verb itself, or by some combination of the two methods.

Exercises **Find the separated parts of the verb.**

A. Make two columns on your paper. Label the first column *Helping Verbs*. Label the second column *Main Verb*. Write the parts of the verb for each of these sentences in the correct column.

Example: Joseph didn't see the curb.

Helping Verbs	**Main Verb**
did	see

1. Our goalie has not blocked any shots.
2. Vicky has never missed a Red Sox game.
3. Would you repeat your answer?
4. The floats were usually awarded prizes.
5. Amanda will probably break the school record in the 100-yard dash.
6. Was the champ resting before the fight?
7. We shouldn't cross the railroad tracks.
8. Leo couldn't believe his eyes.
9. Prisoners have never escaped from that jail.
10. Didn't you bring an umbrella?

B. Follow the directions for Exercise A.

1. I was only joking about your costume.
2. Will winter ever end?
3. Grandma has never missed my birthday party.
4. Winona could barely reach the swing.
5. Barry has almost finished his homework.
6. Have you ever sung in a choir?
7. When does your library card expire?
8. Can you still smell the fish in the kitchen?
9. I don't understand this assignment.
10. Shouldn't the movie start now?

Part 3 Direct Objects of Verbs

In many sentences, a subject and a verb are enough to express a complete thought.

The child fell.
The telephone rang.

In other sentences, the thought is not complete until other words have been added.

Kirk spilled the **glue.**
The class thanked **Jean.**

The word that is needed after the verb to complete the action of the verb is the **direct object of the verb.** *Glue* tells what Kirk spilled. *Jean* tells whom the class thanked. *Glue* and *Jean* are the direct objects in these sentences.

The direct object is the word that receives the action of the verb.

Recognizing Direct Objects

To find the direct object in a sentence, first find the verb. Then place *what* or *whom* after the verb to form a question. If a word answers the question formed with *what* or *whom*, it is the direct object.

Examples: John sharpened his pencil.
John sharpened *what?* his *pencil*
The direct object is *pencil.*

The hockey players cheered their coach.
The players cheered *whom?* their *coach*
The direct object is *coach.*

Direct objects only answer *what* or *whom* after the verb. They do not tell *when* or *where* or *how.* You will see that there

Part 3

Objective

To understand the function of direct objects and to identify them in sentences

Presenting the Lesson

1. Read and discuss pages 331 and 332. Ask students what kind of word a direct object must be if it names a person or thing. Review the definition of a noun. Avoid mentioning pronouns; they will be introduced in Handbook Section 7.

2. Assign and discuss Exercises A and B on page 332. Remind students that to find the direct object, they must ask the question *what*? after the verb.

Individualizing the Lesson

Less-Advanced Students

Point out that all verbs have subjects, but not all have direct objects. Have students list the differences in position and purpose. They should mention that the subject usually comes before the verb, but the direct object comes after. The subject tells who or what did something, while the object tells who or what completes the action of the verb.

Using the following sentences, ask students to underline the verb twice, the subject noun once, and circle the direct object noun.

1. The gym teacher blew his (whistle.)
2. The movers carried the (furniture.)
3. Dale bought (groceries) at the store.
4. Walter Payton scored a (touchdown.)
5. Some pillows have (feathers.)
6. My father vacuumed the (rug.)

Advanced Students

Remind students that direct objects answer questions *what?* or *whom?* after the verb. Have students vary sentences in Exercise A by changing the direct object.

Optional Practice

Direct students to write complete sentences that answer these questions. In their sentences, they should underline the verb twice and circle the direct object. Answers will vary.

1. What does the artist paint?
2. What do seals eat?
3. What does the musician play?
4. What does a doctor use?
5. Whom does the salesperson meet?
6. What do people read?

Extending the Lesson

Remind students that the direct object is a noun or noun phrase that completes the action of the verb. Point out that many verbs are complete and do not need a direct object. Give students the following sentences and have them determine whether or not each verb has a direct object by finding the verb and asking *what* after it.

1. We were riding in the station wagon.
2. Jody dropped a ball out the car window.
3. It hit the truck behind us.
4. The truck skidded to a halt.
5. It bumped the fender of a bus.
6. The police officer blew her whistle.
7. Someone on the bus fainted.
8. People honked their horns.
9. A traffic jam was created.
10. The ball bounced down the street.

are no direct objects in the following sentences.

Andrew plays in the afternoon.
His father drove to Tennessee.

However, there are direct objects in these sentences.

Andrew plays *football* in the afternoon.
His father drove the *truck* to Tennessee.

Exercises Find the direct objects.

A. Copy the following sentences. Underline the verb. Circle the direct object.

Example: Della was riding her bicycle.

1. Teresa broke her ruler.
2. Tim liked the new coach.
3. The fielder should have caught that ball.
4. The conductor will collect tickets.
5. This computer can solve problems.
6. Did you call your parents?
7. My little brothers made a snowman.
8. Phyllis and Mandy were doing a puzzle.
9. Long ago, Indians hunted buffalo here.
10. Lyndon cut the cake into small pieces.

B. Writing Write ten sentences using the following verbs. Put a direct object in each sentence. Circle each direct object. Answers will vary.

1. lost	6. was writing
2. was building	7. covered
3. dropped	8. should have read
4. will fill	9. will eat
5. likes	10. touched

Part 4 Linking Verbs

State-of-being verbs are often called **linking verbs.** Linking verbs connect the subject with a word in the predicate. The word in the predicate tells something about the subject. Read these examples:

Rhonda's dress *was* blue.
The stew *smells* delicious.
Our players *looked* happy.

In the first sentence, *was* connects *blue* with the subject *dress*. What does *blue* tell about *dress?* In the second sentence, *smells* connects *delicious* with the subject *stew.* What does *delicious* tell about *stew?* In the third sentence, *looked* connects *happy* with the subject *players.* What does *happy* tell about *players?*

The most common linking verb is the verb *be. Be* can have many forms:

be	been	is	was
being	am	are	were

The words *seem, look, smell, taste,* and *feel* can also be used as linking verbs.

The words linked to the subject by a linking verb are called **predicate words.** There are *predicate nouns, predicate pronouns,* and *predicate adjectives.* Read these examples:

My mother *is* an **engineer.** (predicate noun)

This *is* **he.** (predicate pronoun)

Yuki *seemed* **nervous.** (predicate adjective)

Part 4

Objective

To understand the concept of linking verbs, and to identify them and the words linked to the subject

Presenting the Lesson

1. Read and discuss page 333. Discuss the meaning of the word *link* (join, connect) and relate it to the function of the linking verb. The word *adjective* is used in the Handbook for the first time on page 333. The term will be defined and discussed thoroughly in Handbook Section 8. At this time, it should be sufficient to explain that an adjective is a describing word. A predicate adjective describes the subject.

2. It is suggested that you do Exercise A on page 334 with the students to be sure they understand the concept of the linking verb. Assign and discuss Exercise B.

3. Read and discuss page 335.

4. It is suggested that you do Exercise A on pages 335 and 336 with the students to be sure they differentiate the direct object from predicate nouns or adjectives. Assign and discuss Exercise B.

Individualizing the Lesson

Less-Advanced Students

Some students may still be having difficulty understanding the difference between linking and action verbs. Work through the following sentences as a group. Have students identify the verb in each sentence. Ask students to state whether any of these sentences have a direct object. Then explain that when the question *who?* or *what?* follows a linking verb, the answer is not a direct object, but a predicate word.

1. You seem tired.
2. The water is too cold.
3. This lemonade tastes very tart.
4. The sky appears cloudy.
5. Yesterday Claire was late for class.
6. Lead is a heavy metal.

Advanced Students

Have the students write a paragraph describing the sights, sounds, tastes and smells of a summer barbeque or picnic. They should underline all predicate words.

Optional Practice

1. Give students the following sentences. Have them underline the predicate word or direct object in each sentence and label it PW or DO.

DO 1. Our town holds a carnival every August.
PW 2. It is the highlight of our summer.
DO 3. We save our allowances for the rides.
PW 4. Some of the rides are very wild.
PW 5. The tilt-a-whirl is my favorite.
DO 6. My little brother likes the merry-go-round.
PW 7. The food always smells delicious.
PW 8. Corn on the cob and ribs are big sellers.
DO 9. Local bands give concerts.
PW 10. It is always great fun.

2. In the following sentences have students underline the linking verb and circle the predicate word.

Example: The tractor is a fairly big machine.

1. The firefighter looks tired.

Exercises Find the linking verbs.

A. Make three columns on your paper. Label the first column *Subject,* the second column *Linking Verb,* and the third column *Word Linked to Subject.* Find these three parts in each sentence below. Write them in the proper columns.

Example: The dancers were energetic.

Subject	Linking Verb	Word Linked to Subject
dancers	were	energetic

1. Ansel Adams is a famous photographer.
2. The trail was rough in spots.
3. That comedian is very clever.
4. Everyone seems sorry about the mix-up.
5. That hot vegetable soup smells good.
6. My old winter coat looks shabby.
7. Our flight to Miami was smooth.
8. Larry has been president of the club.
9. Kris is a varsity swimmer.
10. The coach feels confident about the play-offs.

B. Follow the directions for Exercise A.

1. That new cereal tastes soggy.
2. My sister is the class president.
3. The radio is much too loud.
4. Toby felt nervous at rehearsal.
5. The people were tourists from Germany.
6. Logan Beach looks peaceful today.
7. Casey's aunt has been an aide to Senator Mendez.
8. The topics for speeches seem interesting.
9. Lana was curious about the lineup.
10. The stairs to the attic are creaky.

Direct Object or Predicate Word?

What are the differences between these two sentences?

Bob hit a double. Bob is an outfielder.

You have learned about two kinds of verbs. There are *action verbs* and *linking verbs*. You have also learned about two kinds of words that follow verbs and complete their meaning. There are *direct objects*, and there are *predicate words.*

How can you tell which words are direct objects and which words are predicate words? First, find the verb in a sentence. Is the verb an action verb or a linking verb?

1. If an **action verb** is followed by a noun that tells *what* or *whom*, that noun is a **direct object.**

Examples: Julie studies *Spanish.* Julie ate *lunch* early.

2. If a **linking verb** is followed by a word that tells about the subject, that word is a **predicate noun,** a **predicate pronoun,** or a **predicate adjective.**

Examples: Julie is a *student.* (predicate noun)
This is *she.* (predicate pronoun)
Julie is *hungry.* (predicate adjective)

Now compare these two examples.

Bob hit a double.
Hit is an action verb. *Double* is a direct object.

Bob is an outfielder.
Is is a linking verb. *Outfielder* is a predicate noun.

Exercises Find direct objects and predicate words.

A. Write each of the following sentences. If the sentence contains a linking verb, circle the verb and then circle the predicate word that follows it. If the sentence contains an action verb, underline it and then underline its direct object.

1. The girls formed a band.

2. The bus driver was (friendly.)
3. The garbage smells (awful.)
4. Her birthstone is a (ruby.)
5. That plane is a modern (jet.)
6. Pélé was a (star) in soccer.
7. Those flowers are (tulips.)
8. Joe seems (busy.)
9. The new lamp is (blue.)
10. The weightlifter is (muscular.)

Extending the Lesson

Have students write two sentences for each of the following verbs. In one sentence, the verb is to be used as an action verb. In the second sentence, the verb is to be used as a linking verb, and there must be a predicate word.

look smell taste feel

2. Phil made a metal sculpture.
3. Nicole is a student from France.
4. Roger will design the costumes.
5. *Freaky Friday* is a book by Mary Rodgers.
6. Vanessa is the soprano.
7. This new candy tastes fizzy.
8. My family rented a cabin in the mountains.
9. The weather will be pleasant this spring.
10. That stray dog seems mean.

B. Follow the directions for Exercise A.

1. The dark movie theater was quiet.
2. Blanca's favorite hobby is her computer.
3. We met our cousin for the first time.
4. Kate seems older than her sister.
5. The surrounding farms look prosperous.
6. Josh found his ticket.
7. My brothers built an igloo last winter.
8. Todd feeds his dog every afternoon.
9. Aaron fumbled the pass.
10. After the race, the runners were weary.

Part 5

Objective

To recognize and use the present, past, and future verb tenses

Presenting the Lesson

1. Read and discuss pages 336 and 337. Ask students for sentences using the sample verbs in the different tenses.

2. Assign and discuss Exercises A and B on page 338.

Part 5 Verb Tenses

A verb is a time-telling word. It does not just tell what happens or what *is*. It also tells *when* something happens or *is*. By changing its form, a verb can tell whether an action or state of being happened or *was* in the past, is happening or *is* in the present, or will happen or will *be* in the future. The time expressed by a verb is called **tense.**

The **present tense** tells of an action or state of being that is happening now.

I *work* at school. I *am* a student.

The **past tense** tells of an action or state of being that happened in the past.

I *worked* all last summer. I *was* a library aide.

The **future tense** tells of an action or state of being that will happen in the future.

I *will work* at the pool next year. I *will be* a lifeguard.

Verbs tell time in three ways:

1. By changing their spelling: I **know** now.
   I **knew** then.
2. By adding an ending: We **walk** today.
   We **walked** yesterday.
3. By using helping verbs: She **had decided** last week.
   She **will decide** next week.

Forming the Tenses

Present Tense. The **present tense** of the verb is the same as the name of the verb: *race, call, do, think* (I *race,* you *call,* they *do,* we *think*). Add *-s* or *-es* to the verb when it is used with a singular noun or a pronoun (a word that takes the place of a noun) such as *he, she,* or *it* (he *races,* she *calls,* it *does,* Sara *thinks*).

Past Tense. The **past tense** of most verbs is formed by adding *-d* or *-ed* to the present tense. Verbs that form the past tense in this way are called **regular verbs.**

race—race*d* call—call*ed*

The past tense of some verbs is shown by a change in spelling. Verbs that form the past tense this way are **irregular verbs.**

do → *did* think → *thought*

Future Tense. The **future tense** is formed by using the helping verbs *will* or *shall* with the present tense:

will race *shall* call *will* do *shall* think

Individualizing the Lesson

Less-Advanced Students

To help clarify the difference in tenses, have students use this aid in deciding which tense to use. Fit the appropriate tense into each of the following brief sentences: "Now I _____ . Yesterday I _____ . Tomorrow I _____ ." Completing each in that order will give the student the present, past, and future tense of the verb.

Example: "Now I bake. Yesterday I baked. Tomorrow I shall bake."

Have students write out these three brief sentences, in order, for each of the following verbs.

1. smile	4. order
2. decide	5. plan
3. grab	6. wish

Advanced Students

Have students rewrite the sentences in Exercise A by changing the tense of the verb. They should then write which tense they used after each sentence.

Optional Practice

1. Have students follow the directions for Exercise B for the sentences below. Remind them to check their work by reading the finished sentence to themselves.

1. I no longer (present of *enjoy*) spring showers. enjoy
2. Last night's rain (past of *flood*) our basement. flooded
3. We (future of *work*) all day to clean it. shall/will work
4. The weather (present of *look*) dark and muddy. looks
5. My dad (past of *call*) from out of town. called

2. For each of the following sentences, have students identify the verb. Then have them write the present, past, and future tenses of that verb. Remind students that the present tense form of the verb ends with an *s* when the subject is singular.

Example: The operator answered all the phones.
answered—answers, answered, will answer

1. Magnifying lenses enlarge objects. enlarges, enlarged, will enlarge
2. The computer ran the program in three hours. runs, ran, will run
3. My aunt types faster than anyone else in her office. types, typed, will type
4. A mouse ate the cheese on the table. eats, ate, will eat
5. Lemonade tastes good in hot weather. tastes, tasted, will taste
6. The zoo veterinarian gave the elephant a shot. gives, gave, will give

Extending the Lesson

Have students write at least five sentences describing a party they have attended. All sentences should be in the past tense. Then students should rewrite them in the following manner. First they should pretend they are eyewitness TV reporters describing the scene to the television audience. (present tense) Then they should pretend they are psychics and are describing a party that will happen. (future tense)

Example:
The room was filled with balloons and streamers.
The room is filled with balloons and streamers.
The room will be filled with balloons and streamers.

Exercises Recognize and use verb tenses.

A. Write the verb in each of the following sentences. Then write the tense of each verb.

Example: Superman will stop the runaway train.
will stop, future tense

present 1. We always watch the evening news.
future 2. The crew will build a new gym.
past 3. At midnight we raided the refrigerator.
future 4. Julie will have a slumber party on her birthday.
past 5. Some people dressed in costumes.
present 6. Ken's watch glows in the dark.
future 7. The bus will arrive late today.
present 8. Fresh blueberries taste great on ice cream.
past 9. Someone painted the lockers orange.
past 10. Gail tossed the ball to the catcher for the third out.

B. Write each of the following sentences. Use the tense of the verb asked for in each of the following sentences.

Example: Bill Rodgers (past of *cross*) the finish line first.
crossed

1. Kara (future of *get*) two free throws. will get
2. My sister and I (past of *play*) miniature golf. played
3. Vicky (present of *mow*) her neighbor's lawn. mows
4. The jury (future of *decide*) the sentence. will decide
5. Dad (past of *plant*) pumpkins in the garden. planted
6. I (future of *walk*) to the beach this afternoon. will walk
7. My friends (present of *want*) front-row seats. want
8. Carol (present of *pitch*) with her left hand. pitches
9. Steve (past of *joke*) about his haircut. joked
10. The weather service (past of *warn*) of a tornado. warned

Sentence Patterns The N V N Pattern

A sentence in the **N V N pattern** has three parts. The first *N* stands for the subject noun. The *V* stands for the verb. The second *N* stands for the direct object noun. Read the sentences in the following chart. They are in the N V N pattern.

N	V	N
Cora	writes	songs.
Snakes	lay	eggs.
My friends	planned	a party.
The plumber	fixed	the sink.
Donald	likes	his new bike.

Exercises Use the N V N pattern.

A. Make a chart like the one above. Write these sentences on the chart.

1. Therese plays the flute.
2. Phyllis called Terry.
3. My dog watches TV.
4. Andy took a bow
5. We cheered our goalie.
6. Saturn has ten moons.
7. An arrow hit the target.
8. Martina rode the train.

B. Copy this chart. Add words to complete each sentence in the N V N pattern. Answers will vary.

N	V	N
1. Angela	pushed	__________.
2. __________	measured	__________.
3. James	__________	carrots.
4. __________	answered	the phone.
5. This kitten	chases	__________.

C. Make a chart of your own. Write five sentences on your chart in the N V N pattern.

Sentence Patterns

Objective

To recognize the basic word order in the N V N sentence pattern

Presenting the Lesson

1. Read and discuss page 339. Make it clear that each of the three parts in the N V N pattern may have one or more than one word. Any words that describe the subject noun are grouped in the first noun part. Any words that describe the verb are grouped in the verb part. Any words that describe the object noun are grouped in the second noun part.

2. Assign and discuss Exercises A and C on page 339. Do Exercise B with the class.

Optional Practice

Have students make a chart for the N V N pattern, and fill in the chart with the following sentence parts. They must match the parts to make sensible sentences.

N

1. the hockey player,
2. the baseball player,
3. the basketball player,
4. the tennis player
5. the football player
6. the soccer player

V	N
1 scores	5 the football
4 serves	6 the soccer ball
6 kicks	2 a home run
5 passes	1 a goal
2 hits	3 the basketball
3 dunks	4 the tennis ball

Sentence Patterns

Objective

To recognize the basic word order in the N LV N sentence pattern

Presenting the Lesson

1. Read and discuss page 340. Make it clear that, as with the N V and N V N patterns, each part of an N LV N sentence may have more than one word.

2. Assign and discuss Exercises A, B, and C on page 340.

Optional Practice

Have students make a chart for the N LV N pattern. Tell them to fill in the subject nouns from the following list. For each subject they should chose a linking verb and a noun to follow it. Remind them to capitalize and punctuate where necessary.

N (Subject)	**LV**	**N**
1. flowers	is	fish 5
2. cauliflower	are	cookies 6
3. hamburgers		a vegetable 2
4. rolls		plants 1
5. tuna		bread 4
6. wafers		meat 3

Sentence Patterns

The N LV N Pattern

A sentence in the **N LV N pattern** has three parts. The first *N* stands for the subject noun. *LV* stands for a linking verb. (Remember that *linking verb* is another name for a *state-of-being verb*.) The second *N* stands for the noun that follows the linking verb.

N	V	N
Janet	is	an artist.
Ralph	is	her brother.
The best speller	was	Linn.
Cleopatra	is	my kitten.
My skates	were	a birthday present.

Exercises Use the N LV N pattern.

A. Make a chart like the one above. Write these sentences on the chart.

1. Tomatoes (N) | are (LV) | fruits (N).
2. This game (N) | is (LV) | a challenge (N).
3. Africa (N) | is (LV) | a continent (N).
4. My partner (N) | was (LV) | Reba (N).
5. The boys (N) | were (LV) | friends (N).
6. Larry (N) | is (LV) | a joker (N).
7. Nutmeg (N) | is (LV) | a spice (N).
8. These dogs (N) | are (LV) | poodles (N).

B. Copy this chart. Add words to complete each sentence in the N LV N pattern. Answers will vary.

N	LV	N
1. The last batter	was	________.
2. ________	are	insects.
3. Juan	___	a halfback.
4. ________	was	________.
5. ________	is	a good sport.

C. Make a chart of your own. Label the columns *N*, *LV*, and *N*. Write five sentences on your chart in the N LV N pattern. Answers will vary.

Sentence Patterns The N LV Adj Pattern

Sentences in the **N LV Adj pattern** have three parts. The *N* stands for the subject noun. *LV* stands for the linking verb. *Adj* stands for adjective that follows the linking verb. The sentences in the following chart are in the N LV Adj pattern.

N	LV	Adj
The classroom	is	quiet.
Lemons	taste	sour.
Chris	was	fearless.
This record	sounds	scratchy.
These new boots	look	large.

Exercises Use the N LV Adj pattern.

A. Make a chart like the one above. Write these sentences on the chart.

1. Connie | looks | happy.
2. These roads | are | narrow.
3. Your sweater | feels | soft.
4. Tacos | are | tasty.
5. The radio | sounds | loud.
6. The mail | was | late.
7. The oranges | were | ripe.
8. This radish | tastes | bitter.

B. Copy this chart. Add words to complete each sentence in the N LV Adj pattern. Answers will vary.

N	LV	Adj
1. ______	is	funny.
2. ______	looks	sad.
3. Sandpaper	feels	______.
4. The Halls	______	friendly.
5. ______	was	______.

C. Make a chart of your own. Label the columns *N, LV,* and *Adj.* Write five sentences on your chart in the N LV Adj pattern.
Answers will vary.

Sentence Patterns

Objective

To recognize the basic word order in the N LV Adj sentence pattern

Presenting the Lesson

1. Read and discuss page 341. Remind students that adjectives following linking verbs describe subject nouns before the linking verb.

2. Assign and discuss Exercises A, B, and C on page 341.

Optional Practice

Have students make a chart for the N LV Adj pattern. Tell them to fill in the subject nouns from the following list. They should choose a linking verb, and an adjective to follow it that matches the subject, and fill in the entire sentence. There are several possibilities for correct pairings. Remind students to capitalize and punctuate where necessary.

N (Subject)	**LV**	**Adj**
1. rainbows	is	yellow 5
2. snow	are	crisp 6
3. stop lights		white 2
4. pumpkin		colorful 1
5. the sun		orange 4
6. this apple		red 3

Additional Exercises

These Additional Exercises may be used for additional practice of the concepts presented in this Section. Each exercise focuses on a single concept, and should be used after the page number indicated in parentheses.

Review

If you have not assigned these Additional Exercises before this time, you can also use them as an excellent Section Review.

ADDITIONAL EXERCISES

Using Verbs

A. Action Verbs and State-of-Being Verbs Write the verb in each of the following sentences. Beside the verb, write *Action* or *State-of-Being* to show what kind it is. (Use after page 325.)

SB 1. That classroom was a lunchroom last year.
A 2. Carly made a bowl out of clay.
SB 3. Walt Disney was the creator of Mickey Mouse.
A 4. The doctor put a cast on Mandy's arm.
SB 5. The science experiment was a failure.
A 6. Alex wrote his report in the library.
A 7. During the ride, Carl closed his eyes.
SB 8. Nora is the best player on our team.
A 9. We hung the wallpaper with a thick paste.
SB 10. The tennis courts are wet.

B. Main Verbs and Helping Verbs Write the helping verbs and the main verbs in the following sentences. Underline the helping verbs once and the main verbs twice. (Use after page 330.)

1. The Bears are practicing for the first game.
2. Someone should have called the police.
3. Cindy may visit her grandmother in Minneapolis.
4. Tony was immediately sent to the nurse's office.
5. Ruthie has always liked sports.
6. Carlos is concentrating on his homework.
7. The vice-president didn't attend the meeting.
8. Our team should win this game.
9. Were you reading that magazine?
10. The comedian will be appearing nightly.

C. Verbs and Direct Objects Copy each of the following sentences. Underline each verb. Circle each direct object.

1. The quarterback passed the football.

2. Martin shoveled the driveway.
3. The Pep Club will sponsor a carnival.
4. Can you play the piano?
5. Roberto made chili for dinner.
6. The pirate walked the plank.
7. You can peel the potatoes.
8. The divers recovered some Roman coins.
9. Larry has memorized the poem.
10. The gardener planted the flowers.

D. Linking Verbs Make three columns. Label the first *Subject*, the second *Linking Verb*, and the third *Word Linked to Subject*. Write these parts in the proper columns.

(Use after page 335.)

1. The horses became restless.
2. Margaret was the winner of the contest.
3. This spoon feels greasy.
4. Claude was the goalie.
5. Mr. Cruz will be the new mayor.
6. Those koala bears seem shy.
7. Your desk looks messy.
8. Louise Nevelson is an artist.
9. Keith was happy about the victory.
10. Your projects have always been successful.

E. Verb Tenses Write each verb and its tense.

(Use after page 338.)

present 1. The aquarium displays many types of fish.
future 2. Mr. Vito will change the date of the play.
past 3. Each cast member worked hard.
present 4. Jan always plays the guitar for her friends.
past 5. Larry asked for a different book.
future 6. An usher will take you to your seat.
past 7. Meg brought lemonade to the beach.
past 8. Ms. Brown conducted the band.
present 9. Tony works evenings and weekends.
past 10. I changed my mind.

Mixed Review

These exercises provide review of the concepts presented in this Section. Each exercise challenges the students to apply several of the skills they have acquired during previous study. Because the "mixed" feature of these activities makes them more difficult, the teacher may wish to have less-advanced students do them orally or in small groups.

MIXED REVIEW

Using Verbs

A. Finding action verbs and state-of-being verbs, and identifying tenses Write the verb from each sentence. After it write *Action* or *State-of-Being* to show what kind it is. Then write whether the verb is present, past, or future tense.

1. Hannah plays first base. present
2. Maria is from Mexico City. present
3. The tall clown was Jack. past
4. My brother will drive us to the concert. future
5. Ben will see that movie tomorrow. future
6. Kim and he are twins. present
7. The rabbits ate the lettuce and the marigolds. past
8. Wayne and Lou were the best pitchers this season. past
9. We will be late for the parade. future
10. Beth caught the first fish. past

B. Finding helping verbs, main verbs, and direct objects Make three columns. Label the first *Helping Verbs*, the second *Main Verbs*, and the third *Direct Objects.* Write the verbs and direct objects in the proper columns. Not every sentence will have a helping verb or a direct object.

1. Tim and Darcy are (HV) decorating (MV) the cake.
2. The Olympic gymnast is (HV) practicing (MV) his routine.
3. Have (HV) you ever crossed (MV) the Brooklyn Bridge?
4. Kathryn is (HV) painting (MV) the porch.
5. Drifts of snow covered (MV) the cars.
6. Mrs. Kelly has (HV) been (HV) teaching (MV) violin for seven years.
7. Does (HV) this store sell (MV) wallpaper?
8. The flock of pigeons flew (MV) away.
9. I will (HV) be (HV) taking (MV) Spanish next year.
10. Josh will (HV) attend (MV) a computer camp this summer.

C. Identifying linking verbs and predicate words, and action verbs and direct objects Write the verb in each of the following sentences. Label it *AV* if it is an action verb and *LV* if it is a linking verb. If the verb is an action verb, write its object and label it *DO*. If the verb is a linking verb, write the predicate word and label it *PW*.

1. Ocean water tastes salty.
2. This hat is too big for me.
3. Ants carried crumbs from our picnic.
4. This book about dinosaurs is excellent.
5. Sally Ride is a famous astronaut.
6. The weather has been rainy all week.
7. Fred made a mobile for his room.
8. My brother sailed the boat out of the harbor.
9. In the kitchen we smelled vegetable soup.
10. The building on Oak Street is the new library.

D. Using sentence patterns Write two sentences for each of the following sentence patterns. Answers will vary.

1. N V
2. N V N
3. N LV N
4. N LV Adj

345

Using Grammar in Writing

These challenging and enjoyable activities allow the students to see how the concepts of grammar, usage, and mechanics may be applied in actual writing situations. Each exercise is designed to allow students practice in several of the skills they have acquired in this Section. The activities also provide opportunities for students to write creatively about a wide variety of interesting and unusual subjects.

USING GRAMMAR IN WRITING

Using Verbs

A. What is your favorite TV show? Is it a situation comedy? Is it a detective show or an exciting police series? Imagine that a friend of yours has never seen the show. Pick an episode that you saw recently. Tell your friend what happened in that story. Use strong action verbs to show how exciting it was. Underline all the main verbs once. Underline all helping verbs twice.

B. A company that makes electronic games put this classified ad in the paper:

WANTED

Ideas for new video games. Send us your idea. Describe the game in a paragraph. We will pay $100 for any idea we can use.

You have what you consider a winning idea. Write about it in a paragraph. At least two sentences should contain direct objects. When you are finished, underline all the verbs. Then circle the direct objects.

C. Imagine that your aunt is a skywriter. She writes messages in the sky using the smoke from her plane. Companies hire her to advertise their products. A breakfast cereal company has hired your aunt. She has asked you to help her write the ad. She asks you to write four sentences that would tell about the breakfast cereal. Use linking verbs in your sentences. Underline the linking verbs.

346

Using Irregular Verbs

Part 1 Principal Parts of Verbs

Every verb has many forms. Here are some forms the verb *talk* can have:

talk	talked	will talk
was talking	had talked	have been talking

All of these forms of *talk* are made from the three basic parts of a verb. These three basic parts are called the **principal parts** of a verb. The principal parts of a verb are the **present,** the **past,** and the **past participle.**

Section Objectives

1. To understand the function of the principal parts of the verb in forming the present, past, and other tenses of verbs

2. To form and use the principal parts of regular verbs

3. To differentiate between regular and irregular verbs, and to become familiar with the principal parts of common irregular verbs

4. To use the principal parts of some common irregular verbs correctly

Preparing the Students

Discuss the meanings of the words *regular* (following a certain order, similar) and *irregular* (out of order, different from the normal). Ask students to give examples of regular and irregular things and actions, such as heart beats or swings of a pendulum. Explain that this section will give information about verbs that are regular or irregular. Stress the idea that when the terms *regular* and *irregular* are applied to verbs, they refer only to the form of the verbs, not to their meaning, purpose, or use.

Additional Resources

Mastery Test — pages 43–44 in the test booklet

Additional Exercises — pages 367–368 in the student text

Practice Book — pages 139–144

Duplicating Masters — pages 139–144

Special Populations — See special section at the front of this Teacher's Edition.

Part 1

Objective

To understand the function of the principal parts of the verb in forming the present, past, and other tenses of verbs

Presenting the Lesson

1. Read and discuss pages 347 and 348. Discuss the meanings of the word *principal* (main, most important) in relation to the *principal parts* of verbs.

2. The examples on page 348 illustrate the three major spelling changes involved in adding the *-ed* ending; final *y* changing to *i* (*hurry, hurried*); final *e* being dropped (*paste, pasted*); and final consonant being doubled (*stop, stopped*). Rules concerning these changes are presented in Handbook Section 17.

Part 2

Objective

To identify and use the principal parts of regular verbs

Presenting the Lesson

1. Read and discuss page 348. Have students describe the action in a current movie or TV show. Write on the board, in the present form, the regular verbs they use. Have them tell the past and past participle form for each of these verbs.

2. Assign and discuss Exercises A and B on pages 348 and 349.

Here are some examples:

Present	Past	Past Participle
call	called	(have) called
hurry	hurried	(have) hurried
look	looked	(have) looked
paste	pasted	(have) pasted
stop	stopped	(have) stopped
walk	walked	(have) walked

The *present* part of the verb is used to form the present tense. Add *-s* or *-es* to the verb when it is used with a singular noun or *he, she,* or *it.*

Will or *shall* added to the present part forms the future tense.

The *past* part of the verb is used to form the past tense.

The *past participle* is used with helping verbs to make other forms of the verb. Some of these helping verbs are *has, have, had, will have,* and *shall have.* Here are some examples:

The storms **have stopped.**
Bob **had stopped** at the library.
The team **will have stopped** practicing by then.

Part 2 Regular Verbs

The verbs given in the list of principal parts above are called **regular verbs.** Every verb that is *regular* forms its past tense by adding *-ed* (*call**ed***) or *-d* (*paste**d***) to the present part. The past participle of a regular verb is the same as the past part and is always used with a helping verb. Most English verbs are regular.

Exercises Use principal parts of verbs.

A. Write the verb form indicated for the following regular verbs. Use helping verbs with each past participle.

1. like (past) liked
2. notice (past participle) has/have noticed
3. arrange (present) arrange(s)
4. watch (past participle) has/have watched
5. snow (past) snowed
6. smell (present) smell(s)
7. listen (past participle) has/have listened
8. rock (past participle) has/have rocked
9. use (past) used
10. explain (past) explained

B. Writing Write a sentence for each of the verbs below. Use the verb form indicated.

1. turn (past participle) has/have turned
2. paint (past) painted
3. chase (past participle) has/have chased
4. juggle (present) juggle(s)
5. open (past) opened
6. weigh (present) weigh(s)
7. pound (past) pounded
8. struggle (present) struggle(s)
9. help (present) help(s)
10. order (past participle) has/have ordered

Part 3 Irregular Verbs

Some verbs do not form their pasts and past participles in the regular way. These five verbs are examples:

Present	Past	Past Participle
feel	felt	(have) felt
go	went	(have) gone
know	knew	(have) known
see	saw	(have) seen
think	thought	(have) thought

These verbs are not regular verbs. They are **irregular verbs.** There are only about sixty irregular verbs in the English language. They are important because many of them are verbs you use frequently.

In order to use irregular verbs correctly, you must know their correct past forms and past participles. The best way to learn to use irregular verbs correctly is to memorize as many of these verb forms as possible. A list of the most commonly used irregular verbs is given on page 351.

Optional Practice

In each of the following sentences, have students underline the verb. Next to the sentence, they are to write whether the verb is in the *present, past,* or *past participle* form.

Example: The train roared down the track.—past

Pr 1. That clown laughs all the time.

PP 2. The librarian had ordered the books.

Pr 3. Some flowers bloom early.

P 4. The girl zipped her jacket.

PP 5. The Harlem Globetrotters have played hundreds of basketball games.

P 6. The juggler tossed the balls high in the air.

Part 3

Objective

To differentiate between regular and irregular verbs, and to become familiar with the principal parts of common irregular verbs

Presenting the Lesson

1. Read and discuss pages 349 and 350. Make sure students understand and can make use of the charts on page 350.

2. Present the list of irregular verbs on page 351. You might find it helpful to read the verbs aloud in a rhythmical manner, having students repeat each set after you. If this is successful, you may wish to do it periodically until the students become more familiar with the correct forms of the irregular verbs.

3. Read and discuss the first half of page 352. If students have access to dictionaries, have them look up several verbs in the first column of page 351 to become familiar with the arrangement of principal parts information in an entry.

Individualizing the Lesson

Less-Advanced Students

Point out to the students that there are no rules for irregular verbs. This fact poses many problems for foreigners learning English. The correct forms of irregular verbs are memorized when a child learns to speak. Remind the students to say "Now I _____ . Yesterday I _____ . Tomorrow I _____ ." to tell if the tense is correct. If this fails, refer them to the list of irregular verbs on page 351.

To help students use irregular verbs not on the list, familiarize them with using the dictionary to find irregular forms. Have the students look up the following verbs and copy down their other forms: *become, draw, blow, fly* and *shake.*

Advanced Students

Explain to the students that many of the irregular verbs come from the ancient Germanic language called Anglo-Saxon. Many regular verbs come from French or Latin roots.

Give the students a dictionary that contains the etymology of words. Explain where in the entry this is located. Then have the students look up the following words and ask them if their findings agree with your statement.

When you are using irregular verbs, you should remember these two rules:

1. The past form is always used by itself, *without* a helping verb.
   We *went* to the library last Saturday.
2. The past participle is always used *with* a helping verb.
   We *have gone* to the library every Saturday this month.

Helping Verbs

Forms of *be* and *have* are the helping verbs most often used with past participles. Here are the forms of *be* and *have*.

Be		Present	Past
Singular	I	am	was
	you	are	were
	he, she, it	is	was
Plural	we	are	were
	you	are	were
	they	are	were

Have		Present	Past
Singular	I	have	had
	you	have	had
	he, she, it	has	had
Plural	we	have	had
	you	have	had
	they	have	had

The forms *be, been,* and *being* are helping verbs that must be used with other helping verbs.

He *should be* arriving soon.
Ginny *has been* looking for a job.
They *were being* helped.

Principal Parts of Common Irregular Verbs

Present	Past	Past Participle
begin	began	(have) begun
break	broke	(have) broken
bring	brought	(have) brought
choose	chose	(have) chosen
come	came	(have) come
do	did	(have) done
drink	drank	(have) drunk
eat	ate	(have) eaten
fall	fell	(have) fallen
freeze	froze	(have) frozen
give	gave	(have) given
go	went	(have) gone
grow	grew	(have) grown
know	knew	(have) known
ride	rode	(have) ridden
ring	rang	(have) rung
rise	rose	(have) risen
run	ran	(have) run
say	said	(have) said
see	saw	(have) seen
sing	sang	(have) sung
sit	sat	(have) sat
speak	spoke	(have) spoken
steal	stole	(have) stolen
swim	swam	(have) swum
take	took	(have) taken
teach	taught	(have) taught
throw	threw	(have) thrown
wear	wore	(have) worn
write	wrote	(have) written

German

begin, do, eat, see, steal

French

change, look, paint, surprise

Optional Practice

Put the following sentences on a worksheet or on the board. Have students fill in the blanks with the irregular verb forms called for in the parentheses. All of the verbs are from the list on page 351. Have the students use *has* or *have* as helping verbs.

1. We have known our neighbors a long time. (know—past participle)
2. The ice froze quickly. (freeze—past)
3. The choir has sung that song many times. (sing—past participle)
4. Ben has written a letter to his friend. (write—past participle)
5. The cowgirl rode in the barrel races at the rodeo. (ride—past)
6. Most of the campers have swum before. (swim—past participle)
7. The farmers have grown good corn this year. (grow—past participle)
8. The captains chose their teams during the tryouts. (choose—past)
9. Nancy spoke in the program. (speak—past)
10. The sun rose at 5:47 today. (rise—past)

Extending the Lesson

Have students write five sentences about what happened on a favorite TV show or in a favorite book. (They should note which one.) Have them underline the verb in each sentence twice. Under the sentence they should write the three principal parts of that verb. Lastly, they should write *regular* or *irregular*.

Examples: The detective chased the getaway car.
chase, chased, chased—regular
The car drove quickly through an alley.
drive, drove, driven—irregular

Part 4

Objective

To use the principal parts of some common irregular verbs correctly

Presenting the Lesson

1. Read and discuss pages 352 and 353. Use the Exercise on page 353 as a diagnostic test. It is suggested that you assign only those practice pages each student shows

Using a Dictionary To Find Principal Parts

If you are not sure about a verb form, look it up in a dictionary. If the verb is regular, only one form will usually be listed.

If the verb is irregular, the dictionary will give the irregular forms. It will give two forms if the past and past participle are the same: *say, said.* It will give all three principal parts if they are all different: *sing, sang, sung.*

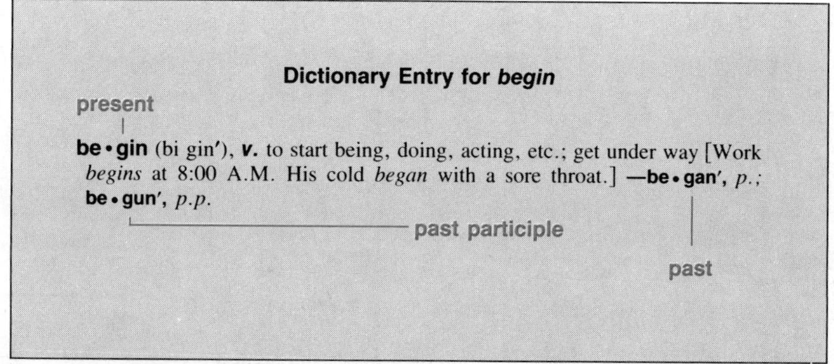

Dictionary Entry for *begin*
present
be•gin (bi gin′), ***v.*** to start being, doing, acting, etc.; get under way [Work *begins* at 8:00 A.M. His cold *began* with a sore throat.] **—be•gan′,** *p.;* **be•gun′,** *p.p.*
past participle
past

Part 4 Practice Pages on Irregular Verbs

A few irregular verbs are especially troublesome. They cause problems in writing and in speaking. Many people get confused about which form is used alone to mean the past, and which form is used with helping verbs.

On pages 354–366, you will find practice sentences for irregular verbs that are used often. To find out which verbs are difficult for you, do the following exercise.

If the exercise shows that you do know these verbs, you may only have to review this section.

If the exercise shows that you need more practice with certain verbs, turn to the pages with exercises for verbs. For each verb there are many sentences that will help you to "say it right," "hear it right," and "write it right."

Exercise Use irregular verbs.

Number your paper from 1 to 20. For each sentence, write the correct verb form from the two given in the parentheses.

1. A relief pitcher has (began, begun) to warm up.
2. That driver has (broke, broken) the law.
3. Joan has (took, taken) her books with her.
4. I have never (saw, seen) a funnier movie.
5. Has Bert (done, did) what he promised?
6. It (took, taken) a long time to find the right house.
7. Christopher has (ate, eaten) a whole pint of blueberries.
8. Jake has (rode, ridden) his bike to the park.
9. Jennifer has (wrote, written) some exciting stories.
10. My brother (ran, run) to catch his bus this morning.
11. Dolores has (gave, given) an excellent report.
12. The Johnsons have (gone, went) on vacation.
13. The sunflower has (grew, grown) five feet high.
14. Barry (knew, known) the rules of the game.
15. The ranch hand (rode, ridden) a wild horse.
16. The students have (took, taken) two tests this week.
17. Your teammates have (ran, run) as fast as you.
18. I (seen, saw) you at the mall.
19. Jan (grew, grown) to like her new school.
20. The fog (began, begun) to clear last night.

a need for. The pages should be assigned over a period of time, rather than in one block.

2. Fourteen common irregular verbs are discussed on pages 354 to 366. If you would like to use the pages for class review, read the *Say It Right, Hear It Right* part of each page, and establish some simple rules for the verb presented. The rules should follow this pattern:

Use *began* by itself.
Use *begun* with helping verbs.

Discuss the *Write It Right* part of the page, or assign it to those students needing practice.

Individualizing the Lesson

Less-Advanced Students

It may be beneficial to do the first part of *Write It Right* aloud with those students who are having great difficulty with irregular verbs. Have them repeat the correct sentence aloud several times to train their ears to the proper use of the verb.

Advanced Students

Some students may be able to skip some of the review section or may complete it rather quickly. Students can then take the extra class time to write a short story or a poem using the three forms of one or more of the irregular verbs listed on page 351.

Use the Right Word

Say It Right   Hear It Right

Say these sentences until the correct use of the verbs sounds natural to you.

1. The little boy *began* to cry.
2. Suddenly the airplane *began* flying in a circle.
3. My mother *has begun* her new job.
4. We *began* by washing the kitchen windows.
5. Alex *had* just *begun* packing for the trip.
6. *Have* you *begun* your social studies report?
7. Many forest fires *are begun* by careless campers.
8. I *have* finally *begun* to get along with my sister.
9. The film *began* with an eerie scene.
10. We *should have begun* the decorations sooner.

Write It Right

Write the correct verb from the two forms given. Check your answer by saying the complete sentence to yourself.

1. We have (began, begun) a new unit in science class.
2. My father (began, begun) cooking lessons last month.
3. By evening the hurricane had (began, begun) to lose force.
4. The next day people (began, begun) returning home.
5. I have (began, begun) to think about a career.
6. Mr. Jansen, have you (began, begun) to correct our tests?
7. Eight people (began, begun) the race, but only three finished.
8. The mayor (began, begun) her speech with a joke.
9. While we set up the tent, it (began, begun) to rain.
10. The hamburgers were ready, so we (began, begun) eating.

354

Say It Right   Hear It Right

Say these sentences until the correct use of the verbs sounds natural to you.

1. What *broke* in the kitchen?
2. Paula *has broken* a plate.
3. My bike *broke* down on the way home.
4. Have you ever *broken* a leg?
5. I once *broke* a finger.
6. The clock radio is *broken*.
7. Ms. Berger *broke* up the argument in the hall.
8. Lorne *had* already *broken* his promise.
9. Carly *broke* the high jump record.
10. What *have* you *broken*?

Write It Right

Write the correct verb from the two forms given. Check your answer by saying the complete sentence to yourself.

1. The chick has (broke, broken) out of the shell.
2. My pencil (broke, broken) again.
3. The sand dollars on the beach are all (broke, broken).
4. The lamp was (broke, broken) into a hundred pieces.
5. His glasses (broke, broken) when he fell.
6. Mitch has finally (broke, broken) in his new hiking boots.
7. The second bus must have (broke, broken) down.
8. All the plates in this box are (broke, broken).
9. We (broke, broken) open the coconut with a hammer.
10. Jim (broke, broken) the eggs into the frying pan.

355

Say It Right Hear It Right

Say these sentences until the correct use of the verbs sounds natural to you.

1. I *did* my homework before dinner.
2. Gerry *had* never *done* any woodworking before.
3. Denise *did* everything she could to help.
4. Who *has*n't *done* the assignment?
5. The cast *did* an extra show.
6. *Have* you ever *done* needlepoint?
7. The cleanup crew *did* a great job.
8. What *was done* about the leaky faucet?
9. Cheryl's science project *has* never *been done* before.
10. Kate *did* her best on the balance beam.

Write It Right

Write the correct verb from the two forms given. Check your answer by saying the complete sentence to yourself.

1. I (did, done) all I could to pass my test.
2. What have you (did, done) with your report card?
3. Those pictures were (did, done) by Carlos.
4. Mary (did, done) the shoveling by herself.
5. I haven't (did, done) a thing about the broken window.
6. We (did, done) most of the work ourselves.
7. Has Mike (did, done) his homework?
8. I should have (did, done) better on my painting.
9. Jack (did, done) more push-ups than anyone else.
10. Faith (did, done) an excellent science project.

356

Say It Right   Hear It Right

Say these sentences until the correct use of the verbs sounds natural to you.

1. What *have* you *eaten* for breakfast?
2. I *ate* eggs and toast this morning.
3. Skip *has eaten* all of the salad.
4. Paula *ate* a delicious slice of watermelon.
5. Johnny *had* never *eaten* oysters before.
6. Hot peppers *are eaten* in Mexico.
7. We *ate* a small lunch before the race.
8. *Have*n't you *eaten* yet?
9. Snails *are eaten* with butter and garlic.
10. Wendy *ate* four apples.

Write It Right

Write the correct verb from the two forms given. Check your answer by saying the complete sentence to yourself.

1. The squirrels have (ate, eaten) all the crumbs.
2. Teddy has (ate, eaten) the last piece of bread.
3. Shelly (ate, eaten) dinner with us last night.
4. Al had just (ate, eaten) breakfast when the phone rang.
5. We should have (ate, eaten) our lunch in a shady spot.
6. Tim has (ate, eaten) the rest of the popcorn.
7. By morning, the raccoons had (ate, eaten) all of our food.
8. Kevin has (ate, eaten) his lunch in a hurry.
9. Why haven't you (ate, eaten) your breakfast?
10. Ruth must have (ate, eaten) one of my sandwiches.

357

Say It Right   Hear It Right

Say these sentences until the correct use of the verbs sounds natural to you.

1. Who *gave* you that book?
2. The roller coaster *has given* me a stomachache.
3. Kim *gave* John some tips on ice skating.
4. The conductor *had given* me the wrong change.
5. Tom *gave* me a ride home yesterday.
6. *Have*n't you *given* your report yet?
7. Our team *gave* a cheer for Coach Long.
8. Ellen *has given* me her new address.
9. Only Susan *had given* the correct answer.
10. Bob *gave* the dog a shampoo.

Write It Right

Write the correct verb from the two forms given. Check your answer by saying the complete sentence to yourself.

1. My mother has (gave, given) me a dollar to buy lunch.
2. Officer Wendell (gave, given) a talk on traffic safety.
3. Calculators were (gave, given) as door prizes.
4. The manager (gave, given) my sister a raise.
5. Linda (gave, given) me a piece of cranberry bread.
6. I was (gave, given) a bike for my birthday.
7. Eric may have (gave, given) the book to Ms. Coleman.
8. The class (gave, given) Sandy a going-away party.
9. I have (gave, given) Bobby my best model car.
10. Has Lois (gave, given) you a copy of the contest rules?

358

Say It Right   Hear It Right

Say these sentences until the correct use of the verbs sounds natural to you.

1. Why *has* Laurie *gone* home early?
2. She *went* home sick.
3. My notebook *is gone* again.
4. Gilbert *went* to the band concert with his cousin.
5. I *had* never *gone* sailing before.
6. Everyone but Pete *went* to the picnic.
7. *Have* you ever *gone* to Missouri?
8. Nina *went* on an errand.
9. Betty *must have gone* fishing in the motorboat.
10. Jeff *went* for a ride on his bike.

Write It Right

Write the correct verb from the two forms given. Check your answer by saying the complete sentence to yourself.

1. Do you know where Ken's family (went, gone)?
2. They have (went, gone) camping again.
3. Fortunately, the hurricane had (went, gone) out to sea.
4. Has Julie (went, gone) already?
5. We haven't (went, gone) to a basketball game lately.
6. Ms. Jamison (went, gone) to the Smoky Mountains last year.
7. My family has always (went, gone) away for Christmas.
8. Last year, we (went, gone) to Washington.
9. The entire class has (went, gone) on a field trip.
10. When we looked, the deer had (went, gone).

359

Use the Right Word

Say It Right Hear It Right

Say these sentences until the correct use of the verbs sounds natural to you.

1. Hank's puppy *has* really *grown.*
2. The injured starfish *grew* a new leg.
3. *Have* you ever *grown* a cactus?
4. The farmer *grew* all sorts of vegetables.
5. The lioness *had grown* too old to hunt.
6. Delicious strawberries *are grown* in Michigan.
7. The noisy crowd *grew* louder and louder.
8. The tomatoes *have grown* rapidly.
9. Terry *grew* pleased with his new school.
10. Country music *has grown* in popularity.

Write It Right

Write the correct verb from the two forms given. Check your answer by saying the complete sentence to yourself.

1. The climbers had (grown, grew) too tired to continue.
2. Mom has (grew, grown) impatient with Larry's practical jokes.
3. The thunder (grew, grown) louder as the storm continued.
4. I have (grew, grown) much closer to my dad.
5. Thick, green ivy has (grew, grown) all over the old house.
6. Rita had finally (grew, grown) tall enough to play basketball.
7. The pollution problem has (grew, grown) even larger.
8. I (grew, grown) weary of reading and fell asleep.
9. Some pineapples are (grew, grown) in Puerto Rico.
10. Palm trees have (grew, grown) all over the island.

360

Know
Knew
Known

Say It Right Hear It Right

Say these sentences until the correct use of the verbs sounds natural to you.

1. Judy *knew* that she had passed the test.
2. Our family *has known* the O'Neills for years.
3. *Had* you *known* that Kurt was worried?
4. North Carolina *is known* for its beauty.
5. We *knew* that the snow would melt by morning.
6. I always *knew* about Frank's talent for painting.
7. How long *have* you *known* Susan?
8. Dogs *are known* for their loyalty.
9. The sportscaster *should have known* the score.
10. Everyone *knew* that the suspect was lying.

Write It Right

Write the correct verb from the two forms given. Check your answer by saying the complete sentence to yourself.

1. Only Gail (knew, known) how to repair the bicycle.
2. John Galvani is (knew, known) as Jackie to his friends.
3. I have never (knew, known) anyone as stubborn as Debra.
4. No one could have (knew, known) that answer.
5. Steve and Carlos have (knew, known) him for years.
6. Our cat Eleanor would have (knew, known) how to protect herself.
7. Dad never (knew, known) his cousin Rosemary very well.
8. If only I had (knew, known) you were home!
9. Everyone had (knew, known) that the work would not be easy.
10. I have always (knew, known) when I could do better.

361

Say It Right   Hear It Right

Say these sentences until the correct use of the verbs sounds natural to you.

1. *Have* you ever *ridden* a horse?
2. The surfer *rode* the waves.
3. We *should have ridden* to school on the bus.
4. Mom's new car *rode* well.
5. The cowboy *has ridden* back to the ranch.
6. The posse *rode* their horses to the badlands.
7. Five people *have ridden* together on this sled.
8. Keith *rode* a train across the country.
9. At night we *rode* with lights on our bikes.
10. In London, horses *are ridden* by some police officers.

Write It Right

Write the correct verb from the two forms given. Check your answer by saying the complete sentence to yourself.

1. The executive (rode, ridden) in the first-class section.
2. Janet (rode, ridden) her bike on the nature trail.
3. Bo (rode, ridden) in his uncle's sailplane.
4. Even the cat (rode, ridden) along on the trip.
5. Ramon has (rode, ridden) the bronco.
6. Portia has (rode, ridden) the roller coaster.
7. Horses were (rode, ridden) by Pony Express carriers.
8. Some people in the parade (rode, ridden) unicycles.
9. The sailors had (rode, ridden) out the storm.
10. The clowns had (rode, ridden) elephants around the ring.

362

Say It Right   Hear It Right

Say these sentences until the correct use of the verbs sounds natural to you.

1. The meeting *ran* late.
2. The grocery store *has run* out of milk.
3. Michelle *ran* for class president.
4. *Have* you ever *run* a mile?
5. We think our cat *ran* away.
6. The old car *had*n't *run* for years.
7. Who *ran* up the stairs?
8. Marathon races *are run* in many cities.
9. Mary *ran* into an old friend from school.
10. The quarterback *should have run* with the ball.

Write It Right

Write the correct verb from the two forms given. Check your answer by saying the complete sentence to yourself.

1. I have never (ran, run) a lawnmower before.
2. Mom stopped baking because she had (ran, run) out of flour.
3. Our gym class hasn't (ran, run) the fifty-yard dash yet.
4. Bicycle races are (ran, run) on a bowl-shaped track.
5. Paul (ran, run) the carousel at the school carnival.
6. The team had (ran, run) out of energy.
7. Cara (ran, run) every morning last summer.
8. The stalled truck must have (ran, run) out of gas.
9. Franklin D. Roosevelt (ran, run) for President four times.
10. Anita will (ran, run) with the track team.

363

Say It Right Hear It Right

Say these sentences until the correct use of the verbs sounds natural to you.

1. *Have* you *seen* Billy?
2. I *saw* him in the gym an hour ago.
3. Angelina *has seen* three plays.
4. We *saw* a mysterious looking man.
5. I thought I *had seen* him somewhere before.
6. Darin *saw* him, too.
7. The suspect *was* last *seen* this morning.
8. Who *has seen* Cindy's gloves?
9. Astronomers *have seen* Mars through their telescopes.
10. Loretta *saw* her mistake in the math problem.

Write It Right

Write the correct verb from the two forms given. Check your answer by saying the complete sentence to yourself.

1. Joey says he once (saw, seen) a UFO.
2. Lana (saw, seen) the tennis match.
3. I have already (saw, seen) that movie.
4. We had (saw, seen) that card trick before.
5. Connie (saw, seen) deer and wild turkey on the island.
6. The Patriots game wasn't (saw, seen) on local TV.
7. Have you ever (saw, seen) the President in person?
8. Terry (saw, seen) her guests to the door.
9. Has anyone (saw, seen) my pencil?
10. No one (saw, seen) Vincent run out the back door.

364

Say It Right   Hear It Right

Say these sentences until the correct use of the verbs sounds natural to you.

1. Kevin *took* the twins to the movies.
2. *Have* you *taken* your vitamins?
3. Tim *took* his sled to Squirrel Hill.
4. This seat *is taken.*
5. What *took* you so long?
6. Ginger *has taken* her sister to school.
7. I *took* first prize in the art fair.
8. Betty *had* often *taken* a taxi before.
9. The prisoner *was taken* to a cell.
10. Lee *took* a course in woodworking.

Write It Right

Write the correct verb from the two forms given. Check your answer by saying the complete sentence to yourself.

1. Shouldn't we have (took, taken) the Taylor Road bus?
2. Keith has (took, taken) out a book about tennis.
3. It has (took, taken) me an hour to get home.
4. Good friends are sometimes (took, taken) for granted.
5. Aunt Charlene (took, taken) me to a double-header.
6. Who could have (took, taken) the clothes to the cleaners?
7. It has (took, taken) you long enough to get ready.
8. Lucy (took, taken) many pictures on her trip.
9. Peter has (took, taken) the baby for a walk.
10. The injured boy was (took, taken) to the nurse's office.

365

Say It Right   Hear It Right

Say these sentences until the correct use of the verbs sounds natural to you.

1. Janie *wrote* the note in green ink.
2. *Has* anyone *written* to Uncle George?
3. I *wrote* to him the other day.
4. The report *was written* neatly.
5. *Have* you *written* your name on your paper?
6. Donna *wrote* another story about her brother.
7. Louis *had* never *written* a poem before.
8. Alexis *wrote* her name in the guest book.
9. The message *is written* in code.
10. Mr. Johnson *wrote* the instructions on the board.

Write It Right

Write the correct verb from the two forms given. Check your answer by saying the complete sentence to yourself.

1. I like the poems that you (wrote, written).
2. Everyone has (wrote, written) his or her name on my cast.
3. Lupé's letter was (wrote, written) in Spanish.
4. My neighbor has (wrote, written) a mystery story.
5. Ms. Jacobson (wrote, written) the year in Roman numerals.
6. Haven't you (wrote, written) to your pen pal?
7. Geraldo should have (wrote, written) in ink.
8. I had (wrote, written) so much that my hand hurt.
9. Have you ever (wrote, written) to a newspaper?
10. I must have (wrote, written) five letters to Sally.

366

ADDITIONAL EXERCISES

Using Irregular Verbs

Irregular Verbs Write the correct verb from the two forms given. Check your answer by reading the sentence to yourself.

1. A loud cheer (began, begun) the pep rally.
2. A thief has (broke, broken) into the safe.
3. Our class (wrote, written) a letter to the mayor.
4. Sherry (gave, given) away the ending of the movie.
5. Bart (did, done) a flip off the diving board.
6. The Davis family (went, gone) on a camping trip last summer.
7. Grandpa could have (ate, eaten) the whole salad.
8. Carrie and Jill (knew, known) how to plant the garden.
9. The usher has (took, taken) our tickets.
10. Kirk (ate, eaten) the rest of the grapes for lunch.
11. The commander (gave, given) an order to the troops.
12. The team has (gone, went) into a huddle.
13. Margie's sunburn (grew, grown) painful.
14. Cindy (knew, known) the magician's secret.
15. The sheik (rode, ridden) a white stallion.
16. Ed has (began, begun) to read an exciting book.
17. All the children have (ran, run) to the ice cream truck.
18. We (saw, seen) the movie at the drive-in.
19. Susan (did, done) a lot of work for the school play.
20. C.S. Lewis has (wrote, written) good science fiction.
21. The glass (broke, broken) in the dishwasher.
22. That avocado pit has (grew, grown) into a plant.
23. Haven't you (rode, ridden) a bicycle?
24. The horses should have (ran, run) around the track.
25. Cliff (saw, seen) that movie on television.

Additional Exercises

These Additional Exercises may be used for additional practice of the concepts presented in this Section. Each exercise focuses on a single concept, and should be used after the page number indicated in parentheses.

Review

If you have not assigned these Additional Exercises before this time, you can also use them as an excellent Section Review.

Mixed Review

These exercises provide review of the concepts presented in this Section. Each exercise challenges the students to apply several of the skills they have acquired during previous study. Because the "mixed" feature of these activities makes them more difficult, the teacher may wish to have less-advanced students do them orally or in small groups.

MIXED REVIEW

Using Irregular Verbs

A. Identifying irregular verbs Write the correct form of the verb from those given in parentheses. After each verb, write *Present, Past,* or *Past Participle*.

1. Dad has (given, gave) me money for the tickets. Past Participle
2. I (known, know) the answer. Present
3. Patti has (took, taken) French for two years. Past Participle
4. The chorus (sang, sung) songs by Stephen Sondheim. Past
5. The storm (damaged, damage) many houses. Past
6. I (seen, saw) Roger at the library. Past
7. The plant has (outgrown, outgrew) its pot. Past Participle
8. The sparrow's eggs were (stolen, stole) from the nest. Past Participle
9. Laura (gone, went) to camp last summer. Past
10. I have (chose, chosen) an album by Men at Work. Past Participle
11. Brad (writes, written) to his grandparents every week. Present
12. We (watch, watched) the fireworks last night. Past
13. Emily has (swam, swum) in two oceans. Past Participle

B. Using irregular verbs Write each of the following sentences, using the form given in parentheses.

1. Carol (past of *give*) us a hand. gave
2. The lake has (past participle of *freeze*). has frozen
3. Terry (past of *run*) all the way home. ran
4. Shelly (present of *speak*) English and Spanish. speaks
5. The baby robins have (past participle of *fly*) away. have flown
6. The runners (past of *drink*) two quarts of lemonade. drank
7. The children have (past participle of *go*) to bed. have gone
8. I have (past participle of *wear*) this jacket before. have worn
9. Doug often (present of *steal*) second base. steals
10. The movie (past of *begin*) on time. began

USING GRAMMAR IN WRITING

Using Irregular Verbs

A. Have you ever bought something and been sorry about it later? Was it a record, a game, or some item of clothing? Was it a ticket to a concert or a movie? Write a short paragraph about what you bought and why it was a mistake. In your paragraph use several of the following irregular verbs. Be sure to use the correct form of each verb.

buy	begin	take
give	see	teach
speak	have	throw
break	ride	wear
do	say	grow

B. Imagine that you just got home from one of the best parties ever. Before you go to sleep, you want to write about it in your journal. Use the past or the past participle form of five or six of the following verbs in your journal entry:

go	swim	take
dance	choose	wear
eat	bring	ride
sing	know	have

C. You have a new cat. Someone has asked why you named your pet "Trouble." Explain why in a paragraph. Use each of the following verbs, in the form shown. Remember to use helping verbs with past participles.

spill (past)	*chase* (past)
drink (past participle)	*break* (present)
scratch (past participle)	*run* (past participle)

Using Grammar in Writing

These challenging and enjoyable activities allow the students to see how the concepts of grammar, usage, and mechanics may be applied in actual writing situations. Each exercise is designed to allow students practice in several of the skills they have acquired in this Section. The activities also provide opportunities for students to write creatively about a wide variety of interesting and unusual subjects.

369

Section Objectives

1. To use the correct forms of the verb *be*

2. To use the correct form of *be* after *there, here,* and *where*

3. To choose the correct verb from verb pairs that are often confused

4. To identify contractions and to use them correctly

5. To identify negatives (*no*-words and *not*-words) and to use them correctly

Preparing the Students

Point out that this is the third section of the Handbook that deals with verbs. This indicates how important verbs are. It also indicates how many problems verbs can cause. These problems can be avoided by knowing about them beforehand. This section takes up some of the most common verb usage problems. The verbs covered in this section are often confused or misused in conversation and writing. Read the introduction to Section 6 on page 370.

Additional Resources

Mastery Test — pages 45–46 in the test booklet

Additional Exercises — pages 383–386 in the student text

Practice Book — pages 145–151

Duplicating Masters — pages 145–151

Special Populations — See special section at the front of this Teacher's Edition.

Using Troublesome Verbs Correctly

There are some verbs that people find troublesome to use correctly. You have studied irregular verbs. In this section, you will learn about other verbs that cause problems. You will then be able to use these verbs correctly, too.

> We was waiting for you.
> Here is some cookies.
> Rodney set down to watch TV.
> The Burtons don't have no pets.

Can you find the trouble spots?

Part 1 Using the Right Form of *Be*

You have already learned that the verb *be* has many forms:

is	was	am	being
are	were	be	been

Some of these forms may be used alone or as helping verbs. Others may be used only *with* helping verbs.

Here are five important rules to remember when using the forms of the verb *be*. Each rule is followed by example sentences. Read each of the sentences aloud. When you hear the verbs used correctly, you will be able to remember the rules more easily.

1. If the subject names one person, place, or thing, use the forms *is* and *was*.

Christine *is* here.	She *is sitting* near me.
Teddy *was* here.	He *was called* away.

2. If the subject names more than one person, place, or thing, use the forms *are* and *were*.

The children *are* late.	They *are riding* their bikes.
The cookies *were* on that plate.	They *were eaten* at lunch.

3. When the subject is *you*, use the forms *are* and *were*.

You *are* my best friend.	*Are* you *coming* with me?
You *were* the fastest swimmer.	You *were doing* a good job.

4. When the subject is *I*, use the forms *am* and *was*.

I *am* here.	I *am studying* English.
I *was* at home.	I *was sleeping* in bed.

5. Use a helping verb before the forms *be, being,* and *been*.

Part 1

Objective

To use the correct forms of the verb *be*

Presenting the Lesson

Read pages 371 and 372. Ask students to explain the difference in meaning and use between the two sets of verbs on page 371. Have them give you other examples using the words in sentences.

Individualizing the Lesson

Less-Advanced Students

Do Exercise A with students, having them give the rule that applies to each sentence. Assign Exercise B and have students write the number of the appropriate rule after each sentence. When correcting the exercise together, read the entire sentence aloud for aural reinforcement.

Advanced Students

Suggest that students write their own sentences to illustrate each rule, putting the number of each rule at the end. They should use the examples given on pages 371 and 372 as a guide.

Optional Practice

Have students follow the directions for Exercise A on page 372, using these sentences.

1. Pierre (is, are) painting the fence.
2. October (am, is) a colorful month.
3. Ralph and Erin (is, are) going to the game today.
4. You (was, were) laughing very loudly.

5. Uncle Matt (been, has been, have been) an explorer.
6. The nurse (were being, being, was being) gentle with the patient.
7. Those pictures (was, were) taken last year.
8. I (is, are, am) going shopping.
9. The custodians (was, were, been) repairing the roof.
10. Our principal (been, was) at a meeting this morning.

Extending the Lesson

Most students are usually aware of rules 1 to 4, so you may find it useful to concentrate on rule 5. Make sure students understand that whether *be, being,* and *been* are helping verbs or main verbs, they may not be used alone. Put these sentences on a worksheet or on the board. Have the students rewrite the sentences correctly, adding a helping verb to the verb in parentheses. They should then underline the whole verb.

Example: Our TV set (being) repaired.
Our TV set is being repaired.

1. Those students [have] (been) working hard.
2. The brown pony [is] (being) difficult.
3. I [have] (been) hungry for the last two hours.
4. The car [will] (be) in the garage until this afternoon.
5. That movie [has] (been) at the theater a long time.
6. That bus driver [has] (been) driving a bus for ten years.
7. The library [will] (be) open until noon.
8. The building on the corner [is] (being) torn down.

Do not use one of these forms alone or as the only helping verb before a main verb.

Karen *will be* here later.
The patient *was being taken* to surgery.
Jeff *has been looking* for you.
These directions *have been* hard to follow.

Exercises Use the right form of *be.*

A. Number your paper from 1 to 10. Write the correct form of *be* from the two given in parentheses.

1. George and Eileen (is, are) my neighbors.
2. I (is, am) a forward on the basketball team.
3. (Is, Are) you the team captain?
4. The TV (been, has been) on for several hours.
5. You (was, were) blocking my view.
6. (Was, Were) Craig and Janet going roller skating?
7. The Great Dane (being, was being) playful.
8. Your backpack (is, are) loaded with books.
9. Nancy (be, is) a figure skater.
10. The boys (been, were) practicing for the band concert.

B. Follow the directions for Exercise A.

1. Tammy and I (is, are) building a bird feeder.
2. I (am, is) just guessing his age.
3. (Is, Are) you a good sport when you lose?
4. Jorge (be, is) feeding the fish in the science lab.
5. I (am, be) helping by cooking dinner tonight.
6. Eric and Sam (been, have been) at the beach.
7. The haunted house (was, were) torn down.
8. They (was, were) building a fort in the snow.
9. You (was being, were being) silly.
10. (Is, Are) the passengers boarding the plane?

Part 2 Using the Right Verb After *There, Here,* and *Where*

Many sentences begin with the words *There is* or *There are.* How can you tell when to use each?

First find the subject of the sentence. The word *there* is never the subject. When a sentence begins with *there,* the subject usually comes after the verb.

> There is a squirrel in the tree. (*Squirrel* is the subject)
> There are the boats. (*Boats* is the subject)

Next, find out whether the subject names one person, place, or thing, or more than one. Then follow the rules for the forms of the verb *be.*

Can you decide which form to use in each of these sentences?

> There (is, are) a motor in that boat.
> There (is, are) papers on the floor.

The subject in the first sentence is *motor.* The subject names one thing. You should have chosen *is.* The subject in the second sentence is *papers.* Since this names more than one thing, you should have chosen *are.*

The words *here* and *where* are also used to begin sentences. They cause the same problem as *there.* When should you say *Here is* or *Where is?* When should you say *Here are* or *Where are?*

You can tell by finding the subject. *Here* and *where* are never the subject. In sentences beginning with *here* or *where,* the subject comes after the verb. If the subject names one thing, use *is*. If the subject names more than one thing, use *are.*

> Here *is* the *trail.* (*Trail* is the subject of the verb *is.*)
> Where *is* the *door?* (*Door* is the subject of the verb *is.*)
> Here *are* the *pens.* (*Pens* is the subject of the verb *are.*)
> Where *are* the *books?* (*Books* is the subject of the verb *are.*)

Part 2

Objective

To use the correct form of *be* after *there, here,* and *where*

Presenting the Lesson

1. Read and discuss page 373. If necessary, remind students that a subject is not always at the beginning of a sentence (Section 1, Part 7). Ask students for additional examples of sentences using *there, here,* and *where,* with a verb. Discuss the subjects of those sentences and how they govern their verbs.

2. Assign and discuss Exercises A and B on page 374.

Individualizing the Lesson

Less-Advanced Students

Explain that because *here, there,* and *where* seem singular, one may expect to follow each of them with a singular verb. But if you turn the sentence around, putting the subject at the beginning, you can easily see which verb to use. Have students reorder the four sentences at the bottom of page 373 to illustrate this.

Advanced Students

Have students write six questions, three beginning with "Where" and three beginning with "How many." Have them trade sentences with their neighbor and have each write an answer to the questions. They should circle the subject in the question and in the answer.

Optional Practice

Have students make the following phrases into complete sentences. They should underline the subject.

Answers will vary.

1. There is
2. There was
3. There are
4. There were
5. Here is
6. Here are
7. Here was
8. Here were
9. Where is
10. Where was
11. Where are
12. Where were

Extending the Lesson

Have students complete the following sentences by adding a verb. They should choose from *is, are, was* and *were*.

1. There is your sister's kitten.
2. Where are/were David's socks?
3. Where is the latest issue of this magazine?
4. Here are the new members of the club.
5. There was no more grape juice.
6. Here are the news headlines.

Part 3

Objective

To choose the correct verb from verb pairs that are often confused

Exercises **Use the right verb after *There, Here,* and *Where.***

A. Copy these sentences, using the correct form of *be*.

1. Where (is, are) your friends?
2. There (is, are) five magazines on the table.
3. Where (is, are) the two broken bicycles?
4. There (is, are) a strong wind from the west.
5. Here (is, are) the oldest trees in the park.
6. There (was, were) a letter for Rick in the mailbox.
7. There (is, are) several students in the library.
8. Where (is, are) the Big Dipper?
9. (Was, Were) there any more apples on the tree?
10. Here (is, are) the computer program you need.

B. Follow the directions for Exercise A.

1. Where (is, are) my math book?
2. There (is, are) six tomatoes left.
3. Here (is, are) several old photographs.
4. Where (is, are) the keys for the car?
5. Here (is, are) a box of your old clothes.
6. There (is, are) a good reason for my mistake.
7. Here (is, are) the tracks of a big animal.
8. Where (is, are) my old blue jeans?
9. Here (is, are) the folder of papers you lost.
10. There (is, are) my two best friends.

Part 3 Some Confusing Pairs of Verbs

Some pairs of verbs cause trouble because they are alike in meaning. In this section you will learn how to use these verbs.

Learn and *Teach*

Learn means "to understand" or "to gain knowledge."

Everyone should *learn* to swim.

Teach means "to show how" or "to explain."

Can you *teach* me how to swim?

The principal parts of these verbs are:

learn, learned, learned **teach, taught, taught**

Say these sentences until they sound correct and natural.

Learn

Present: The students *learn* new words by reading.
Past: Britt *learned* to read a compass.
Past Participle: I *have learned* some of the customs of India.

Teach

Present: Trained instructors *teach* diving.
Past: Ms. Voss *taught* us science last year.
Past Participle: My sister *has taught* me how to play Scrabble.

Exercise Use *learn* and *teach* correctly.

Write the correct verb from the two given in parentheses.

1. Will you (teach, learn) me to play chess?
2. Ms. Casey (teaches, learns) eighth-graders.
3. I have (taught, learned) to operate our school's computer.
4. Mr. Dior (teaches, learns) ballet classes at his studio.
5. My sister has (taught, learned) me to ride a horse.
6. Beginners can (teach, learn) the game by watching.
7. By reading, Al has (taught, learned) about other lands.
8. Your parents (taught, learned) you good manners.
9. Ms. Fairbanks (taught, learned) our class about the birth of the solar system.
10. These students have (taught, learned) about programming.

Presenting the Lesson

1. Read pages 374 and 375. Ask students to explain the difference in meaning and use between the two sets of verbs on page 375. Have them give you other examples using the words in sentences.

2. Assign and discuss the Exercise on page 375.

3. Read page 376. Discuss the same questions as for page 375. You may want to take more time with *let* and *leave* since it is sometimes more difficult to differentiate between them.

4. If the distinctions appear to be understood, assign and discuss the Exercise on page 376. Otherwise, it is suggested that you do part of the Exercise with the class first.

5. Follow steps 1 and 2 above for page 377.

6. Follow steps 3 and 4 above for page 378.

7. Assign and discuss the *Review Exercise* on page 379, or use it as a mastery quiz.

Individualizing the Lesson

Less-Advanced Students

1. Remind students that these verbs are confusing to many people, and that they may hear adults misusing them, especially in areas where dialects are strong. ("Set a spell," "Leave me be," "Learn him a thing or two.") This lesson should be viewed as a challenge.

2. Give students the following helpful hints. You may wish to do this as each pair of words is covered.

a. Point out that usually people or animals *sit;* things get *set.*

b. Point out that *let* means "permit" and both words end in the letter *t. Let me go* means *Permit me to go. Mom lets us have a snack* means *Mom permits us to have a snack.*

c. Read this dialogue to show the difference between *may* and *can.*

"Mother," Ron asked greedily, "can I have that extra piece of pie?"

"Of course you CAN," answered Mother as she took the plate away, "but you MAY not. This is for your father. There are many things you CAN do but you MAY not do. Now you MAY be excused."

d. Point out that someone else can *teach* you, but you have to *learn* for yourself. Ask for sentences showing this.

Optional Practice

1. Direct students to fill in the blanks with one of the verbs written above each group of sentences.

sit—set

1. Sit on the ground.
2. Set the glass down.
3. Sit in the bleachers.
4. Sit on the curb.
5. Set the pitcher on the table.

may—can

1. May I borrow your crayons?
2. Most people can learn to dance.
3. Everyone may have more dessert.
4. Can you ride a horse?
5. May I use your bike?

let—leave

1. Let the baby bird go when it can fly.
2. Leave the mail next door.
3. Leave the money in the bank.
4. Let me walk home with you.
5. Leave enough cereal for breakfast.

Let and *Leave*

Let means "to permit."

Will you *let* me borrow a pencil?

Leave means "to go away from."

The bus *will leave* in an hour.

The principal parts of these verbs are:

let, let, let **leave, left, left**

Say these sentences until they sound correct and natural.

Let

Present: *Let* me go!
Past: Tracy *let* her dog jump into the icy water.
Past Participle: My parents *have let* me decide that myself.

Leave

Present: *Leave* me alone.
Past: Kerry *left* the house in a hurry.
Past Participle: The girls *have left* us with the clean-up chores.

Exercise Use *let* and *leave* correctly.

Write the correct verb from the two given in parentheses. Check by reading each sentence to yourself.

1. Don't (let, leave) the toast burn.
2. Our guests will (let, leave) soon.
3. Sometimes Dad has (left, let) me win at backgammon.
4. (Let, Leave) your suggestions in the box.
5. Have you (let, left) your gym shoes at school?
6. (Let, Leave) Earl choose the music for our videotape.
7. Will you (let, leave) your brother help us?
8. (Let, Leave) my books in the classroom.
9. Will Mom (let, leave) you attend camp this summer?
10. Ben and Molly have (let, left) their bikes in the yard.

376

May and *Can*

May refers to permission, or to something that is possible. *Might* is another form of *may*. There are no principal parts. Both *may* and *might* are used only as helping verbs.

You *may* go to the beach. We *might* see Frank there.

Can means "to be able to do something." *Could* is another form of *can*. There are no principal parts. *Can* and *could* are usually used as helping verbs.

Tim *could* have done better. I *can* speak Spanish.

Say these sentences until they sound correct and natural.

May

You *may* check out only five books.
May we use the gym after school?
Might I help?

Can

This ladder *can* reach the roof.
The dolphins *could* jump through hoops.
That librarian *could* have helped Al.

Exercise Use *may* and *can* correctly.

Write the correct verb from the two given in parentheses.

1. (May, Can) I borrow your ruler?
2. Magnets (may, can) attract metals.
3. Most magicians (may, can) make things disappear.
4. Lionel (may, can) fix anything.
5. Yes, you (may, can) have some dessert now.
6. Cats (may, can) see in the dark.
7. (Can, May) you tell me what time it is?
8. You (may, can) try my new camera.
9. No one (may, can) shout in the library.
10. (May, Can) we please feed the animals?

teach—taught—learn

1. Teach me how to play the guitar.
2. The sailor will learn how to tie knots.
3. The tailor taught his assistant to sew.
4. I had to learn to be patient.
5. Will the champion teach us to throw the Frisbee?

2. Have students underline the correct verb from the two given in parentheses.

1. Don't (sit, set) your glasses on that chair!
2. The baby will (sit, set) in the high chair.
3. Who (sit, set) the wet glass on my dresser?
4. (Let, Leave) me do it by myself.
5. Dad will (let, leave) me go to the show tonight.
6. It's warm enough to (let, leave) the windows open.
7. Will you (let, leave) us at the beach today?
8. (May, Can) I go to the park with Leroy?
9. (Can, May) you sew this button on my coat?
10. After school (may, can) Angela go uptown with me?
11. No one (may, can) drive through a red light.
12. Do you think I could (learn, teach) to knit?
13. I could (learn, teach) you to play chess.
14. My uncle (taught, learned) my cousin to play backgammon.
15. Sarah has just (learned, taught) how to swim from the lifeguard.

Extending the Lesson

Have students think up a scene which shows the meaning of a pair of the confusing verbs covered in this lesson. They should then perform it for the class, using a partner if necessary.

Example: A pair of students could act out a scene in which one is a well-known tennis star teaching the other how to play tennis. They should use dialogue which incorporates the pair of words *teach* and *learn*.

Set and *Sit*

Set means "to place something somewhere."

Set the grocery bags on the counter.

Sit means "to rest in one place."

I usually *sit* in the front seat.

The principal parts of these verbs are:

set, set, set   **sit, sat, sat**

Say these sentences until they sound correct and natural.

Set

Present: The machine *sets* the crates on end.
Past: Chuck *set* his books on the desk.
Past Participle: The stage crew *has set* the props in place.

Sit

Present: Kyle *sits* in the back row.
Past: Connie *sat* in an inner tube.
Past Participle: The girls *have sat* by the fireplace all evening.

Exercise Use *set* and *sit* correctly.

Write the correct verb from the two given in parentheses. Check by reading each sentence to yourself.

1. I will (set, sit) the plates on the table.
2. Please (set, sit) in this chair.
3. We (set, sat) in the front row.
4. (Set, Sit) that heavy carton on the counter.
5. In music class we (set, sit) in small groups.
6. Margie (set, sat) the vase on the piano.
7. My dog will (set, sit) by my side.
8. Don't (set, sit) the ice cream on the stove.
9. Anne will (set, sit) under the hairdryer.
10. Did the old man (set, sit) his hat down?

Review Exercise **Use the right verb.**

Write the correct verb from the two given in parentheses. Check your answer by reading the sentence to yourself.

1. (May, Can) whales live underwater?
2. We will (let, leave) the campgrounds tomorrow.
3. (Set, Sit) your cards in front of you.
4. Beth has (taught, learned) me the words to the song.
5. (May, Can) we please open the gifts now?
6. Don't (let, leave) the water run.
7. Tall people should have (set, sat) in back.
8. Nobody (teaches, learns) babies to talk.
9. Sarah (may, can) stand on her head without help.
10. The coach will (let, leave) us rest now.
11. (May, Can) I see your new bike?
12. You should never have (let, left) your parrot out of its cage.
13. Henry (taught, learned) us the rules for basketball.
14. The movers will (set, sit) the furniture in place.
15. (Teach, Learn) me that card trick, Raoul.

Part 4 Using Contractions

Sometimes a verb is combined with another word to make one word. These shortened forms are called **contractions.** Here are some examples:

is not	=	isn't	that is, that has	=	that's
were not	=	weren't	will not	=	won't
I have	=	I've	where is, where has	=	where's
she would	=	she'd	can not	=	can't

When you write a contraction, use an **apostrophe** to show where letters have been left out.

Part 4

Objective

To identify contractions and to use them correctly

Presenting the Lesson

1. Read and discuss page 379. You may find it helpful to talk about possible meanings for the base word *contract* (agreement, to pull together). A word contraction is a coming together of a verb and another word to make a shortened form. Stress that there is no change of meaning. Ask students to tell the missing letters for the examples.

2. Assign and discuss Exercises A and B on page 380.

Individualizing the Lesson

Less-Advanced Students

Before doing Exercise A, have students identify the two words in each contraction and tell which letters are missing.

Advanced Students

Point out that contractions are often used in advertising to make a phrase catchy or to help the beat of a sentence. ("We're number one!" "You've come a long way, baby.") Have students think of more examples of contractions in ads. Ask them to consider whether or not the ad would be as effective without the contraction.

Optional Practice

Put the contractions listed below on the board. Have the students copy them, putting the apostrophe where it belongs. Then have the students write the words for which the contraction stands.

1. I'm I am
2. you're you are
3. what's what is
4. it's it is
5. we're we are
6. where's where is

Part 5

Objective

To identify negatives (*no*-words and *not*-words) and to use them correctly

Exercises **Make contractions correctly.**

A. Copy each contraction below. Place the apostrophe where it belongs.

1. I've
2. we'll
3. they've
4. can't
5. there's
6. aren't
7. don't
8. he's
9. that's
10. I'm
11. here's
12. isn't

B. Writing Copy the following sentences. Make a contraction of the underlined words in each sentence.

1. You are the first to arrive. You're
2. Francis has not eaten lunch yet. hasn't
3. They are all ready to go to the beach. They're
4. We are on Debra's softball team. We're
5. I will help you carry these books. I'll
6. What has happened here? What's
7. I think she would like to go. she'd
8. Beth will not go near snakes. won't
9. Where is the bike pump? Where's
10. It is Bill's football. It's

Part 5 Using Negatives Correctly

Some contractions are made by joining *not* with certain verbs, like this: *is* + *not* = *isn't*.

The **apostrophe (')** takes the place of the *o* in *not*. These contractions are called *not*-words.

have + not = haven't	is + not = isn't
were + not = weren't	do + not = don't
would + not = wouldn't	could + not = couldn't

The *no*-words are different. You can see *no* in all but one:

no	nobody	none	never
no one	nothing	nowhere	

Together, the *not*-words and the *no*-words are called **negatives.**

Two negatives used together make what is called a **double negative.** Do not ever use double negatives. They are always incorrect.

Wrong: Melvin does**n't** do **nothing.**

Correct: Melvin does**n't** do anything.

or

Correct: Melvin does **nothing.**

The sentences below show the right way to use negatives. Read the sentences aloud until they sound correct and natural to you:

There is**n't** any flour left.
There is **no** flour left.

Do**n't** ever do that again!
Never do that again!

We have**n't** gone anywhere this week.
We have gone **nowhere** this week.

Have**n't** you ever ridden in a plane?
Have you **never** ridden in a plane?

Exercises Use negatives correctly.

A. Copy these sentences. Choose the correct word from the two given in parentheses. Then read the completed sentence to yourself.

1. Doesn't (nobody, anybody) want to play tennis?
2. Don't those boys have (anything, nothing) to do?
3. Haven't you (never, ever) been to the ocean?

Presenting the Lesson

1. Discuss the meaning of the word *negative*. Point out that *not* is a form of *no* and is also negative. Ask students to give you examples of things they consider to be negative (things that should *not* be done). Read and discuss pages 380 and 381.

2. You may find it helpful to do Exercise A on pages 381 and 382 with the students. Discuss the reasons for the answers and have students point out *no*-words and *not*-words. Have them check each sentence to be sure it has only one negative. Assign and discuss Exercise B.

Individualizing the Lesson

Less-Advanced Students

Put the following equation on the board: $-2 \times -2 = 4$. Point out that in multiplication and other areas of life two negatives can make a positive. Therefore, if someone says, "I don't want no more trouble," it means that he or she *does* want trouble. In order to express a negative, only *one* negative should be used: "I don't want any trouble," or $-2 \times 2 = -4$.

Advanced Students

Have students write themselves five New Year's resolutions. They should use five of the following words: *won't, shouldn't, never, nothing, no one, nobody* or *isn't.* The resolutions may be realistic or fanciful. Example: "I resolve that there isn't anything that will make me get up early on Saturdays." Remind students not to use double negatives.

Optional Practice

Put the ten sentences below on a worksheet or on the board. Tell students that five of them are correct and that five contain double negatives. If the sentence is correct, they should put a *C* to the right of it; if it is not, they should use *X*. You might want to have your more advanced students rewrite the double negative sentences correctly.

X 1. Paul won't never eat so much again. (will never/won't ever)

C 2. No one is allowed to go into that room.

C 3. I don't think anyone knows my secret.

X 4. My pen doesn't have no ink left. (has no / doesn't have any)

C 5. There aren't any basketballs in the gym.

C 6. We didn't see anything better on the menu.

X 7. No one couldn't hit a home run. (No one could)

C 8. My brother can't drive a car yet.

X 9. Why wouldn't nobody go on the trip? (wouldn't anybody/would nobody)

X 10. There wasn't no orange juice left. (wasn't any/was no)

Extending the Lesson

Point out that sentences containing a *not*-word may also contain these words:

any	anybody	anywhere
anyone	anything	ever

Have students write a sentence for each of these words, using a *not*-word in each sentence.

Example: I don't want any more dinner.

Then show that many of these examples can be written in a second way, without the meaning being changed.

I want no more dinner.

4. There isn't (none, any) of the stew left for us.
5. Adam doesn't go (nowhere, anywhere).
6. Isn't there (no one, anyone) we could ask?
7. There weren't (any, no) prizes left for Jason and her.
8. I guess no one (is, isn't) coming.
9. (Does, Doesn't) nobody want to sing along?
10. (Weren't, Were) none of you at the picnic?

B. Write the correct word from the two given in parentheses. Check your answer by reading the sentence to yourself.

1. There won't be (anything, nothing) left for lunch.
2. Those girls don't do (nothing, anything) wrong.
3. Nothing was (never, ever) said about the broken window.
4. We didn't hear (anybody, nobody) crying.
5. Doesn't (nothing, anything) ever go wrong at camp?
6. We don't want (any, no) trouble.
7. I couldn't see (nothing, anything) on the stage.
8. Isn't there (any, no) milk left in the carton?
9. The bus didn't have (no, any) empty seats.
10. Manuel's glasses (were, weren't) nowhere to be found.

ADDITIONAL EXERCISES

Using Troublesome Verbs Correctly

A. The Right Form of *Be* Write the correct form of *be* from the two given in parentheses.

1. Lois (is, be) in the library.
2. Gregg and Jan (is, are) the goalies.
3. (Was, Were) you late for class?
4. The tomatoes (is, are) on the windowsill.
5. You (is, are) the first one here.
6. I (was, were) waiting for you.
7. Sue (be, has been) studying for the test.
8. The twins (was, were) absent today.
9. I (is, am) working tonight.
10. The cat (be, is) chasing the mouse.

B. The Right Verb After *There, Here,* and *Where* Write the correct form of *be* from the two given in parentheses.

1. There (is, are) two reasons for our delay.
2. Here (is, are) the best map of the area.
3. Where (was, were) the children hiding?
4. There (was, were) no commercials on that station.
5. Here (is, are) the scripts for the show.
6. There (was, were) a message for you.
7. Here (is, are) the ambulance.
8. Where (is, are) the jello salad?
9. There (is, are) seven candles on the table.
10. Where (is, are) the jars of paste?

C. Confusing Pairs of Verbs Write the correct verb.

1. Will you (learn, teach) me the school song?
2. Barb (let, left) her gym shoes in her locker.

Additional Exercises

These Additional Exercises may be used for additional practice of the concepts presented in this Section. Each exercise focuses on a single concept, and should be used after the page number indicated in parentheses.

Review

If you have not assigned these Additional Exercises before this time, you can also use them as an excellent Section Review.

3. (May, Can) we please take the subway downtown?
4. Bev and Gloria (set, sat) together on the bus.
5. Ms. Barnes (let, left) us choose our project topics.
6. (Let, Leave) Grace help herself.
7. You (may, can) have some cheese.
8. Eric (set, sat) his tray on the table.
9. Chuck (taught, learned) me how to drive the boat.
10. You (may, can) be excused now.

D. Contractions Make a contraction of the underlined words.

1. We are writing a news article. We're
2. Roberto has not watered that plant for days. hasn't
3. I will never trust Freddie again. I'll
4. What has been discussed in student council? What's
5. Dad said he would take us bowling. he'd
6. Maria does not want dessert. doesn't
7. They have already left. They've
8. I could not eat the squid. couldn't
9. Steve should not have gone. shouldn't
10. I have caught a cold. I've

E. Negatives Write the correct word.

1. The curtain hasn't (never, ever) gone up on time.
2. I have (any, no) money left.
3. (Does, Doesn't) no one recycle aluminum cans here?
4. Report cards show (nothing, anything) but grades.
5. Haven't you (never, ever) attended a play?
6. We can't go (anywhere, nowhere) without a car.
7. (Weren't, Were) none of you listening?
8. Isn't (anybody, nobody) leaving soon?
9. There isn't (no one, anyone) on the stage.
10. Don't buy (no, any) more of these pens.

MIXED REVIEW

Using Troublesome Verbs Correctly

A. Using the right form of *be* after *there, here,* and *where* Make two columns on your paper. Label one *Subject* and the other *Verb*. Write the subject of each sentence below in the *Subject* column. Then choose the correct form of the verb given in parentheses and write it in the *Verb* column.

1. Here (is, are) your photographs.
2. Where (is, are) the library?
3. There (was, were) ten people in line.
4. Where (is, are) my track shoes?
5. Here (is, are) the list of names.
6. There (was, were) a flock of geese over the lake.
7. Here (is, are) the notes for my report.
8. There (is, are) a new program at school for children.
9. Where (is, are) the buried treasure?
10. Here (is, are) the answer to the problem.

B. Using the correct verb Write the correct verb for each sentence below.

1. (Learn, Teach) me that new dance.
2. Let's (set, sit) down and rest.
3. (May, Can) I borrow your pen?
4. We should (leave, let) Jay work by himself.
5. Don't (set, sit) your glass on this table.
6. Carrie (let, left) her bike out in the rain.
7. I (may, can) need your help.
8. My cousin (learned, taught) me to speak German last summer.
9. Please (let, leave) your boots outside the door.
10. Our class (set, sat) in the balcony.

Mixed Review

These exercises provide review of the concepts presented in this Section. Each exercise challenges the students to apply several of the skills they have acquired during previous study. Because the "mixed" feature of these activities makes them more difficult, the teacher may wish to have less-advanced students do them orally or in small groups.

C. Using contractions and negatives correctly Copy each of the following sentences. Write the underlined words as a contraction. Choose the correct word of the two in parentheses.

1. Erin did not do (anything, nothing) wrong.
2. I have not (never, ever) used Dad's camera.
3. Chuck could not think of (anything, nothing) to write.
4. We can not find (anybody, nobody) to play shortstop.
5. This desert does not get (no, any) rain.
6. She is not doing (anything, nothing) this evening.
7. Do not (never, ever) play with fire.
8. The king will not listen to (anyone, no one).
9. There were not (no, any) empty seats in the theater.
10. Does not (anybody, nobody) want another taco?

D. Using verbs correctly Six of the following sentences contain errors in the use of verbs. If a sentence contains an error, rewrite it correctly. If a sentence is already correct, write *Correct*.

1. We set near the water.
2. Karen learned me the magic trick.
3. Mr. Fisher taught the lesson well.
4. Where is my keys?
5. I be tired from swimming.
6. The bus left without Leon.
7. There were many questions about the assignment.
8. Here are another bag of plums.
9. Can I please look at your map?
10. Dan let me borrow his bike.

386

USING GRAMMAR IN WRITING

Using Troublesome Verbs Correctly

A. Do you ever feel that there are disadvantages to being a teenager? Write a paragraph telling about two or three things that are hard about being your age. Begin two sentences with the words *There is* or *There are,* and *Here is* or *Here are.* In the other sentences, include at least two of the following verbs. Use the correct form of each verb.

learn—teach let—leave—left may—can

B. The following story was turned in to the sports editor of your school paper. The editor was too busy to rewrite it. She has asked you to do the job. She wants you to change any verbs followed by negative words into contractions. Be sure all other contractions are punctuated correctly. She also wants you to make sure there are no double negatives.

Friday's game ~~was not~~ wasn't the best I have ever seen. Our basketball team ~~was not~~ wasn't in peak form. No one could~~n't~~ score. None of our opponents missed a shot. That isn't ~~no~~ any exaggeration, either.

Three of our best players ~~were not~~ weren't playing because they had the flu. That is not the worst part. Forward "Ace" Green sprained his ankle. There wasnt ' ~~no~~ any replacement for him.

We haven't ~~never~~ ever played so badly. I hope we will not repeat the performance ~~neither.~~ either.

Using Grammar in Writing

These challenging and enjoyable activities allow the students to see how the concepts of grammar, usage, and mechanics may be applied in actual writing situations. Each exercise is designed to allow students practice in several of the skills they have acquired in this Section. The activities also provide opportunities for students to write creatively about a wide variety of interesting and unusual subjects.

387

Section Objectives

1. To understand the function of the pronoun, and to identify pronouns in sentences

2. To use pronouns correctly as subjects of sentences, particularly in compound subjects

3. To use pronouns correctly after state-of-being verbs

4. To use pronouns correctly as objects in sentences, particularly in compound objects

5. To use *we* and *us* correctly

6. To identify possessive pronouns and to use them correctly

Preparing the Students

Choose a picture from a student text that shows several people. Ask students to tell you about the picture. Perhaps write on the board some of the sentences or noun phrases they use. Then repeat those same sentences or phrases, using pronouns to substitute for the nouns. Ask them how they know what the pronouns refer to. Stress that they need to know the noun referred to in order to understand the meaning of the pronoun.

Additional Resources

Diagnostic Test — page 4 in the test booklet

Mastery Test — pages 47–48 in the test booklet

Additional Exercises — pages 400–404 in the student text

Practice Book — pages 152–158

Duplicating Masters — pages 152–158

Special Populations — See special section at the front of this Teacher's Edition.

Using Pronouns

Part 1 Substituting Pronouns for Nouns

Read the two paragraphs below. Which paragraph sounds more natural?

> *Ned* and *Carla* wanted to earn money to buy an aquarium. *Ned* and *Carla* asked *Ned* and *Carla's* mother for a job. *Ned* and *Carla's* mother told *Ned* and *Carla* that *Ned* and *Carla* could paint the garage. *Ned* and *Carla* worked hard. *Ned* and *Carla* earned enough money for the aquarium.

> *Ned* and *Carla* wanted to earn money to buy an aquarium. *They* asked *their* mother for a job. *She* told *them* that *they* could paint the garage. *Ned* and *Carla* worked hard. *They* earned enough money for the aquarium.

Did you decide that the second paragraph sounds more natural? How did the second paragraph avoid using the names *Ned* and *Carla* too often? Try to find the places where the following words were used instead of those names: *they, their, them.* Can you find where *she* was used instead of *Ned and Carla's mother?*

The words *they, their, them,* and *she* are **pronouns.** Using pronouns in the second paragraph did not change the meaning of the paragraph, but it did improve the sound.

A pronoun is a word used in place of a noun.

You use pronouns to do three things.

1. To refer to yourself.
   I asked *my* mother to give *me* a ride.
2. To refer to the person you are talking to:
   Did *you* bring *your* camera?
3. To refer to other persons, places, or things:
   The people ran from the lion. *They* were afraid of *it.*

Like nouns, pronouns can be singular or plural. Study this chart:

The Forms of Pronouns

Singular Pronouns			
Person Speaking:	I	me	my, mine
Person Spoken To:	you	you	your, yours
Other Persons, Places, and Things:	he she it	him her it	his her, hers its
Plural Pronouns			
Persons Speaking:	we	us	our, ours
Persons Spoken To:	you	you	your, yours
Other Persons, Places, and Things:	they	them	their, theirs

Part 1

Objective

To understand the function of the pronoun, and to identify pronouns in sentences

Presenting the Lesson

1. Read and discuss pages 388 and 389. Point out that the second sample paragraph on page 388 not only sounds better, but is easier to write and say. Ask students for sentences using the pronouns listed on page 389.

2. Assign and discuss Exercises A and B on page 390.

Individualizing the Lesson

Less-Advanced Students

Before assigning the exercises, direct students' attention to the two paragraphs on page 388. Have them substitute *Ned and Carla* with *Brad*. Then go over the second paragraph together, noting the words that must change form. When finished, have students write out the second paragraph using *I* and then *Emma* instead of *Ned and Carla*.

Advanced Students

Give students several newspaper headlines. Have them choose one and write several sentences they think might follow. Have them underline all pronouns.

Optional Practice

1. Have students follow the directions for Exercise A on page 390, using these sentences.

1. He found his lost tape cassette.
2. Did Karla and he go with you?

3. She played on her guitar.
4. We saw them on television.
5. You must have cut your hair.
6. Carl and I will lend you our notes.
7. Did Cameron invite me to his party?
8. They put their books on my desk.
9. Carmine and she deposited their money in the bank.
10. I found my sweater where I left it.

2. Have students follow the directions for Exercise B on page 390 for these sentences.

1. Edna washed ~~Edna~~'s hair. (her)
2. When Adam went to school, ~~Adam~~ (he) forgot ~~Adam's~~ (his) lunch.
3. Yesterday the girls cooked sloppy joes for ~~the girls'~~ family. (their)
4. The cat washed ~~the cat's~~ (its) whiskers with ~~the cat's~~ (its) paw.
5. Brett and I are Boy Scouts. ~~Brett and I~~ (We) are in the same troop.
6. Mother knitted a sweater. ~~Mother~~ (She) used wool yarn.
7. The crowd saw the actor leave the theater. ~~The crowd~~ (They) cheered ~~the actor.~~ (him, her)
8. Henry, will ~~Henry~~ (you) give me ~~Henry's~~ (your) phone number, please?
9. The gardener covered the plants to keep ~~the plants~~ (them) warm.
10. Today the weather is hot, but yesterday ~~the weather~~ (it) was cold.

Extending the Lesson

Have students list five people they know (such as family members, friends, or neighbors), and five things in their houses or apartments. Then have them write five sentences linking the people they have named with the things they have listed.

Example: My Aunt Julie set up her new computer.

Exercises Find the pronouns.

A. Write the pronouns used in each sentence below.

Example: He gave me a new watch.
He, me

1. I wore my new boots today.
2. Katy displayed her model ships in our classroom.
3. Steve, do you read comic books?
4. Dad brought me to the roller rink.
5. The horse tugged at its reins.
6. Roger told us a secret.
7. She took the rock and skipped it across the water.
8. The waitress asked them for their order.
9. Carrie threw snowballs at him and me.
10. We rubbed our hands to keep them warm.

B. Copy the sentences below. Use pronouns instead of nouns where they will make the sentences sound better.

Example: Geno was riding Geno's bike.
Geno was riding his bike.

1. Ted ran in the 50-yard dash. ~~Ted~~ (He) was the winner.
2. Maria likes baseball, and ~~Maria~~ (she) plays every Saturday.
3. The building is closed. ~~The building~~ (It) is very old.
4. The men saw Jim walking down the road. ~~The men~~ (They) waited for ~~Jim~~ (him).
5. Betty brought ~~Betty's~~ (her) new book to school.
6. Tom and I are neighbors. ~~Tom and I~~ (We) walk to school together.
7. The boys wore ~~the boys'~~ (their) best suits for the program.
8. Sam is Lisa's brother. ~~Sam~~ (He) is two years older than ~~Lisa.~~ (she)
9. We ate the fruit. ~~The fruit~~ (It) was cold and sweet.
10. Toni, would ~~Toni~~ (you) lend me ~~Toni's~~ (your) pencil, please?

Part 2 Using Pronouns as Subjects

You remember that the subject of a sentence tells who or what does something. Find the subject in each of these sentences:

I visited my uncle. He has a motorcycle.
We drove along River Road.

Did you find that the subjects were the pronouns *I, he,* and *we?* These are three of the pronouns often used as subjects. Four others are *you, she, it,* and *they.*

Usually you will have no trouble using these pronouns as subjects. However, when the subject is compound, sometimes you may get confused.

Which of these sentences is correct?

Rita and *she* played together.
or
Rita and *her* played together.

To decide which pronoun to use in a compound subject, use this simple test. Try each pronoun separately with the verb.

She played. Her played.

You can hear that *she* is the correct pronoun. So the correct sentence is *Rita and she played together.*

Use the same test when there are two pronouns in the subject.

Example: (She, Her) and (I, me) took piano lessons.
Try: *She* took piano lessons. *Her* took piano lessons.
Try: *I* took piano lessons. *Me* took piano lessons.

Now you know the correct pronouns:

She and *I* took piano lessons.

Here are two important rules for using pronouns as the subject of a sentence.

1. Only these pronouns may be used as the subject:

Part 2

Objective

To use pronouns correctly as subjects of sentences, particularly in compound subjects

Presenting the Lesson

1. Read and discuss pages 391 and 392. Ask students for other examples of sentences using pronouns as subjects.

2. You may find it helpful to do Exercise A on page 392 with the students. Have students try each part of the subject in each example separately as the text suggests. Assign and discuss Exercise B.

Individualizing the Lesson

Less-Advanced Students

1. Point out that in compound subjects containing *I*, it is a matter of courtesy to put the other person's name first. To say "I and Jeff" or "I and Julie" puts yourself in the position of importance rather than honoring your friend.

2. Read the following sentences aloud to the students. Have them tell you what is wrong and how the sentences should be corrected.

1. Becky and ~~me~~ I look like sisters.
2. ~~I and he~~ He and I will be there on time.
3. The teacher and ~~us~~ we listened to the announcement.
4. ~~Him~~ He and I are walking home.
5. The farmer and ~~her~~ she fed the chickens.
6. Ann and ~~them~~ they ran to the window.
7. ~~Him~~ He and ~~her~~ she were the fastest runners.
8. He and ~~me~~ I plan to enter the contest together.

9. You and him should enter, too.
10. They and us have a chance to win the top prizes.

Advanced Students

Give students a brief comic strip or have them bring one to class. Tell them to write a description of what happens. When finished, they should circle all the pronouns they used as subjects.

Optional Practice

Have students insert a subject pronoun that makes sense in the blank in each sentence.

1. My brother looked for his watch. ___It___ was under the chair.
2. Those are library books. ___They___ are on the top shelf.
3. My sister sews. ___She___ made a dress for herself.
4. My mother likes to barbeque. ___She___ does a good job.
5. ___I___ asked my friend to go with me.
6. ___We___ won our baseball game yesterday.
7. Our neighbors just moved in. ___They___ asked to borrow our mower.
8. ___You___ should cover your mouth when you yawn.
9. Margie runs fast. ___She___ is on the track team.
10. ___I___ clean my room by myself every week.

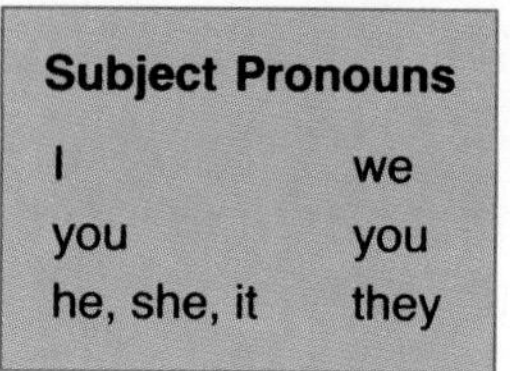

Subject Pronouns

I	we
you	you
he, she, it	they

2. If the pronoun *I* is used with one or more nouns or pronouns as the subject of a sentence, put *I* last.

Robert and I were in Boston. *He and I* saw the marathon.

Exercises Use pronouns as subjects.

A. Choose the correct words from those in parentheses.

1. Frances and (I, me) are going to a party.
2. Jane and (her, she) will be there.
3. Donald and (them, they) visit me often.
4. Philip and (he, him) went to the circus.
5. (Juan and I, I and Juan) ate the oranges.
6. You and (I, me) make a good team.
7. Ms. Coburn and (we, us) saw a movie yesterday.
8. Eva and (me, I) will finish the work.
9. (He, Him) and his mother painted his room.
10. (I and Donna, Donna and I) watched the parade.

B. Follow the directions for Exercise A.

1. Lydia and (I, me) started arguing.
2. Rusty and (them, they) don't play fairly.
3. Elena and (she, her) demonstrated a cartwheel.
4. Someday you and (me, I) will play on the varsity team.
5. (Me and Joanne, Joanne and I) apologized to Kim.
6. My parents, my teachers, and (I, me) had a meeting.
7. Uncle Jerry and (we, us) ate dinner at Ruth's house.
8. Alex and (he, him) are best friends.
9. Julie and (they, them) raced for the front seat.
10. (She, Her) and Carl caught two trout.

Part 3 Using Pronouns After Linking Verbs

Read these two sentences:

The doctor is *she.* *She* is the doctor.

These sentences mean the same thing. As you can see, the pronoun following the linking verb *is* can be used as the subject without changing the meaning of the sentence.

Pronouns used after linking verbs are called predicate pronouns. Predicate pronouns are the same as those pronouns used as subjects. Read these sentences.

The best player was he.
He was the best player.

The semifinalists were Dan and I.
Dan and I were the semifinalists.

The newest members are she and Chris.
She and Chris are the newest members.

Remember to use only these pronouns after linking verbs:

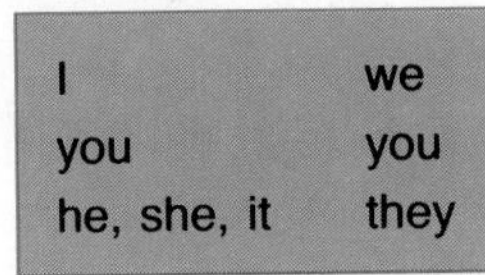

I	we
you	you
he, she, it	they

Exercises Use pronouns after linking verbs.

A. Write the correct pronoun from the two given in parentheses.

1. The new library aides are Darla and (he, him).
2. Tim's closest neighbors are Lee and (I, me).
3. The family's best golfers are (her, she) and Dad.
4. The only shoppers left were (them, they).

Part 3

Objective

To use pronouns correctly after state-of-being verbs

Presenting the Lesson

1. Read and discuss page 393. If necessary, review the term *linking verb* and the most common linking verbs, the foms of *to be.*

2. Assign and discuss Exercises A and B on pages 393 and 394.

Individualizing the Lesson

Less-Advanced Students

Remind students of the concept of linking verbs as equal signs. Then point out that the pronouns used after linking verbs are the same ones used as subjects. Illustrate this point by doing Exercise A on pages 393–394 as a group.

Advanced Students

Have students write sentences using the pronouns listed on page 393. They should first use each of the pronouns as a subject and then use each as a predicate pronoun.

Optional Practice

Have students follow the directions for Exercise A on pages 393–394, using these sentences.

1. The park rangers are Sam and (him, he).
2. The librarians will be Mrs. Blanco and (her, she).
3. The best Frisbee throwers were Noah and (them, they).
4. The cooks will be Joan and (me, I).
5. The new store owners are Mrs. Howard and (she, her).

6. The people in the boat are Ramon and (they, them).
7. The two hikers in the walk-a-thon were Karen and (her, she).
8. The best artists in the school are Abigail and (he, him).
9. The best students this semester were Booker and (they, them).
10. Your new partner is (me, I).

Extending the Lesson

Write the following sentences on the board. Have students rewrite them, putting the pronoun before the state-of-being verb.

Example: The boy is he.
He is the boy.

1. The fastest swimmers are they.
2. The best singer is she.
3. The contest winners were she and I.
4. The crossing guards are Mr. Jones and she.
5. The clerks at the grocery are Mrs. Allan and he.
6. A polite tour guide is he.
7. The best mechanics are they.
8. The last to arrive were Judy and I.
9. The chefs were Dad and he.
10. The tired player was I.

Part 4

Objective

To use pronouns correctly as objects in sentences, particularly in compound objects

Presenting the Lesson

Read and discuss pages 394 and 395. Because students have not been introduced to the terms *indi-*

5. Your biggest fans are Deena and (me, I).
6. The lifeguards are Melissa and (I, me).
7. The first people in line were (her, she) and Rose's brother.
8. The co-captains are Stewart and (I, me).
9. The cooks for the banquet are Candy and (him, he).
10. My dad's bosses are (she, her) and Mr. Jones.

B. Follow the directions for Exercise A.

1. Kim's ski instructors were (her, she) and Tim.
2. The newest teachers are Mr. Reynolds and (she, her).
3. The fastest runners are (he, him) and Tony.
4. The newspaper's editor is (her, she).
5. The crossing guards are Vanessa and (he, him).
6. One of the disc jockeys is (her, she).
7. Our biggest rivals are (they, them).
8. Judith's lab partners are Jon and (he, him).
9. My favorite comedians are (she, her) and Bill Cosby.
10. The most reliable bus drivers are Curt and (her, she).

Part 4 Using Pronouns as Objects

Which pronoun should be used in each of these sentences?

1. The cat scratched (they, them).
2. Eddie asked Rachel and (she, her) a question.
3. Divide the candy among (we, us) now.

If you are not sure which pronoun to use in a sentence, first decide whether the missing pronoun is the subject or follows a state-of-being, or linking, verb. You know that if the pronoun is the subject or follows a linking verb, you use, *I, you, he, she, it, we, you,* and *they.*

If a pronoun is not used as the subject or as a predicate pronoun, use *me, you, him, her, it, us, you,* and *them.* These pronouns are called the **object pronouns.** Notice that the pronouns *you* and *it* stay the same as subject or object pronouns.

Object Pronouns	
me	us
you	you
him, her, it	them

In Example 1, the subject is *cat.* Since the missing pronoun is not the subject, you cannot use *they.* The correct sentence is: *The cat scratched* **them.**

In Example 2, what is the subject? Is the missing pronoun the subject? Since the missing pronoun is not the subject, you cannot use *she.* The correct sentence is: *Eddie asked Rachel and* **her** *a question.*

In Example 3, *you* is the understood subject. The missing pronoun is not the subject. Which pronoun did you choose? The correct sentence is *Divide the candy among* **us** *now.*

Exercises Use pronouns as objects.

A. Write the correct pronoun from the two given in parentheses. Then read the sentence to yourself.

1. Eduardo's mother called (him, he) and his brother.
2. The baseball coach called Bill and (I, me).
3. Would you like to visit Pete and (we, us)?
4. Sue chose Brian and (she, her) for the team.
5. Mort made dinner for Hal and (she, her).
6. Louella finally found Marion and (they, them).
7. Telephone Mike and (I, me) after the game.
8. Jan saw Mary Lou and (me, I) at the store.

rect object and *object of the preposition,* and this distinction is not important at this time, the text simply distinguishes between subjects and all objects.

Individualizing the Lesson

Less-Advanced Students

Before assigning Exercise B, make sure that students will recognize when the pronoun is used as part of a compound object. Ask them to rewrite each sentence in Exercise A as two sentences, using one part of the compound object in each.

Example:
Eduardo's mother called him and his brother.
Eduardo's mother called him.
Eduardo's mother called his brother.

Advanced Students

Have students pretend that they are going hiking with three friends. Have them describe the preparations in six sentences using pronouns in compound objects. Example: "I asked Sabina and her to pack the food."

Optional Practice

Have students follow the directions for Exercise A on page 395, using these sentences:

1. The duet was played by Andre and (him, he).
2. The kites got away from Ralph and (them, they).
3. Alejandro visited Uncle Juan and (him, he).
4. Mother will drive Tracy and (him, he) to the science fair.
5. Please come skating with Leroy and (we, us).

6. When will you come to see Andrea and (I, me)?
7. Mr. Wang will make breakfast for Alice and (they, them).
8. Tony went swimming with Julio and (us, we).
9. The flowers were sent by Aunt Grace and (I, me).
10. The lost ring was found by Lee and (she, her).

Part 5

Objective

To use *we* and *us* correctly

Presenting the Lesson

1. Read and discuss pages 396 and 397. Remind students that *we* is a subject pronoun (used when a subject pronoun should be used); and *us* is an object pronoun (used when an object pronoun should be used).

2. It is suggested that you do Exercise A on page 397 with the class. Have students read each sentence, leaving out the noun used in combination with the pronoun. Then

9. Did you see Ann and (I, me) at the track meet?
10. Can you give Arlene and (she, her) your address?

B. Follow the directions for Exercise A.

1. The letter surprised Joan and (us, we).
2. Jody's father sent (he, him) a postcard from Kansas City.
3. My sister helped Ellen and (she, her) with the work.
4. Did you meet Valerie and (she, her) at the park?
5. I made hamburgers for (them, they) and me.
6. A loud crash frightened Angelo and (we, us).
7. The officer handcuffed Mills and (he, him).
8. Hit some fly balls to Emily and (me, I).
9. Mrs. Johnson settled the argument between Jason and (I, me).
10. Show Roberto and (she, her) to their seats.

Part 5 Using *We* and *Us*

Read each pair of sentences. In each pair, which sentence is correct?

1. We boys are going hiking.

   or

   Us boys are going hiking.

2. Have you ever seen us girls in a hockey game?

   or

   Have you ever seen we girls in a hockey game?

Read the sentences without the word *boys* or the word *girls*. You will see that in the first example the pronoun is part of the subject. *We* is the correct pronoun. The correct sentence is: *We* boys are going hiking.

In the second example, the pronoun is part of the object. *Us* is the correct choice. The sentence is: Have you ever seen *us* girls in a hockey game?

Whenever you have trouble choosing pronouns, try each pronoun alone in the sentence.

Exercises Use *we* and *us* correctly.

A. Write the correct pronoun for each sentence below. Check by reading each sentence to yourself.

1. (We, Us) girls went to the gym.
2. Mother sent (we, us) boys to the grocery store.
3. (We, Us) cyclists took our lunch with us.
4. In the woods (we, us) hikers saw a deer.
5. The new band costumes are for (we, us) two.
6. After lunch, (we, us) gardeners rested for a long time.
7. The coach praised (we, us) girls for our victory.
8. Terence told (we, us) Scouts about his climb.
9. The food was divided among (we, us) four.
10. Mr. Scott, this present is from (we, us) students.

B. Follow the directions for Exercise A.

1. (We, Us) girls took the bus downtown.
2. The gentle pony nuzzles (we, us) visitors.
3. (We, Us) boys had a tug-of-war.
4. Finally, Jamie spotted (we, us) wanderers.
5. (We, Us) six planned a farewell party.
6. A net fell on top of (we, us) girls.
7. The child asked (we, us) bystanders for help.
8. The girls challenged (we, us) boys.
9. Together (we, us) swimmers pulled the boat to shore.
10. An acrobat performed for (we, us) boys.

have them write the complete sentence, using the pronoun that was chosen by itself. Assign and discuss Exercise B on page 397.

Individualizing the Lesson

Less-Advanced Students

Before doing Exercise A on page 397, review the difference between a subject and an object. Then have students tell whether the correct pronoun in each sentence is a subject pronoun or an object pronoun.

Advanced Students

Ask students to write a sentence using *we* and a sentence using *us* correctly in combination with each of the following words: *shoppers*, *players*, and *runners*.

Optional Practice

Have students follow the directions for Exercise A on page 397, using these sentences.

1. Are those apples for (we, us) trick-or-treaters?
2. At the hospital (us, we) aides enjoy our work.
3. (We, Us) swimmers won the relay race.
4. At the party (we, us) guests made our own tacos.
5. (We, Us) carpenters will fix the fence.
6. The new rackets are for (us, we) tennis players.
7. In the kitchen (us, we) chefs made fruit salad.
8. Did you bring the boards for (us, we) surfers.
9. The lunch was spread out among (us, we) picnickers.
10. At the gift shop (we, us) tourists bought souvenirs.

Part 6

Objective

To identify possessive pronouns and to use them correctly

Presenting the Lesson

1. Read and discuss page 398. You may want to review the concept of possession and the mechanics of contractions.

2. Assign and discuss Exercises A and B on page 399.

Individualizing the Lesson

Less-Advanced Students

To be sure that students fully understand the concept of possession, have them write each of these expressions in a shorter way.

Example: the notebook belongs to you (your notebook)

1. the coats belonging to them (their coats)
2. the tail belonging to it (its tail)
3. the pen belonging to him (his pen)
4. the ring belonging to her (her ring)
5. the car belonging to us (our car)
6. the cat belonging to me (my cat)

Advanced Students

Tell students to pretend that they are unpacking after a trip for which everyone contributed something. Now it is time to get everything back to its rightful owner, even though it has been a long trip and there is bound to be confusion. Have students write a list of objects to be divided up. They should then write at least six sentences using as many possessive pronouns as possible.

Example: Is this lounge chair yours or ours?

Part 6 Possessive Pronouns

To make the possessive form of a noun, you add an apostrophe or an apostrophe and *s* to the noun. Pronouns have special possessive forms. These forms do not use apostrophes at all.

Here are the possessive pronouns.

Possessive Pronouns	
my, mine	our, ours
your, yours	your, yours
his, her, hers, its	their, theirs

Now read these sentences that use possessive pronouns:

This is *my* coat.
The coat is *mine.*

Is that *your* hat?
Is that *yours?*

Here is *his* dog.
The dog is *his.*

Where is *her* cat?
This cat is *hers.*

We have *our* tickets.
These tickets are *ours.*

Are those *your* books?
Are those *yours?*

Do you like *their* pets?
The pets are *theirs.*

Its and *It's*

The major problem most people have with possessive pronouns is confusing the possessive *its* with the contraction *it's.*

Its (without the apostrophe) is the possessive form of *it.*

Example: That book is missing *its* cover.
(The cover belongs to the book)

It's (with the apostrophe) means *it is* or *it has.*

Example: *It's* a library book.
(*It is* a library book.)

Exercises Use possessive pronouns and *it's.*

A. Copy these sentences. Include a possessive pronoun according to the information in the parentheses.

Example: I found ______ notebook. (The notebook belongs to him.)

I found his notebook.

1. My handwriting can be read easily. (The handwriting belongs to me.)
2. Did you see their faces? (The faces belong to them.)
3. Those keys are yours. (The keys belong to you.)
4. Next comes his turn. (The turn belongs to him.)
5. The error is hers. (The error was made by her.)
6. The reward is ours. (The reward belongs to us.)
7. This is our chance. (The chance belongs to us.)
8. That was my mistake. (The mistake was made by me.)
9. The fingerprints are his. (The fingerprints belong to him.)
10. The pictures are theirs. (The pictures belong to them.)

B. Copy the following sentences. Insert apostrophes where they are needed.

1. It's a home run!
2. It's been raining for two days.
3. The leopard chased its prey through the tall grass.
4. What is its title?
5. The puppy wagged its tail when we came home.
6. My mother makes bread, and it's delicious.
7. The railroad stopped its service to Clinton.
8. Our school has its own hockey team.
9. Grandpa has a beard. It's white and thick.
10. It's too early to buy tickets for the game.

Optional Practice

Have students divide a paper into two columns: personal pronouns and possessive pronouns. Tell them to write each pronoun from the following list in the proper column. One pronoun *(her)* should be put in both columns.

I, it, yours, him, theirs, its, she, you, our, them, hers, we, his, my, they, her, mine, us, your, he, their, me, ours

Extending the Lesson

Discuss the differences between *your* and *you're,* and *their, there,* and *they're.* Be sure that the students understand the difference in meaning and usage by having them complete the following sentences.

1. I think (your, you're) right.
2. Raise (your, you're) right hand.
3. I will be (there, their, they're) by nine o'clock.
4. Did your friends bring (their, they're, there) skates?
5. I know that (they're, their, there) here somewhere.

Bring to class some examples of correct and incorrect use of the above words from a current newspaper or magazine. Point out that such mistakes occur even in well-written articles and ads. Ask students to proofread a section, or an issue, of a newspaper or magazine to look for incorrect usage of apostrophes with possessive pronouns, or confusion of *its* and *it's, their, there* and *they're,* or *your, you're.*

Additional Exercises

These Additional Exercises may be used for additional practice of the concepts presented in this Section. Each exercise focuses on a single concept, and should be used after the page number indicated in parentheses.

Review

If you have not assigned these Additional Exercises before this time, you can also use them as an excellent Section Review.

ADDITIONAL EXERCISES

Using Pronouns

A. Recognizing Pronouns Write the pronouns in the following sentences. (Use after page 390.)

1. Have you seen my algebra book?
2. Do you want to watch the football game with us?
3. Paul watered their plants while they were away.
4. Coach Ryan gave her a special award.
5. She and I have earned our lifesaving badges.
6. Cheryl showed me her stamp collection.
7. Our skating club meets Wednesday at 3:00.
8. Your brother, Darren, found it for me.
9. His handwriting is similar to mine.
10. Chris and he share a locker.

B. Subject Pronouns Write the correct pronouns. (Use after page 392.)

1. Cora and (I, me) babysat for the triplets.
2. (Him, He) and his brother traded baseball cards.
3. (Her, She) and her sister work as cashiers.
4. The other team and (we, us) lined up for the kickoff.
5. Suzanne and (me, I) agreed on a plan.
6. You and (I, me) are on the same team.
7. Mark and (he, him) painted the garage.
8. Jill and (they, them) split the prize.
9. The horse and (she, her) walked around the ring.
10. (Clark and I, I and Clark) play in the jazz band.

C. Pronouns After Linking Verbs Write the correct pronouns. (Use after page 394.)

1. The men in uniform were (him, he) and Dad.
2. Our school's nurse is (her, she).

3. The best dancers were George and (she, her).
4. The co-pilots are Jackie Miller and (he, him).
5. The only people in the audience were (us, we).
6. The leaders are Sara and (I, me).
7. The dance contest winners are (they, them).
8. Two new students are (she, her) and Joyce.
9. The masked pirates were Dennis and (he, him).
10. Our best runner is (she, her).

D. Object Pronouns Write the correct pronouns.

(Use after page 396.)

1. Geraldo gave directions to (they, them).
2. Francie invited (we, us) to her party.
3. Cathy split a banana with (me, I).
4. Brooke showed Mark and (her, she) the ballet steps.
5. A taxi took Diane and (he, him) to the airport.
6. The bus driver gave Adele and (I, me) directions.
7. Mom brought Lill and (she, her) to the movie theater.
8. The kangaroo punched (they, them) several times.
9. Give John and (I, me) some popcorn, please.
10. Craig lent the book to Gary and (he, him).

E. Using *We* and *Us* Write the correct pronoun for each sentence. Check by reading each sentence to yourself.

(Use after page 397.)

1. (We, Us) runners must train every day.
2. Ms. Stevens gave (we, us) students a special assignment.
3. (We, Us) three built a model of Sears Tower.
4. The pilot spoke to (we, us) passengers.
5. Without the map, (we, us) hikers would have been lost.
6. The tourists asked (we, us) guides for information.
7. Together (we, us) girls can move these desks.

401

8. Next year, (we, us) band members will have new uniforms.
9. The gym was decorated by (we, us) art students.
10. The platform will not hold all of (we, us) boys.

F. Possessive Pronouns Copy the following sentences. Where there is a blank, write the correct possessive pronoun.
(Use after page 399.)

1. Bill injured __his__ ankle. (The ankle belongs to Bill.)
2. The company hires __its__ own guards. (The guards belong to the company.)
3. The sketches are __hers__. (The sketches belong to her.)
4. The car has kept __its__ shine. (The shine belongs to the car.)
5. All of the ideas were __theirs__. (The ideas belong to them.)
6. That backpack is __mine__. (The backpack belongs to me.)
7. Those are __your__ new books. (The books belong to you.)
8. This garage is __ours__. (The garage belongs to us.)
9. Marcy completed __her__ report. (The report belongs to Marcy.)
10. Alex stapled __his__ papers together. (The papers belong to Alex.)

402

MIXED REVIEW

Using Pronouns

A. Using pronouns as subjects and objects Write the correct pronoun from those given in parentheses. After each answer write S if the pronoun is used as a subject or O if the pronoun is used as an object.

S 1. (He, Him) babysits on Friday nights.
O 2. The coach gave (she, her) the trophy.
S 3. Ben and (I, me) painted the fence.
S 4. You and (she, her) are tied for first place.
O 5. Joel brought (I, me) the newspaper.
S 6. (He, Him) and I are tennis partners.
O 7. I will ride with (they, them).
S 8. (We, Us) live in the same building.
O 9. The stage manager showed (we, us) the dressing rooms.
O 10. Karla got a birthday card from Liz and (she, her).

B. Using pronouns correctly Write the correct pronoun from those given in parentheses.

1. The sound scared (they, them) and me.
2. Ms. McAllister and (they, them) chose the script.
3. The teachers were proud of (we, us) students.
4. You and (she, her) sang well together.
5. The winners are Christy and (I, me).
6. (We, Us) girls can play soccer on the south field.
7. We found (she, her) in the library.
8. Two members of the committee were Sandy and (he, him).
9. The stray dog followed Tim and (I, me) home.
10. I'll cheer for (they, them) at the game.

Mixed Review

These exercises provide review of the concepts presented in this Section. Each exercise challenges the students to apply several of the skills they have acquired during previous study. Because the "mixed" feature of these activities makes them more difficult, the teacher may wish to have less-advanced students do them orally or in small groups.

C. Using subject, object, and possessive pronouns Change the underlined nouns to pronouns in the following sentences. After each new pronoun you write, write *S* (Subject), *O* (Object), or *P* (Possessive) to show what kind it is.

S 1. Carla is my younger sister. She
S 2. Rob and Sam are finished with their project. He
S 3. Sue and Katy are happy in their new home. she
S 4. Jeff and I found it under your bed. He
O 5. Jack gave his tickets to Rick and Tom. him
P 6. It is Rita's turn to bat. her
P 7. Greg showed me Greg's coin collection. his
P 8. Paul told us about Paul's vacation. his
O 9. Did you lend John and Kelly your books? him
O 10. I bought it for Nancy. her

D. Using possessive pronouns correctly Six of the following sentences use possessive pronouns incorrectly. Rewrite those six sentences correctly. If a sentence is already correct, write *Correct.*

1. It's time for lunch.
2. The musical instruments are their's. theirs
C 3. His dog and our cat got into a fight.
C 4. It's too late to call.
5. Are these records your's? yours
C 6. The raccoon dipped its food in the water.
7. It's their anniversary today.
C 8. The store closes its doors at six o'clock.
9. The video recorder is our's. ours
10. It's a very funny movie.

404

USING GRAMMAR IN WRITING

Using Pronouns

A. Almost everyone likes going to the zoo to watch the animals. Have you ever wondered how the animals feel? Imagine that you are an animal at the zoo. You might be a monkey. Perhaps you're an elephant, or a penguin. If you could talk, what would you say about the *people* you see at the zoo? Write a paragraph about what you would say. Use a number of different pronouns in your sentences. Underline each pronoun that you use.

B. You may have heard the saying, "You can't judge a book by its cover." This means our first impressions of something or someone may be wrong. For example, once you may have met someone that you didn't like at first. Later, he or she may have become a good friend. Write about an experience like this. In some sentences use a pronoun as the subject. In other sentences, use a pronoun as a direct or an indirect object. Use at least one possessive pronoun in your paragraph.

C. Imagine that you are running for president of your class. Write a short speech explaining why the students should vote for you. Mention the changes you would make in your school. Use at least four subject pronouns in your paragraph. Underline all the pronouns you use.

D. Imagine that after reaching your destination by airplane you and two friends can't find your luggage. You walk to the baggage claim booth to ask about your luggage and the luggage of the others in your group. Write the conversation that takes place. Use a possessive pronoun in each sentence.

Using Grammar in Writing

These challenging and enjoyable activities allow the students to see how the concepts of grammar, usage, and mechanics may be applied in actual writing situations. Each exercise is designed to allow students practice in several of the skills they have acquired in this Section. The activities also provide opportunities for students to write creatively about a wide variety of interesting and unusual subjects.

Section Objectives

1. To understand the function of adjectives, and to identify those adjectives that tell *what kind, how many,* and *which ones*

2. To identify articles and to use them correctly

3. To identify predicate adjectives and to use them correctly

4. To identify proper adjectives and to use them correctly

5. To differentiate between *them* and *those,* and to use the demonstrative adjectives with the words *kind* and *kinds* correctly

6. To form the comparative and superlative forms of adjectives and to use them correctly

Preparing the Students

Discuss a textbook picture. Have students tell what they see. Write the common nouns on the board. Then ask for words that describe those things. Point out that a common noun could refer to any member of a large group. However, once that noun is described more fully, it applies to a narrower group. Those descriptive words identify what someone is talking about.

Additional Resources

Diagnostic Test — page 5 in the test booklet

Mastery Test — pages 49–50 in the test booklet

Additional Exercises — pages 422–426 in the student text

Practice Book — pages 159–168

Duplicating Masters — pages 159–168

Special Populations — See special section at the front of this Teacher's Edition.

Using Adjectives

Part 1 What Are Adjectives?

What do you see in your mind when you read this sentence?

I saw dogs.

The sentence expresses a complete idea, but it does not make the idea clear. It needs words to describe *dogs* more exactly. Here are four ways the sentence could be made clearer. What do you see when you read these sentences?

I saw huge, furry dogs. I saw vicious, wild dogs.
I saw small, playful dogs. I saw four lovable dogs.

The words *huge, furry, small, playful, vicious, wild, four,* and *lovable* tell more about *dogs.* They make the meaning of the word more exact. These words are called **adjectives.**

Adjectives are used with nouns and pronouns. They may come before the noun or pronoun they describe.

I saw *brown* and *black* dogs.

They may also come after the word they describe. Sometimes adjectives follow a linking verb and describe the subject.

The dogs were *friendly*.   They were *restless*.

Notice how differently the word *dogs* is described in these two sentences:

I saw small, playful dogs.
I saw vicious, wild dogs.

You can see that adjectives change, or *modify*, the meaning of the word they describe. For this reason, adjectives are called **modifiers.**

An adjective is a word that modifies a noun or pronoun.

Usually, when you use two or more adjectives together, you separate them with commas. Adjectives that tell *how many* do not have to follow this rule.

The *friendly, lovable* dogs belonged to *two young* children.
Several dangerous alligators lived in the *warm, murky* pond.

Exercise Find the adjectives.

In each of the following pairs of sentences, only the adjectives have been changed. For each pair of sentences, list the nouns that are modified. After each noun, write the adjectives that modify it.

Example: a. The short *man* lifted the heavy *box*.
b. The strong *man* lifted the huge *box*.
man—short, strong   *box*—heavy, huge

1. a. The small girl ran through the grassy field. girl—small, careless
   b. The careless girl ran through the muddy field.
   field—grassy, muddy

Part 1

Objective

To understand the function of adjectives, and to identify those adjectives that tell *what kind, how many,* and *which ones*

Presenting the Lesson

1. Read and discuss pages 406 and 407. At this time, the text does not discuss articles as adjectives. Articles will be introduced and discussed fully in Part 2.

2. There are various ways to identify an adjective. These ways, listed below, are based on what linguists have discovered about the structure of a word and the order of words in a sentence. It is suggested that this be used to point out additional ways in which adjectives function.

Ways To Identify Adjectives

1. Adjectives change form to show comparison. Adjectives of more than two syllables usually show comparison by using the words *more* and *most*.

bright brighter brightest
good better best
beautiful more beautiful most beautiful

2. Adjectives are often preceded by words such as *very, quite,* or *much*.

very bright
quite good
much better

3. Adjectives usually occur before nouns.

Rosa has a *beautiful* ring.
Juan has the *best* idea.

3. Assign and discuss the Exercise on pages 407 and 408.

4. Read and discuss page 408. Point out that most adjectives fall into the *what kind* category. Ask students for other adjectives with the adjective endings listed in the text. Can they think of other adjective endings and at least two examples of each ending?

5. Assign and discuss Exercises A and B on pages 408 and 409.

6. Read and discuss page 409. Point out that some adjectives that tell *how many* give specific amounts (*six, three*), while others are general (*many, few*).

7. Assign and discuss Exercises A and B on pages 409 and 410. You may wish to have students change each specific adjective to a general one and vice versa after they have completed the exercises.

8. Read and discuss page 410. Point out that these adjectives do not describe the nouns they modify, but serve to point them out. Make sure students recognize that *this* and *these* refer to objects close at hand, while *that* and *those* refer to objects at a distance.

More information about demonstratives will be presented in Part 5 of this Section.

9. Assign and discuss the Exercise on pages 410 and 411.

10. Read and discuss the summary on page 411.

11. You may wish to use Exercise A on page 411 as an oral review. Have students first identify all the adjectives that tell *what kind*, then all adjectives that tell *how many*, and last all the adjectives that tell *which ones*. Assign and discuss Exercise B.

2. a. Twenty clowns wore colorful costumes. clowns—twenty, wacky
   b. Wacky clowns wore silly costumes. costumes—colorful, silly
3. a. Many children won different prizes. children—many, lucky
   b. Lucky children won valuable prizes. prizes—different, valuable
4. a. Soft music played on an old radio. music—soft, classical
   b. Classical music played on a new radio. radio—old, new
5. a. The large vase was filled with red flowers. vase—large, silver
   b. The silver vase was filled with fresh flowers. flowers—red, fresh

Some Adjectives Tell *What Kind*

Most of the adjectives used so far in this section describe *what kind.* Here are some adjectives used so far to tell *what kind:*

huge	brown	furry	vicious	playful
small	black	murky	dangerous	lovable
wild	warm	young	friendly	restless

In the last three columns, you can see five endings often found on adjectives: *-y, -ous, -ful, -able,* and *-less.*

Exercises Use adjectives that tell *what kind.*

A. Read each sentence. Write each adjective that tells *what kind.*

1. Joyful shouts came from the stands.
2. Mr. Chalmers is a capable carpenter.
3. Jed wore his warm, red parka.
4. We sang funny songs on the long trip.
5. Marguerite threw out the old, dirty sneakers.
6. Cecilia put a large poster on the blank wall.
7. The spare room is a hopeless mess.
8. Max drew furry, monstrous creatures.
9. Long, colorful streamers hung from the ceiling.
10. A beautiful sunset lit the rosy sky.

B. Writing In this exercise, you will write your own sentences using adjectives that tell *what kind.* The following list gives ten nouns with an adjective modifying each noun. Write at least five sentences. Use two of the adjective-noun combinations in each of your sentences. You may add some adjective-noun combinations of your own in any of your sentences. Answers will vary.

fearless captain	loud music
spicy pizza	helpful doctor
dark room	silky shirt
rocky ground	poisonous air
friendly face	thoughtful friend

Some Adjectives Tell *How Many*

Some adjectives tell *how many*. Here are examples of adjectives that tell *how many:*

six animals	*many* birds	*several* people
three stores	*few* lions	*more* insects

Exercises Find adjectives that tell *how many.*

A. Read each sentence. Write the adjectives that tell *how many.*

1. Two jets power the plane.
2. Eight children raced past our house.
3. A trainer groomed four horses.
4. We waited for the bus for forty minutes.
5. Curt read several books about China.
6. Lucinda put nine daisies in one vase.
7. The question has many answers.
8. The girls made a dozen candles.
9. Jupiter has many moons.
10. Few people knew the song.

Individualizing the Lesson

Less-Advanced Students

1. To give students more practice in adjective placement, put the following sentences on the board:

1. I saw the (*adjective*) (*noun*).
2. Where are the (*adjective*) (*adjective*) (*noun*)?

Have students complete the sentences using the following nouns, adding descriptive adjectives: *cats, balloons, bikes,* and *stars.*

2. Have students write five adjectives that describe themselves.

Advanced Students

Give students the following lifeless paragraph and have them rewrite it with descriptive adjectives.

A man went into a restaurant. He sat at a table. A waitress took his order. A waiter dropped a tray on the floor. A busboy cleaned up with a mop. The man's order came. He ate his soup. Then he drank his glass of juice and ate his pie. He left a tip and went out the door.

Optional Practice

1. Have students identify every phrase containing an adjective that tells how many. Ask them to rewrite the other phrases so that each of them will contain a *how many* adjective.

1. a noisy drill
2. several cement mixers
3. the heavy truck
4. ten yellow telephones
5. some shiny tubas
6. several red vans
7. the biggest drums
8. more electric guitars
9. many famous artists
10. the narrow kayaks

2. Discuss the use of *this* and *these* to refer to something close by, and of *that* and *those* for something farther away. Have students look around the room at things they can see and first list ten things that are close to them, using *this* with five and *these* with five; then list ten things farther away, using *that* with five and *those* with five.

Extending the Lesson

1. In each of the following pairs of sentences, only the adjectives have been changed. Have students write both sentences as one sentence, using all the adjectives. They should use commas when needed.

Example: a. The red book is on the top shelf.
b. The small book is on the wooden shelf.
The small, red book is on the top, wooden shelf.

1. a. The huge dog licked the tiny kitten.
   b. The furry dog licked the gray kitten.
2. a. The colorful fireworks filled the dark sky.
   b. The bright fireworks filled the summer sky.
3. a. The sidewalk sale attracted eager customers.
   b. The yearly sale attracted many customers.
4. a. The young poet used descriptive adjectives.
   b. The famous poet used precise adjectives.
5. a. The skillful robot piloted the interplanetary spaceship.
   b. The alien robot piloted the large spaceship.

B. For each sentence below, write the adjectives that tell *how many.*

1. Both eggs hatched.
2. The program lasts thirty minutes.
3. We picked three bushels of apples.
4. Mother bought a dozen doughnuts.
5. Ken did twenty push-ups.
6. Seven cars were damaged in the accident.
7. Few people were at the movie.
8. I have six dollars in my wallet.
9. Dee had one scoop of strawberry ice cream.
10. There are thirty students and only twenty-five desks.

Some Adjectives Tell *Which Ones*

Some adjectives tell *which one* or *which ones.* Here are four adjectives in this group that are used often:

this team   *these* mitts
that field   *those* players

Adjectives that point to persons, places, and things always come before the words they point to.

Exercise **Find the adjectives that tell *which ones.***

For each sentence below, write the adjective that tells *which ones.* Then write the noun that it modifies.

1. These jackets have pockets.
2. Those colors are my favorites.
3. This house has nine rooms.
4. Will this salad serve six people?
5. This book has many pages.
6. Several sandwiches are in that bag.
7. This record player has three speeds.

410

8. That octopus in the picture has only seven arms.
9. We bought sourdough bread at that bakery.
10. Some swans swim on that pond.

You have learned that adjectives modify nouns and pronouns. You have also learned that adjectives tell three different things about the nouns and pronouns they modify. Study this chart. It will help you to recognize adjectives and to use them correctly.

An adjective tells

what kind
how many
which one

about the noun or pronoun it modifies.

Exercises Recognize adjectives.

A. Write each adjective and the noun it modifies.

1. Put these three blue boxes on that empty shelf.
2. We had several sheets of green paper.
3. Many young people crowded into one tiny room.
4. Look at that silver tray of delicious sandwiches.

B. Follow the directions for Exercise A.

1. Does that noisy dog herd this flock of sheep?
2. This tall lighthouse warns stray ships of dangerous rocks.
3. Hand me that old purple sweatshirt with long sleeves.
4. Two stocky men with dark beards rescued the weary campers.

2. To play "Adjective Riddles" each student chooses some object that can be found in the classoom and thinks of five adjectives that describe the object. For example, adjectives for a window might be *rectangular*, *glass*, *large*, *open*, and *clear*. Each student in turn tries to stump the class on the identity of the assigned object by asking *What is* _____, _____, _____, _____, *and* _____? (filling in the blanks with the list of adjectives). Whoever names the object gets the next turn. If the class cannot discover the object from five adjective clues, the first student tells the answer and chooses the student who gets the next turn.

411

Part 2

Objective

To identify articles and to use them correctly

Presenting the Lesson

1. Read and discuss page 412. Explain that the article *a* is used before the long *u* sound (*a* uniform, not *an* uniform).

2. Hearing the article-noun combination may help students to remember the rules. Do Exercise A on page 412 orally. Assign and discuss Exercise B.

Individualizing the Lesson

Less-Advanced Students

Put these pairs of words on the board and have students add either *a* or *an* in the blank.

_a_ flower	_an_ unusual flower
_an_ oyster	_a_ raw oyster
_a_ jewel	_a_ unique jewel
_a_ salesman	_an_ honest salesman

Advanced Students

Have students come up with rhyming pairs of words in which one word uses *a* and the other uses *an*. They may also use adjective-noun combinations.

Examples: a fox, an ox
an old toy, a happy boy
an ugly goat, a yellow boat

Optional Practice

Divide the class into two parts, one side representing the article *a*, the other, *an*. Make flash cards with the words and phrases listed below. Show the cards one at a time to the

Part 2 Articles

The words *a, an,* and *the* are called **articles.** Since they always modify nouns, they are also adjectives.

You may use the word *the* before singular or plural nouns beginning with any letter.

the alphabet   *the* sentences   *the* onion   *the* record

You may use the words *a* and *an* before singular nouns only. Follow these rules in choosing the correct article:

1. Use *a* before words beginning with consonant sounds:

   a person   *a* fresh egg   *a* story   *a* black olive

2. Use *an* before words beginning with vowel sounds:

   an average person   *an* egg   *an* impossible story

Some words begin with a silent *h*. In these words, you do not say the *h* sound. Instead, you begin the word with a vowel sound. Therefore, you follow the second rule, and use *an*.

an hour   *an* honor   *an* honest child

Exercises Use articles.

A. Copy these sentences. Fill in the blanks with *a* or *an.*

1. Do you keep __a__ diary?
2. Judge Rogers is __an__ honorable judge.
3. Sarah held __a__ brush and __a__ comb.
4. Gordon got __a__ haircut.
5. The train left __an__ hour ago.
6. __A__ dachshund has __a__ long body.
7. Diana tossed __a__ horseshoe.
8. __An__ old woman opened __an__ umbrella.
9. I had __a__ nightmare last night.
10. The forester carried __an__ ax and __a__ saw.

B. Writing There are eight nouns below. Write eight sentences, using one noun in each sentence. Place an article (*a, an,* or *the*) and another adjective before each noun.

Answers will vary.

1. wolf 3. movie 5. book 7. idea
2. lunch 4. team 6. sister 8. friend

Part 3 Predicate Adjectives

When an adjective follows a linking verb like *is* or *feels,* it is part of the predicate. However, it often modifies a noun or pronoun in the subject. Look at these examples:

The slopes looked *icy.* Jill is *right.*

The patient seems *upset.* They were *rude.*

When an adjective follows a linking verb and modifies the subject, it is called a **predicate adjective.**

Exercises Use predicate adjectives.

A. Writing Copy these sentences. Put a predicate adjective in each blank. Draw an arrow from the predicate adjective to the word it modifies. Answers will vary.

1. Joel seemed ______ yesterday.
2. The buzzer on my alarm clock is too ______.
3. Our gym is ______ and spacious.
4. The strings on this tennis racket are ______.
5. This album is ______.
6. This country road is very ______.
7. A swan dive looks ______.
8. The sky was ______ and gray.
9. The price of those skis is too ______.
10. The berries on that tree are ______.

class. Read a card to the class. If the word or phrase should have *a* before it, then that side of the room should stand and say *a* and the word or phrase. If it should be *an,* the *an* side of the room should respond.

airplane, old calendar, afternoon tour, addition problem, animal catcher, answer, arm, army, aunt of mine, earful, hourly chime, human being, office worker, orange peel, uncle, hourly rate, able seaman, angry bee, early bird, easy problem, empty basket, important lesson, inside curve, happy laugh, high note, open door, understanding

Part 3

Objective

To identify predicate adjectives and to use them correctly

Presenting the Lesson

1. Read and discuss page 413. Ask students to give examples of sentences using a linking verb and a predicate adjective.

2. Assign and discuss Exercises A and B on pages 413–414.

Individualizing the Lesson

Less-Advanced Students

Using the following sentences, have students underline the predicate adjective or predicate noun in each sentence, and write which it is.

PA 1. The blue stick in the drawer was dry.
PA 2. The third story in that book is terrible.
PA 3. The snowy mountains are magnificent.
PN 4. Those men in the hangar are pilots.

Advanced Students

Have students write five sentences using these words as predicate adjectives: *exciting, horrible, spooky, slippery, impossible.*

Optional Practice

Have students complete the following sentences by adding predicate adjectives. Answers will vary.

1. The spaceship is
2. Our TV antenna is
3. The snow blower is
4. The soccer players are

Part 4

Objective

To identify proper adjectives and to use them correctly

Presenting the Lesson

1. Read and discuss pages 414–415. Ask students for other examples of proper nouns and adjectives that are formed from them.

2. Do Exercise A on page 415 as a class activity. Assign and discuss Exercise B.

B. Write the predicate adjective in each sentence below.

1. Unless we hurry, we will be late.
2. That film is scary.
3. I will be nervous on stage.
4. CB radios are popular with truckers.
5. The food in the cafeteria tastes spicy.
6. The fruit on the tree looked ripe.
7. After dinner, Megan felt better.
8. Several of the records seem unbeatable.
9. The new fashions look weird.
10. The TV picture looks hazy.

Part 4 Proper Adjectives

In this section, you have already used many adjectives formed from common nouns: *furry, playful, lovable.* **Proper adjectives** are adjectives formed from proper nouns.

You know that a proper noun names a particular person, place, or thing. By adding adjective endings to some proper nouns, you change them into proper adjectives. Here are some examples:

Proper Noun	**Proper Adjective + Noun Modified**
Spain	Spanish music
China	Chinese food
Mexico	Mexican jewelry
Bible	Biblical verse

Very often a proper name is used as an adjective without the addition of an adjective ending. Here are some examples of the second kind of proper adjective:

Ford engine	Cinderella story
Hitchcock thriller	Beethoven symphony

414

A proper adjective is an adjective that has been made from a proper noun.

A proper adjective begins with a capital letter.

Exercises Use proper adjectives.

A. Write each proper adjective that you find in these sentences. Capitalize the proper adjectives.

1. Ms. Ames wears french perfume.
2. Jonathan asked for swiss cheese on rye.
3. Grandpa sent us a bushel of florida oranges and california avocados.
4. Scientists studied the martian soil.
5. We purchased a bushel of idaho potatoes to make german potato salad.
6. Paula wears italian shoes.
7. Do you enjoy mexican food?
8. Sue prefers dannon yogurt.
9. Nadia's brother has a dodge truck.
10. Two british ships docked in the harbor.

B. Follow the directions for Exercise A.

1. Carol sang an english folk song.
2. The french soldiers marched in long lines.
3. Some african countries export oil.
4. Are there guards at the canadian border?
5. Have you ever eaten german chocolate cake?
6. Some indian jewelry is made from turquoise and silver.
7. Drew is training for the olympic track team.
8. Many hollywood actors make commercials.
9. Craig's brother has a honda motorcycle.
10. The democratic candidate won the election.

Individualizing the Lesson

Less-Advanced Students

To be sure that students understand the concept of proper adjectives, have them complete the following sentences.

1. This blanket is from Mexico. It is a Mexican blanket.
2. In Africa he photographed many African animals.
3. My aunt is from Sweden. She makes great Swedish meatballs.
4. People living in Texas are called Texans.

Advanced Students

Have students write two sentences each for the words below. The first sentence should use the word as a proper noun, and the second should use it as a proper adjective.

California	Franklin
July	Dickens

Optional Practice

Have students follow the directions for Exercise A on page 415, using these sentences:

1. The north american climate was cooler than normal this year.
2. A new cambodian restaurant opened last week.
3. Many houses along the hudson river bank are quite old.
4. The latest paris fashions went on sale downtown last week.
5. We saw egyptian mummies at the museum.
6. Did you study for the test on greek city-states?
7. Dad put a pennsylvania dutch sign on the barn.
8. Is that dog an irish setter?

Part 5

Objective

To differentiate between *them* and *those*, and to use the demonstrative adjectives with the words *kind* and *kinds* correctly

Presenting the Lesson

1. Read and discuss page 416. Remind students that *them* is a plural pronoun and takes the place of plural nouns used as objects only. It is never used as an adjective.

2. Ask students for sample sentences using *those, them, this kind, that kind, these kinds,* and *those kinds*.

3. It is suggested that you do Exercise A on page 417 as a class activity. Assign and discuss Exercise B.

Individualizing the Lesson

Less-Advanced Students

Point out that when it means "sort" or "type," the word *kind* should be treated like other nouns. Do not use a singular adjective to describe a plural noun and vice versa. Put the following chart on the board:

Singular		Plural	
Adjective	Noun	Adjective	Noun
this	kind	these	kinds
that	thing	those	things

Tell students to close their eyes and picture this scene in a shoe store.

Salesman #1: This kind of shoe is better than those kinds of shoes.

Salesman #2: No. These kinds of shoes are better than that kind of shoe.

Part 5 Using Adjectives Correctly

Four adjectives that tell *which one* or *which ones* are *this, that, these,* and *those.* When they modify nouns and pronouns, they point out specific things.

This book is more interesting than *that* one.
These pencils are sharper than *those* pencils.

Using *Them* and *Those*

Look at these sentences carefully.

I saw *those* men on the airplane.
Jeanie saw *them,* too.

The word *those* is an adjective. It tells *which* men. The word *them* is not an adjective. It is never used to point to a noun. *Them* is a pronoun. It is used *in place of a noun.*

We found *those books* in the pack.
Someone left *them* there.

Using *This Kind* and *That Kind*

The word *kind* sometimes causes problems. It means just *one kind.* If you want to speak of more than one kind, say *kinds.*

When you use an adjective to point to *kind,* use *this* or *that.* Never say "those kind" or "them kind."

When you use an adjective to point to *kinds,* use *these* or *those.*

Study the sentences below to see how these words are used.

I like *this kind* of bicycle.
I wore *that kind* of hat last year.
Those kinds of tapes are the best.
I like *those kinds* of books.

Exercises Choose the right word.

A. Write the correct word for each sentence. Check your choice by reading the sentence to yourself.

1. We like (them, those) plaid shirts best.
2. Do you have any of (those, them) magazines?
3. (This, Them, These) kind of tire is safest.
4. (Them, These) kinds of problems are very hard.
5. I use (that, those, them) kind of pen at school.
6. We read (those, them) books last summer.
7. (This, Them, These) kind of story appeals to me.
8. Will you take (those, them) packages to the office?
9. Where can I see (them, those) kinds of monkeys?
10. (Them, Those) clothes must be washed.

B. Follow the directions for Exercise A.

1. (Those, Them) firecrackers exploded.
2. (That, Those) kind of apple is tart.
3. Do (them, those) gloves keep you warm?
4. Audrey always makes (this, these) kind of tennis shot.
5. I am allergic to (that, them, those) kind of fruit.
6. (Those, Them) reins control the horse.
7. Queen Elizabeth wore (them, those) jewels.
8. Terry likes (this, these) kinds of projects.
9. Many farmers in the U.S. grow (them, those) grains.
10. Marietta builds (that, those) kind of model airplane.

Part 6 Making Comparisons with Adjectives

You often use adjectives to compare people, places, and things. The adjectives used to describe must be changed slightly when they are used to compare.

Advanced Students

Have students write sentences using each of the following words correctly: *this kind, that kind, these kinds, those kinds, them, those.*

Optional Practice

Have students follow the directions for Exercise A, on page 417, using these sentences:

1. Try (them, these) granola bars.
2. (This, Them, These) TV program is most exciting!
3. (That, Those, Them) kind of program is not as good.
4. Some of (them, those) video games are really fun!
5. (This, These) kinds of jets are supersonic.

Extending the Lesson

Have students identify those sentences in which the italicized word or phrase can be replaced by *them.* They should revise the sentences they identify, using the word *them* instead of the phrase.

1. I enjoy ~~*those kinds of movies*~~ them.
2. We bought them ~~*those new tennis balls*~~ there.
3. *These* puzzles confuse me.
4. The young kitten clawed ~~*the new drapes*~~ them.

Part 6

Objective

To form the comparative and superlative forms of adjectives, and to use them correctly

Presenting the Lesson

1. Read and discuss pages 417 to 420. If students are familiar enough with the concept of syllables, you may find it helpful to define a long adjective as one with more than two syllables. Ask for more examples for each rule. Spelling changes will be discussed more thoroughly in Handbook Section 17.

2. You may wish to refer back to the chart for identifying adjectives on page 407.

3. You may wish to do Exercise B on page 420 with the class. Assign and discuss Exercise A on page 420 and Exercise C on page 421.

Individualizing the Lesson

Less-Advanced Students

Before doing the exercises give these words to students and have them decide whether to use *-er*, *-est*, or *more, most:*

-er, -est gentle	more, most expensive
more, most cheerful	-er, -est bright
-er, -est old	more, most unusual
-er, -est blue	-ier, -iest funny
more, most colorful	more, most delicious
-er, -est tame	-er, -iest tiny

Advanced Students

Point out to students that in addition to *good* and *bad* there are some other adjectives that are irregular. Have students form the comparative and superlative of the following words, checking their work in the dictionary: *little, many, ill.* Then have them use each form in a sentence.

Optional Practice

1. Have students follow the directions for Exercise A on page 420, using these words:

For example, you could describe two students with these sentences:

Marilyn is *tall.*
Frank is *tall.*

What if you want to compare the two, and to say that they are not the same size? You would use one of these sentences:

Marilyn is *taller* than Frank.
Frank is *taller* than Marilyn.

Now, suppose you want to compare a third student with Frank and Marilyn. Charles is taller than Frank, and taller than Marilyn. What would you say?

You probably gave this sentence:

Charles is the *tallest.*

Here are the rules for using short adjectives in comparisons:

1. When you compare two people, places, or things, you usually add *-er* to the adjective.

tall + er = taller	happy + er = happier
large + er = larger	funny + er = funnier

If the adjective ends in *e*, drop the *e* before adding *-er.* If the adjective ends in *y* following a consonant, change the *y* to *i* before adding *-er.*

2. When you compare more than two people, places, or things, you usually add *-est* to the adjective.

tall + est = tallest	happy + est = happiest
large + est = largest	funny + est = funniest

If the adjective ends in *e*, drop the *e* before adding *-est.* If the adjective ends in *y* following a consonant, change the *y* to *i* before adding *-est.*

Using *More* and *Most* in Comparisons

You do not always add *-er* or *-est* to make comparisons. If the adjective is a long one, use *more* and *most* instead of adding *-er* and *-est.*

> Ted has been *more careful* since the accident.
> Barbara was the *most careful* of the three girls.
>
> My puzzle is *more difficult* than yours.
> This is the *most difficult* dive of all.

Here are the rules for using long adjectives in comparisons:

1. Use *more* when comparing two persons, places, or things.

more difficult　　more terrible　　more dangerous

2. Use *most* when comparing more than two persons, places, or things.

most difficult　　most terrible　　most dangerous

Use only one form of comparison at a time. If you use *-er* or *-est,* do not use *more* or *most* in the same comparison. You would not say, "my brother is *more bigger* than I am." Instead, you would say, "My brother is *bigger* than I am." You would not say, "Our dog is the *most smartest* dog on the block." You would say, "Our dog is the *smartest* dog on the block."

The Forms of *Good* and *Bad*

A few adjectives change to become completely new words when they are used in comparisons. Here are two important adjectives of this kind:

good	better	best
bad	worse	worst

1. smart (-er, -est)
2. strong (-er, -est)
3. wise (-er, -est)
4. delicious (more, most)
5. white (-er, -est)
6. sharp (-er, -est)
7. favorite (more, most)
8. fierce (more, most)
9. narrow (-er, -est)
10. safe (-er, -est)
11. large (-er, -est)
12. horrible (more, most)
13. sunny (-ier, -iest)
14. poisonous (more, most)
15. independent (more, most)
16. playful (more, most)

2. Have students follow the directions for Exercise B on pages 420 and 421, using these sentences:

1. The front door is (wider, more wider) than the back door.
2. Which of the two projects took (more, most) work?
3. Is the park slide or the school slide the (longer, longest)?
4. Your monster picture is (more scary, scarier) than mine.
5. Juan ate the (riper, ripest) peach of all.
6. The accident was the (most terrible, terriblest) one at that intersection.
7. My mother fixes my (favoritest, favorite) food on my birthday.
8. I was much (more comfortable, comfortabler) when I got over the flu.
9. The blue whale is the (most large, largest) mammal.
10. It's much (warmer, more warmer) inside.
11. This is the (most hot, hottest) weather we've had.
12. Yesterday I had the (worst, baddest) cold!
13. Which is the (taller, tallest) building of all?
14. This is the (brighter, brightest) of the two light bulbs.
15. My brother is always the (hungriest, most hungriest) person at the table.

Extending the Lesson

Have students choose one or more of the sets of animals below and write six sentences comparing them, using *-er* or *more* with adjective forms. Have them head their papers with the names of the animals they have chosen, then write the first three sentences comparing the first animal with the second, and the next three sentences comparing the second animal with the first.

Answers will vary.

Example: a brown bear and a wolverine

a. A brown bear is bigger than a wolverine.

b. A wolverine has a longer tail than a brown bear.

1. a kangaroo and a camel
2. a giraffe and a moose
3. a skunk and a porcupine
4. an elephant and a polar bear
5. an eagle and a rabbit
6. a frog and a snake

Read these examples:

My father is a *good* bowler.
Doug is a *better* pitcher than Dan.
Is Patty the *best* swimmer in the class?

The weather is *bad* today.
Will tomorrow's storm be *worse* than this?
The blizzard in Chicago was the *worst* storm this year.

Exercises **Make comparisons with adjectives.**

A. Some of the following adjectives add *-er* and *-est* when they are used in comparisons. Others are used with *more* and *most.* Copy each adjective. Then write the two forms it uses in comparisons.

Examples: slow
slow, slower, slowest
colorful
colorful, more colorful, most colorful

1. helpful (more helpful, most helpful)
2. dark (darker, darkest)
3. dangerous (more dangerous, most dangerous)
4. pretty (prettier, prettiest)
5. hard (harder, hardest)
6. intelligent (more intelligent, most intelligent)
7. wonderful (more wonderful, most wonderful)
8. silly (sillier, silliest)
9. curious (more curious, most curious)
10. great (greater, greatest)

B. Write the correct adjective form for each sentence below. Check your choice by reading each sentence to yourself.

1. The cheetah is the (most fastest, fastest) animal of all.
2. A whale is (larger, more large) than an elephant.
3. Laura is the (most happy, happiest) baby I've seen.
4. This map is (more useful, usefuller) than the globe.
5. Pat is (carefuller, more careful) than Tom.
6. Darren is the (fastest, most fast) runner of all.

7. The lake is (more clean, cleaner) than it was last year.
8. Your house is (more large, larger) than ours.
9. The last math problem was also the (most hard, hardest).
10. This is the (most delicious, deliciousest) salmon I have ever eaten.

C. Follow the directions for Exercise B.

1. Which of the two pails is (larger, largest)?
2. I picked the (smaller, smallest) of the three packages.
3. This piece of cloth is the (biggest, bigger) of the two.
4. In our dance class, who is the (more graceful, most graceful)?
5. Was Harry's the (worse, worst) injury of the race?
6. I read the (longer, longest) of the three books.
7. Of the thirty flavors, which is (better, best)?
8. The (bigger, biggest) of the two packages was mine.
9. Which of the two ponies is (gentler, gentlest)?
10. In Jane's family, her mother is the (better, best) athlete.

421

Additional Exercises

These Additional Exercises may be used for additional practice of the concepts presented in this Section. Each exercise focuses on a single concept, and should be used after the page number indicated in parentheses.

Review

If you have not assigned these Additional Exercises before this time, you can also use them as an excellent Section Review.

ADDITIONAL EXERCISES

Using Adjectives

A. Recognizing Adjectives Write the adjectives in the following sentences. Beside each adjective, write the noun it modifies. Put the noun in parentheses. Ignore *a, an,* and *the.*

(Use after page 411.)

Example: The young skater won two medals.
young (skater), two (medals)

1. The teacher spoke in a quiet voice.
2. Jessica paints with vivid colors.
3. Those four magazines are for young people.
4. A large, muddy dog bounded into the full classroom.
5. David made a special sauce for the raw vegetables.
6. The new committee had several foolish plans.
7. That dentist uses modern equipment.
8. Many tall buildings line those elegant streets.
9. That boy has curly blond hair.
10. Jean wore one bracelet and four rings.

B. Articles Number your paper from 1 to 10. Write the correct article for each sentence. (Use after page 412.)

1. The committee made (a, an) announcement about the art contest.
2. Susan found (a, an) unusual old coin.
3. Has anyone ever seen (a, an) live dinosaur?
4. (A, An) elevator is sometimes called a lift.
5. I'll be back in about (a, an) hour.
6. Our cat discovered (a, an) mouse in the basement.
7. The squirrel buried (a, an) acorn near its nest.
8. (A, An) taxi will cost too much.

9. The bride carried (a, an) bouquet of white flowers.
10. Beth has grown (a, an) inch this year.

C. Predicate Adjectives Write the predicate adjective in each sentence. (Use after page 414.)

1. That style of jacket is popular.
2. Our victory over the Wildcats was lucky.
3. The crowd in the street seems orderly.
4. The winners were grateful.
5. Everyone in class looked happy.
6. Is the sidewalk slippery?
7. These turnips taste bitter.
8. That book was enjoyable.
9. These shoes are tight.
10. The battery in the car is new.

D. Proper Adjectives Write the proper adjectives in the following sentences. Capitalize them correctly. (Use after page 415.)

1. The bread was made with california raisins.
2. Danny's favorite candy is english toffee.
3. The orchestra played music by german composers.
4. Todd prefers american cheese to swiss cheese.
5. A russian ballet company performed at the auditorium.
6. The museum has a display of american folk art.
7. Her songs have a nashville sound.
8. Please pass the french bread.
9. Honey and nuts covered the greek pastries.
10. The plane crashed in the brazilian jungle.

E. Using Adjectives Correctly Write the correct word from those given for each of the following sentences. (Use after page 417.)

1. Read (them, those) reports immediately.
2. (This, Them, These) kind of cloth is waterproof.

423

3. (Those, Them) kinds of flowers are hardy.
4. Look at (them, those) ducks on the pond.
5. Matt usually wears (this, these, them) kind of jacket.
6. Kelly saw (those, them) shoes on sale.
7. Aunt Julia likes (that, them, those) kind of soup.
8. Do you like (these, them) kinds of flowers?
9. (This, Them, Those) kind of knife is for cleaning fish.
10. Who has (those, them) newspaper articles?

F. Adjectives in Comparisons Write the correct form of the adjective from the two given. (Use after page 421.)

1. Of the four questions, this one is (harder, hardest).
2. The sun seems (hotter, more hot) today than yesterday.
3. That measurement is (accuratest, most accurate).
4. This licorice is the (chewier, chewiest) I've ever had.
5. Is Sally (younger, youngest) than Ray?
6. Which of the two photographs is (older, oldest)?
7. The loss was their (worse, worst) defeat in three years.
8. Ron is the (better, best) speaker in our class.
9. That ladder is (sturdier, more sturdy) than this one.
10. That clown has the (saddest, most saddest) face of all!

424

MIXED REVIEW

Using Adjectives

A. Using articles and predicate adjectives Copy these sentences. Choose the correct word from the two given in parentheses. Write an adjective where the blank space is.

Adjectives will vary.

1. (A, An) owl is ______.
2. (A, An) rainy day feels ______.
3. (A, An) costume can be ______.
4. (A, An) old friend is ______.
5. (A, An) taco tastes ______.
6. (A, An) igloo must be ______.
7. (A, An) haunted house seems ______.
8. (A, An) ocean breeze feels ______.
9. (A, An) game of basketball is ______.
10. (A, An) spy story is ______.

B. Using adjectives that tell *how many, which ones* and *what kind* Make four columns on your paper. Label them *How Many, Which Ones, What Kind,* and *Noun Modified.* Write the adjectives from the following sentences in the correct columns. Write the noun that each adjective modifies on the same line as that adjective.

1. Several good players were injured in that game.
2. Dad will hang yellow and white wallpaper in the large bedroom.
3. This old sled has rusty runners.
4. Many customers complained about the slow service.
5. Jill used five quarts of blue paint.
6. He ordered two large glasses of orange juice.
7. I haven't seen that movie for several years.
8. Those girls weren't frightened by the big green bug.

Mixed Review

These exercises provide review of the concepts presented in this Section. Each exercise challenges the students to apply several of the skills they have acquired during previous study. Because the "mixed" feature of these activities makes them more difficult, the teacher may wish to have less-advanced students do them orally or in small groups.

9. The new mayor won by a few thousand votes.
10. Did you make these colorful pillows?

C. Using adjectives correctly For each sentence, write the correct adjective from the two given in parentheses. After each adjective, write the noun it modifies.

1. Darren's handwriting is the (better, best) in the class.
2. I like (them, those) grey mittens.
3. (This, These) kinds of flowers grow wild here.
4. A shark is (more dangerous, dangerouser) than a barracuda.
5. (This, These) box is heavier than (that, those) box.
6. What is the (most useful, usefulest) tool for this job?
7. These are the (worse, worst) strawberries I have ever eaten.
8. Jenny bought (those, this) kind of sweater.
9. George's score was (worse, badder) than mine.
10. Who is the (faster, fastest) player on the team?

426

USING GRAMMAR IN WRITING

Using Adjectives

A. You have just heard about a contest, called "I Scream for Ice Cream!" The sponsor, a dairy, is looking for a new flavor that everyone will "scream" for. Write a description of your new ice cream flavor. Tell why it's better than other flavors. Use as many vivid adjectives as you can. Use at least two adjectives in the comparative form. Underline all the adjectives. Circle any articles you use.

B. Imagine that you have been given permission to design and decorate a room of your own at home. What colors would the room be? What kind of furniture would it have? Would it contain any special equipment? Be creative. Write a paragraph to describe your wonderful new room. Include at least two predicate adjectives. Underline all the adjectives in your description. Draw an arrow from each adjective to the noun it modifies.

C. Your next door neighbor is a science fiction writer. Yesterday she told you that she is fresh out of ideas. She asked you to help her. She wants you to write about an imaginary planet for her next book. You will have to describe any forms of life on the planet. Include adjectives that tell *what kind, how many,* and *which ones.* Underline all the adjectives you use.

D. Make a proper adjective from each of the following proper nouns. Look in a dictionary if you need help with the spelling. Then use each proper adjective in a sentence: *Italy, Texas, Germany, Midwest, Japan.*

Using Grammar in Writing

These challenging and enjoyable activities allow the students to see how the concepts of grammar, usage, and mechanics may be applied in actual writing situations. Each exercise is designed to allow students practice in several of the skills they have acquired in this Section. The activities also provide opportunities for students to write creatively about a wide variety of interesting and unusual subjects.

Section Objectives

1. To understand the function of adverbs and to identify them in sentences

2. To form the comparative forms of adverbs and to use them correctly

3. To differentiate between adverbs and adjectives and to make the correct choice in sentences

Preparing the Students

Using a picture that shows people in action, ask the students for words that tell about the action. Write the verbs and related adverbs on the board. Point out that in these phrases, verbs are described. Tell students that this section will inform them about the group of words used to describe words other than nouns.

Additional Resources

Diagnostic Test — page 6 in the test booklet

Mastery Test — pages 50–51 in the test booklet

Additional Exercises — pages 437–440 in the student text

Practice Book — pages 169–173

Duplicating Masters — pages 169–173

Special Populations — See special section at the front of this Teacher's Edition.

Using Adverbs

Part 1 What Are Adverbs?

In **Section 8,** you learned that adjectives are modifiers that tell *what kind, how many,* or *which ones* about nouns and pronouns.

There is another kind of modifier called an **adverb.** Study the examples below.

The students worked **quietly.**
The pigeons flew **away.**
My train leaves **soon.**
The clerk was **very** helpful.

Adverbs tell *how, where, when,* or *to what extent.* Adverbs can modify verbs, adjectives, or other adverbs.

Adverbs Modify Verbs

The baby crawled.

How? The baby crawled *quickly.*

Where? The baby crawled *everywhere.*

When? The baby *sometimes* crawled.

Adverbs Modify Adjectives

That box is heavy.

How heavy? That box is *terribly* heavy.

This is an interesting book.

How interesting? This is an *extremely* interesting book.

Adverbs Modify Other Adverbs

Dale eats hamburgers often.

How often? Dale eats hamburgers *very* often.

He never eats pizza.

To what extent? He *almost* never eats pizza.

An adverb modifies a verb, an adjective, or another adverb.

It tells *how, where, when,* or *to what extent.*

Many adverbs are formed by adding *-ly* to an adjective, as in these examples:

quick—quickly	happy—happily	powerful—powerfully
slow—slowly	sad—sadly	careless—carelessly

Here are some other examples of words often used as adverbs:

How? well, hard, fast, much
Where? here, there, everywhere
When? now, never, always, often
To what extent? very, too, quite, almost

Part 1

Objective

To understand the function of adverbs and to identify them in sentences

Presenting the Lesson

1. In addition to what is presented in the text, there are other ways to identify an adverb, based on the structure and order of words in a sentence. Below is a list of these ways. The information in this list can be used to point out ways adverbs function.

Ways To Identify Adverbs

1. Adverbs are often difficult to separate from adjectives. One of the best ways to identify adverbs is by their positions in sentences. They are most often found at the end of a sentence.

   She walked *slowly*.
   He worked *quickly*.

2. Adverbs can also be found in other places in a sentence.

   At the Beginning
   Now the race begins.
   Between Subject and Verb
   The vegetables *here* are fresh.
   Within Verb Phrases
   I can *always* eat dessert.
   Before an Adjective
   The box is *extremely* heavy.

3. Look for words that fit the blank in this test sentence:

   He did it ______.

4. Look for words ending in *-ly:*

   bad + ly = badly
   quick + ly = quickly

2. Read and discuss pages 428 to 430. Ask for other adverbs belonging to each of the four groups. Have the students change the sample sentences by substituting their adverbs for those given.

3. Assign and discuss Exercises A and B on pages 430–431. In Exercise A, every adverb modifies a verb. In Exercise B, adverbs modify verbs, adjectives, and other adverbs. When checking Exercise B, you might find it helpful to have the students identify each word modified by adverbs and identify which of the three types it is.

Individualizing the Lesson

Less-Advanced Students

Explain that while adjectives usually come before the noun, adverbs can move around. Have the students find the adverb in the following sentences.

The sun rose quickly.
The sun quickly rose.
Quickly rose the sun.
I am now tired.
Now I am tired.
I am tired now.

Advanced Students

Have the students write five examples of instructions or directions using adverbs. Answers will vary.

Examples: Drive slowly around this corner.
Open the box cautiously.

Optional Practice

Have students divide their papers into four columns: *how, when, where, to what extent.* Ask students to list each of the following adverbs in the correct columns:

If you are not sure whether a word is an adverb, ask yourself two questions. Does the word modify a verb, an adjective, or another adverb? Does it tell *how, where, when,* or *to what extent?* If you can answer *yes* to these questions, the word is an adverb.

Study this chart to help you recognize adverbs and to use them correctly.

An adverb tells

how
when
where
to what extent

about a verb, an adjective, or another adverb.

Exercises Use adverbs.

A. In these sentences the words in *italics* are adverbs. Find the verb that each adverb modifies.

1. Trigger whined *sadly,* but Luke left him behind.
2. Luke started *slowly* up the mountain.
3. He *carefully* watched where to put his feet.
4. One of the rocks slipped *suddenly.*
5. Luke scrambled *wildly* for a footing.
6. Then blackness surrounded him *completely.*
7. When he awoke, his head throbbed *painfully.*
8. He moved *slowly* in the darkness.
9. A cold nose touched his cheek *lightly.* It was Trigger!
10. Trigger barked *happily.*

B. Write every adverb used in each sentence.

1. The bikers were hopelessly lost.
2. The hunters never found the deer.
3. This watch is always wrong.
4. The new hobby store opens tomorrow.

5. The driver instantly stopped the car.
6. Debbie tugged quite hard on the rope.
7. Leroy outgrew his clothes very quickly.
8. My canteen is almost empty.
9. The bus nearly hit the sign.
10. Merle peered timidly around the corner.

Part 2 Making Comparisons with Adverbs

Adverbs, like adjectives, can be used in comparisons.

John Henry worked *harder* than the steam engine.
He worked the *hardest* of all the drillers.

There are three ways adverbs change to show comparisons.

1. Some short adverbs add *-er* when two persons or things are being compared. They add *-est* when more than two are compared.

hard	harder	hardest	early	earlier	earliest
fast	faster	fastest	soon	sooner	soonest

2. Most adverbs that end in *-ly* use the word *more* in comparing two persons or things. They use *most* in comparing more than two.

carelessly	more carelessly	most carelessly
quickly	more quickly	most quickly

3. Some adverbs change their forms completely when they are used in comparisons.

well	better	best
badly	worse	worst
much	more	most
little	less	least

up, suddenly, too, outside, never, hard, loudly, much, easily, cheerfully, painlessly, very, there, silently, often, quiet, down, inside, continuously, well, sometimes, outdoors, here, early, actively, yearly, late, tightly, always, weekly, briefly, now, almost, peacefully, seldom, correctly, fast

Extending the Lesson

Have students imagine a supermachine they would like to invent, give it a name, and write at least five sentences, each telling something different that it does. Students should use an adverb in each sentence to describe the action.

Part 2

Objective

To form the comparative forms of adverbs and to use them correctly

Presenting the Lesson

1. Read and discuss page 431. Point out that the rules for making the comparative form of adverbs are the same as for adjectives. Ask for sentences using all three forms of the sample adverbs correctly.

2. Assign and discuss Exercise A on page 432. You may wish to do Exercise B with the class to be sure that the students understand the forms. Assign Exercise C.

Individualizing the Lesson

Less-Advanced Students

To help the student see the relationship between the different forms, read aloud the following sentences and have the class form the comparative and superlative for each adverb they hear.

1. My paper airplane flies fast. faster, fastest
2. Our side cheered loudly. louder, loudest
3. She dances well. better, best
4. This bulb shines brightly. brighter, brightest
5. Your frog jumped high. higher, highest

Advanced Students

Put three pictures of action scenes in a place where they can be easily viewed by the students. Have the students write six sentences comparing the pictures, using at least one comparative adverb in each. Be sure to label the pictures 1, 2, and 3.

Optional Practice

1. Have the students follow the directions for Exercise A page 432, using these words.

1. sharply sharper, sharpest	7. dimly dimmer, dimmest
2. soon sooner, soonest	8. wisely wisest, wiser
3. loosely looser, loosest	9. gently gentler, gentlest
4. much more, most	10. deep deeper, deepest
5. exactly more, most exactly	11. proudly prouder, proudest
6. angrily more, most angrily	12. sadly sadder, saddest

2. Make copies of the sentences below or put them on the board. Have students copy the sentences, putting a comparative adverb in the blank. Next to the sentence, they should write the verb it describes. Answers will vary.

Example: The cat meowed louder at night. meowed

1. The huge elephant trumpeted louder than the baby elephant.
2. The chattering monkeys swung higher on the ropes than before.
3. The old hippopotamus wallowed longer in the mud than the young one.

Exercises Make comparisons with adverbs.

A. Copy each adverb below. Then write the two forms it uses in comparisons. Use the guidelines on page 431 to help you.

1. rapidly more rapidly, most rapidly	5. fast faster, fastest	9. loudly more loudly, most loudly
2. little less, least	6. carefully more carefully, most carefully	10. well better, best
3. happily more happily, most happily	7. brightly more brightly, most brightly	
4. naturally more naturally, most naturally	8. badly worse, worst	

B. For each sentence below, write the correct adverb form from the two given in parentheses.

1. Please wake me (earlier, more early) tomorrow.
2. Louise pushed (hardest, harder) than Dan.
3. The squirrel came (more near, nearer) to Jan than to Rob.
4. The new toaster works (more well, better) than the old one.
5. Of the two girls, Anna jumped (higher, highest).
6. Colin runs (faster, more fast) than I can.
7. Jess swam (better, best) today than yesterday.
8. The team played (best, bestest) in the finals.
9. Of the three cereals, I like Wheaties (least, littlest).
10. The large fish ate (most greedily, more greedily) of all.

C. Follow the directions for Exercise B.

1. Anna writes (neatlier, more neatly) than I do.
2. This sailboat finished the race (sooner, soonest) than that one.
3. Sequoias grow (taller, more tall) than other trees.
4. The swift flies (fastest, most fast) of all birds.
5. The fog spread (lower, more low) over the city.
6. This train rides (more smoothly, smoother) than any other.

7. Which of the two movies ends (most happily, more happily)?
8. Of the two girls, Donna was dressed (more warmly, most warmly).
9. Trish draws (better, best) of all the artists.
10. Train travel costs (less, least) than air travel.

Part 3 Adjective or Adverb?

Adjectives tell about nouns and pronouns. Adverbs tell about verbs, adjectives, and other adverbs. Sometimes it is hard to tell which modifier to use. This confusion happens because many adverbs and adjectives look alike.

Many adverbs are made by adding *-ly* to an adjective. See how this works:

Adjective: The *loud* music bothered me.
Adverb: We sang *loudly*.

Adjective: Traffic was *slow* tonight.
Adverb: Traffic moved *slowly* tonight.

Now look at this sentence:

My brother Jim drives (*careful, carefully*).

Would you use *careful* or *carefully* in the sentence?

To find the answer, ask what you are trying to say. Are you trying to say:

how many Jim drives?
which one Jim drives?
what kind Jim drives?

Or are you trying to say:

how Jim drives?

You are trying to say *how*. The kind of word that tells how something happened or how something was done is an adverb.

4. The sleek jaguar ran faster than its prey.
5. The thin greyhound ran fastest of all the dogs.

Extending the Lesson

Ask the students to think about three people they know and make a list of actions these people have in common such as *talk, run, sit, watch*. They should then write several sentences comparing the way these people perform their actions.

Part 3

Objective

To differentiate between adverbs and adjectives and to make the correct choice in sentences

Presenting the Lesson

1. Read and discuss pages 433–434.

2. It is suggested that you do Exercise A on pages 434–435 with the class. Assign and discuss Exercise B on page 435.

3. Read and discuss pages 435–436. Ask students for other sentences using *good* and *bad*, and *well* and *badly*.

4. You might find it helpful to do Exercise A on page 436 with the class. Assign Exercise B.

Individualizing the Lesson

Less-Advanced Students

1. The adverb most frequently misused in conversation is *real* instead of *really*. Give students practice in saying and hearing the correct word in each of the following sentences.

1. That halfback runs really fast.
2. Really loud music can damage the eardrum.
3. You are going to be really late.
4. This is a really tasty sandwich.
5. My brother was a really big baby.

2. Students should underline the correct use of good/well and bad/badly in each sentence.

1. Tina tap-danced (good/well) tonight.
2. Jeff needs a haircut (bad/badly).
3. The whole class did (good/well) on the exam.
4. It was a (good/well) day to sleep late.
5. Fredrick acted (bad/badly) at the party, but his brother behaved (good/well).
6. My sister took the news (bad/badly).

Advanced Students

Point out to the students that some words can be both adjectives or adverbs, depending on what words they are modifying. *More* is an adjective when modifying a noun such as *more candles*. It is an adverb when modifying an adjective such as *more careful*, or an adverb such as *more quickly*. Have the students write two sentences for each of the following words using the word as an adjective in the first sentence and as an adverb in the second:

little, best, much

Optional Practice

1. Have the students follow the directions for Exercise A on page 434, using the following sentences.

This adverb modifies the verb *drives*. You would use the adverb *carefully* in this sentence.

My brother Jim drives *carefully*.

When you are choosing the correct modifier, ask yourself:

1. Which word does the modifier tell about?
2. What does the modifier tell?

This chart will help you to answer these questions.

An adverb tells	An adjective tells
how when where to what extent	what kind how many which one
about a verb, an adjective, or another adverb.	**about a noun or pronoun.**

Exercises **Choose the right modifier.**

A. Copy each sentence below. Choose the correct modifier from the two given in parentheses. Draw an arrow from the modifier to the word it modifies. Then write *Adjective* or *Adverb* to show how the modifier is used.

Examples: The batter hit the ball (solid, solidly).
The batter hit the ball *solidly*. Adverb
Carol was (hopeful, hopefully) about the test.
Carol was *hopeful* about the test. Adjective

Adv. 1. I see (perfect, perfectly) without glasses.
Adv. 2. Ramon ran (quick, quickly) to the corner.
Adj. 3. Janet was (eager, eagerly) for the play to begin.
Adv. 4. My father handles his tools (careful, carefully).
Adv. 5. Harriet won the game (fair, fairly).

Adj. 6. The sky was (clear, clearly).
Adv. 7. Faith decorated the room (colorful, colorfully).
Adv. 8. The old turtle moved (slow, slowly) through the grass.
Adv. 9. The sun shone (bright, brightly).
Adv. 10. A group of students talked (quiet, quietly) in class.

B. Follow the directions for Exercise A.

Adv. 1. The younger children ran (noisy, noisily) to the gym.
Adj. 2. The dinner smells (deliciously, delicious)!
Adv. 3. The tractor moved (slowly, slow) across the field.
Adv. 4. Dale spoke (soft, softly) on the phone.
Adv. 5. The racer turned the corner (sharp, sharply).
Adj. 6. The prospector made a (careful, carefully) search of the area.
Adv. 7. Your serve is (near, nearly) perfect.
Adj. 8. To their trainer, the animals seemed (hungry, hungrily).
Adj. 9. Paul was (shy, shyly) with the strangers.
Adv. 10. Lance stitched the seam (perfect, perfectly).

Using *Good* and *Bad*, and *Well* and *Badly*

You will have no trouble with the words *good* and *bad* if you follow this rule:

Use *good* and *bad* to describe nouns or pronouns. These words are adjectives.

Examples: Jane has a *good* clarinet. (what kind)
Jim has a *bad* cold. (what kind)

Follow this rule for using *well* and *badly:*

Well and *badly* are used with verbs to tell how something is done. When used in this way, these words are adverbs.

Examples: Jane plays the clarinet *well.* (*how* she plays)
Jim behaved *badly.* (*how* he behaved)

1. The truck came to a (sudden, suddenly) stop. Adj.
2. The truck (suddenly, sudden) stopped. Adv.
3. (Loudly, Loud) the rain beat down on the roof. Adv.
4. The (shining, shiningly) sun warmed us. Adj.
5. Bart's dog followed him (faithful, faithfully). Adv.
6. The fans cheered (loud, loudly). Adv.
7. (Joyous, Joyously) the crowd celebrated the victory. Adv.
8. A (piercing, piercingly) scream rang out. Adj.
9. Mother smiled (tender, tenderly) at the baby. Adv.
10. Angelica tied the bow (loose, loosely). Adv.

2. Present the following lists of words on the board or on a worksheet. Students are to identify each word: noun, verb, adjective, or adverb. Then they should choose a word from the *Adjectives and Adverbs* column that can describe a word in the *Nouns and Verbs* column and write the combination phrase either by itself or in a sentence. Answers will vary.

	Nouns and Verbs	Adjectives and Adverbs	
N	1. hamburger	a. helpful	Adj.
V	2. ran	b. narrow	Adj.
V	3. searched	c. easily	Adv.
V	4. behaves	d. raw	Adj.
N	5. advice	e. solid	Adj.
V	6. walked	f. closely	Adv.
V	7. sat	g. oddly	Adv.
N	8. stereo	h. comfortably	Adv.

Extending the Lesson

Have students think of a job: firefighter, policeman, policewoman, baseball player, secretary, etc. Tell them to write six sentences. Three sentences should have adjectives to describe different things a person in that occupation needs or uses, and three sentences should have adverbs to describe actions a person in that occupation does. Students should identify the adjectives and adverbs they use, and tell what word each modifies.

Examples: A secretary uses *modern* equipment. (modifies *equipment*)
A secretary works *quickly*. (modifies *works*)

Well can also be used after a linking verb to mean "in good health." In this case, *well* is a predicate adjective.

I feel *well* today.

Exercises Use *good* and *bad*, and *well* and *badly*.

A. Copy each sentence. Draw an arrow from each underlined modifier to the word it modifies. Then write Adjective or Adverb to tell how each modifier is used.

Example: You are good at spelling.

You are good at spelling. Adjective

Adj. 1. Dark clouds are a bad sign.
Adj. 2. Tina has good news.
Adv. 3. Hank draws very well.
Adj. 4. The ferris wheel is a good ride.
Adj. 5. Rosa is good at playing comic roles.
Adj. 6. That bike is in bad shape.
Adj. 7. John feels well despite a nagging cold.
Adj. 8. A bad storm delayed the shuttle launch for hours.
Adj. 9. Last spring Matt had the worst cold ever.
Adv. 10. Marva performs well on the balance beam.

B. Follow the directions for Exercise A.

Adv. 1. The other team played badly.
Adj. 2. Did you eat a good breakfast?
Adv. 3. We planned the party well.
Adj. 4. Tony has a bad temper.
Adj. 5. My friend writes good letters.
Adv. 6. The old car rattles badly.
Adj. 7. A bad drought plagued the Midwest.
Adv. 8. Jeff skated badly after he sprained his ankle.
Adj. 9. Tim decided the rainbow was a good sign.
Adj. 10. Rick felt well after a restful night.

436

ADDITIONAL EXERCISES

Using Adverbs

A. Recognizing Adverbs Copy each sentence. Circle the adverb. Draw an arrow from the adverb to the word it modifies. (Use after page 430.)

Example: Paint spilled everywhere.

Paint spilled everywhere.

1. The cards were hidden somewhere.
2. The fly ball landed far in the outfield.
3. A new movie opened yesterday.
4. A snow plow slowly cleared the streets.
5. Grease from the pan splattered everywhere.
6. Our friends called later.
7. We arrived too late for the movie.
8. Janice almost forgot her club dues.
9. Brian practices the piano often.
10. Marla completed the puzzle quickly.

B. Adverbs in Comparisons Write the correct form of the adverb. (Use after page 432.)

1. One actor spoke (more softly, most softly) than the other.
2. Jake walks the dog (more often, most often) than Beth does.
3. The train leaves (earlier, more early) on Tuesdays than on Mondays.
4. Of the three shirts, this one fits (better, best).
5. A helicopter flies (lower, lowest) than a jet.
6. Sue guessed the song title (faster, fastest) than I did.
7. Norman prints (more neatly, neatlier) than he writes.

Additional Exercises

These Additional Exercises may be used for additional practice of the concepts presented in this Section. Each exercise focuses on a single concept, and should be used after the page number indicated in parentheses.

Review

If you have not assigned these Additional Exercises before this time, you can also use them as an excellent Section Review.

437

8. The teachers dressed (more formally, most formally) than the students.
9. Of all the movies I've seen, that is my (least favorite, less favorite).
10. My bike stops (faster, more fast) than yours.

C. Adjective or Adverb? Write the correct modifier for each. (Use after page 434.)

1. The police followed the suspect (close, closely).
2. Todd read that mystery (quick, quickly).
3. The accident happened quite (sudden, suddenly).
4. Last night's snowfall seems (light, lightly).
5. The downhill slope looked (dangerous, dangerously).
6. The scientist measured the chemicals (careful, carefully).
7. All of the contestants looked (nervous, nervously).
8. The pickles tasted (bitter, bitterly).
9. Ms. Rogers was (grateful, gratefully) for the help.
10. The pilot landed the jet (smooth, smoothly).

D. Using *Good* and *Bad*, and *Well* and *Badly* Write the correct modifier for each. (Use after page 436.)

1. Marta has a (good, well) ten-speed bike.
2. She rides the bike (good, well).
3. Larry's bike has (bad, badly) brakes.
4. This radio sounds (bad, badly).
5. Vicky rides a horse very (good, well).
6. Mark has a (bad, badly) bruise on his arm.
7. Grandmother isn't feeling (good, well) today.
8. That cafe serves (good, well) food.
9. The new antenna works (good, well).
10. Rehearsal today went (bad, badly).

438

MIXED REVIEW

Using Adverbs

A. Finding and using adverbs Write the adverbs used in the following sentences. After each adverb, write the words it modifies. Write *how, where, when,* or *to what extent* to show what each adverb tells. Two sentences have two adverbs.

1. The swimmer glided easily through the water. how
2. Do you always shop here? here—where, always—when
3. We searched everywhere for the ring. where
4. Karen was quite honest about her mistake. to what extent
5. Ted often forgets his homework. when
6. The crew landed the aircraft smoothly. how
7. Clara eats too fast. too—to what extent, fast—how
8. I never saw the first Superman movie. when
9. Paula quickly read the instructions. how
10. Write your name here. where

B. Making comparisons with adverbs Read each sentence below. Write the correct modifier from the two given in parentheses. Tell whether the modifier is an adjective or an adverb. Then write the word it modifies.

adv. 1. Julie knows (more, most) about computers than Ray. knows
adv. 2. Of the three dogs, Patch behaves (better, best). behaves
adv. 3. Lynn runs (faster, more fast) than anyone on the team. runs
adv. 4. Of the planets, Venus shines (most brightly, brightliest). shines
adj. 5. Which animal is the (most smart, smartest)? animal
adv. 6. The good news spread (more quickly, quicklier) through Rob's class than Marilyn's. spread
adv. 7. Amy reads (better, best) than I do. reads
adv. 8. No one was hurt (bad, badly) in the accident. hurt
adv. 9. Of all the players, Skip plays the (hardest, most hard). plays
adv. 10. Steve did his swan dive (perfectly, perfect). did

Mixed Review

These exercises provide review of the concepts presented in this Section. Each exercise challenges the students to apply several of the skills they have acquired during previous study. Because the "mixed" feature of these activities makes them more difficult, the teacher may wish to have less-advanced students do them orally or in small groups.

Using Grammar in Writing

These challenging and enjoyable activities allow the students to see how the concepts of grammar, usage, and mechanics may be applied in actual writing situations. Each exercise is designed to allow students practice in several of the skills they have acquired in this Section. The activities also provide opportunities for students to write creatively about a wide variety of interesting and unusual subjects.

USING GRAMMAR IN WRITING

Using Adverbs

A. Following are two mini-poems. Notice that the subjects and verbs in each are the same. It is the adverbs that make the big difference in meaning. They tell how the action was done.

I	II
Softly I walked,	**Boldly** I walked,
Slowly I talked,	**Loudly** I talked,
Finally I stopped.	**Suddenly** I stopped.

Now write two mini-poems of your own. Use the subjects and verbs below in each poem. Put an adverb in front of each subject and verb. Then change the adverbs in the second poem. Make the two poems as different as possible. Do not use any of the adverbs that were used in the two poems above.

_______ I ran
_______ I leaped
_______ I danced
_______ I tripped
_______ I fell

B. It's Saturday afternoon, and you have to take care of your neighbor's two children. You take them to the park. They love to swing, to play on the slide, to ride the merry-go-round and the see-saw, and to climb on the jungle gym. Describe the children as they play. Use adverbs that tell *when, where, how,* and *to what extent* an action happened. Include one or more adverbs in the comparative form. Also include at least one sentence in which you use *good* or *well.* Include another sentence that uses *bad* or *badly.*

Using Prepositions and Conjunctions

In this section you will learn about prepositions and conjunctions. These are words that have little meaning in themselves. They are used to connect words and groups of words. They are also used to show how one word in a sentence is related to another. Prepositions and conjunctions are important because they show relationships and combine ideas.

Section Objectives

1. To understand the function of prepositions, and to identify prepositions and prepositional phrases in sentences

2. To identify and use nouns and pronouns as objects of prepositions

3. To differentiate between the use of a word as a preposition and its use as an adverb

4. To avoid confusion caused by misplaced prepositional phrases

5. To identify conjunctions and to understand their function

Preparing the Students

Write this sentence on the board and ask the students to identify the types of words in it: *The red telephone in the office rang loudly.* Students should have no trouble identifying the nouns *(telephone, office),* verb *(rang),* adjectives *(the, red, the),* and adverb *(loudly).* Ask students what the remaining word, *in,* does. Make sure they see that it does not function like any of the other four groups, but is a new type of word.

Additional Resources

Diagnostic Test — page 7 in the test booklet

Mastery Test — pages 52–53 in the test booklet

Additional Exercises — pages 455–461 in the student text

Practice Book — pages 174–179

Duplicating Masters — pages 174–179

Special Populations — See special section at the front of this Teacher's Edition.

Part 1

Objective

To understand the function of prepositions, and to identify prepositions and prepositional phrases in sentences

Presenting the Lesson

1. Read and discuss page 442. Make sure that the students recognize how the relationship stated in the sample sentence changes when the preposition changes. Ask them to substitute other prepositions from the list to see other possible relationships.

2. Point out that *pre-* means *before* and that the position of a preposition is always before the noun. It is important for the students to remember that the preposition is always followed by an object.

3. Have students give other examples of prepositional phrases, using some of the prepositions from the list on page 442. Ask them to find those prepositions on the list that show location and those that show time. Stress the fact that a preposition is always found in a prepositional phrase.

4. Assign and discuss Exercises A and B on page 443.

5. Read *Using Prepositional Phrases* on page 444. Before assigning Exercise A, study the example with the class. Point out that there are two prepositional phrases in a row. Have the students identify which words belong to the first phrase and which belong to the second.

6. You may wish to do Exercise A with the class. Assign and discuss

Part 1 What Are Prepositions?

Prepositions are words that show relationships. A preposition stands before its object. It shows how the object is related to another word in the sentence. Read this sentence:

The jet flew over Mexico.

In this sentence, *over* is the preposition. It stands before its object, *Mexico. Over* relates *Mexico* to *flew.*

The following prepositions are in italics. Find the object of each preposition and the word the object is related to.

Melanie walked *across* the playground.
Harry studied *before* the test.

In the first sentence, the preposition is *across.* Its object is *playground. Across* relates *playground* to *walked.*

In the second sentence, the preposition is *before.* Its object is *test. Before* relates *test* to *studied.*

A preposition is a word that relates its object to some other word in the sentence. It may show time, location, or people and things in special relationships.

Words Often Used as Prepositions

about	behind	except	on	to
above	below	for	onto	toward
across	beneath	from	out	under
after	beside	in	outside	until
against	between	inside	over	up
along	beyond	into	past	upon
among	but (*except*)	like	since	with
around	by	near	through	within
at	down	of	throughout	without
before	during	off		

Exercises **Find the prepositions and their objects.**

A. Number your paper from 1 to 10. Write the preposition and its object in each of the following sentences.

1. There is gum on my shoe.
2. Jeff opened his book to the index.
3. Our team can't compete under the new rules.
4. This portrait of George Washington is two hundred years old.
5. Louisa May Alcott wrote about her own times.
6. The cans on this shelf are dented.
7. We went bowling with my cousins.
8. The Plains Indians depended upon the buffalo.
9. The pinch hitter rifled the ball into left field.
10. Everybody in my family has blue eyes.

B. Writing Read each sentence. How many different prepositions can you find that fit each blank space? Refer to the list on page 442 to help you choose. Write at least two prepositions for each sentence.

Answers may vary. Suggested answers are given.

Example: Put the bench ______ the table.

near, under, beside, behind

1. B. J.'s dog was playing ______ the house. in, outside
2. Cornelia heard a strange noise ______ the hall. in, down
3. A flock of birds flew ______ the river. over, beyond
4. Who put the butter ______ the oven? in, on
5. An American flag flew ______ the house. over, beside
6. We found these coins ______ the bookcase. behind, on
7. The pen ______ the desk is mine. on, behind
8. The winners of the contest will travel ______ Alaska. to, through
9. You'll find the sugar bowl on the shelf ______ the sink. beside, under
10. The clown jumped ______ the platform. on, onto

Exercise B on page 445 for individual completion.

Individualizing the Lesson

Less-Advanced Students

1. When assigning Exercise A on page 444, remind the students to refer to the list of prepositions on page 442. The words which immediately follow the preposition make up the rest of the phrase which they are to locate.

2. Reinforce the idea of changing relationships shown by prepositional phrases. Use an object large enough for the students to see, such as an eraser. Put the object in several different places and have the students describe the location with a prepositional phrase. Some examples are: *under your foot*, *in the drawer*, *against the window*, *among the books*. You may wish to have the students think up some locations and write them in sentences such as "I put the eraser behind the door."

Advanced Students

Have the students describe a place in the school using at least ten prepositional phrases in several complete sentences. Tell them not to name the place but to see whether the reader can guess the location from the description.

Optional Practice

Have the students underline the preposition and circle the prepositional phrases in the following sentences:

1. We laughed at the jokes in the book.
2. Jeri found the book on a shelf in the library.

3. She brought it to class.
4. Arnie read jokes to us.
5. Then he put the book under his chair.
6. My dad took us to a ballgame last week.
7. I sat between my brothers.
8. Before the game we watched the warmups.
9. Some players were talking with the fans.
10. Around seven o'clock the game started.
11. We could see the players inside the dugout.
12. A foul ball sailed toward our seats during the fifth inning.
13. It landed in my lap!
14. Our catcher hit a grand slam outside the park.
15. The home team won by four runs.

Extending the Lesson

1. Have students identify the prepositional phrase in each of the following sentences. They should write the phrase and next to it write *time*, *location*, or *other relationship*, according to its use in the sentence.

Example: The book is on the table.
on the table—location.

O 1. Greg climbed the face of the mountain.
L 2. The traffic moved slowly down the street.
T 3. The movie lasted for three hours.
L 4. The pipe below the sink was leaking.
O 5. We walked against the wind.
L 6. Clarissa did a perfect swan dive into the pool.
L 7. The pitcher threw the ball to first base.
O 8. All of my cousins are here.

Using Prepositional Phrases

The group of words that includes a preposition and its object is called a **prepositional phrase.** All the words that modify the object are also part of the phrase.

Example: We rode *in the bus.*
We rode *in an old, broken-down bus.*

Gail was waiting *for dessert.*
Gail was waiting *for the special chocolate dessert.*

If a preposition has more than one object, all the parts of the object are included in the prepositional phrase.

Example: Weeds grew *in the lawn, the flower garden, and the vegetable garden.*

Some sentences have more than one prepositional phrase.

Bob works in the cafeteria with his friends.
Every member of the team will play during the game.

Exercises Find the prepositional phrases.

A. Write the prepositional phrase or phrases that you find in each of the following sentences.

Example: The yarn was stuck to the paper with glue.
to the paper
with glue

1. Everybody in the classroom saw the accident.
2. The doll beside the teddy bear has eyes made of black buttons.
3. We found a good spot for our picnic.
4. Maureen and her little brother played on the swings for hours.
5. Donald plays clarinet in the orchestra at school.

6. The acrobat balanced on the tightrope stretched between two buildings.
7. Mary Ann waited near the school|until four o'clock.
8. Put the keys on the hook|in the hall.
9. The apartment across the hall has been empty for a month.
10. Mother hung a clock with a flower design|above the door.

B. Follow the directions for Exercise A.

1. During its journey, the space probe will travel past Venus.
2. Rosa tied a ribbon around the present|for her cousin.
3. The puppy slept on a rug|in the corner.
4. Janet finished her painting of the willow trees|along the river.
5. Tell me about the characters|in that story.
6. After the hurricane, the river spilled over its banks.
7. A squirrel ran up the maple tree|outside my window.
8. You may choose among the last three items|on the menu.
9. Dave shopped at the drugstore|beside the new restaurant.
10. The team from El Paso plays against us|before Thanksgiving.

Part 2 Objects of Prepositions

Using Nouns as Objects of Prepositions

You have seen that nouns may be used as subjects or objects of verbs. Nouns also are used as objects of prepositions. Here are some examples of objects of prepositions:

O 9. My scarf of blue silk is missing.
T10. We are going swimming after school.

2. Have the students complete the following sentences three ways using three different prepositional phrases. The first phrase should be a *time* phrase, the second a *location* phrase, and the third some *other relationship* phrase. Answers will vary.

1. We camped_____.
2. Two cats were fighting_____.
3. Our class picnic was held_____.
4. Louise painted_____.

Part 2

Objective

To identify and use nouns and pronouns as objects of prepositions

Presenting the Lesson

1. Read and discuss pages 445–446.

2. Assign and discuss the Exercise on page 446.

3. Read and discuss pages 446–447. Ask students for other examples of sentences using pronouns as objects of prepositions. Stress the choice of pronouns in compounds by first considering the pronoun as a single object.

4. You may wish to do Exercise A on page 448 with the class. Assign and discuss Exercise B on page 448.

Individualizing the Lesson

Less-Advanced Students

Ask students to complete the following sentences by filling in each blank with an object pronoun. Point out that there is more than one possible answer, so students should try to use different pronouns in the different sentences. Answers will vary.

1. The librarian showed the books to ______.
2. My dog ran around ______ in circles when I came home from school.
3. We passed beside ______ on the street.
4. People took pictures of ______ during the show.
5. The adults played baseball with ______ at the park.
6. John takes the bus with Dan and ______.
7. The huge dog growled at Julie and ______ when we walked by.
8. Can we all go with Roberto and ______ to the game?

Advanced Students

Ask the students to think up as many song, book, or film titles as they can that have prepositional phrases in them. Then have them

The campers pitched their tents *near the* **river.**
Mickey left his gym shoes *in his* **locker.**
The winning run was scored *by* **Bonita.**
The movie showed the arrival *of* **aliens** *on* **earth.**

Exercise **Find nouns used as objects of prepositions.**

Number your paper from 1 to 10. For each sentence, write each prepositional phrase and underline the noun that is the object of the preposition.

1. We all cleared the dishes from the table.
2. These Civil War photographs are by Matthew Brady.
3. Nobody in that movie is well known.
4. Elizabeth Blackwell began the study of medicine here.
5. The new computer will be delivered before Friday.
6. The temperature went below zero last night.
7. The lid on this jar won't budge.
8. When was gold discovered in California?
9. Around the Christmas tree were piled many presents.
10. The football sailed over the goal posts and into the stands.

Using Pronouns as Objects of Prepositions

When a pronoun is used as the object of a preposition, its object form must be used. The object forms are these:

Object Pronouns	
me	us
you	you
him, her, it	them

Examples: The prize was awarded *to us.*
Was there a message *for me?*
Laura's mother was looking *for her.*

Using Pronouns in Compound Objects of Prepositions

Usually you make few mistakes in using the object form of a pronoun as the object of a preposition. However, you may become confused when the object of a preposition is compound. Read the examples to yourself.

Simple Object	Compound Object
I talked *with* **her.** We stood *near* **him.** Give that *to* **me.**	I talked *with* **Darren** *and* **her.** We stood *near* **Jackie** *and* **him.** Give that *to* **her** *and* **me.**

If you are not sure which form to use, say the sentence with the pronoun alone following the preposition. Then say the complete sentence.

Example: We're waiting for James and (she, her).
We're waiting for *her.*
We're waiting *for James and her.*

Using *Between* and *Among*

Often people use the prepositions *between* and *among* as if there were no difference between them. There is a difference that you should know, so that you can use them correctly.

Use *between* to speak of two persons or things or two groups of persons or things.

Choose **between** *these two programs.*
The next game is **between** *the Jefferson High team and our team.*

Use *among* to speak of more than two. Here are examples:

We will divide the jobs **among** *Nancy, you, and me.*
There was a three-way tie **among** *the Yankees, the Red Sox, and the Indians.*

make up their own unique titles by changing the objects of the prepositions and their modifiers if needed.

Examples: *Gone with the Wind*
Gone with My French Fries
Somewhere Over the Rainbow
Somewhere Over the Gymnasium

Optional Practice

1. Have the students follow the directions for the exercise on nouns as objects on page 446 using these sentences.

1. My grandmother lives in a small town near Cleveland.
2. I visited her during spring vacation.
3. Her house was built around 1900.
4. Inside her closet, I found stairs to the attic.
5. An old trunk was in the corner under some clothes.
6. I called to my grandmother.
7. She said I could look inside the trunk.
8. I read clippings from old newspapers about my grandfather.
9. I discovered much family history among those old papers.

2. Have the students choose the correct word from the two given in parentheses and then write the complete prepositional phrase.

1. These gifts are for Barbara and (she, her).
2. Divide the crayons (between, among) Billy, Craig and Tom.
3. The crows hovered above Carrie and (me, I).
4. I almost ran into Mr. Rossetti and (he, him).
5. Everyone is going outside except you and (he, him).

6. Wally received a funny card from Evelyn and (they, them).
7. Don't come without Kelly and (him, he).
8. The orange can be shared (between, among) Jose and you.
9. You are supposed to stand behind Crystal and (I, me).
10. Is the argument (between, among) you and Carlton serious?

Extending the Lesson

Have students make three columns on their papers, headed *preposition, modifiers,* and *noun object.* Tell them to write the parts of each phrase below in the appropriate columns.

1. over the thick wall (P M NO)
2. across the busy street (P M NO)
3. on time (P NO)
4. near the open window (P M NO)
5. until the sad ending (P M NO)
6. down the steep slide (P M NO)
7. behind the huge tractor (P M NO)
8. beside the antique vases (P M NO)
9. during the intermission (P NO)
10. on the high trapeze (P M NO)

Exercises Use pronouns as objects of prepositions.

A. Choose the correct pronoun from the two given in parentheses. Write the complete prepositional phrase.

Example: The villain shot at Superman and (he, him).
at Superman and him

1. The coach called on Leo and (I, me).
2. The roof over Marcia and (them, they) started to leak.
3. Carrie lives near Juan and (she, her).
4. Will you sit beside your mother and (me, I)?
5. The car behind Beverly and (us, we) broke down.
6. A firecracker exploded near Timothy and (we, us).
7. My advice to Norita and (him, he) was ignored.
8. The wolves howled at Thompson and (they, them).
9. The album by James Taylor and (her, she) went on sale today.
10. The rivalry between Ohio State and (them, they) started years ago.

B. Follow the directions for Exercise A.

1. On your cue, turn toward Ms. Bennett and (she, her).
2. As Paula hurried past Brian and (him, he), she waved.
3. Mr. Washington was looking at Jason and (I, me).
4. The puppy's high-pitched whine went right through Ginny and (we, us).
5. Terrence's kite flew above the boys and (he, him).
6. That car almost bumped into Gayle and (they, them).
7. I ordered a cheese and mushroom pizza for Susan and (her, she).
8. Everyone but Peter and (us, we) has had a turn.
9. The paper carried an article about (they, them) and the marching band.
10. My pet duck waddles after my friends and (I, me).

Part 3 Preposition or Adverb?

Several words used as prepositions are also used as adverbs.

Example: We looked *up.* (adverb)
We looked *up the chimney.* (preposition)

If you aren't sure whether a word is an adverb or a preposition, study the way it is used in the sentence. If it begins a phrase and has an object, it is probably a preposition. If it is used alone, it is probably an adverb.

Exercises Find prepositions and adverbs.

A. The word in italics is used both as an adverb and as a preposition. Number your paper from 1 to 10. After each number, write *a.* and *b.* After each letter, write *Preposition* or *Adverb* depending on which you find in that sentence.

Example: a. Look *out*! b. Look *out* the window.
a. Adverb b. Preposition

1. a. There was litter all *around* the store. b. There was litter all *around.*
2. a. Don't come *near*! b. Don't come *near* the cliff!
3. a. Can you get *past* the barrier? b. Can that big Cadillac get *past?*
4. a. Those cans should be stored *underneath* the cabinet. b. Those cans should be stored *underneath.*
5. a. Miguel will soon be coming *along.* b. Miguel is coming *along* the path.
6. a. Please stand *by.* b. Please stand *by* the window.
7. a. *Above* the fog, the lights glowed. b. *Above,* the lights glowed.
8. a. A hiker climbed *up.* b. A hiker climbed *up* the hill.
9. a. We've met *before* today. b. We've met *before.*
10. a. Puffs of white smoke drifted *up.* b. White smoke drifted *up* the chimney.

Part 3

Objective

To differentiate between the use of a word as a preposition and its use as an adverb

Presenting the Lesson

1. Read and discuss page 449. It may be helpful to review briefly the definition and use of an adverb. Remind students that if there is no object used with the word in question, it is probably an adverb.

2. It is suggested that you do Exercise A on page 449 with the class. Assign and discuss Exercise B on page 450.

Individualizing the Lesson

Less-Advanced Students

Point out to the students that it is impossible to tell whether a word like *over* or *by* is an adverb or preposition unless the word is used in a sentence.

Give the students the following sentences and be sure that they understand the meaning of the adverb in each. Then have the students add objects and modifiers to the sentences so as to change the adverbs to prepositions. Answers will vary.

1. A plane flew over.
2. The cars sped by.
3. Angelo strolled outside.
4. The officer stood near.

Advanced Students

After the students have completed the exercises, have each of them write three pairs of original sentences like those in the exercises. Remind them that in one sentence of the pair the word must be used as a preposition and have an object.

Optional Practice

Have the students follow the directions for Exercise A on page 449 using the following sentences:

A 1. a. Wash the suds off.
 P b. Wash the suds off the dishes.
P 2. a. Leave the box outside the door.
 A b. Leave the box outside.
A 3. a. The magic city lay beyond.
 P b. The magic city lay beyond the dark forest.
A 4. a. Don't let the soup boil over.
 P b. Don't let the soup boil over the pan.
A 5. a. Jessie fell down.
 P b. Jessie fell down the steep stairs.
P 6. a. Crowds passed by the new statue.
 A b. Crowds passed by.
P 7. a. Gnats swarmed about the bright lights.
 A b. Gnats swarmed about.
A 8. a. The passengers watched the clouds below.
 P b. The passengers watched the clouds below the plane.

Part 4

Objective

To avoid confusion caused by misplaced prepositional phrases

Presenting the Lesson

1. Read and discuss pages 450–451. Point out the humorous effects,

B. Follow the directions for Exercise A.

1. a. Agatha took her coat *off.* [A] b. Agatha took her coat *off* [P] the hanger.
2. a. Many children walked *behind* [P] the parade. b. Many children walked *behind.* [A]
3. a. *Beyond,* [A] the sea stretched to the horizon. b. *Beyond* [P] the rocky shore, the sea stretched to the horizon.
4. a. Cut the cake into layers and spread the filling *between.* [A] b. Spread the filling *between* [P] the layers.
5. a. My friends are waiting *outside* [P] the house. b. My friends are waiting outside. [A]
6. a. A DC-10 flew *over.* [A] b. A DC-10 flew *over* [P] the playground.
7. a. The stuntman fell *down* [P] the chute. b. The stuntman fell *down.* [A]
8. a. Don't just stand *around!* [A] b. Don't just stand *around* [P] the kitchen!
9. a. Abigail opened the freezer and put the meat *inside.* [A] b. Abigail put the meat *inside* [P] the freezer.
10. a. When the light changes, you can get *across.* [A] b. When the light changes, you can get *across* [P] the intersection.

Part 4 Using Prepositional Phrases in the Right Places

Some prepositional phrases may be moved from one position in a sentence to another without changing the meaning of the sentence. Here is an example:

We visited Meramec Cavern during our vacation.

During our vacation we visited Meramec Cavern.

To give your writing variety, begin a sentence with a prepositional phrase now and then. However, always placing a prepositional phrase at the beginning of a sentence can become boring. Try to begin sentences in a variety of ways.

Some prepositional phrases do not move easily from one position in a sentence to another. The position of the phrase can make a great deal of difference in the meaning of the sentence.

Example: Walter touched the flower with purple petals.

With purple petals, Walter touched the flower.

The second sentence suggests that Walter used purple petals to touch the flower. This prepositional phrase should not be moved away from flower, the word it describes.

Example: Gerri called the dog with a loud voice.

With a loud voice, Gerri called the dog.

The second sentence puts the prepositional phrase where it belongs, next to *Gerri*. This position makes the meaning much clearer. A prepositional phrase should be placed as close as possible to the word it tells about.

Exercises Use prepositional phrases correctly.

A. The following sentences are confusing. By changing the position of one prepositional phrase in each sentence, you can make the meaning clear. Rewrite each sentence to make it clear.

1. Bill put the bowl on the table of potato chips.
2. The clock has Roman numerals over the mantel.
3. On the roof Marian spotted a squirrel.
4. Do you have the keys with you to the house?
5. Everybody signed Lisa's photo on the team.
6. With a torn cover, Gordon found an old math book.

as well as the confusion, caused by putting words in the wrong order in sentences.

2. You may find it helpful to do Exercise A on pages 451–452 with the class. Assign and discuss Exercise B.

Individualizing the Lesson

Less-Advanced Students

Point out that the placement of modifiers must be planned in order to avoid misleading or confusing the reader. It is important to first know which word is to be modified. Before doing Exercise A, have the students identify the misplaced phrase and then underline the word that the misplaced phrase should modify. You may wish them to do the same with Exercise B.

Advanced Students

Have each of the students create three sentences with humorously misplaced prepositional phrases. They are to then exchange papers with their neighbors and have them correct the placement.

Optional Practice

Have the students follow the directions for Exercise A on page 451, using the following sentences:

The horse ate the oats in the pail.
1. In the pail, the horse ate the oats.

On her way to church, Alice saw your lost cat.
2. Alice saw your lost cat on her way to church.

The salesman with a red tie sold us a vacuum cleaner.
3. The salesman sold us a vaccuum cleaner with a red tie.

The thunder made me jump under my covers.
4. Under my covers, the thunder made me jump.

With a bat, he hit a ball to his dog.
5. He hit a ball to his dog with a bat.

From the parking lot, we heard the choir sing.
6. We heard the choir sing from the parking lot.

The bull with the ring in his nose chased the farmer.

7. The bull chased the farmer with the ring in his nose.

The baby drank her milk from the bottle.

8. From the bottle, the baby drank her milk.

The horse without a saddle jumped over the fence.

9. The horse jumped over the fence without a saddle.

Mom made a banana cake without frosting.

10. Without frosting, Mom made a banana cake.

Extending the Lesson

Put the exercise below on the board or on a worksheet. Have students rewrite the sentences, inserting the preposition phrase where it will make sense.

1. The rocket was launched. (from Cape Canaveral)
2. The seagulls picked upon the oyster shells. (on the beach)
3. The escalator in the store is being repaired. (by the candy section)
4. There were weird monsters roaming the earth. (in the science fiction movie)
5. The paintings were exhibited last week. (of the artist)
6. I could see the band formations on the field. (from the highest seat)

Part 5

Objective

To identify conjunctions and to understand their function

Presenting the Lesson

1. Read and discuss pages 452–453. Explain to the students that a junction is a station where different railroad lines connect. Just as the station connects railroad lines, con-

7. On the clothesline, Thelma saw a chickadee.
8. The book isn't mine in my locker.
9. The pencils should be sharp on my desk.
10. From her aunt, Jennifer put away the hat.

B. Follow the directions for Exercise A.

1. A painting hung on the wall of a sunset.
2. Under the car, Dorothy noticed the softball.
3. Penelope made a puzzle in her room of the United States.
4. Albert wrote a story for the class about his cat.
5. With a curly red wig, Mr. Morgan watched the clown.
6. I have buttons on my dress of gold.
7. There is a beautiful carved mask in the museum of an Indian chief.
8. People for breakfast eat lots of eggs.
9. The special effects deserve a prize in that movie.
10. The crew in the distance sighted a whale.

Part 5 What Are Conjunctions?

You have learned that prepositions show relationships between words in a sentence. Relationships are also shown by another kind of word: a **conjunction.**

How is the word *and* used in each of these sentences?

Tracy **and** *Deborah* went to the movie.
The class *wrote* **and** *performed* the play.
Allen's puppy *broke his leash* **and** *ran away.*
Yastrzemski hit a *double* **and** two *singles* in the game.

Do you see that in each sentence, *and* connects words or groups of words of the same type? In the first example, *and* joins two subjects. In the second example, *and* joins two verbs.

In the third example, *and* connects two predicates. In the last example, *and* connects two direct objects. The word *and* is a conjunction.

A conjunction is a word that connects words or groups of words.

Two other conjunctions you use often are *but* and *or.* Like *and,* they may be used to connect sentence parts.

> **Andrew** *or* **Ginny** will bring the potato chips.
> (compound subject)
>
> Our forward **shot** *but* **missed.**
> (compound verb)
>
> The class **could see a movie** *or* **study the science chapter.**
> (compound predicate)
>
> Please buy **bread** *or* **rolls.**
> (compound direct object)
>
> The package was **bulky** *but* **light.**
> (compound predicate adjective)
>
> The orchestra performed for the **faculty** *and* **parents.**
> (compound object of a preposition)

Exercises Use conjunctions correctly.

A. For each of the following sentences, write the compound sentence parts and their conjunction. Circle the conjunction. Tell what kind of compound words you found. Write *Compound Subject, Compound Verb, Compound Predicate, Compound Direct Object,* or *Compound Object of a Preposition.*

> Example: The Mets survived that season but finished last.
>
> survived that season (but) finished last
>
> compound predicate

CS 1. The snow (and) ice made the roads impassable.
CDO 2. For breakfast, Lorraine likes eggs (or) oatmeal.

junctions connect parts of a sentence.

2. Assign and discuss Exercises A and B on pages 453–454.

Individualizing the Lesson

Less-Advanced Students

Make sure the students can identify the words being connected by conjunctions in each of the examples and the role of those words in the sentence. Ask the students to supply alternate words or phrases to replace the ones in boldface print.

Advanced Students

Have students write a sentence using each of the following phrases, and circle each conjunction.

1. sing or dance
2. bass drums and kettle drums
3. inside or outside
4. run and jump
5. north but not south

Optional Practice

Have the students rewrite the two sentences as one using the conjunctions *and, but* or *or.* After each sentence have them identify what part of the sentence they joined.

> *Example:*
> The phone rang. It woke the baby.
> The phone rang and woke the baby.
> (compound predicate)

1. We cleaned the kitchen, and ~~We cleaned~~ the family room.
2. Eat your dinner, or You will get no dessert.
3. The horses ~~are in the meadow.~~ and The cows are in the meadow.
4. Our school won the swimming trophy, but ~~Our school did~~ not ~~win~~ the baseball game.

5. The announcement will be heard on the radio. and ~~The announcement will be heard~~ on TV.
6. Tuesday was sunny. but ~~Tuesday was~~ bitter cold.

CP 3. The wind shook the windows and whistled down the chimney.

COPrep 4. I wrote a message on the box and the card.

CS 5. Our television and stereo were stolen last night.

CP 6. Gerald takes piano lessons but doesn't practice.

CV 7. The puppy yawned and stretched.

CS 8. Football and soccer are Lennie's favorite sports.

CDO 9. Trudy accidentally splashed Doug and me with her paint.

CS 10. Tecumseh and his brother led their forces against the U.S. Army.

B. Write sentences with compound subjects, verbs, predicates, direct objects or objects of a preposition as the directions state. Use *and, but,* or *or.*

Example: Compound direct object. Use a noun and a pronoun.

Please take **Amy** *and* **me** to the library.

Answers will vary.

1. Compound subject. Use a noun and a pronoun.
2. Compound verb.
3. Compound direct object. Use two nouns.
4. Compound object of a preposition. Use two nouns.
5. Compound predicate.

ADDITIONAL EXERCISES

Using Prepositions and Conjunctions

A. Prepositional Phrases Write the prepositional phrases in each of the following sentences. Circle each object of the preposition. Some sentences have more than one prepositional phrase. (Use after page 446.)

1. My birthday is in September.
2. Eddie found these shells on the beach.
3. There is a telephone call for Nerissa.
4. Jessica volunteers at the hospital during the summer.
5. When will *Star Wars* be on television?
6. Laina wants mint sherbet with raspberries.
7. We shone the flashlights into the cave.
8. Are you going to the sale on Saturday?
9. In California, winters are mild.
10. After lunch, we shopped for a gift.

B. Pronouns as Objects of Prepositions Choose the correct pronoun from the two given. Write the complete prepositional phrase. (Use after page 448.)

1. The taxi splashed water onto Joan and (I, me).
2. Two FBI agents explained their work to (us, we).
3. A tall man sat in front of Chris and (I, me).
4. The scenery was designed by Lee and (she, her).
5. The play-offs are between the Tigers and (us, we).
6. The surprise party for (they, them) was postponed.
7. Clyde shares his locker with Brian and (he, him).
8. The messages were for Helen and (they, them).
9. Give your entry blank to Ms. Lee or (she, her).
10. The gift is from my brother and (I, me).

Additional Exercises

These Additional Exercises may be used for additional practice of the concepts presented in this Section. Each exercise focuses on a single concept, and should be used after the page number indicated in parentheses.

Review

If you have not assigned these Additional Exercises before this time, you can also use them as an excellent Section Review.

C. Preposition or Adverb? In each sentence, there is an adverb or a preposition. Write the adverb or preposition on your paper and tell which it is. (Use after page 450.)

1. The runners jumped over the hurdles.
2. Below the deck the crew was working.
3. The Dodgers fell behind.
4. A light breeze rippled across the countryside.
5. We sang the national anthem and sat down.
6. The cats played outside.
7. Come in and relax.
8. The parakeet flew around the room.
9. The little girl blew the candles out.
10. Oil spilled onto the floor.

D. Placement of Prepositional Phrases The following sentences are confusing. By changing the position of one phrase in each sentence, you can make the meaning clear. Rewrite each sentence to make it clear. (Use after page 452.)

1. In the pot, Paul placed the vegetables and the chicken broth.
2. The locket has my initials engraved in silver on it around my neck.
3. With a wagging tail, Lance saw the dog.
4. Myra bought the towel at the bazaar for her grandmother.
5. The crack is widening in the sidewalk.
6. Mr. Klein told a story to the students with a surprise ending.
7. Jesse in the wishing well saw a silver dollar.
8. Everybody sent a card to Joan in the class on her birthday.
9. From the teakettle Martin saw steam rising.
10. There is a model in the gift shop of the Sears Tower.

456

E. Conjunctions and Compound Sentence Parts Write each compound sentence part with its conjunction. Circle the conjunction. (Use after page 454.)

1. This game requires skill and practice.
2. Cheryl or Denny will help me.
3. An omelette should be light and fluffy.
4. Carter read the paper but skipped the comics.
5. Ben dashed outside without a hat or gloves.
6. Meg can play the piano and the violin.
7. Band members and chorus members will be excused early.
8. The airline offered chicken or lasagne on the noon flight.
9. We mowed the lawn and weeded the garden.
10. Is the letter from Jenny or Sue?

457

Mixed Review

These exercises provide review of the concepts presented in this Section. Each exercise challenges the students to apply several of the skills they have acquired during previous study. Because the "mixed" feature of these activities makes them more difficult, the teacher may wish to have less-advanced students do them orally or in small groups.

MIXED REVIEW

Using Prepositions and Conjunctions

A. Finding prepositions and objects of prepositions Make two columns on your paper. Label one *Prepositions* and the other *Objects of Prepositions.* For each sentence, write the preposition and its object in the correct columns. Some sentences have more than one preposition and object.

1. The cash register on the counter is made of brass.
2. For hot-air balloons, races are tests of accuracy.
3. The jockey on Daredevil wiped mud from his eyes.
4. There is a mass of wires behind the TV screen.
5. A wagon drawn by horses plodded through the snow.
6. Into the spotlight stepped the master of ceremonies.
7. Mom placed a bag of ice on my sprained ankle.
8. The sailboat glided under the bridge and into the harbor.
9. The box of old clothes is on the shelf in that closet.
10. The blimp flew over the stadium during the game.

B. Finding adverbs and prepositional phrases Make one column on your paper and label it *Adverbs.* Make a second column and label it *Prepositional Phrases.* Write each adverb and prepositional phrase that you find in the following sentences in the correct column. Every sentence does not have one of each.

1. You can sit beside me.
2. The flock of gulls flew away.
3. We drove past Independence Hall.
4. The skater fell down.
5. Walk carefully near those thorny bushes.
6. We stayed inside during the storm.
7. The movie was over at nine o'clock.

8. Tanya wished upon a star.
9. Keith hid behind an old locomotive in the station.
10. Did you let the cat out?

C. Using prepositional phrases correctly Nine of the following sentences do not use prepositional phrases correctly. In some, the prepositional phrase is in the wrong place. In others, the pronoun used as the object of the preposition is in the wrong form. Correctly rewrite any sentences containing errors. If a sentence is already correct, write *Correct.*

C 1. There's a robin's nest under the eaves.
2. The money is for the delivery person in the drawer.
3. We discussed our plans with Mr. Jacobs and they.
C 4. The mechanic crawled under the car.
5. Lisa told us about her trip to California at lunch.
6. David spread on the hot dog catsup and mustard.
7. Several students visited our school from Germany.
C 8. Don't leave without an umbrella.
C 9. I saw a bird with yellow wings.
10. In the file drawer Mrs. Dobbs neatly arranged the papers.
11. Jeannie sat in the bleachers with Paul and I.
C 12. I got a birthday card from her.
13. Without Eric and he, our team can't play.
C 14. We enjoyed the cool breeze from the lake.
15. The books are mysteries on this shelf.

D. Finding conjunctions and compound sentence parts Write any compound subjects, compound verbs, compound predicates, compound direct objects, or compound objects of prepositions from the following sentences. Label each one. Underline the conjunction that connects the parts of each compound.

CP 1. Jeff climbed the mountain and enjoyed the view.

459

CO 2. Street vendors sell hot dogs and pretzels in the city.
CP 3. The girls made their own Chinese kite and flew it.
COP 4. These bushes provide food for birds and squirrels.
CS 5. Ben or Molly will represent our class in the meet.
CV 6. The wild horse pranced and reared.
CO 7. Wendy found a fossil and an old coin among the ruins.
CS 8. My mother and I made this quilt from scraps of old clothing.
CV 9. The audience cheered and applauded.
CP 10. Sylvia took the test and passed it.
CP 11. Rosa borrowed my skateboard but did not return it.
COP 12. We planted a lilac bush between the porch and the garage.

460

USING GRAMMAR IN WRITING

Prepositions and Conjunctions

A. It is your job to plan a treasure hunt to take place in your classroom. You are to write five clues. Each clue should contain one prepositional phrase. Use some of these prepositions:

above	behind	by	in	near
against	below	down	down	of
among	beneath	over	inside	off
around	beside	through	into	onto
upon	between	under	to	outside

Don't make your clues too easy. When you finish your sentences, write one more sentence that tells what the treasure is and where you hid it.

B. You have a whole day off from school. You can spend it as you like. Will you go to the shopping mall? Will you take a hike or a bike ride? Perhaps you will just stay home and listen to records. Tell about your day off. Use at least five prepositional phrases as you describe it. Underline each preposition you use. Circle the object of each preposition.

C. Describe two people in your class. You may first want to ask them some questions to get information. In your description, use most of the following conjunctions: *and, but, or, both-and, either-or, neither-nor.*

Using Grammar in Writing

These challenging and enjoyable activities allow the students to see how the concepts of grammar, usage, and mechanics may be applied in actual writing situations. Each exercise is designed to allow students practice in several of the skills they have acquired in this Section. The activities also provide opportunities for students to write creatively about a wide variety of interesting and unusual subjects.

Section Objectives

1. To learn about the eight parts of speech

2. To recognize the use of a single word as different parts of speech

Preparing the Students

Discuss how each word in a sentence has a particular job to do. Ask students to tell you the part of speech and function of each word in the following sentence.

John and I raced quickly across the wide field.

List the seven groups of words. Explain that almost every word can be placed in one of these groups, or the last group to be studied.

Additional Resources

Mastery Test — pages 54–55 in the test booklet

Additional Exercises — pages 467–471 in the student text

Practice Book — pages 180–182

Duplicating Masters — pages 180–182

Special Populations — See special section at the front of this Teacher's Edition.

Part 1

Objective

To learn about the eight parts of speech

Presenting the Lesson

1. Read and discuss pages 462–463. Ask students for other examples of interjections and why they

Using the Parts of Speech

Part 1 The Parts of Speech

You have studied verbs, nouns, pronouns, adjectives, adverbs, prepositions, and conjunctions. You have been learning to recognize these kinds of words and to use them correctly in sentences. The name used for these groups of words is **parts of speech.** There are eight parts of speech. In this section, you will review the parts of speech you have studied. You will also learn about another part of speech called **interjections.**

What Are Interjections?

In addition to the seven parts of speech you have studied, there is another part of speech called **interjections.**

An interjection is a word or short group of words used to express strong feeling.

An interjection may express surprise, joy, anger, or sadness. An interjection is often followed by an exclamation mark (!).

Look at these examples of interjections:

No way! I'm not singing by myself.
Congratulations!
Ouch! That hurts.
Great!

Now you have learned about all eight parts of speech.

The Parts of Speech

nouns	verbs	adverbs	conjunctions
pronouns	adjectives	prepositions	interjections

A word fits into one of these groups because of the way it is used in a sentence.

Exercises Recognize the parts of speech.

A. Write each underlined word. Beside each word, write what part of speech it is.

noun 1. Hamburgers were cooking on the grill.
adj. 2. Gail keeps her jewelry in a blue box.
pron. 3. I need a ride to town.
adv. 4. Luis smiled warmly at his friends.
interj. 5. Never! I wouldn't jump from here!
conj. 6. Tracy and Chuck can't keep secrets.
prep. 7. Vinnie peered at the sky through a telescope.

should be followed by exclamation marks.

2. You may wish to do Exercise A on pages 463–464 with the class. Assign and discuss Exercise B on page 464.

Individualizing the Lesson

Less-Advanced Students

To be sure that the students remember the meaning of each part of speech, have them define each part orally and give an example of each. If students are still having difficulty after this review, have them write out the definition of each part of speech to use as a reference.

Advanced Students

One word is missing in each of the sentences below. Students are to fill in a word that makes the sentence complete and then write the part of speech of that word.

(Answers will vary.)

1. Did you _____ your paper?
2. The bottles were put _____ the table.
3. Marsha's _____ bracelet is lost.
4. Paul _____ I are working on this project together.
5. _____! The bathtub is over flowing!
6. Do you have any _____?

Optional Practice

Put this exercise on a worksheet. Have students underline the words called for in each sentence.

nouns

1. My mother baked cookies, breads, and rolls for the sale.
2. Pistons, rods, and cylinders are parts of engines.

pronouns

1. We went with Bob and her to see the tennis match.
2. Kim and she roller skated to school with Carol and him.

verbs

1. Yolanda danced and sang at the talent show.
2. The scientists tested the invention and were eager for the results.

adjectives

1. The shiny, silver train roared past the old station.
2. Sensors detected a large monster.

adverbs

1. The dolphins swam slowly and evenly through the water.
2. The children jumped up and down.

prepositions

1. In the valley, the cows in the field rested contentedly in the shade.
2. Around the corner and on the other side of the street is a store.

conjunctions

1. The alligator and the crocodile have large and frightening teeth.
2. Luis and John said they would ride or walk with us to the drugstore.

interjections

1. Yes! Now I see how you did it.
2. Oh! No! Never! Don't ask again!

Part 2

Objective

To recognize the use of a single word as different parts of speech

Presenting the Lesson

1. Read and discuss pages 464–465. Ask students to give sentences using each word in two ways:

claim dance paper water wall

noun 8. *The Farmer's Almanac* predicts the weather.

adv. 9. The tiger moved suddenly into sight.

noun 10. Our group climbed sand dunes all morning.

B. Follow the directions for Exercise A.

Interj. 1. Oh, no! It's raining.

pron. 2. Do you remember your dreams?

prep. 3. Hans is worried about the math test.

adv. 4. Later we will have a sing-along.

noun 5. Too many people crowded onto the bus.

adj. 6. These lights warn of approaching trains.

adj. 7. Lisa's birthday cake had twelve candles.

conj. 8. You can get candy or gum from the machine.

verb 9. The arrow hit the bullseye.

prep. 10. A water snake skimmed across the pond.

Part 2 Using Words as Different Parts of Speech

You cannot tell what part of speech a word is until you see how the word is used in a sentence. Many words can be used as different parts of speech.

In **Section 10,** you learned that the same word could be used as either an adverb or a preposition. Read this pair of sentences:

Climb up.

(In this sentence, *up* is an adverb. It modifies the verb *climb.*)

Climb up the ladder.

(Here, *up* is a preposition. Its object is the noun *ladder.*)

Other words may be used as different parts of speech. Here are more examples for you to study.

Please clear the table.
(Here, *clear* is used as a verb.)

The day was clear and sunny.
(And here, *clear* is used as a predicate adjective. It follows the linking verb *was* and it describes the noun *day*.)

Farmers plant wheat in the spring.
(In this sentence, *plant* is used as a verb.)

This plant grows best in light, sandy soil.
(In this sentence, *plant* is used as a noun.)

My father is a plant foreman.
(Here, *plant* is used as an adjective. It describes the noun *foreman*.)

I feel very well.
(Here, *well* is used as a predicate adjective. It follows the linking verb *feel* and describes the pronoun *I*.)

You skate very well.
(In this sentence, *well* is an adverb. It describes the action verb *skate* by telling *how*.)

When a word is used as a certain part of speech, it follows the rules for that part of speech. For example, when you use *plant* as a noun, you form the plural by adding *-s: plants*. When you use it as a verb, you form the past tense by adding *-ed: planted*.

There is only one sure way to decide what part of speech a word is. Check to see how the word is used in the sentence.

Exercises Recognize the part of speech.

A. In each pair of sentences that follows, one word is used as two different parts of speech. Number your paper from 1 to 10. After each number, write *a.* and *b.* After each letter, write the word in italics and tell how it is used. It may be a noun, a verb, an adjective, an adverb, or a preposition.

1. a. I *brush* (verb) my hair. b. This *brush* (noun) is plastic.
2. a. *Name* (verb) your favorite foods. b. What's your *name* (noun)?
3. a. The bus turned *around* (adv.). b. Joggers run *around* (prep.) the block.

2. It is suggested that you do Exercise A on pages 465–466 with the class. Assign and discuss Exercise B on page 466.

Individualizing the Lesson

Less-Advanced Students

As an in-class exercise, have the students make up two sentences for each of the words below. In the first sentence they should use the word as a noun, and in the second they should use it as a verb. Write the sentences on the chalkboard for reinforcement.

1. cry	4. cook
2. turn	5. call
3. kick	6. ring

Advanced Students

Reinforce the idea that a single word may be used different ways. Have the students look up the word *top* in the dictionary. Then have someone read the definitions of *top* noting the three different parts of speech. Have the students make up a sentence for each use. Then have the students come up with as many words as they can that are used as two or more parts of speech.

Optional Practice

Have the students follow the directions for Exercise A using the following sentences.

N 1. a. The *strike* has lasted for three weeks.
Adj b. A *strike* vote was taken last night.
V c. *Strike* the match quickly.
N 2. a. A lawyer knows how to draw up a *will*.
V b. *Will* you help wash the car?
Adj c. I have no *will* power when it comes to dessert.

V 3. a. I helped Dad *tar* the driveway.

Adj b. Have you visited the *tar* pits in Los Angeles?

N c. Michelle got *tar* on her shoes.

Adj 4. a. The *back* cover of this book is missing.

N b. I hurt my *back* playing football.

Adv c. Move *back*, please.

N 5. a. When does the *cast* on your arm come off?

V b. The sculptor *cast* the statue in bronze.

Adj c. After the play there was a great *cast* party.

V 6. a. I *wish* it would snow.

Adj b. A catalogue is sometimes called a *wish* book.

N c. Close your eyes and make a *wish*.

Extending the Lesson

Have students look in some of their other texts or in other books or magazines and list at least ten words. Next to each word, have them write what part of speech the word was used as. They should end up with examples of all eight parts of speech.

4. a. The store is *open* [adj.]. b. *Open* [verb] this box.
5. a. *Place* [verb] the book on the desk. b. Where is a quiet *place* [noun]?
6. a. She must take the *late* [adj.] bus. b. The speaker arrived *late* [adv.].
7. a. Carol fixed a *light* [adj.] snack. b. Turn on the *light* [noun].
8. a. Hold your arms *high* [adv.]. b. *High* [adj.] waves hit the ship.
9. a. A motorbike zoomed *past* [adv.]. b. I rode *past* [prep] your house.
10. a. *Flag* [verb] down that car. b. Which *flag* [noun] is blue and green?

B. Follow the directions for Exercise A.

1. a. We have a *color* [adj.] TV. b. What *color* [noun] is this?
2. a. The *last* [adj.] act is best. b. Which float comes *last* [adv.]?
3. a. Rita has a new *watch* [noun]. b. I *watch* [verb] the news every night.
4. a. Sunday was a *fine* [adj.] day. b. Does the judge *fine* [verb] people?
5. a. It's time for a *rest* [noun]. b. Horses *rested* [verb] in the stable.
6. a. I asked for *more* [adj.] milk. b. Jody practices *more* [adv.] often than Ed.
7. a. The young boys dashed *off* [adv.]. b. Randy flipped *off* [prep.] the balance beam.
8. a. The ship *sails* [verb] soon. b. One *sail* [noun] was ripped.
9. a. We followed a *dirt* [adj.] path. b. *Dirt* [noun] covered the floors.
10. a. A small cart trailed *behind* [adv.]. b. The cat lay *behind* [prep.] a bush.

ADDITIONAL EXERCISES

The Parts of Speech

Parts of Speech Read each sentence. Write the underlined words. Then write what part of speech each of those words is.

Prep. 1. Rena stuffed her notebook <u>into</u> a backpack.
Noun 2. Our entire class flew <u>kites</u> on the beach.
Adj. 3. That movie was the <u>true</u> story of the discovery of radium.
Noun 4. The <u>treasure</u> was hidden underwater.
Adj. 5. <u>Three</u> trees were uprooted during the tornado.
Prep. 6. Allen found his friends <u>at</u> the baseball park.
Pron. 7. Adam learned to type when <u>he</u> was ten.
Conj. 8. We can reach the island by plane <u>or</u> ferry.
Interj. 9. <u>Hooray!</u> School's out for the summer!
Adj. 10. <u>That</u> campground has been closed since the dam burst.
Interj. 11. <u>Help!</u> This boat is sinking!
Noun 12. <u>Maggie</u> removed the horse's saddle.
Verb 13. <u>Did</u> anybody <u>bring</u> the hot dog buns?
Verb 14. The cowhand finally <u>roped</u> the steer.
Adv. 15. A hot-air balloon drifted <u>slowly</u> above the countryside.
Adv. 16. The boat sailed <u>away</u>.
Conj. 17. The newsstand sells magazines <u>and</u> comic books.
Adj. 18. What are the <u>key</u> issues in the campaign?
Adv. 19. Finally, the storm blew <u>over</u>.
Verb 20. Jamie <u>tossed</u> a pillow at her brother.
Adj. 21. Give <u>this</u> letter to Mr. Scott.
Pron. 22. Can we help <u>them</u> with their work?
Adv. 23. You left the car door <u>open</u>.
Adj. 24. They attended a <u>music</u> festival.
Verb 25. <u>Do</u> you <u>shop</u> at the new mall in Hazeltown?

Additional Exercises

These Additional Exercises may be used for additional practice of the concepts presented in this Section. Each exercise focuses on a single concept, and should be used after the page number indicated in parentheses.

Review

If you have not assigned these Additional Exercises before this time, you can also use them as an excellent Section Review.

467

Mixed Review

These exercises provide review of the concepts presented in this Section. Each exercise challenges the students to apply several of the skills they have acquired during previous study. Because the "mixed" feature of these activities makes them more difficult, the teacher may wish to have less-advanced students do them orally or in small groups.

MIXED REVIEW

The Parts of Speech

Identifying the parts of speech Write the underlined word or words in each of the following sentences. Then write its part of speech.

Adv. 1. She climbed cautiously up the stairs to the dark attic.
Verb 2. Mom caught three rainbow trout.
Interj. 3. No way! I washed the dishes last night.
Prep. 4. Scott can swim under water for two minutes.
Noun 5. These jeans are too short for me.
Adj. 6. Karla has brown eyes and wavy black hair.
Conj. 7. They are going to Tennessee and Kentucky during their vacation.
Pron. 8. He can sit in the back with his friends.
Noun 9. Marc planted twenty tulip bulbs last fall.
Adj. 10. Kit's bike needs a new chain.
Prep. 11. The runner slid into third base.
Pron. 12. We met them after the concert.
Conj. 13. The store will reopen in September or October.
Adv. 14. All the water leaked out.
Verb 15. We were lost without a map.
Adj. 16. Patti is fourteen years old.
Prep. 17. Liz can only babysit during the day.
Interj. 18. Wow! I can't wait until Saturday.
Conj. 19. She hurried but missed the bus.
Noun 20. Dad refinished this old rocking chair.

468

USING GRAMMAR IN WRITING

Using Parts of Speech

A. Read the following advertisement. Notice the underlined words in it. Make a list of those words and write the part of speech of each word as it is used in the advertisement.

> You will love the new Mighty Bike! Its design is outstanding. Its wheels grip the hills. It climbs faster and performs better than any other dirt bike. Mighty Bike has power, speed, and control. Stop in today at your nearest bike shop to test drive it!

Now, choose any five words from the list. Use each word in a sentence.

B. Many people, especially poets, enjoy playing with words. They like to rhyme words. They also like to use words in different ways—as different parts of speech, for example. Here are two lists of rhyming words. Choose one of the lists and write a four-line poem. Each line should end with one of the rhyming words. Write the part of speech of each rhyming word you use.

Now, write one sentence for each of the rhyming words you used. Write what part of speech each rhyming word is used as in each sentence.

brick	glow
kick	slow
trick	hoe
pick	low
sick	row
tick	show

Using Grammar in Writing

These challenging and enjoyable activities allow the students to see how the concepts of grammar, usage, and mechanics may be applied in actual writing situations. Each exercise is designed to allow students practice in several of the skills they have acquired in this Section. The activities also provide opportunities for students to write creatively about a wide variety of interesting and unusual subjects.

469

Cumulative Review

These exercises are designed to cover broad areas of grammar, usage, and mechanics. They require the application of skills taught thus far in the text. The exercises may be used for testing purposes, or as an excellent resource for review.

CUMULATIVE REVIEW

The Parts of Speech

A. Identifying parts of speech There are twenty underlined words in the following paragraph. Decide what part of speech each word is used as. Number your paper from 1 to 20. Write *Noun, Verb, Pronoun, Adjective, Adverb, Preposition,* or *Conjunction* for each word. Be sure to check *how* the word is used in the sentence.

A new water event (1, noun) was introduced at (2, prep.) the 1984 Summer Olympics in (3, prep) Los Angeles. This exciting sport is called (4, verb) boardsailing. A small (5, adj.), colorful sail is attached to an ordinary (6, adj.) surfboard. The boardsailor (7, noun) must hold the sail (8, noun), control her direction, and stay up (9, adv.). Wind and water provide (10, verb) the fun (11, noun) and challenge. Boardsailing is not very (12, adv.) difficult to learn, but (13, conj.) it (14, pro.) is necessary to have an instructor (15, noun). Anyone who weighs (16, verb) sixty-five pounds or (17, conj.) more can learn this sport. If you (18, pro.) are interested, be prepared for many dunkings. Boardsailors say you must fall (19, verb.) five hundred times before you master the (20, adj.) technique!

B. Recognizing how words are used Each of the following sentences contains an underlined word. Decide how that word is used. Number your paper from 1 to 15. Write *Subject, Verb, Direct Object, Object of the Preposition, Predicate Noun,* or *Predicate Adjective* to show what each word is.

1. Patti asked a difficult question. (DO)

470

2. After the party, the cleanup committee [S] began its work.
3. Ron performed [V] several card tricks.
4. Sandra's hair becomes lighter [PA] in the sun.
5. Jenna's dog is a Shelty [PN].
6. Our class found several fossils [DO] in the rock.
7. Has your film [S] been developed yet?
8. The trees behind the barn are silver maples [PN].
9. We [S] visited the Okefenokee swamp.
10. The farmers are hoping [V] for more rain.
11. Ms. Beck showed us a film [DO] about first aid.
12. The river looks clean [PA] and clear.
13. The hurricane raged [V] for five days.
14. Todd is usually tired after hockey practice [OP].
15. Nicola is Luke's sister [PN].

471

Section Objectives

1. To understand and apply the rules for making the subject and the verb agree

2. To use correct forms of verbs with problem subjects

Preparing the Students

Discuss the fact that the subject and the verb are the most important parts of the sentence. It is important that they should be put together correctly to avoid confusion.

List these words on the board:

mechanic / mechanics	repair, repairs
governor / governors	agree, agrees
artist / artists	draw, draws

Ask students to match the correct verbs with the nouns, and see if they can distinguish the pattern for singular subjects + singular verb forms, and plural subjects + plural verb forms. Read and discuss the introduction on page 472.

Additional Resources

Mastery Test — pages 56–57 in the test booklet

Additional Exercises — pages 483–486 in the student text

Practice Book — pages 183–189

Duplicating Masters — pages 183–189

Special Populations — See special section at the front of this Teacher's Edition.

Making Subjects and Verbs Agree

Do these sentences sound correct to you?

> The ham sandwich are good.
> One star shine in the sky.
> My friends is coming with me.
> Many families goes on vacations.

If you listen carefully, these four sentences should sound incorrect to you. Each one of them breaks a basic rule of English grammar: The subject and verb in a sentence must agree.

Part 1 Rules for Making the Subject and Verb Agree

When a noun or pronoun names one thing, it is **singular** in number.

friend bus country he

When a noun or pronoun names more than one thing, it is **plural** in number.

friends buses countries they

Verbs, too, can be singular or plural in number. An *s* at the end of a verb shows that the verb is singular in number.

sings crawls speaks

If there is no *s* at the end of the verb, the verb is plural in number.

sing crawl speak

When a subject noun or pronoun in a sentence is singular, the verb in that sentence must also be singular. If the subject noun or pronoun is plural, the verb must be plural. When the subject and the verb in a sentence are both singular or both plural, the subject and verb are said to **agree in number.**

Read these examples:

Singular	**Plural**
Jane sings in the choir.	Some **girls sing** alto parts.
The **baby crawls** everywhere.	Most **babies crawl.**
Al speaks Spanish.	Those **boys speak** French.

Remember these rules:

1. The subject and verb in a sentence must agree in number.
2. If the subject is singular, use the singular form of the verb.
3. If the subject is plural, use the plural form of the verb.

Part 1

Objective

To understand and apply the rules for making the subject and the verb agree

Presenting the Lesson

1. Read and discuss pages 473–474. Point out that agreement problems occur primarily in the present tense. Emphasize the *-s* ending as the mark of the singular form of regular verbs.

2. Assign and discuss Exercises A and B on pages 474–475.

3. Read and discuss page 475. Put the following chart on the board and discuss it.

	Singular	Plural
Present Tense	is has does	are have do
Past Tense	was had did	were had did

Discuss also the negative contractions of the words on the chart: *isn't, hasn't*, etc. Ask the students which of the verbs and negative contractions may be used with *he, she, we,* and *they*.

4. Assign and discuss Exercises A and B on pages 475–476.

Individualizing the Lesson

Less-Advanced Students

Point out to the students that the most common problem in agreement is discovering the subject of the verb. It is often separated from the verb. Give the students the following sentences and have them state the verb and then the subject.

1. The feathers in the hat were red.
2. Your supplies for your art classes have arrived.
3. Men in uniform led the parade.
4. Those pieces of cake are stale.
5. The key to all of these locks is missing.
6. The tusks of the elephant are made of ivory.

Advanced Students

Have the students write eight sentences describing occupations using the following words: *is, are, was, were, do, does, have, has.*

Optional Practice

1. Have the students choose the correct word from the two in parentheses.

1. A swarm of mosquitoes (were, was) in our yard last night.
2. Ellie and I (was, were) almost eaten alive.
3. Our town (don't, doesn't) have a spraying program.
4. Those bugs (have, has) a way of destroying a party.
5. However, several cans of bug spray usually (do, does) the trick.
6. (Have, Has) you or Alex ever heard of liquid air?
7. It (has, have) a temperature of −315°F.
8. Bottles of liquid air (is, are) too cold to handle.
9. Liquid air (look, looks) like boiling water.
10. Scientists in a laboratory (uses, use) liquid air to freeze things.

Prepositional Phrases After the Subject

Be careful with prepositional phrases that come between the subject and the verb. Remember, the verb must agree in number *only* with the subject. The subject of the verb is never found in a prepositional phrase.

Read this sentence. Which verb would you choose?

The members of the team (practices, practice) every day.

In this sentence, *members* is the subject of the verb. *Of the team* is just a prepositional phrase describing *members*. Because *members* is plural in number, the verb must also be plural in number. *Practice* is the correct verb for this sentence.

The members of the team *practice* every day.

Here's another example. Which verb would you choose?

A flock of geese (visits, visit) this lake each spring.

In this sentence, *flock* is the subject of the verb. *Of geese* is just a prepositional phrase describing *flock*. Because *flock* is singular in number, the verb must also be singular in number. *Visits* is the correct verb for this sentence.

A flock of geese *visits* this lake each spring.

Exercises Recognize singular and plural forms.

A. On your paper, write the subjects listed below. After each subject, write *Singular* or *Plural* to tell whether it will take the singular or the plural form of the verb.

S 1. typewriter	S 6. lesson
P 2. kittens	S 7. menu
S 3. ambulance	P 8. members
P 4. ravens	P 9. teachers
P 5. fingers	S 10. treehouse

B. Write the subject and verb in each sentence. Write whether they are singular or plural.

S 1. The movie shows a strange creature.
S 2. This truck rides well over dirt roads.
S 3. Today's newspaper contains a good editorial.
P 4. The books on the bookcase fell.
S 5. A box of apples sits in the corner.
P 6. The nurses in the hospital work hard.
S 7. One package of raisins lasts all week.
P 8. Monica's parents camp frequently in Yellowstone.
P 9. The girls on our block play basketball after school.
S 10. A string of firecrackers makes a loud noise.

Special Forms of Certain Verbs

A few verbs have special forms that you should keep in mind.

Is, Was, Are, Were. The verb forms *is* and *was* are singular. The forms *are* and *were* are plural.

Singular: The bus *is* here. The bus *was* here.
Plural: Our buses *are* here. Our buses *were* here.

Has, Have. The verb form *has* is singular. *Have* is plural.

Singular: Paula *has* a plan.
Plural: They *have* a plan.

Does, Do. The verb form *does* is singular. *Do* is plural.

Singular: Joe *does* the cooking.
Plural: They *do* the cooking.

Exercises Use the correct verb.

A. Write the correct verb from the two given.

1. New York City (has, have) a large population.
2. Every Sunday my family (have, has) a big breakfast.
3. The travelers (has, have) a lot of luggage.

2. Have the students correct the verb in the following sentences.

1. They always was [were] a crazy bunch.
2. Practical jokes of any kind has [have] been their specialty.
3. I, for one, doesn't [don't] like that kind of humor.
4. People always is [are] getting hurt by them.
5. You, I hope, has [have] more sense.
6. Games of skill is [are] fun to play.
7. We all has [have] fun playing checkers.
8. It really do [does] liven up a party.

Extending the Lesson

1. Put the following exercise on the board or on a worksheet. Have students write the correct present tense form of the verb next to the nouns underneath.

1. *cook*	2. *do*
cooks the pizza	does an elephant
cook we	does Superman
cook men	do machines
cooks your aunt	does milk
cook children	do pictures
3. *has*	4. *is*
have schools	is Arnie
has my teacher	are they
has a bus	are cars
have glasses	is the insurance
have verbs	are companies
5. *travel*	6. *ring*
travel people	rings the mail carrier
travel geese	rings the bell
travels a jet	ring we
travel rockets	rings my neighbor
travel my cousins	rings the girl

2. Have the students copy the following *Subject* column from the board, or distribute it on a worksheet. Tell students to underline the subject in each phrase, chose a verb from the *Verb* column that will complete it, and write the verb next to the phrase.

(A verb may be used more than once.) Caution students to distinguish the subject nouns from the nouns in the prepositional phrases.

(Verbs will vary.)

Subjects	Verbs
1. the champion weightlifter	provide, provides
2. the rain in the desert	cost, costs soak, soaks
3. the statues in the garden	
4. the clothes in the washer	
5. the lakes of the earth	
6. the rings in the window	

Part 2

Objective

To use correct forms of verbs with problem subjects

Presenting the Lesson

1. Read and discuss pages 476–477. Point out that in the words *everyone* and *anyone* is the singular word *one*, and in the words *everybody* and *nobody* is the singular word *body*.

2. It might be helpful to do Exercise A on page 477 with the class. Assign and discuss Exercise B.

4. Notre Dame (was, were) ahead at the half.
5. Franklin (does, do) his homework after school.
6. This ice-cream shop (has, have) twenty flavors.
7. Jan's left leg (is, are) in a cast.
8. These carpenters (does, do) a good job.
9. (Is, Are) calculators always right?
10. The winners of the tournament (is, are) proud.

B. Follow the directions for Exercise A.

1. Runners usually (does, do) warm-up exercises.
2. (Does, Do) the gymnasts use the rings?
3. Jerry (does, do) a great Eddie Murphy imitation.
4. The crate of oranges (is, are) heavy.
5. The waves in the Pacific (is, are) best for surfing.
6. This stack of letters (has, have) no addresses.
7. The bags by the door (has, have) gifts inside.
8. The dogs (is, are) in the kennel.
9. This batch of brownies (does, do) taste good.
10. Those pinball machines (was, were) fun to play.

Part 2 Special Problems with Subjects

Sometimes making subjects and verbs agree can be a little difficult. Some subjects are tricky to use. You can learn to use these tricky subjects with the correct verbs.

Certain Pronouns

The words listed below are singular pronouns. Each is used with a singular verb form.

each	either	everyone	anyone
one	neither	everybody	nobody

Read these sentences several times until they sound correct and natural to you.

Each of my sisters *sings* well.
One of the gymnasts *is practicing.*
Is either of you *coming?*
Neither of the stories *is* long.
Everyone does homework.
Is anyone home?
Nobody leaves early.

Be especially careful when a singular pronoun is used as a subject followed by a prepositional phrase. If the object of the preposition is plural, don't make the mistake of using a plural verb form. Remember, the verb must agree *only* with the subject.

Neither of the cars (is, are) new.
What is the complete subject? *Neither of the cars*
What is the prepositional phrase? *of the cars*
What is the subject? *Neither*
Neither is singular, so the verb must be singular.
Neither of the cars *is* new.

Exercises Use the right verb form.

A. Copy these sentences, choosing the right form of the verb from the two given in parentheses. Circle the prepositional phrase that comes between the subject and the verb.

Example: Neither of the movies (were, was) good.

Neither (of the movies) was good.

1. Neither (of the bikes) (works, work) well.
2. One (of the library books) (are, is) overdue.
3. Either (of those routes) (is, are) fast.
4. Each (of the pets) (need, needs) special care.
5. Everyone (in our class) (like, likes) a good joke.

3. Read and discuss page 478. You may find it helpful to review Handbook Section 6, Part 2.

4. It is suggested that you do Exercise A on page 479 with the class. Assign and discuss Exercise B on page 479.

5. Read and discuss pages 479–480. Stress the difference in approach between a compound subject using *and* and a compound subject using *or.* Pay particular attention to the sentences using *or.*

6. It may be helpful to do Exercise A on page 480 with the class. Assign and discuss Exercise B on pages 480–481.

7. Read and discuss page 481. Point out that *I* and *you* are particular pronouns that need particular verbs.

8. Assign and discuss Exercises A and B on pages 481–482.

Individualizing the Lesson

Less-Advanced Students

You should do Exercise A in each section aloud with the students to spot problem areas. Have the students state the simple subject and simple verb after each sentence is completed.

Advanced Students

Have the students make up ten imaginary newspaper headlines using the pronouns on page 476. Remind them to be sure that the subject and verb agree.

Examples:
Someone Will Win World Series!
Nobody Watches Six O'Clock News!
One of the States Is Missing!

Optional Practice

1. Have the students choose the correct verb and underline the simple subject in each of the following sentences.

1. Neither of these cakes (was, were) made with sugar.
2. Each of them (is, are) delicious.
3. There (is, are) many different ways to cut down on sweets.
4. You don't (have, has) to use any added sugar on foods.
5. Fruits and cheese (makes, make) excellent snacks.
6. Here (are, is) a list of nutritious foods.
7. (Does, Do) anyone enjoy getting cavities?
8. Too many sweets and not enough brushing (causes, cause) tooth decay.
9. I really (has, have) changed my eating habits.
10. Everyone in the world (need, needs) to be aware of what he or she eats.

2. Put the words below on index cards. Put the cards in a box and have each of the students take one. (You may need to make more cards or duplicates.) Ask one of the questions listed on page 479 and have students respond in complete sentences using the words on their cards as subjects.

Words for cards:

each of the boys	Jake and Willie
one of the girls	I
either of the twins	you
neither of my sisters	nobody
everyone	everybody
anyone	Maria and I
Sarah and Julie	You and Joe

6. Either (of these radios) (works, work) well.
7. Neither (of the magazines) (has, have) poetry.
8. One (of the clues) (leads, lead) to the treasure.
9. Everyone (on the horses) (ride, rides) well.
10. Each (of the players) (try, tries) hard.

B. Choose the right form of the verb for each sentence and write it.

1. Everybody on the bus (get, gets) off at Maple Avenue.
2. One of the phones (is, are) always busy.
3. Everyone in the cafeteria (eat, eats) with friends.
4. Each of the speed-skaters (deserve, deserves) to win.
5. Each of the boys (carve, carves) wooden figures.
6. Either of the computers (prints, print) out responses.
7. Everybody in the art studio (studies, study) drawing.
8. Neither of the squad cars (patrol, patrols) this area.
9. Everybody in the stands (cheers, cheer) loudly.
10. Neither of the radios (have, has) a powerful sound.

There Is, Where Is, Here Is

Many sentences begin with *There, Where,* or *Here.* These words are never subjects. In sentences beginning with these words, the subject usually comes after the verb.

Before you can choose the right verb form, you have to know what the subject is. You have to know whether it is singular or plural.

There are your parents. (*Parents* is the subject; the plural form *are* is correct.)

Here is the trail. (*Trail* is the subject; the singular form *is* is correct.)

Where do the dishes belong? (*Dishes* is the subject; the plural form *do belong* is correct.)

Exercises Use the right verb form.

A. Write the correct form of the verb from the two given.

1. There (is, are) no rules for this game.
2. Where (does, do) the ticket line start?
3. Here (is, are) the dugout for the players.
4. There (was, were) no boots in my size.
5. Here (is, are) my fishing license.
6. Where (is, are) the nearest phone?
7. There (is, are) scratches on that antique desk.
8. Here (is, are) the pizzas we ordered.
9. Where (is, are) the chess pieces?
10. Here (is, are) the girls' lockers.

B. Follow the directions for Exercise A.

1. Where (has, have) the salespeople gone?
2. Here (is, are) the relief pitcher.
3. There (is, are) poster paints for the project.
4. Where (does, do) your parents work?
5. Where (was, were) the President's bodyguards?
6. Where (is, are) the road to Springfield?
7. Here (is, are) the sandwiches you ordered.
8. Where (is, are) the batteries for the flashlight?
9. There (is, are) a club for model airplane buffs.
10. Here (is, are) the thief's fingerprints.

Compound Subjects

When the parts of a compound subject are joined by the conjunction *and,* use the plural form of the verb.

The *judge* and the *lawyers* **were** in a meeting.
Are my *hat* and *coat* upstairs?

Questions:

Who sings well?
Who likes coconut?
Who is going to the dance?
Who has his or her homework?
Who needs a pencil?

Extending the Lesson

Put these subjects on the board.

were 1. the office and the school
were 2. dinosaurs
was 3. I
were 4. the breads in the bakery
was 5. the report on stars and planets
was 6. everybody
were 7. neither the captain nor his men
was 8. nobody in the classes
were 9. you
was 10. anyone in movies
was 11. each of the library books
were 12. an apple and an orange
was 13. the picture of the mountains
were 14. the people in the theater
was 15. either you or I

Have the students decide which subjects can use *was* as a verb and which must use *were*.

When the parts are joined by *or, either—or,* or *neither—nor,* use the form of the verb that agrees in number with the subject noun or pronoun nearer to it.

> Tom or *Dick* **is driving.**
> Neither Aunt Ginny nor my *cousins* **are** here.
> Either ten pencils or one *pen* **costs** a dollar.

Exercises Use the right verb form.

A. Write each sentence, choosing the right form of the verb from the two given in parentheses. If a conjunction with *or* or *nor* is used in the subject, circle the part of the compound subject nearer the verb you chose.

1. Neither Kelly nor Jason (plays, play) soccer.
2. Either the roast or the potatoes (is, are) burning.
3. Neither Lee nor her sisters (wants, want) that dress.
4. Martha and her brother (speaks, speak) Norwegian.
5. Both the costumes and sets (is, are) Ben's creations.
6. Either milk or fruit juice (is, are) available.
7. Neither the stadium nor the park (holds, hold) enough fans for the championship game.
8. Either the books or the shelf (is, are) labeled wrong.
9. (Is, Are) Hal's bike and my scooter missing?
10. Neither he nor his brothers (likes, like) that program.

B. Follow the directions for Exercise A.

1. (Is, Are) the snow and ice melting?
2. Neither my dog nor my other pets (eats, eat) much.
3. Either the Scouts or another club (is, are) selling cookies.
4. Either the stereo or the records (is, are) damaged.
5. Neither the park nor the back lot (has, have) a baseball diamond.
6. Chess and checkers (is, are) similar in some ways.

7. Either Bob or his sister (has, have) the keys to the bike shed.
8. Either the head lifeguard or her assistant (sits, sit) here.
9. Neither our clothes nor our furniture (has, have) been delivered.
10. (Is, Are) candy or flowers the usual Valentine's Day gift?

Using *I*

Although *I* stands for a single person, it does not usually take a singular verb form. The only singular verb forms used with it are *am* and *was*.

I **am** the shortstop. I **was** in our garage.

Otherwise, the verb form used with *I* is the same as the plural form.

I **do** the dishes every day. I **have** a friend in Mexico.

Using *You*

The word *you* can stand for one person or for several persons. It may be either singular or plural. Whether it is singular or plural, always use the plural verb form with the pronoun *you*.

You **were** the only *person* with a bike.
You **were** the only *students* in the hall.

Exercises Use the right verb form.

A. Write the correct verb form from those given.

1. You (was, were) the biggest vote-getter.
2. I (is, are, am) watching a TV special on China.

3. I (makes, make) candles and paper flowers in craft class.
4. (Was, Were) you courteous to all of the customers?
5. (Has, Have) you tried bagels and cream cheese?
6. After everyone left, I (was, were) lonely.
7. You (was, were) nervous before the exam on Monday.
8. You (has, have) a fine stamp collection.
9. I (was, were) sad when my best friend moved away.
10. I (draws, draw) cartoons for the school paper.

B. Follow the directions for Exercise A.

1. I (was, were) a crossing guard last year.
2. (Is, Are) you hungry after our long hike?
3. You (makes, make) delicious fudge.
4. I (am, is) cold after shoveling all that snow.
5. (Has, Have) you read *Johnny Tremain?*
6. With that hat on, you (looks, look) silly.
7. Greg, you always (loses, lose) your ticket.
8. On Mondays I (takes, take) the train into the city.
9. I (am, is, are) using my new hockey stick.
10. During the last game, you (was, were) the dealer.

482

ADDITIONAL EXERCISES

Making Subjects and Verbs Agree

A. Making Subjects and Verbs Agree Write the correct form of the verb for each sentence.

1. Our albums (contains, contain) many photos.
2. TV detectives always (solves, solve) the crime.
3. This sports story (quotes, quote) our coach.
4. The hand brakes on my bike (sticks, stick).
5. This bunch of wildflowers (comes, come) from the woods.
6. The booth for refreshments (stands, stand) behind the fence.
7. The lions at the zoo (is, are) fed at two o'clock.
8. A swarm of ants (has, have) raided our picnic.
9. (Does, Do) this book of ghost stories scare you?
10. This pair of skates (does, do) not fit.

B. Using Problem Subjects Write the correct form of the verb for each subject.

1. Each of my shirts (is, are) dirty.
2. Neither of the skis (has, have) been waxed.
3. Everybody in the cast (likes, like) the director.
4. There (is, are) several days of vacation this month.
5. Here (is, are) the deepest snowdrifts.
6. Coffee and some colas (contains, contain) caffeine.
7. Neither the showers nor the pool (is, are) heated.
8. Either rain or high winds (has, have) delayed the flight.
9. I (believes, believe) that flying saucers do exist.
10. You (was, were) the strongest hitter on the team.

Additional Exercises

These Additional Exercises may be used for additional practice of the concepts presented in this Section. Each exercise focuses on a single concept, and should be used after the page number indicated in parentheses.

Review

If you have not assigned these Additional Exercises before this time, you can also use them as an excellent Section Review.

Mixed Review

These exercises provide review of the concepts presented in this Section. Each exercise challenges the students to apply several of the skills they have acquired during previous study. Because the "mixed" feature of these activities makes them more difficult, the teacher may wish to have less-advanced students do them orally or in small groups.

MIXED REVIEW

Making Subjects and Verbs Agree

Making subjects and verbs agree Copy each of the following sentences. Choose the correct form of the verb from the two in parentheses. Underline the subject once and the verb twice.

1. The plants in that windowbox (need, needs) water.
2. One of my best friends (is, are) captain of the rugby team.
3. This bag of plums (weigh, weighs) one pound.
4. Everyone in my family (has, have) brown eyes.
5. Joe's cousins (live, lives) in Austin, Texas.
6. The dishes in the dishwasher (is, are) clean.
7. Nobody in our class (understand, understands) the assignment.
8. This book (has, have) less than two hundred pages.
9. Here (is, are) my medical forms.
10. My cousin and I (has, have) a secret code.
11. I (is, am) the best candidate for the office.
12. Where (is, are) your nearest neighbors?
13. (Has, Have) you seen today's headlines?
14. The girl in the yellow sweater (look, looks) like you.
15. Neither of these dresses (fits, fit) me.
16. There (is, are) some talented students in our class.
17. I (has, have) an identical twin brother.
18. You (keep, keeps) your room very neat.
19. Luis or Tony (are, is) the best qualified candidate.
20. Neither Beth nor Sara (has, have) arrived yet.

USING GRAMMAR IN WRITING

Making Subject and Verbs Agree

A. Everyone has had experiences that are embarrassing. Often those experiences seem very funny a day or a week later. Think of a time when you were embarrassed. Then see if you can remember what seemed funny about it later. Write about your experience. Use *I* to tell the story, and be sure to make all subjects and verbs agree. Then write the story again, but pretend it happened to someone else. Use *He* or *She* instead of *I*. Remember, when you change the subject of a sentence, the form of the verb may change.

B. Think of two people you know. They may be relatives, friends, or even characters in a TV series. Think about the ways they are alike and the ways they are different. Write about their similarities and differences. Use at least five of the following words as subjects. Be sure that the verb agrees with its subject in each sentence.

Each	She/He	Everyone
Both	One	The other
Neither	Nobody	They
Either	No one	Anybody

C. Write six sentences about the last day of school. Use the following words and phrases as subjects of sentences. Then label each subject and verb as either singular or plural.

1. the last day of school
2. students
3. principal
4. books of the entire class
5. school assembly
6. all of the lockers

Using Grammar in Writing

These challenging and enjoyable activities allow the students to see how the concepts of grammar, usage, and mechanics may be applied in actual writing situations. Each exercise is designed to allow students practice in several of the skills they have acquired in this Section. The activities also provide opportunities for students to write creatively about a wide variety of interesting and unusual subjects.

Cumulative Review

These exercises are designed to cover broad areas of grammar, usage, and mechanics. They require the application of skills taught thus far in the text. The exercises may be used for testing purposes, or as an excellent resource for review.

CUMULATIVE REVIEW

Usage

A. Choosing the correct word Write the correct word from the two given in parentheses.

1. Lemonade tastes (good, well) on a hot summer day.
2. (Leave, Let) the bird go when (its, it's) wing has healed.
3. You speak French very (good, well).
4. (May, Can) I use (your, you're) eraser?
5. (Their, They're) team lost a close game last Sunday.
6. This is a (good, well) day to (lie, lay) in the sun.
7. (Them, Those) kinds of books are my favorite.
8. (Its, It's) too late to call Amy.
9. (Their, They're) working on (their, they're) oral presentation.
10. The situation looked (bad, badly).

B. Using words correctly Twenty words are underlined in the following paragraph. Ten of the underlined words contain errors in the use of verbs, nouns, pronouns, adverbs, and adjectives. Ten of the words are correct. Rewrite, correcting the errors.

Martha looked sad [sadly] at her rusty old bike. Wouldn't anyone never [ever] buy it from she [her]? Ads in the paper hadn't worked. Neither had notes posted on her school's bulletin board's [boards], reading "Bike for Sale—Handywoman's Delight." It were [was] not possible to trade it in for a newest [newer] model. Al, the bike shop's owner, only excepted [accepted] bikes in working condition. Martha's bike looked badly [bad]. It needed a fresh coat of paint, a chain, and a new seat. She decided then and there to get them [those] things fixed. She sanded the front fender and plan [planned] her next ad: "Bike for Sale—Completely Remodeled".

Using Compound Sentences

Part 1 A Review of the Sentence

Throughout this book you have been studying sentences. Now is a good time to review what you have learned.

A **sentence** has two basic parts, a subject and a predicate.

Subject	Predicate
Girls	hike.
Those four girls	hike.
Those four girls	hike every summer.
Those girls from Atlanta	hike in the forest every summer.

The **subject** of a sentence tells *who* or *what* the sentence says something about. The **predicate** tells *what the subject did, what the subject is,* or *what happened to the subject.*

Section Objectives

1. To understand the definition of a simple sentence

2. To understand the definition of a compound sentence, and to use correct punctuation in a compound sentence

Preparing the Students

Review the meaning of the word *compound* (Section 1). Ask students to tell you what parts of the sentence they already know can be compound. You may also want to discuss the meaning and purpose of three main conjunctions: *and* (addition), *but* (contrast), and *or* (choice). Ask students to give you examples.

Additional Resources

Mastery Test — pages 58–59 in the test booklet

Additional Exercises — pages 494–499 in the student text

Practice Book — pages 190–193

Duplicating Masters — pages 190–193

Special Populations — See special section at the front of this Teacher's Edition.

Part 1

Objective

To understand the definition of a simple sentence

Presenting the Lesson

1. Read and discuss pages 487–488. Emphasize the idea of a simple sentence with compound parts.

2. Assign and discuss Exercises A and B on pages 488–489.

Individualizing the Lesson

Less-Advanced Students

Stress that any *part* of a sentence can be compound yet the sentence itself remains simple. Be sure that the students understand compound parts by completing the following sentences with the compound part stated. Answers will vary.

1. *Compound subject* are going to Wyoming this summer.
2. The paramedics *compound verb* the injured man's arm.
3. The custodians *compound predicate*.
4. There are *compound subject* in the next booth.
5. These dresses are *compound adjective*.
6. The boat sailed *compound adverb* into the harbor.

Advanced Students

Have the students describe in simple sentences how to get from school to their homes. They should underline any compound parts used.

Optional Practice

Have the students follow the directions for Exercise A on pages 488–489 using these sentences.

1. My aunt and uncle| visited Rome this summer.
2. They| sent several postcards to my sister and me.
3. My favorite cards| pictured the Trevi Fountain and St.Peter's Square.
4. The Swiss Guards| were marching at St. Peter's.
5. The statues and columns there| are made of marble.
6. Many people| throw coins into the Trevi Fountain for good luck.
7. I| had given my aunt three dimes.

Compound Parts of the Sentence

You have also learned that all parts of the sentence may be **compound.** That is, all the parts of the sentence may have more than one part.

Compound Subject:

Carla and *Dave* sit closest to the teacher.

Compound Verb:

Lena *has read* and *studied* all morning.

Compound Predicate:

The Earth *has one moon* and *revolves around the sun.*

Compound Direct Object:

The principal asked *Rob* and *Laura* to the meeting.

Compound Object of a Preposition:

Settlers drove the wagons across *prairies* and *deserts.*

A Definition of the Sentence

You can see that each of these example sentences expresses one main idea. These sentences, like all of those you have been studying, are called **simple sentences.**

A simple sentence is a sentence with two basic parts, subject and predicate. The subject and the predicate, or any part of the subject and predicate, may be compound.

Exercises Review simple sentences.

A. Write each sentence. Draw a vertical line between the subject and the predicate.

488

1. The planet Jupiter|has many moons.
2. The roller rink|rents skates.
3. The rings in a tree trunk|tell its age.
4. Roberto and Ken|are bowling this evening.
5. The dentist|cleans teeth and fills cavities.
6. The mice|escaped from the cage in the biology lab.
7. The people of Mexico|are proud of their culture.
8. Athena and Diana|are goddesses in Greek mythology.
9. The door to the hallway|slammed shut.
10. The school|is much larger than the library.

B. Follow the directions for Exercise A.

1. The lumberjack|cuts down trees for the sawmill.
2. Corn, tomatoes, and spinach|grow in our garden.
3. A blizzard|stopped traffic and closed the airport.
4. The space shuttle|glided to a smooth landing.
5. Yesterday's game|had two overtimes.
6. Some trains|travel over one hundred miles an hour.
7. The roads|were slippery and dangerous after the ice storm.
8. Charles Dickens|wrote stories for magazines.
9. Ellen|raked the leaves and bagged them for the trash collectors.
10. The gymnast|did flips and cartwheels on the mat.

Part 2 What Are Compound Sentences?

Sometimes two sentences are so closely related in thought that you join them together. You can join them by using the conjunctions *and, but,* and *or.* Then you have a different kind of sentence. You have a sentence with two closely related main ideas. Each main idea has its own subject and predicate. This is called a **compound sentence.**

8. Aunt Gemma|threw my coins into the fountain for me.

Extending the Lesson

Have students write the compound part of the following sentences. They should write whether the compound part is a subject, predicate, adjective, or adverb. Stress that all the sentences are simple, but each has a compound part.

Example: Carla and Juan saw camels at the zoo.
Carla and Juan—compound subject

P 1. The pencil sharpener shaves and sharpens pencils.
S 2. The hero and his enemy fought a duel early in the morning.
P 3. The pinball machines buzz loudly and show the score.
Adv 4. The pitcher threw the ball high and outside.
Adv 5. Julia drives safely and carefully.
Adj 6. The ancient and spooky castle was high on the hill.
S 7. Rubies and diamonds are birthstones.
Adj 8. Young and old fishermen entered the casting contest.
Adv 9. Cast your fishing line carefully and accurately.
S 10. Batman and Spiderman are comic book characters.

Part 2

Objective

To understand the definition of a compound sentence, and to use correct punctuation in a compound sentence

Presenting the Lesson

1. Read and discuss pages 489–490. Make sure the students notice that the chart lists subjects of the verb, not complete subjects, and verbs, not predicates. Remind them that the subject of the verb is the most important part of the complete subject, and the verb is the most important part of the predicate.

Put the chart from page 490 on the board and ask for other compound sentences to add to it. Make it clear that the two simple sentences joined in a compound sentence must have some relation to each other. A compound sentence is not merely two or more distinct sentences strung together with *and's* or other conjunctions.

2. You might find it helpful to do Exercise A on page 491 with the class. Assign and discuss Exercise B on pages 491–492.

3. Read and discuss page 492. Have students suggest examples of both long and short compound sentences.

4. It is suggested that you do Exercise A on page 492 with the class. Assign and discuss Exercises B and C.

Individualizing the Lesson

Less-Advanced Students

Remind the students that a comma is necessary in a compound sentence unless the sentence is very short. Duplicate the following sentences for the students and have them identify the compound sentences and place the comma correctly.

CS 1. I wasn't cold, but I put on my coat to go out.

Ernie Banks was elected to the Baseball Hall of Fame **and** he was thrilled.

My family arrived at the airport on time, **but** the storm delayed our flight.

The bread must be baked for one hour, **or** it will be soggy.

Now look at the parts of these compound sentences:

Subject	Verb	Conjunction	Subject	Verb
Ernie Banks	was elected	and	he	was
family	arrived	but	storm	delayed
bread	must be baked	or	it	will be

A compound sentence consists of two or more simple sentences joined together.

Why Write Compound Sentences?

Why would you want to write compound sentences? Why not use only simple sentences? You will know the answer as soon as you read this paragraph.

> I tried to water-ski last summer. I put on the water-skis. They fell off. Finally, I found the proper skis. The boat stalled. We had to get a different boat. I jumped into the water. I tried to get up on the skis. I tried at least twenty-five times. Each time I fell. At last, I succeeded. Skimming the water felt terrific. All the effort was worthwhile.

You can see that these sentences are very short and sound choppy when you read them. Many of these sentences are closely related in thought. Combined into compound sentences, they read much more smoothly.

> I tried to water-ski last summer. I put on the water-skis, but they fell off. Finally, I found the proper skis, but then the boat stalled. We had to get a different boat. I jumped into the water, and I tried to get up on the skis. I tried at least twenty-five times, but each time I fell. At last, I succeeded. Skimming the water felt terrific, and all the effort was worthwhile.

Exercises Use compound sentences.

A. Make three columns on your paper. Label them *Subject/Verb, Conjunction,* and *Subject/Verb.* Fill in the columns with the correct words from each of the following sentences.

Example: Dana went to the movie, but I stayed home.

Subject / Verb	Conjunction	Subject / Verb
Dana went	but	I stayed

1. Lori got new shoes, but they hurt her.
2. Last summer Mom grew vegetables, and we picked them daily.
3. The forest is very dry, and everyone worries about fires.
4. Tracy pumped water, and we drank it immediately.
5. The food must be eaten, or it will spoil.
6. A dog barked loudly, and it scared us away.
7. The rocket roared into life, and the flight to the moon was underway.
8. Jo Ellen used the water wings, and Kate had the inner tube.
9. Connie went to the doctor, and she had allergy tests.
10. These tickets were expensive, but the seats are terrible.

B. Follow the directions for Exercise A.

1. Wendy made the team, but she is on the second string.
2. The game was tough, and it ended in a tie.
3. Do you like hamburgers, or would you prefer a pizza?
4. Linda is very friendly, and she is always cheerful.
5. Two boats capsized, but the others reached the shore.
6. The defense is strong, but the offense is weak.
7. Katy had braces, and now her teeth are straight.

CS 2. We were all starving, but Jill had some sandwiches for us.

CS 3. The light burned out, and it was impossible to see anything.

CS 4. You stay and I'll go.

5. The mouse ran out and scared me.

CS 6. The floor was wet, and I slipped on it.

Advanced Students

Have students find examples of compound sentences in the newspaper. Have them underline the subjects and circle the verbs.

Optional Practice

1. Have students copy the following sentences. Next to each one, have students write *simple,* if it is a simple sentence, or *compound,* if it is a compound sentence. Then have them underline the subject(s) once and the verb(s) twice. They should also insert any necessary commas.

S 1. Lunch and dinner are my two favorite meals.

C 2. The ambulance sounded its siren, and cars moved over to the side of the street.

S 3. The typewriter and the computer work smoothly now.

C 4. The mail was delivered, but nothing came for Dora.

S 5. We moved out of an apartment and into a house.

C 6. I like scary movies, but my little brother dislikes them.

2. Ask students to choose a subject/verb combination from the first group of words, a conjunction from the second, and a subject/verb combination from the third. Have them put the parts together into a compound sentence, with correct punctuation. Remind them that compound sentences must contain related ideas.

Subject/Verb:

1. The message contained secret writing
2. The slumber party was a success
3. We can eat now
4. Fireflies lit up in the evening
5. The batter hit a hard ball to second base
6. We had noisemakers and balloons at the party

Conjunction:
and, but, or

Subject/Verb:
the spy broke the code.
we can order pizza later.
everyone had a good time.
we tried to catch some.
later we played games.
the runner was tagged out.

Extending the Lesson

Give the students the paragraph below and have them rewrite it using compound sentences. Tell them to combine sentences where logical, using *or, and,* or *but* and commas. Answers will vary.

We visited my friend Lee. He took us to a Chinese New Year parade. His family is from Taiwan. Lee was born in California. We left his house at seven. The buses were running late. Lee was afraid we would miss the parade. We got there on time. We were hungry. Lee suggested we buy some traditional Chinese food. The red bean popsicles we ate were delicious. The singing rice was fun to eat. I will never forget the parade. It was a wonderful way to end my trip.

8. Keith is a good actor, but he didn't get the part.
9. Do you bring your lunch, or do you buy it at school?
10. Tom rolled the bowling ball, and he scored a strike.

Punctuating Compound Sentences

Because compound sentences contain more than one idea, they can be confusing. To help the reader keep the closely related thoughts clear, put a **comma** before the conjunction in a compound sentence. The comma alerts the reader to the end of the first idea, and it prepares the reader for the second idea.

I hit the ball and my brother fielded it.
I hit the ball**,** *and* my brother fielded it.

You may leave out the comma only when the two sentences that you join are very short.

Dinner was served and we ate.
The sun shone and the birds sang.

Exercises Punctuate compound sentences.

A. Copy the following compound sentences. Add a comma wherever one is needed. Circle the conjunction that joins the parts of the sentence.

1. You must hold the lid, or the popcorn will pop out.
2. The math test is tomorrow, but I haven't studied yet.
3. The sun was hot but the breeze was refreshing.
4. Carol climbed the snowbank, and Julie followed her.
5. Down jackets are warm, and they are lightweight, too.
6. Pam met her friends in the cafeteria, and they ate together.
7. Sue lost her shoe, but she finished the race.
8. Dan shot for the goal, but he missed it by a foot.
9. Kim sawed and I hammered.
10. Did you make that glider, or did you buy it?

B. Follow the directions for Exercise A.

1. The sky was hazy, (but) I got a sunburn anyway.
2. Doors slammed (and) windows shook.
3. Sarah shaped the clay, (and) then she fired it in the kiln.
4. Mom selected the lumber, (and) she made the bookcase.
5. The helicopter landed (and) three people got out.
6. Brad enjoys math, (but) science is his favorite subject.
7. Is Gilda in the hospital, (or) has she recovered?
8. Two outfielders ran for the ball, (but) neither caught it.
9. Jeff walks to school, (and) Ramona rides her bike.
10. Candy learned some magic tricks, (and) she does them well.

C. Writing Write a paragraph about a pet. Use three compound sentences in your paragraph. Underline the subject once and the verb twice in each part of each compound sentence. Circle the conjunction that joins both parts of the sentence. Be sure to use a comma. Answers will vary.

493

Additional Exercises

These Additional Exercises may be used for additional practice of the concepts presented in this Section. Each exercise focuses on a single concept, and should be used after the page number indicated in parentheses.

Review

If you have not assigned these Additional Exercises before this time, you can also use them as an excellent Section Review.

ADDITIONAL EXERCISES

Using Compound Sentences

A. Simple Sentences Write the subjects and verbs in these simple sentences. Some parts may be compound.

(Use after page 489.)

1. Once again, Emily searched for the book.
2. Don and Liz made vases with the clay.
3. The baby squirmed and cried in the highchair.
4. Cathy played well at her piano recital.
5. Elliot closed his locker and hurried to class.

B. Compound Sentences Copy each sentence. For both parts of the compound sentence, underline the subject once and the verb twice. Then add the punctuation needed to make the sentence correct. (Use after page 493.)

1. Bill subscribes to *Tennis Monthly*, and he reads every article.
2. Sandy lives in the city, but she likes the country better.
3. One station plays jazz, but the rest play rock music.
4. Are you hungry, or have you eaten dinner?
5. The TV set is on, but nobody is watching it.
6. Dad has a moustache, and Uncle Joe has a beard.
7. First the swimmers warm up, and then they race.
8. The house is empty, but eerie sounds come from it.
9. Rain fell for days, and the rivers overflowed.
10. Hal plays chess often but he always loses.
11. I start crossword puzzles, and my sister finishes them.
12. Have you missed practice, or was it canceled?
13. The train stopped and we got off.
14. This horse is gentle, but she runs very fast.
15. The pitcher threw a curve ball, and the batter doubled.

MIXED REVIEW

Using Compound Sentences

A. Recognizing simple and compound sentences Copy each of the following sentences. If a sentence is simple, write *S*. If it is compound, write *C*. Underline the subjects once and the verbs twice. If a sentence is compound, be sure to underline both sets of subjects and verbs.

C 1. Do you walk to school, or do you take the bus?
S 2. After dinner, we all washed and dried the dishes.
S 3. Chris needs plywood and wire for his project.
C 4. Mom cut the flowers, and we arranged them in vases.
C 5. Vera addressed the envelopes, but I mailed them.
S 6. Bob sings and plays the guitar in a rock group.
C 7. This weather is beautiful, but we need rain.
C 8. Rick walks but Liz rides.
S 9. Dana and Keith learned sign language.
S 10. Kristen applied for a paper route and got one.

B. Combining sentences Combine the following pairs of simple sentences into compound sentences. Use the conjunctions *and, but,* or *or*. Punctuate them correctly.

Suggested answers are given.

1. Gail served the ball. I returned it. *Gail served the ball, and I returned it.*
2. Eric likes cats. He is allergic to them. *Eric likes cats, but he is allergic to them.*
3. You can borrow my book. You can get one from the library. *You can borrow my book, or you can get one from the library.*
4. Dennis dusted the furniture. Larry vacuumed the rug. *Dennis dusted the furniture, and Larry vacuumed the rug.*
5. Sally might buy that dress. She might make one just like it. *Sally might buy that dress, or she might make one just like it.*
6. I enjoy music. I have no talent. *I enjoy music, but I have no talent.*
7. We gave Jan a surprise party. She wasn't surprised. *We gave Jan a surprise party, but she wasn't surprised.*
8. Juan entered the photo contest. He won second prize. *Juan entered the photo contest, and he won second prize.*
9. Do you just watch sports? Do you participate? *Do you just watch sports, or do you participate?*
10. These records are old. They are in good condition. *These records are old, but they are in good condition.*

Mixed Review

These exercises provide review of the concepts presented in this Section. Each exercise challenges the students to apply several of the skills they have acquired during previous study. Because the "mixed" feature of these activities makes them more difficult, the teacher may wish to have less-advanced students do them orally or in small groups.

Using Grammar in Writing

These challenging and enjoyable activities allow the students to see how the concepts of grammar, usage, and mechanics may be applied in actual writing situations. Each exercise is designed to allow students practice in several of the skills they have acquired in this Section. The activities also provide opportunities for students to write creatively about a wide variety of interesting and unusual subjects.

USING GRAMMAR IN WRITING

Using Compound Sentences

A. Do you sometimes wish you had special powers like Superman or Superwoman? If you had special abilities, how would you use them? Write about what you would do. In your paragraph, include at least one sentence with a compound subject. Include at least one with a compound verb. Underline each compound subject once. Underline each compound verb twice.

B. You work at a Chinese fortune cookie factory. It is your job to compose the fortunes. Fortunes tell what will happen in the future. They tell about life, love, fame, fortune, health, happiness, and friendship. You must write six fortunes. Each fortune must be a compound sentence. Use *and, but,* and *or* to connect the parts of the compound sentences.

Example: You will find a great treasure, *but* you will lose it through carelessness.

C. Imagine that you have volunteered for a scientific experiment. You will be able to travel through time. You can choose where you would like to go. You could go hurtling into the future or spinning back in time. Write about the choice you make. Tell what you saw and did during your day in the past or the future. One sentence should contain a compound subject and one a compound verb. Include two compound sentences.

CUMULATIVE REVIEW
The Sentence

A. Identifying kinds of sentences Copy the following sentences. Insert the correct punctuation. After each sentence, write *D* for declarative, *INT* for interrogative, *IMP* for imperative, or *E* for exclamatory. Underline each subject once and each verb twice.

INT 1. Has the mayor arrived yet?
E 2. Water is pouring into the basement!
D 3. This flat tire cannot be repaired.
IMP 4. Fasten your seat belt. (You)
D 5. The choir sang beautifully.
INT 6. Did you lock the bikes securely?
E 7. What an unusual fish you caught!
D 8. Mark designed and built that birdhouse.
IMP 9. Read the directions on the box. (You)
E 10. There's a bear outside our tent!

B. Understanding agreement in sentences Number your paper from 1 to 15. Write the correct word from the two given in parentheses.

1. The milk in these cartons (is, are) leaking out.
2. The apartments in our building (was, were) remodeled last year.
3. Each of the students had (his or her, their) picture taken for the yearbook.
4. Here (is, are) the plates and napkins.
5. Books about history (interest, interests) Ted.
6. One of my best friends (is, are) moving to Arizona.
7. Either Sam or his brothers (knows, know) how to fix your bike.

Cumulative Review

These exercises are designed to cover broad areas of grammar, usage, and mechanics. They require the application of skills taught thus far in the text. The exercises may be used for testing purposes, or as an excellent resource for review.

8. They (don't, doesn't) understand Spanish.
9. Each of the girls chooses (her, their) own position on the team.
10. Most of Roger's poems (describe, describes) nature.
11. The squirrels buried (its, their) acorns near this tree.
12. Where (is, are) the tools for the job?
13. Have the robins returned to (their, its) nest?
14. The rose and the petunias (need, needs) more water.
15. You (is, are) the first guest here.

C. Correcting fragments and run-on sentences The following paragraph contains fragments and run-on sentences. Rewrite the paragraph. Use capitalization and punctuation to correct the fragments and run-ons. Do not add or change any words.

It seems strange to me that so many people ski. For fun and relaxation. It snows all the time. In my state. I use my skis to run errands and to deliver the newspapers on my route I also use them to get to school. The history of this sport. Proves that I am not alone. In the past, skis have been used by messengers, mail carriers, and even armies, skiing as a sport came much later. What do I do? For fun and relaxation? I sit by a blazing fire and read about warmer climates.

D. Writing good sentences Rewrite each of the following sentences. Follow the directions in the parentheses.

Some answers may vary.

Kevin writes stories about talking animals for young children.

1. Kevin writes stories for young children. (Add the prepositional phrase *about talking animals*.)
2. Lynn will play on the hockey team. She will join the basketball team. (Combine these two simple sentences into a compound sentence using **, or**.)
3. Marcella found her ring. (Add the prepositional phrase *near third base*.)

498

4. The carpenters built the new deck. (Add the prepositional phrase *on Thursday*.) On Thursday, the carpenters built the new deck.
5. Maurice Sendak wrote that book. He illustrated it. (Combine these two simple sentences into one with a compound verb.) Maurice Sendak wrote and illustrated that book.
6. Grant studied the code, but he couldn't understand it. (Combine these two simple sentences into a compound sentence using **, but**.)
7. Karen is a friendly girl. (Change this N LV N sentence into one with a N LV ADJ pattern.) Karen is friendly.
8. Anita tried to catch the ball. Scott tried, too. (Combine these two simple sentences into one with a compound subject.) Anita and Scott tried to catch the ball.
9. The cocoa is too hot to drink. (Add the prepositional phrase *in that pot*.) The cocoa in that pot is too hot to drink.
10. Sylvia cleaned yesterday. (Change this NV sentence to one with a NVN pattern.) Sylvia cleaned the house yesterday.

499

Section Objectives

1. To understand the purpose of diagraming

2. To diagram verbs and their subjects

3. To diagram subjects in unusual order

4. To diagram questions

5. To diagram imperative sentences

6. To diagram sentences with *There*

7. To diagram compound subjects and verbs

8. To diagram sentences with direct objects

9. To diagram sentences with predicate nouns

10. To diagram sentences with predicate adjectives

11. To diagram sentences with adjectives

12. To diagram sentences with possessive nouns

13. To diagram sentences with adverbs

14. To diagram compound sentences

Preparing the Students

Ask the students if they have ever seen a drawing of the inside of an engine. Explain that sentence diagrams are similar. They show how the parts of a sentence fit together, and function.

Additional Resources

Mastery Test — pages 60-61 in the test booklet

Additional Exercises — pages 516-520 in the student text

Special Populations — See special section at the front of this Teacher's Edition.

Diagraming the Sentence

Part 1 What Is Diagraming?

A **diagram** of a sentence is a picture of the parts of a sentence. A diagram shows how the parts of a sentence work together and how they are related.

When you make diagrams, you follow patterns. It is important to follow the patterns exactly. You will need to put words in the right places. You will need to make vertical lines, horizontal lines, and slanted lines. Copy words exactly as they appear in a sentence, with capital letters or without them. Do not copy any punctuation marks except the apostrophes within a word.

In this section, you will be learning how to diagram sentences. Diagraming can help you to see how the parts of a sentence work together to express an idea.

Part 2 Diagraming Verbs and Their Subjects

A sentence diagram always begins on a horizontal line. A vertical line cuts the horizontal line in two. It separates the subject from the verb. The subject is placed to the left of the line. The verb is placed to the right side of the line.

Roosters crow.

Dorothy Taylor sang.

Exercise Diagram verbs and their subjects.

Diagram the verb and its simple subject in each of the following sentences. (Ignore all other words.)

1. The jet | climbed.
2. Rhonda | hesitated.
3. The fireworks | exploded.
4. Penguins | waddle.
5. The candle | drips.
6. A rainbow | appeared.
7. The room | darkened.
8. The bus | swerved.
9. JoAnn | went to the door.
10. My book | dropped into the mud.

Presenting the Lesson

Read and discuss the explanatory material for each section with the class. You may need to review the definitions of the different types of sentences and parts of speech covered in each section. It would also be helpful to diagram on the board a few examples that the students create. Then assign the exercises.

Individualizing the Lesson

Less-Advanced Students

Be sure that the definitions and use of each part to be covered are clear to the students. Do the first half of each exercise on the board with the students. Then assign the rest of the exercise to be done by the students individually.

Advanced Students

After the students have completed the exercise in each section, have them compose five original sentences that follow the pattern of the sentence covered. They should then diagram those sentences.

Extending the Lesson

To add challenge and excitement to diagraming, have the class play *Diagraming Relays.* Divide the class into teams. Have one student from each team go to the board and write out a sentence you read. Then at the word *Go* each participant should diagram the sentence. The first to finish correctly wins three points, the second wins two points and the third wins one point. Then the next person on the team goes to the board and the race continues.

Part 1

Objective

To understand the purpose of diagraming

Presenting the Lesson

Read and discuss the material on page 500. Ask the students to compare any other sort of diagrams and patterns they can think of.

Part 2

Objective

To diagram verbs and their subjects

Optional Practice

Have the students diagram the verb and its subject in each sentence of Exercises A and B on pages 282–283.

Part 3

Objective

To diagram subjects in unusual order

Optional Practice

Have students diagram the verb and its subject in each sentence of Exercises A and B on pages 284–285. Mention that this kind of

Part 3 Diagraming Subjects in Unusual Order

In some sentences, the subject and verb are in an unusual order. Their position on a diagram, however, does not change.

Down our street came the parade.

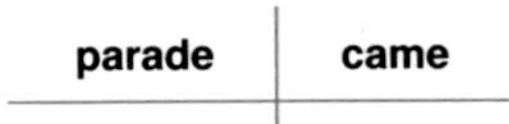

High above our heads flew the kites.

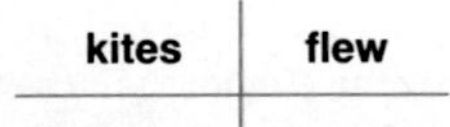

Exercise Diagram subjects in unusual order.

Diagram the subjects and verbs in the following sentences. (Ignore all other words.)

1. Around the curve came the cars. cars | came
2. Under the car hid the kitten. kitten | hid
3. In the field grazed some cows. cows | grazed
4. Onto the floor tumbled the tomatoes. tomatoes | tumbled
5. Over the beach flew the helicopter. helicopter | flew
6. Into the pool dove Sandra. Sandra | dove
7. From the woods came a deer. deer | came
8. Through the yard raced a rabbit. rabbit | raced
9. Down the street zoomed a motorcycle. motorcycle | zoomed
10. Around in circles went the Tilt-a-Whirl. Tilt-a-whirl | went

Part 4 Diagraming Questions

When you diagram a question, put the subject and verb in normal order. Remember that you capitalize only the words that are capitalized in the sentence.

Have you heard the news?

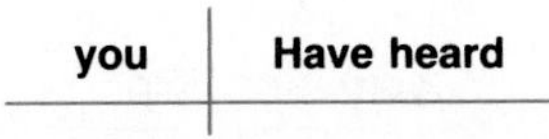

Does Jim help with the chores?

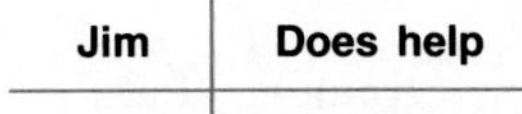

Exercise Diagram questions.

Diagram the subject and verb in each of the following questions. (Ignore all other words.)

1. Does the snake bite? snake | Does bite
2. Should we feed the cat? we | Should feed
3. Did Mary lock the gate? Mary | Did lock
4. Did you solve the mystery? you | Did solve
5. When did the fire begin? fire | did begin
6. Have you ever seen a ghost? you | Have seen
7. Do you babysit at night? you | Do babysit
8. Has the aquarium arrived? aquarium | Has arrived
9. Where are volcanos located? volcanos | are located
10. Will the runner steal third base? runner | Will steal

sentence often begins with an adverb or a prepositional phrase, and that it may be helpful to turn the sentence around mentally to *subject—verb* order.

Part 4

Objective

To diagram questions

Optional Practice

Have the students diagram the subjects and verbs of the questions in Exercises A and B on page 274. Again remind them to turn the sentence around mentally to a *subject—verb* order.

503

Part 5

Objective

To diagram imperative sentences

Optional Practice

Have the students diagram the subjects and verbs of the sentences in Exercises A and B on pages 285–286.

Part 5 Diagraming Imperative Sentences

When the subject of an imperative sentence is understood, show it on your diagram by writing (*you*).

Fold your paper in half.

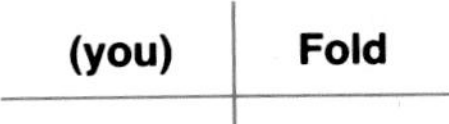

Put this gift under the tree.

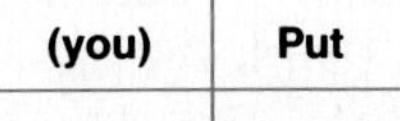

Exercise Diagram imperative sentences.

Diagram the subjects and verbs in the following imperative sentences. (Ignore all other words.)

1. Explain this problem. (you) | Explain
2. Keep that smile on your face. (you) | Keep
3. Find some more clues. (you) | Find
4. Read at your own pace. (you) | Read
5. Have a good time. (you) | Have
6. Open that old trunk. (you) | Open
7. Whisper in the library. (you) | Whisper
8. Ride your bike on the street. (you) | Ride
9. Try a new approach. (you) | Try
10. Enter through the side door. (you) | Enter

Part 6 Diagraming Sentences with *There*

There is often just an "extra" word. It is placed on a separate line above the subject in a sentence diagram.

There are twenty students in this class.

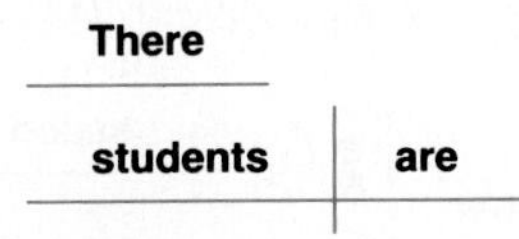

Were there many people at the dance?

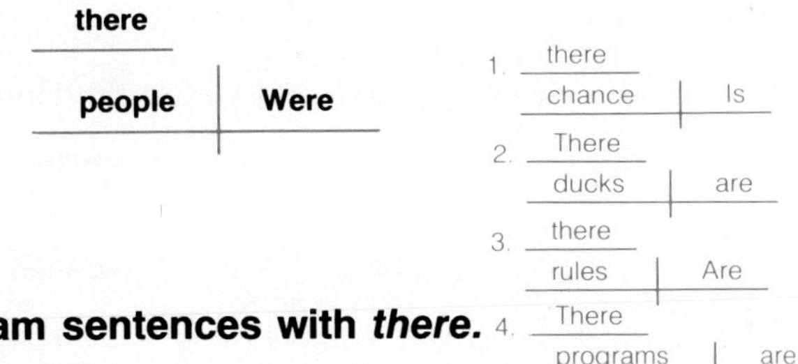

Exercise **Diagram sentences with *there*.**

Diagram the subjects and verbs in the following sentences with *there*.

1. Is there a chance of rain?
2. There are only seven ducks on the pond.
3. Are there new rules for this game?
4. There are two good programs on TV tonight.
5. There is a purpose for each lesson.
6. Were there footprints by the window?
7. There were several leaks in the ceiling.
8. There was a thunderstorm last night.
9. Are there any books on that subject?
10. Is there time for another tennis match?

5. There / purpose | is
6. there / footprints | Were
7. There / leaks | were
8. There / thunderstorm | was
9. there / books | Are
10. there / time | Is

Part 6

Objective

To diagram sentences with *There*

Optional Practice

Have the students diagram the subjects and verbs of the sentences beginning with *There* in Exercises A and B on page 374. Mention that, as a general rule, *there* is an extra word when it appears as the first or second word of a sentence. However, it is an adverb when it answers the question *where?*, as in *John sat there.* In such sentences, *there* is diagramed as an adverb; this will be covered in Part 13 of this section.

Part 7

Objective

To diagram compound subjects and verbs

Optional Practice

Have students diagram the compound subjects and verbs in Exercise A on pages 287–288, and Exercise A on page 289.

Part 7 Diagraming Compound Subjects and Verbs

To diagram the two or more parts of a compound subject, split the subject line. Put the conjunction on a connecting dotted line.

Jill and her father sailed the boat.

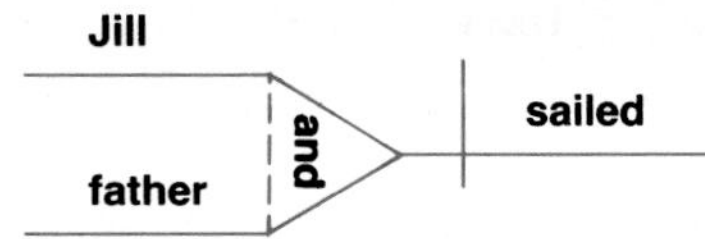

To diagram the two or more parts of a compound verb, split the predicate line. Put the conjunction on a connecting dotted line.

Sam swept, washed, and waxed the floor.

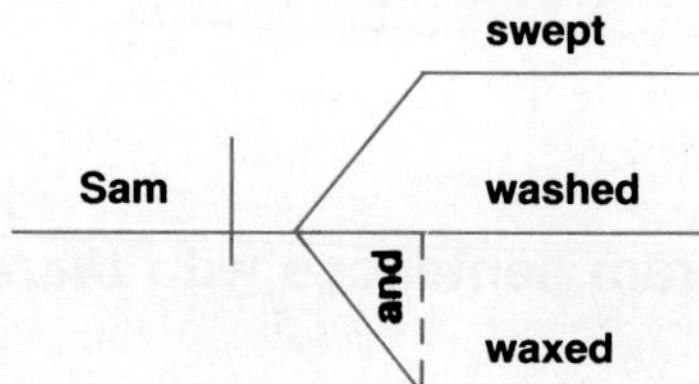

Exercise Diagram compound subjects and verbs.

Diagram the compound subjects and verbs.

See pages T17–T26 at the back of this Teacher's Edition.

1. Tara designed and built a small table.
2. Smoke and fumes pollute the air.
3. Chris waters, feeds, and prunes her plants.
4. The newscaster and sports reporter gave their reports.
5. Have Steve and Lisa visited the museum?
6. The wild animals gathered and drank at the stream.
7. There are sandwiches and fruit in the picnic basket.
8. We fished from the riverbank and caught three fish.

506

9. Toward the finish line dashed Judy and Carmen.
10. Rangers survey the forest and watch for danger.

Part 8 Diagraming Sentences Containing Direct Objects

When you diagram a sentence, place a direct object on the horizontal line following the verb. Separate it from the action verb by a vertical line that does not cut through the subject-verb line.

My parents bought a new car.

For compound direct objects, continue the horizontal line a little way beyond the verb and then split it. Make as many parallel direct-object lines as you need. Put the vertical line before the split, to show that all the words that follow are direct objects.

We met Laura, Dawn, and Billy at the bus stop.

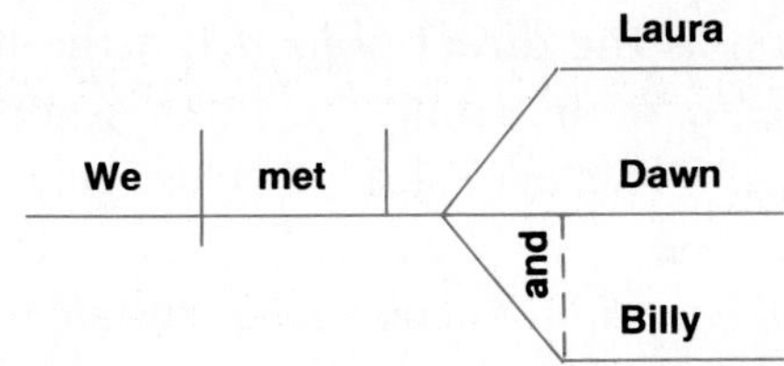

Exercise Diagram sentences containing direct objects.

Diagram the subjects, action verbs, and direct objects in these sentences. (Some direct objects may be compound.)

See pages T17–T26 at the back of this Teacher's Edition.

1. The puppy took a nap.

Part 8

Objective

To diagram sentences with direct objects

Optional Practice

Have the students diagram the subjects, verbs, and direct objects in the sentences of Exercise A on page 332.

2. He made a beautiful drawing.
3. We recycle bottles, cans, and newspapers.
4. Get a subscription to this magazine.
5. Ernest collects stamps and coins.
6. The hikers ate lunch on a hilltop.
7. Did the class plan a party?
8. Beth and Rochelle played Scrabble.
9. We bought apples, plums, and strawberries.
10. The magician hypnotized two people in the audience.

Part 9

Objective

To diagram sentences with predicate nouns

Optional Practice

Have the students diagram the subjects, verbs, and predicate nouns in the sentences in Exercises A and B on page 334. Remind them not to confuse predicate nouns and predicate adjectives.

Part 9 Diagraming Sentences Containing Predicate Nouns

The diagram for a sentence containing a predicate noun is different from that for a sentence containing a direct object.

Dr. Sarah Powers is our dentist.

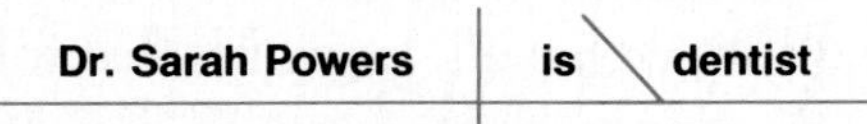

Notice that the predicate noun is on the horizontal line in the same position as the direct object. But the line that separates the predicate noun from the linking verb slants back toward the subject. This is to show its close relationship to the subject.

For sentences containing **compound predicate nouns,** use parallel lines. Put the slanting line after the verb and before the main line is split.

Duke was a good pet but a poor watchdog.

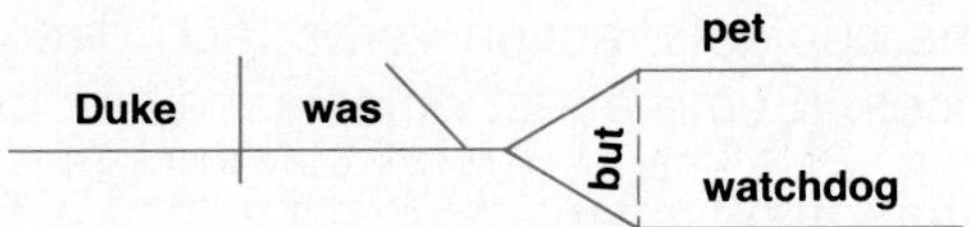

Exercise Diagram sentences containing predicate nouns.

Diagram the subjects, linking verbs, and predicate nouns in the following sentences.

See pages T17–T26 at the back of this Teacher's Edition.

1. The Pizza Palace is a new restaurant.
2. A tandem is a bicycle for two people.
3. Is Buddy the pitcher today?
4. Dolphins are mammals.
5. Are Sam and Dick best friends?
6. Spaghetti is an Italian dish.
7. Three string instruments are the violin, the cello, and the bass.
8. Two useful knots are the half-hitch and the butterfly.
9. Gwendolyn Brooks is a famous poet.
10. Ben Franklin was a writer, an inventor, and a statesman.

Part 10 Diagraming Sentences Containing Predicate Adjectives

You show predicate adjectives on diagrams just as you show predicate nouns. Place them on the horizontal line following the linking verb, and separate them from the verb by a line slanting back toward the subject.

That platform seems unsafe.

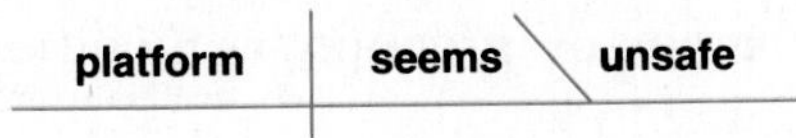

Part 10

Objective

To diagram sentences with predicate adjectives

Optional Practice

Have the students diagram the subjects, verbs, and predicate adjectives of the sentences in Exercises A and B on page 334. Remind them not to confuse predicate adjectives with predicate nouns.

For sentences with compound predicate adjectives, use parallel lines. Put the slanting line after the verb and before the main line is split.

The hikers were cold and tired.

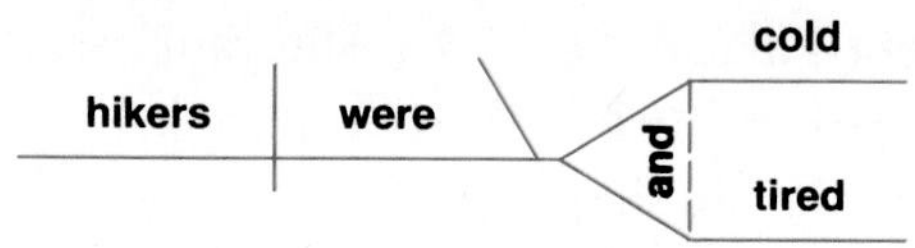

Exercise **Diagram sentences containing predicate adjectives.**

Diagram the subjects, linking verbs, and predicate adjectives in the following sentences.

See pages T17–T26 at the back of this Teacher's Edition.

1. The races were fun.
2. Diamonds are extremely hard.
3. Computers are quick and accurate.
4. Be careful.
5. My backpack is empty.
6. That watermelon is ripe, sweet, and juicy.
7. The moon is full tonight.
8. These tomatoes and cucumbers are very fresh.
9. Soccer is fast and rough.
10. Is Sherry happy in her new neighborhood?

Part 11 Diagraming Sentences Containing Adjectives

On a diagram, an adjective is shown on a line that slants down from the noun or pronoun it modifies. (Articles are shown the same way.)

Part 11

Objective

To diagram sentences with adjectives

Optional Practice

Have the students follow the directions for the Part 11 Exercise, using the sentences in Exercise A on page 422.

That new cook made a thick, lumpy gravy.

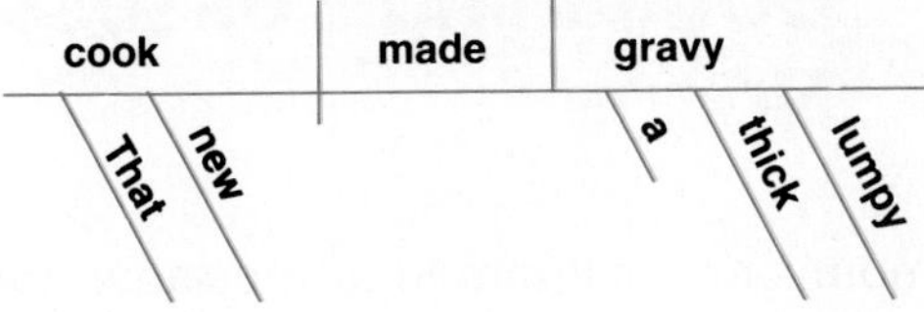

Mrs. Holmes is a patient, friendly teacher.

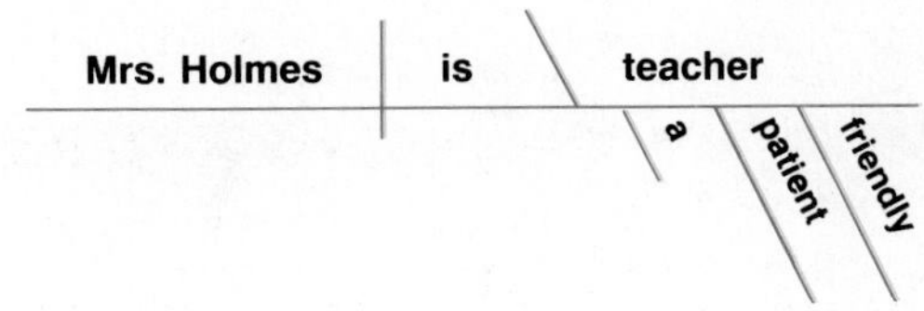

Exercise Diagram sentences containing adjectives.

Diagram the subjects, verbs, articles, and adjectives in the following sentences. Also diagram any direct objects, predicate nouns, or predicate adjectives.

See pages T17–T26 at the back of this Teacher's Edition.

1. Kirstin heard strange, squeaky noises.
2. The large group sang patriotic songs.
3. That antique clock is beautiful and accurate.
4. Kathleen wrote those short, humorous poems.
5. The hefty weightlifter raised the heavy barbell.
6. Does this album contain old snapshots?
7. Ten acrobats walked the high tightrope.
8. The politician made an angry, forceful speech.
9. The lemon is a small, yellow, sour fruit.
10. An alert neighbor spotted the dangerous sparks.

511

Part 12

Objective

To diagram sentences with possessive nouns

Optional Practice

Have the students diagram the subjects, verbs, and correct possessive nouns in Exercises A and B on page 315.

Part 12 Diagraming Sentences Containing Possessive Nouns

Possessive nouns are diagramed in the same way that adjectives are. They are written on lines slanting down from the nouns with which they are used.

These are Ellen's books.

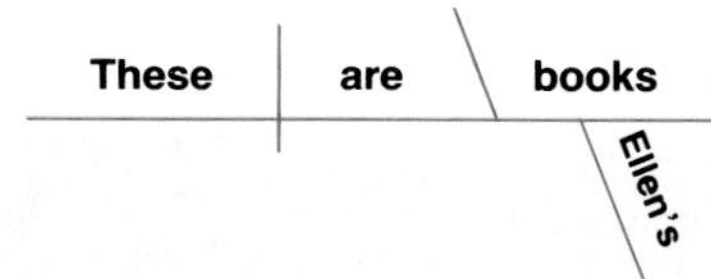

We heard the minister's sermon.

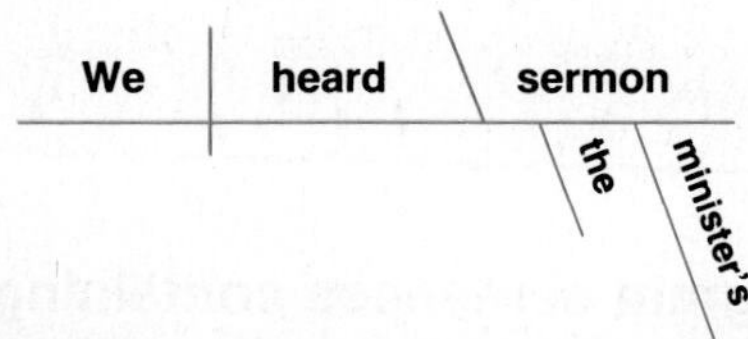

Exercise Diagram sentences containing possessive nouns.

Diagram the subjects, verbs, and possessive nouns in the following sentences. Also diagram any direct objects, predicate nouns or predicate adjectives, articles, and adjectives.

See pages T17–T26 at the back of this Teacher's Edition.

1. The Riveras' black cat followed me.
2. Kendra's mother is an excellent pianist.
3. Bruce's serve is strong and fast.
4. Read Jack London's stories.
5. Cathy's dog found Dad's brown slippers.
6. The girls' chorus sang Andy's original songs.
7. Ms. Mason's class toured museums and historic places.
8. Did Douglas borrow Elena's new album?

9. The town's mayor proposed several laws.
10. The siren's shrill wail filled the air.

Part 13 Diagraming Sentences Containing Adverbs

Adverbs, like adjectives, are shown on diagrams on slanting lines attached to the words they modify. The following diagram shows an adverb modifying a verb.

Finally, the shy boy raised his hand.

The next diagram shows one adverb modifying a verb, another modifying an adjective, and a third modifying another adverb.

Some fairly young children play musical instruments very well.

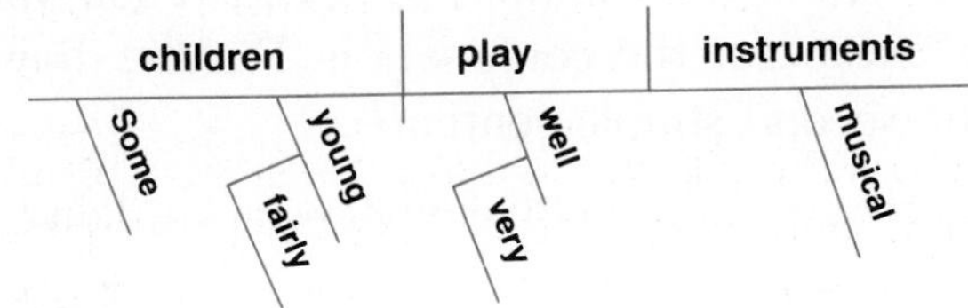

Notice how *fairly* is attached to *young*. Notice how *very* is attached to *well*.

Exercise **Diagram sentences containing adverbs.**

Diagram the subjects, verbs, and adverbs in the following sentences. Also diagram adjectives, articles, predicate adjectives or predicate nouns, and direct objects.

See pages T17–T26 at the back of this Teacher's Edition.

Part 13

Objective

To diagram sentences with adverbs

Optional Practice

Have the students follow the directions for the Part 13 Exercises, using the sentences in Exercises A and B on pages 430–431. Remind the students that adverbs telling *how, when,* or *where* usually modify the verb. Adverbs that tell *to what extent* may modify adjectives or other adverbs.

513

1. The climber moved upward quickly.
2. Finally, the police caught the suspect.
3. Fans wildly cheered the team's victory.
4. The butcher rapidly trimmed the steaks.
5. Tomorrow Al will referee the hockey game.
6. This train is too noisy.
7. This yellow is an extremely vivid color.
8. Did most students study hard?
9. They usually ride their bikes.
10. Very few stations play classical music.

Part 14

Objective

To diagram compound sentences

Optional Practice

Have the students follow the directions for the Part 14 Exercise, using the sentences of Exercises A and B, on pages 491–492.

Part 14 Diagraming Compound Sentences

It is not difficult to diagram compound sentences if you can already diagram simple sentences. A compound sentence is just two or more simple sentences joined together. First, you draw the diagram for the first simple sentence. Then you draw a dotted line "step" for the conjunction. Finally, draw the diagram for the second simple sentence.

Daniel slept soundly, but the other campers didn't close their eyes.

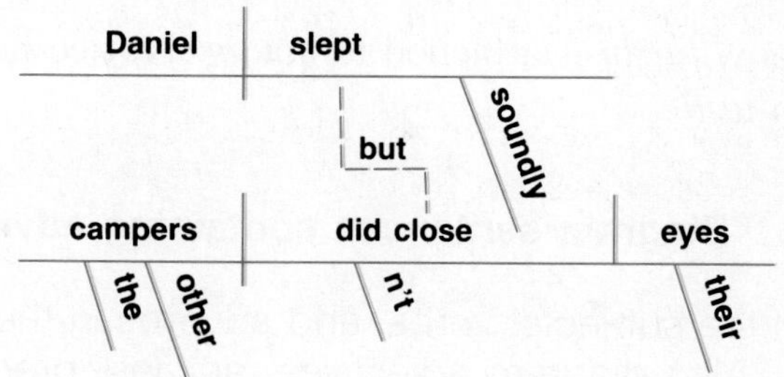

514

Sally is a strong swimmer, and she has won many races.

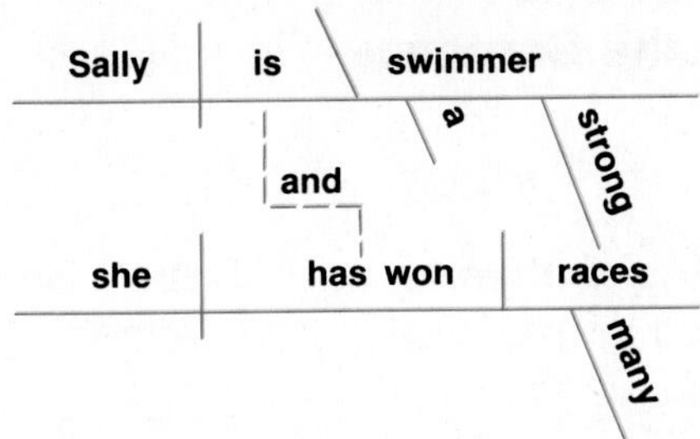

Exercise **Diagram compound sentences.**

Diagram the following compound sentences. Diagram each part of the sentence. Then join the parts.

See pages T17–T26 at the back of this Teacher's Edition.

1. Winston hid Heather's mittens, but she found them.
2. The flowers are growing, but the weeds are growing faster.
3. Stacey arrived late, and she left early.
4. Did Dan walk, or did he ride his bike?
5. The door opened, but nobody entered.
6. Hop aboard, or you will miss the train.
7. Noah is a fair player, but he is tough.
8. Jan found a shiny silver ring, and he kept it.
9. Liz always takes out the garbage, but she never dries the dishes.
10. Badminton and volleyball are outdoor sports, but they are also played indoors.

515

Additional Exercises

These Additional Exercises may be used for additional practice of the concepts presented in this Section. Each exercise focuses on a single concept, and should be used after the page number indicated in parentheses.

Review

If you have not assigned these Additional Exercises before this time, you can also use them as an excellent Section Review.

ADDITIONAL EXERCISES

Diagraming the Sentence

A. Diagraming Subjects and Verbs Diagram the subjects and verbs in the following sentences. Ignore any other words. See pages T17–T26 at the back of this Teacher's Edition.

1. Elizabeth answered.
2. Over the roof flew the robin.
3. Can the baby walk?
4. Try harder.
5. There is a squirrel in the attic.
6. Cars and trucks blocked the entrance.
7. The builders sawed and hammered.
8. Did our team win?
9. I swept, washed, and waxed the floor.
10. Watch the screen.

B. Diagraming Direct Objects and Predicate Words Diagram the subjects, verbs, direct objects, and predicate words in each of the following sentences.

See pages T17–T26 at the back of this Teacher's Edition.

1. Karen, Dennis, and Juan organized the picnic.
2. Yolanda brought food, a blanket, and a radio.
3. Tanya is our candidate.
4. Don't forget your boots and umbrella.
5. Is Mr. Holmes your teacher?
6. The wrestlers were breathless and weak.
7. Two popular evergreens are pine and spruce.
8. Does this book seem mysterious?
9. Rebecca is a fine dancer.
10. Lou entered the math competition.

C. Diagraming Modifiers Diagram the subjects, verbs, direct objects, predicate words, and modifiers in the following sentences. See pages T17–T26 at the back of this Teacher's Edition.

1. Choose a bright, cheerful card.
2. Can the farmer's heavy tractor plow this rocky field?
3. Randi washed Evan's shaggy dog.
4. Very few people play this complex game correctly.
5. A fierce, hot wind swept the plains.
6. Everyone enjoyed Karen's funny story.
7. They never heard the final score.
8. We ate crisp, buttery popcorn.
9. Tony read the latest report very carefully.
10. The wooden raft drifted lazily downstream.

D. Diagraming Compound Sentences Diagram the following sentences. See pages T17–T26 at the back of this Teacher's Edition.

1. Nancy Lopez is a golfer, and she has won many prizes.
2. Will you call, or will you write?
3. We roasted the corn, and we ate it hungrily.
4. Is that lovely fruit real, or is it wax?
5. The clouds are dark, and it will rain soon.
6. Ted missed the movie, but he can see it tomorrow.
7. The porch is wide, and the windows are large.
8. Sue planted beans, and Jerry planted squash.
9. We caught three trout, and Dad grilled them.
10. Did Gary and Elsa ride horses, or did they take their bikes?

517

Mixed Review

These exercises provide review of the concepts presented in this Section. Each exercise challenges the students to apply several of the skills they have acquired during previous study. Because the "mixed" feature of these activities makes them more difficult, the teacher may wish to have less-advanced students do them orally or in small groups.

MIXED REVIEW

Diagraming the Sentence

Diagraming sentences Diagram the following sentences.

See pages T17–T26 at the back of this Teacher's Edition.

1. The ten campers wore bright red shirts.
2. The audience cheered and applauded wildly.
3. There aren't enough plates.
4. The boys rented a canoe.
5. The bacon sizzled and the coffee perked.
6. Are you the new captain?
7. Did Abby finish that difficult puzzle?
8. Williamsburg is an old, historic city.
9. Carol and Ben wrote the play, and our class performed it.
10. The kitten ran and hid.
11. Did Lennie believe your story?
12. Call again later.
13. The church choir sang Handel's *Messiah.*
14. Lawrence saw a UFO, and he reported it.
15. Jamie collects coins, stamps, and postcards.
16. We could hardly hear the lovely music.
17. Our cellar is cool and damp.
18. The coals are still hot, but we have eaten all the marshmallows.
19. Beverly Cleary is my favorite author.
20. Debbie walks, but her friends take the bus.

USING GRAMMAR IN WRITING

Diagraming the Sentence

A. Your friend has written you a message. She didn't want her nosey younger brother to read it, so she put the message in "code." She wrote it entirely in sentence diagrams. To find out what she said, you must "de-code" the diagrams.

Josh and Jenny are having a Halloween party next Saturday.

1.

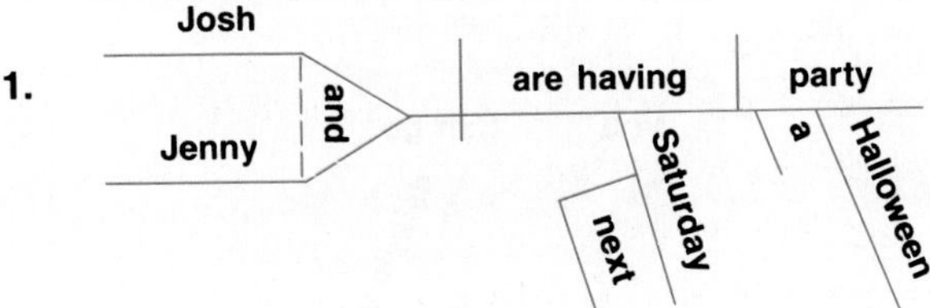

There will be about twenty people there.

2.

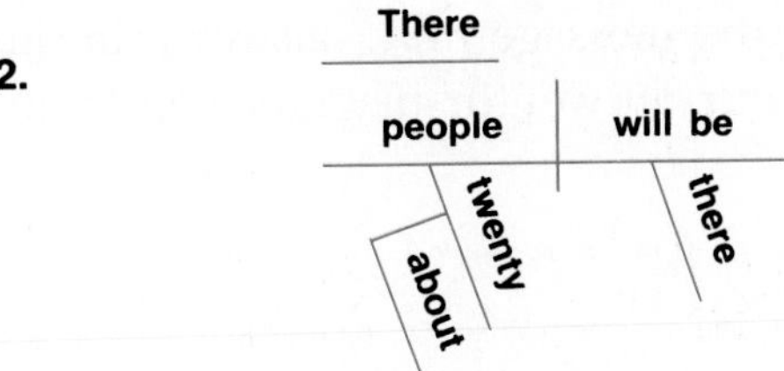

Your costume should be a total secret.

3.

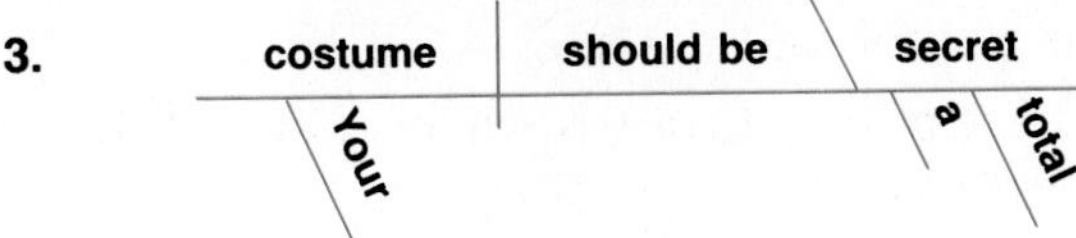

Terry will probably bring some good tapes and records.

4.

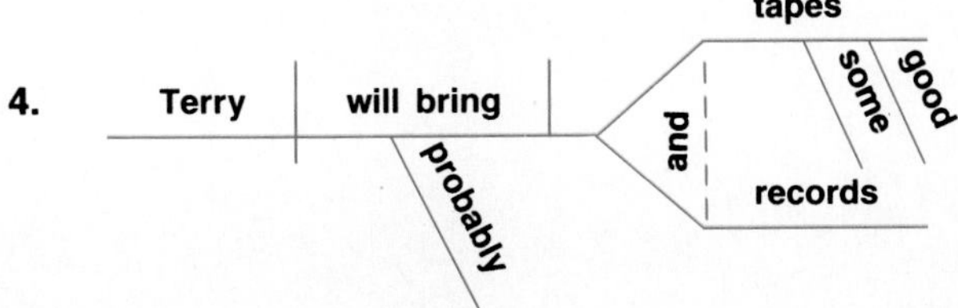

Using Grammar in Writing

These challenging and enjoyable activities allow the students to see how the concepts of grammar, usage, and mechanics may be applied in actual writing situations. Each exercise is designed to allow students practice in several of the skills they have acquired in this Section. The activities also provide opportunities for students to write creatively about a wide variety of interesting and unusual subjects.

5.

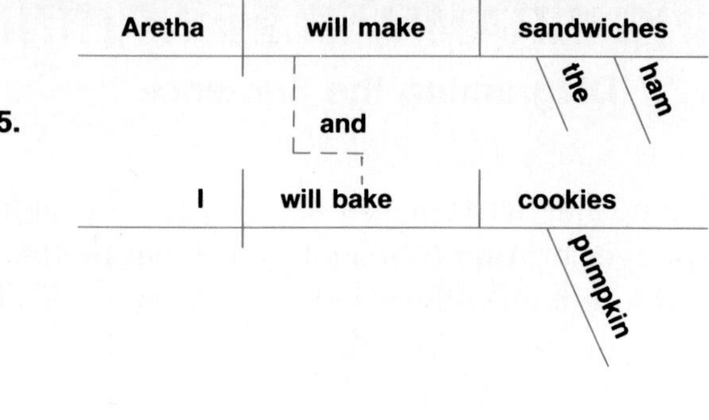

6.

Can you definitely go?

you | Can go

definitely

B. After you decode the message in *A*, answer it in three or four sentences. Put your answer in diagram code like your friend's message.

520

Capitalization

The use of capital letters is called **capitalization.** When you use a capital letter at the beginning of a word, you *capitalize* the word.

Capital letters are used to call attention to the beginnings of sentences and to certain special words. Using capital letters makes everything easier to read.

In this section you will be learning rules for capitalization. Study the rules and their examples. Refer to them whenever you have a question about capitalization.

Section Objectives

1. To understand and apply the general rules for capitalizing proper nouns and adjectives, and the first-person pronoun

2. To understand and apply the rules for capitalization of first words and for capitalization in titles

Preparing the Students

It might be helpful to discuss why capitalization is used: to point out something specific, to name something particular (a person's name, a month of the year). Ask students for examples of capitalization usage. Put the examples on the board, and see if students can group them and make any general rules from them.

Read and discuss the introduction on page 521.

Additional Resources

Diagnostic Test — page 8 in the test booklet

Mastery Test — pages 62–63 in the test booklet

Additional Exercises — pages 536–540 in the student text

Practice Book — pages 194–200

Duplicating Masters — pages 194–200

Special Populations — See special section at the front of this Teacher's Edition.

Proper Nouns and Proper Adjectives

Objective

To understand and apply the general rules for capitalizing proper nouns and adjectives, and the first-person pronoun

Presenting the Lesson

1. Read and discuss page 522. Point out how the sample common nouns are made more specific by the sample proper nouns *(planet, Mars)* and how these proper nouns are changed to proper adjectives *(Martian)*.

2. Assign and discuss the Exercise on page 523.

3. Read and discuss pages 523–524.

4. You may wish to do Exercise A on pages 524–525 with the class. Assign and discuss Exercise B.

5. Read and discuss pages 525–526. Ask students for further examples. Point out that the two-letter state abbreviations are written without periods.

6. Assign and discuss Exercise A and B on pages 526–527.

7. Read and discuss pages 527–528.

8. It is suggested that you do Exercise A on page 528 with the class. Assign and discuss Exercises B and C.

Individualizing the Lesson

Less-Advanced Students

Point out to the students that some of the rules for capitalization are con-

Proper Nouns and Proper Adjectives

A **common noun** is a general name for a person, place, or thing.

hero   country   planet

A **proper noun** is the name of one particular person, place, or thing.

Hercules   **S**witzerland   **M**ars

Begin every proper noun with a capital letter.

The words below are proper nouns. Some of them are made up of two words. Both words are parts of the proper noun. Both begin with capital letters.

Independence **D**ay	**S**outh **A**merica	**F**ebruary
Exton **M**all	**L**ake **E**rie	**M**ary **S**helley

A **proper adjective** is an adjective made from a proper noun.

***H**erculean* strength	***S**wiss* cheese	***M**artian* atmosphere
(from ***H**ercules*)	(from ***S**witzerland*)	(from ***M**ars*)

Begin every proper adjective with a capital letter. Proper adjectives are often used with common nouns. Do not capitalize the common noun.

Proper Noun	Proper Adjective	Adjective and Noun
England	**E**nglish	**E**nglish language
Rome	**R**oman	**R**oman numerals
Canada	**C**anadian	**C**anadian mountains
Indian	**I**ndian	**I**ndian corn

Most pronouns are treated like common nouns and are not capitalized. The pronoun *I*, however, is always capitalized.

Exercise **Use capital letters.**

Number your paper from 1 to 15. Copy each word below, changing small letters to capitals where necessary. After each word, write the group that the word belongs to: *Common Noun, Proper Noun,* or *Proper Adjective.* Some words can belong to more than one category.

P,PA	1. boston Boston	C	9. park
C	2. city	C	10. actress
PA	3. french French	P,PA	11. los angeles Los Angeles
P	4. mississippi river Mississippi River	C	12. woman
P,PA	5. kentucky Kentucky	P	13. disney world Disney World
P	6. pete rose Pete Rose	P	14. carrie fisher Carrie Fisher
PA	7. texan Texan	C	15. school
C	8. singer		

Names and Initials

Capitalize the names of people and pets.

Carla **M**ichael **S**noopy

Begin every word in a person's name with a capital letter.

Dan **R**ather **S**andra **D**ay **O'C**onnor **M**artin **L**uther **K**ing, **J**r.

Capitalize an initial and follow it with a period. An **initial** is the first letter of a name. An initial stands for a name.

Susan **B.** Anthony **S. F. B.** Morse
P. T. Barnum **O. J.** Simpson

Capitalize words for family relations when they are used as names of specific people.

Father **M**other **A**unt **E**m
Dad **M**om **U**ncle **H**enry
Pa **M**a **G**randma

fusing and may have to be memorized. However, all rules will be clearer if students understand the difference between common and proper nouns.

Make sure the students see the differences in the following sentences:

I saw Dad at school.
I saw my dad at school.
Mom made cookies.
Sue's mom made cookies.

Stress that words like *mom, dad,* and *uncle* are capitalized only when they are used in direct address or as names.

Go over the sentences below before assigning the exercises. Have the students tell you which nouns should be capitalized.

1. a. Where is our family doctor?
   b. Where is Doctor Taylor?
2. a. We go to church every Sunday.
   b. We go to the First Baptist Church every Sunday.
3. a. Is my uncle here yet?
   b. Is Uncle Frank here yet?
4. a. We went fishing in the river.
   b. We went fishing in the Rio Grande River.

Advanced Students

After the students have finished the exercises, have them look through magazines and find at least twenty examples of proper nouns, adjectives or titles. Have them copy the examples.

Optional Practice

1. Distribute copies of the list below, or put the list on the board. Have students number their papers from one to thirteen. Explain that they are to find on the list a common noun and a proper noun that match.

They are to write the two nouns together on the same line (common noun first), and to capitalize where needed.

Example: month—December

dog, city, truman, buick, asia, Lassie, comic book character, holiday, philadelphia, president, car, continent, tuesday, ocean, spanish, pacific, explorer, tires, balboa, uniroyal, language, state, spiderman, day, south dakota, thanksgiving

2. Have students copy the following list, changing small letters to capital letters where necessary.

1. all my aunts, including aunt georgina
2. queen elizabeth, the queen of england
3. the doctor at the clinic, dr. t. j. calloway
4. grandma moses, a famous painter
5. the superintendent of schools, ms. bessie clark
6. the head nurse, mrs. arlene grover
7. prime minister winston churchill
8. smokey the bear, the forest rangers' friend

3. Distribute copies of the paragraph below. Have students find errors in capitalization, and write the words correctly.

My family lives in missouri. Every summer we spend a week with my cousins in sioux falls, south dakota. We usually arrive on july 3, the day before independence day. Last year we visited mt. rushmore, where the heads of famous men have been carved in granite out of the side of the mountain. The men are presidents george washington, thomas jefferson, abraham lincoln, and theodore roosevelt. I like the head of president lincoln the best. The carvings are so immense that they make me feel very small.

However, if you use a possessive noun or pronoun before the word stating a relationship, do not capitalize the word.

Meet **A**unt **K**ate.	*but* Meet Sally's aunt.
Today **D**ad took the bus.	*but* Today my dad took the bus.

Titles and Their Abbreviations

You may have noticed that many people have special words before their names. Your dentist has the word *Doctor* before his or her name. So has your doctor. These special words are titles. Titles that are followed by names are capitalized. Titles used by themselves are not capitalized.

Doctor Rosen will see you now.	*but*	The doctor will see you now.
Marcia wrote to **G**overnor Happ.	*but*	Marcia wrote to the governor.

Many titles have short forms. A shortened form of a word is an **abbreviation.** Abbreviations for titles are capitalized and followed by a period. Never use an abbreviation unless you follow it with a name.

Doctor = **D**r. Brown Governor = **G**ov. Johnson
Reverend = **R**ev. Clements

Always capitalize the titles *Mr.*, *Mrs.*, *Ms.*, and *Miss.* Be aware that *Ms.* has no long form and that *Miss* has no short form.

Capitalize titles and their abbreviations when you use them with names. Follow an abbreviation with a period.

Exercises Use capital letters correctly.

A. Copy the following sentences. Change small letters to capital letters wherever necessary.

1. We live next door to dr. l. e. brown.
2. My brother luis met superintendent julia f. jones.

3. The mayor presented an award to miss allen.
4. My father knows judge mercedes blake and senator steven thomas.
5. Last Thursday senator phyllis r. grimes and professor a. e. ames visited our school.
6. The writer charles lutwidge dodgson used the pen name lewis carroll.
7. Perhaps i'll name my new puppies pepper and salt.
8. The best players on rhonda's team are rhonda and i.
9. Some famous indian leaders were chief joseph, sitting bull, and cochise.
10. At the convention, clara and her cousin b. j. met governor ridge.

B. Follow the directions for Exercise A.

1. Katy moran's mom produces a television show.
2. Yes, aunt aretha and i met dr. cooley.
3. My neighbor, mrs. avellini, repairs cars.
4. A dog named benji adopted us.
5. Did you see the program with steve martin?
6. One champion golfer is judy rankin.
7. The bill was introduced by senator hernandez.
8. "Stamp out forest fires," smokey tells us.
9. Yesterday, grandma and my brother jeremy made soup.
10. Timothy bottoms and joseph bottoms are brothers.

Months, Days, and Holidays

Capitalize the names of months, days, and holidays.

Do not capitalize names of seasons, such as spring and summer.

Extending the Lesson

1. You may want to have your more advanced students work this exercise in small groups. Give students copies of the following list of countries. Instruct the students to write the proper nationality adjective that describes people and things of each country. Make sure they know where they can look to find the information (dictionary, social studies text). Remind them to capitalize when necessary. After everyone is finished, discuss the answers.

china, mexico, austria, norway, japan, iran, sweden, italy, france, spain, turkey, ireland, britain, australia, brazil, africa, israel, poland, canada, india, portugal, vietnam, egypt, jamaica, russia

2. You may want to divide the students into small groups for this exercise. Distribute copies of the following lists of states and two-letter mailing abbreviations. Direct students to match each state with its abbreviation, and to write the abbreviation next to the state, using proper capitalization. Then have the students look up the capital city of each state and write it after the state abbreviation.

	States		Abbreviations	
d	1. kentucky	a.	me	Augusta
e	2. missouri	b.	co	Denver
b	3. colorado	c.	or	Salem
j	4. idaho	d.	ky	Frankfort
h	5. delaware	e.	mo	Jefferson City
a	6. maine	f.	az	Phoenix
g	7. georgia	g.	ga	Atlanta
i	8. minnesota	h.	de	Dover
c	9. oregon	i.	mn	St. Paul
f	10. arizona	j.	id	Boise

l 11. arkansas — k. tx Austin
t 12. michigan — l. ar Little Rock
q 13. indiana — m. vt Montpelier
o 14. iowa — n. wy Cheyenne
n 15. wyoming — o. ia Des Moines
p 16. utah — p. ut Salt Lake City
s 17. florida — q. in Indianapolis
m 18. vermont — r. ri Providence
r 19. rhode island — s. fl Tallahassee
k 20. texas — t. mi Lansing

My birthday is **S**eptember 1.
We observe **L**incoln's **B**irthday on **F**ebruary 12.
Next **F**riday is the first day of summer.

Particular Places and Things

Capitalize the names of cities, states, and countries.

Did you live in **K**ansas **C**ity, **K**ansas, or **K**ansas **C**ity, **M**issouri?
The **U**nited **S**tates shares borders with **M**exico and **C**anada.

Capitalize both letters of the two-letter abbreviations for states, used in addresses on all mail.

California = **CA** Maine = **ME** Wisconsin = **WI**

Capitalize the names of streets, bridges, and buildings, such as schools.

Chambers **E**lementary **S**chool is on **S**haw **A**venue.
The **O**akland **B**ay **B**ridge was being repainted.

Capitalize geographical names.

Also capitalize such words as *north, south, east,* and *west* when they refer to a section of the country. Do not capitalize them when they are used as directions.

The explorers traveled *south* along the **M**ississippi **R**iver.
The **W**est is beautiful country.
The storm is moving *east* over the **A**tlantic **O**cean.

Exercises Use capital letters correctly.

A. Copy the following sentences. Change small letters to capital letters wherever necessary.

1. Cactus grows in the southwest. (S)
2. Vacation begins on tuesday. (T)
3. The danube river flows into the black sea. (D, R, B, S)
4. My friend miya osaka has relatives in japan. (M, O, J)

5. On may 5, harper school will hold a carnival.
6. A time for picnics is independence day, july 4.
7. The international peace bridge connects canada and the united states.
8. Norman's little sister, linda, wrote to big bird at 123 sesame street, new york, new york.
9. Last saturday terry and i saw a ball game at comiskey park.
10. The aleutian islands are southwest of alaska.

B. Follow the directions for Exercise A.

1. The swedish ship passed through the panama canal.
2. Huge tortoises live on the galapagos islands.
3. The pentagon is the world's largest building.
4. The first monday in september is labor day.
5. Ms. e. e. stefano is the librarian at the carver public library.
6. Did you know that elm street is made of bricks?
7. On may 5, 1961, alan shepard became the first american to travel in space.
8. Last summer dad and i crossed the golden gate bridge.
9. The paddlewheel boat toured the missouri river.
10. Union troops were led by general u. s. grant of illinois.

Religions, Nationalities, and Languages

Capitalize the names of religions, nationalities, and languages.

Three major faiths are **C**hristianity, **J**udaism, and **I**slam.
Many **M**exicans speak both **S**panish and **E**nglish.

Clubs, Organizations, Businesses

Capitalize the names of clubs, organizations, and businesses.

527

Mary Ann belongs to the **J**unior **P**hotographers' **C**lub.

The **C**ampfire **G**irls took a tour of the **B**ell **T**elephone **C**ompany offices downtown.

Exercises **Use capital letters correctly.**

A. Copy these sentences, using correct capitalization.

1. Did o. j. simpson play for the buffalo bills?
2. Last december russian dancers performed here.
3. Juan martinez speaks spanish at home and english at school.
4. The national geographic society has a fascinating magazine.
5. Yes, uncle tony, schwinn builds ten-speed bicycles.
6. Did you see the beautiful indian cloth and jewelry?
7. A store called go fly a kite at 1434 third avenue sells kites.
8. Many chinese people practice buddhism.
9. Jeb and i read about the israeli leader golda meir.
10. The sierra club holds nature outings each summer.

B. Follow the directions for Exercise A.

1. My sister jeannine has posters of british monarchs.
2. The polish scientist madame curie discovered radium.
3. In october, logan school started the snowflake club.
4. Cathy stover has folk dolls from portugal and brazil.
5. The springfield bicycle league held a race on august 5.
6. The museum is open from october to june.
7. During the christmas season, f.a.o. schwarz is a busy store.
8. The spanish explorer balboa discovered the pacific ocean.
9. The white house is at 1600 pennsylvania avenue.
10. Last spring mom and i flew a delta jet to atlanta.

528

C. Writing Copy this paragraph, using correct capitalization.

Our teacher, ms. abbott, told us about woodrow wilson the other day. At princeton university, professor wilson taught politics. He later became president of princeton university. Then he was known as doctor wilson. In 1912, the people elected him to the presidency of the united states. After that he was called president wilson.

First Words

Any word is capitalized if it appears in certain places in written work.

Sentences

Capital letters are important sentence signals. They tell when a new sentence begins.

Capitalize the first word of every sentence.

My brother likes mushrooms on his pizza.
Does February have twenty-nine days this year?
Look out!

Direct Quotations

When you write the exact words somebody else said, you are **quoting** that person. The words are a **direct quotation.**

Capitalize the first word of a direct quotation.

"**T**oday we can expect two inches of snow," said the forecaster.

First Words

Objective

To understand and apply the rules for capitalization of first words and for capitalization in titles

Presenting the Lesson

1. Read and discuss pages 529–530. Give particular attention to the use of two capital letters in a sentence ending with a direct quotation.

2. Assign and discuss Exercises A and B on page 530. Stress the importance of copying the punctuation (commas, end marks, and quotation marks) exactly as shown in the text.

3. Read and discuss pages 531–532. Point out that most poems that rhyme also use capital letters to begin each line; poems that do not rhyme often do not use capital letters in this way. Make sure that students notice the last example under *Letters*. Stress that they capitalize only the first word in the closing of a letter.

4. Assign and discuss Exercises A and B on pages 532–533.

5. Read and discuss page 534. Have the students copy the example titles, using underlining and quotation marks as shown.

6. Assign and discuss Exercises A and B on pages 534–535.

Individualizing the Lesson

Less-Advanced Students

Do Exercise A on page 530 orally with these students.

Advanced Students

Create a short dialogue between two people, leaving out all capitalization. The students should add capital letters where they are needed.

Optional Practice

Play *Capital Riddle.*

Give the students the sentences below and have them capitalize the words that need capitalization. Tell them to copy down, in order, each letter they capitalize and they will come up with the answers to the riddle.

Riddle: Why did the elephant wear a plaid jacket?

(*Answer:* His tuxedo was at the cleaners.)

Sentences:

1. harry and i watched star trek on television.
2. uncle xavier visited us at easter.
3. dr. ogden set wayne's broken arm.
4. all of seventh avenue was flooded tuesday.
5. tami's family is celebrating hanukkah this week.

Usually, when you are writing what a person has said, you use explaining words like *he said* or *she asked*, before or after the direct quotation. If these explaining words come before the direct quotation, capitalize the first explaining words. Then capitalize the first word of the direct quotation.

"**I**t's raining," my brother said.
My mother asked, "**I**s the cake still in the oven?"

Exercises Use capital letters correctly.

A. Copy these sentences using correct capitalization.

1. giant reptiles roamed the earth in prehistoric times.
2. "a robot has no brain," mr. rodriguez said.
3. maria asked, "may i use the microscope?"
4. "would you like to take a bike trip?" roosevelt asked.
5. wildflowers grow in the forest.
6. i explained, "a spaceship has landed on the surface of mars."
7. a kayak is similar to a canoe.
8. mother reminded me, "your fish must be fed."
9. mona asked, "have you seen my sweater?"
10. the teacher said, "admiral byrd was the first person to fly over the south pole."

B. Writing These sentences belong in one paragraph. Write them as a paragraph. Indent the first line. Use correct capitalization.

many years ago lanterns were used to light the streets of big cities.
candles were used in the lanterns.
the people in each house had to hang out a lantern.
in paris, in 1666, nearly three thousand lanterns gleamed in the streets.
isn't it strange to think of a city street lighted by candlelight?

530

Poetry

Capitalize the first word in most lines of poetry.

Cats sleep fat and walk thin.
Cats, when they sleep, slump;
When they wake, pull in—
And where the plump's been
There's skin.
Cats walk thin.

—ROSALIE MOORE, from "Catalogue"

Sometimes, the lines of a poem do not begin with capital letters.

Foghorns

The foghorns moaned
in the bay last night
so sad
so deep
I thought I heard the city
crying in its sleep.

—LILIAN MOORE

Outlines

Capitalize the first word of each line of an outline.

The major ideas of an outline are marked with Roman numerals (I, II, III). The secondary ideas are marked with capital letters (A, B, C).

Systems of **M**easurement

I. **T**he British system
- **A.** **I**nch, foot, yard, mile
- **B.** **O**unce, pound, ton
- **C.** **C**up, pint, quart, gallon

II. **T**he metric system
- **A.** **M**eter
- **B.** **G**ram
- **C.** **L**iter

E C
6. everyone asked, "can you lift that?"

L E
7. london is one of the largest cities in europe.

A N
8. annie is seeing her brother in nashville this fall.

E
9. eddie read a book on shipwrecks.

R S
10. robb's mother was born in sweden.

Extending the Lesson

Give the students the list of "headlines" below. As a group, identify them as nursery rhymes, and then have students write out the titles with the correct capitalization.

1. Flock of Birds Found in Pastry (Sing a Song of Sixpence)
2. Spider Terrorizes Petite Woman (Little Miss Muffet)
3. Rodents Attack Farm Woman (Three Blind Mice)
4. Shepherd Found Sleeping on Job (Little Boy Blue)
5. Sheep Invades School (Mary Had a Little Lamb)
6. Lunar Cow Makes Dog Hysterical (Hey Diddle Diddle)
7. Five Porkers Go Separate Ways (This Little Piggy)
8. Young Boy Finds Object in Pie (Little Jack Horner)
9. Missing Sheep Upset Girl (Little BoPeep)
10. Boy Arrested for Waking Neighbors (Wee Willie Winkie)
11. Pig Thief Caught Leaving Scene of Crime (Tom, Tom, the Piper's Son)
12. Boy Retires Wearing Pants (Diddle Diddle Dumpling)
13. Senior Citizen Tries to Save Starving Dog (Old Mother Hubbard)
14. Two Children Injured in Water Mishap (Jack and Jill)
15. Jubilant King Demands Entertainment (Old King Cole)

Letters

Capitalize the greeting and the first word of the closing of a letter.

Dear **S**ir: **D**ear **L**ucy, **S**incerely, **Y**our friend,

Exercises **Use capitals correctly.**

A. Capitalize the following poem, outline, and letter.

1. (poem) **The Steam Shovel**

the steam digger
is much bigger
than the biggest beast i know.
he snorts and roars
like the dinosaurs
that lived long years ago.

—ROWENA BENNETT

2. (outline) The Lewis and Clark Expedition

I. why it was needed
a. the Louisiana Purchase of 1803
b. lack of good maps

II. why Lewis and Clark were chosen
a. achievements of Meriwether Lewis
b. achievements of William Clark

3. (letter)

euclid park school
cleveland, ohio 44112
march 17, 1985

dear ms. lopez,

we enjoyed your lesson about how to use a videotape camera. it was fun to see ourselves on television. in the future we will be able to videotape plays and other activities in our classroom.

sincerely yours,
william hodges

532

B. Follow the directions for Exercise A.

1. (poem)

How To Tell the Top of a Hill

the top of a hill
is not until
the bottom is below.
and you have to stop
when you reach the top
for there's no more UP to go.

—JOHN CIARDI

2. (outline)

Planning a Vegetable Garden

I. choose a good spot
   a. enough sunshine
   b. good soil
   c. proper drainage

II. choose your crops
   a. tasty vegetables
   b. easily grown vegetables

III. draw a garden plan

3. (letter)

november 2, 1985

dear sarah,

i am sending you a photo i took of my newest pet. panda is a beagle and a very playful puppy. by next summer she should be ready to go on our long hikes. whatever we do at the lake, panda will do, too. i know you'll like her.

your friend,

marie

533

Capitalizing Titles

Capitalize the first word and all important words in chapter titles, titles of magazine articles, titles of short stories or single poems, and titles of songs.

Use quotation marks for these titles.

Chapter:	Chapter 3, "**O**ur **S**olar **S**ystem"
Magazine article:	"**S**afety on **S**kateboards"
Short story:	"**T**he **L**egend of **S**leepy **H**ollow"
Poem:	"**C**atalog"
Song:	"**A**merica the **B**eautiful"

Capitalize the first word and all important words in titles of books, newspapers, magazines, movies, and television programs.

Underline these titles. (When these titles are printed, they are *italicized.*)

Book:	*Abe Lincoln Grows Up*
Newspaper:	*Chicago Tribune*
Magazine:	*National Geographic*
Movie:	*King Kong*
Television program:	*Nova*

Do not capitalize words such as *the, in, for, from, by, at, a,* or *an,* unless they come first or last in a title.

Exercises Use capital letters correctly.

A. Copy the following titles. Capitalize them correctly.

1. *i am the cheese* (book)
2. "east of the sun and west of the moon" (story)
3. *little house on the prairie* (book)
4. *and now miguel* (book)
5. "the lady or the tiger?" (short story)

534

6. "the life of the pioneers" (chapter title)
7. "the top ten on television" (magazine article)
8. *creative computing* (magazine)
9. "the horses of the sea" (poem)
10. *willie wonka and the chocolate factory* (book and movie)

B. Follow the directions for Exercise A.

1. *m.c. higgins, the great* (book)
2. *wall street journal* (newspaper)
3. "a visit from st. nicholas" (poem)
4. *the lord of the rings* (book and movie)
5. "the highwayman" (poem)
6. "building better kites" (magazine article)
7. *wild, wild world of animals* (television program)
8. "the star-spangled banner" (song)
9. *freedom train* (book)
10. "casey at the bat" (poem)

535

Additional Exercises

These Additional Exercises may be used for additional practice of the concepts presented in this Section. Each exercise focuses on a single concept, and should be used after the page number indicated in parentheses.

Review

If you have not assigned these Additional Exercises before this time, you can also use them as an excellent Section Review.

ADDITIONAL EXERCISES

Capitalization

A. Proper Nouns and Proper Adjectives Copy each of the following sentences. Change small letters to capital letters wherever necessary.

1. Do wesley and craig phillips live on cherry street?
2. Last summer aunt rhoda studied mexican art.
3. Lloyd j. curtis sails his yacht on lake michigan.
4. Last tuesday governor scott was re-elected.
5. My teacher, mr. olsen, rides a bike to school.
6. The first day of spring is march 21.
7. This wednesday, february 14, is valentine's day.
8. Last may the mason family moved to georgia.
9. Alicia plays the french horn in our school orchestra.
10. The principal of skiles middle school is ms. j. e. clark.
11. Is salt lake city west of the rocky mountains?
12. The boys clubs of america sponsor service projects.
13. The founder of buddhism was a teacher from india.
14. We buy spanish magazines at books galore on oak street.
15. Does the colorado river flow through arizona?
16. Last summer i took the train to minneapolis, minnesota.
17. The bill from dr. bates arrived on tuesday.
18. An important jewish holiday is yom kippur.
19. Beth speaks english, russian, and italian.
20. Our tour began at the united nations building in manhattan.

B. First Words and Titles Copy each of the following items. Change small letters to capital letters when necessary.

1. terry asked, "has the bell rung?"

536

2. "estes national park is terrific!" jenny said.
3. he has a heart of gold beneath
   but the lion just can't trust his teeth.

   —JOHN CIARDI, from "Why Nobody Pets the Lion at the Zoo"
4. *the jungle book* was written by rudyard kipling.
5. one very popular movie was *return of the jedi.*
6. mr. grant asked, "where are those reports?"
7. kinds of business ownership
   - I. corporation
     - a. privately held
     - b. publicly held
   - II. partnership
   - III. individual ownership
8. ms. irwin assigned the book *the chocolate war.*
9. laura memorized the poem "mending wall" by robert frost.
10. dear sharon,

    meet me in the library at 4:00. i found the book you need for your report.

    your friend,
    nancy
11. watch out! there's a pothole in the street.
12. jim said, "let's try out for the diving team."
13. "what is that sculpture supposed to be?" asked ted.
14. **the termite**

    some primal termite knocked on wood
    and tasted it, and found it good,
    and that is why your cousin May
    fell through the parlor floor today.

    —OGDEN NASH
15. mr. johnson announced, "we will see the movie *the red pony* tomorrow."

537

Mixed Review

These exercises provide review of the concepts presented in this Section. Each exercise challenges the students to apply several of the skills they have acquired during previous study. Because the "mixed" feature of these activities makes them more difficult, the teacher may wish to have less-advanced students do them orally or in small groups.

MIXED REVIEW

Capitalization

A. Using capital letters correctly Copy the following sentences. Change small letters to capital letters wherever necessary.

1. the ancient romans spoke latin.
2. dad and i will visit the san diego zoo this summer.
3. when walking in a tiny rain
   across a vacant lot,
   a pup's a good companion—
   if a pup you've got.

   —GWENDOLYN BROOKS, from "Vern"
4. orphan annie has a dog named sandy.
5. "did you read *sounder*?" asked marge.
6. john lennon was a rock singer from england.
7. the students at lincoln school will celebrate chinese new year this tuesday.
8. have you ever attended a hawaiian luau?
9. president ronald reagan was once the governor of california.
10. nathan asked, "are you going to los angeles this friday?"
11. Have you read the article "don't be shy" in *scholastic magazine*?
12. The beck family canoed down the eagle river.
13. the chorus sang "what do the simple folk do?" from the play *camelot*.
14. "oh, yes! we'd love to go sledding!" exclaimed the children.
15. my uncle enjoys watching *masterpiece theatre* each week.

16. dear sir:

enclosed is a donation for the american heart association.

sincerely,
jerry lipke

17. "do you have the july, 1981, issue of *national geographic?*" asked mike.
18. i am in the seventh grade at tuley junior high.
19. "we're going to aunt jane's house for thanksgiving," said mother.
20. are you going to try out for the tiger's pom-pom club?

B. Using capital letters correctly in proofreading Proofread the following letter. Rewrite it, changing small letters to capital letters where necessary.

december 31, 1985

Hi brad,

greetings from the north. I remember the great send-off i received from my friends at prairie school when I left Kansas. It helped me to get through my first minnesota winter. i think snow was invented just for Minneapolis. cross-country skiing around Lake nikomas keeps me in shape the way running did in kansas city. my family is planning a return visit for memorial day weekend. Say hello to pat, terry, and the rest of the gang for me.

see you in may,
marc

539

Using Mechanics in Writing

These challenging and enjoyable activities allow the students to see how the concepts of grammar, usage, and mechanics may be applied in actual writing situations. Each exercise is designed to allow students practice in several of the skills they have acquired in this Section. The activities also provide opportunities for students to write creatively about a wide variety of interesting and unusual subjects.

USING MECHANICS IN WRITING

Capitalization

A. Your pen pal in another country is very interested in popular American music. He or she has written a letter asking what songs, singers, and groups you enjoy most. Write to your pen pal about the music you like. Include at least two names of groups, two performers, and three album titles. Tell what new song is your favorite. Be sure to use capital letters correctly.

B. Think about a country you would like to visit. Look up that country in an encyclopedia. Write down the names of the country's capital and its major cities. Also write the names of major rivers, lakes, mountain ranges, or other geographic features. Write a paragraph telling some facts about this country. Remember to use capital letters correctly.

C. Choose five interesting places in your city or town. These places could include streets, buildings, museums, and parks. Write a paragraph about these places. In your paragraph, tell where each place is and why it is interesting. Remember to capitalize all of the proper nouns you use.

D. Make a list of your three favorite books. Write the author of each book. Then make a list of your three favorite TV shows. Include the names of the characters.

Then write two paragraphs. One paragraph should tell about your favorite books. Tell who wrote them and why you like them. The second paragraph should be about your favorite TV shows. Explain why they are your favorites. Tell who stars in them. Use capital letters correctly.

Punctuation

Punctuation marks are signals. They signal the ends of sentences. They also signal pauses inside sentences. A punctuation mark can signal a direct quotation, a question, or an exclamation. Punctuation helps you to write clearly. It helps your readers understand what you have written.

In this section, you will learn rules for punctuating correctly. Study the rules and their examples. Whenever you are writing, use this section to make sure you are using punctuation marks correctly.

Section Objectives

1. To use the period correctly
2. To use the question mark correctly
3. To use the exclamation mark correctly
4. To use the comma correctly
5. To use the apostrophe correctly to form possessives and contractions
6. To use the hyphen correctly to divide words at the end of a line
7. To use quotation marks correctly in direct quotations, and to use quotation marks and underlining in titles

Preparing the Students

It is suggested that you present this section periodically rather than as a single unit. Have students use this chapter as a reference independently during the year.

When introducing the chapter, ask students for specific examples of material in which incorrect or missing punctuation would make writing confusing and difficult to understand. Then read and discuss the introduction on page 541.

Additional Resources

Diagnostic Test — page 9 in the test booklet

Mastery Test — pages 64–65 in the test booklet

Additional Exercises — pages 561–566 in the student text

Practice Book — pages 201–211

Duplicating Masters — pages 201–211

Special Populations — See special section at the front of this Teacher's Edition.

Using the Period

Objective

To use the period correctly

Presenting the Lesson

1. Read and discuss pages 542–544. Review the definition and use of the declarative sentence and the imperative sentence. Explain that the period is used at the end of any imperative sentence that does not show strong emotion. Ask students to give examples for each rule.

2. Assign and discuss Exercises A, B, and C on page 545.

Individualizing the Lesson

Less-Advanced Students

Give students a piece of paper divided into 35 squares—7 across and 5 down. Tell the students to create a calendar for their favorite month. Have them label the month and days and fill in events with initials and abbreviations.

Advanced Students

To emphasize the use of periods with abbreviations, give students the following directions and have them put periods where needed.

Follow these directions and win a prize!

Start at 123 S. 1st Ave. on the S.E. corner this Sat. at 12:00 P.M. Walk 3 blks. to the U.S. P.O. and pick up a letter addressed to I.M.A. Contestant. Go a doz. steps up the blvd. Turn l. and walk 12 ft. to the 8th St. fruit stand. Buy 1 lb. 8 oz. of apples. Take 2 apples dwtn. to the R.R. tracks. Give one apple and the letter to a man wearing an L.A. Dodgers hat. He will give you your reward.

Using the Period

When you write, you use a **period (.)** for different purposes. Here are four uses of the period.

The Period at the End of a Sentence

A period is used at the end of a declarative sentence and at the end of an imperative sentence. The period is a signal that the sentence has ended. When you are reading aloud, the period tells you to drop your voice.

Declarative: Navaho Indians built homes called hogans.

Imperative: Help me find my sweater.

Use a period at the end of a declarative sentence and at the end of an imperative sentence.

The Period After an Initial

An **initial** is the first letter of a name. An initial is always capitalized and followed by a period.

Nancy L. Kassebaum John F. Kennedy

Use a period after an initial.

The Period After an Abbreviation

An **abbreviation** is a short form of a word. An abbreviation is usually followed by a period.

Here are abbreviations for the days of the week.

Sun. Mon. Tues. Wed. Thurs. Fri. Sat.

Here are abbreviations for months of the year:

Jan. Feb. Mar. Apr. Aug. Sept. Oct. Nov. Dec.

What three months are left out? Why? A word that is short in its regular form does not usually have an abbreviation.

Some abbreviations stand for more than one word and have more than one period.

D.C. District of Columbia	P.O. Post Office
A.M. *(ante meridiem)* means before noon	B.C. Before Christ
P.M. *(post meridiem)* means after noon	A.D. *(Anno Domini)* means in the year of the Lord

Below is a list of common abbreviations.

Titles

Mr. Mister	Mrs. Mistress	Ms. (no long form)
Dr. Doctor	Rev. Reverend	

Geographic Terms

Rd. Road	Ave. Avenue	U.S.A. United States of America
Blvd. Boulevard	St. Street	

English Measure

oz. ounce(s)	lb. pound(s)	in. inch(es)	doz. dozen
yd. yard	mi. mile	ft. foot (or feet)	

Not all abbreviations use periods. Here are some examples:

mph miles per hour	UN United Nations	ZIP Zone Improvement Plan

Use a period after most abbreviations.

Optional Practice

1. Have students copy the names and addresses listed below, inserting periods where needed.

Example: Supt. M. R. Richardson
10 Apple Tree Ln.
Chattanooga, Tenn. 37401

1. Rev. Caleb R. Zimmerman
129 Cottonwood Rd.
Los Angeles, Calif. 90053
2. Mr. John H. Kingston
209 E. 9th St.
New York, N.Y. 10003
3. Mrs. H. L. Crawford
2312 S. E. Washington Blvd.
Louisville, Ken. 40222
4. Ms. Janet S. Reed
1633 N. Ashland Ave.
Chicago, Ill. 60622
5. Prof. Irma G. Hanson
63 Circle Dr.
Kalamazoo, Mich. 49001
6. Dr. Joseph E. Scanlon
14320 S. Dixie Hwy.
Miami, Fla. 33161

2. Have students abbreviate the days and months below. Remind them to check the dictionary if they are unsure of the abbreviation.

1. Tuesday, February 10 Tues., Feb. 10
2. Wednesday, July 29 Wed., Jul. 29
3. Monday, January 2 Mon., Jan. 2
4. Saturday, August 17 Sat., Aug. 17
5. Thursday, September 8 Thurs., Sept. 8
6. Friday, April 30 Fri., Apr. 30
7. Sunday, October 12 Sun., Oct. 12
8. Tuesday, March 8 Tues., Mar. 8
9. Friday, November 5 Fri., Nov. 5
10. Wednesday, December 28 Wed., Dec. 28

3. Have the students follow the directions for Exercise A using these sentences.

1. President John F. Kennedy was the youngest elected U.S. president.

2. E B White wrote *Stuart Little*.
3. This package came C.O.D.
4. Send your entries to P.O. Box 38, Boston, MA.
5. The rehearsal will begin at 2:30 P.M.
6. Steven J.Spielberg was the director of the movie *E.T.*
7. The note said, "Meet at 49th St.and Fifth Ave. in N.Y.C."
8. Karen Christine is called K.C.
9. My brother is Mr. Perry D. Howard Jr.
10. Rev. Wiley visited the U.N. this spring.

4. Have students follow the directions for Exercise C.

School Sports
I. Fall Sports
A. Football
B. Cross Country
C. Soccer
II. Winter Sports
A. Basketball
B. Hockey
III. Spring Sports
A. Baseball
B. Track

Extending the Lesson

Give the students the following paragraph. There are 28 missing periods they are to place correctly.

My name is T.J. McGill. I was born on April 8, 1971 A.D. Yesterday I was walking to a 10 A.M. appointment when I saw Sgt. Cory. He is a friendly man who always tells us about his adventures on the U.S.S. Merimac. Now he is a painter. He showed me the sign he was finishing for a building. It read

Dr. Wm. B. Schultz D.D.S.
Hrs. by appt. only

Mary E. White Esq.
Attorney-at-Law

I wanted to stay and watch but I had to go in and have my braces tightened by Dr. Schultz. I wished it were 10 P.M.

Using Abbreviations Correctly

Abbreviations may be used in lists, addresses, arithmetic problems, or other special forms of writing. You should not use abbreviations in sentences, paragraphs, and compositions. For example, on an application for a library card, or on an envelope, you may write your address in this way:

2176 So. Taylor Rd.

In a sentence, you should write this:

I live at 2176 South Taylor Road.

As a general rule, the only abbreviations you should use in sentences are *A.M.* and *P.M.*, *B.C.* and *A.D.*, and titles with names, such as *Dr. Perez.*

The Period After Each Numeral or Letter in an Outline

Use a period after each numeral or letter that shows a division of an outline.

How the Months Got Their Names

I. Months named for real people
A. July
B. August
II. Months named for gods
A. January
B. March
C. May
D. June
III. Other months

Exercises **Use periods correctly.**

A. Copy these sentences, using periods where needed.

1. The Rev. Lydia Marshall spoke at our church.
2. Capt. James Cook sailed across the ocean.
3. Ms. Sue Schneider refereed the game.
4. J. Fred Muggs was a famous chimpanzee.
5. Ask Dr. Jean Casey for an appointment.
6. Be sure to bring warm mittens.
7. Capt. B. J. Hunnicutt talked to Gen. Sherman Potter.
8. Make yourself comfortable.
9. Send your questions to Mr. Thomas N. Sane.
10. Author P. L. Travers wrote about Mary Poppins.

B. Copy the following, putting periods where necessary.

1. 1301 Ridge Ave.
2. 260 B. C.
3. 4:15 P. M.
4. 4 Pond St. Winthrop, MA 02152
5. P.O. Box 253
6. Dec. 15, 1985
7. 20 lb.
8. Dr. C. G. Opaskar
9. 5 ft. 7 in.
10. 55 mi.

C. Copy this outline, putting periods where necessary.

Abraham Lincoln

I. Before becoming President
  A. Childhood
  B. Early career
II. As President
  A. Civil War
  B. Emancipation Proclamation

545

Using the Question Mark

Objective

To use the question mark correctly

Presenting the Lesson

1. Read and discuss page 546. Review the definition and use of the interrogative sentence.

2. Assign and discuss Exercises A and B on pages 546–547.

Individualizing the Lesson

Less-Advanced Students

Have the students write two questions beginning with each of the following interrogative words: *who, what, where, when, why, how.*

Advanced Students

Tell students that a UFO has landed and that they are to compose 10 questions to ask the extra-terrestrial beings on board.

Optional Practice

Have students follow directions for Exercise A using these sentences.

1. Do you like plums?
2. Is that an oyster or a clam?
3. Mom wants to know when you will be home.
4. Where is Independence Hall?
5. Please take that away.
6. Have you lost weight?
7. Are sapphires blue or green?

Extending the Lesson

Give students a short list of people, places, events, and things from

Using the Question Mark

A **question mark (?)** is used at the end of every interrogative sentence. It is a signal that a question has been asked. When you are reading aloud, the question mark tells you to raise the pitch of your voice.

Are you ready to go? What did you say?

Use a question mark at the end of every interrogative sentence.

Exercises **Use question marks correctly.**

A. Copy these sentences. Use either a period or a question mark at the end of each sentence.

1. I built a bookshelf in shop class.
2. Does Jason collect stamps?
3. Look at that printing press.
4. What is batik?
5. Can you grow a plant from orange seeds?
6. How does this camera work?
7. Mom made the costumes for our play.
8. Do all of the problems on this page.
9. When was the Battle of Gettysburg fought?
10. Do you have this album?

B. Follow the directions for Exercise A.

1. Sam plays the saxaphone.
2. Are you babysitting for the Mayberry children?
3. Measure the length and width of the room.
4. I make animals and flowers from paper scraps.
5. Can you tie a half-hitch knot?
6. Come and join our softball game.
7. Have you ever made granola?

8. Recycle glass bottles to save natural resources.
9. What is that sound in the engine?
10. The motor is racing.

Using the Exclamation Point

An **exclamation point (!)** is used at the end of an exclamatory sentence and after words or phrases that show strong feeling. An exclamation point tells the reader that the sentence or words should be read with strong feeling. The exclamation point signals surprise, joy, fear, excitement, or shock.

Don't open that door!

Help! Fire!

Good grief!

Use an exclamation point at the end of an exclamatory sentence or word.

Exercises Use the exclamation point correctly.

A. Copy these sentences. Use a period, a question mark, or an exclamation point where it is needed.

1. Do you have a sweet tooth?
2. Hooray! We won!
3. Oh, no! The bus has gone.
4. When does the dance begin?
5. Where is your prize?
6. We went to the new house.
7. Let's play these records.
8. May I use the shovel?
9. Start with a simple project.
10. Halt!

their other studies, or have them make their own list. Ask them to write a question beginning with *who, what, where,* or *when* for each item and to write an answer for the question. Use the questions for a review in that subject, or for a contest.

(Answers will vary.)

Examples:
a. larynx
What is your larynx?
The larynx is your voice box.
b. July 4, 1776
What happened on July 4, 1776?
The Declaration of Independence was adopted on July 4, 1776.

Using the Exclamation Point

Objective

To use the exclamation point correctly

Presenting the Lesson

1. Read and discuss page 547. Review the exclamatory sentence. Point out that an imperative sentence showing strong emotion is punctuated like an exclamatory sentence.

Imperative: Stop that dog!

2. Assign and discuss Exercises A and B on pages 547–548.

Individualizing the Lesson

Less-Advanced Students

Have the students read the sentences in Exercise A with proper intonation. Direct them to be conscious of the way their voices rise and/or drop, depending on the type of sentence.

Advanced Students

Have the students create five exclamatory sentences using the following emotions: surprise, excitement, joy, shock, and caution.

Optional Practice

Have students follow the directions for Exercise A.

1. Watch out for that snake !
2. Peanuts are actually beans .
3. This is very hot !
4. Did you see that skunk ?
5. How delicious this shrimp is !

Using the Comma

Objective

To use the comma correctly

Presenting the Lesson

1. Read and discuss pages 548–550. Point out how confusing our written language would be without commas. Ask students for additional examples of each rule concerning the use of commas. Stress that the comma before or after a direct quotation is placed *before* the quotation marks.

2. You may find it helpful to do Exercise A on page 550 with the class. Assign and discuss Exercises B and C.

Individualizing the Lesson

Less-Advanced Students

Caution students against using an unnecessary comma after the final word in a series. For example, "The

B. Writing Number your paper from 1 to 5. Write an exclamation to express your feeling about five imaginary events.
Answers will vary.

Example: *Event*—I received a 10-speed bicycle.
Exclamation—This is just what I wanted!

Using the Comma

The **comma (,)** generally signals a pause in a sentence, or a separation between related ideas. When you are reading aloud, the comma tells you to pause briefly.

There are eight uses of the comma that you should know.

Use a comma to separate the day of the month from the year.

Thomas Jefferson died on July 4, 1826.

The stock market crashed on October 29, 1929.

If the date appears in the middle of the sentence, place a comma after the year, also.

Peace came on November 11, 1918, to the nations of Europe.

On August 9, 1974, President Nixon resigned.

Use a comma to separate the name of a city from the state or country in which it is located.

Toronto, Canada   Detroit, Michigan

Miami, Florida   Tokyo, Japan

If the name appears in the middle of a sentence, place a comma after the state or country.

We lived in Cherry Valley, Ohio, for several years.

Every year in Rutland, Vermont, there is a county fair.

Use a comma to set off the name of a person spoken to.

Will you close the door, Juan?

Miss Bristol, may I leave early today?

I think, Nancy, that I'll be late today.

Use a comma after introductory words, such as *yes* and *no*.

No, planets are not stars.

Yes, we will meet you before the game.

Use a comma to set apart words or names in a series.

Two words or names are not a series. There are always more than two in a series.

We had watermelon and sherbet for dessert. (no series)

We had apples, pears, and cheese for dessert. (series)

Read and punctuate a series carefully.
How many girls are named in each sentence below?

I invited Mary, Louise, Sue, Ann, and Jean.

I invited Mary Louise, Sue Ann, and Jean.

You see that changing the number of commas changes the number of girls from five to three.

Use a comma before or after a direct quotation.

The crowd shouted, "Run to third base!"

"I like swimming best," Ted replied.

Use a comma after the greeting of a friendly letter and the closing of any letter.

Dear Joseph,   Yours truly,

large, brown, and shaggy, dog" is incorrect. Remind them that words in a series must be of the same type and there is one less comma than the number of words in the series.

Have the students put commas in the following sentences:

1. Our school colors are blue, white, and orange.
2. We were hot, tired, and sweaty after gym.
3. After lunch I have math, reading, and science.
4. I just want some peace and quiet.
5. You will need thread, buttons, pins, and needles to fix this jacket.

Advanced Students

Have the students write a sentence illustrating each of the rules for commas. Encourage them to be original.

Optional Practice

Have students copy the following phrases from the board or a worksheet, inserting commas when necessary.

1. *Dates:* January 1, 1979
   October 25, 1792
   June 3, 1903
   April 10, 1686
   February 29, 1970
2. *Cities and Countries:*
   Acapulco, Mexico
   Buenos Aires, Argentina
   Geneva, Switzerland
   Dublin, Ireland
   Tokyo, Japan
3. *Series:* planets, stars, and moons
   eye, ear, nose, and throat
   movies, books, television programs, and articles
   sugar, honey, jam, and jelly
   soccer, football, baseball, and hockey

Extending the Lesson

1. This project may be done during another exercise or with small groups. Give one person in the group/class the first line of a story such as "Once upon a time there was a man who was rich, but he could never stay in one place." Each student is to add a sentence containing at least one comma to the story. The story can be silly, but each sentence should build on the ones before it. When all have contributed, the story can be duplicated and the commas identified.

2. Tell the students that the printer who made the following signs did not have his stencil for commas and that they are to supply the commas where missing.

1. State Fair, August 29, 30, 31
2. Shoppers, don't miss the Springhill Mall!
3. If you care, do your share.
4. Grand Hotel, located in downtown Centerville, Ohio
5. For better goverment, vote for Elliot Jones.
6. Speedy Bee says, "Use Fast Freight Delivery Service."
7. Try our breakfast special—ham, eggs, toast, jelly, and juice.
8. Yes, everyone loves Fun City!
9. Say folks, want to save money?
10. Eye, ear, nose, and throat clinic just ahead

Use a comma in a compound sentence.

Place the comma before the conjunction.

Casey struck out, and the game was over.

The cookies burned, but we ate them anyway.

Exercises **Use commas correctly.**

A. Copy the following sentences. Put in commas where they are needed. Be ready to explain the reason for each comma you put in.

1. Dad, where did you find my gloves?
2. Julie, answer this riddle.
3. The Declaration of Independence was signed on July 4, 1776.
4. Amelia Earhart was born in Atchison, Kansas, on July 24, 1898.
5. Yes, you may have another glass of apple juice.
6. A Kentucky Derby winner must be bold, fast, and strong.
7. Do you always stop, look, and listen at crossings?
8. "You'll feel better after a rest," the nurse said.
9. The birdcage fell, and my parakeet screeched.
10. Courtney said, "Pick a card."

B. Follow the directions for Exercise A.

1. No, I'd rather have soup.
2. Stacey said, "Try this magic trick."
3. The Astrodome is in Houston, Texas.
4. This lake is cool, deep, and clear.
5. The guide arrived early, but the tour began late.
6. Debbie, did you see the seahorse?
7. "I'll be outside," Larry said.
8. We had planned a picnic, but it rained all day.

9. The fielder caught, dropped, and recovered the ball.
10. Sputnik was launched on October 4, 1957.

C. Writing Copy the following note, using necessary commas.

Dear Kate,
Yes, my parents said that I may visit you and your family in Little Rock on the weekend of July 4. I am so excited! I cannot wait to see you, Kate. I will be arriving by bus on July 2, at 2:30 P.M. Be sure to give my best to Jodie, Sara, Maggie, and your parents.

Your friend,
Ginny

Using the Apostrophe

The **apostrophe (')** is used for two different purposes. When you are reading aloud, it has no effect on how you say the word in which it appears.

The Apostrophe To Show Possession

A **possessive** is a word that shows that someone or something owns something else.

To form the possessive of a singular noun, add an apostrophe and an *s*.

The tent that belongs to James is James's tent.

The car that belongs to his mother is his mother's car.

To form the possessive of a plural noun that does not end in *s*, add an apostrophe and an *s*.

The toys of the children are the children's toys.

The hats that belong to men are men's hats.

Using the Apostrophe

Objective

To use the apostrophe correctly to form possessives and contractions

Presenting the Lesson

1. Read and discuss pages 551–552. If necessary, review briefly the definition and use of possession in Section 3, Part 4.

2. Assign and discuss Exercises A and B on page 552.

3. Read and discuss pages 552–553.

4. Assign and discuss Exercises A and B on page 554.

Individualizing the Lesson

Less-Advanced Students

Remind the students that there is one rule for making singular words possessive but two for plural words. Give the students the following two columns of words and have them make each possessive.

Singular	Plural
1. a lady's watch	many ladies' watches
2. a cat's paw	many cats' paws
3. a sheep's wool	many sheep's wool
4. a girl's room	many girls' rooms
5. a soldier's hat	many soldiers' hats
6. a mouse's tail	many mice's tails
7. a gentleman's hat	many gentlemen's hats
8. a tree's trunk	many trees' trunks
9. a boss's car	many bosses' cars
10. a leaf's color	many leaves' colors

Advanced Students

Give the students the following phrases and have them rewrite them using possessive forms. Remind them to be careful in their placement of *s* and an apostrophe.

Example: The dog of my sister
my sister's dog

1. the records of Leo Leo's records
2. the mothers of the babies babies' mothers
3. the horns of the deer deer's horns
4. the caps of the sailors sailors' caps
5. the smell of the cookies cookies' smell
6. the boots of the boys boys' boots
7. the pages of the book book's pages
8. the ties of the men men's ties
9. the votes of the people people's votes
10. the cage of the walrus walrus's cage

Optional Practice

Have the students write the possessive form for the following words:

1. Carmen's	6. fish's
2. bus's	7. child's
3. swimmers'	8. fox's
4. hats'	9. Gus's
5. dress's	10. bees'

To form the possessive of a plural noun that ends in *s*, add only an apostrophe.

The cages of the tigers are the tigers' cages.

The costumes of the actresses are the actresses' costumes.

Exercises **Use apostrophes to show possession.**

A. Write the possessive form of these words.

1. Maria's	5. boss's	9. the Smiths'
2. our class's	6. woman's	10. tribe's
3. people's	7. workers'	11. ranchers'
4. puppies'	8. Chris's	12. hostess's

B. Copy the groups of words below. Make the underlined word in each group show possession.

1. the <u>kittens'</u> mother	6. your <u>grandparents'</u> house
2. the <u>catcher's</u> mitt	7. the <u>captain's</u> orders
3. bus <u>drivers'</u> uniforms	8. the <u>woman's</u> office
4. <u>Ann's</u> cousin	9. <u>Geraldo's</u> uncle
5. the <u>children's</u> library	10. the <u>canary's</u> cage

The Apostrophe in Contractions

Do you often use the word *don't*? It is a short way of saying *do not*. The apostrophe shows that a letter has been left out.

A word made up of two words combined into one by leaving out one or more letters is called a **contraction.**

Common Contractions

is not = isn't	it is = it's
does not = doesn't	I will = I'll
do not = don't	I am = I'm
cannot = can't	they are = they're
will not = won't	we are = we're
have not = haven't	you have = you've
would not = wouldn't	I would or I had = I'd

Use an apostrophe in a contraction, to show where one or more letters have been omitted.

Be especially careful with *it's* and *its.* Remember:

It's (with an apostrophe) always means *it is* or *it has.*
It's time for lunch.

Its (without the apostrophe) is the possessive of *it.*
The kitten played with *its* rubber mouse.

Remember also that no apostrophe is used with the possessive pronouns *hers, yours, ours,* and *theirs.*

This guitar is *hers.* *Ours* is the best team.
That one is *yours.* *Theirs* is losing now.

Here are some contractions and other words that are often confused.

Who's means *who is* or *who has.*
Who's been eating my porridge?

Whose is the possessive of *who.*
Whose coat is this?

You're means *you are.*
You're the first person to give the right answer.

Your is the possessive of *you.*
I'll put *your* paper on the bulletin board.

They're means *they are.*
They're on the plane to Oregon now.

Their is the possessive form of *they.*
The band members played *their* instruments well.

There means a place, or it is used to begin sentences.
I am going *there* later. *There* is someone at the door.

Extending the Lesson

Point out to the students that possessive personal pronouns *(his, hers, its, ours, yours, theirs)* do not use apostrophes yet indefinite pronouns (*everyone*, *anyone*, *someone* etc.) do require an apostrophe. Give the students the following sentences and have them choose the correct word in parentheses.

1. The dog lost (its, it's) owner.
2. This could be (anyone's, anyones) pencil.
3. I think these books are (hers, her's).
4. (Somebodys, Somebody's) car has (its, it's) lights on.
5. Is this camera (your's, yours) or (hers, her's)?
6. It was (anybody's, anybodys) game after the field goal.
7. Those parking spaces are (theirs, their's), but these are (ours, our's).

Exercises **Use apostrophes to show contractions.**

A. Write each pair of words. Beside each pair, write its contraction.

1. have not (haven't)
2. does not (doesn't)
3. it is (it's)
4. was not (wasn't)
5. would not (wouldn't)
6. were not (weren't)
7. I am (I'm)
8. did not (didn't)
9. are not (aren't)
10. had not (hadn't)
11. you are (you're)
12. she would (she'd)

B. Copy the following sentences, inserting apostrophes where they are needed.

1. Isn't that racket yours?
2. Who's building the fire?
3. I can't play chess.
4. Doesn't your city have a children's museum?
5. You'll enjoy Lisa's new records.
6. Vic's house is full of pets.
7. It's a picture of a lion's den.
8. The kittens are Mandy's and hers.
9. They're in Mr. Baxter's art class.
10. The box won't fit on this shelf.

Using the Hyphen

Often when you are writing you run out of space at the end of a line and cannot fit in all of the next word. When this happens, you write part of the word, followed by a **hyphen (-)**, on that line. You write the rest of the word at the beginning of the next line.

Use a hyphen to divide a word at the end of a line.

In prehistoric times, the dinosaur roamed the earth.

Using the Hyphen

Objective

To use the hyphen correctly to divide words at the end of a line

Presenting the Lesson

1. Read and discuss pages 554–555. Stress the importance of referring to the dictionary for help in deciding where to divide a word.

2. It is suggested that Exercise A on page 555 be done as a class activity. Assign and discuss Exercise B.

554

Only words of two or more syllables can be divided at the end of a line. Never divide words of one syllable, such as *pound* or *might*. If you are in doubt about dividing a word, look it up in a dictionary.

A single letter must not be left at the end of a line. For example, this division would be wrong: *a-part*. A single letter must not appear at the beginning of a line either. It would be wrong to divide *dictionary* like this: *dictionar-y*.

Exercises Use the hyphen.

A. Decide whether you can divide each of these words into two parts. Each part should have more than one letter. Check the word in a dictionary to be sure. If a word can be divided, write it as you would if the word occurred at the end of a line. Add the necessary hyphen. If the word can be divided into two parts in more than one way, show both ways. If the word cannot be divided, just copy it.

Examples: a. arithmetic
arith- or *arithme-*
metic *tic*

b. able
able

1. bury
2. ad|ven|ture
3. sail
4. mu|sic
5. owl
6. copy
7. gro|cer|ies
8. mar|bles
9. live
10. hon|est
11. to|geth|er
12. hun|gry

B. Follow the directions for Exercise A.

1. ban|ner
2. col|lec|tion
3. strange
4. po|ny
5. equal
6. his|to|ry
7. sketch
8. ama|zing
9. body
10. mea|sure
11. neigh|bor|hood
12. crafts

Individualizing the Lesson

Less-Advanced Students

Review the methods that dictionaries use to divide words, such as dots, slashes or spaces between syllables. Do Exercise A aloud, having students use the dictionary.

Advanced Students

After they have completed the exercises, have students find several words in the dictionary that may appear to be two syllables but are actually one and cannot be divided.

Examples: played, yelled

Optional Practice

Using a spelling or vocabulary list, have students identify the words that may be divided at the end of a line. Ask them to list those words, and then divide each word according to the rules discussed in **Using the Hyphen.**

Extending the Lesson

Have students number their papers from one to sixteen. Put the following list of words on the board or on a worksheet. If the word is hyphenated correctly, students should write a *C*. If it is not, they should rewrite the word hyphenated correctly, or copy it without a hyphen if it cannot be divided. Remind students to check the dictionary.

1. ca-lendar (cal-en-dar)
2. hy-phen C
3. punctua-tion (punc-tu-a-tion)
4. secre-t (se-cret)
5. manu-facture (man-u-fac-ture)
6. a-partment (a-part-ment)
7. lot-tery (lot-ter-y)
8. tele-vision (tel-e-vi-sion)
9. wri-te (write)
10. resta-urant (res-tau-rant)
11. nin-th (ninth)
12. e-qual C
13. to-day C
14. smi-le (smile)
15. di-vide C
16. tac-os (ta-cos)

Using Quotation Marks

Objective

To use quotation marks correctly in direct quotations, and to use quotation marks and underlining in titles

Presenting the Lesson

1. Read and discuss pages 556–557. Point out that quotation marks are always used in pairs.

2. It is suggested that you do Exercise A on page 557 with the class. Assign and discuss Exercises B and C on pages 557–558.

3. Read and discuss page 558. Stress that quotation marks enclose only what is actually spoken. Explain that if the actual quotation is one sentence, it should be treated as one sentence even if it is interrupted by phrases such as *she said* or *he replied.* If there are two sentences, they should be treated as two standard sentences, both beginning with capital letters and ending with proper punctuation.

4. It is suggested that Exercise A on page 559 be done as a class activity. Assign and discuss Exercise B.

5. Read and discuss pages 559–560.

6. Assign and discuss the Exercise on page 560.

Individualizing the Lesson

Less-Advanced Students

Tell the students to think of a quotation as a sentence within a sentence. In addition to the four rules on page 556, tell the students that asking the following questions

Using Quotation Marks

When you write the exact words that someone said, you are quoting that person. The person's exact words are called a direct quotation. **Quotation marks (" ")** are the sign that someone is being quoted exactly.

Use quotation marks before and after the words of every direct quotation.

Read this sentence carefully:

Molly called, "**T**he game starts in ten minutes."

Notice these things about the sentence above:

1. There is a comma (,) before the quotation.
2. Only the speaker's exact words are placed inside the quotation marks.
3. The quotation begins with a capital letter.
4. The punctuation at the end of the sentence is placed *inside* the quotation marks.

Study each of these sentences. See how each one follows the four rules.

Kenneth yelled, "**T**here is a fire in the kitchen**!**"

Della asked, "**D**id anybody find a red glove**?**"

The director insisted, "**S**peak slowly and clearly**.**"

A Quotation at the Beginning of a Sentence

Sometimes a quotation is placed at the beginning of a sentence.

"**T**his plant needs water," Mr. Crockett said.

Notice that the comma ending the quotation is placed inside the quotation marks. Notice that the punctuation ending each of the following quotations is also placed inside the quotation marks. Notice, too, the punctuation at the end of each sentence.

> "**T**here is a fire in the kitchen**!**" yelled Kenneth.
>
> "**D**id anybody find a red glove**?**" Della asked.
>
> "**S**peak slowly and clearly," the director insisted.

Exercises Punctuate quotations correctly.

A. Copy these sentences. Punctuate them correctly.

1. "Make up your mind," Dennis urged.
2. "I finished the puzzle," he announced.
3. JoAnn asked, "Is that a sparrow?"
4. The zookeeper warned, "Don't disturb the panda."
5. "Where is the North Star?" she asked.
6. "What causes a storm?" Lauren asked.
7. "Mom raises bees," said Jeff.
8. "A chameleon changes color," Terri noted.
9. Dad asked, "Where are your gloves?"
10. Mr. Owens said, "Sing that verse again."

B. Follow the directions for Exercise A.

1. "What happened to my room?" Caroline asked.
2. The doctor shouted, "I need a bandage!"
3. "Put your feet in the stirrups," she said.
4. "Here's the entrance!" Kyle yelled.
5. Charlene asked, "What's your favorite color?"
6. "The monarch is a butterfly," Alonzo explained.
7. Steve shouted, "My kite string broke!"
8. Emily said, "I have a Venus' flytrap."
9. I asked, "Have you read the comic strips?"
10. "Where is the Nancy Drew book?" Alison asked.

about a sentence should make it easier to punctuate.

1. Who is the speaker?
2. What are the speaker's exact words?
3. Where do the quotation marks go?

Advanced Students

Ask the students to recall a conversation that they had in the last twenty-four hours. Have them write at least five sentences from that conversation with correct punctuation and speaker identification.

Optional Practice

1. Have the students punctuate the following sentences.

1. "What are you doing?" I asked.
2. "Cutting glass for my window," Louis answered.
3. "Which window," I inquired, "is that?"
4. Louis replied, "I make stained glass windows."
5. "Can I watch you work?" I asked.
6. "Sure," Louis said, "but watch out for glass bits."
7. "Is this," I asked, "a soldering gun?"
8. "Yes," Louis replied. "It is used to join the lead together."
9. "Now I am cementing the glass into the lead," Louis continued.
10. I exclaimed, "This is beautiful!"

2. You may want to put this exercise on a worksheet. Leave enough space between pairs of sentences so that students have room to rewrite one of the sentences. Explain that one of the two sentences in each pair is correct, but that the other needs quotation marks and may also need capitalization. Students should write *C* after the correct sentence in each pair. In the

557

space below each pair, students should rewrite correctly the sentence containing errors.

Example: a. Roger wanted to know where Eric was. C
b. Why couldn't Eric play baseball? Roger asked.
"Why couldn't Eric play baseball?" Roger asked.

1. a. He asked me if I wanted to go. C
   b. He asked, "Do you want to go?"
2. a. The baby cried, "Waaa! Waaa!"
   b. The baby cried when he was hungry. C
3. a. "I can fix the computer," the robot said.
   b. It was the robot that fixed the computer. C
4. a. The librarian asked if I liked to read biographies.
   b. The librarian asked, "Do you like to read biographies?"
5. a. One of the questions on the test was about the planet Saturn.
   b. "Do you know which planets have rings around them?" the teacher asked.
6. a. My mother yelled to my little sister, "Stay out of the street!"
   b. My mother yelled at my little sister to stay out of the street. C
7. a. The conductor on the train said, "Tickets, please."
   b. The conductor on the train asked us for our tickets. C
8. a. The announcer said that the center fielder had fumbled the ball. C
   b. The announcer said, "The center fielder fumbled the ball."
9. a. The imaginary lion won't scare us. C
   b. "I'll try not to scare you," roared the imaginary lion.
10. a. The ski instructor told us to bend our knees. C
    b. "Bend your knees," directed the ski instructor.

C. Writing Each of these five sentences has one mistake in it. Write the sentences correctly.

1. "Mary said, "I will be home soon."
2. "Do you deliver the newspaper" Ms. Conklin asked the girl on the bicycle.
3. Jeff yelled, "look out for the car!"
4. Lydia said, "You may use my skateboard".
5. "My watch broke," Spencer" complained.

Divided Quotations

Sometimes a quotation is divided by explaining words. These are words like *she said* or *he asked* that come in the middle of the quotation.

"After three hamburgers," Vic said, "pie would be too much."

Divided quotations follow the same capitalization and punctuation rules that you have already studied. Here are three more rules for divided quotations:

1. Use two sets of quotation marks.
2. Use a comma or a period after the explaining words. Use a comma if the second part of the quotation does not begin a new sentence. Use a period if the second part of the quotation is a new sentence.

"Did you know," Katherine asked, "that mammoths once lived here?"

"Turn off the TV," Larry suggested. "**N**othing good is on now."

3. If the second part of the quotation begins a new sentence, capitalize the first word. This was done in the second example above. Otherwise, do not capitalize the first word.

Exercises **Punctuate divided quotations correctly.**

A. Copy these divided quotations. Add punctuation and capital letters where they are needed.

1. "Some people," Josh noted, "don't laugh much."
2. "I'm tired," Suzanne said. "let's rest."
3. "After you move," Jeff asked, "will you write to me?"
4. "During the summer," Amy said, "we make ice cream."
5. "What's cooking?" I asked. "it smells good."
6. "We're late," Mom said. "the show has started."
7. "When does camp start?" Sonia asked. "I'm ready."
8. "I have a layout," Bill said, "for a model railroad."
9. "For my project," Tom said, "I made soap sculptures."
10. "We've looked at stars," Lynn said. "we used a telescope."

B. Follow the directions for Exercise A.

1. "My favorite ballplayer," Kelly said, "is Pete Rose."
2. "Drop the anchor," Sandra called. "we'll fish here."
3. "The space shuttle *Columbia*," Marilyn reported, "has been reused many times."
4. "Drumbeats," our guide noted, "are a way of sending messages."
5. "Thread the needle," Dad said. "then make a knot."
6. "Eric made a film," I explained, "of our science project."
7. "Try this sauce," my sister said. "it's very good."
8. "Throw the boomerang," Judith said. "it will return."
9. "What's a tangram?" Joe asked. "is it a puzzle?"
10. "What," asked Elena, "can we learn from fossils?"

Using Quotation Marks for Titles

Use quotation marks to enclose chapter titles, titles of magazine articles, titles of short stories or single poems, and titles of songs.

Extending the Lesson

1. Your more-advanced students may enjoy this activity. Have students write an imaginary interview with a favorite character from a book, movie, or television program. They should write six questions and answers using phrases such as *I said, I asked,* or *he replied,* each time someone talks. Ask students to write each question and answer in a separate paragraph.

2. Have students choose three chapters from their textbooks, three articles from a newspaper, and three articles from a magazine, and write a sentence for each according to the pattern of the example below. They must use capital letters, quotation marks, and underlining correctly.

Example: "Yankee Doodle" is the title of a chapter from the book, *American History*.

Chapter: Chapter 7, "The Civil War"
Magazine article: "Finding Summer Jobs"
Short story: "The Tell-Tale Heart"
Poem: "How To Eat a Poem"
Song: "The Battle Hymn of the Republic"

Underlining

When you are writing or typing, underline the titles of books, newspapers, magazines, movies, and television programs.

The Incredible Journey   Kansas City Star
Rocky   Sports Illustrated

When these titles are printed, they are printed in *italics*, rather than underlined.

Book: *The Incredible Journey*
Newspaper: *Kansas City Star*
Magazine: *Sports Illustrated*
Movie: *Rocky*
Television program: *Good Morning, America*

Exercise Punctuate titles correctly.

Copy the following titles. Use quotation marks or underlining to make each title correct.

1. "Babe, the Blue Ox" (short story)
2. The Moonspinners (movie)
3. "How To Train Your Dog" (magazine article)
4. Hot Rod (magazine)
5. Karen (book)
6. Seattle Times (newspaper)
7. "Women in America" (chapter title)
8. "You Are My Sunshine" (song)
9. Nightline (TV program)
10. "Annabel Lee" (poem)

560

ADDITIONAL EXERCISES

Punctuation

A. The Period Write the following items, adding periods where they are needed. (Use after page 545.)

1. E. B. White wrote several famous children's books.
2. The bus will leave Washington, D. C. at 4:30 P. M.
3. Write me at P. O. Box 640, Ada, Ohio, after June 1.
4. Ms. K. L. Waverly visited the UN building.
5. The Battle of Hastings was fought in A. D. 1066.
6. Dr. F. T. Richards
   800 Austin St.
   Evanston, IL 60202
7. Salads
   I. Fruit salads
      A. Waldorf salad
      B. Hawaiian salad
   II. Vegetable salads
8. Mr. John J. Lynk works for Data Control, Inc.
9. The note read, "Meet me at 9:00 A. M., Thurs., Jan. 28."
10. Gen. George S. Patton lead U. S. Army troops during World War II.

B. The Period, the Question Mark, and the Exclamation Point Copy these sentences. Put either a period, a question mark, or an exclamation point where it is needed. (Use after page 547.)

1. When does the play begin?
2. Transplant this rosebush to the back yard.
3. Oh no! The kitten has climbed a tree.
4. Joseph mailed the basket of fruit and cheese to Aunt Evelyn.
5. Where is my ski cap?
6. How are pearls formed?

Additional Exercises

These Additional Exercises may be used for additional practice of the concepts presented in this Section. Each exercise focuses on a single concept, and should be used after the page number indicated in parentheses.

Review

If you have not assigned these Additional Exercises before this time, you can also use them as an excellent Section Review.

7. Julie practiced the piano after school.
8. Ouch! I burned my finger.
9. Cliff scored sixteen points in the basketball game.
10. Congratulations! You won the race.

C. The Comma Write the following sentences or phrases, adding commas where they are needed. (Use after page 551.)

1. On June 28, 1919, the treaty was signed in Versailles.
2. No, Sharla, I've never been to Toledo, Ohio.
3. The interviewer asked, "Mr. Cassidy, what are your plans?"
4. Yes, they sell blueberry, raspberry, and strawberry yogurt.
5. Dad made apple pancakes, and they were terrific.
6. Well, Ms. Baker, John plays the tuba, and I play the saxophone.
7. "This car needs a battery, tires, and a paint job," said the mechanic.
8. Craig, are you going to visit Springfield, Illinois, or Springfield, Massachusetts?
9. The chef said, "The recipe calls for fresh tomatoes, green peppers, and onions."
10. Dear Roger,

    I will arrive at the airport in Atlanta, Georgia, at 8:00 P.M. on June 13, 1985. Let me know if you can meet me.

    Your friend,
    Jeff

D. The Apostrophe Write each sentence, adding an apostrophe where it is needed. (Use after page 554.)

1. James's brother built a model of a space station.
2. This theater's prices have increased again.
3. Aren't the boys' lockers just like ours?

562

4. Who's the women's diving champion?
5. I'm surprised that you're here.
6. Doesn't the children's matinee begin at 2:00 P.M.?
7. Can't you go, or don't you want to?
8. Claire's cousin couldn't attend the meeting.
9. It's the pilot's voice on the intercom.
10. We're going to the Taylor's house.

E. The Hyphen Decide whether you can divide each of these words into two parts. Each part should have more than one letter. If a word can be divided, write it as you would if the word occurred at the end of a line. Add the necessary hyphen. If the word can be divided into two parts in more than one way, show both ways. If the word cannot be divided, just copy it. Use a dictionary to check your work. (Use after page 555.)

1. hob|by
2. can|dle
3. ra|zor
4. mis|be|have
5. pil|low
6. plate
7. li|brary
8. cac|tus
9. so|fa
10. drafty

F. Quotation Marks Write each sentence, adding quotation marks where they are needed. (Use after page 560.)

1. Jessica asked, "How are pickles made?"
2. "The next holiday is Halloween," Maria said.
3. "We had a picnic," Olivia said, "beside a lake."
4. "That tunnel goes through the mountains," Steven said.
5. Eve Merriam wrote the poem called "Cheers."
6. "Who wants pepperoni," asked Vic, "and who wants mushrooms?"
7. Mr. Barker remarked, "The traffic is heavy today."
8. "Hold that line!" shouted the cheerleaders.
9. At midnight the band played "Good Night, Ladies."
10. "Give me two burgers," ordered the waiter, "but no fries."

563

Mixed Review

These exercises provide review of the concepts presented in this Section. Each exercise challenges the students to apply several of the skills they have acquired during previous study. Because the "mixed" feature of these activities makes them more difficult, the teacher may wish to have less-advanced students do them orally or in small groups.

MIXED REVIEW

Punctuation

A. Using punctuation correctly Copy the following sentences, adding periods, question marks, exclamation points, apostrophes and commas where necessary.

1. Did you read the book *Extra Cash for Kids* before starting your business?
2. Yes, I visited EPCOT Center in March, 1984.
3. The baby played in the mud, the sand, and the water.
4. On July 8, 1985, we will move to Mobile, Alabama.
5. The Smithsonian Institute is in Washington, D.C.
6. Susan B. Anthony worked for women's rights.
7. "I looked," said Ray, "but I can't find the hamster."
8. "Dr. Kramer will see you at 10:00 A.M.," said Gail.
9. "I'm cheering for the Giants," said Alison. "I hope they win."
10. "Jeff, isn't this your notebook?" I asked.

B. Using punctuation correctly in letters Copy the following letter. Add the punctuation that is needed.

Camp We-Ha-Kee
Winter, WI 53714
July 20, 1985

Dear Molly,

You were right! I'm so busy with my activities here that I hardly have time to miss you and the folks. Archery, sailing, and riding are my favorites. Our drama group will be performing The Princess and the Pea for Parents' Weekend. Are you coming too? I hope you're keeping my side of the room clean, Molly!

Your sister,

Jennifer

C. Proofreading for correct punctuation Proofread the following paragraph. Most of the punctuation in it is missing. Rewrite the paragraph, adding the correct punctuation.

Throughout history, people have built many amazing things. The Great Wall of China is one of them. The Great Wall of China was built more than 2,000 years ago. It's almost 4,000 miles long and it is the only structure on earth that astronauts in outer space can see. The Great Wall was built to protect the Chinese people against invaders. Wouldn't you like to visit this wonder of the world? Prof. Hsang from the university will lead a tour starting July, 1985. The tour will depart from Chicago, Illinois. You can read more about the Great Wall in the article "China's Amazing Wall" in this month's *Adventure* magazine.

565

Using Mechanics in Writing

These challenging and enjoyable activities allow the students to see how the concepts of grammar, usage, and mechanics may be applied in actual writing situations. Each exercise is designed to allow students practice in several of the skills they have acquired in this Section. The activities also provide opportunities for students to write creatively about a wide variety of interesting and unusual subjects.

USING MECHANICS IN WRITING

Punctuation

A. Imagine that you are out riding your bike one day. A blinding white light suddenly appears. Then the light disappears. On the ground is a glowing object. As you look closer, you see that it is an electronic message. The words are in English, but there is no punctuation. You must punctuate it in order to make sense out of it.

> Hello, earthlings. We are friendly beings from another galaxy. We know your language, but we are not sure you know ours. That's why we are writing in English. We are curious about life on your planet. How interesting it seems! We want to learn more about you, and we are eager to tell you about life on our planet Polaria. Would you like to communicate? If so, write your name, age, and address on this scroll. We will come for it at 8:30, Mon., Nov. 12 in front of Lincoln's statue in the park. Don't be afraid.

B. You dialed the phone number of your best friend. For some reason, you got the Twilight Zone instead. A famous person from history answers the phone. Write down the unusual conversation you have with this person. Use quotation marks correctly in recording your dialogue.

Spelling

When you speak, you never have to think about how a word is spelled. When you write, however, correct spelling is absolutely necessary. Because you want your writing to make sense, you want to be a good speller.

You can become a better speller by developing a few good habits and understanding a few basic rules. These habits and rules will help you to write clearly. In this section you will learn the most important habits and rules of good spelling.

Section Objectives

1. To develop habits for good spelling
2. To understand and apply common spelling rules
3. To distinguish between homonyms and other words often confused, and to use them correctly

Preparing the Students

Read and discuss the introduction on page 567. Bring up the fact that the rules discussed in this chapter will not tell how to spell every word, but will make most words easier to figure out. The rules will also give clues to help students find the more difficult words in the dictionary.

It might be more helpful to do parts of this section periodically so that students will not have too many spelling rules to learn all at once; instead, they can concentrate on a few at a time. You can coordinate learning some of the rules with other spelling lessons or vocabulary work.

Additional Resources

Diagnostic Test — page 10 in the test booklet

Mastery Test — pages 66–67 in the test booklet

Additional Exercises — pages 583–586 in the student text

Practice Book — pages 212–220

Duplicating Masters — pages 212–220

Special Populations — See special section at the front of this Teacher's Edition.

Plan Your Study of Spelling

Objective

To develop habits for good spelling

Presenting the Lesson

1. Read and discuss pages 568–570. Ask students for examples of words they find difficult to spell correctly. Write them on the board and ask other students if they can think of any memory devices that would help someone remember the correct spelling. Using a few of the most difficult words on the board, have the class go through the *Steps for Mastering Specific Words* together. Erase the words and test the class on them. Let students check their own papers to help each one discover personal strengths or weaknesses.

2. You may find it helpful to do Exercise A on page 570 as a class activity. Discuss why people frequently misspell those particular words. Assign and discuss Exercises B and C.

Individualizing the Lesson

Less-Advanced Students

Attitude is often a major problem with poor spellers. You should try to help those with a defeatist attitude by constantly encouraging them to make use of the seven improvement habits.

Remind students that correct spelling is difficult because there are no rules that cover all words and there are countless exceptions to rules that do exist. Therefore present spelling as a challenge, but an

Plan Your Study of Spelling

There may always be a few words that you will have trouble spelling. However, you will be able to master most words quickly if you work at developing the following habits.

Habits for Improving Your Spelling

1. Make a habit of looking at words carefully.

When you come to a new word, be sure you know its meaning. If you are not certain, look up the word in a dictionary.

Practice seeing every letter. Many people see a word again and again but don't really look at it. When you see a new word, or a tricky word, like *government*, look at all the letters. To help you remember them, write the word several times.

2. When you speak, pronounce words carefully.

Some people spell words wrong just because they do not pronounce them right. If you leave out certain sounds, you will have a hard time spelling words correctly.

Here is a list of words that cause trouble because they are often pronounced wrong. The letters in dark print are the letters that are often left out in spelling because they are left out in pronouncing the words.

Feb**r**uary	diff**e**rent	gover**n**ment
lib**r**ary	groc**e**ry	fam**i**ly
hund**r**ed	hist**o**ry	proba**b**ly
sev**e**ral	fun**e**ral	ev**ery**body

3. Find out your own spelling enemies and attack them.

Look over your papers and make a list of the misspelled words. Also keep a list of new words that are difficult for you. Study these words until you can spell them correctly and easily.

4. Find memory devices to help with problem spellings.

Some words are difficult to remember. In these cases, a memory device may help you. A memory device is a trick, or a catchy sentence about the word, that you can remember easily. The device tells you how to spell the word. Here are two examples:

friend *I* will be your fri*end* to the *end.*
believe There is a *lie* in be*lie*ve.

5. Proofread what you write.

To make sure that you have spelled all words correctly, reread your work. Examine it carefully, word for word. Don't let your eyes race over the page and miss incorrectly spelled words.

6. Use a dictionary.

You don't have to know how to spell every word. No one spells everything correctly all the time. A good dictionary can help you to be a better speller. Use a dictionary whenever you need help with your spelling.

7. Study the few important spelling rules given in this section.

Steps for Mastering Specific Words

When you notice that you are having trouble with a certain word, take a few minutes to study it carefully. Give it all your attention. If you spend the time and energy to learn it correctly once, you will save yourself all the trouble of correcting it many times.

Follow these steps to master a specific word.

important one that will make a difference in the way they communicate with others.

Be sure to write on the board any useful memory aids that the students devise, for all to share.

Examples:
1. The "princi*pal*" is your *pal.*
2. *"Loose"* rhymes with *moose.*
3. "Capitol" is often a round building—like the letter *o.*
4. "Except" means to leave out or "X" out.
5. "Dessert" has two *s's* like *strawberry shortcake.*

Advanced Students

Good spellers should be challenged to become even better spellers. You may wish to use an advanced list of spelling words and have the students use them in sentences or quiz each other in spelling. An alternate exercise is to have students copy words they may use in any of their classes but have trouble spelling, and make their own list of difficult words to master.

Optional Practice

Divide the class into small groups. Have each student list five words he or she finds difficult to spell, circling each trouble spot. The groups should discuss ways that might be helpful for students to remember the correct spellings. They should compile a group list, making a copy for each group member. Any suggestions that were made to help remember the spellings should be noted next to the word on the list. Before the students study the entire list, check the words to see that they are practical. The students should

569

then take their lists home and study the words according to the directions in the text. Have the groups form again later for post-tests.

Extending the Lesson

Combine all the lists from each group from the optional exercise above and use them for a spelling bee. Distribute copies to students for study beforehand.

Steps for Mastering Specific Words

1. **Look at the word and say it to yourself.**
   Pronounce it carefully. If it has two or more syllables, say it again, one syllable at a time. Look at each syllable as you say it.

2. **Look at the letters and say each one.**
   If the word has two or more syllables, pause between syllables as you say the letters.

3. **Without looking at the word, write it.**

4. **Now look at your book or list to see if you have spelled the word correctly.**
   If you have, write it once more. Compare it with the correct spelling again. For best results, repeat the process once more.

5. **If you have misspelled the word, notice where the error was.**
   Then repeat steps 3 and 4 until you have spelled the word correctly three times in a row.

Exercises **Develop good habits.**

A. Here are some words that are often pronounced carelessly and then misspelled. Look at each letter of every word. Pronounce the words correctly to yourself. Write the words in alphabetical order.

1. regular [7]
2. Saturday [9]
3. general [4]
4. ruin [8]
5. police [6]
6. different [2]
7. diamond [1]
8. poem [5]
9. violet [10]
10. finally [3]

B. Writing Write five of the words listed in Exercise A in good sentences. Check your spelling when you write the words. Sentences will vary.

C. Read through some of your recent papers to find words you have misspelled. Make a list of five to ten of your personal spelling enemies. Then study them, following the **Steps for Mastering Specific Words.**

Rules for Spelling

Many words in our language follow certain spelling patterns. Studying the following rules should help you with these words.

Spelling Words with *ie* and *ei*

Many students find it hard to tell whether *i* comes before or after *e* in spelling certain words. When the sound is long *e* ($\bar{e}$), the following rhyme provides some rules which will help you.

I before *e*
Except after *c*,
Or when sounded like *a*
As in n*ei*ghbor or w*ei*gh.

This rhyme does help. Look at the words below. Decide which lines of the rhyme work for each of these words.

believe	receive	weigh
niece	conceit	weight
relief	ceiling	eight

The rule will help you with most words. But you will have to study and remember these four words. They do not follow the rule. They are **exceptions** to the rule.

either neither seize weird

Rules for Spelling

Objective

To understand and apply common spelling rules

Presenting the Lesson

1. Read and discuss page 571. Ask students for other examples of *ie* and *ei* words.
2. Assign and discuss the Exercise on page 572.
3. Read and discuss pages 572–573. Ask students for examples of other prefixes, and other words that follow the two suffix rules.
4. Assign and discuss the Exercise on page 573.
5. Read and discuss page 574. Make sure the students recognize and can use the words listed as examples and exceptions.
6. Assign and discuss the Exercise on page 574.
7. Read and discuss pages 574–575. Ask students for examples of other words ending in *y* to which suffixes may be added. Have the students tell whether the *y* in each of those words will be changed to *i*.
8. Assign and discuss the Exercise on page 575.

9. Read and discuss the bottom of page 575 and the top of page 576. Ask students for examples of other words that need the final consonant doubled, and words that do not.

10. Assign and discuss the Exercise on 576.

11. Assign and discuss Review Exercises A and B on pages 576–577.

Individualizing the Lesson

Less-Advanced Students

Point out to students that spelling rules are often needed for easier pronunciation. Illustrate on the board what would happen to some words if rules were *not* followed.

- *babyes* looks like *bab yes*
- *storyes* looks like *stor yes*
- *carful* is a *full car*
- *fliing* is unrecognizable
- *boies, toies, buier* have too many vowels
- *swiming, spining, fater* all get the vowel sound changed from short to long

You may wish to put the above words on the board and have the students point out what rule each is violating.

Advanced Students

1. Give the students the following words and have them decide which rule each follows. (Have them use a dictionary for any word they don't know.)

1. robber	6. immature
2. illegal	7. heir
3. pierce	8. disappoint
4. studying	9. shyly
5. lovable	10. grief

Exercise **Write words with *ie* and *ei*.**

Writing Write ten sentences using words with *ie* or *ei*. (You may use more than one such word in each sentence.) Underline each of the *ie* or *ei* words you use. Answers will vary.

Example: My *niece received eight* presents.

Adding Prefixes

A **prefix** is a syllable or group of syllables that is added to the beginning of a word to change its meaning. Here are some common prefixes and examples of their use:

Prefix		Base Word		New Word
re- (again)	+	write	=	rewrite (write again)
dis- (not)	+	approve	=	disapprove (not approve)
un- (not)	+	able	=	unable(not able)
in- (not)	+	formal	=	informal (not formal)
im- (not)	+	possible	=	impossible (not possible)
counter- (against)	+	act	=	counteract (act against)
pre- (before)	+	view	=	preview (see before)
mis- (incorrectly)	+	spell	=	misspell (spell incorrectly)

When a prefix is added to a word, the spelling of the word stays the same.

Adding the Suffixes *-ly* and *-ness*

A **suffix** is a letter or syllable added to the end of a word to change its meaning. For example, the suffix *-s* is added to a singular noun to make it plural. The suffix *-ed* is added to a verb to change the action to the past. Adding a suffix sometimes adds a spelling problem to a word.

The suffix *-ly* added to an adjective changes it to an adverb.

Adjective	**Adverb**
The *total* price is ten dollars.	The car was *totally* ruined.
This puzzle is a *real* challenge.	This puzzle is *really* difficult.
My mother is a *careful* driver.	My mother drives *carefully.*

When the suffix *-ly* is added to a word ending with *l*, both *l*'s are kept.

The suffix *-ness* added to an adjective changes it to a noun.

Adjective	**Noun**
Kirk is *open* and honest.	I admire Kirk's *openness.*
Meat with little fat is called *lean.*	Look for *leanness* when you buy bacon.

When the suffix *-ness* is added to a word ending with *n*, both *n*'s are kept.

Exercise Add prefixes and suffixes.

Find the misspelled word in each of these sentences and spell it correctly.

1. I liked the eveness of Tammy's haircut.
2. Spencer thoughtfuly brought a gift to the graduation party.
3. A dog is unnable to climb a tree.
4. Winding this watch is unecessary.
5. The thiness of this pencil makes it hard to hold.
6. Some people misstrust cats.
7. We admired the salesperson's openess.
8. Those hints were awfuly misleading.
9. Holmes uncovered a totaly new clue.
10. We usualy see movie previews.

2. Have the students do the same with these exceptions to the rules.

1. science
2. busily
3. emptiness
4. height
5. judgment

Optional Practice

1. Have students complete these words with *ie* or *ei.*

1. br_ie_f	14. w_ie_rd
2. rec_ei_ve	15. c_ei_ling
3. f_ie_ld	16. s_ie_ze
4. _ei_ther	17. gr_ie_f
5. fr_ei_ght	18. y_ie_ld
6. n_ie_ce	19. bel_ie_ve
7. ch_ie_f	20. misch_ie_f
8. conc_ei_t	21. w_ei_ght
9. rec_ei_pt	22. sl_ei_gh
10. w_ei_gh	23. th_ie_f
11. dec_ei_ve	24. rel_ie_f
12. _ei_ght	25. n_ei_ther
13. th_ei_r	26. v_ei_n

2. Point out that large words are often simple roots with prefixes or suffixes added on. Give the students the following lists and have them build larger words. When they are finished they should check the spelling in the dictionary.

Prefixes	**Roots**	**Suffixes**
dis-	color	-ing
un-	write	-ly
re-	person	-able
in-	end	-ness
	comfort	-ed
	correct	-ful
	mind	
	respect	
	friend	
	predict	
	direct	
	work	
	agree	
	break	
	accept	

Extending the Lesson

1. Have students write the base word and a brief definition for each word in the list below.

1. staring (stare) starring (star)	4. planed (plane) planned (plan)
2. hoping (hope) hopping (hop)	5. riding (ride) ridding (rid)
3. scaring (scare) scarring (scar)	6. hatter (hat) hater (hate)

2. On the board, write a list of words recently studied with the letters scrambled. Have the students rearrange the letters into their proper spelling. You may wish to make this exercise a race or have the students work in teams.

Adding Suffixes to Words Ending in Silent e

Notice what happens when you add suffixes beginning with vowels to words that end in silent *e*.

hope + ing = hoping	fame + ous = famous
refuse + al = refusal	pale + er = paler
expense + ive = expensive	like + able = likable

When a suffix beginning with a vowel is added to a word ending in silent e, the e is usually dropped.

Now see what happens when you add suffixes beginning with consonants to words that end in silent *e*.

care + ful = careful	move + ment = movement
lone + ly = lonely	same + ness = sameness
score + less = scoreless	bore + dom = boredom

When a suffix beginning with a consonant is added to a word ending in silent e, the e is usually kept.

The following words are exceptions to these two rules:

truly argument ninth wholly

Exercise Add suffixes correctly.

Add the suffix given for each word. Write each new word correctly.

1. place + ing	5. hope + ful	9. like + ly
2. use + able	6. come + ing	10. save + ing
3. sure + ly	7. make + er	11. desire + able
4. confuse + ion	8. safe + ty	12. remove + al

Adding Suffixes to Words Ending in *y*

See what happens when you add suffixes to words that end in *y* following a consonant.

574

baby + es = babies	lazy + ness = laziness
empty + er = emptier	carry + ed = carried
happy + ly = happily	story + es = stories

When a suffix is added to a word that ends with *y* following a consonant, the *y* is usually changed to *i*.

However, the *y* is not changed when the suffix *-ing* is added.

empty + ing = emptying	carry + ing = carrying
fly + ing = flying	apply + ing = applying

Notice too, what happens when you add suffixes to words that end in *y* following a vowel.

boy + s = boys	play + ed = played
buy + er = buyer	stay + ing = staying

When a suffix is added to a word that ends with *y* following a vowel, the *y* usually is not changed.

The following words are exceptions: *paid, said.*

Exercise **Add suffixes correctly.**

Add the suffix given for each word. Write each new word correctly.

1. hurry + ing	6. play + er	11. carry + ed
2. story + es	7. fly + ing	12. happy + ness
3. heavy + est	8. sky + es	13. early + est
4. fly + er	9. ready + ness	14. toy + s
5. enjoy + ed	10. easy + ly	15. cry + ing

Doubling the Final Consonant

What happens to these words when you add suffixes?

spin + ing = spinning	fat + er = fatter
hot + est = hottest	scrub + ed = scrubbed

575

You can see that the last letter is doubled when suffixes beginning with a vowel are added to these words.

In words of one syllable that end with a consonant following one vowel, double the final consonant before adding *-ing*, *-ed*, *-en*, *-er*, or *-est*.

The final consonant is **not** doubled when it follows two vowels.

trail + er = trailer	shout + ed = shouted
steam + ing = steaming	float + er = floater
peel + ed = peeled	shoot + ing = shooting

Exercise Double the final consonant.

Decide whether or not the final consonant should be doubled. Add the suffix as shown. Write the new word correctly.

1. fat + est
2. stop + ed
3. sad + er
4. hear + ing
5. pat + ed
6. bit + en
7. soon + est
8. get + ing
9. plan + ed
10. big + est
11. put + ing
12. hot + er
13. leak + ed
14. rot + en
15. hop + ed

Review Exercises Use the spelling rules.

A. Find the misspelled words in these sentences and spell them correctly. (In some of the sentences, more than one word is misspelled.)

1. The surface of this desk is very iregular.
2. The wagons moved into the openess of the plains.
3. Beth recieved a carefuly wrapped gift.
4. Mom ordered a birthday cake especialy for Terry's party.
5. I copied the poem on a clean peice of paper.
6. I beleive I hear a mysteryous sound.

576

7. The theif opened the safe easyly.
8. Shopers spoted the bargains.
9. We're geting excited about the upcomeing play.
10. Hikeing and bikeing are two camp activities.

B. Add the suffix given for each word below and write the new word.

1. bite + ing
2. stay + ed
3. play + ing
4. try + ed
5. heat + er
6. shop + ed
7. make + ing
8. enjoy + s
9. waste + ing
10. fry + ed
11. hope + ing
12. tiny + est
13. sit + ing
14. big + er
15. hope + ful
16. fat + en
17. stumble + ing
18. live + able
19. worry + ing
20. run + ing

Homonyms and Other Words Often Confused

Sometimes while you are writing, you may get confused by words that look almost the same. It is not always easy to know which word to use.

Much of this confusion is caused by homonyms. **Homonyms** are words that sound the same, or nearly the same, but that are spelled differently and have different meanings. Here are some examples of homonyms:

by The parade passed *by* my house.
buy I want to *buy* that game.

meat Pork, beef, and lamb are kinds of *meat.*
meet Cara wants to *meet* her new neighbors.

threw Bob *threw* the ball to the shortstop.
through The laser burned a hole *through* the wood panel.

Before you can use homonyms correctly, you must know what each one means. You cannot depend on spelling rules to help you. The best approach is to memorize which spelling goes with which meaning.

Homonyms and Other Words Often Confused

Objective

To distinguish between homonyms and other words often confused, and to use them correctly

Presenting the Lesson

1. Read and discuss pages 577–581. Have students note those words in the list with which they have no difficulty. Try to find a reason for the difficulties with other words.

After going through the list, part by part, have students close their books. Read the definition and sentence for each word. Have students spell the word orally and then write it correctly.

2. You may wish to do Exercise A on pages 581–582 with the class. Assign and discuss Exercises B and C on page 582.

Individualizing the Lesson

Less-Advanced Students

Two of the most often misused words are *its* and *it's*. Remind the students that if "it is" or "it has" will fit into the sentence, they should use the apostrophe.

Give the students the following sentences and have them tell you whether or not *its* uses an apostrophe.

1. It's time to go.
2. The dog buried its bone.
3. The flower lost its petals.
4. I'm glad it's finally spring.
5. The cat knows it's time for its dinner.

Advanced Students

After they have completed the exercises, ask the students to add the words below to their knowledge of homonyms. Have them look up the words in the dictionary and then use each in a sentence that shows its meaning.

1. a. alter
   b. altar
2. a. break
   b. brake
3. a. course
   b. coarse
4. a. dessert
   b. desert
5. a. minor
   b. miner
6. a. waist
   b. waste

Optional Practice

1. Follow the directions for Exercise C.

1. (Which, Witch) shoes match this dress?
2. Who (won, one) the game?
3. (Their, There, They're) order is over (their, they're, there).
4. Don't (accept, except) the package without a receipt.

Following is a list of homonyms and other words that are frequently confused. Study the sets of words. Try to connect each word with its correct meaning. Refer to the list if you have further problems with these words.

accept means to agree to something or to receive something willingly.

Ms. Daly will not *accept* excuses.

except means to leave out, or leaving out.

Everyone *except* Carl won a prize.

all ready means completely prepared.

The party decorations are *all ready*.

already means previously or before.

The hikers have *already* returned.

capital means chief or important. It also means the city or town that is the official seat of government of a state or nation.

Begin every sentence with a *capital* letter.
Lincoln is the *capital* of Nebraska.

capitol is the building where a state legislature meets.

The *capitol* in Lincoln is a new building.

the Capitol is the building in Washington, D.C. in which the United States Congress meets. This *Capitol* is always capitalized.

The nation's lawmakers meet at the *Capitol.*

hear means to listen to.

I *hear* a drumbeat.

here means in this place.

Drop your fishing line *here*.

its shows ownership or possession.

We studied Mexico and *its* people.

it's is the contraction for *it is* or *it has*.

We visited Calico. *It's* a ghost town.

knew means understood or was familiar with.

Sherry *knew* many card tricks.

new is the opposite of old and means fresh or recent.

The horse has a *new* saddle.

know means to understand or to be familiar with.

The pilots *know* their flight patterns.

no is a negative word meaning *not* or *not any*.

This snowman has *no* hat.

lead (lĕd) is a heavy, gray metal.

The pipes were made of *lead*.

lead (lēd) means to go first, to guide.

The general will *lead* his army.

led (lĕd) is the past form of lead (lēd).

Pioneers *led* the way west.

loose means free or not tight.

My brother pulled his *loose* tooth.

lose means to mislay or suffer the loss of something.

If you leave, you will *lose* your place in line.

peace is calm or stillness or the absence of disagreement.

The rival tribes enjoyed a time of *peace*.

piece means a portion or part.

Liz molded the *piece* of clay.

5. I ate (two, too, to) much (dessert, desert).
6. We (all ready, already) saw this episode.
7. I (know, no) they can't (here, hear) us.
8. The (led, lead) pipe came (loose, lose) during the cleanup.
9. Is this (you're, your) (piece, peace) of pie?
10. The (principal, principle) took a (plane, plain) to a conference.
11. The defendant entered two guilty (please, pleas).
12. At noon the bells began to (peal, peel).
13. The fireplace (great, grate) was full of ashes.
14. You have every (write, right) to be here.
15. We met our state representative in the (capital, capitol) at Springfield.

2. Tell students that six of the following sentences use the wrong word, and four use the correct one. If the sentence is correct, they should put a *C* after the number of the sentence. If it is not, they should rewrite the sentence, using the correct word.

1. The library is usually a quite [quiet] place.
2. Their [They're] going shopping after lunch.
3. C Do you need some plain paper?
4. C The principal color in that painting is orange.
5. A.J. Foyt, the race car driver, passed the cars on the write [right].
6. C Its [It's] the best zoo we've visited yet.
7. The workmen were sandblasting the capitol.
8. The whether [weather] forecaster said it would rain today.
9. Ricardo and his brother no [know] how to fix televisions and air conditioners.
10. C My sister accepted the package from the delivery man.

Extending the Lesson

Pick pairs of homonyms and other words from pages 577–581. Have students, either in groups or individually, write one sentence for each of the words, or one sentence using both words in the pair. You may wish to add the pairs below.

presence	precede	sense
presents	proceed	since

plain means clear or simple. It also means an expanse of land.

Trish put a decal on the *plain* T-shirt.
Horses roamed across the *plain*.

plane refers to a woodworking tool. It also is the short form of *airplane*.

A *plane* is useful in carpentry.
The small *plane* landed in a field.

principal means first or most important. It also refers to the head of a school.

The *principal* purpose of TV is to entertain.
Our school *principal* talked to parents.

principle is a rule, truth, or belief.

Superman's *principle* is justice for all.

quiet means free from noise or disturbance.

The rabbit is a *quiet* pet.

quite means truly or almost completely.

Those acrobats are *quite* daring.

right means proper or correct. It also means the opposite of left. A third meaning refers to a fair claim.

Maria found the *right* key for the safe.
Hebrew is read from *right* to left.
The colonists felt freedom was their *right*.

write refers to forming words with a pen or pencil.

We must *write* a thank-you note.

their means belonging to them.

The children took *their* rafts to the beach.

there means at that place.

Plant the tomato seeds *there*.

they're is the contraction for *they are.*

They're taking the train to Cleveland.

to means in the direction of.

Snowflakes drifted *to* the ground.

too means also or very.

My sister wants to come, *too.*

two is the whole number between one and three.

The moose had *two* huge antlers.

weather is the state of the atmosphere, referring to wind, moisture, temperature, and other such conditions.

Tornadoes usually occur during warm *weather.*

whether indicates a choice or alternative.

Jon asked *whether* wood sinks or floats.

who's is the contraction for *who is* or *who has.*

Who's throwing those snowballs?

whose is the possessive form of *who.*

Whose house is closest to school?

your is the possessive form of *you.*

Did *your* wish come true?

you're is the contraction for *you are.*

You're looking at a haunted house.

Exercises **Use homonyms and other confusing words correctly.**

A. Write the correct word from those given in parentheses.

1. A dog can (hear, here) high-pitched sounds.
2. There are (know, no) lifeboats on this ship.

581

3. Did you (loose, lose) your library card?
4. (Their, There, They're) making stained glass.
5. Who knows the (right, write) answer?
6. This church is cool and (quiet, quite).
7. (Who's, Whose) banging those cymbals?
8. Penny has (all ready, already) finished her drawing.
9. No one (accept, except) Ramón had seen the bear.
10. Gravity is a (principal, principle) of science.

B. Follow the directions for Exercise A.

1. The bike trail begins (hear, here).
2. A giraffe raised (its, it's) head.
3. The collectors (knew, new) about foreign stamps.
4. An elephant (lead, led) the circus parade.
5. Our cabin has (to, too, two) portholes.
6. The runners are (all ready, already) for the race.
7. I borrowed (your, you're) radio.
8. The artist started with a (plain, plane) white canvas.
9. Which city is the (capital, capitol, Capitol) of Texas?
10. Joe tied the rowboat with a (peace, piece) of rope.

C. Choose the correct homonym from the two or three in parentheses. If you are not sure which word is correct, look up each homonym in the dictionary. Then write the correct word.

1. What is the (some, sum) of five plus seven?
2. The dog followed the (heard, herd) of cattle.
3. May I borrow a (pair, pare, pear) of scissors?
4. The carnation is the state (flour, flower) of Ohio.
5. How do you control the (brakes, breaks) on the bike?
6. Rhea hates to (waist, waste) time waiting for people.
7. For this macramé project, I tied a special (knot, not).
8. When Kenny fell, he complained of the (pain, pane).
9. The snowmobiles (road, rode) over the frozen marsh.
10. Gum is stuck to the (heal, heel) of my left shoe.

582

ADDITIONAL EXERCISES

Spelling

A. Spelling Look at each sentence carefully. Find the misspelled words. Write each word correctly. (Use after page 576.)

1. Pat recieved many Valentines.
2. My neice is actualy older than I am.
3. It is immpossible to reset this watch.
4. We noticed the eveness of Fred's writing.
5. This new ink is realy eraseable.
6. A furyous bull charged into the field.
7. Whistleing happyly, Carlos finished his project.
8. Jason hurryed to the nearest phone.
9. Kelly's bating average is amazeing.
10. Jenny riped the letter and tosed it into the garbage.

B. Homonyms and Words Often Confused Write the correct word from the two words in parentheses. (Use after page 581.)

1. Jody Turner (accepted, excepted) the nomination.
2. I (hear, here) the music starting.
3. The plant lost (its, it's) leaves.
4. This parade has (know, no) end!
5. How did you (loose, lose) your voice?
6. Please have a (peace, piece) of cake.
7. The horses tossed (their, they're) heads.
8. Lyle wondered (weather, whether) the team had won or lost.
9. (Who's, Whose) speech is next?
10. (Your, You're) garden is filled with weeds.

Additional Exercises

These Additional Exercises may be used for additional practice of the concepts presented in this Section. Each exercise focuses on a single concept, and should be used after the page number indicated in parentheses.

Review

If you have not assigned these Additional Exercises before this time, you can also use them as an excellent Section Review.

Mixed Review

These exercises provide review of the concepts presented in this Section. Each exercise challenges the students to apply several of the skills they have acquired during previous study. Because the "mixed" feature of these activities makes them more difficult, the teacher may wish to have less-advanced students do them orally or in small groups.

MIXED REVIEW

Spelling

A. Spelling words correctly Pick out the words that are spelled incorrectly in the following sentences. Write them correctly. Some sentences have more than one misspelled word.

1. Everyone at the party recieved a prize.
2. Dad tryed an unusual recipe.
3. His meaness made him unpopular.
4. Our forth bater struck out.
5. Is cleanlyness important to you?
6. The bicycle seat is to lose.
7. The stale bread is still useable.
8. The butcher is triming the meet.
9. Carolyn wrote the sillyest limerick.
10. Don't go swiming buy yourself.

B. Proofreading for correct spelling Proofread the following paragraph. It contains twelve spelling errors. Rewrite the paragraph, spelling all the words correctly.

I enjoy going to the libary and reading storys about famous explorers. Last Saturday I red about the British explorer Captain James Cook. During the 1770's, Cook led three voyages in the South Pacific. He discovered and explord many islandes that Europeans did not no about. These included the Cook Islands, New Zealand, and Hawaii. During one voyage, Cook searched for a knew continent. Geographers beleived it was south of Australia. The whether was bitter, and icebergs towered over Cook's boat. Dense fog and harsh winds made sailing immpossible. Finaly, the explorers had to give up there search. It wasn't until 1840 that Charles Wilkes discovered this continent—Antarctica.

584

USING MECHANICS IN WRITING

Spelling

A. The English language is full of spelling demons. Spelling demons are words that are tricky to spell. Try to outwit the demons in this writing assignment. Remember the spelling rules and hints you have learned. Also remember the exceptions!

Here are fifteen words. Seven of them are misspelled. Correct the misspelled words. Then write a story using any ten of the fifteen words. The story can be funny or serious.

confusion	steaming	cieling (ceiling)	Febuary (February)
hurrying	fameous (famous)	police	funeral
flying	immpossible (impossible)	diffrent (different)	totaly (totally)
realy (really)	believe	seize	

B. Mr. Spellright taught English for thirty years. His students remembered him for one thing: he always drilled them on homonyms. He would get quite upset when a student wrote *hear* for *here*, or *too* for *to*.

When Mr. Spellright died, his students sent a wreath of flowers. On it they wrote, "Rest in Piece, Deer Mr. Spellright." When Mr. Spellright's ghost read that, he began moaning. Legend says that if any student can use ten of the following words correctly in a story, Mr. Spellright will stop moaning. See if you can send Mr. Spellright back to his eternal rest.

except	it's	lose	write	whether
already	knew	peace	their	who's
capitol	know	plane	they're	whose
hear	no	principle	to	your
its	lead	quite	two	you're
knot	led	quiet	too	waste

Using Mechanics in Writing

These challenging and enjoyable activities allow the students to see how the concepts of grammar, usage, and mechanics may be applied in actual writing situations. Each exercise is designed to allow students practice in several of the skills they have acquired in this Section. The activities also provide opportunities for students to write creatively about a wide variety of interesting and unusual subjects.

Cumulative Review

These exercises are designed to cover broad areas of grammar, usage, and mechanics. They require the application of skills taught thus far in the text. The exercises may be used for testing purposes, or as an excellent resource for review.

CUMULATIVE REVIEW

Capitalization, Punctuation, and Spelling

A. Using capitalization, punctuation, and spelling correctly Copy the following sentences, correcting the errors in capitalization, punctuation, and spelling.

1. Los angeles Montreal St. louis and mexico city have all hosted the Summer olympics
2. We could not here the speech accept for the end of it
3. Bjorn borg, a fameous swedish tennis pro, has one quiet a few titles at wimbledon
4. "havent you renewed you're subscription two national geographic" asked diane
5. Was philadelphia once the capitol of the united states
6. "Did jrr tolkien right the book The hobbitt" asked Joe
7. These knew tapes were realy inexpenseive
8. Ive all ready seen the movie star wars eight times
9. What an unbeleivably beautiful picture that is
10. "I fryed the fish said Tim. Lee choped the vegetables"

B. Using proofreading skills Proofread the following paragraph. Copy it, correcting the errors in capitalization, punctuation, and spelling.

Do you ever, have difficulty makeing decisions or solveing arguments. I did then i discovered that the toss of a coin can usualy solve this problem. its quick and simple. Most People do knot argue, with the results of a toss. For centurys, coins have been used for trade. Tossing was an early use two. did you no, that orville and Wilbur wright actualy tossed a coin, at Kitty hawk North carolina, They wanted to decide who would pilot the first Airplain. Orville one that toss. So practice tossing catching and fliping the coin. Heads or tails may help you solve an arguement or make a decision.

A

a, an, the. See Articles
in book titles, 534
before nouns, 412
Abbreviations
capitalization of, 524
definition, 524
in dictionary entries, 23
for note taking, 224–225
period with, 542–544
punctuation of, 524, 542–544
of states, 526
using correctly, 544
Accent mark, 27
accept/except, 578
Action verbs, 98–99, 321–322
Additional exercises. *See* end of each lesson.
Addresses
in business letters, 242
on envelopes, 237–239
Adjectives, 108–109, 406–427
adverbs or, distinguishing, 433–435
articles, 412
commas with, 407
comparative forms of, 418
making comparisons with, 417–421, 424
compound predicate, 453–454
correct use of, 416–417
definition of, 406–407
in descriptive paragraphs, 108–109
diagraming, 510–511
predicate, 413
proper, 414–415, 522–523
definition of, 414–415
that tell how many, 409
that tell what kind, 408
that tell which ones, 410–411
Adverbs, 428–439
adjectives or, distinguishing, 433–435
comparisons with, 431–433, 437
definition of, 428–430
diagraming, 513–514
exercises, 430–431, 432–433, 435, 436, 437–440, 458
prepositions or, distinguishing, 449–450, 464
Agreement of subject and verb, 472–482
compound subjects, 479–481
exercises, 474, 475–476, 477–478, 480, 481–482, 483–486, 497–498
prepositional phrases after subject, 474
pronouns, 476–477
rules for, 473
tricky subjects, 476–477
using *I,* 481–482
using *you,* 481–482
all ready/already, 578
Alphabetical order
of dictionary words, 22, 24
of encyclopedia articles, 210–212
of fiction books, 204, 206
of titles in card catalog, 207–208
already/all ready, 578
among/between, 447–448
Announcements, 252–255
Antonyms, 9–10, 28, 29
Apostrophe
in contractions, 379, 552–554

587

in possessives, 314–315, 551–552
Articles, 412, 534
Assignments, understanding, 214–215
Audience, of a speaker, 256
Author card in card catalog, 207–208
Auxiliaries. *See* Helping verbs.

B

bad/badly, 486
bad/good, 419–420
Base words, 12–13
be, forms of, 323, 326–327, 333, 350. *See also is, was, are, were.*
between/among, 447–448
Bibliographies, 194–195
Body of business letter, 242
Body of composition, 132–133, 138, 144–145
Body of friendly letter, 234–236
Books, finding and using in library. *See* Library, using the.
Borrowed words, 2
Brainstorming, 64–65, 70–71
Bread and butter notes, 239–241
Brittanica Junior Encyclopedia, 211
Business letters, 242–244
  block form, 242–244
  modified block form, 242–244
buy/by, 577

C

Call numbers of library books, 205
can/may, 377
capital/capitol, 578
Capitalization, 521–540
  abbreviations, 524
  businesses, 527–528
  clubs, 527–528
  days, 525–526
  direct quotations, 529–530
  first words
    of outlines, 531
    of poetry lines, 531
    of quotations, 529–530
    of sentences, 529
  holidays, 525–526
  I, 522
  initials, 523–524
  languages, 527
  in letters, 234, 532
  months, 525–526
  names, 523–524
  nationalities, 527
  organizations, 527–528
  places and things, 526
  proper adjectives, 522–523
  proper nouns, 522–523
  religions, 527
  rules for, 521–534
  titles of persons and their abbreviations, 524
  written works, 534
Card catalogs, 207–209
  author card, 207
  subject card, 208
  title card, 208
Characters, 148–149
Charts. *See* Graphic aids.
Chronological order, 72–73, 92–93, 151
  in narrative compositions, 92–93
  in paragraphs, 72–73
Closing of letters, 234–236, 244
  commas with, 549
Collier's Encyclopedia, 211
Commas, 548–551
  with adjectives, 407

588

with city, state, country, 548
in compound predicates, 288–289
in compound sentences, 492–493, 495, 550
with dates, 548
with direct address, 549
with direct quotations, 549
with introductory words, 549
in letters, 549
rules for use, 548–550
in a series, 549
after *yes, no,* 549
Common nouns, 522
Comparisons
of adjectives, 417–421, 424
of adverbs, 431–433, 437
Completion or fill-in-the-blank tests, 230–231
Complete predicate of sentence, 279
Complete sentences, 271–272
Complete subject of sentence, 279
Compositions, 131–145
body in, 132–133, 138, 144–145, 166–167
characters in, 148
choosing topics for, 134–135
conclusion in, 132–133, 138, 144–145
definition of, 132–133
descriptive, 163–171
details in, 164–165
development of, 144–145
explanatory, 173–181
final copy of, 142–143
first drafts of, 138–139
first-person point of view in, 152–153
introduction in, 132–133, 138, 144–145
logical order in, 176–177, 254
narrative, 147–161
omniscient point of view in, 152–153
organizing ideas, 136–137
parts of, 132, 166–167
planning, 148–149
plot in, 150–151
point of view in, 152–153
revision of, 140–141, 145, 170–171, 180–181
sensory details in, 164–165
setting in, 148–149
step-by-step order, 176–177
third-person point of view in, 152–153
time sequence in, 150–151
title for, 142, 144
transitions in, 158–159, 178–179
See also Writing and Pre-writing.
Compound direct object, 453–454
Compound object of preposition, 453–454
Compound object of verb, 453–454
Compound predicate, 288–290
Compound predicate adjective, 453–454
Compound predicate noun, 453–454
diagraming, 508–509
Compound sentences, 487–499
commas with, 492–493, 495, 550
definition of, 489–490
diagraming, 514–515
punctuation of, 492–493, 495, 550
Compound subjects, 286–288
diagramming, 506–507
Compound verb, 453–454
diagraming, 506–507
Compound words, 2
Computers, 18

589

Conclusions, in composition, 132–133, 138, 144–145, 155, 168–169, 190
Conclusions, in paragraphs, 76–77
Conflict, in stories, 148, 149
Conjunctions, 452–455
  in compound sentence parts, 452–454
  in compound sentences, 489–493
  definition of, 452–453
  exercises, 453–454, 457, 459–461
Context
  defined, 4
  learning word meanings from
    by definition, 6–7
    in dictionary entries, 30–31
    by examples, 8–9
    by restatement, 6–7
Contractions, 379–380
  apostrophe in, 379–380, 552–554
  definition, 379
  list of, 379
  negatives, 380–382
  n't not included in verb, 329–330
Cumulative review,
  capitalization, punctuation, spelling, 586
  parts of speech, 470–471
  sentence, 497–499
  usage, 486

D

Dates
  capitalization of, 525
  commas with, 548
Declarative sentences, 273–274
  defined, 273
  exercises for, 275–276, 291
  periods with, 275–276
Definition, as context clue to meaning of word, 6–7
Definitions, 12–13, 14–15, 16–17, 24–29, 30–31
Definitions in dictionary, 28–31
Demonstrations, 252–253, 254–255
Descriptions, 101–109, 163–171
Descriptive compositions, 163–171
Descriptive paragraph
  gathering sensory details, 102–103
  revising, 108–109
  using spatial order, 104–105
  using transitional words, 106–107
Details, 42, 56–57, 83, 90–91, 102–103
  organizing, 72–73
  in paragraphs, 56–57
  sensory, 164–165
  in speeches, 254–255
Dewey Decimal System, 204–206
Diagraming, 500–520
  adjectives, 510–511
  adverbs, 513–514
  compound sentences, 514–515
  compound subjects and verbs, 506–507
  direct objects, 507–508
  imperative sentences, 504
  possessive nouns, 512–513
  predicate adjectives, 509–510
  predicate nouns, 508–509
  questions, 503
  sentences, 500–519
  sentences with *there*, 505
  subjects in unusual order, 502
  verbs and their subjects, 501
Diagrams, *See* Graphic aids.
Dialogue, 156–157
Dictionary, 21–31

590

abridged, 22
alphabetical order in, 22
abbreviations and symbols, 23
definition of, 22, 24
definitions in, 30–31
entries, information in
antonyms, 28
colloquial meaning, 28
definitions, 28
origin, or history, 27
part of speech, 27
pronunciation, 27
special forms or endings, 27
syllables, 28
synonyms, 28
entry word, 27
guide words, 25–26
irregular verbs in, 352
meaning, choosing right one, 30–31
plurals in, 312
pronunciation in, 27
special forms or endings in, 27
types of, 22
unabridged, 22
using to find plurals, 312
See also Words and Vocabulary.
Directions, 41, 252–253
following, 216–217
giving, 254–255
reading forms, 248–249
spoken, 216–217
written, 216–217
Direct objects, 331–332
compound, 453–454
definition of, 331
diagraming, 507–508
exercises, 332–345
nouns as, 331–332
predicate words or, distinguishing, 335–336
pronouns as, 394–395, 447
recognizing, 331–332
Direct quotations, 556
and capitalization, 529–530
and commas, 549
punctuation of, 556,–557
Divided quotations, 558–559
punctuation of, 558
Double negatives, 381

E

either-or, neither-nor, or with compound subjects, 479–481
empty sentences, 42–43
Encyclopedia, 186, 210–212
articles, 210–211
guide words, 210
Ending in compositions. *See* Conclusion in composition.
Ending sentence in "why" paragraph, 126
English language
as a living language, 2–3, 18–19
nonstandard, 34–35
number of words, 22
slang, 36–37
standard, 34–35
English language words. *See* Words.
Envelope, address, 237–239
Essay tests, 230–231
Example(s)
as context clue to meaning of word, 8–9
used to develop paragraph, 56–57, 70–71
except/accept, 578
Exclamation mark, or point, 547–548
with exclamatory sentences, 275–276
with interjections, 463–464
with quotation marks, 556

591

Exclamatory sentences, 273–274, 275–276, 291
defined, 273
See also Compositions, explanatory.
Explanatory compositions, 173–181
Explanatory paragraphs, 111–119, 121–129
"how," 58–59, 111–119
revising, 118–119
step-by-step order, 114–115
using transitional words, 116–117
"why," 58–59, 121–129
developing an opinion, 122–123
organizing an opinion, 124–125
revising, 128–129
using transitional words, 126–127

F

Fact, defined, 198
Facts and figures in paragraphs, 56–57
Fact and opinions, 198–199
Fiction books, 204
Final copy of composition, 142–143
First drafts, 74–75
of compositions, 138–139
of descriptive writing, 106–107, 158–159, 166–167
ending sentences in paragraphs, 76–77
of explanatory writing, 126–127, 178–179
of narrative writing, 96–97, 154–155, 156–157
as part of a process, 61–63, 84–85
of reports, 190–191
First-person point of view,
in compositions, 152–153
in paragraphs, 94–95
Forms, filling out, 248–249
Fragments, 270, 272, 299–300
exercises, 272, 291, 296, 300–301, 304–307, 498
Friendly letters, *See* Letters, friendly.

G

Geographical names
capitalization of, 526
Goals, for study, 220–221
good/bad, 419–420
good/well, 486
Graphic aids, 226–227
Graphs, *See* Graphic aids.
Greetings, commas with, 549
Guide words, 25–26
in dictionary, 25–26
in encyclopedia, 210–211

H

has/have, 475
Heading in letters, 234–236, 244
hear/here, 578
Helping verbs, 326–330
Homonyms, 577–582
"How" compositions, 173–181
"How" paragraphs, 58–59, 112–119
Hyphen, 554–555

I

I
and agreement with verb, 481
capitalization of, 522

592

with first-person point of view, 94–95, 152–153
ie, ei, 571–572
Imaginary narrative compositions (stories), 148–149
Imaginary subjects for paragraphs, 90–91
Imperative sentences, 273–274, 275–276, 285–286, 291
defined, 273
diagraming, 504
period with, 275–276
you as understood subject in, 285–286
Importance of reasons, order of, in "why" paragraphs, 72–73
Indenting first line of paragraphs in letters, 234
Initials
capitalization of, 522
defined, 523
periods with, 522–523, 542
Inside address of business letters, 242–244
Interjections, 463–464
Interrogative sentences, 273
defined, 273
diagraming, 503
exercises for, 275–276, 291
question mark with, 275–276
Introductions in compositions, 132–133, 144–145
Invitations, *See* Letters.
Irregular verbs, 349–369
agreement with subject, 476–478
begin, 354
break, 355
do, 356
eat, 357
give, 358
go, 359
grow, 360
and helping verbs, 350
is, are, was, were, 475
know, 361
list of principal parts, 351
ride, 362
rules for, 350
run, 363
see, 364
take, 365
after *there, here, where,* 478–479
write, 366
Italics, underlining for, 560
its/it's, 486

J

Journal as source of ideas for writing, 134
Journal writing, 64

K

knew/new, 579
know/no, 579

L

Languages, capitalization of, 527
lay/lie, 486
lead/led, 579
learn/teach, 375
leave/let, 376
led/lead, 579
let/leave, 376
Letters, 233–249
business, 242–244
of complaint, 242
examples of, 244
forms for, 242–244
to order products, 242
parts of, 242–244
punctuation in, 242

593

of request, 245–247
capitalization in, 532
envelopes, addressing, 237–238
ZIP code in, 237–238
friendly, 234–236
capitalization in, 234
examples of, 235
parts of, 234, 236
punctuation in, 234
social notes, 239–241
of invitation, 239
R.S.V.P., 239
thank-you
for gift, 239
for hospitality (bread and butter), 239
Letters of request, 245–247
Library, using the, 203–212
call numbers, 205–206
card catalog, 207–209
classification and arrangement of fiction and nonfiction books, 204
Dewey Decimal System, 204–205
encyclopedias, 210–212
Linking verbs, 333–334
Listening, 262–263
and judging a talk, 264–265
content guidelines for, 264
presentation guidelines for, 264
Logical order in compositions and paragraphs
chronological, 72–73, 92–93, 150–151
order of importance of reasons, 72–73
spatial, 72–73, 104–105
step-by-step, 114–115, 176–177, 254
lose/loose, 579

M

Magazines, 186
Main idea
in compositions, 132–133
listening for, 262
in paragraphs, 50–51
in speeches, 256
See also Topic sentence.
Main verbs, 326–327
Maps. *See* Graphic aids.
Matching tests, 228–229
may/can, 377
meat/meet, 577
Mixed review. *See* end of each lesson.
Modifiers. *See* Adjectives, Adverbs, Prepositional phrases.
Mood in paragraphs
created with adjectives, 108–109
created with specific verbs, 98–99
more/most
with adjectives, 419–420
with adverbs, 431
Multiple-choice tests, 228–229

N

Narrative compositions, 147–161
elements of, 148–149
Narrative paragraphs, 89–99
Nationalities
capitalization of, 527
Negatives, 380–382
defined, 381
double, 381
n't not part of verb, 329–330
new/knew, 579
Newspapers, 186
no/know, 579
no words, *not* words. *See* Negatives.
Nonfiction books, 204

594

Nonstandard English, 33–35
Notes, social, *See* Letters.
Notetaking, 186–187, 224–225
  cards, 186–187
  organizing notes, 188–189
Nouns, 308–320
  as compound objects
    of prepositions, 453–454
    of verbs, 453–454
  as compound subjects, 286–288
  common, 310, 522
  definition of, 308
  as objects of prepositions, 446
  as objects of verbs, 331–332
  plural forms of, 311–312
  possessive forms of, 313–315
  predicate, 333
  proper, 310, 522–523
    capitalization of, 522
  in sentence patterns, 316, 339–341
  singular forms of, 311–312
  as subject of the verb, 281–286
Number of verb, defined, 472

O

Objective tests, 228–229
Object of the preposition, 445–446
Object of the verb, 331–332
Object pronouns, 394–395, 447
Observation, 70–71, 102–103
Omniscient point of view, 152–153
Opinion, 122–125
  defined, 198
  and facts, 198–199
  supporting, 200–201
Opinion, in "why" paragraph, 122–123
Order of writing
  chronological, 72–73, 92–93
  importance, 72–73
  spatial, 72–73, 104–105, 164–165
  step-by-step, 114–115, 176–177, 254
Organizations
  capitalization of, 527–528
Outlines, 531
  capitalization in, 531
  periods in, 544

P

Padded sentences 44–45
Paragraphs, 49–130
  adjectives in, 108–109
  chronological order in, 72–73, 92–93
  definition of, 50–51
  descriptive, 58–59, 101–109
  details in, 56–57, 90–91, 102–103, 108–109
  developing, 56–57
  ending a sentence in, 76–77
  examples in, 56–57
  explanatory, 58–59, 111–119, 121–129
    "how," 58–59, 112–119
    "why," 58–59, 122–129
  facts and figures in, 56–57
  first-person point of view in, 94–95
  kinds of, 58–59
  logical order in, 72–73, 92–93, 104–105, 114–115
  main idea in, 50–51
  narrative, 58–59, 89–99
  narrowing topics for, 66–67
  natural order in, 72–73
  opinion in, 121–130
  order of importance of reasons in, 72–73
  organizing, 72–73
  personal point of view in, 94–95

595

point of view in, 94–95
process of writing, 61–79
sensory details in, 102–103
spatial order in, 72–73, 104–105
specific verbs in, 98–99
step-by-step order in, 114–115
third-person point of view in, 94–95
time sequence in, 72–73
topic for, narrowing, 66–67
topic sentence in, 54–55, 68–69
transitions in, 96–97, 106, 116–117, 126–127
unity in, 52–53
Parts of speech, 27, 28, 29, 462–471
definition of, 462
as shown in dictionary entries, 27–29
using words as different, 464–466
See also Adjectives, Adverbs, Conjunctions, Interjections, Nouns, Prepositions, Pronouns, Verbs.
Past participles of verbs, 348
Past tense of verbs, 337–338
peace/piece, 579
Period, 542–545
in abbreviations, 524, 542–544
and declarative sentences, 275–276
and imperative sentences, 275–276
after initials, 523–524, 542
in outlines, 544
with quotation marks, 556
in sentences, 542
Personal observation to attain information, 70–71
Personal point of view. *See* First-person point of view.
piece/peace, 579
plain/plane, 580
Plot in stories, 148, 149, 150–151
Plural forms
of nouns, 311–312
shown in dictionary entries, 312
of pronouns, 389
of verbs, 472–482
Poetry lines,
capitalization of first words in, 531
Point of view, 94–95, 152–153
first-person, 94–95, 152–153
omniscient, 152–153
third-person, 94–95, 152–153
Possessive nouns, 313–315
diagraming, 512–513
Possessive pronouns, 398–399
Predicate
complete, 279
compound, 288–289
definition of, 277–278
exercises, 278, 280, 282, 289, 292, 293, 295, 296, 297
simple, 279–281
Predicate adjectives, 334–336, 413–414
compound, 453–454
definition of, 413
diagraming, 509–510
Predicate nouns, 334–336
compound, 453–454
definition of, 333
diagraming, 508–509
Predicate pronouns, 333–336
Predicate words
definition of, 333
or direct objects, 335–336
exercises, 335–336
Prefixes, 14–15
and spelling, 572, 573

596

Prepositional phrases, 444, 450–452
Prepositions, 441–452
adverbs or, distinguishing, 449–450, 464
between/among, 447–448
compound objects of, 453–454
definition of, 442
exercises, 443, 444–445, 446, 448, 449–450, 451, 455, 456, 458–459, 461
list of, 442
objects of, 445–447
nouns as, 445–446
pronouns as, 446–447
Present tense of verbs, 337
Pre-Writing, 82–83
as part of a process, 62–63, 82–83
choosing a subject, 64–65
choosing a topic, 134–135
for compositions, 136–137
definition of, 63
for descriptive writing, 102–105, 164–165
for explanatory writing, 112–115, 122–125, 174–177
gathering ideas, 70–71
guidelines, 144
for narrative writing, 89–100, 148–149, 150–151, 152–153
developing a paragraph, 90–91
choosing point of view, 94–95
revising, 98–99
using chronological order, 92–93
using transitional words, 96–97
narrowing a topic, 66–67
organizing paragraphs, 72–73
chronological order, 72–73
order of importance, 72–73
spatial order, 72–73
for reports, 184–187
writing a topic sentence, 68–69
principal/principle, 580
Process of writing
pre-writing, 62–63
revising, 62–63
steps in a, 112–115, 174–175
writing the first draft, 62–63
See also Writing.
Pronouns, 388–405
as compound objects of prepositions, 453–454
definition, 389
after linking verbs, 393–394
as objects, 394–395, 447
of prepositions, 445–446
of verbs, 331–332
plural, 389
possessive, 398–399
predicate, 333–334, 393–394
singular forms of, 476–477
as subjects, 391–392
agreement with verbs, 476–478
with point of view
first-person, 94–95, 152–153
third-person, 94–95, 152–153
substituting nouns, 388–389
we/us, 396–397
Pronunciation of words, shown in dictionary entries, 27–29
Proofreading, 86, 192–193, 569
forms, 248–249
symbols, 85
Proper adjectives, 414, 522
capitalization of, 415, 522–523
Proper nouns, 310, 522–523
capitalization of, 522–523

597

Punctuation, 541–566
accent mark, 27
apostrophe, 314–315, 379, 551–554
comma, 549–551
in compound sentences, 492–493
at end of sentence, 542, 546–548
exclamation mark, or point, 547–548
exercises, 275, 276, 561–566
hyphen, 554–555
in letters, 234, 242
period, 542–545
question mark, 546–547
quotation marks, 556–560
and sentences, 275–276
as a signal, 541
and underlining, 560

Q

Question mark, 546–547
and interrogative sentences, 275–276
Questions. *See* Interrogative sentences.
Quotations
capitalization in, 529–530
definition of, 556
direct, 549, 556–559
divided, 558
punctuation with, 556–560
Quotation marks, 556–560
commas with, 556
end punctuation with, 556
with divided quotations, 558
with titles, 559–560

R

Real life narrative compositions, 148

Real life subjects for paragraphs, 90–91
Regular verbs, 337, 348–349
Religions
capitalization of, 527
Reports, 183–195
choosing a topic, 184–185
first draft, 190–191
gathering information, 186–187
listing sources, 194–195
organizing information, 188–189
revising, 192–193
Research, 70–71
gathering information for speeches, 256
See also Study and research skills.
Restatement, as context clue to meaning of word, 6
Return address on envelopes, 237
Revision, 62–63, 85, 140–141
definition of, 63
of compositions, 145
of descriptive writing, 108–109, 170–171
of explanatory writing, 118–119, 128–129, 180–181
of a first draft, 78–79, 85
of narrative writing, 98–99, 160–161
as part of a process, 62–63
of a report, 192–193
Rewriting paragraphs and compositions, 140–141, 145, 170–171, 180–181
right/write, 580
R.S.V.P., 239
Run-on sentences, 299, 302
exercises, 302–303, 304–307, 498

S

s'/'s, 313–314
Salutation in letters, 234–236, 242–244
Schedules
  for study, 220–221
Senses, as base for detail in writing, 102–108
Sensory details, 102
Sentence fragments, 270, 272, 299–300
Sentence patterns,
  N LV Adj., 341
  N LV N, 340
  NV, 316
  NVN, 339
Sentences, 39–47, 269–297
  capitalization in, 529
  combining, 46–47
  complete, 271–272
  complete predicate in, 279
  complete subject in, 279
  compound, 487–499
  compound predicate in, 288–290
  compound subject in, 286–288
  correct use of, 299–307
  declarative, 273–274
  definition of, 40–41, 270, 488
  diagraming, 500–519
  empty, 42–43
  ending, in paragraphs, 76–77
  end punctuation in, 542, 546–548
  exclamatory, 273–274
  exercises, 272, 291, 296, 298, 497–499
  fragments of, 270, 272, 299–301
  imperative, 273–274
  interrogative, 273–274
  kinds of, 273
  padded, 44–45
  in paragraphs, 50–51, 52–53
  parts of, 276–289
  patterns of, 316, 339–341, 345
  punctuation of, 275–276, 542
  run-on, 299, 302–303
  simple, 488–489
  simple predicate (the verb) in, 277, 279–281
  simple subject in, 277, 281–283
  topic, 68–69, 167
  writing, 39–48
set/sit, 378
Setting in stories, 148, 149
Short answer tests, 230–231
Signature in letters, 234–236, 244
Simple predicate (the verb), 277, 279–281
Simple sentences, 488–489
  definition of, 488
Singular forms
  of nouns, 311–312
  of pronouns, 476–477
  of verbs, 472–482
sit/set, 378
Skimming, 248–249
Slang, 36–37
Social notes. *See* Letters.
Source cards, 186–187
Special order in a composition, 164–165
Specific verbs, 98–99
Speech, 251–265
  choosing topics, 256
  and eye contact, 258–259
  formal, 252–253, 256–257
    choosing a topic, 256
    deciding your purpose, 256
    gathering information, 256
    knowing the audience, 256
    organizing information, 256
  and gestures, 258–259
  guidelines for content, 264–265

599

guidelines for presentation, 264–265
informal, 252–253, 254–255
announcements, 254
demonstrations, 254
directions, 254
introductions, 254
informal and formal, 252–253
and posture, 258–259
and practice, 260–261
and visual aids, 258–259
and voice, 258–259
Spelling, 567–586
habits for improving, 568–569
memory devices, 569
homonyms, 577–582
proofreading, 569
rules for
adding prefixes, 572–573
adding suffixes, 572–576
words with *ie* or *ei,* 571–572
steps for mastering, 569–570
words often confused, 577–582
SQ3R study method, 222–223
Standard English, 34–35
State-of-being verbs (linking verbs), 323–324
Step-by-step order
in "how" compositions, 176–177
in "how" paragraphs, 114–115
Stories, writing, 90–91, 148–149
Study and research skills, 213–231
assignments, understanding, 214–215
directions, 216–217
guidelines for following, 216
graphic aids, 226–227
SQ3R study method, 222–223
study plans, 220–221
taking notes, 224–225
test taking, 228–229, 230–231
time and place to work, 218–219
Subject card in card catalog, 208
Subject pronouns, 391
Subject of the sentence, 276–278
agreement with verb, 472–485
complete, 279
compound, 286–288, 479–481, 488
definition of, 277
diagraming, 501–502
exercises, 278, 282, 284, 286, 288, 292, 293, 294, 296, 297
following *there is, where is,* or *here is,* 478–479
in imperative sentences, 285–286
nouns as, 281–286
pronouns as, 391
simple, 281–283
special problems, 476–481
in unusual positions, 283–285
of the verb, 281–283
Suffixes, 16–17
and spelling, 572–576
Syllables
as shown in dictionary entries, 27–30
dividing words into, 554–555
Synonyms, 9–10
Synonyms in dictionary, 28–29

T

Tables. *See* Graphic aids.
Talks. *See* Speech.
teach/learn, 375
Tense of verbs, 336–338
Test taking
objective, 228–229
matching, 228–229
multiple-choice, 228–229
true-false, 228–229
written, 230–231

600

completion or fill-in-the blank, 230–231
essay, 230–231
short answer, 230–231
Thank-you notes. *See* Letters.
that kind/this kind, 416
their/they're/there, 486, 553, 581
them/those, 486
there, here, where, introducing sentences, 478–479
there/they're/their, 553, 581
Thinking clearly, 197–201
Third-person point of view
in compositions, 152–153
in paragraphs, 94–95
this kind/that kind, 416
those/them, 486
threw/through, 577
Time sequence
in compositions, 150–151
in paragraphs, 72–73, 92–93
Title card in card catalog, 208
Titles
capitalization of, 524, 534
of compositions, 142, 145
of persons, 524–525
of written works,
quotation marks with, 559–560
underlining for italics, 560
to/too/two, 581
Topic, choosing a, 134–135
Topic, narrowing the
for compositions, 134–135
for paragraphs, 66–67
Topic sentences, 68–69, 167
in compositions, 166–167, 168
in paragraphs, 54–55
writing lively, 68–69
Transitions, 96–97, 106, 116–117, 126–127, 158–159, 178–179
showing chronological order, 72–73, 92–93
showing order of importance of reasons, 72–73
showing spatial order, 72–73, 104–105, 164–165
showing step-by-step order, 114–115, 176–177
True-false tests, 228–229
two/to/too, 581

U

Underlining certain titles for italics, 560
Understood subject (you), 285–286
Unity in paragraphs, 52–53
Usage, 486. *See also* Agreement.
Using grammar in writing. *See* end of each lesson.
Using mechanics in writing
capitalization, 540
punctuation, 566
spelling, 585

V

Verb, the (simple predicate), 278–281
Verbs, 321–345
action, 321–322
after *here,* 373
after *there,* 373
after *where,* 373
agreement with subjects, 472–485
be, 371
compound, 488
confusing pairs, 374–379
in contractions, 379–380
definition of, 327
diagraming, 501
direct objects of, 331–332

601

exercises for, 278, 280, 282, 289, 292, 293, 295, 296, 297, 322, 323–324, 325, 327, 328–329, 334, 338, 342–346, 348, 349, 372, 374, 379, 381–387
future tense, 337–338
helping, 326–330
irregular, 347–369
linking, 333–334
main, 326–327
in negative contractions, 380–382
number, defined, 473
object of, 331–332
past part of, 348
past participle of, 348
past tense, 337–338
plural forms, 472–482
present part, 348
present tense, 336–337
principal parts of, 347
regular, 337, 348–349
in sentences, using, 324–325
separated parts of, 329–330
simple predicate, 279–281
singular forms of, 472–482
specific, in writing, 98–99
special forms, 475
state-of-being, 323–324
subjects of, 281–283
tenses, 336–338
troublesome, 370–387
using verbs, 324–325
See also Irregular verbs.
Vocabulary, 1–19
antonyms, 9–10
base words, 12–13
context clues, 4–5, 6–7, 8–9
definition and restatement, 6–7
for special fields, 18–19
synonyms, 10–11
See also Words and Dictionary.

W

we/us, 396–397
weather/whether, 581
well/good, 486
whether/weather, 581
who's/whose, 553, 581
"Why" paragraphs, 58–59, 121–129
Word endings, shown in dictionary entries, 27–28
Word parts, 12–17,
base words, 12–13
prefixes, 14–15
suffixes, 16–17
Words, English language
antonyms, 9–10, 28–29
borrowed, 2–3
compound, 2–3
context clues to meaning of, 6–8
from names, 2–3
number of, 22
as different parts of speech, 464–466
origins, 27
slang, 36–37
transitional, 96–97, 106–107, 116–117, 126–127, 158–159
See also Vocabulary and Dictionary.
World Book Encyclopedia, 211
write/right, 580
Writing
choosing a subject, 64–65
compositions, 131–196
definition of, 63
final copy, 87
first drafts, 74–75, 84, 96–97, 106–107, 126–127, 154–155, 156–157, 158–159, 166–167, 178–179, 190–191
letters, 233–247
narrowing a topic, 66–67

602

paragraphs, 61–79
pre-writing, 64–65
as a process, 62–63, 82–87, 144–145
proofreading, 85
revising, 62–63
sentences, 39–48
See also Composition and letters.
Written tests, 230–231
completion or fill in the blank, 230–231
essay, 230–231
short answer, 230–231

Y

you
as understood subject, 285–286
and agreement with verb, 481–482
your/you're, 553, 581

Z

ZIP code, 237–239

603

Acknowledgments

Johnny Hart and News Group Chicago, Inc.: For BC cartoon; copyright © 1971 Publishers Newspaper Syndicate; copyright © 1977 by Fawcett Publications, Inc. The New Yorker Magazine, Inc.: For "Catalogue" by Rosalie Moore; copyright © 1940, 1968, The New Yorker Magazine, Inc.

Photographs

Jim Whitmer, ii, xvi, 32, 48, 80, 100, 110, 146, 162, 196, 202, 250, 266; Jacqueline Durand, 20; James L. Ballard, 38, 60, 172, 182, 212, 232; Brent Jones, 88, 120; Hillstrom Stock/Tom McCarthy, 130.

Cover

Sinjerli Variation I, 1977. Frank Stella. Petersburg Press, London and New York. © Vert Foncé, 1977.

Editorial Credits

Editor-in-Chief: Joseph F. Littell
Administrative Editor: Kathleen Laya
Managing Editor: Geraldine Macsai
Senior Editor: Bonnie Dobkin
Editors: James M. LiSacchi, Mary Schafer
Associate Designer: Mary E. MacDonald
Cover Design: Joy Littell, Mary E. MacDonald

84 85 86 87 / 9 8 7 6 5 4 3 2 1

604

Handbook Section 14: Additional Answers

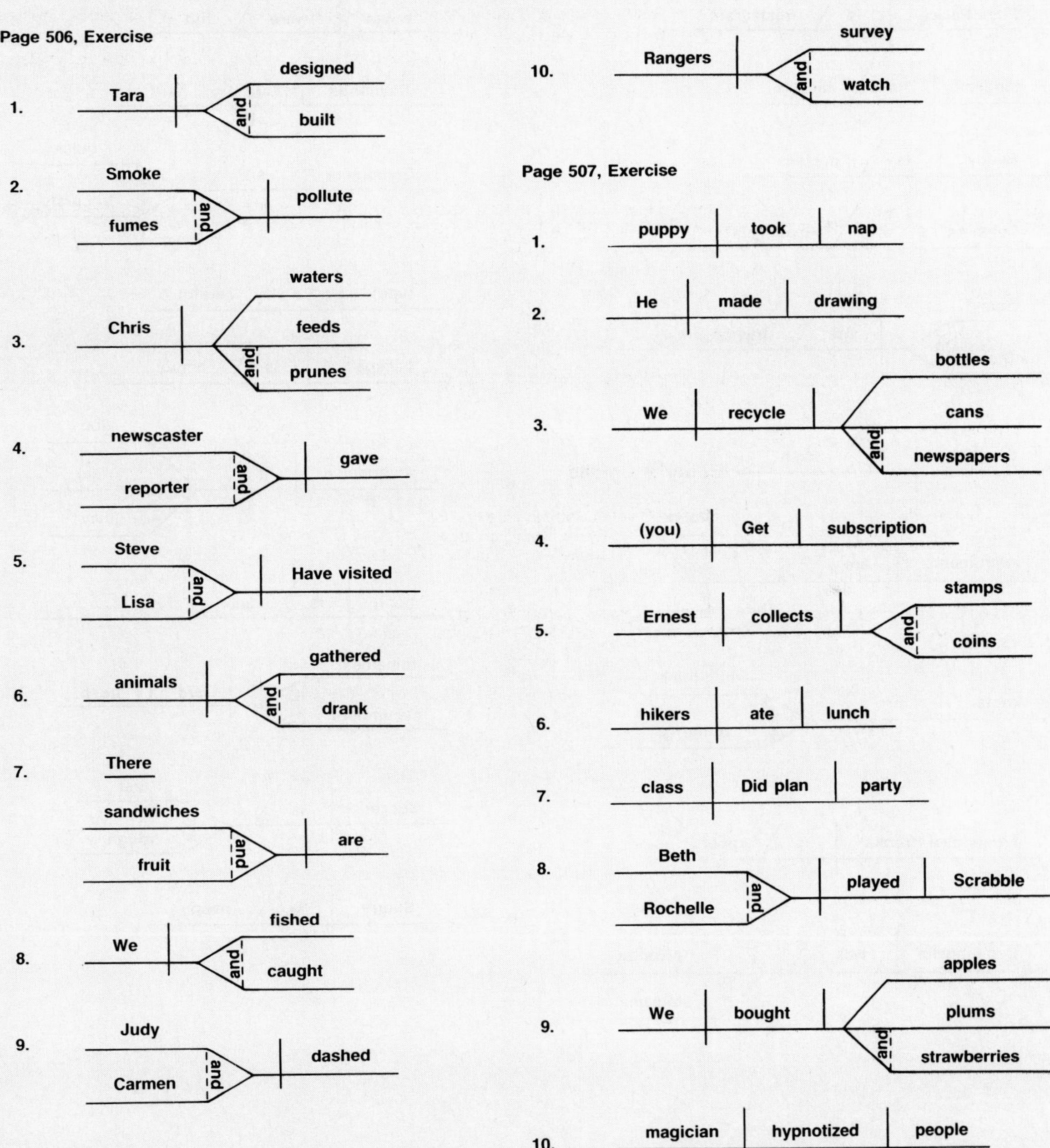

Page 509, Exercise

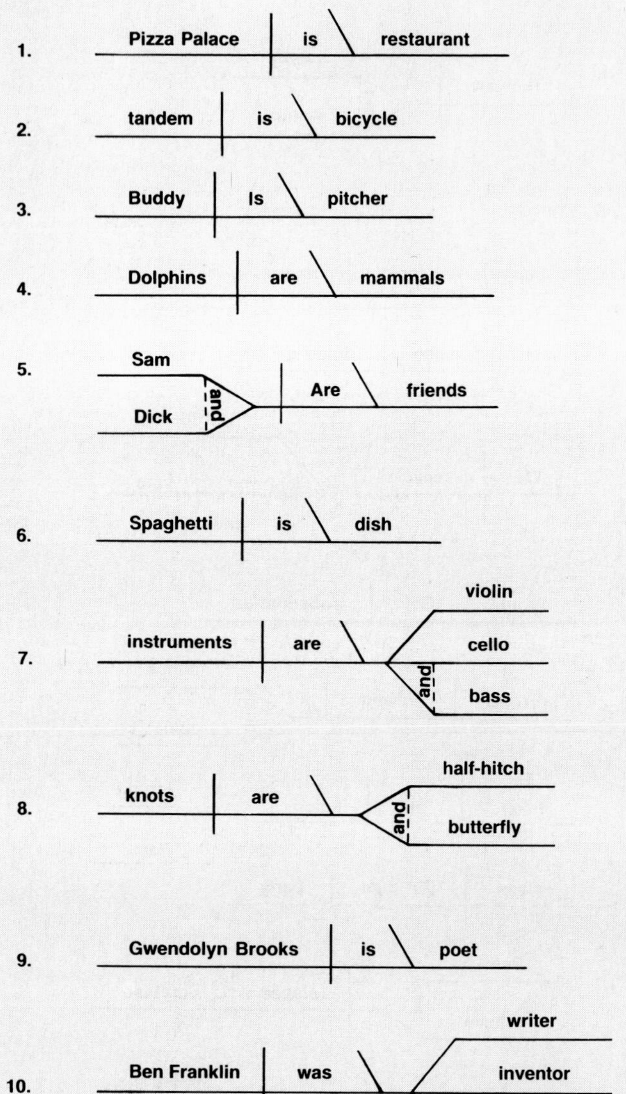

Page 510, Exercise

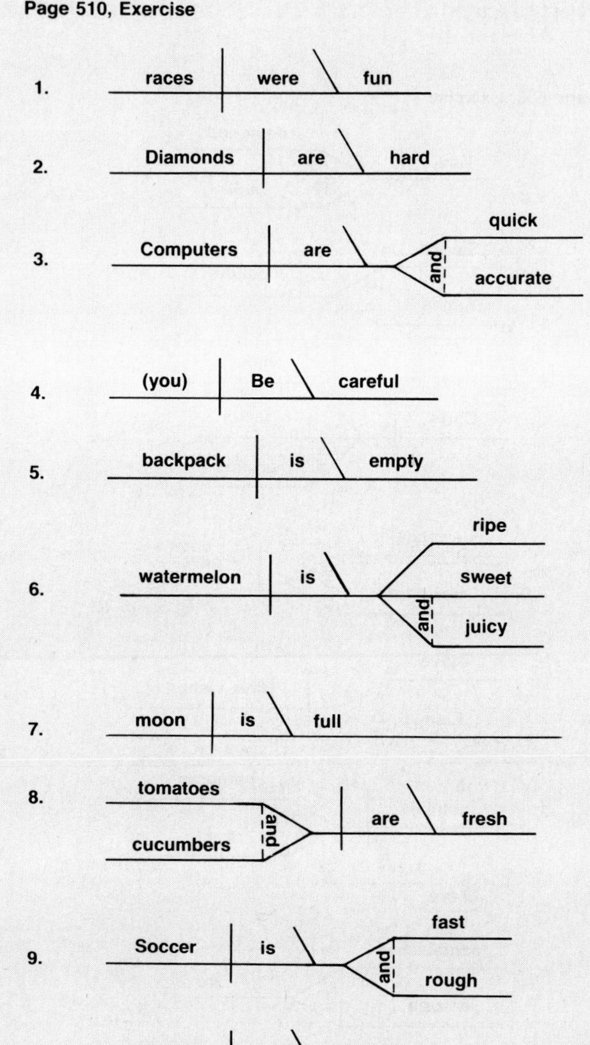

Page 511, Exercise

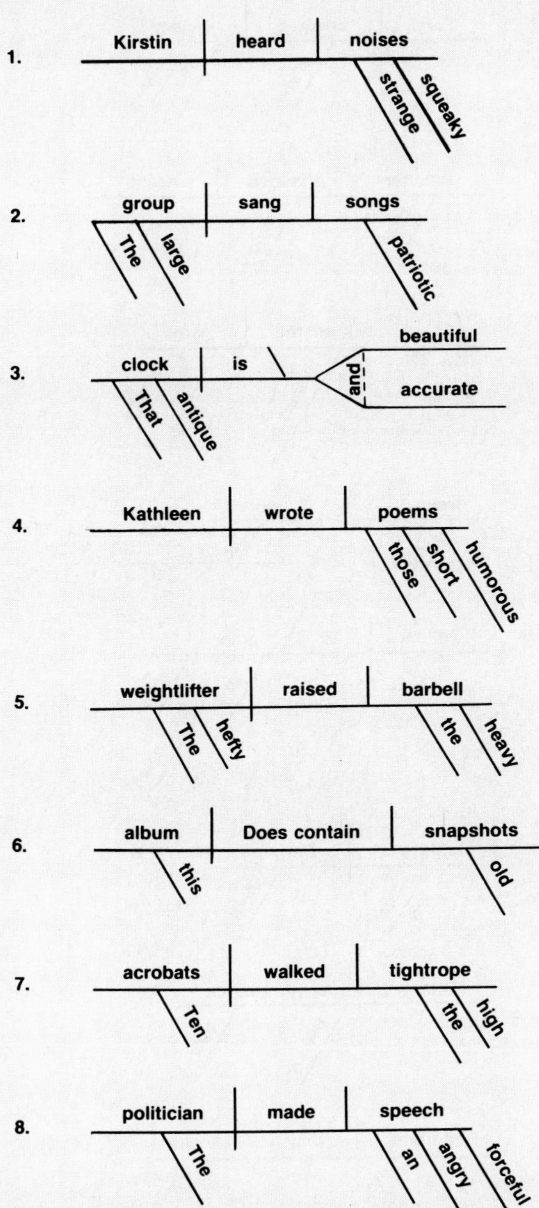

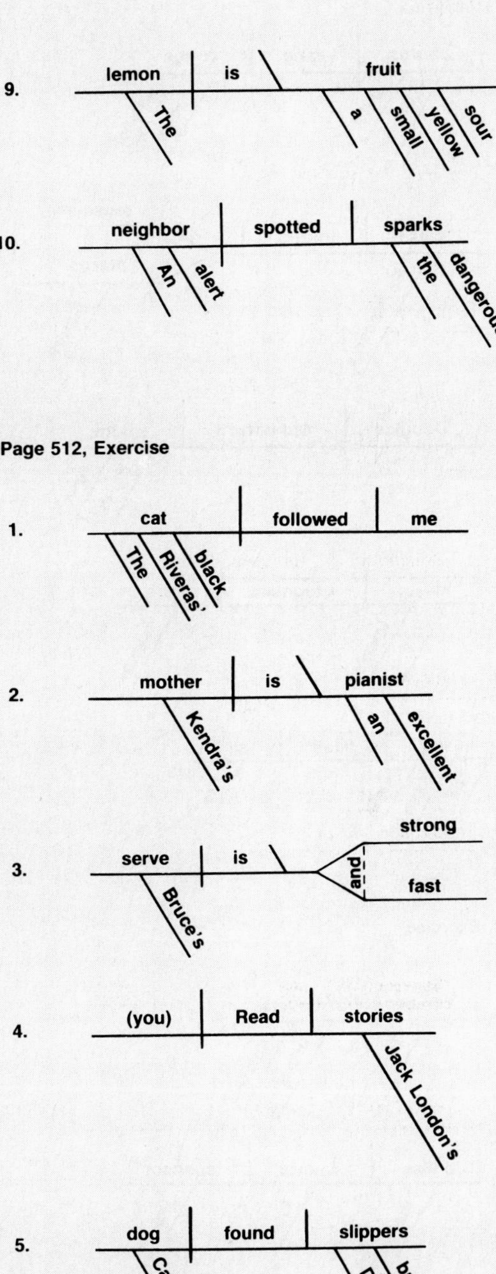

Page 512, Exercise

6.

7.

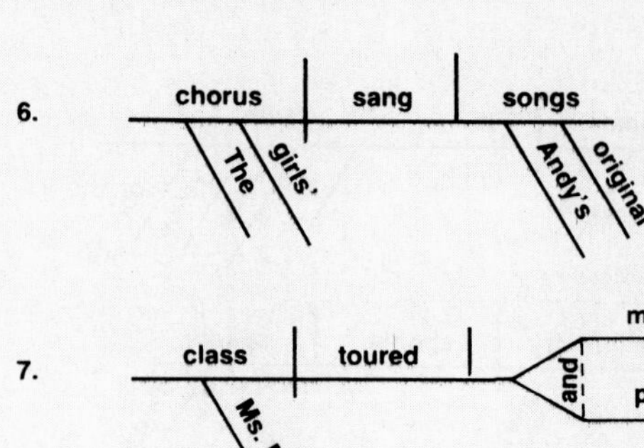

8.

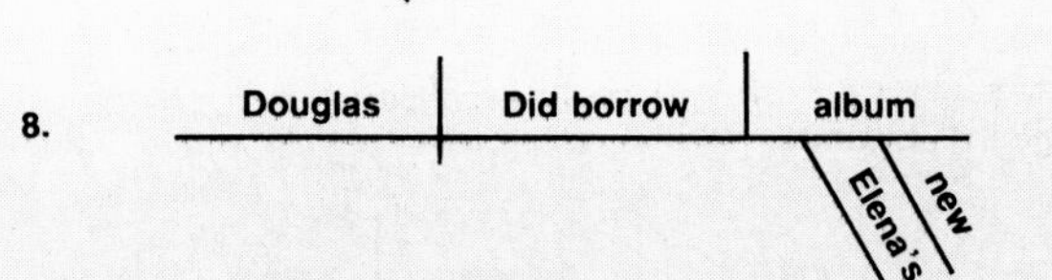

9.

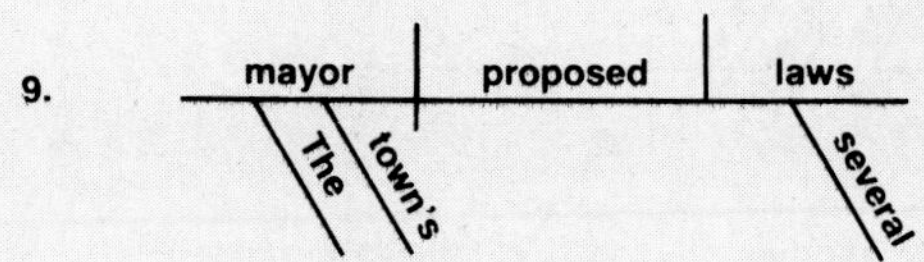

10.

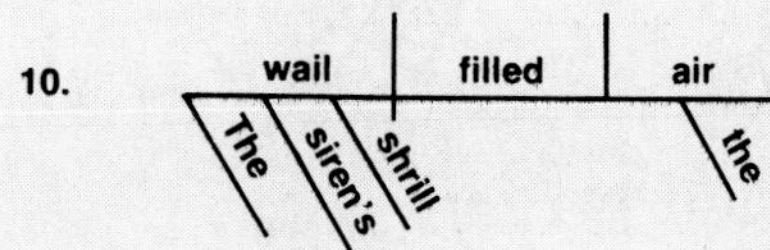

Page 513, Exercise

1.

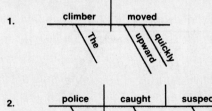

climber
moved
The
upward
quickly

2.

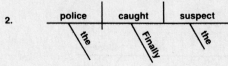

police
caught
suspect
the
Finally
the

3.

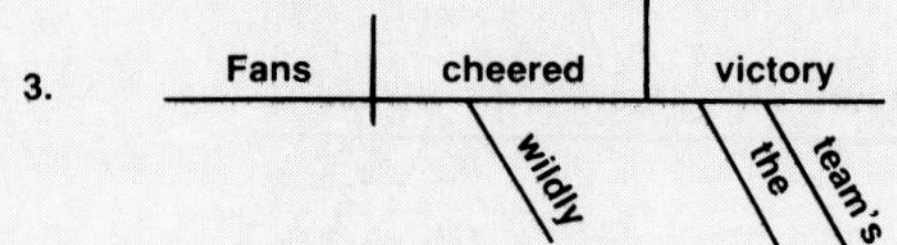

4.

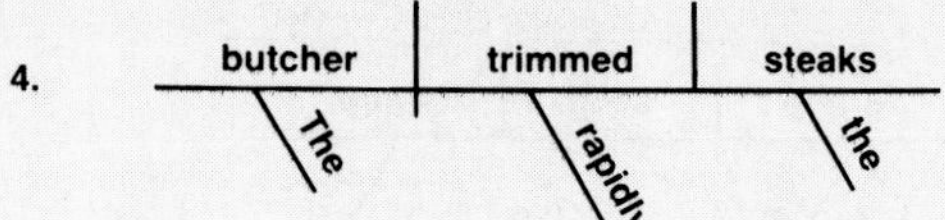

5.

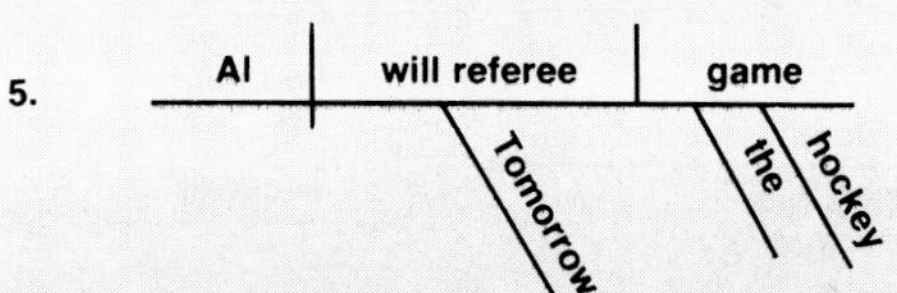

6.

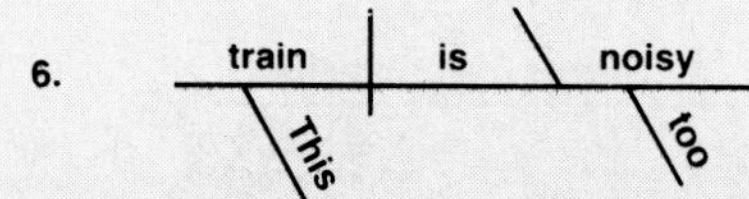

7.

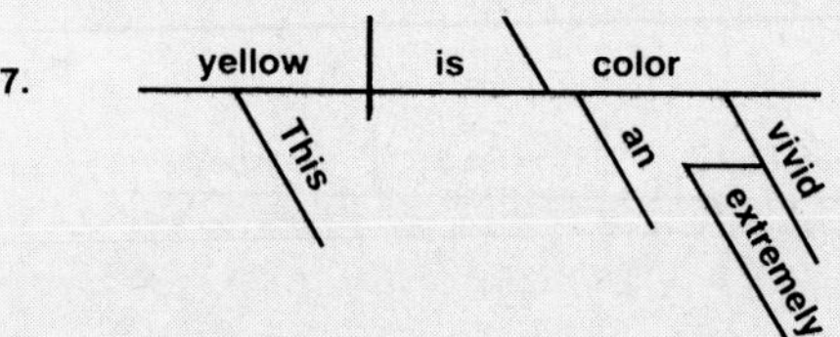

8.

students
Did study
most
hard

9.

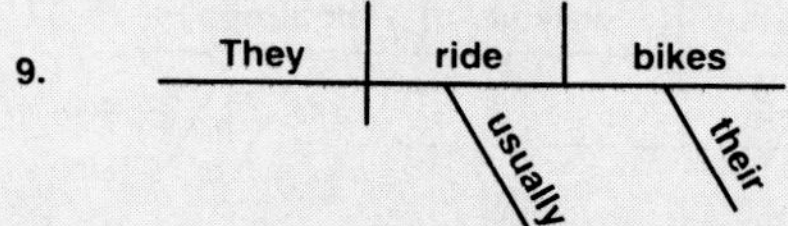

10.

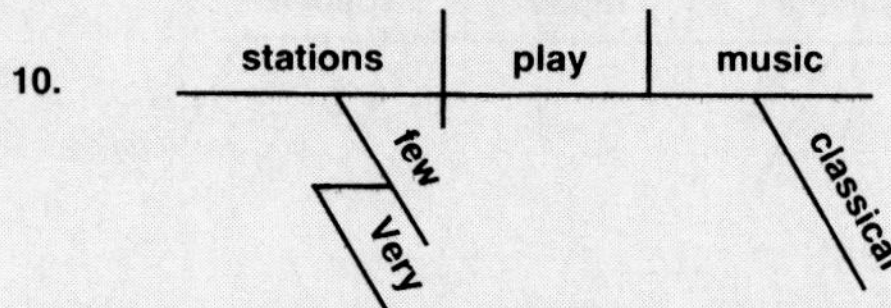

Page 514, Exercise

1.
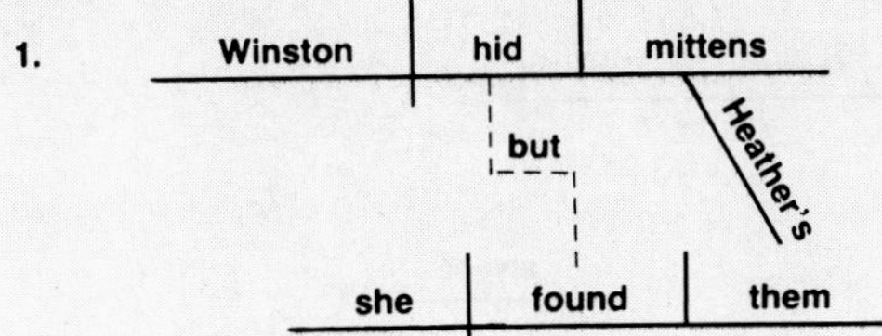

2.
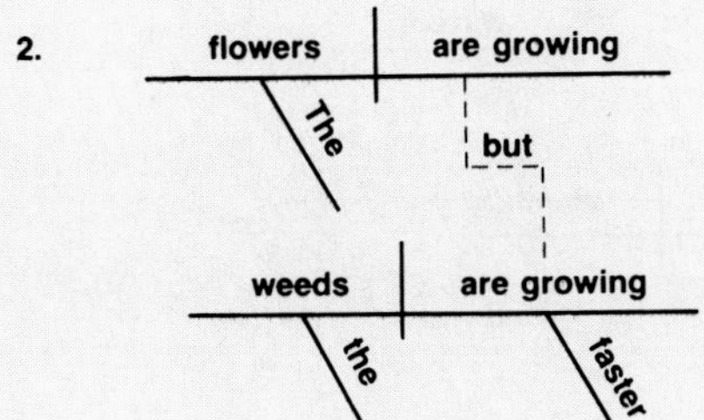

3.
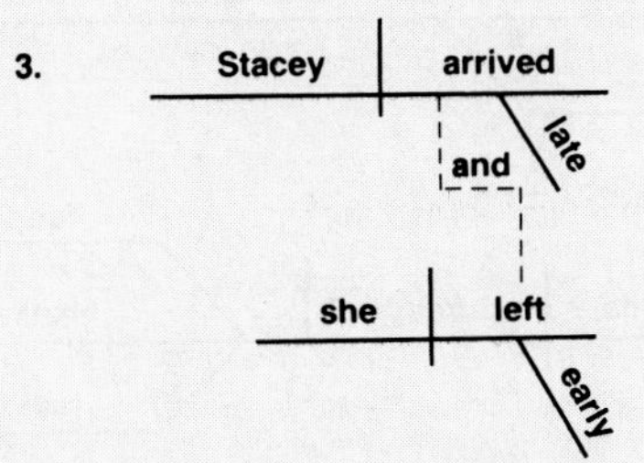

4.
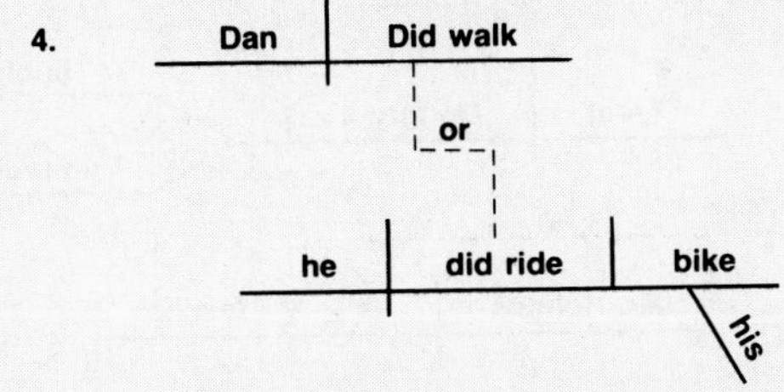

5.
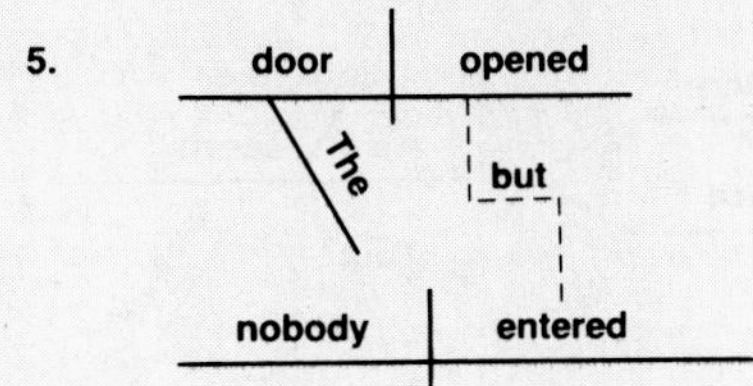

6.
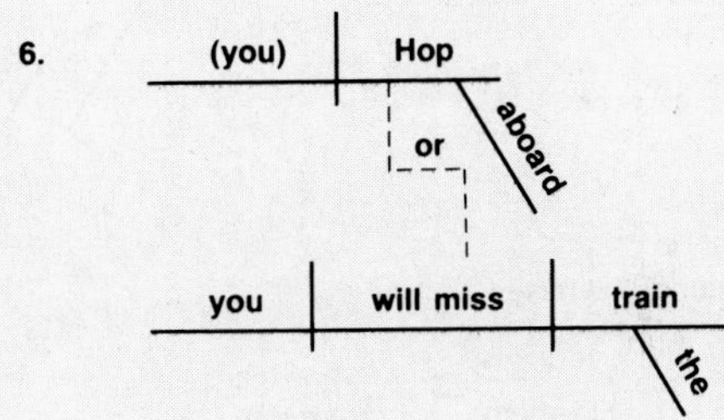

7.
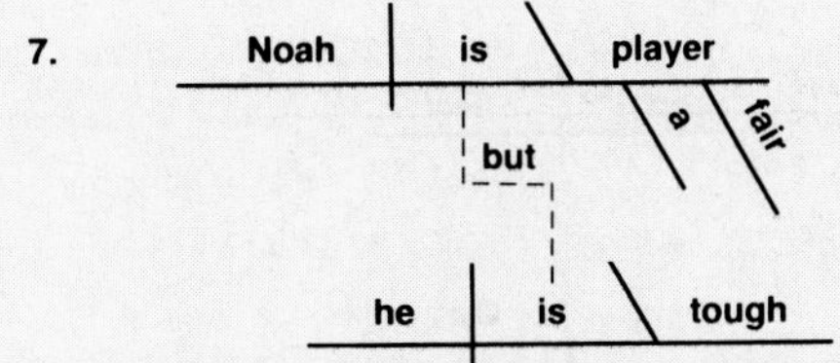

8.
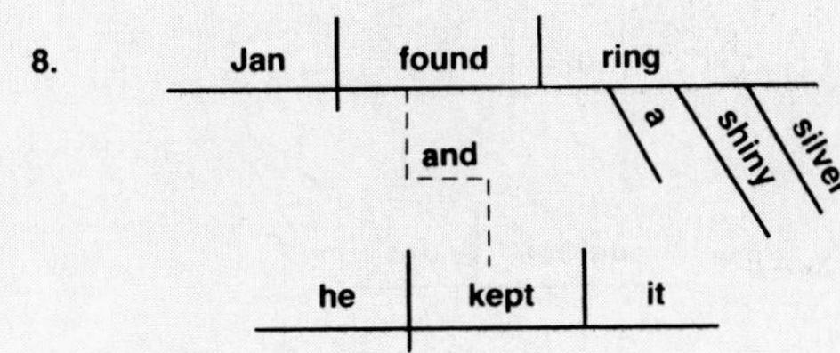

9.
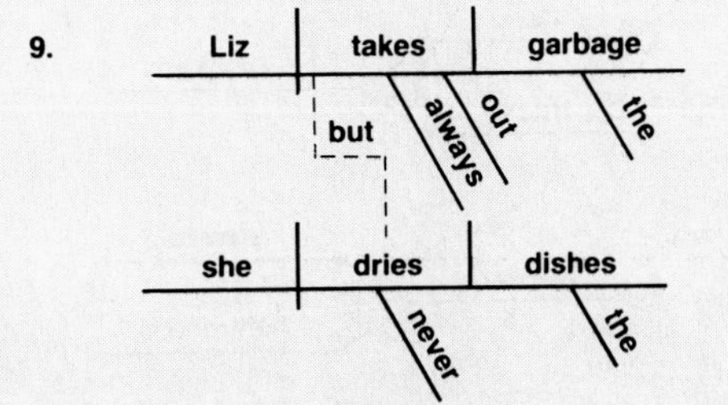

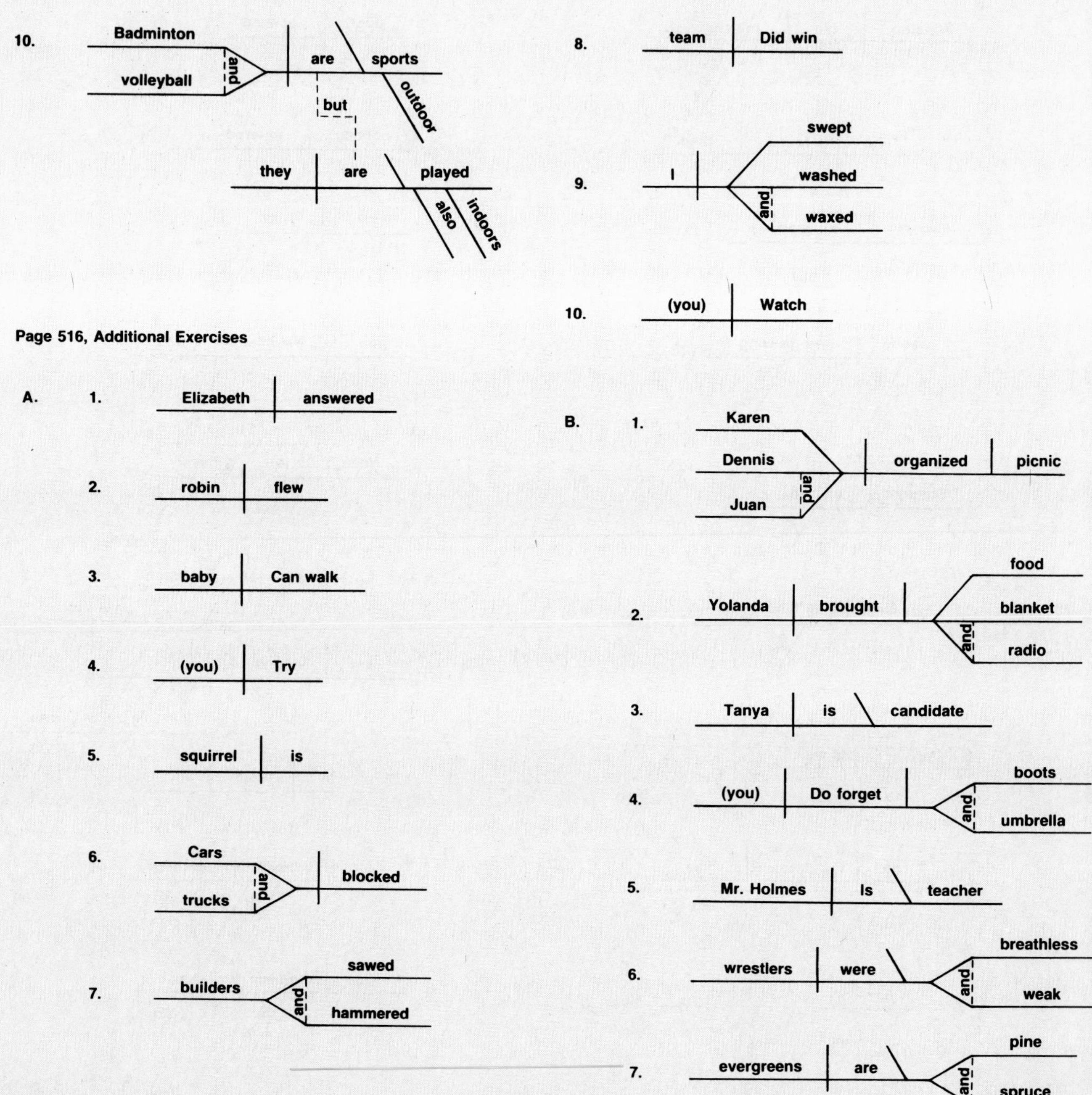
10.
Badminton
volleyball
and
are
sports
outdoor
but
they
are
played
also
indoors
8.
team
Did win
9.
I
swept
washed
and
waxed
10.
(you)
Watch
Page 516, Additional Exercises
A.
1.
Elizabeth
answered
2.
robin
flew
3.
baby
Can walk
4.
(you)
Try
5.
squirrel
is
6.
Cars
trucks
and
blocked
7.
builders
sawed
and
hammered
B.
1.
Karen
Dennis
and
Juan
organized
picnic
2.
Yolanda
brought
food
blanket
and
radio
3.
Tanya
is
candidate
4.
(you)
Do forget
boots
and
umbrella
5.
Mr. Holmes
Is
teacher
6.
wrestlers
were
breathless
and
weak
7.
evergreens
are
pine
and
spruce

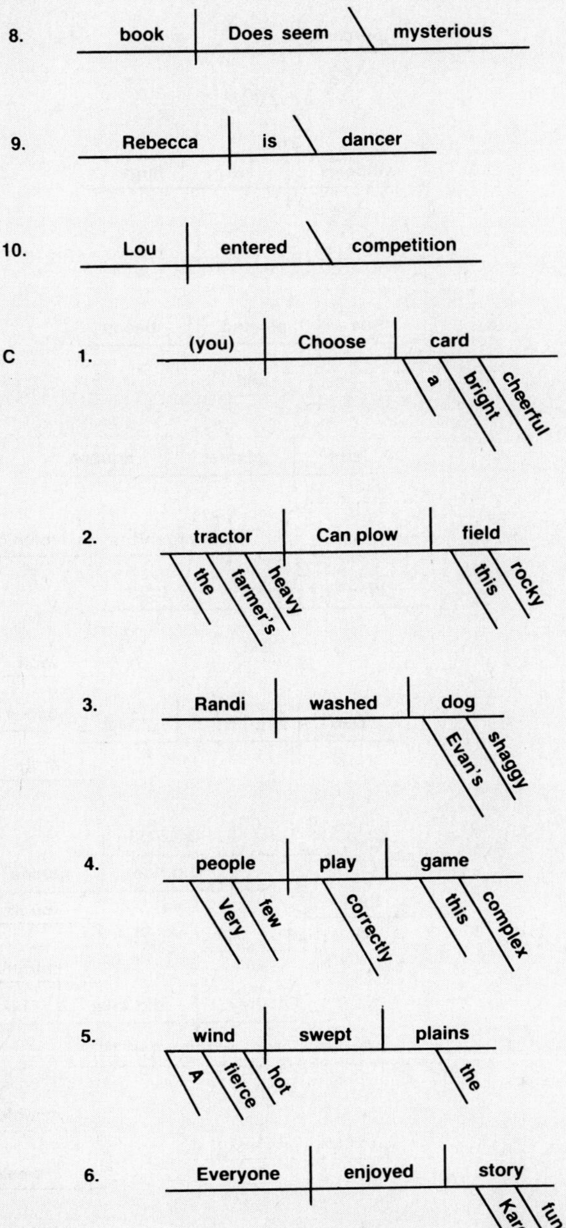

8.
book
Does seem
mysterious
9.
Rebecca
is
dancer
10.
Lou
entered
competition
C
1.
(you)
Choose
card
a
bright
cheerful
2.
tractor
Can plow
field
the
farmer's
heavy
this
rocky
3.
Randi
washed
dog
Evan's
shaggy
4.
people
play
game
Very
few
correctly
this
complex
5.
wind
swept
plains
A
fierce
hot
the
6.
Everyone
enjoyed
story
Karen's
funny

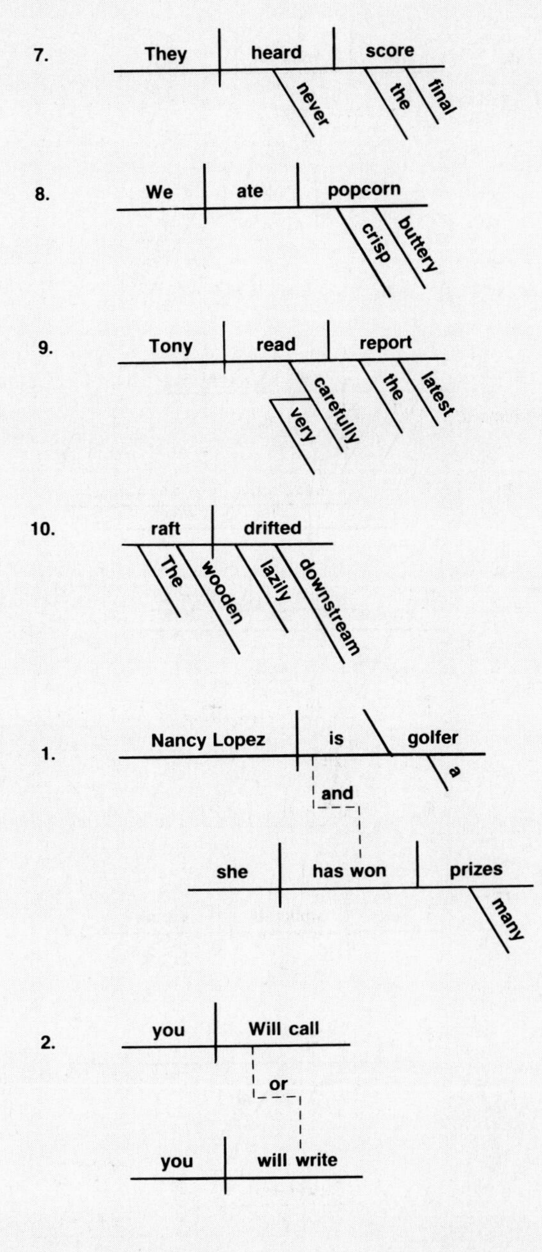

7.
They
heard
score
never
the
final
8.
We
ate
popcorn
crisp
buttery
9.
Tony
read
report
carefully
very
the
latest
10.
raft
drifted
The
wooden
lazily
downstream
D.
1.
Nancy Lopez
is
golfer
a
and
she
has won
prizes
many
2.
you
Will call
or
you
will write

3.

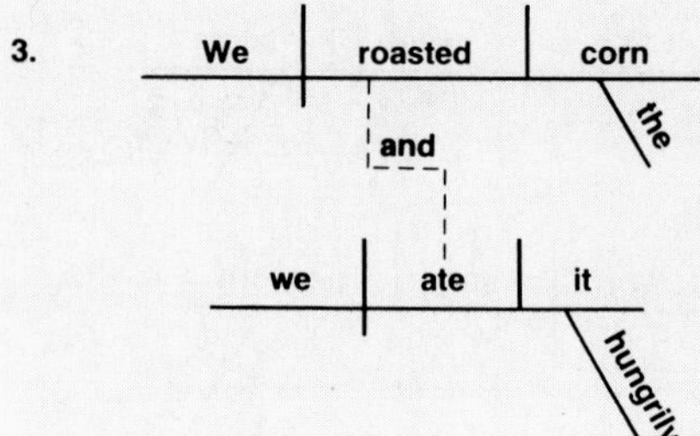
We
roasted
corn
the
and
we
ate
it
hungrily

4.

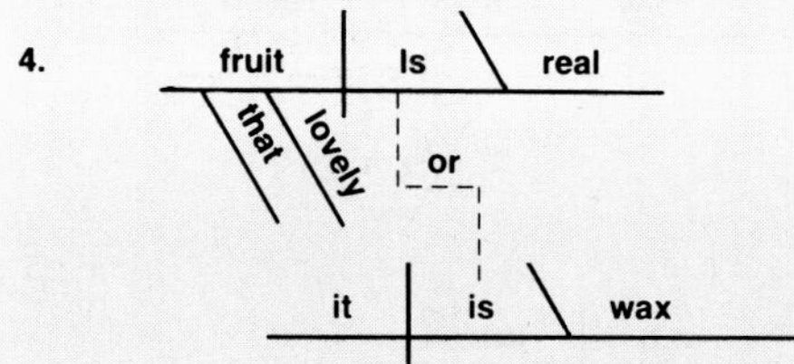
fruit
Is
real
that
lovely
or
it
is
wax

5.

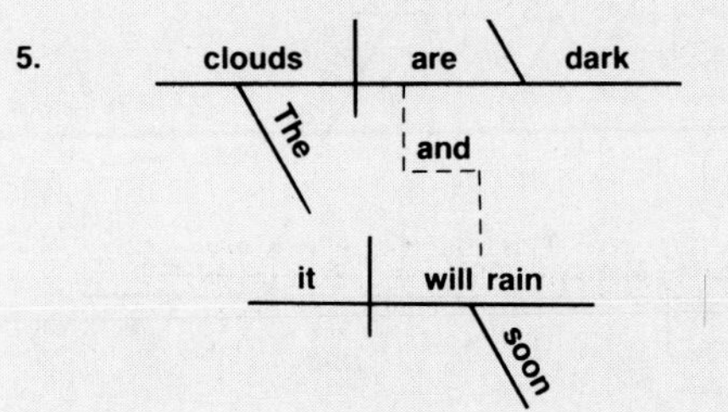
clouds
are
dark
The
and
it
will rain
soon

6.

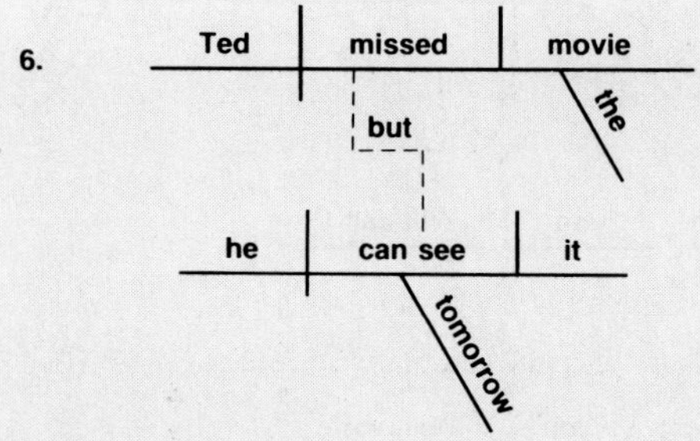
Ted
missed
movie
the
but
he
can see
it
tomorrow

7.

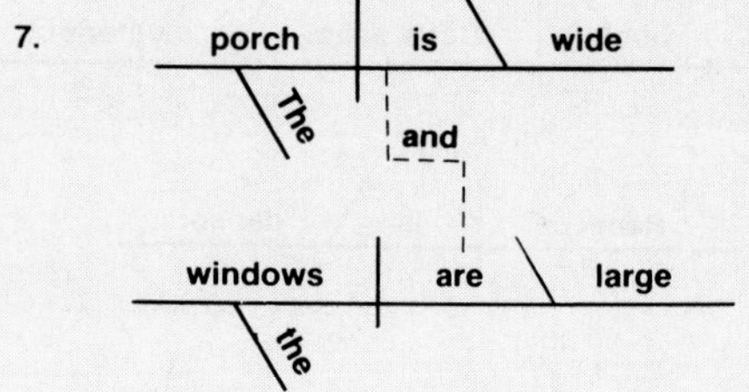
porch
is
wide
The
and
windows
are
large
the

8.

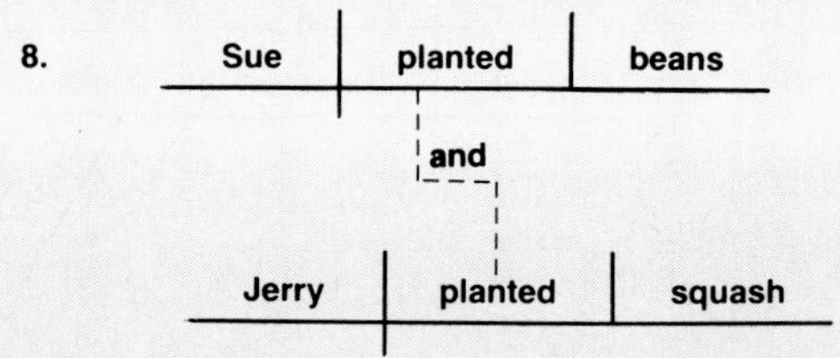
Sue
planted
beans
and
Jerry
planted
squash

9.

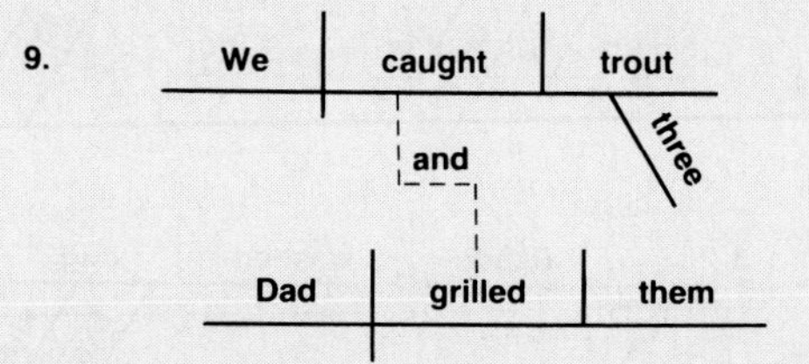
We
caught
trout
three
and
Dad
grilled
them

10.

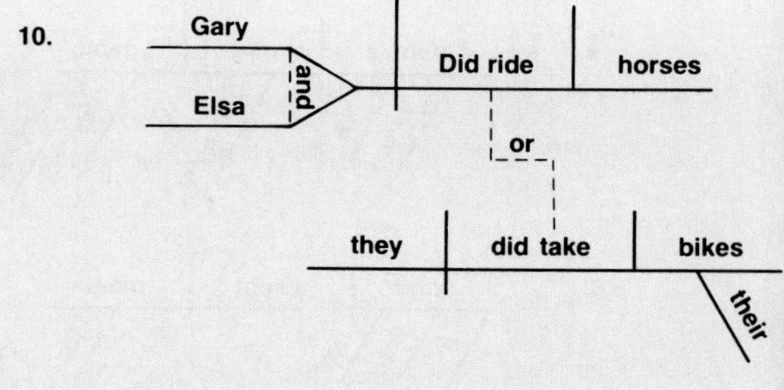
Gary
Elsa
and
Did ride
horses
or
they
did take
bikes
their

Page 518, Mixed Review

1. 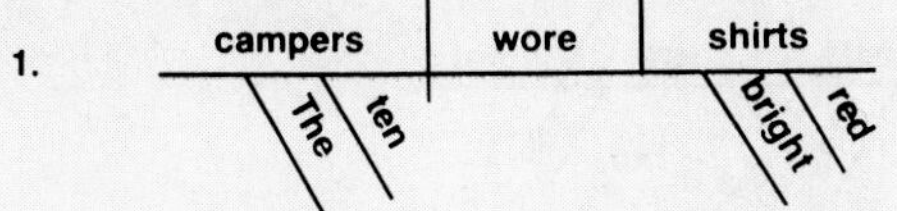

2. 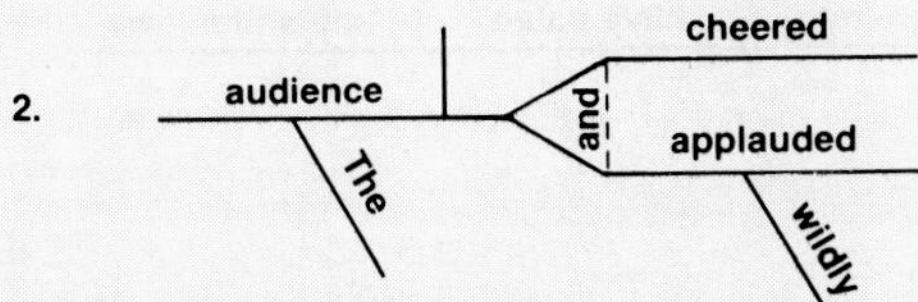

3. 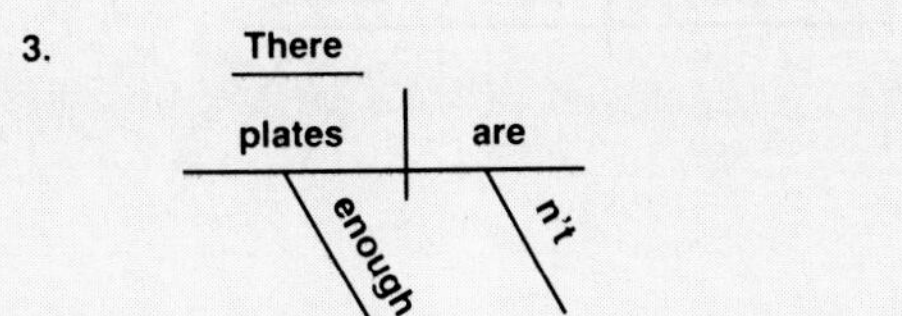

4. 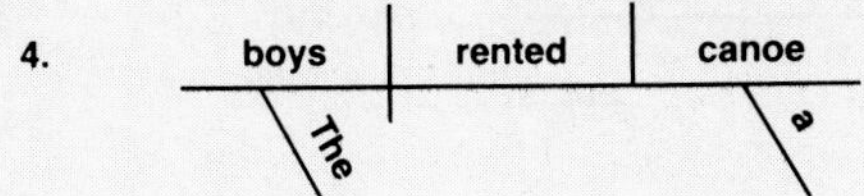

5. 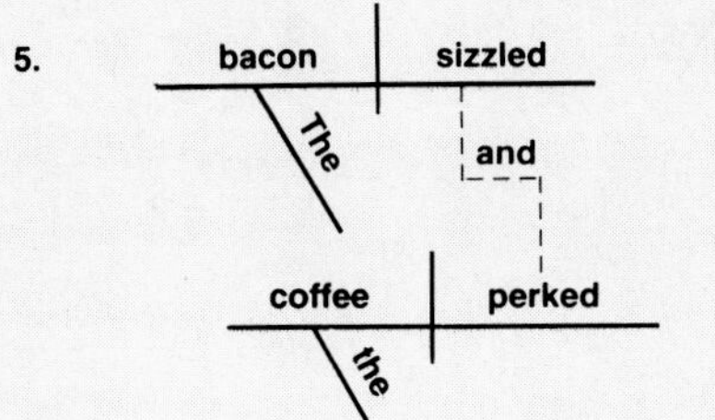

6. 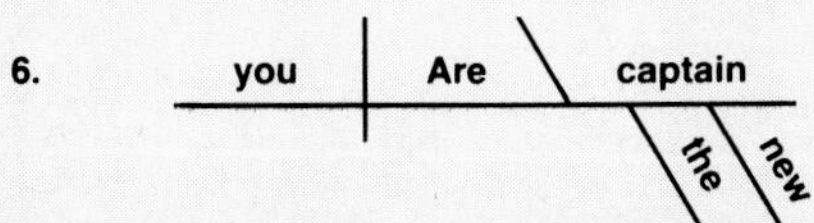

7. 

8. 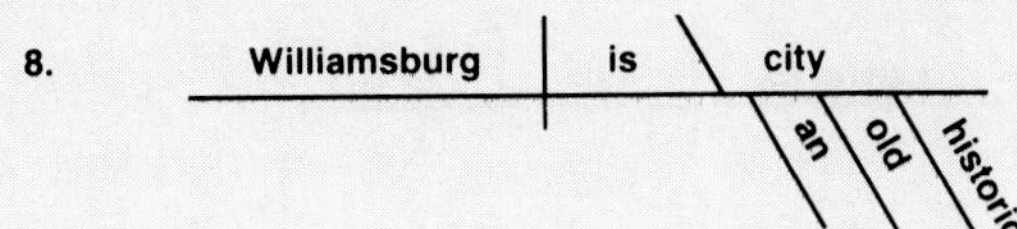

9. 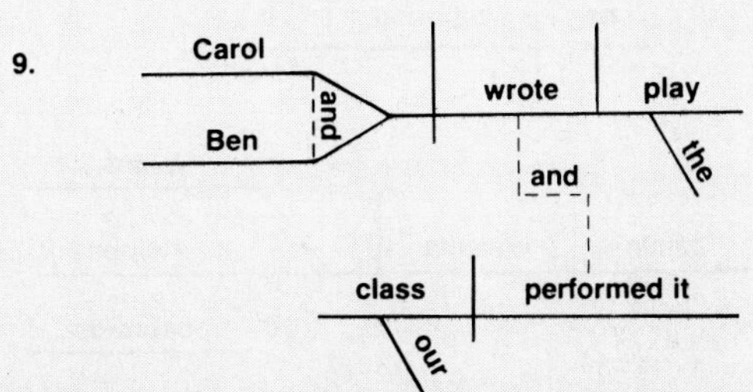

10. 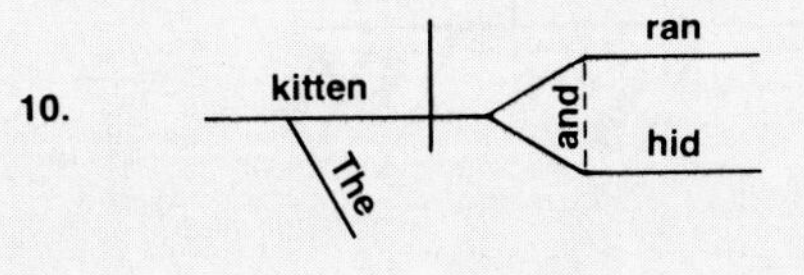

11. 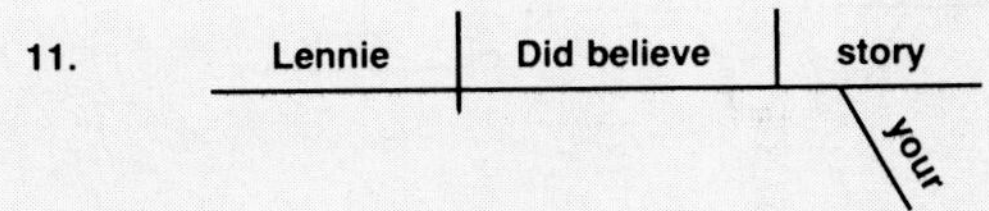

12. 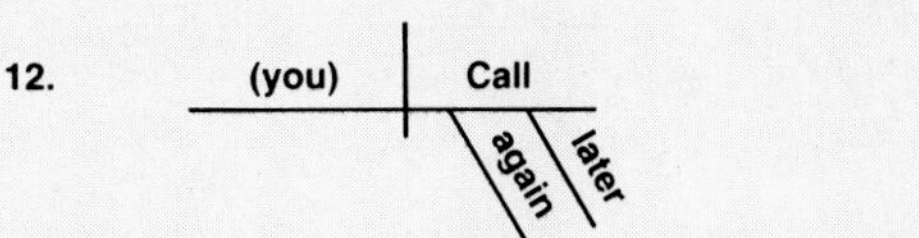

13. 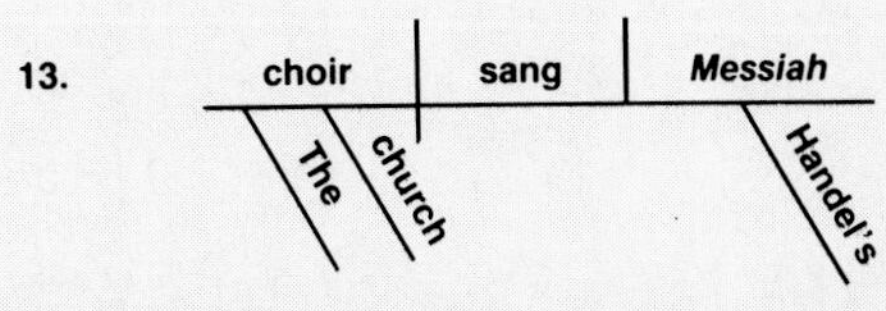

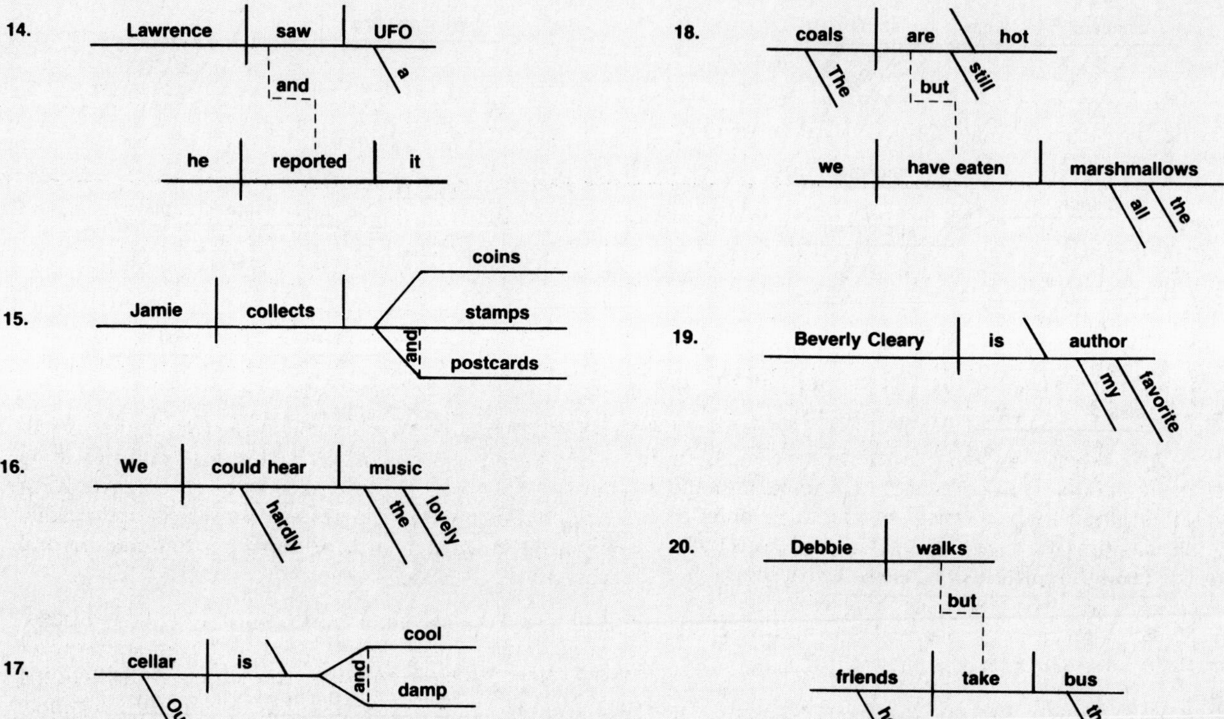

14.
Lawrence
saw
UFO
a
and
he
reported
it
15.
Jamie
collects
coins
stamps
and
postcards
16.
We
could hear
music
hardly
the
lovely
17.
cellar
is
Our
and
cool
damp
18.
coals
are
hot
The
still
but
we
have eaten
marshmallows
all
the
19.
Beverly Cleary
is
author
my
favorite
20.
Debbie
walks
but
friends
take
bus
her
the

Section 1: Learning About Sentences

LD LD students will find it easier to distinguish sentences from fragments if you stress that a fragment contains only part of an idea. Demonstrate this by using, first, an incomplete request.

EXAMPLE: Please lift. (incomplete)
Please lift this box.

Explain that this request can be completed only when expressed in full.

ESL ESL students will have trouble distinguishing sentence fragments from sentences, as their command of syntax is likely to be poor. Provide extra practice using the diagrams on page 271 and the questions *who*? and *what*? until the difference is clear. Use a scrambled sentence exercise; give sentences with scrambled word order (*is pencil there desk a on the*) and have students unscramble them (*there is a pencil on the desk*).

Stress word order in each of the four types of sentences. Demonstrate differences in intonation.

Practice with scrambled sentences and substitution drills. In the latter, the teacher provides a model sentence; students substitute cue words (from the teacher) to make new sentences.

MODEL: My sister talked to Helen yesterday.
CUES: walked school
STUDENTS RESPONSE: My sister walked to school yesterday.

Stress the logic of punctuation, which is common to all languages.

ESL students will find the English verb system confusing. Demonstrate usage and correct form, and provide practice as needed. Give additional practice placing *who*? or *what*? before the verb in order to identify the subject. Stress the exercises in which the students must find the subject in unusual positions, and add to them if possible.

NSD NSD students frequently have difficulty choosing the correct form of verbs, especially the forms of the verb *be*. Use the exercises on finding verbs as an oral reinforcement of the standard verbal forms.

Section 2: Using Sentences Correctly

LD and ESL Because LD and ESL students will do a number of the exercises in this text orally, it will be helpful to spend some time on the lesson *Avoiding Run-on Sentences*. Run-on errors, which are readily apparent in written work, are not easy to detect in oral work.

When teaching ESL students, see comments in preceding section. Identifying fragments and run-ons requires comprehension of examples. Check for understanding of vocabulary. ESL students may not be able to generate their own sentences. Provide them with native English-speaking partners, or help them yourself.

Section 3: Using Nouns

LD LD students may have difficulty using dictionaries to find plurals of nouns. Thus frequent repetition and reinforcement will be necessary when teaching singular and plural nouns, particularly for irregular examples.

ESL ESL students will understand proper and common nouns and possessives more readily through comparisons and contrasts with their own languages. They will need extra practice with forming plurals, the irregular ones in particular. Using a dictionary may be beyond their skill; again, a partner could help.

Word order will continue to be a problem. Be alert for negative transfer from the student's native language: for example, placing an adjective after a noun, or placing a verb near the beginning of a sentence.

NSD NSD students will need to spend some additional time working on *Singular and Plural Nouns.* Encourage these students to use a dictionary. You may wish to work through or review the lesson **Using a Dictionary** (Writing Section 2) before attempting this section.

Section 4: Using Verbs

LD LD students may require additional explanation and drill in order to master state-of-being verbs. Instructions for exercises may have to be more explicit. These students will need more explanation and examples of separated parts of verbs and predicate word in order to complete the exercises.

ESL ESL students frequently omit forms of *be*, drop *s* from third-person singular present tense, or drop *ed* from regular past tense. Go over rules very carefully and provide extra practice: scrambled sentences, fill-in sentences, substitution drills.

In some languages the pronoun is indicated in the verb ending, so these students may omit the pronoun in English. As far as possible, compare English forms with forms in other languages.

ESL students will have many difficulties with helping verbs. Extensive practice of these verbs may be necessary.

In some languages, gender and number determine the form of the predicate word. Explain that English relies on the meanings of the subject and the predicate word to establish their relationship. Give oral practice before requiring written responses. Extensive use of the sentence pattern chart will benefit ESL students; be sure, however, that they first recognize parts of speech.

NSD NSD students have many difficulties with main verbs and helping verbs. Use Part 2 of this section to concentrate on specific problems. Be especially aware of the faulty use of *be*.

Section 5: Using Irregular Verbs

LD LD students will require extensive practice in using irregular verbs correctly. Additional exercises can be found in this book and in the Practice Book.

ESL ESL students may have trouble distinguishing between past and past participle forms. Provide extensive oral drills and substitution drills. These students will not be good judges of what "sounds right." Give supplementary oral practice before assigning written exercises, or do some written exercises together as a class.

NSD Many NSD students will be more familiar with deviant than with standard usage of irregular verbs. They may not be able to distinguish aurally between standard and non-standard usage. Emphasis must be placed on both the written and the oral exercises. Repetition and patience will be essential when attempting to modify linguistic habits.

Section 6: Using Troublesome Verbs Correctly

ESL Allow ESL students ample time for practice with confusing pairs of verbs. Contractions may be entirely unfamiliar to ESL students. Review, practice, and encourage reference to the list of contractions on page 379.

Double negatives are required in some languages. Compare the form in the ESL student's language and mark out the extra negative to show the difference. Practice with substitution drills and fill-in sentences.

NSD This lesson is of particular importance to NSD students. Many non-standard dialects use double negatives and original contractions of the verb *to be*. Many NSD students will also regularly substitute one verb for another similar verb. (Example: *lay* for *lie*). Remember that the students are obeying their own dialect's semantic rules. If necessary, spend extra time on this lesson.

Section 7: Using Pronouns

LD LD students should be allowed to do several exercises orally, to make sure that they understand the directions.

ESL ESL students will find this section difficult because pronouns are much more complicated in English than in many other languages. These students are likely to mistake case and gender and to omit pronouns. Review the rules, stressing that pronouns are not dropped in English. Provide extensive practice: scrambled sentences, cloze exercises, substitution drills.

ESL students cannot usually judge what "sounds natural." Encourage reference to the charts in this Section. Practice possessive pronouns, especially *its*, extensively.

Some ESL students will substitute a pronoun for the verb *to be* forming a double subject. (*Mary, she nice.*) Be aware of this problem, too, when teaching linking verbs.

NSD NSD students will have difficulty determining when to use the object form and when to use the subject form of pronouns. Pay particular attention to Parts 2, 3 and 4 of this lesson.

Section 8: Using Adjectives

LD LD students will have trouble generating and writing sentences as instructed in Exercise B on page 409. Either omit the exercise or do it as a group exercise.

ESL ESL students will have trouble using articles and placing adjectives in the sentences correctly. Practice with scrambled sentences and expansion drills. In an expansion drill, the teacher gives a base sentence (*The sky is blue*), the student repeats it, the teacher gives a new word (*always*), and the student inserts it in the correct place in the sentence (*The sky is always blue*).

Make sure that these students know the vocabulary in this section, and also concepts like *what kind, how many, which ones,* etc.

Agreement in gender and number between an adjective and the noun it modifies is much simpler in English than in many languages. Point out that English does not require distinct forms for gender and number (except for demonstratives *this, these, that,* and *those*).

Give many examples of predicate adjectives, and use arrows, as on page 413, to indicate the word modified.

ESL students may be slow to master English conventions governing proper adjectives, but experience will eventually teach them. Unlearning the rules from their native language may be harder than learning new ones. Parts 5 and 6 will be most accessible to these students if taught with ample supplementary illustration (*That chair over there is smaller than this one over here*).

Section 9: Using Adverbs

ESL ESL students may confuse adverbs and predicate adjectives, especially when they are used with linking verbs. Focus on the words modified. As you present the examples and the exercises, ask the questions *how, when, where* or *to what extent,* and encourage the students to do so. Give these students ample practice (scrambled sentences, fill-in sentences) using adjectives and adverbs before moving on to comparative forms.

NSD NSD students often use *more* and *most* with adverbs as an emphatic statement (*most slowest, more earlier*). Provide extra examples of correct usage.

Section 10: Using Prepositions and Conjunctions

ESL For ESL students the functions of prepositions and conjunctions in English may be very confusing because their native languages use them quite differently. Contrast the usages whenever possible, and emphasize memorizing the list on page 442. Pace this material very cautiously, as the concepts presented are numerous and difficult to see in relation to one another. Correct placement of prepositional phrases may require more sensitivity to English word order than these students have developed. Do many of the sentences orally, discussing the relationships among sentence parts and, when possible, the contrasts with the native language. You may need to review terminology and give additional examples. You may also have to review *and, but,* and *or*.

Section 11: Using the Parts of Speech

LD LD students will require some review of parts of speech before they can do the first exercise. You can use the exercise as the basis for an oral review.

ESL ESL students will find this review very helpful. Stress the material on multiple functions of words, which is very important for non-native speakers.

Section 12: Making Subjects and Verbs Agree

LD For LD students, emphasize the rules. Use examples to illustrate conditional statements such as "If a subject is plural, use the plural form of the verb."

ESL ESL students may need some review. The concepts *singular* and *plural* will be familiar, but the students may need to be reminded of specific examples. Third person singular present tense verbs end in *s* as do plural nouns, a fact which may cause confusion. Practice with substitution drills and fill-in sentences.

Special verb forms and compound subjects may require extra practice; encourage use in classroom conversation.

There is, here is and *where is* should be familiar from Section 6; use these sentences as review. The explanation of "Using I" may be confusing to ESL students. If necessary write all six verb forms on the board to illustrate (*I have, you have, he/she/it has, we have, you have, they have*).

NSD Stress the necessity of agreement between subject and verb, especially the state-of-being verbs.

Section 13: Using Compound Sentences

ESL ESL students may need careful explanation of the relationships of the uncombined sentences before they can combine them with the correct conjunction. Review uses of *and, but,* and *or.*

Section 14: Diagraming the Sentence

LD You may want to limit your LD students to the simple subject-verb diagrams. Introduce other elements only when and if your students are ready for them.

ESL ESL students will find this section especially helpful because it provides visual representations of difficult syntactical patterns. The pace may have to be slowed to allow time for extra practice and monitoring.

Section 15: Capitalization

LD LD students will have trouble copying all the sentences. Assign fewer sentences, or allow these students to complete them orally.

ESL ESL students will find some personal titles, proper nouns, outline/letter forms, and literary titles unfamiliar. Have these students work with native speaking partners who can explain this material. The rules must be practiced to be learned.

Section 16: Punctuation

LD LD students will have trouble copying all the sentences. Assign fewer sentences, or allow these students to complete them orally.

ESL ESL students will benefit from emphasis on the logic which governs punctuation. Point out any marks whose use may be unfamiliar, such as the hyphen or the apostrophe in possessives, and give extra practice in using them. A native English speaking partner may be helpful, especially in using the dictionary.

Section 17: Spelling

ESL ESL students must learn English spelling through written use and practice. Discuss the rules at a leisurely pace, using a multi-sensory approach: see, hear, say, write.

NSD Most likely NSD students will need additional work in spelling. Encourage the use of the dictionary through dictionary drills. Spelling Bees are also helpful.

Guidelines for Evaluating Composition

Adapted from Teaching and Evaluating Student Writing,

Types of Evaluation

In order to give student writers the constant practice and feedback they need, teachers must have a practical method of evaluation. Obviously, if the student will be writing constantly, a teacher cannot be expected to evaluate each piece in a line-by-line, word-by-word manner. Nor would such an evaluation necessarily be useful to the developing writer. It is therefore suggested that a teacher learn to use two different evaluation methods—the holistic method and the more detailed analytic method.

Holistic evaluation of writing is a quick, guided method of rating pieces of writing. It can best be used to evaluate daily writing samples or first drafts of more complex pieces. With holistic evaluation, an evaluator reads the written piece as a whole, considers certain features, and immediately assigns a grade. The grade may be a single rating for the entire piece of writing or a set of ratings for the different features being considered.

Analytic evaluation should occur only when the student has turned in the clean, final copy of a piece of writing. In this detailed type of evaluation, the teacher analyzes each aspect of a piece of writing, including both content and mechanics.

Evaluators

The evaluation process can be utilized by three types of evaluators: the writer of the piece, other students, and the teacher. Each type of evaluation offers unique benefits to the developing writer.

1. Self-Evaluation. In this type of evaluation, a writer comments on his or her own work, noting which parts were successful and which unsuccessful.

2. Peer Evaluation. Evaluating the writing of others is often a strong learning experience. In peer evaluation, students work together in small groups to improve a piece of writing. Student evaluators should always be given a list of specific criteria that the writing is expected to meet, and should then comment on how well each paper succeeds.

3. Teacher Evaluation. The teacher's comments and suggestions may be incorporated at any point in the writing process. Studies indicate that evaluation by the teacher is most successful when it is done in combination with self- and peer evaluation. The evaluation that follows provides for such a combination of evaluation procedures.

Teacher evaluation should also involve direct communication with every student. Such help can be provided in student-teacher conferences.

Keeping a Record of Improvement

Both the teacher and students benefit when writing folders are maintained throughout the school year. A piece of writing from early in the year, along with its evaluations, can be compared with later pieces. Progress from one piece to the next will be erratic, as the writer takes risks using new techniques and appears to move backwards until gaining mastery of each new technique. However, over the course of the year, progress should be evident.

BIBLIOGRAPHY

Cooper, Charles R. and Lee Odell, eds. *Evaluating Writing: Describing, Measuring, Judging.* Urbana, Illinois: National Council of Teachers of English, 1977.

Graves, Donald H. *Balance the Basics: Let Them Write.* New York: The Ford Foundation, 1978.

Murray, Donald M. *A Writer Teaches Writing: A Practical Method of Teaching Composition.* Boston: Houghton Mifflin, 1968.

Payne, Lucile Vaughn, *The Lively Art of Writing.* Chicago: Follett, 1965.

Using the Evaluation Form

The following form for composition evaluation may be used at any stage of the writing process, and may be re-used after each revision.

The form should be filled out by the student and turned in with the writing. There is also space on the form for peer evaluation, if desired. The teacher may ask students to turn in only final copies, or may ask to see work in progress. The student states whether the submitted writing is the final copy.

On the evaluation form, content may be rated at any point; mechanics should be graded only on a final copy.

Self-Evaluation: Besides the questions on the form, the student can ask himself or herself the questions concerning revising listed in the relevant composition chapter. The student may use 1, 3, and 5 subjectively.

Peer Evaluation: Members of the peer group should rate each feature as objectively as possible. In order to focus on ideas and organization, the group should evaluate content only.

Teacher Evaluation: The following standards for evaluating composition are provided to assist the teacher in rating papers with objectivity and consistency. In a conference, the teacher might discuss one or two of these areas in detail.

Standards for Evaluation

Content

	1—Low	3—Average	5—High
1	Unclear, unimaginative writing.	Understandable but unimaginative writing.	Imaginative, interesting writing.
2	Boring or poorly defined topic.	Topic adequately limited and defined.	Well-chosen, precisely developed topic.
3	Purpose unclear, or not achieved in the writing.	Purpose defined adequately. Not completely achieved.	Clear, well-defined purpose. Writing achieves purpose successfully.
4	Writing so lacking in detail that topic remains undeveloped.	Incomplete development. More information needed.	Topic thoroughly covered. Writing is rich in detail and supporting information.
5	Many irrelevant sentences or details.	Few irrelevant sentences or details.	Well-chosen, relevant sentences and details.
6	Disjointed ideas. No transitional words, phrases, or ideas.	Inconsistent flow. Some transitional devices.	Ideas flow well. Good use of transitional devices.
7	Lack of any logical organization of ideas.	Some organization of ideas evident.	Well-organized ideas. Type of organization suited to topic and purpose.
8	Dull, general words, poorly chosen. Inappropriate to audience.	Suitable but unimaginative language. Generally appropriate to audience.	Specific, vivid language. Appropriate to audience.

Mechanics

1	Many fragments and run-on sentences. Frequent mistakes in the use of nouns, verbs, pronouns, and subject-verb agreement.	Few fragments and run-ons. Some mistakes in the use of nouns, verbs, pronouns, and subject-verb agreement.	No fragments or run-ons. Few mistakes in the use of nouns, verbs, pronouns, and subject-verb agreement.
2	Frequent mistakes in capitalization.	Occasional mistakes in capitalization.	Infrequent mistakes in capitalization.
3	Punctuation marks frequently misused or missing.	Punctuation marks usually used correctly.	Infrequent mistakes in punctuation.
4	Frequent mistakes in spelling, without any indication of awareness of spelling patterns.	Occasional misspellings, usually indicating an approximation of the correct spelling and an awareness of spelling patterns.	Infrequent spelling mistakes.
5	Paragraphs not indented. Writing illegible. Incorrect headings or margins.	Some carelessness or inconsistency in form. Occasionally hard to read.	Correct form. Neat, legible handwriting.

Composition Evaluation Form

Writer ______________________ **Date** ______________

Title ______________________ **Circle one:** Unfinished Final Copy

Evaluation Symbols
1 Needs a great deal of work
3 Acceptable—could be improved
5 Very good. Needs no further revision.

Content	Writer's Opinion	Peer Group Opinion	Teacher's Evaluation	Teacher's Comments
1. **Interest.** Is the writing interesting and understandable? Does it hold the reader's attention?				
2. **Topic.** Is the topic a good one? Has it been narrowed sufficiently?				
3. **Purpose.** Is the purpose of the writing clear? Has the writer accomplished this purpose?				
4. **Development.** Has the topic been developed well? Is there sufficient information?				
5. **Unity.** Are all ideas and details related to the topic? Do they all help to develop or strengthen the main idea?				
6. **Continuity.** Do ideas flow smoothly? Has the writer avoided any breaks in thought?				
7. **Organization.** Were ideas arranged in a logical order? Does this order suit the purpose of the writing?				
8. **Language.** Is the language appropriate to the writing? Does it suit the audience? Are the words vivid?				
Additional Guidelines				

Mechanics (to be graded by teacher on final copy only)

Mechanics	Writer's Opinion	Peer Group Opinion	Teacher's Evaluation	Teacher's Comments
1. **Grammar and Usage.** Are there any fragments or run-ons? Is the correct form of every pronoun or verb used? Are adjectives and adverbs used correctly?				
2. **Capitalization.** Are all first words, initials, proper nouns, proper adjectives, and titles capitalized?				
3. **Punctuation.** Does each sentence have the proper end mark? Are all punctuation marks used correctly?				
4. **Spelling.** Are all words spelled correctly? Are plurals and possessive forms spelled correctly?				
5. **Form.** Is the writing legible? Is the heading correct? Are there sufficient margins?